# Popular Culture

# Popular Culture

## A Reader

Raiford Guins and Omayra Zaragoza Cruz

**SAGE** Publications
London • Thousand Oaks • New Delhi

First published 2005

SAGE Publications Ltd
1 Oliver's Yard
55 City Road
London EC1Y 1SP

SAGE Publications Inc.
2455 Teller Road
Thousand Oaks, California 91320

SAGE Publications India Pvt Ltd
B-42, Panchsheel Enclave
Post Box 4109
New Delhi 110 017

**British Library Cataloguing in Publication data**

A catalogue record for this book is available
from the British Library

ISBN 0-7619-7471-7
ISBN 0-7619-7472-5 (pbk)

**Library of Congress Control Number available**

Typeset by C&M Digitals (P) Ltd., Chennai, India
Printed in Great Britain by Cromwell Press Ltd, Trowbridge, Wiltshire

# Contents

Entangling the Popular: An Introduction to *Popular Culture: A Reader*     1

Omayra Cruz and Raiford Guins

    *I.  DELINEATING*: CULTURE–MASS–POPULAR     19

1.  **Raymond Williams. 'Culture' and 'Masses'**     25

From: *Keywords: A Vocabulary of Culture and Society.*
London: Fontana Press, 1976.

2.  **F.R. Leavis. 'Mass Civilisation and Minority Culture'**     33

From: *Mass Civilisation and Minority Culture.* Cambridge:
Minority Press, 1930.

3.  **Dwight Macdonald. 'A Theory of Mass Culture'**     39

From: *Mass Culture: The Popular Arts in America.*
Ed. Bernard Rosenberg and David Manning White. New York:
The Free Press, 1957.

4.  **Tania Modleski. 'Femininity as Mas[s]querade:
    A Feminist Approach to Mass Culture'**     47

From: *High Theory/Low Culture: Analyzing Popular Television
and Film.* Ed. Colin MacCabe. Manchester: Manchester
University Press, 1986.

5.  **Morag Shiach. 'The Popular'**     55

From: *Discourses on Popular Culture: Class, Gender and History
in Cultural Analysis, 1730 to the Present.* London: Polity Press, 1989.

6.  **Stuart Hall. 'Notes on Deconstructing "The Popular"'**                                       64

    From: *People's History and Socialist Theory.*
    Ed. Raphael Samuel. London: Routledge, 1981.

7.  **Juan Flores. ' "Pueblo Pueblo": Popular Culture in Time'**                                    72

    From: *From Bomba to Hip-Hop: Puerto Rican Culture
    and Latino Identity.* New York: Columbia
    University Press, 2000.

       II.  *COMMODIFYING*: THE COMMODITY,
            CULTURE AND SOCIAL LIFE                                                                 83

8.  **Karl Marx. 'The Fetishism of Commodities and the Secret Thereof'**                           89

    From: *Capital: Volume One. A Critical Analysis of
    Capitalist Production* (Orig. 1867). Reprinted in
    *The Marx-Engels Reader.* R. Tucker (ed). London:
    W.W. Norton & Co, 1972.

9.  **Walter Benjamin. 'The Work of Art in the Age of Mechanical Reproduction'**                    96

    From: *Illuminations.* Ed. H. Arendt and trans. H. Zohn.
    London: Fontana, 1992 (orig. 1936).

10. **Theodor W. Adorno. 'Culture Industry Reconsidered'**                                          103

    From: *The Culture Industry: Selected Essays on Mass Culture.*
    London: Routledge, 1991 (orig. English trans., 1975).

11. **Guy Debord. 'The Commodity as Spectacle'**                                                    109

    From: *Society of the Spectacle.* Detroit, MI: Black
    and Red, 1970.

12. **Fredric Jameson. 'Reification and Utopia in Mass Culture'**                                   115

    From: *Signature of the Visible.* London: Routledge, 1990.

13. **Lisa Lowe and David Lloyd. 'Introduction to**
    ***The Politics of Culture in the Shadow of Late Capital'***   129

    From: *The Politics of Culture in the Shadow of Late Capital.*
    Ed. Lisa Lowe and David Lloyd. Durham, NC:
    Duke University Press, 1997.

    III.   *MARKETING*: SOCIO-ECONOMIC CONSIDERATIONS
           OF POPULAR CULTURE                                       147

14. **Paul Smith. 'Tommy Hilfiger in the Age**
    **of Mass Customization'**                                      151

    From: *No Sweat: Fashion, Free Trade, and the Rights of
    Garment Workers.* Ed. Andrew Ross. New York: Verso, 1997.

15. **Ellis Cashmore. 'America's Paradox'**                         159

    From: *The Black Culture Industry.* London: Routledge, 1997.

16. **Inderpal Grewal. 'Traveling Barbie: Indian**
    **Transnationality and New Consumer Subjects'**                 168

    From: *positions* 7.3, 1999.

17. **Janet Wasko. 'Corporate Disney in Action'**                   184

    From: *Understanding Disney: The Manufacture of Fantasy.*
    Cambridge: Polity, 2001.

18. **Henry Yu. 'How Tiger Lost His Stripes:**
    **Post-Nationalist American Studies as a History of Race,**
    **Migration, and the Commodification of Culture'**              197

    From: *Post-Nationalist American Studies.* Ed. J.C. Rowe. Berkeley, CA:
    University of California Press, 2000.

    IV.   *PRACTICING*: POPULAR TASTES AND
          WAYS OF CONSUMING                                         211

19. **John Fiske. 'Popular Discrimination'**                        215

    From: *Modernity and Mass Culture.* Ed. James Naremore
    and Patrick Brantlinger. Bloomington, IN:
    Indiana University Press, 1991.

20.   **Laura Kipnis. '(Male) Desire and (Female) Disgust:
      Reading *Hustler*'**                                                223

      From: *Cultural Studies.* Ed. Lawrence Grossberg et al.
      London: Routledge, 1992.

21.   **Paul Willis. 'Symbolic Creativity'**                             241

      From: *Common Culture: Symbolic Work at Play in the Everyday
      Cultures of the Young.* Milton Keynes: Open University Press, 1990.

22.   **Henry Jenkins. '*Star Trek* Rerun, Reread, Rewritten:
      Fan Writing as Textual Poaching'**                                 249

      From: *Close Encounters: Film, Feminism, and Science
      Fiction.* Ed. Constance Penley et al. Minneapolis, MN:
      University of Minnesota Press, 1991.

23.   **Joan Hawkins. 'Sleaze Mania, Euro-Trash
      and High Art: The Place of European Art Films
      in American Low Culture'**                                         263

      From: *Film Quarterly* 53.2, 2000.


              *V.   VOICING*: IDENTITIES AND ARTICULATION                 279


24.   **Stuart Hall. 'What is this "Black" in Black
      Popular Culture?'**                                                285

      From: *Black Popular Culture.* Ed. Gina Dent. Seattle, WA:
      Bay Press, 1992.

25.   **Gayatri Gopinath. '"Bombay, UK, Yuba City":
      Bhangra Music and the Engendering of Diaspora'**                   294

      From: *Diaspora* 4.3, 1995.

26.   **Lauren Berlant. 'The Face of America and
      the State of Emergency'**                                          309

      From: *The Queen of America Goes to Washington City: Essays on
      Sex and Citizenship.* Durham, NC: Duke University Press, 1997.

27.   **José Esteban Muñoz. 'Pedro Zamora's Real World of
      Counterpublicity: Performing an Ethics of the Self'**              324

      From: *Disidentifications: Queers of Color and the Performance of
      Politics.* Minneapolis, MN: University of Minnesota Press, 1999.

28. **Richard Fung. 'Looking for My Penis: The Eroticized Asian in Gay Video Porn'**   338

    From: *How Do I Look? Queer Film and Video.* Ed. Bad-Object Choices. Seattle, WA: Bay Press, 1991.


    *VI.   STYLING*: SUBCULTURE AND POPULAR PERFORMANCE   349

29. **Dick Hebdige. 'Subculture'**   355

    From: *Subculture: The Meaning of Style.* London: Routledge, 1979.

30. **Angela McRobbie. 'Second-Hand Dresses and the Role of the Ragmarket'**   372

    From: *Zoot Suits and Second-Hand Dresses: An Anthology of Fashion and Music.* Ed. Angela McRobbie. Boston, MA: Unwin Hyman, 1988.

31. **Sarah Thornton. 'The Media Development of "Subcultures" (or the Sensational Story of "Acid House")'**   383

    From: *Club Cultures: Music, Media and Subcultural Capital.* Hanover, NH: Wesleyan University Press, 1996.

32. **Tricia Rose. 'A Style Nobody Can Deal With: Politics, Style and the Postindustrial City in Hip Hop'**   401

    From: *Microphone Fiends: Youth Music and Youth Culture.* Ed. Andrew Ross and Tricia Rose. New York and London: Routledge, 1994.

33. **Cynthia Fuchs. 'If I Had a Dick: Queers, Punks, and Alternative Acts'**   417

    From: *Mapping the Beat: Popular Music and Contemporary Theory.* Ed. Thomas Swiss, John Sloop and Andrew Herman. Oxford: Blackwell Publishers, 1998.

34. **Judith Halberstam. 'Drag Kings: Masculinity and Performance'**   429

    From: *Female Masculinity.* Durham, NC: Duke University Press, 2000.

*VII.   LOCATING*: SPACE, PLACE, AND POWER                441

**35.  Michel de Certeau. 'Walking in the City'**                449

From: *The Practice of Everyday Life.* Berkeley, CA:
University of California Press, 1984.

**36.  Michael Nevin Willard. 'Séance, Tricknowlogy,
Skateboarding, and the Space of Youth'**                462

From: *Generations of Youth: Youth Cultures and History in
Twentieth-Century America.* Ed. Joe Austin and Michael Nevin
Willard. New York: New York University Press, 1998.

**37.  Victor Hugo Viesca. '*Straight Out the Barrio*: Ozomatli and
the Importance of Place in the Formation of Chicano/a
Popular Culture in Los Angeles'**                479

From: *Cultural Values* 4.4 (October), 2000.

**38.  Paul Gilroy. 'Wearing Your Art on Your Sleeve: Notes
Towards a Diaspora History of Black Ephemera'**                495

From: *Small Acts: Thoughts on the Politics of Black Cultures.*
London: Serpent's Tail, 1993.

**39.  George Lipsitz. 'Diasporic Noise: History, Hip Hop,
and the Post-Colonial Politics of Sound'**                504

From: *Dangerous Crossroads: Popular Music, Postmodernism and
The Poetics of Place.* New York and London: Verso, 1994.

**40.  Lisa Nakamura. 'Head-Hunting on the Internet: Identity
Tourism, Avatars, and Racial Passing in Textual and
Graphic Chat Spaces'**                520

From: *Cybertypes: Race, Ethnicity, and Identity on the Internet.*
London: Routledge, 2002.

**Index**                534

# Entangling the Popular: An Introduction to *Popular Culture: A Reader*

Parallel to the ever ubiquitous presence of 7 Eleven and just behind a *tacqueria*, we came across a most unusual façade in a city known for bewildering visual landscapes. Whether driving, waiting for a bus, or walking, one can't help but notice this tattered front. There is a haphazard mixture of grafittied words, stickers, and massive posters glued to its walls. Upon first glance, one immediately asks: 'What is this place?' The immense 'Obey' poster of Andre the Giant's face next to a poster of Angela Davis circa early 1970s, and a mural of Vladimir Lenin in now common Obey-esque graphics, and a virtually unreadable banner flapping over the forbidding entrance to … . Oh yes, there is one more sign. It is small, hand painted, and barely visible. The wooden placard reads: 'It's a skate shop!' A second glance, now that we've been enlightened as to the nature of this structure, still doesn't reveal any obvious connection between the products sold and its façade. The flapping banner does provide what we now understand to be the name of this elusive place. 'Juvee'. And the banner does contain an image, not of a skateboard but of a young turntablist. The only blatant relation to skateboards and skate equipment is found in the form of stickers wallpapering the open door. Juvee certainly does not present either its products or its sense of place in the marketing rhetoric of 'extreme' sports, Gen X sport star endorsements, and culture industry caricatures that range from video games to Hollywood film, from fast food (for example, Stouffers' 'Maxaroni') to soft drinks (Mountain Dew's marketing slogan – 'Do the Dew').

Juvee entangles its subject. What does the act of skating have to do with Lenin? The black power movement? These are hardly iconic in the world of Tony Hawk video games and ESPN2's X-Games! On the surface of Juvee skating, youth culture, urban space, Los Angeles geographies, street graphics, and the history of radical politics mix. Like the hands of the cartoon DJ depicted over its threshold, Juvee's façade mixes political ideology, style, and commerce. The function of these 'samples' is not immediately apparent, yet they demand that the subject of skating, or perhaps popular culture in general, be understood as configurations that are neither smooth nor always obvious. The messy blend of signs that Juvee uses to create its public face are hardly silenced once Juvee announces its actual purpose to be the sale of skate gear. If anything, its semantically complicated and irreducible façade alerts us that the study of popular culture requires a mindset that can handle such complexity and even contradiction.

Our description of the richness of this particular cultural composite is intended to serve as an illustration of the equally rich composite of the popular that the essays in this book promote. *Popular Culture: A Reader* provides a range of scholarly approaches to its subject matter. Its purpose is to show how such interventions have played a key role in shaping what we understand by the concept. This presents a major challenge because what gives the study of popular culture its richness also makes it a rather unwieldy subject. Specifically, any careful consideration of popular culture's intellectual histories will show that it reflects neither a unified way of thinking nor an easily mapped path of development. Formal interest in popular culture may be heavily rooted in European thought – the 'Great Tradition' of literary critique, the Frankfurt Institute for Social Research, and the interdisciplinary workings of the Birmingham Centre for Contemporary Cultural Studies, to name a few highly influential examples – but it far from envelops the ways that popular culture has been theorized. A great deal of influential work has also emerged from North America. Michael Denning, for example, makes a compelling argument for the interwar emergence of the popular front as a wide-scale 'laboring of culture'. According to Denning, 'the heart of this cultural front was a new generation of plebian artists and intellectuals who had grown up in the immigrant and black working-class neighborhoods of the modernist metropolis' (1997: xv). Considerations of diaspora and the intercultural regional dynamics of areas like the black Atlantic, the Pacific Rim, and the Caribbean have further enriched the means by which we can recognize and understand the workings of popular culture.

Moreover, popular culture has frequently been considered from diverse disciplinary perspectives. Unlike the study of poetry, more or less predictably housed in language departments, the study of popular culture has taken place under the rubrics of sociology, music, communications, media studies, cinema studies, history, economics, and so on. Matters are further complicated in the USA because popular culture's common home within cultural studies has frequently been an extension of literary studies. In conjunction with disciplinary bounds, the study of popular culture in the classroom is ever burdened with the imposing challenge of generational divide and the related issue of canon formation. Carla Freccero's *Popular Culture: An Introduction* (1999) accurately points out that contemporary students do not share a standardized cultural canon, the type of canon that has frequently served as a counterpoint for critics of popular culture in the past. Far in advance of Freccero's observation, Marshall McLuhan recalls an early teaching experience of comparable significance. The following story is recounted in a 1967 interview with G.E. Stearn in *McLuhan Hot & Cool*:

In 1936, when I arrived at Wisconsin, I confronted classes of freshmen and I suddenly realized that I was incapable of understanding them. I felt an urgent need to study their popular culture: advertising, games, movies. It was a pedagogy, part of my teaching program. To meet them on their grounds was my strategy in pedagogy: the world of pop culture. (1967: 303)

In recognition of such challenges, this *Reader* adopts a proviso elaborated within Stuart Hall and Paddy Whannel's *The Popular Arts* (1964): in order to best meet the needs of 'media-saturated pupils', teaching practices should engage popular forms. Our introductory essay surveys key words such as mass, popular, and culture to determine both how they have been understood and the context of their analysis. As we touch upon approaches to these key words, we discuss a range of related concepts and schools of thought that have been recognized as markers of pivotal transformation in the way that the distinctly modern phenomenon of popular culture and the issues that it informs have been conceived. Our gloss of the competing intellectual projects that have shaped the study of popular culture begins with the late nineteenth-century and extends only to the 1970s because this period forms the backdrop for the bulk of material contained within this *Reader*. Since most of the selections that we include reflect developments in the study of popular culture since the 1980s, commentary on recent work is treated in detail in the short introductions that precede each section of the book. The general introduction offers students a general sense of how we got here.

The danger of such an approach, one that recounts the development of a canon, is that it can very easily replicate that canon. Nevertheless, recognition of the processes that create a canon can be remarkably useful.[1] Within them are traces of the social, economic and political factors that have shaped discussions of the popular. Our approach emphasizes that scholarship on popular culture has not emerged in a vacuum. Theorists and critics have actively considered and often responded to social and material developments in their environments through their work on popular culture. It also stresses that the study of popular culture has been heterogeneous and in foregrounding both the context of its production and the competing projects that have endeavored to define it, we hope to provide the sort of textured survey of popular culture's intellectual history that shows the specificity and impact of its gender, class, and racial assumptions.

A commonly held view on popular culture is that it is simultaneously incredibly easy to talk about (Juvee is after all a skateshop) and incredibly difficult to talk about (a skateshop that associates skating with histories of urban radical politics). Reasons for this apparently paradoxical view are that the popular is astonishingly pervasive and that intellectual polemics have targeted popular culture as an overwhelming influence on historical perceptions of, and social relations to, culture. *Popular Culture: A Reader* remains sensitive to this pervasiveness. It addresses the combination of economic, technological, political, social and cultural shifts that shape our ability to define popular culture. The essays that it contains provide a sense of the stakes and complexities that characterize the realm of the popular as well as its material and ideological expression in our daily lives. In other words, the famous maxim by Raymond Williams that 'culture' is one of 'the two or three most complicated words in the English language' (1976: 87) is no doubt as true today as when first uttered in 1976. The etymology of 'culture', as Williams and others have shown, is a complex assemblage produced through distinct Western philosophical and literary traditions. Antiquity understood 'culture' (*colere*) and 'civilization' (*civis*) to act in similar ways: as both a socialization process of 'cultivation', and membership of and identification with the *polis*. 'Civilizing' was a political, moral, and ethical process premised upon 'an achieved state, which could be contrasted with 'barbarism' [and] an achieved state *of development*, which implied historical process and progress' (Williams, 1976: 13). In contrast, Richard Drinnon argues that modern writers have *not* used the terms so interchangeably. His book, *Facing West: The Metaphysics of Indian Hating and Empire Building*, explains that in making a distinction between 'culture' and 'civilization' writers like Sigmund Freud have employed the latter 'to distinguish Western superculture, or the one true "civilization", from so-called primitive cultures' (1990: xxviii). This semantic shift, whereby civilization comes to connote a unity that contrasts the plurality of cultures that abound, has infused debates over culture in general and popular culture in particular with potentially ethnocentric hierarchies. Much recent scholarship on the subject has worked to uncover and, in some cases, to counter the implications embedded within these connotations.

Certain nineteenth-century developments have played a particularly prominent role in constituting today's understanding of culture as a special enclave of a society's values.[2] Most notably, a powerful literary tradition characterized by new ideas on culture emerged in response to the industrialization of the epoch and the social transformations for which it was responsible. Romantic works like Samuel Taylor Coleridge's *Constitution of Church and State* (1837) and Thomas Carlyle's *Signs of the Times* (1829) actively engage the social, economic, political, and technological changes transforming culture and humanity within the modern age. Coleridge draws a distinction between the concepts of 'culture' and 'civilization'. 'Culture' becomes an active, spiritual, process ('cultivation'), whereas 'civilization' is associated with the violence of modernization. Carlyle argues that the reorganization of the social through the 'mechanical age' of industrialization and capitalism demanded human culture to seek refuge in a literary elite. Both writers place 'culture' in the hands of a vanguard, a literary intelligentsia called on to protect and preserve its integrity. Influenced by Coleridge as well as Plato's *Republic*, Matthew Arnold's *Culture and Anarchy* (1869) defines 'culture' as 'the best that has been thought and said in the world', thus continuing to equate 'culture' with 'goodness'. The latter is, in turn, conceived as 'a study of perfection'. The pursuit of perfection (or 'cultivated inaction') exists in opposition to the unrefined working-class culture of the 'populace'. This culture of the populace, emanating from 'the raw and unkindled masses', is for Arnold dangerous and destructive. He goes so far as to brand it 'anarchy'. Like Coleridge and Carlyle, Arnold demands an intervention: the State and the institution of education would have to function as policing agents to civilize the populace.

If 'culture' is indeed as complicated a word as Williams claims, what then are students to make of its numerous antecedent adjectives like 'folk', 'mass' and 'popular'? How might they come to terms with even more recent pairings like 'counterculture', 'subculture', 'common culture', or 'mainstream culture'? Popular, in particular, has heralded heated debate because (like Juvee) it is not always necessarily clear what we're looking at when we look to popular culture. Its definitions are historically contingent and therefore frequently incongruous. It draws from the connotations of 'folk culture' often evoked to conceptualize the cultural practices and forms (for instance, the folksongs of an oral tradition, dance, and material culture) circulating in pre-industrial and pre-urban societies, and is notoriously irreverent of the boundaries meant to distinguish mass-produced culture from more 'organic' or ostensibly 'rooted' culture. For these reasons, it is worth taking the time to elaborate on the development of these words' interconnected meanings.

The influence of Carlyle, Coleridge, and Arnold's complementary views helped establish a hierarchy for making sense of culture – a hierarchy premised upon separations between culture and civilization, the equation of 'culture' with perfection and goodness, and social progress/order (cultural preservation) through education – that has lasted well into the twentieth century. This is evidenced as recently as the publication of Allan Bloom's *The Closing of the American Mind* (1987) and E.D. Hirsch's *Cultural Literacy* (1992), though the most prominent examples of this legacy are consolidated in the works of F.R. Leavis, Q.D. Leavis and Denys Thompson. An additional proponent of this trajectory has been T.S. Eliot.[3] Like Arnold, Eliot maintains a Platonic view of society: the cultural decline of his period is attributed to a leveling of social classes, the democratization of high culture, erosion of religious faith, and the degradation of culture brought about by the 'lower standards' produced through mass education. The mass or 'substitute' culture of Eliot's period takes the blame for gradual destruction of the high class or 'elite' culture within which 'goodness', 'cultural heritage', and 'tradition' work in accordance with Christian values to maintain a 'whole way of life'. For the Leavises, culture presented itself via two forms: a 'minority culture' that preserves and transmits the literary tradition indicative of Arnold's 'best that has been thought and said' and through commercial culture aimed at an uneducated mass ('mass civilization'). The mass media of the press, popular novels, radio, and film were thought to be expressive of the 'cultural leveling' that the Leavises feared would replace the influence of minority culture. Like their nineteenth-century predecessors, these critics called for a vanguard to house and protect culture from the influences of the masses and mass culture. An organic view of culture unobstructed by industrial society, commercial interests, and mass media colors their respective works. Folk culture, derived from the German word *volk* for 'people', 'common people', or 'the masses', signals a form of culture thought to originate from the elusive category 'the people'. It is often regarded as culture *made by* or *of* 'the people' and, for this reason, has been thought to serve the needs and interests of its producers. Critics of mass-produced culture like Eliot predictably champion (and mourn the posited loss of) folk culture of an imagined pre-industrial epoch as a homogeneous, more 'authentic', and 'organic' experience in contradistinction to capitalist society. With this maneuver, they simultaneously idealize folk culture of earlier epochs, and place it in opposition to the supposed 'cultural decline' of the interwar period.[4]

Clearly, a great deal of political and social investment typifies claims about mass culture. Williams, whose entry on this word appears in this collection, explains that powerful positive and negative connotations of the term vie for prominence: mass as 'something amorphous and indistinguishable' and mass as 'an avoidance of unnecessary division or fragmentation and thus an achievement of unity'. Historically, mass culture has been deemed contrary to both the posited authenticity of culture untarnished by reproduction and high culture premised upon social and cultural hierarchies. Mass-produced commodities have been regarded as inauthentic, formulaic, simplistic, and banal. Because they are designed to appeal to global commercial markets rather than reflect the specificity of unique cultural expression, many have and continue to argue that such objects neither challenge aesthetically, morally or spiritually, nor promote active engagement and critical contemplation. Where the German intellectual tradition of the nineteenth century invested in the concept of *kultur* as emblematic of creative achievements in the arts and humanities, the opposite can be said to inform mass culture. If *kultur* addresses 'high' or 'elite' European culture, mass (*masse*) covers the gambit of the 'low', 'common' or 'plebian'. It is culture for the uneducated and the uncultured, a purportedly indiscriminate consuming majority.

In the interwar period, Max Horkheimer and Theodor Adorno's collaboration produced a highly influential approach to mass culture. Their work on the culture industry (a neologism meant to suggest a paradox in that 'culture' was thought to be antithetical to 'industry') asserts that this institution 'has molded people as a type unfailingly reproduced in every product' (1944: 127).[5] Not just products, but themselves as product called consumer, is what the culture industry offers its audience.[6] Miriam Bratu Hansen makes this point abundantly clear as she points out that in *Dialectic of Enlightenment*, 'Horkheimer and Adorno ascribe the effectivity of mass-cultural scripts of identity not simply to the viewers' manipulation as passive consumers, but rather to their very solicitation as experts, as active readers' (1997: 89). Particular to the culture industry, however, 'is that the irreconcilable elements of culture, art and distraction, are subordinated to one end and subsumed under one false formula: the totality of the culture industry' (1997: 136). Art critic Clement Greenberg shared Adorno and Horkheimer's disdain for mass culture. His 'Avant-Garde and Kitsch', which originally appeared in the *Partisan Review* (1939) criticizes mechanical reproduction and the mass production of culture. 'Kitsch', his term of choice for mass culture, is used in a derogatory sense. It connotes a tawdry and tasteless absence of aesthetic purpose: it is cultural production dismissed as inferior and designed to appeal only to the popular tastes believed to epitomize mass markets. As kitsch, mass culture marks a crisis in the separation between high and low culture, which leads Greenberg to describe it as 'a spreading epidemic' that replaces the dominant role of the avant-garde as gatekeepers of taste and culture.

While associated with the Frankfurt School, Walter Benjamin's deliberations on culture mark a break from the distrustful position of his contemporaries. The theorization of mass culture that he advances in 'The Work of Art in the Age of Mechanical Reproduction' (1992 [1936]) attributes a potentially powerful political element to the consumption of mass culture. For example, Benjamin focuses on mechanical reproduction, the means by which capitalism mass-produces commodities, in order to posit a participatory, potentially democratic relationship to consumption, rather than the negative and authoritarian understanding maintained by the culture industry thesis. The passivity assigned to the consumption of mass culture is transformed, such that 'mechanical reproduction of art changes the reactions of the masses towards art'. In other words, mechanical reproduction's ability to change our relationship to art by making it more accessible (which Benjamin argues also makes it less auratic) pressures a reconceptualization of the function and nature of art rather than appraisal of mass culture from the privileged perspective of high culture. A great deal of subsequent cultural criticism has swung between the contrasting though not at all unrelated positions of the Frankfurt School.

The potential of popular culture has also been powerfully theorized by Antonio Gramsci. Gramsci, who was both a writer (an essayist in particular) and a political activist, played a leading role in the Italian Socialist Party. Until his death in 1937 Gramsci produced a body of work (over 2,000 pages of articles, essays, and fragments), some of which has been collected in *Selections from the Prison Notebooks* (1971). One of the most influential themes to develop within the *Notebooks* is that of hegemony. Above all, hegemony represents Gramsci's answer to economic reductionism. As Chantal Mouffe writes, hegemony comes to represent the 'complete fusion of economic, political, intellectual and moral objectives

which will be brought about by one fundamental group and group
it *through the intermediary of ideology* when an ideology manages
throughout the whole of society not only united economic and political
but also intellectual and moral unity'" (1979: 181, italics in original). T
enables a hegemonic class to articulate the interests of other social gro
own by means of ideological struggle.[7] From the perspective of hegemony theory,
popular culture is a contradictory mix of competing interests, values and shifting
balances; yet Gramsci's concept came into prominence as a major theoretical tool
for explaining popular culture's position within power relations long after his
death. For example, it has played a major role in the development of British
cultural studies and is clearly evident in Stuart Hall and Tony Jefferson's edited
collection, *Resistance through Rituals: Youth Subcultures in Post-war Britain*
(1976) and Dick Hebdige's *Subculture: The Meaning of Style* (1979);[8] while Ranajit
Guha has adapted Gramsci's theory of hegemony to considerations of colonialism
in *Dominance without Hegemony: History and Power in Colonial India* (1998).

In the immediate post-war period, work on mass-produced culture reflected both
a new set of concerns and new ways of thinking about the relationship of culture
and society. The advance of the Cold War greatly impacted conceptualizations of
culture. Recognition of popular culture's *overt* political role heightened substantially and distress over the effects of 'Americanization' abounded. The type of cultural criticism produced significantly broadened the scope of earlier debates on
mass culture. Attempts to determine and maintain distinctions between mass and
high culture persisted, yet they also gave way to far broader considerations of culture than had previously been entertained.[9] The analytical tools brought to bear
on these expanded deliberations were drawn from disciplines like linguistics,
communications, and anthropology.

For example, Gary Genosko, author *of McLuhan and Baudrillard: The Masters
of Implosion* (1999), claims that the publication of Marshall McLuhan's *The
Mechanical Bride: Folklore of Industrial Man* (1951), Roland Barthes' *Mythologies*
(1957), and Richard Hoggart's *The Uses of Literacy* (1957) marked a shift in
cultural criticism of post-war popular forms. He emphasizes that each writer
expresses a 'sense of regret' about: 'the emergence of a mythic consciousness whose
distinguishing feature was that it did not want to be identified and that it erased
itself in order to more fully and powerfully perfuse and influence social and
cultural life: French bourgeois ideology ex-nominates itself; American magazines
offer satisfyingly comprehensive attitudes and opinions to their readers; and
the emerging mass form is a "faceless", "classless" and "characterless" culture'
(Hoggart, 1957: 31–2). McLuhan, therefore, opens his preface to *The Mechanical
Bride* with a new and striking metaphor – that of a whirlpool – through which to
conceive of mass media. If mass media is a whirlpool, then McLuhan advocates
that we ride the current, rather than attempt to hold our hands up against the
onslaught of the deluge. For it is precisely in such a critical appropriation of the
cultural material in circulation that new strategies for dealing with mass culture
can be created, or as McLuhan himself queries: 'Why not use the new commercial
education as a means to enlightening its intended prey?' (1951: v). Barthes, who
approached the whirlpool from the perspective of Marxian semiology, sought to
understand the *mélange* of signs that informed the ideological structure of cultural
meaning and meaningfulness that he refers to as 'myth'. His purpose, as stated in
the Preface to the 1957 edition of *Mythologies*, was 'to reflect regularly on some

myths of French daily life' (11); a task that he carried out on phenomena as diverse as wrestling, toys, film, automobiles, and food. Barthes' work infused analyses of culture with new dimensions and analytical possibilities, for it maintained that the most powerful work of mass culture was carried out not at the level of primary signification (or what it denotes), but at the level of its secondary signification (or connotation). The intelligibility of secondary signification, in turn, rests on the culture at large in the same way that a word means something in relation to the language of which it is a part.[10] Hoggart, who focuses his attention on the British working class, explores the idea that culture might include a wide array of common activities. He interprets such activities by way of literary paradigms, and in doing so effects quite a dramatic break from the emphasis of early twentieth-century debates on the superiority of high culture. As Graeme Turner spells out in *British Cultural Studies: An Introduction*:

> *The Uses of Literacy* observes conflicting social and theoretical allegiances: to both the culture and civilization tradition from which its ideological assumptions and analytical practices proceed, and to a working-class cultural and political tradition that acknowledges significance in the *whole* of the cultural field. (1996: 45)

The emphasis that Hoggart places on the cultural character of the working class, a unity based on shared traditions, rituals, speech and status, feeds an admitted nostalgia for a vision of organic working-class culture as a way of life, a nostalgia that stems from concerns over the effects of Americanization and mass culture on the cohesion of this way of life.

These and other authors took up a range of concerns that emanated from major shifts in the organization of political power across the globe. For example, although not included in Genosko's survey of 1950s cultural criticism, Raymond Williams added his voice to Hoggart's call for a broad yet thoroughly nuanced understanding of culture as the fabric of social life. Williams' work charted a path that variously unsettled and reinforced aspects of the early twentieth century's literary and aesthetic position on mass culture. This is especially apparent in the statement that 'culture is ordinary', which was the basis of an article published in Norman McKenzie's *Convictions* (1958) and further developed in Williams' *The Long Revolution* (1961).[11] Henri Lefebvre also effected a considerable contribution to the development of intellectual work on mass culture in his analyses of the French 'everyday' and 'everyday life'.[12] For Lefebvre, a Marxist humanist who was greatly concerned over American influence on French culture, the everyday is a concept that refers to several things: reified and alienated life under capitalism, pleasure and resistance by members of a community, and a psychic relationship between objects and persons. Such a focus on the everyday emanates from a desire to foreground the importance of transforming consciousness by changing the routines and material elements of daily life, and from the belief that: 'In order to change life, society, space, architecture, even the city must change' (1987: 73). As Kristin Ross points out in 'French Quotidian': 'In the 1950s and 60s, something that could be called Americanism (or multinational capital, in another formulation) was insinuating itself into France not by means of any heavy-handed ideological takeover but precisely through the quotidian: blue jeans, car culture, cleaning products' (1997: 22). The concept of 'everyday life' was in no way restricted to the 1950s and 1960s. The English translation of Michel de Certeau's *The Practice of Everyday Life* (1984) reintroduced the concept along with an influential study of everyday practices ('ways of operating') that ranged from walking in cities to reading tactics. These ideas were incorporated into the study of popular culture in the USA through work on media fandom, audience, and the active pleasures of discriminating consumption.[13]

This brings us to a point where we might begin to understand how competing positions over what constitutes culture, and the role of mass culture and folk culture in these positions, come to inform a working understanding of the popular. The term 'popular' houses a broad range of meanings. Incorporating folk culture's link to organic community – of the people – as well as mass culture's status – being well liked or merely widely available – popular culture brings together diverse and sometimes contradictory associations. As many essays contained within this *Reader* will attest, the word 'popular' is often dismissed outright as vulgar or cheap, used interchangeably with or in place of 'mass', or popular culture is championed as a term synonymous with 'the people's' experiences with and discriminating uses of mass-produced commodities. For example, in his 'A Theory of Mass Culture' (1957 [1953]) Dwight Macdonald opts to use 'mass' rather than 'popular', since being 'solely and directly an article for mass consumption' (p. 59) renders an object unworthy of the title 'popular'. Andrew Ross, when working through US post-war mass culture debates in *No Respect: Intellectuals and Popular Culture* (1989) prefers 'popular' to 'mass' because of the connotations of elitism that mark 'mass'. And John Fiske diligently distinguishes 'folk' from 'popular' when he writes that 'popular culture is made out of industrially produced and distributed commodities that must, in order to be economically viable and thus to exist at all, offer a variety of cultural potentialities to a variety of social formations' (1989: 170).

Most profoundly, however, the intellectual shifts that pressed toward a reckoning of the popular have sought to understand how it is a site of struggle where the ability to create meaning is recognized as a significant form of power. Such work on popular culture, which has grown exponentially since the 1960s, also actively reflects social and political transformations, including but not limited to a wide array of interconnected political interventions ranging from new feminisms, civil rights activities, decolonization and class-based movements. For example, the mass political mobilization of workers and students in 1968 is frequently hailed as a watershed event, particularly for French intellectuals, and by extension their contribution to the shape of scholarly inquiry into popular culture.[14] These events indelibly marked a generation of scholars, scholars like Louis Althusser, Michel Foucault, Jean Baudrillard, Gilles Deleuze, Félix Guattari, Guy Debord, and Henri Lefebvre, who wrote about and theorized the period as well as its implications for future political and intellectual work.[15]

In the USA, the late 1960s and early 1970s were characterized by fierce countercultural movements, anti-war protest, and radical political activism. Examples include the efforts of the Black Power movement, emergent Chicano/a nationalism (frequently linked with pronounced labor advocacy), gay and lesbian rights campaigns, disability awareness, and new dimensions of feminist protest. There was also change within the academy itself. The social and political transformations of the post-war era ushered in a diversity of scholars, including more people of color and from working-class origins. These scholars' experience impacted what would be studied and how. Ethnic studies, postcolonial studies and cultural studies would not exist today without this influx of scholars, for as traditional organizations of power were challenged so too were traditional ways of organizing knowledge. Ultimately, this created the basis for profound breaks in the constitution of authority that connected a commitment to radical change and social justice with the production of new knowledge.

The late twentieth century witnessed a great diversification of issues and approaches that structured intellectual engagements with popular culture. For example, the Birmingham Centre for Contemporary Cultural Studies focused much of its energies on what analyses of youth could tell us about meaning and agency in the post-war cultural realm.[16] The British journal *Screen* utilized Lacanian psychoanalysis and Althusserian elaboration of ideology to explore the relationship between identity, visual media and power at approximately the same time. Feminist film criticism and analyses of other forms of cultural production – from television to romance novels and from pornography to subculture – powerfully transformed how the politics of culture are perceived to operate.[17] Considerations of gender and sexuality have, in turn, been fruitfully informed by the significant epistemological and historical work of queer theory.[18]

The study of popular culture also came to supplement the analyses of the everyday, audience, and pleasure mentioned earlier in relation to de Certeau with detailed considerations of postmodernism (Fredric Jameson (1991) *Postmodernism, or, the Cultural Logic of Late Capitalism*; Jim Collins (1989) *Uncommon Culture: Popular Culture and Post-Moderism*; Angela McRobbie (1994) *Postmodernism and Popular Culture*; George Lipsitz (1990) *Time Passages: Collective Memory and American Popular Culture*; E. Ann Kaplan (1987) *Rocking Around the Clock: Music Television, Postmodernism and Consumer Culture*) and fandom (Constance Penley (1997) *Nasa/Trek: Popular Science and Sex in America*; Henry Jenkins (1992) *Textual Poachers: Television Fans and Participatory Culture*; Lisa A. Lewis (ed.) (1992) *The Adoring Audience: Fan Culture and Popular Media*). Concurrently, a shift in emphasis toward the role of globalization (Arjun Appadurai (2001) *Globalization*; John Tomlinson (1999) *Globalization and Culture*; Fredric Jameson and Masao Miyoshi (eds) (1998) *The Cultures of Globalization*; Reinhold Wagnleitner and Elaine Tyler May (eds) (2000) *Here, There and Everywhere: The Foreign Politics of American Popular Culture*) and diaspora (Rey Chow (1993) *Writing Diaspora: Tactics of Intervention in Contemporary Cultural Studies*; George Lipsitz (1994) *Dangerous Crossroads: Popular Music, Postmodernism and the Poetics of Place*; Paul Gilroy (1993) *The Black Atlantic: Modernity and Double Consciousness*) along with renewed interest in the study of imperialism (Edward Said (1993) *Culture and Imperialism*; Amy Kaplan and Donald Pease (eds) (1994) *Cultures of United States Imperialism*) has contributed to more intricate engagements with identity. Work on visual and material culture (Lynn Spigel (1992) *Make Room for TV*; Anna McCarthy (2001) *Ambient Television: Visual Culture and Public Space*; Dick Hebdige (1988) *Hiding in the Light: On Images and Things*; Jeffrey Sconce (2000) *Haunted Media*), as well as new media (Lisa Nakamura (2002) *Cybertypes: Race, Ethnicity and Identity on the Internet*; Justine Cassell and Henry Jenkins (eds) (1998), *From Barbie to Mortal Kombat: Gender and Computer Games*; Paul Théberge (1997) *Any Sound You Can Imagine*; Alondra Nelson, Thuy Linh N. Tu and Alisa Headlam Hines (eds) (2001) *Technicolor: Race, Technology and Everyday Life*; Noah Wardrip-Fruin and Pat Harrigan (eds) (2004) *First Person: New Media as Story, Performance and Game*) account for the changes to media that impact contemporary experiences of the popular. In brief, there is no longer a clearly dominant paradigm. Like Juvee's façade, it takes time to digest the 'mixed-bag' approach that we operate with today. As Freccero insisted, there is no popular canon that students possess, and there is no canon by which scholars of popular culture abide. Biography works alongside ethnography. Textual analysis accompanies studies of economics.

Our *Reader* welcomes this moment. And it does so by acknowledging the relationship between historically situated debates on mass/popular culture and the wide range of knowledge production on the subject of popular culture today. We hope that the preceding paragraphs demonstrate just how much popular culture has been characterized by change, for this is precisely what we try to illustrate through our selection and organization of diverse subject matter. As a result, the presentation of popular culture tendered by this *Reader* begins with and rests on a key premise: that popular culture is the site of a dynamic process – a zone of interaction, where relationships are made and unmade to produce anything from meaning to pleasure, from the trite to the powerful. Three factors in this dynamic that most frequently structure developments in and experiences of popular culture include its status as a product of industry, an intellectual object of inquiry, and an integral component of people's lives. Considerations of production, conceptualization and practice are therefore brought together to promote an engaging and informative elucidation of the subject.

This structure illuminates the motives behind this book's organization. It speaks to why specific scholarly interventions have been highlighted to represent the significance that popular culture currently commands. More specifically, *Popular Culture: A Reader* is composed of edited articles and chapters from fields within the humanities, such as cultural studies, media studies, queer theory, American studies, and ethnic studies, that assemble a cross-section of trans-Atlantic popular practices examined from a number of perspectives. This heterogeneous group of interventions mark general turning points in the shape of popular culture study in the USA and the UK.

Essays are placed within seven complementary thematic sections, each framed by a brief expository introduction. Each section combines essays that engage, extend, and critique the specific conceptual actions being explored within this book. The seven thematic sections are:

Delineating: Culture–Mass–Popular
Commodifying: The Commodity, Culture and Social Life
Marketing: Socio-economic Considerations of Popular Culture
Practicing: Popular Tastes and Ways of Consuming
Voicing: Identities and Articulation
Styling: Subculture and Popular Performance
Locating: Space, Place, and Power

Let us explain exactly why we have organized the *Reader* in such a manner. To organize the essays into useful themes through which to analyze specific aspects of popular culture, we have opted to categorize them according to seven present participles. Each of the verbs we have chosen signifies an action or a process, and in applying familiar language in a verb form we hope to speak to the present condition of popular culture's uses as well as the array of actions that it carries out.

Although the titles are not intended to exhaust the diverse actions of the essays that they name, they do give a fair indication of relationships between the essays. They offer a flexible yet recognizable means of helping readers who may be grappling, perhaps for the first time, with the study of popular culture. We hope that you will find this decision an illuminating and intentionally self-reflexive example of the collection's project.

On the one hand, we do not feel that a *Reader* on popular culture for a twenty-first-century student body can be organized into sections premised upon specific media. Topics like 'mass literature', 'motion pictures', 'television and radio' may have successfully allowed the critics of *Mass Culture: The Popular Arts in America* (Rosenberg and White, 1957) to consider popular phenomena of their day; however in the epoch of media convergence, new media, digital technology and remediation, this separation becomes increasingly difficult and far from desirable. Popular culture is experienced, produced, practiced, marketed, lived, and consumed ubiquitously due to the ever-increasing presence of media technology in all aspects of everyday life and the entertainment industry's cross-market repurposing practices. (Herein lies the main significance of our emphasis on the commodity form!)[19] Contemporary popular culture's presence is not defined by a single medium, which means that considerations of media within a collection on popular culture should, and in this *Reader* do, traverse and interconnect all sections.

On the other hand, and in an attempt to forgo historical or paradigmatic hierarchy, the conceptual actions are designed to be fundamentally pluralistic. Each actively endeavors to engineer a minute, *site-specific* consideration of broad intellectual categories such as Marxism, structuralism and postmodernism because adherence to such categories can easily push discourses on feminism, race, ethnicity, and sexuality to sideline positions. The latter may appear as brief chapters or subsections within a larger normative tale of popular culture's history overdetermined by Western literary traditions and their investments in British and American cultural studies. For us, it is of the utmost importance that the social histories and processes behind the experience of identity are central to any understanding of the stakes and operations of popular culture. To consider popular culture as a dynamic process is to stress a set of axiomatic principles. First, all aspects of popular culture are political. Secondly, the caliber of engagement with popular culture that we are calling for requires an understanding of both the history and development of the commodity form. And thirdly, the significance of popular culture is impacted by its relation to social movements and transformations in social consciousness. For this reason, considerations of racialization, gender, sexuality and class also run through each section of the book.

Lastly, *Popular Culture: A Reader* provides its users with a 'play list' at the end of each section introduction. Borrowing from the performance set of live music and the arrangement of self-produced compilation cassette tapes, CDs and MP3 libraries, the play lists extend the performance of this *Reader*'s ideas and contents. They are composed of familiar academic texts (books, edited collections, articles) dedicated to the study of popular culture, films and music that have been discussed within the section as well as media that address the specific section's emphasis, and popular texts (magazines, fanzines, web pages) that critically speak from within and to popular culture phenomena. Meant to stand in for and enlarge the function of the standard 'suggested readings' included in similar collections, our play lists take a step toward acknowledging the diverse media and disparate practices through which popular culture is expressed. Though obviously bound by the limitations of print media (not least of which are binding and general production expenses), we hope that the play lists will surpass aspects of the book's restrictions and allow the user to study the popular *across* culture.

## Notes

1. After such an exegesis it is important to note that there are many ways to narrate the history of approaches to popular culture. One might, for example, be inclined to trace the way we think about popular culture to antiquity. Plato or Aristotle's pronouncements on the popular reception of drama and their subsequent impact on the shape of modern views of culture would be useful for an analysis of the popular that focuses on aesthetics (formalism, taste, etc.). In contrast, Henry Jenkins, Tara McPherson and Jane Shattuc organize their introduction to *Hop on Pop* (2002), a collection of new work on the subject of popular culture, according to the field's initial anthropological cast, followed by an account of commercialization and the impact of taste and power relations on the way that popular culture has been understood. These points are followed by Marxist perspectives on the popular as well as their legacy in the form of critical theory. Ultimately, the introduction to popular culture provided by *Hop on Pop* speaks to the volume's investment in the politics of pleasure that motivate a major contemporary trajectory in the study of the popular. What we are trying to demonstrate by this account of the ways that popular culture can be approached is that although the history of the study of popular culture has attained the status of doctrine that the initiated can rattle off with ease, what is compelling about the study of popular culture is that each addition to the conversation has the potential to radically transform the way that the concept and field, as well as the stakes that animate it, function.

2. The roots of these ideas may also be said to extend to antiquity. For example, in Aristotle's *Nicomachean Ethics,* 'the good' is expressed through fulfillment of a teleology, or essential purpose. The essential purpose of human beings is to realize their nature, which he identifies as the correspondence of the soul and reason. Human culture is thus an expression of this self-realization. The function and character of culture have since been continually reshaped and successive views on humanity have generated their own position on the role of culture in human development.

3. See F.R. Leavis (1930) *Mass Civilisation and Minority Culture,* included in this volume; Q.D. Leavis (1978) *Fiction and the Reading Public;* F.R. Leavis and Denys Thompson (1933) *Culture and Environment;* and T.S. Eliot (1948) *Notes Towards the Definition of Culture.*

4. Such work paints specific pictures of what folk culture looks like in contrast to the culture of mass civilization. According to Eliot, culture includes 'all the characteristic activities and interests of a people: Derby Day, Henley Regatta, Cowes, the twelfth of August, a cup final, the dog races, the pin table, the dart board, Wensleydale cheese, boiled cabbage cut into sections, beetroot in vinegar, nineteenth-century Gothic churches and the music of Elgar' (1948: 31). The 'loss' recorded in Leavis and Thompson's *Culture and Environment* presents itself in the following way: 'Folk-songs, folk-dances, Cotswold cottages and handicraft products are signs of expressions of something more: an art of life, a way of living ...' (1933: 1–2).

5. Such a claim is very much in keeping with the work of Siegfried Kracauer, one of Adorno's philosophical mentors. Kracauer's work on the mass ornament develops the idea of the mass as entity offered up to itself in *The Mass Ornament* (1995 [1926]).

6. Further to this, Adorno writes: 'By reproducing [the reified consciousness of the audience] with hypocritical subservience, the culture industry in effect changes this

consciousness all the more, that is, for its own purposes. ... The consumers are made to remain what they are: consumers.'

7. Gramsci distinguishes two main ways of achieving hegemonic status. These are transformism – or passive revolution which neutralizes non-dominant interests – and expansive hegemony – whereby an active and direct consensus develops between the hegemonic class and the interests of popular classes. This consensus creates a genuine 'national-popular will'.

8. For a more detailed discussion of Gramsci's impact on British cultural studies, see Tony Bennett, Colin Mercer and Janet Woolacott (eds), *Culture, Ideology and Social Process* (London: Batsford, 1981) or Stuart Hall's 'Gramsci's Relevance for the Study of Race and Ethnicity' (*Journal of Communication Inquiry* 10.2: 5–27, 1986) and 'Notes on Deconstructing "The Popular"' (1981) contained within this *Reader*.

9. For example, a very lively debate (well represented in the work of Dwight Macdonald, whose 'A Theory of Mass Culture' (1957) is included in this book) sprang up to probe the implications of mass culture on US life. This debate is evident in Bernard Rosenberg and David Manning White's *Mass Culture: The Popular Arts in America* (1957). Rosenberg and White admit that one of their major challenges as editors was to secure work that spoke to the potential of mass culture because the fact that 'there have been far more excoriators of mass culture than defenders became readily apparent to us as we sought representative selections for both points of view' (v). In contrast to and as evidence of the type of approach that later came to characterize the study of popular culture is the 1964 publication of Stuart Hall and Paddy Whannel's *The Popular Arts*. This book diverges from the majority of earlier works on popular culture in that it calls for an exploration of the possibilities rather than the negative impact of electronic communication and culture. Hall and Whannel also advocate a shift away from what they consider to be false distinctions used to discuss new media (such as serious versus popular and entertainment versus values) as poor frameworks for reference and judgment (45), and maintain that new media are linked to social change (45). Largely geared toward educators, its rationale is that in order to best meet the needs of media-saturated pupils, didactic practice should engage popular forms rather than dismiss them wholesale.

10. Barthes is especially indebted to the work of Swiss linguist Ferdinand de Saussure, whose *Course in General Linguistics* (1983 [1916]) elaborated on a proposed new science dedicated to 'the life of signs within society' and proposed a structural approach to language that emphasized the arbitrary relationship between signifier and signified. The name that Saussure chose to describe this science was semiology (from the Greek *semeîon*, or 'sign') (16). For a discussion of semiology in the context of cultural studies, see: Kaja Silverman (1983) *The Subject of Semiotics;* and Richard Harland (1987) *Superstructuralism: The Philosophy of Structuralism and Post-Structuralism.*

11. An especially important concept to subsequent work on popular culture is Williams' elaboration of 'structures of feeling' in *Marxism and Literature* (1977). Through this term, Williams theorizes the relationship between transformations of meaning and change: 'it is a structured formation which, because it is at the very edge of semantic availability, has many characteristics of a pre-formation, until specific articulations – new semantic figures – are discovered in material practice: often, as it happens, in relatively isolated ways, which are only later seen to compose a significant (often in fact minority) generation: this is often, in turn, the generation that substantially connects to its successor' (134).

12. Henri Lefebvre's approach to cultural criticism as published in *Critique de la vie quotidienne I* (1946) and *Critique de la vie quotidienne II* (1962) did not become widely available in English until the publication of Sacha Rabinovitch's translation of the work as *Everyday Life in the Modern World* (1984). Nevertheless, the work has exerted a not inconsiderable influence both through its role in the emergence of a French cultural studies tradition and the impact of this tradition on cultural studies in other locations.

13. Particularly in debt to de Certeau's work are: John Fiske (1989) *Understanding Popular Culture*; and Henry Jenkins (1992) *Textual Poachers: Television Fans and Participatory Culture.*

14. For commentary on these events see: Les Evans (ed.) (1968) *Revolt in France: May–June 1968 – A Contemporary Record*; Ronald Fraser (1988) *1968: A Student*

*Generation in Revolt*; D.L. Hanley and A.P. Kerr, (eds) (1989) *May '68: Coming of Age*; Henri Lefebvre (1969) *The Explosion: Marxism and the French Upheaval*; Keith A. Reader and Khursheed Wadia (1993) *The May 1968 Events in France: Reproductions and Interpretations*; Patrick Seale and Maureen McConville (1968) *Red Flag/Black Flag: French Revolution 1968*; Situationist International (1974) *Ten Days that Shook the University*; Alain Touraine (1971) *The May Movement: Revolt and Reform*; Immanuel Wallerstein (1989) '1968, Revolution in the World-System: Theses and Queries'.

15. In addition, many continental works that have come to be central to the formation of cultural studies were translated into English during this period and impacted the way that UK and US scholars would approach the subject of popular culture. Much of Karl Marx's work was translated in the 1970s, and Antonio Gramsci's *Prison Notebooks* was made available to English-speaking audiences in 1971. Jacques Lacan's *Four Fundamental Concepts of Psycho-analysis* and *Écrits,* which expounded upon theories of subjectivity that were to have a profound effect on the shape of feminist film studies, both appeared in English in 1977.

16. What has come to be known as British cultural studies, often associated with the Centre for Contemporary Cultural Studies at Birmingham, built on the legacy of sociology and Marxism to promote class-conscious analyses and empirical studies of the large-scale changes that characterized the post-war era. Prominent members and affiliated scholars included the likes of Richard Hoggart, E.P. Thompson, Raymond Williams, Stuart Hall, Tony Jefferson, Phil Cohen, John Clarke, Paul Willis, and Dick Hebdige. Important revision of the scope of British cultural studies was ushered in by the criticism of scholars like Angela McRobbie and Paul Gilroy whose work sought to account for the ways in which gendered and racialized experience was part and parcel of, though not exhausted by, the categories of class, generational or national identity.

17. Roughly concurrent with the consolidation of British cultural studies was the emergence of an energetic new focus in *Screen,* which came to represent a branch of analysis known as 'Screen Theory'. Originally an educational journal from the Society for Education in Film and Television in the 1950s, *Screen* published work on a variety of new developments in cinema studies. For example, it provided a forum for work that explored the implications of structuralism, semiotics and ideology on our understanding of cinema. *Screen* also became the preeminent site of exploration of the relationship between subjectivity, sexuality and cinema in the 1970s and 1980s. Drawing heavily from psychoanalytic and feminist theory, *Screen* pressed readers to consider the ways that visual experience created gendered subject positions. Yet these subjects were far from neutral in that they reinforced repressive power structures. For example, Laura Mulvey's foundational 'Visual Pleasure and Narrative Cinema' (1975) argues that narrative cinema, especially in its creation of a complacent form of identification, underscores 'the way the unconscious of patriarchal society has structured film form'. Emphases within this period of *Screen*'s publication history also include the role of stereotype in representations and contestations of both sexual and, to a lesser extent, racial difference. Additional theorizations of gender, sexuality and the popular have been developed by a variety of scholars including, but not limited to, Janice Radway, Meaghan Morris, Judith Butler, Ella Shohat, Tania Modleski, Angela McRobbie, Teresa de Lauretis, Linda Williams, Lauren Berlant, Ian Ang, Laura Kipnis, Angela Davis, Mary Ann Doane, Jane Gaines, bell hooks, Carol Clover, Barbara Creed, Annette Kuhn, Kaja Silverman, Elizabeth Cowie, Pam Cook, Jacqueline Rose, Griselda Pollock, Gaylyn Studlar, and Constance Penley.

18. The following scholars have made particularly influential contributions to the advance of queer theory: José Esteban Muñoz, Judith Halberstam, Sue-Ellen Case, Eve Sedgwick, Philip Brian Harper, Alexander Doty, Chris Straayer, Richard Fung, Richard Dyer, Rhona J. Berenstein, Marlon Riggs, Kobena Mercer, Judith Butler, Judith Mayne, Ann Cvetkovitch, Samuel Delaney, Lisa Duggan, Lee Edelman, Diana Fuss, Martin Manalansan, Jay Prosser, Adrienne Rich, Jackie Stacey. There is, of course, a great deal of overlap between scholars of heterosexual and same-sex identity formations, especially given the

extent to which theorizations of gender and sexuality have highlighted the relational core of both. Many of the scholars noted previously have thus made contributions to the development of queer theory and vice versa.

19. For example, reflecting on his collaboration with Max Horkheimer on the *Dialectic of Enlightenment,* Theodor Adorno clarifies their decision to substitute the phrase 'mass culture' with their neologism 'culture industry'. The latter excludes 'from the outset the interpretation agreeable to its advocates: that it is a matter of something like a culture that arises spontaneously from the masses themselves …'. For our purposes, however, there is no necessary incompatibility between the terms 'culture' and 'industry'. Their relationship is actually the *sine qua non* of the popular as it is conceived and presented in this volume. This is the reason that we dedicate two sections of the *Reader* to the socio-economic impact of the commodity form and marketing practices. If we hold out for an ideal of the popular as that which resists commodification, then we fail to understand the interrelated complexities of either.

# References

Appudurai, A. (2001) *Globalization.* Durham, NC: Duke University Press.

Arnold, M. (1993 [1869]) *Culture and Anarchy and Other Writings.* Ed. S. Collini. Cambridge: Cambridge University Press.

Barthes, R. (1993 [1957]) *Mythologies.* Trans. Annette Lavers. London: Vintage.

Benjamin, W. (1992 [1936]) *Illuminations.* Ed. H. Arendt and trans. H. Zohn. London: Fontana.

Bennett, T., Mercer, C. and Woolacott, J. (eds) (1981) *Culture, Ideology and Social Process.* London: Batsford.

Bloom, A. (1987) *The Closing of the American Mind.* London: Penguin Books.

Carlyle, T. (1858 [1829]) 'Signs of the Times', in *The Collected Works of Thomas Carlyle.* London: Chapman and Hall.

Cassell, J. and Jenkins, H. (eds) (1998) *From Barbie to Mortal Kombat: Gender and Computer Games.* Cambridge, MA: MIT University Press.

Chow, R. (1993) *Writing Diaspora: Tactics of Intervention in Contemporary Cultural Studies.* Bloomington, IN: Indiana University Press.

Coleridge, S.T. (1972 [1837]) *On the Constitution of the Church and State According to the Idea of Each.* Ed. with an introduction by John Barrell. London: Dent.

Collins, J. (1989) *Uncommon Culture: Popular Culture and Post-Modernism.* London: Routledge.

De Certeau, M. (1984) *The Practice of Everyday Life, Volume 1.* Trans. S. Rendall. Berkeley, CA: University of California Press.

Denning, M. (1997) *The Cultural Front: The Laboring of American Culture in the Twentieth Century.* London: Verso.

Drinnon, R. (1990) *Facing West: The Metaphysics of Indian Hating and Empire Building.* New York: Schocken.

Eliot, T.S. (1948) *Notes Towards the Definition of Culture.* London: Faber & Faber.

Evans, L. (ed.) (1968) *Revolt in France: May–June 1968 – A Contemporary Record.* New York: Les Evans.

Fiske, J. (1989) *Understanding Popular Culture.* New York: Routledge.

Fraser, R. (1988) *1968: A Student Generation in Revolt.* London: Chatto & Windus.

Freccero, C. (1999) *Popular Culture: An Introduction.* New York: New York University Press.

Genosko, G. (1999) *McLuhan and Baudrillard: The Masters of Implosion.* London: Routledge.

Gilroy, P. (1993) *The Black Atlantic: Modernity and Double Consciousness.* Cambridge, MA: Harvard University Press.

Gramsci, A. (1971) *Selections from the Prison Notebooks.* New York: International Publishers.

Greenberg, C. (1939) 'Avant-Garde and Kitsch', *Partisan Review* 6: 34–49.

Guha, R. (1998) *Dominance without Hegemony: History and Power in Colonial India.* Cambridge, MA: Harvard University Press.

Hall, S. (1981) 'Notes on Deconstructing "The Popular"', in *People's History and Socialist Theory.* Ed. Raphael Samuel. London: Routledge.

Hall, S. (1986) 'Gramsci's Relevance for the Study of Race and Ethnicity', *Journal of Communication Inquiry* 10.2: 5–27.

Hall, S. and Jefferson, T. (1976) *Resistance through Rituals: Youth Subcultures in Post-war Britain.* London: Hutchinson.

Hall, S. and Whannel, P. ( 1964) *The Popular Arts.* London: Hutchinson.

Hanley, D.L. and Kerr, A.P. (eds) (1989) *May '68: Coming of Age.* London: Macmillan.

Hansen, M.B. (1997) 'Mass Culture as Hieroglyphic Writing: Adorno, Derrida, Kracauer', in *The Actuality of Adorno: Critical Essays on Adorno and the Postmodern.* Ed. M. Pensky. New York: SUNY Press.

Harland, R. (1987) *Superstructuralism: The Philosophy of Structuralism and Post-Structuralism.* London: Routledge.

Hebdige, D. (1979) *Subculture: The Meaning of Style.* London: Routledge.

Hebdige, D. (1988) *Hiding in the Light: On Images and Things.* London: Routledge.

Hirsch, E.D. (1992) *Cultural Literacy: What Every American Needs to Know.* Boston: Houghton Mifflin.

Hoggart, R. (1957) *The Uses of Literacy.* London: Chatto & Windus.

Horkheimer, M. and Adorno, T. (1973 [1944]) *Dialectic of Enlightenment.* Trans. J. Cumming. New York: Continuum.

Jameson, F. (1991) *Postmodernism or, the Cultural Logic of Late Capitalism.* Durham, NC: Duke University Press.

Jameson, F. and Miyoshi, M. (eds) (1998) *The Cultures of Globalization.* Durham, NC: Duke University Press.

Jenkins, H. (1992) *Textual Poachers: Television Fans and Participatory Culture.* New York and London: Routledge.

Jenkins, H. et al. (2002) *Hop on Pop: The Politics and Pleasures of Popular Culture.* Durham, NC: Duke University Press.

Kaplan, E. (1987) *Rocking Around the Clock: Music Television, Postmodernism and Consumer Culture.* London: Methuen.

Kaplan, A. and Pease, D. (eds) (1994) *Cultures of United States Imperialism.* Durham, NC: Duke University Press.

Kracauer, S. (1995 [1926]) *The Mass Ornament.* Trans. Thomas Y. Levin. Cambridge, MA: Harvard University Press.

Lacan, J. (1977) *Ecrits: A Selection.* Trans. A. Sheridan. London: Tavistock.

Lacan, J. (1994 [1977]) *Four Fundamental Concepts of Psycho-analysis.* ed. J.A. Miller, trans. A. Sheridan, introduction D. Macey. London: Penguin.

Leavis, F.R. (1930) *Mass Civilisation and Minority Culture.* Cambridge: Minority Press.

Leavis, F.R. and Thompson, D. (1933) *Culture and Environment.* London: Chatto & Windus.

Leavis, Q.D. (1978 [1932]) *Fiction and the Reading Public.* London: Chatto & Windus.

Lefebvre, H. (1969) *The Explosion: Marxism and the French Upheaval.* New York: Monthly Review Press.

Lefebvre, H. (1984 [1946, 1962]) *Everyday Life in the Modern World.* Trans. S. Rabinovitch. New Brunswick, NJ: Transaction Books.

Lefebvre, H. (1987) 'The Everyday and Everydayness', trans. C. Levich et al. *Yale French Studies* 73: 7–11.

Lewis, L. (ed.) (1992) *The Adoring Audience: Fan Culture and Popular Media.* London: Routledge.

Lipsitz, G. (1991) *Time Passages: Collective Memory and American Popular Culture.* Minneapolis, MN: University of Minnesota Press.

Lipsitz, G. (1994) *Dangerous Crossroads: Popular Music, Postmodernism and the Poetics of Place.* London: Verso.

McCarthy, A. (2001) *Ambient Television: Visual Culture and Public Space*. Durham, NC: Duke University Press.

Macdonald, D. (1957) 'A Theory of Mass Culture', in *Mass Culture: The Popular Arts in America*. Eds B. Rosenberg and D.M. White. New York: The Free Press.

McKenzie, N. (ed.) (1958) *Convictions*. London: MacGibbon and Kee.

McLuhan, M. (1951) *The Mechanical Bride: Folklore of Industrial Man*. London: Routledge and Kegan Paul.

McRobbie, A. (1994) *Postmodernism and Popular* Culture. London: Routledge.

Mouffe, C. (ed.) (1979) *Gramsci and Marxist Theory*. London: Routledge and Kegan Paul.

Mulvey, L. (1975) 'Visual Pleasure and Narrative Cinema', *Screen* 16(3): 6–18.

Nakamura, L. (2002) *Cybertypes: Race, Ethnicity and Identity on the Internet*. London: Routledge.

Nelson, A. and Thuy Linh N. Tu with Alicia Headlam Hines. (eds) (2001) *Technicolor: Race, Technology, and Everyday Life*. New York: NYU Press.

Penley, C. (1997) *Nasa/Trek: Popular Science and Sex in America*. London: Verso.

Reader, K.A. and Wadia, K. (1993) *The May 1968 Events in France: Reproductions and Interpretations*. London: Macmillian.

Rosenberg, B. and White, D.M. (eds) (1957) *Mass Culture: The Popular Arts in America*. New York: The Free Press.

Ross, A. (1989) *No Respect: Intellectuals and Popular Culture*. New York: Routledge.

Ross, K. (1997) 'French Quotidian', in *The Art of the Everyday: The Quotidian in Postwar French Culture*. Ed. L. Gumpert. New York: New York University Press.

Said, E. (1993) *Culture and Imperialism*. London: Chatto & Windus Ltd.

Saussure, F. de (1983 [1916]) *Course in General Linguistics*. Ed. C. Bally et al., trans. R. Harris. London: Duckworth.

Sconce, J. (2000) *Haunted Media: Electronic Presence from Telegraphy to Television*. Durham, NC: Duke University Press.

Seale, P. and McConville, M. (1968) *Red Flag/Black Flag: French Revolution 1968*. New York: G.P. Putnam's Sons.

Silverman, K. (1983) *The Subject of Semiotics*. Oxford: Oxford University Press.

Situationist International (1974) *Ten Days that Shook the University*. New York: Black and Red Publications.

Spigel, L. (1992) *Make Room For TV: Television and the Family Ideal in Postwar America*. Chicago: University of Chicago Press.

Stearn, G.E. (ed.) (1967) *McLuhan Hot & Cool: A Critical Symposium*. New York: Dial Press.

Théberge, P. (1997) *Any Sound You Can Imagine: Making Music/Consuming Technology*. Hanover and London: Wesleyan University Press.

Tomlinson, J. (1999) *Globalization and Culture*. Chicago: University of Chicago Press.

Touraine, A. (1971) *The May Movement: Revolt and Reform*. New York: Random House.

Turner, G. (1996) *British Cultural Studies: An Introduction* (2nd edn). London: Routledge.

Wagnleitner, R. and May, E.T. (eds) (2000) *'Here, There and Everywhere': The Foreign Politics of American Popular Culture*. Hanover and London: University Press of New England.

Wallerstein, I. (1989) '1968, Revolution in the World-System: Theses and Queries', *Theory and Society 18*, Norwell, MA: Kluwer, pp. 431–49.

Wardrip-Fruin, N. and Harrigan, P. (eds) (2004) *First Person: New Media as Story, Performance, and Game*. Cambridge, MA: MIT University Press.

Williams, R. (1961) *The Long Revolution*. London: Chatto & Windus.

Williams, R. (1976) *Keywords: A Vocabulary of Culture and Society*. London: Fontana Press.

Williams, R. (1977) *Marxism and Literature*. Oxford: Oxford Paperbacks.

# PART ONE

# DELINEATING

# CULTURE–MASS–POPULAR

To delineate marks an action. It outlines. It traces. It does not, however, represent. Because of its process-based rather than exhaustive sense, delineation is preferred over the arduous, and often questionable task of definition. Simply stated, the articles in this *Reader* present not a definitive statement regarding the nature of popular culture, but a thread. The understanding of popular culture that this *Reader* advances involves tensions between ideologies, needs, and interests that characterize contemporary social life, political culture, and identity. The essays collected in this particular section span the twentieth century to trace varying engagements with key terms and concepts as well as developments in historical approaches to culture, broadly defined, and popular culture in particular as the basis for an understanding of the fundamentals of inquiry that have organized approaches to the study of popular culture. Special attention is dedicated to how processes of delineation are effected through the vocabularies and insights that have generated dialogue and debate over the popular. This is not to suggest that the study of popular culture resembles a clean or easy progression. If anything, the essays chosen demonstrate the extent to which breaks from established approaches and new angles of convergence impact the ways that popular culture is known. In other words, this section considers the difficulty of 'defining' as a generative site from which to initiate a critical inquiry into the popular. In its organization and content, this section does not purport to arrive at a definitive meaning, so much as it strives to make readers aware that it is in contestation over words such as 'culture', 'mass', and 'popular' that much meaning has been generated. Readers are asked to begin with this outline in order to successfully place forthcoming sections into the provided lineage as well as develop new maps across the unstable, and ever shifting terrain of popular culture.

Raymond Williams is considered a founding figure of British cultural studies. *Culture and Society, 1780–1950* (London: Chatto & Windus, 1958), *The Long Revolution* (London: Chatto & Windus, 1961), *Television: Technology and Cultural Form* (London: Fontana, 1974), and *Marxism and Literature* (Oxford: Oxford University Press, 1977), to name a few of his works, expand the ways that we can think about culture as a way of life and contribute a great deal to the interrelations of social and political forms that characterize Marxist cultural theory. In his invaluable, *Keywords: A Vocabulary of Culture and Society* (1976), Williams provides an accessible etymology of the keywords, **'Culture'** and **'Masses'**, that have been and continue to be a vantage point from which to examine ideas of the 'popular' and 'popular culture'. His statement that 'Culture is one of the two or three most complicated words in the English language' marks a beginning to the study of popular culture practiced within this *Reader*.

Indebted to Matthew Arnold's *Culture and Anarchy* (Cambridge: Cambridge University Press, 1993 [1869]) and sharing views on the subject of culture later expressed by T.S. Eliot's *Notes Towards the Definition of Culture* (London: Faber & Faber, 1948), F.R. Leavis's polemical **'Mass Civilisation and Minority Culture'** (1930) insists that as a hierarchy of value culture is fast eroding: an elitist, classed, cultural vanguard is threatened by supposed democratic commercial culture. As a result, according to Leavis, culture has become split into two oppositional camps: minority culture and mass civilization. The cultural authority of an educated/literary minority culture ('In any period it is upon a very small minority that the discerning appreciation of art and literature depends') is compromised by, and is feared to be replaced by, the mass press and commercial culture's influences on the general public. Leavis's essay, along with Q.D. Leavis's *Fiction and the Reading Public* (London: Chatto & Windus, 1978 [1932]) and his collaboration with Denys Thompson in *Culture and Environment* (London: Chatto & Windus, 1933), responds to industrialization as well as changes to class dynamics prevalent in the early twentieth century, and constitutes the basis of the 'culture and civilization' tradition against which many subsequent theorizations of popular culture have been a critical response.

A contributor to the landmark collection, *Mass Culture: The Popular Arts in America* edited by Bernard Rosenberg and David Manning White, Dwight Macdonald's work on mass culture, as well as the other essays that appeared within the 1957 volume, 'contained' (Andrew Ross's *No Respect: Intellectuals and Popular Culture* (1989) frames US cold-war policy, ideology, and critiques of mass culture in terms of 'containment') how mid-century US mass culture could be understood. Post-war 'mass culture debates', as the concentration of commentary became known, sought to specify the threats to 'high culture' enacted by 'low culture' (a 'threat' cast in epidemic terms in Clement Greenberg's 'Avant-Garde and Kitsch' (*Partisan Review*, 1939)) in the form of magazines, pulp fiction, comic books, films, television and radio, as well as US cold-war concerns that enveloped conceptualizations of 'the masses' and 'mass culture' ascribed to the Soviet Union. In other words, Macdonald's intervention attests to the impact of a new political landscape on considerations of culture and its relationship to nation. Macdonald's **'A Theory of Mass Culture'** (1957 [1953]) is the second version of his argument: an exemplary espousal of the debates of the era that stood 'against the spreading ooze of Mass Culture'. The first appeared in 1944 as 'A Theory of Popular Culture' and the last, a reworking of how the term 'mass' had been previously used, appeared in 1962 as 'Masscult and Midcult'.

'I want to show how our ways of thinking and feeling about mass culture are so intricately bound up with notions of the feminine that the need for a feminist critique becomes obvious at every level of the debate.' This powerful statement, taken from Tania Modleski's **'Femininity as Mas[s]querade: A Feminist Approach to Mass Culture'**, marks a crucial intervention in debates on mass culture and how mass culture has been understood within the Western academy as undifferentially gendered. Modleski's contribution to Colin MacCabe's edited collection, *High Theory/Low Culture: Analyzing Popular Television and Film* (1986), examines the condemnation of mass culture. It claims that this charge couches the subject in terms of a threat; one often assigned to femininity and carried out through troubling analogies that dismiss mass culture as feminizing. In its purportedly 'feminine' capacity, mass culture is accused of devaluing and sentimentalizing culture overall. A sample of Modleski's other work on women, feminism, and mass culture includes: *Feminism Without Women: Culture and Criticism in a 'Postfeminist' Age* (London: Routledge, 1991), *Studies in Entertainment: Critical Approaches to Mass Culture* (editor, Bloomington, IN:Indiana University Press, 1986), *Loving with a Vengeance: Mass-Produced Fantasies for Women* (Hamden, CT: Archon Books, 1982).

Like Raymond Williams, Morag Shiach provides working definitions relevant to this *Reader's* project. Shiach's book, *Discourse on Popular Culture: Class, Gender and History in Cultural Analysis, 1730 to the Present* (1989), acknowledges Williams' enormous influence and underscores that the word **'Popular'** is one of those 'most complicated words in the English language' through a lengthy etymology. Shiach relays the transformations of the term 'popular' from its legal connotations to the idea of a 'general public'. A fascinating issue raised by this etymology is the extent to which traces of these definitions inform contemporary conceptualizations and practices of the popular.

Stuart Hall's **'Notes on Deconstructing "The Popular"'** (1981) begins where Shiach's address of the term concludes. It critically focuses on 'popular culture' within the poles of containment and resistance. 'When you put the two terms ['popular' and 'culture'] together', he suggests, 'the difficulties can be pretty horrendous'. Hall, whose impact and influence have been exceptional (see, for example, his collaboration with Paddy Whannel, *The Popular Arts* (London: Hutchinson, 1964), and numerous contributions to edited collections dedicated to culture, media, identity and politics, as well as *Working Papers in Cultural Studies*, *New Socialist* and *Marxism Today*), constructs an essay that is certainly 'required reading' for any student of popular culture. In Hall's piece, popular culture is carefully considered in relation to one of its most enigmatic definitions: 'the people'. Indebted to both Antonio Gramsci and Raymond Williams, Hall's work on popular culture approaches culture as a 'way of life' to conceive culture as a 'way of struggle': 'Popular culture is one of the sites where this struggle for and against a culture of the powerful is engaged: it is also the stake to be won or lost *in* that struggle.'

Many first became aware of Juan Flores's work on popular culture and Puerto Rican identity in 'Puerto Rican and Proud, Boy-ee!', his contribution to Andrew Ross and Tricia Rose's *Microphone Fiends: Youth Music and Youth Culture* (London: Routledge, 1994). Since then his work has also appeared in Amritjit Singh and Peter Schmidt's collaborative rethinking, *Postcolonial Theory and the United States: Race, Ethnicity, and Literature* (Jackson, MS: University Press of Mississippi, 2000). The selection presented here, **'*"Pueblo Pueblo"*: Popular Culture in Time'** from his book, *From Bomba to Hip Hop: Puerto Rican Culture and Latino Identity* (2000), works through an exegesis of the concept of popular culture, referencing many of the arguments that precede his in this *Reader*, to arrive at a challenging question: 'Does the household term *popular culture* still bear any substantive content, or has it become so replete with referents to every aspect and detail of social experience as to have been depleted of any and all specificity?' To gauge this question Flores turns to Johannes Fabian's notion of 'moments of freedom' and Michel de Certeau's 'arts of timing' to support historical awareness for the study of popular culture in time: 'for historical rather than preponderantly spatial contexts' and 'the enactment and the "capturing" of popular culture as the establishing of temporal relations, associations fashioned by acts of memory and imagination'.

# Play List

Bennett, Tony (1981) *Popular Culture: Themes and Issues.* Milton Keynes: Open University Press.

Bennett, Tony, Mercer, Colin and Woollacott, Janet (eds) (1986) *Popular Culture and Social Relations.* Milton Keynes: Open University Press.

Berger, Arthur Asa (1973) *Pop Culture.* Dayton, OH: Pflaum/Standard.

Bigsby, C.W.E. (1976) *Approaches to Popular Culture.* Bath: Edward Arnold.

Brantlinger, Patrick (1983) *Bread and Circuses – Theories of Mass Culture as Social Decay.* New York: Cornell University Press.

Burke, Peter (1978) *Popular Culture in Early Modern Europe.* London: Maurice Temple Smith Ltd.

Chambers, Iain (1986) *Popular Culture: The Metropolitan Experience.* London: Methuen.

Creekmur, Corey K. and Doty, Alexander (eds) (1995) *Out In Culture: Gay, Lesbian, and Queer Essays on Popular Culture.* Durham, NC: Duke University Press.

Dent, Gina (ed.) (1992) *Black Popular Culture.* Seattle, WA: Bay Press.

Doty, Alexander (1993) *Making Things Perfectly Queer: Interpreting Mass Culture.* Minneapolis, MN: University of Minnesota Press.

Ellison, Ralph (1986) *Going to the Territory.* New York: Random House.

Fiske, John (1989) *Understanding Popular Culture.* New York: Routledge.

Freccero, Carla (1999) *Popular Culture: An Introduction.* New York: New York University Press.

Gans, Herbert (1999) *Popular Culture and High Culture: An Analysis and Evaluation of Taste.* New York: Basic Books.

Grossberg, Lawrence (1997) 'Re-placing Popular Culture.' In *The Clubcultures Reader: Readings in Popular Cultural Studies.* Steve Redhead (ed.) Oxford: Blackwell.

Hall, Stuart and Whannel, Paddy (1964) *The Popular Arts.* London: Hutchinson.

James, C.L.R. (1993 [1950]) *American Civilization.* Ed. Anna Grimshaw and Keith Hart. Oxford: Blackwell.

Jenkins, Henry McPherson, Tara and Shattuc, Jane (eds.) (2002) *Hop on Pop: The Politics and Pleasures of Popular Culture.* Durham, NC: Duke University Press.

Lipsitz, George (1990) 'Listening to Learn and Learning to Listen: Popular Culture, Cultural Theory, and American Studies.' *American Quarterly.* Vol. 42, No. 4 (December), pp. 615–636.

MacCabe, Colin (ed.) (1986) *High Theory/Low Culture: Analyzing Popular Television and Film* Manchester: Manchester University Press.

McLuhan, Marshall (1951) *The Mechanical Bride: The Folklore of Industrial Man.* New York: Vanguard Press.

McLuhan, Marshall (1994 [1964]) *Understanding Media: The Extensions of Man.* Cambridge, MA: MIT Press.

Miller, Toby and McHaul, Alex W. (1998) *Popular Culture and Everyday Life*. London: Sage.

Mukerji, Chandra and Schudson, Michael (1991) *Rethinking Popular Culture: Contemporary Perspectives in Cultural Studies.* Berkeley, CA: University of California Press.

Naremore, James and Brantlinger, Patrick (1991) *Modernity and Mass Culture*. Bloomington, IN: Indiana University Press.

Rosenberg, Bernard and White, David Manning (1957) *Mass Culture: The Popular Arts in America.* New York: Free Press.

Ross, Andrew (1989) *No Respect: Intellectuals and Popular Culture*. New York: Routledge.

Storey, John (1993) *An Introductory Guide to Cultural Theory and Popular Culture*. New York: Harvester Wheatsheaf.

Streeby, Shelley (2002) *American Sensations: Class, Empire, and the Production of Popular Culture.* Berkeley, CA: University of California Press.

Strinati, Dominic (1995) *An Introduction to the Theories of Popular Culture*. New York: Routledge.

Thompson, Denys (ed.) (1964) *Discrimination and Popular Culture*. Baltimore, MD: Penguin Books.

Warshow, Robert (1970 [1946]) *The Immediate Experience: Movies, Comics, Theater & Other Aspects of Popular Culture*. New York: Atheneum.

# Chapter 1

# Raymond Williams

## 'Culture' and 'Masses'

## Culture

Culture is one of the two or three most complicated words in the English language. This is so partly because of its intricate historical development, in several European languages, but mainly because it has now come to be used for important concepts in several distinct intellectual disciplines and in several distinct and incompatible systems of thought.

The fw is *cultura*, L, from rw *colere*, L. *Colere* had a range of meanings: inhabit, cultivate, protect, honour with worship. Some of these meanings eventually separated, though still with occasional overlapping, in the derived nouns. Thus 'inhabit' developed through *colonus*, L to *colony*. 'Honour with worship' developed through *cultus*, L to *cult*. *Cultura* took on the main meaning of cultivation or tending, including, as in Cicero, *cultura animi*, though with subsidiary medieval meanings of honour and worship (cf. in English culture as 'worship' in Caxton (1483)). The French forms of *cultura* were *couture*, oF, which has since developed its own specialized meaning, and later *culture*, which by eC15 had passed into English. The primary meaning was then in husbandry, the tending of natural growth.

Culture in all its early uses was a noun of process: the tending *of* something, basically crops or animals. The subsidiary *coulter* – ploughshare, had travelled by a different linguistic route, from *culter*, L – ploughshare, *culter*, oE, to the variant English spellings *culter, colter, coulter* and as late as eC17 culture (Webster, *Duchess of Malfi,* III, ii: 'hot burning cultures'). This provided a further basis for the important next stage of meaning, by metaphor. From eC16 the tending of natural growth was

From: Raymond Williams, *Keywords: A Vocabulary of Culture and Society.* London: Fontana, 1976.

extended to a process of human development, and this, alongside the original meaning in husbandry, was the main sense until lC18 and eC19. Thus More: 'to the culture and profit of their minds'; Bacon: 'the culture and manurance of minds' (1605); Hobbes: 'a culture of their minds' (1651); Johnson: 'she neglected the culture of her understanding' (1759). At various points in this development two crucial changes occurred: first, a degree of habituation to the metaphor, which made the sense of human tending direct; second, an extension of particular processes to a general process, which the word could abstractly carry. It is of course from the latter development that the independent noun culture began its complicated modern history, but the process of change is so intricate, and the latencies of meaning are at times so close, that it is not possible to give any definite date. Culture as an independent noun, an abstract process or the product of such a process, is not important before lC18 and is not common before mC19. But the early stages of this development were not sudden. There is an interesting use in Milton, in the second (revised) edition of *The Readie and Easie Way to Establish a Free Commonwealth* (1660): 'spread much more Knowledg and Civility, yea, Religion, through all parts of the Land, by communicating the natural heat of Government and Culture more distributively to all extreme parts, which now lie num and neglected'. Here the metaphorical sense ('natural heat') still appears to be present, and *civility* is still written where in C19 we would normally expect culture. Yet we can also read 'government and culture' in a quite modern sense. Milton, from the tenor of his whole argument, is writing about a general social process, and this is a definite stage of development. In C18 England this general process acquired definite class associations though cultivation and cultivated were more commonly used for this. But there is a letter of 1730 (Bishop of Killala, to Mrs Clayton; cit Plumb, *England in the Eighteenth Century*) which has this clear sense: 'it has not been customary for' persons of either birth or culture to breed up their children to the Church'. Akenside (*Pleasures of Imagination*, 1744) wrote: '... nor purple state nor culture can bestow'. Wordsworth wrote 'where grace of culture hath been utterly unknown' (1805), and Jane Austen (*Emma*, 1816) 'every advantage of discipline and culture'.

It is thus clear that culture was developing in English towards some of its modern senses before the decisive effects of a new social and intellectual movement. But to follow the development through this movement, in lC18 and eC19, we have to look also at developments in other languages and especially in German.

In French, until C18, culture was always accompanied by a grammatical form indicating the matter being cultivated, as in the English usage already noted. Its occasional use as an independent noun dates from mC18, rather later than similar occasional uses in English. The independent noun *civilization* also emerged in mC18; its relationship to culture has since been very complicated. There was at this point an important development in German: the word was borrowed from French, spelled first (lC18) *Cultur* and from C19 *Kultur*. Its main use was still as a synonym for *civilization*: first in the abstract sense of a general process of becoming 'civilized' or 'cultivated'; second, in the sense which had already been established for *civilization* by the historians of the Enlightenment, in the popular C18 form of the universal histories, as a description of the secular process of human development. There was then a decisive change of use in Herder. In his unfinished *Ideas on the Philosophy of the History of Mankind* (1784–91) he wrote of *Cultur*: 'nothing is more indeterminate than this word, and nothing more deceptive than its application to all nations and periods'. He attacked the assumption of the universal histories that 'civilization' or 'culture' – the historical self-development of humanity – was what we would now call a unilinear process, leading to the high and dominant point of C18 European culture. Indeed he attacked what he called European subjugation and domination of the four quarters of the globe, and wrote:

> Men of all the quarters of the globe, who have perished over the ages, you have not lived solely to manure the earth with your ashes, so that at the end of time your posterity should be made happy by European culture. The very thought of a superior European culture is a blatant insult to the majesty of Nature.

It is then necessary, he argued, in a decisive innovation, to speak of 'cultures' in the plural: the specific and variable cultures of different nations and periods, but also the specific and variable cultures of social and economic groups within a nation. This sense was widely developed, in the Romantic movement, as an alternative to the orthodox and dominant '*civilization*'. It was first used to emphasize national and traditional cultures, including the new concept of folk-culture. It was later used to attack what was seen as the 'MECHANICAL' character of the new civilization then emerging: both for its abstract rationalism and for the 'inhumanity' of current industrial development. It was used to distinguish between 'human' and 'material' development. Politically, as so often in this period, it veered between radicalism and reaction and very often, in the confusion of major social change, fused elements of both. (It should also be noted, though it adds to the real complication, that the same kind of distinction, especially between 'material' and 'spiritual' development, was made by von Humboldt and others, until as late as 1900, with a reversal of the terms, culture being material and *civilization* spiritual. In general, however, the opposite distinction was dominant.)

On the other hand, from the 1840s in Germany, *Kultur* was being used in very much the sense in which *civilization* had been used in C18 universal histories. The decisive innovation is G.F. Klemm's *Allgemeine Kulturgeschichte der Menschheit* – 'General Cultural History of Mankind' (1843–52) – which traced human development from savagery through domestication to freedom. Although the American anthropologist Morgan, tracing comparable stages, used 'Ancient *Society*', with a culmination in *Civilization,* Klemm's sense was sustained, and was directly followed in English by Tylor in *Primitive Culture* (1870). It is along this line of reference that the dominant sense in modern social sciences has to be traced.

The complexity of the modern development of the word, and of its modern usage, can then be appreciated. We can easily distinguish the sense which depends on a literal continuity of physical process as now in 'sugar-beet culture' or, in the specialized physical application in bacteriology since the 1880s, 'germ culture'. But once we go beyond the physical reference, we have to recognize three broad active categories of usage. The sources of two of these we have already discussed: (i) the independent and abstract noun which describes a general process of intellectual, spiritual and aesthetic development, from C18; (ii) the independent noun, whether used generally or specifically, which indicates a particular way of life, whether of a people, a period, a group, or humanity in general, from Herder and Klemm. But we have also to recognize (iii) the independent and abstract noun which describes the works and practices of intellectual and especially artistic activity. This seems often now the most widespread use: culture is music, literature, painting and sculpture, theatre and film. A Ministry of Culture refers to these specific activities, sometimes with the addition of philosophy, scholarship, history. This use, (iii), is in fact relatively late. It is difficult to date precisely because it is in origin an applied form of sense (i): the idea of a general process of intellectual, spiritual and aesthetic development was applied and effectively transferred to the works and practices which represent and sustain it. But it also developed from the earlier sense of process; cf. 'progressive culture of fine arts', Millar, *Historical View of the English Government,* IV, 314 (1812). In English (i) and (iii) are still close; at times, for internal reasons, they are indistinguishable as in Arnold, *Culture and Anarchy* (1869); while sense (ii) was decisively introduced into English by Tylor, *Primitive Culture* (1870), following Klemm. The decisive development of sense (iii) in English was in lC19 and eC20.

Faced by this complex and still active history of the word, it is easy to react by selecting one 'true' or 'proper' or 'scientific' sense and dismissing other senses as loose or confused. There is evidence of this reaction even in the excellent study by Kroeber and Kluckhohn, *Culture: a Critical Review of Concepts and Definitions* [1963, New York: Vintage Books], where usage in North American anthropology is in effect taken as a norm. It is clear that, within a discipline, conceptual usage has to be clarified. But in general it is the range and overlap of meanings that is significant. The complex of senses indicates a complex argument about the relations between general human development and a particular way of life, and between both and the works and practices of art and intelligence. It is especially interesting that in archaeology and in *cultural anthropology* the reference to culture or a culture is primarily to *material* production, while in history and *cultural studies* the reference is primarily to *signifying* or *symbolic* systems. This often confuses but even more often conceals the central question of the relations between 'material' and 'symbolic' production, which in some recent argument – cf. my own *Culture* – have always to be related rather than contrasted. Within this complex argument there are fundamentally opposed as well as effectively overlapping positions; there are also, understandably, many unresolved questions and confused answers. But these arguments and questions cannot be resolved by reducing the complexity of actual usage. This point is relevant also to uses of forms of the word in languages other than English, where there is considerable variation. The anthropological use is common in the German, Scandinavian and Slavonic language groups, but it is distinctly subordinate to the senses of art and learning, or of a general process of human development, in Italian and French. Between languages as within a language, the range and complexity of sense and reference indicate both difference of intellectual position and some blurring or overlapping. These variations, of whatever kind, necessarily involve alternative views of the activities, relationships and processes which this complex word indicates. The complexity, that is to say, is not finally in the word but in the problems which its variations of use significantly indicate.

It is necessary to look also at some associated and derived words. Cultivation and cultivated went through the same metaphorical extension from a physical to a social or educational sense in C17, and were especially significant words in C18. Coleridge, making a classical eC19 distinction between civilization and culture, wrote (1830): 'the permanent distinction, and occasional contrast, between cultivation and civilization'. The noun in this sense has effectively disappeared but the adjective is still quite common, especially in relation to manners and tastes. The important adjective cultural appears to date from the 1870s; it became common by the 1890s. The word is only available, in its modern sense, when the independent noun, in the artistic and intellectual or anthropological senses, has become familiar. Hostility to the word culture in English appears to date from the controversy around Arnold's views. It gathered force in lC19 and eC20, in association with a comparable hostility to *aesthete*. Its association with class distinction produced the mime-word *culchah*. There was also an area of hostility associated with anti-German feeling, during and after the 1914–18 War, in relation to propaganda about *Kultur*. The central area of hostility has lasted, and one element of it has been emphasized by the recent American phrase culture-vulture. It is significant that virtually all the hostility (with the sole exception of the temporary anti-German association) has been connected with uses involving claims to superior knowledge, refinement (*culchah*) and distinctions between 'high' art (culture) and popular art and entertainment. It thus records a real social history and a very difficult and confused phase of social and cultural development. It is interesting that the steadily extending social and anthropological use of culture and cultural and such formations as sub-culture (the culture of a distinguishable smaller group) has, except in certain areas (notably popular entertainment), either bypassed or effectively diminished the hostility and its associated unease and embarrassment. [...]

## Masses

Mass is not only a very common but a very complex word in social description. The masses, while less complex, is especially interesting because it is ambivalent: a term of contempt in much conservative thought, but a positive term in much socialist thought.

Terms of contempt for the majority of a people have a long and abundant history. In most early descriptions the significant sense is of *base* or *low*, from the implicit and often explicit physical model of a society arranged in successive stages or layers. This physical model has determined much of the vocabulary of social description; compare *standing, status, eminence, prominence* and the description of social *levels, grades, estates* and *degrees*. At the same time more particular terms of description of certain 'low' groups have been extended: *plebeian* from Latin *plebs; villein* and *boor* from feudal society. COMMON added the sense of 'lowness' to the sense of mutuality, especially in the phrase 'the common people'. *Vulgar* by C16 had lost most of its positive or neutral senses and was becoming a synonym for 'low' or 'base'; a better derived sense was preserved in *vulgate. The people* itself became ambiguous, as in C17 arguments which attempted to distinguish the 'better sort' of people from the *meaner* or *basest*. The grand ratifying phrase, *the people,* can still be applied, according to political position, either generally or selectively.

Terms of open political contempt or fear have their own history. In C16 and C17 the key word was *multitude* [...]. Although there was often reference to *the vulgar* and *the rabble*, the really significant noun was *multitude,* often with reinforcing description of numbers in *many-headed*. There were also *base multitude, giddy multitude, hydra-headed monster multitude* and *headless multitude*. This stress on large numbers is significant when compared with the later development of mass, though it must always have been an obvious observation that the most evident thing about 'the common people' was that there were so many of them.

*Base* is an obvious sense, ascribing lowness of social condition and morality. *Idiot* and *giddy* may have originally overlapped, from 'ignorant' and 'foolish' to the earlier sense of *giddy* as 'crazed' (it had signified, originally, possession by a god). But the sense of *giddy* as 'unstable' became historically more important; it is linked with the Latin phrase *mobile vulgus* – the unstable common people, which by lC17 was being shortened to English *mob*. […]. The common C16 and C17 *multitude* was steadily replaced, from C18, by *mob,* though with continuing support from the usual battery of *vulgar, base, common* and *mean. Mob* has of course persisted into contemporary usage, but it has been since eC19 much more specific: a particular unruly crowd rather than a general condition. The word that then came through, for the general condition, was mass, followed by the masses.

Mass had been widely used, in a range of meanings, from C15, from fw *masse,* F and *massa,* L – a body of material that can be moulded or cast […] and by extension any large body of material. Two significant but alternative senses can be seen developing: (i) something amorphous and indistinguishable; (ii) a dense aggregate. The possible overlaps and variations are obvious. There was the use in *Othello*: 'I remember a masse of things, but nothing distinctly'. There is the significant use in Clarendon's *History of the Rebellion,* on the edge of a modern meaning: 'like so many atoms contributing jointly to this mass of confusion now before us'. Neutral uses of mass were developing in the physical sciences, in painting and in everyday use to indicate bulk. […] But the social sense can be seen coming through in lC17 and eC18: 'the Corrupted Mass' (1675); 'the mass of the people' (1711); 'the whole mass of mankind' (1713). But this was still indeterminate, until the period of the French Revolution. Then a particular use was decisive. As Southey observed in 1807: 'the levy in mass, the telegraph and the income-tax are all from France'. Anna Seward had written in 1798: 'our nation has almost risen in mass'. In a period of revolution and open social conflict many of the things that had been said, during the English Revolution, about *the multitude* were now said about the mass, and by the 1830s, at latest, the masses was becoming a common term, though still sometimes needing a special mark of novelty. A sense of the relation of the term to the INDUSTRIAL REVOLUTION appears to be evident in Gaskell's 'the steam engine has drawn together the population into dense masses' (*The Manufacturing Population of England,* 6; 1833). Moore in 1837 wrote: 'one of the few proofs of good Taste that 'the masses', as they are called, have yet given', and Carlyle, in 1839: 'men … to whom millions of living fellow-creatures … are 'masses', mere 'explosive masses for blowing down Bastilles with', for voting at hustings for *us*'. These two examples neatly illustrate the early divergence of implication. Moore picked up the new word in a cultural context, to indicate 'lowness' or 'vulgarity' as distinct from TASTE. Carlyle was aware of the precise historical reference to the revolutionary *levée en masse* but was also sufficiently aware of the established usage in physical science to carry through the metaphor of explosion. He also, significantly, linked the revolutionary usage, which he condemned as manipulative, with the electoral or parliamentary usage – 'voting at hustings for *us*' – which was given the same manipulative association.

The senses are thus very complex, for there is a persistence of the earlier senses (i) and (ii) of mass. Sense (i), of something amorphous and indistinguishable, persisted especially in the established phrase in the mass, as in Rogers (1820): 'we condemn millions in the mass as vindictive'; or Martineau (1832): 'we speak of society as one thing, and regard men in the mass', where what is implied is a failure to make necessary distinctions. Increasingly, however, though less naturally in English than in either French or German, the positive sense (ii), of a dense aggregate, was given direct social significance, as in the directly comparable *solidarity*. It was when the people acted together, 'as one man', that they could effectively change their condition. Here what had been in sense (i) a lack of necessary distinction or discrimination became, from sense (ii), an avoidance of unnecessary division or fragmentation and thus an achievement of unity. Most English radicals continued to use *the people* and its variations – *common people, working people, ordinary people* – as their primary positive terms, though in lC19 there was a common contrast between the masses and '*the classes*': 'back the masses against the classes' (Gladstone, 1886). Masses and its variants – the broad masses, the working masses, the toiling masses – have continued to be specifically used (at times in imperfect translation) in the revolutionary tradition.

In the modern social sense, then, masses and mass have two distinguishable kinds of implication. Masses (i) is the modern word for *many-headed multitude* or *mob:* low, ignorant, unstable. Masses (ii) is a description of the same people but now seen as a positive or potentially positive social force. The distinction became critical in many of the derived and associated forms. Mass meeting, from mC19, was sense (ii): people came together for some common social purpose (though the derogatory like a mass meeting is significant as a reaction). But sense (i), as in 'there are very few original eyes and ears; the great mass see and hear as they are directed by others' (S. Smith, 1803), has come through in C20 in several formations: mass society, mass suggestion, mass taste. Most of these formations have been relatively sophisticated kinds of criticism of DEMOCRACY, which, having become from eC19 an increasingly respectable word, seemed to need, in one kind of thought, this effective alternative. Mass-democracy can describe a manipulated political system, but it more often describes a system which is governed by uninstructed or ignorant preferences and opinions: the classical complaint against *democracy* itself. At the same time several of these formations have been influenced by the most popular among them: mass production, from USA in the 1920s. This does not really describe the process *of production,* which in fact, as originally on an assembly line, is multiple and serial. What it describes is a process of *consumption,* the mass market, where mass is a variation of sense (i), *the many-headed multitude* but now a *many-headed multitude* with purchasing power. Mass market was contrasted with *quality market,* retaining more of sense (i), but by extension mass production came to mean production in large numbers. The deepest difficulty of C20 uses of mass is then apparent: that a word which had indicated and which still indicates (both favourably and unfavourably) a solid aggregate now also means a very large number of things or people. The sense of a very large number has on the whole predominated. Mass communication and the mass media are by comparison with all previous systems not directed at masses (persons assembled) but at numerically very large yet in individual homes relatively isolated members of audiences. Several senses are fused but also confused: the large numbers reached (*the many-headed multitude* or *the majority of the people*); the mode adopted (*manipulative* or *popular*); the assumed taste (*vulgar* or *ordinary*); the resulting relationship (*alienated and abstract* or a *new kind of social communication*).

The most piquant element of the mass and masses complex, in contemporary usage, is its actively opposite social implications. To be engaged in mass work, to belong to mass organizations, to value mass meetings and mass movements, to live wholly in the service of the masses: these are the phrases of an active revolutionary tradition. But to study mass taste, to use the mass media, to control a mass market, to engage in mass observation, to understand mass psychology or mass opinion: these are the phrases of a wholly opposite social and political tendency. Some part of the revolutionary usage can be understood from the fact that in certain social conditions revolutionary intellectuals or revolutionary parties do not come from *the people,* and then see 'them', beyond themselves, as masses with whom and for whom they must work: masses as object or mass as material to be worked on. But the active history of the *levée en masse* has been at least as influential. In the opposite tendency, mass and masses moved away from the older simplicities of contempt [...]. The C20 formations are mainly ways of dealing with large numbers of people, on the whole indiscriminately perceived but crucial to several operations in politics, in commerce and in culture. The mass is assumed and then often, ironically, divided into parts again: *upper* or *lower* ends of the mass market; the *better kind* of mass entertainment. Mass society would then be a society organized or perceived in such ways; but, as a final complication, mass society has also been used, with some relation to its earlier conservative context, as a new term in radical and even revolutionary criticism. Mass society, massification (usually with strong reference to the mass media) are seen as modes of disarming or incorporating the *working class,* the *proletariat,* the masses: that is to say, they are new modes of alienation and control, which prevent and are designed to prevent the development of an authentic *popular* consciousness. It is thus possible to visualize, or at least hope for, a mass uprising against mass society, or a mass protest against the mass media, or mass organization against massification. The distinction that is being made, or attempted, in these contrasting political uses, is between the masses as the SUBJECT and the masses as the *object* of social action.

It is in the end not surprising that this should be so. In most of its uses masses is a cant word, but the problems of large societies and of collective action and reaction to which, usually confusingly, it and its derivatives and associates are addressed, are real enough and have to be continually spoken about.

# Chapter 2

# F.R. Leavis

# Mass Civilisation and Minority Culture

And this function is particularly important in our modern world, of which the whole civilisation is, to a much greater degree than the civilisation of Greece and Rome, mechanical and external, and tends constantly to become more so.

Matthew Arnold, *Culture and Anarchy.* 1869.

For Matthew Arnold it was in some ways less difficult. I am not thinking of the so much more desperate plight of culture to-day,[1] but (it is not, at bottom, an unrelated consideration) of the freedom with which he could use such phrases as 'the will of God' and 'our true selves.' To-day one must face problems of definition and formulation where Arnold could pass lightly on. When, for example, having started by saying that culture has always been in minority keeping, I am asked what I mean by 'culture,' I might (and do) refer the reader to *Culture and Anarchy*; but I know that something more is required.

In any period it is upon a very small minority that the discerning appreciation of art and literature depends: it is (apart from cases of the simple and familiar) only a few who are capable of unprompted, first-hand judgment. They are still a small minority, though a larger one, who are capable of endorsing such first-hand judgment by genuine personal response. The accepted valuations are a kind of paper currency based upon a very small proportion of gold. To the state of such a currency the possibilities of fine living at any time bear a close relation. There is no need to elaborate the metaphor: the nature of the relation is suggested well enough by this passage from Mr. I. A. Richards, which should by now be a *locus classicus:*

From: F.R. Leavis, *Mass Civilisation and Minority Culture*. Cambridge: Minority Press, 1930.

But it is not true that criticism is a luxury trade. The rearguard of Society cannot be extricated until the vanguard has gone further. Goodwill and intelligence are still too little available. The critic, we have said, is as much concerned with the health of the mind as any doctor with the health of the body. To set up as a critic is to set up as a judge of values. ... For the arts are inevitably and quite apart from any intentions of the artist an appraisal of existence. Matthew Arnold, when he said that poetry is a criticism of life, was saying something so obvious that it is constantly overlooked. The artist is concerned with the record and perpetuation of the experiences which seem to him most worth having. For reasons which we shall consider ... he is also the man who is most likely to have experiences of value to record. He is the point at which the growth of the mind shows itself.[2]

This last sentence gives the hint for another metaphor. The minority capable not only of appreciating Dante, Shakespeare, Donne, Baudelaire, Hardy (to take major instances) but of recognising their latest successors constitute the consciousness of the race (or of a branch of it) at a given time. For such capacity does not belong merely to an isolated aesthetic realm: it implies responsiveness to theory as well as to art, to science and philosophy in so far as these may affect the sense of the human situation and of the nature of life. Upon this minority depends our power of profiting by the finest human experience of the past; they keep alive the subtlest and most perishable parts of tradition. Upon them depend the implicit standards that order the finer living of an age, the sense that this is worth more than that, this rather than that is the direction in which to go, that the centre[3] is here rather than there. In their keeping, to use a metaphor that is metonymy also and will bear a good deal of pondering, is the language, the changing idiom, upon which fine living depends, and without which distinction of spirit is thwarted and incoherent. By 'culture' I mean the use of such a language. I do not suppose myself to have produced a tight definition, but the account, I think, will be recognised as adequate by anyone who is likely to read this pamphlet.

It is a commonplace to-day that culture is at a crisis. It is a commonplace more widely accepted than understood: at any rate, realisation of what the crisis portends does not seem to be common. [...]

It seems, then, not unnecessary to restate the obvious. In support of the belief that the modern phase of human history is unprecedented it is enough to point to the machine. The machine, in the first place, has brought about change in habit and the circumstances of life at a rate for which we have no parallel. The effects of such change may be studied in *Middletown,* a remarkable work of anthropology, dealing (I am afraid it is not superfluous to say) with a typical community of the Middle West. There we see in detail how the automobile (to take one instance) has, in a few years, radically affected religion,[4] broken up the family, and revolutionised social custom. Change has been so catastrophic that the generations find it hard to adjust themselves to each other, and parents are helpless to deal with their children. It seems unlikely that the conditions of life can be transformed in this way without some injury to the standard of living (to wrest the phrase from the economist): improvisation can hardly replace the delicate traditional adjustments, the mature, inherited codes of habit and valuation, without severe loss, and loss that may be more than temporary. It is a breach in continuity that threatens: what has been inadvertently dropped may be irrecoverable or forgotten.

To this someone will reply that Middletown is America and not England. And it is true that in America change has been more rapid, and its effects have been intensified by the fusion of peoples. But the same processes are at work in England and the western world generally, and at an acceleration. It is a commonplace that we are being Americanised, but again a commonplace that seems, as a rule, to carry little understanding with it. Americanisation is often spoken of as if it were something of which the United States are guilty. But it is something from which Lord Melchett, our 'British-speaking'[5] champion, will not save us even if he succeeds in rallying us to meet that American enterprise which he fears, 'may cause us to lose a great structure of self-governing brotherhoods whose common existence is of infinite importance to the future continuance of the Anglo-Saxon race, and of the gravest import to the development of all that seems best in our modern civilisation.'[6] For those who are most defiant of America do not propose to reverse the processes consequent upon the machine. We are to have greater efficiency, better salesmanship, and more mass-production and standardisation. Now, if the worst effects of mass-production and standardisation were represented by Woolworth's there would be no need to despair. But there are effects that touch the life of the community more seriously. When we consider, for instance, the processes of mass-production and standardisation in the form represented by the Press, it becomes obviously of sinister significance that they should be accompanied by a process of levelling-down. [...]

It applies even more disastrously to the films: more disastrously, because the films have a so much more potent influence.[7] They provide now the main form of recreation in the civilised world; and they involve surrender, under conditions of hypnotic receptivity, to the cheapest emotional appeals, appeals the more insidious because they are associated with a compellingly vivid illusion of actual life. It would be difficult to dispute that the result must be serious damage to the 'standard of living' (to use the phrase as before). All this seems so obvious that one is diffident about insisting on it. And yet people will reply by adducing the attempts that have been made to use the film as a serious medium of art. Just as, when broadcasting is in question, they will point out that they have heard good music broadcasted and intelligent lectures. The standardising influence of broadcasting hardly admits of doubt, but since there is here no Hollywood engaged in purely commercial exploitation the levelling-down is not so obvious. But perhaps it will not be disputed that broadcasting, like the films, is in practice mainly a means of passive diversion, and that it tends to make active recreation, especially active use of the mind, more difficult.[8] [...]

Contemplating that deliberate exploitation of the cheap response which characterises our civilisation we may say that a new factor in history is an unprecedented use of applied psychology. This might be thought to flatter Hollywood, but, even so, there can be no room for doubt when we consider advertising, and the progress it has made in two or three decades. [...] 'It ought to be plain even to the inexperienced,' writes an authority, Mr. Gilbert Russell, (in *Advertisement Writing*), 'that sucessful copywriting depends upon insight into people's minds: not into individual minds, mark, but into the way average people think and act, and the way they react to suggestions of various kinds.' And again: 'Advertising is becoming increasingly exact every day. Where instinct used to be enough, it is being replaced by inquiry. Advertising men nowadays don't say, 'The public will buy this article from such and such a motive': they employ what is called market research to find out the buying motives, as exactly as time and money and opportunity permit, from the public itself.'

So, as another authority, Mr. Harload Herd, Prinicpal of the Regent Institute, says (*Bigger Results from Advertising*): 'Now that advertising is more and more recruiting the best brains of the country we may look forward to increasingly scientific direction of this great public force.'

Mr. Gilbert Russell, who includes in his list books for 'A Copy Writer's Bookshelf' the works of Shakespeare, the Bible, *The Forsyte Saga, The Oxford Book of English Verse, Fiery Particles* by C.E. Montague and Sir Arthur Quiller-Couch's *The Art of Writing,* tells us that:

> Competent copy cannot be written except by men who have read lovingly, who have a sense of the romance of words, and of the picturesque and the dramatic phrase; who have versatility enough and judgment enough to know how to write plainly and pungently, or with a certain affectation. Briefly, competent copy is a matter not only of literary skill of a rather high order, but also skill of a particular specialised kind.'

The influence of such skill is to be seen in contemporary fiction. For if, as Mr. Thomas Russell (author of 'What did you do in the Great War, daddy?'), tells us, 'English is the best language in the world for advertising,' advertising is doing a great deal for English. It is carrying on the work begun by Mr. Rudyard Kipling, and, where certain important parts of the vocabulary are concerned, making things more difficult for the fastidious. For what is taking place is not something that affects only the environment of culture, stops short, as it were, at the periphery. This should be obvious, but it does not appear to be so to many who would recognise the account I have given above as matter of commonplace. Even those who would agree that there has been an overthrow of standards, that authority has disappeared, and that the currency has been debased and inflated, do not often seem to realise what the catastrophe portends. My aim is to bring this home, if possible, by means of a little concrete evidence. I hope, at any rate, to avert the charge of extravagant pessimism. [...]

There seems every reason to believe that the average cultivated person of a century ago was a very much more competent reader than his modern representative. Not only does the modern dissipate himself upon so much more reading of all kinds: the task of acquiring discrimination is much more difficult. A reader who grew up with Wordsworth moved among a limited set of signals (so to speak): the variety was not overwhelming. So he was able to acquire discrimination as he went along. But the modern is exposed to a concourse of signals so bewildering in their variety and number that, unless he is especially gifted or especially favoured, he can hardly begin to discriminate. Here we have the plight of culture in general. The landmarks have shifted, multiplied and crowded upon one another, the distinctions and dividing lines have blurred away, the boundaries are gone, and the arts and literatures of different countries and periods have flowed together, so that, if we revert to the metaphor of 'language' for culture, we may, to describe it, adapt the sentence in which Mr. T.S. Eliot describes the intellectual situation: 'When there is so much to be known, when there are so many fields of knowledge in which the same words are used with different meanings, when every one knows a little about a great many things, it becomes increasingly difficult for anyone to know whether he knows what he is talking about or not.'

We ought not, then, to be surprised that now, when a strong current of criticism is needed as never before, there should hardly be in England a cultivated public large enough to support a serious critical organ. [...]

The prospects of culture, then, are very dark. There is the less room for hope in that a standardised civilisation is rapidly enveloping the whole world. The glimpse of Russia that is permitted us does not afford the comfort that we are sometimes invited to find there. Anyone who has seen Eisenstein's film, *The General Line,* will appreciate the comment made by a writer in the *New Republic* (June 4, 1930) comparing it with an American film:

> One fancies, thinking about these things, that America might well send *The Silent Enemy* to Russia and say, 'This is what living too long with too much machinery does to people. Think twice, before you commit yourselves irrevocably to the same course.'

But it is vain to resist the triumph of the machine. It is equally vain to console us with the promise of a 'mass culture' that shall be utterly new. It would, no doubt, be possible to argue that such a 'mass culture' might be better than the culture we are losing, but it would be futile: the 'utterly new' surrenders everything that can interest us.[9]

What hope, then, is there left to offer? The vague hope that recovery *must* come, somehow, in spite of all? Mr. I.A. Richards, whose opinion is worth more than most people's, seems to authorise hope: he speaks of 'reasons for thinking that this century is in a cultural trough rather than upon a crest'; and says that 'the situation is likely to get worse before it is better.'[10] 'Once the basic level has been reached,' he suggests, 'a slow climb back may be possible. That at least is a hope that may be reasonably entertained.'[11] But it is a hope that looks very desperate in face of the downward acceleration described above, and it does not seem to point to any factor that might be counted upon to reverse the process.

Are we then to listen to Spengler's[12] (and Mr. Henry Ford's[13]) admonition to cease bothering about the inevitable future? That is impossible. Ridiculous, priggish and presumptuous as it may be, if we care at all about the issues we cannot help believing that, for the immediate future, at any rate, we have some responsibility. We cannot help clinging to some such hope as Mr. Richards offers; to the belief (unwarranted, possibly) that what we value most matters too much to the race to be finally abandoned, and that the machine will yet be made a tool.

It is for us to be as aware as possible of what is happening, and, if we can, to 'keep open our communications with the future.'

## Notes

1. 'The word, again, which we children of God speak, the voice which most hits our collective thought, the newspaper with the largest circulation in England, nay with the largest circulation in the whole world, is the *Daily Telegraph!*' – *Culture and Anarchy.*

It is the *News of the World* that has the largest circulation to-day.

2. Richards, I.A. (1924) *The Principles of Literary Criticism*, p. 61. London: Routledge and Kegan Paul.

3. '... the mass of the public is without any suspicion that the value of these organs is relative to their being nearer a certain ideal centre of correct information, taste and intelligence, or farther away from it.' – *Culture and Anarchy.*

4. 'One gains a distinct impression that the religious basis of all education was more taken for granted if less talked about thirty-five years ago, when high school 'chapel' was a religio-inspirational service with a 'choir' instead of the 'pep session' which it tends to become to-day.' Lynd, R.S. and Lynd, H.M. (1929) *Middletown: A Study in Modern America*, p. 204. Orlando, FL: Harcourt Brace and Company. This kind of change, of course, is not due to the automobile alone.

5. 'That would be one of the greatest disasters to the British-speaking people, and one of the greatest disasters to civilisation.' – LORD MELCHETT, *Industry and Politics*, p. 278.

6. Ibid., p. 281.

7. 'The motion picture, by virtue of its intrinsic nature, is a species of amusing and informational Esperanto, and, potentially at least, a species of aesthetic Esperanto of all the arts; if it may be classified as one, the motion picture has in it, perhaps more than any other, the resources of universality. ... The motion picture tells its stories directly, simply, quickly and elementally, not in words but in pictorial pantomime. To see is not only to believe; it is also in a measure to understand. In theatrical drama, seeing is closely allied with hearing, and hearing, in turn, with mental effort. In the motion picture, seeing is all – or at least nine-tenths of all.' – *Encyclopedia Britannica*, 14th Ed. – 'Motion Pictures: A Universal Language.'

The *Encyclopedia Britannica*, 14th Ed., is itself evidence of what is happening: 'humanised, modernised, pictorialised,' as the editors announce.

8. Mr. Edgar Rice Burroughs (creator of Tarzan) in a letter that I have been privileged to see, writes: 'It has been discovered through repeated experiments that pictures that require thought for appreciation have invariably been box-office failures. The general public does not wish to think. This fact, probably more than any other, accounts for the success of my stories, for without this specific idea in mind I have, nevertheless, endeavoured to make all of my descriptions so clear that each situation could be visualised readily by any reader precisely as I saw it. My reason for doing this was not based upon a low estimate of general intelligence, but upon the realisation that in improbable situations, such as abound in my work, the greatest pains must be taken to make them appear plausible. I have evolved, therefore, a type of fiction that may be read with the minimum of mental effort.' The significance of this for my argument does not need comment. Mr. Burroughs adds that his books sell at over a million copies a year. There is not room here to make the comparisons suggested by such documents as the *Life of James Lackington* (1791).

9. '... indeed, this gentleman, taking the bull by the horns, proposes that we should for the future call industrialism culture, and then of course there can be no longer any misapprehension of their true character; and besides the pleasure of being wealthy and comfortable, they will have authentic recognition as vessels of sweetness and light.' – *Culture and Anarchy*.

10. Richards, I.A. (1929) *Practical Criticism*, p. 320. Orlando, FL: Harcourt Brace and Company.

11. Ibid., p. 249.

12. 'Up to now everyone has been at liberty to hope what he pleased about the future. Where there are no facts, sentiment rules. But henceforward it will be every man's business to inform himself of what *can* happen and therefore of what with the unalterable necessity of destiny and irrespective of personal ideals, hopes or desires, will happen.' – Spengler, O. (1923 [1918]) *The Decline of the West*, Vol. I, p. 39. London: Alfred Knopf, Inc.

13. 'But what of the future? Shall we not have over-production? Shall we not some day reach a point where the machine becomes all powerful, and the man of no consequence?

No man can say anything of the future. We need not bother about it. The future has always cared for itself in spite of our well-meant efforts to hamper it. If to-day we do the task we can best do, then we are doing all that we can do.

Perhaps we may over-produce, but that is impossible until the whole world has all its desires. And if that should happen, then surely we ought to be content.' – Ford, H. (1926) *To-day and To-morrow*, pp. 272–273. New York: Productivity Press.

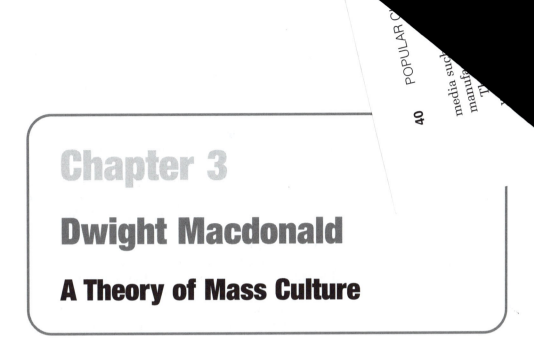

# Chapter 3

# Dwight Macdonald

# A Theory of Mass Culture

For about a century, Western culture has really been two cultures: the traditional kind – let us call it 'High Culture' – that is chronicled in the textbooks, and a 'Mass Culture' manufactured wholesale for the market. In the old art forms, the artisans of Mass Culture have long been at work: in the novel, the line stretches from Eugène Sue to Lloyd C. Douglas; in music, from Offenbach to Tin-Pan Alley; in art from the chromo to Maxfield Parrish and Norman Rockwell; in architecture, from Victorian Gothic to suburban Tudor. Mass Culture has also developed new media of its own, into which the serious artist rarely ventures: radio, the movies, comic books, detective stories, science fiction, television.

It is sometimes called 'Popular Culture,'[1] but I think 'Mass Culture' a more accurate term, since its distinctive mark is that it is solely and directly an article for mass consumption, like chewing gum. A work of High Culture is occasionally popular, after all, though this is increasingly rare. [...]

## The Nature of Mass Culture

The historical reasons for the growth of Mass Culture since the early 1800's are well known. Political democracy and popular education broke down the old upper-class monopoly of culture. Business enterprise found a profitable market in the cultural demands of the newly awakened masses, and the advance of technology made possible the cheap production of books, periodicals, pictures, music, and furniture, in sufficient quantities to satisfy this market. Modern technology also created new

From: *Mass Culture: The Popular Arts in America*. Ed. Bernard Rosenberg and David Manning White. New York: The Free Press, 1957.

as the movies and television which are specially well adapted to mass
...cture and distribution.

...e phenomenon is thus peculiar to modern times and differs radically from
what was hitherto known as art or culture. It is true that Mass Culture began as,
and to some extent still is, a parasitic, a cancerous growth on High Culture. As
Clement Greenberg pointed out in 'Avant-Garde and *Kitsch*' (*Partisan Review*,
Fall, 1939): 'The precondition of *kitsch* (a German term for 'Mass Culture') is the
availability close at hand of a fully matured cultural tradition, whose discoveries,
acquisitions, and perfected self-conscious *kitsch* can take advantage of for its own
ends.' [...] *Kitsch* 'mines' High Culture the way improvident frontiersmen mine
the soil, extracting its riches and putting nothing back. Also, as *kitsch* develops,
it begins to draw on its own past, and some of it evolves so far away from High
Culture as to appear quite disconnected from it.

It is also true that Mass Culture is to some extent a continuation of the old Folk
Art which until the Industrial Revolution was the culture of the common people,
but here, too, the differences are more striking than the similarities. Folk Art grew
from below. It was a spontaneous, autochthonous expression of the people, shaped
by themselves, pretty much without the benefit of High Culture, to suit their own
needs. Mass Culture is imposed from above. It is fabricated by technicians hired
by businessmen; its audiences are passive consumers, their participation limited
to the choice between buying and not buying. The Lords of *kitsch,* in short, exploit
the cultural needs of the masses in order to make a profit and/or to maintain their
class rule – in Communist countries, only the second purpose obtains. (It is very
different to *satisfy* popular tastes, as Robert Burns' poetry did, and to *exploit* them,
as Hollywood does.) Folk Art was the people's own institution, their private little
garden walled off from the great formal park of their masters' High Culture. But
Mass Culture breaks down the wall, integrating the masses into a debased form of
High Culture and thus becoming an instrument of political domination. If one had
no other data to go on, the nature of Mass Culture would reveal capitalism to be
an exploitative class society and not the harmonious commonwealth it is sometimes alleged to be. The same goes even more strongly for Soviet Communism and
*its* special kind of Mass Culture.

## Mass Culture: U.S.S.R.

'Everybody' knows that America is a land of Mass Culture, but it is not so generally recognized that so is the Soviet Union. Certainly not by the Communist leaders, one of whom has contemptuously observed that the American people need not
fear the peace-loving Soviet state which has absolutely no desire to deprive them
of their Coca-Cola and comic books. Yet the fact is that the U.S.S.R. is even more
a land of Mass Culture than is the U.S.A. This is less easily recognizable because
their Mass Culture is *in form* just the opposite of ours, being one of propaganda
and pedagogy rather than of entertainment. None the less, it has the essential
quality of Mass, as against High or Folk, Culture: it is manufactured for mass consumption by technicians employed by the ruling class and is not an expression of
either the individual artist or the common people themselves. Like our own, it
exploits rather than satisfies the cultural needs of the masses, though for political

rather than commercial reasons. Its quality is even lower: our Supreme Court building is tasteless and pompous, but not to the lunatic degree of the proposed new Palace of the Soviets – a huge wedding cake of columns mounting up to an eighty-foot statue of Lenin; Soviet movies are so much duller and cruder than our own that even the American comrades shun them; the childish level of *serious* Soviet magazines devoted to matters of art or philosophy has to be read to be believed, and as for the popular press, it is as if Colonel McCormick ran every periodical in America.

## Gresham's Law in Culture

The separation of Folk Art and High Culture in fairly watertight compartments corresponded to the sharp line once drawn between the common people and the aristocracy. The eruption of the masses onto the political stage has broken down this compartmentation, with disastrous cultural results. Whereas Folk Art had its own special quality, Mass Culture is at best a vulgarized reflection of High Culture. And whereas High Culture could formerly ignore the mob and seek to please only the *cognoscenti*, it must now compete with Mass Culture or be merged into it.

The problem is acute in the United States and not just because a prolific Mass Culture exists here. If there were a clearly defined cultural *élite,* then the masses could have their *kitsch* and the *élite* could have its High Culture, with everybody happy. But the boundary line is blurred. A statistically significant part of the population, I venture to guess, is chronically confronted with a choice between going to the movies or to a concert, between reading Tolstoy or a detective story, between looking at old masters or at a TV show; i.e., the pattern of their cultural lives is 'open' to the point of being porous. Good art competes with *kitsch,* serious ideas compete with commercialized formulae – and the advantage lies all on one side. There seems to be a Gresham's Law in cultural as well as monetary circulation: bad stuff drives out the good, since it is more easily understood and enjoyed. It is this facility of access which at once sells *kitsch* on a wide market and also prevents it from achieving quality.[2] Clement Greenberg writes that the special aesthetic quality of *kitsch* is that it 'predigests art for the spectator and spares him effort, provides him with a shortcut to the pleasures of art that detours what is necessarily difficult in genuine art' because it includes the spectator's reactions in the work of art itself instead of forcing him to make his own responses. Thus 'Eddie Guest and the Indian Love Lyrics are more "poetic" than T.S. Eliot and Shakespeare.' And so, too, our 'collegiate Gothic' such as the Harkness Quadrangle at Yale is more picturesquely Gothic than Chartres, and a pinup girl smoothly airbrushed by Petty is more sexy than a real naked woman.

When to this ease of consumption is added *kitsch's* ease of production because of its standardized nature, its prolific growth is easy to understand. It threatens High Culture by its sheer pervasiveness, its brutal, overwhelming *quantity.* The upper classes, who begin by using it to make money from the crude tastes of the masses and to dominate them politically, end by finding their own culture attacked and even threatened with destruction by the instrument they have thoughtlessly employed. (The same irony may be observed in modern politics, where most swords seem to have two edges; thus Nazism began as a tool of the big bourgeoisie and the army *Junkers* but ended by using *them* as *its* tools.)

## Homogenized Culture

Like nineteenth-century capitalism, Mass Culture is a dynamic, revolutionary force, breaking down the old barriers of class, tradition, taste, and dissolving all cultural distinctions. It mixes and scrambles everything together, producing what might be called homogenized culture, after another American achievement, the homogenization process that distributes the globules of cream evenly throughout the milk instead of allowing them to float separately on top. It thus destroys all values, since value judgments imply discrimination. Mass Culture is very, very democratic: it absolutely refuses to discriminate against, or between, anything or anybody. All is grist to its mill, and all comes out finely ground indeed. [...]

## Academicism and Avantgardism

Until about 1930, High Culture tried to defend itself against the encroachments of Mass Culture in two opposite ways: Academicism, or an attempt to compete by imitation; and Avantgardism, or a withdrawal from competition.

Academicism is *kitsch* for the *élite*: spurious High Culture that is outwardly the real thing but actually as much a manufactured article as the cheaper cultural goods produced for the masses. It is recognized at the time for what it is only by the Avantgardists. A generation or two later, its real nature is understood by everyone and it quietly drops into the same oblivion as its franker sister-under-the-skin. [...]

The significance of the Avantgarde movement (by which I mean poets such as Rimbaud, novelists such as Joyce, composers such as Stravinsky, and painters such as Picasso) is that it simply refused to compete. Rejecting Academicism – and thus, at a second remove, also Mass Culture – it made a desperate attempt to fence off some area where the serious artist could still function. It created a new compartmentation of culture, on the basis of an intellectual rather than a social *élite*. The attempt was remarkably successful: to it we owe almost everything that is living in the art of the last fifty or so years. In fact, the High Culture of our times is pretty much identical with Avantgardism. [...]

## A Merger has been Arranged

In this new period, the competitors, as often happens in the business world, are merging. Mass Culture takes on the color of both varieties of the old High Culture, Academic and Avantgarde, while these latter are increasingly watered down with Mass elements. There is slowly emerging a tepid, flaccid Middlebrow Culture that threatens to engulf everything in its spreading ooze. Bauhaus modernism has at last trickled down, in a debased form of course, into our furniture, cafeterias, movie theatres, electric toasters, office buildings, drug stores, and railroad trains. Psychoanalysis is expounded sympathetically and superficially in popular magazines, and the psychoanalyst replaces the eccentric millionaire as the *deus ex machina* in many a movie. T.S. Eliot writes *The Cocktail Party* and it becomes a Broadway hit. [...]

All this is not a raising of the level of Mass Culture, as might appear at first, but rather a corruption of High Culture. There is nothing more vulgar than sophisticated *kitsch*. Compare Conan Doyle's workmanlike and unpretentious Sherlock Holmes stories with the bogus 'intellectuality' of Dorothy M. Sayers, who, like many contemporary detective-story writers, is a novelist *manquée* who ruins her stuff with literary attitudinizing. Or consider the relationship of Hollywood and Broadway. In the twenties, the two were sharply differentiated, movies being produced for the masses of the hinterland, theatre for an upper-class New York audience. The theatre was High Culture, mostly of the Academic variety (Theatre Guild) but with some spark of Avantgarde fire (the 'little' or 'experimental' theatre movement). The movies were definitely Mass Culture, mostly very bad but with some leaven of Avantgardism (Griffith, Stroheim) and Folk Art (Chaplin and other comedians). With the sound film, Broadway and Hollywood drew closer together. Plays are now produced mainly to sell the movie rights, with many being directly financed by the film companies. The merger has standardized the theatre to such an extent that even the early Theatre Guild seems vital in retrospect, while hardly a trace of the 'experimental' theatre is left. And what have the movies gained? They are more sophisticated, the acting is subtler, the sets in better taste. But they too have become standardized: they are never as awful as they often were in the old days, but they are never as good either. They are better entertainment and worse art. [...]

## The Problem of the Masses

Conservatives such as Ortega y Gasset and T.S. Eliot argue that since 'the revolt of the masses' has led to the horrors of totalitarianism (and of California roadside architecture), the only hope is to rebuild the old class walls and bring the masses once more under aristocratic control. They think of the popular as synonymous with cheap and vulgar. Marxian radicals and liberals, on the other hand, see the masses as intrinsically healthy but as the dupes and victims of cultural exploitation by the Lords of *kitsch* – in the style of Rousseau's 'noble savage' idea. If only the masses were offered good stuff instead of *kitsch*, how they would eat it up! How the level of Mass Culture would rise! Both these diagnoses seem to me fallacious: they assume that Mass Culture is (in the conservative view) or could be (in the liberal view) an expression of *people*, like Folk Art, whereas actually it is an expression of *masses*, a very different thing.

There are theoretical reasons why Mass Culture is not and can never be any good. I take it as axiomatic that culture can only be produced by and for human beings. But in so far as people are organized (more strictly, disorganized) as masses, they lose their human identity and quality. For the masses are in historical time what a crowd is in space: a large quantity of people unable to express themselves as human beings because they are related to one another neither as individuals nor as members of communities – indeed, they are not related *to each other* at all, but only to something distant, abstract, nonhuman: a football game or bargain sale in the case of a crowd, a system of industrial production, a party or a State in the case of the masses. The mass man is a solitary atom, uniform with and undifferentiated from thousands and millions of other atoms who go to make up 'the lonely crowd,' as David Riesman well calls American society. A folk or a people, however, is a community, i.e., a group of individuals linked to each other by common interests, work, traditions, values, and sentiments; something like a family, each of whose members has a special place and function as an individual while at the same time sharing the group's interests (family budget) sentiments (family quarrels), and culture (family jokes). The scale is small enough so that it 'makes a difference' what the individual does, a first condition for human – as against mass–existence. He is at once more important as an individual than in mass society and at the same time more closely integrated into the community, his creativity nourished by a rich combination of individualism and communalism. [...] In contrast, a mass society, like a crowd, is so undifferentiated and loosely structured that its atoms, in so far as human values go, tend to cohere only along the line of the least common denominator; its morality sinks to that of its most brutal and primitive members, its taste to that of the least sensitive and most ignorant. And in addition to everything else, the scale is simply too big, there are just *too many people*.

Yet the collective monstrosity, 'the masses,' 'the public,' is taken as a human norm by the scientific and artistic technicians of our Mass Culture. They at once degraded the public by treating it as an object, to be handled with the lack of ceremony and the objectivity of medical students dissecting a corpse, and at the same time flatter it, pander to its level of taste and ideas by taking these as the criterion of reality (in the case of questionnaire-sociologists and other 'social scientists') or of art (in the case of the Lords of *kitsch*). When one hears a questionnaire-sociologist talk about how he will 'set up' an investigation, one feels he regards people as a herd of dumb animals, as mere congeries of conditioned reflexes, his calculation being which reflex will be stimulated by which question. At the same time, of necessity, he sees the statistical majority as the great Reality, the secret of life he is trying to find out; like the *kitsch* Lords, he is wholly without values, willing to accept any idiocy if it is held by many people. The aristocrat and the democrat both criticize and argue with popular taste, the one with hostility, the other in friendship, for both attitudes proceed from a set of values. This is less degrading to the masses than the 'objective' approach of Hollywood and the questionnaire-sociologists, just as it is less degrading to a man to be shouted at in anger than to be quietly assumed to be part of a machine. But the *plebs* have their dialectical revenge: complete indifference to their human *quality* means complete prostration before their statistical *quantity*, so that a movie magnate who cynically 'gives the public what it wants' – i.e., assumes it wants trash – sweats with terror if box-office returns drop 10 per cent.

## The Future of High Culture: Dark

The conservative proposal to save culture by restoring the old class lines has a more solid historical base than the Marxian hope for a new democratic, classless culture, for, with the possible (and important) exception of Periclean Athens, all the great cultures of the past were *élite* cultures. Politically, however, it is without meaning in a world dominated by the two great mass nations, U.S.A. and U.S.S.R. and becoming more industrialized, more massified all the time. The only practical thing along those lines would be to revive the *cultural élite* which the Avantgarde created. As I have already noted, the Avantgarde is now dying, partly from internal causes, partly suffocated by the competing Mass Culture, where it is not being absorbed into it. Of course this process has not reached 100 per cent, and doubtless never will unless the country goes either Fascist or Communist. There are still islands above the flood for those determined enough to reach them, and to stay on them: as Faulkner has shown, a writer can even use Hollywood instead of being used by it, if his purpose is firm enough. But the homogenization of High and Mass Culture has gone far and is going farther all the time, and there seems little reason to expect a revival of Avantgardism, that is, of a successful countermovement to Mass Culture. Particularly not in this country, where the blurring of class lines, the absence of a stable cultural tradition, and the greater facilities for manufacturing and marketing *kitsch* all work in the other direction. The result is that our intelligentsia is remarkably small, weak, and disintegrated. One of the odd things about the American cultural scene is how many brainworkers there are and how few intellectuals, defining the former as specialists whose thinking is pretty much confined to their limited 'fields' and the latter as persons who take all culture for their province. Not only are there few intellectuals, but they don't hang together, they have very little *esprit de corps*, very little sense of belonging to a community; they are so isolated from each other they don't even bother to quarrel – there hasn't been a really good fight among them since the Moscow Trials.

## The Future of Mass Culture: Darker

If the conservative proposal to save our culture via the aristocratic Avantgarde seems historically unlikely, what of the democratic-liberal proposal? Is there a reasonable prospect of raising the level of Mass Culture? In his recent book, *The Great Audience*, Gilbert Seldes argues there is. He blames the present sad state of our Mass Culture on the stupidity of the Lords of *kitsch*, who underestimate the mental age of the public; the arrogance of the intellectuals, who make the same mistake and so snobbishly refuse to work for such mass media as radio, TV and movies; and the passivity of the public itself, which doesn't insist on better Mass Cultural products. This diagnosis seems to me superficial in that it blames everything on subjective, moral factors: stupidity, perversity, failure of will. My own feeling is that, as in the case of the alleged responsibility of the German (or Russian) people for the horrors of Nazism (or Soviet Communism), it is unjust to blame social groups for this result. Human beings have been caught up in the inexorable workings of a mechanism that forces them, with a pressure only heroes can resist [...] into its own pattern. I see Mass Culture as a reciprocating engine, and who is to say, once it has been set in motion, whether the stroke or the counterstroke is 'responsible' for its continued action?

The Lords of *kitsch* sell culture to the masses. It is a debased, trivial culture that voids both the deep realities (sex, death, failure, tragedy) and also the simple, spontaneous pleasures, since the realities would be too real and the pleasures too *lively* to induce what Mr. Seldes calls 'the mood of consent,' i.e., a narcotized acceptance of Mass Culture and of the commodities it sells as a substitute for the unsettling and unpredictable (hence unsalable) joy, tragedy, wit, change, originality and beauty of real life. The masses, debauched by several generations of this sort of thing, in turn come to demand trivial and comfortable cultural products. Which came first, the chicken or the egg, the mass demand or its satisfaction (and further stimulation) is a question as academic as it is unanswerable. The engine is reciprocating and shows no signs of running down.

Indeed, far from Mass Culture getting better, we will be lucky if it doesn't get worse. [...] Since Mass Culture is not an art form but a manufactured commodity, it tends always downward, toward cheapness – and so standardization – of production. Thus, T.W. Adorno has noted, in his brilliant essay 'On Popular Music' (*Studies in Philosophy and Social Science,* New York, No. 1, 1941) that the chorus of every popular song *without* exception has the same number of bars, while Mr. Seldes remarks that Hollywood movies are cut in a uniformly rapid tempo, a shot rarely being held more than forty-five seconds, which gives them a standardized effect in contrast to the varied tempo of European film cutting. This sort of standardization means that what may have begun as something fresh and original is repeated until it becomes a nerveless routine. [...] The only time Mass Culture is good is at the very beginning, before the 'formula' has hardened, before the money boys and efficiency experts and audience-reaction analysts have moved in. Then for a while it may have the quality of real Folk Art. But the Folk artist today lacks the cultural roots and the intellectual toughness (both of which the Avantgarde artist has relatively more of) to resist for long the pressures of Mass Culture. [...] Whatever virtues the Folk artist has, and they are many, staying power is not one of them. And staying power is the essential virtue of one who would hold his own against the spreading ooze of Mass Culture.

## Notes

Reprinted from *Diogenes,* No. 3, Summer, 1953, pp. 1–17, by permission of the author and the publisher. (Copyright, 1953, by Intercultural Publications, Inc.)

1. As I did myself in 'A Theory of Popular Culture' (*Politics,* February, 1944) parts of which have been used or adapted in the present article.

2. The success of *Reader's Digest* illustrates the law. Here is a magazine that has achieved a fantastic circulation – some fifteen millions, much of which is accounted for by its foreign editions, thus showing that *kitsch* by no means appeals only to Americans – simply by reducing to even lower terms the already superficial formulae of other periodicals. By treating a theme in two pages which they treat in six, the *Digest* becomes three times as 'readable' and three times as superficial.

# Chapter 4

# Tania Modleski

## Femininity as Mas(s)querade: A Feminist Approach to Mass Culture

In closing remarks given at the weekend seminar on popular culture John Caughie referred in passing to an 'absence of feminist work around popular culture'. Another participant, Simon Frith, pointed out that women have indeed addressed questions of popular culture, but that when women talk about it, it is not generally considered popular culture. Frith referred to Rosalind Coward's book *Female Desire,* which analyses fashions, romances, women's magazines, and a whole host of specifically feminine cultural artifacts and practices. In effect, he was pointing to the critical double standard which has been as pervasive in popular culture studies as it has been in studies of high culture – a double standard I discuss in the first chapter of my own work on women and popular culture, *Loving with a Vengeance: Mass-produced Fantasies for Women.* Although women have spoken, then, they have not always been heard, and one of the tasks for feminism is continually to insist upon recognition, as well as upon the priority of its work.

Beyond this important role that must be assigned to feminist criticism, however, lies an even larger role – the necessity of showing that the entire issue of gender is of much larger significance than has previously been acknowledged in discussions of mass culture. Gender has typically been theorised as simply one positioning among many, one possible point of resistance to mass culture's attempts to homogenise social reality. Thus Fredric Jameson says:

From: *High Theory/Low Culture: Analyzing Popular Television and Film.* Ed. C. MacCabe. Manchester: Manchester University Press, 1986.

> The only authentic cultural production today has seemed to be that which can draw on the collective experience of marginal pockets of the social life of the world system: black literature and blues, British working-class rock, women's literature, gay literature, the *roman québecois,* the literature of the Third World; and this production is possible only to the degree to which these forms of collective life or collective solidarity have not yet been fully penetrated by the market and by the commodity system.[1]

Orthodox Marxism today abandons its exclusive reliance on the working class as agents of revolutionary change, and grants women and a few other groups a token importance as well. The invocation of the women's movement occurs towards the end of an essay with no feminist perspective, and women are brought in at the last to be offered as one of the few rays of hope in what has been portrayed as a bleak situation. Indeed, the very measure of its bleakness, it is implied, is that women, gays, and rock groups – these 'marginal pockets' of social life – *are* our best hope.

But the issue of gender in relation to mass culture goes much deeper and ramifies in a number of quite surprising directions. By looking at several different kinds of discourse, I want to show how our ways of thinking and feeling about mass culture are so intricately bound up with notions of the feminine that the need for a feminist critique becomes obvious at every level of the debate. To begin with, women find themselves at the centre of many historical accounts of mass culture, damned as 'mobs of scribbling women', in Hawthorne's famous phrase, and held responsible for the debasement of taste and the sentimentalisation of culture. As the example of Hawthorne suggests, historians of culture are not the only ones who blame women for creating the conditions of what Ann Douglas calls 'the cultural sprawl that has increasingly characterised post-Victorian life'.[2] Artists themselves adopt this view, which holds such sway not because of its truth value but because it rests on powerful stereotypes, habits of language, and unexamined – because unconscious – psychic associations.

In this chapter I want first to examine the orthodox position of the literary historian for the way in which mass culture is condemned as a 'feminised' culture. Then I will discuss the work of two other contemporaries, an artist (Manuel Puig) and a theorist (Jean Baudrillard) who, far from condemning mass culture because it is 'effeminate', try to re-evaluate and to some extent affirm it precisely on the grounds of its association with or resemblance to the feminine. This is certainly an interesting twist to the old debate, though it must be remembered that the feminine has always been a term alternately denigrated and exalted. Whether the latest development represents a gain for women or for feminism remains to be seen.

The orthodox view can be found in its sternest form in *The Feminization of American Culture* by critic, literary historian, and professed feminist, Ann Douglas. The book was a major publishing event and a resounding critical success in America. [...] With all the fervour of one converted to, rather than born in the patriarchal faith, Douglas not only judges the writings of the majority of nineteenth-century women to be of inferior quality when measured against the artistic achievements of a Herman Melville; she also holds them entirely accountable for the advent of modern mass culture. Discussing Little Eva in Harriet Beecher Stowe's *Uncle Tom's Cabin* as the archetypal heroine of women's fiction and Little Eva's death as the archetypal event, Douglas writes:

Stowe's infantile heroine anticipates that exaltation of the average which is the trademark of mass culture. Vastly superior as she is to most of her figurative off-spring, she is nonetheless the childish predecessor of Miss America, of 'Teen Angel', of the ubiquitous, everyday, wonderful girl about whom thousands of popular songs and movies have been made ... In a sense, my introduction to Little Eva and to the Victorian scenes, objects and sensibility of which she is suggestive was my introduction to consumerism. The pleasure Little Eva gave me provided historical and practical preparation for the equally indispensable and disquieting comforts of mass culture. (2–3)

Instigating the Civil War was obviously not the last charge for which Stowe would be answerable. Despite Douglas's homage in the book to a masculine kind of intel-lectual 'toughness', what is remarkable about this passage is its reliance on impres-sionistic associations. Out of such associations are generated a causal sequence and a history. The last line of the passage is ironic in the light of Douglas's repeated castigations of the women for their narcissism, of which Little Eva is the chief exemplar. Somehow Douglas's private pleasure metamorphoses into an *ex post facto* 'historical preparation' for the national and increasingly global phenomenon of mass culture itself. Nowhere does she consider the question of who profits from Miss America, nor does she acknowledge the extent to which the image of the 'teen angel' antedates Stowe and the vast majority of women writers.

Little Eva's death from 'consumption' would appear to take on a retroactively symbolic significance. But rather than examine the forces that conspire to con-demn women to be the pre-eminent consumers in consumer society, the literary historian often assumes women's habit of consumption to be nearly as unavoid-able as death. In an illuminating passage, Douglas remarks that 'content was *not* the most important aspect of their work. Ministerial and feminine authors were as involved with the method of consumption as with the article consumed'. Thus, in an extraordinary move, Douglas manages to transform even women's production of texts into an act of consumption, or, in Roland Barthes' terminology, their writing of books into a readerly practice.

Douglas goes on to contrast the nineteenth-century minister, who preferred 'light reading' (i.e. fiction and poetry), to the well-educated eighteenth-century minister of Calvinism [...]. The latter read 'dense argumentative tracts' that 'forced him to think, not to 'read' in our modern sense; metaphorically speaking, he was produc-ing, not consuming'. Finally, Douglas speaks of the 'countless Victorian women' who 'spent much of their middle-class girlhoods prostrate on chaise-longues with their heads buried in "worthless novels"'. Douglas's evidence is taken from the writings of contemporary 'observers' contrasting these girls unfavourably with their supposedly more industrious grandmothers who 'spent their time studying the Bible and performing useful household chores'. Now, 'evidence' of this kind should clearly be treated with considerable caution by the tough-minded historian. But it is not the truth value of these observations that counts. It is the vivid *image* of girls prostrate on chaise-longues, immersed in their worthless novels, that has provided historical preparation for the practice of countless critics who persist in equating femininity, consumption, and reading, on the one hand, and masculinity, production, and writing on the other.

The wilfulness of these connections is indicated by the fact that Douglas singles out Stowe's *Uncle Tom's Cabin* [...] to indict for introducing the pleasures of consumerism. Far from being a work that simply participates in a kind of 'complicated mass dream life', which for Douglas means that such books are readerly even in their writing, recent criticism has shown how carefully crafted and controlled the novel actually is. Moreover, feminist analysis has revealed that its Utopian vision is based upon an ideal *of feminine* production in the home which gets extended into an ideal for national and international government. As Jane Tompkins notes, the home 'is conceived as a dynamic center of activity, physical and spiritual, economic and moral, whose influence spreads out in ever widening circles'.[3] Feminist criticism of this sort leads us to re-evaluate and clarify our terms and to rid our selves of some of the unconscious associations they carry. Too often politically-oriented criticism invokes 'production' as an ideal pure and simple, without concerning itself with what is being produced. Thus, the Calvinist minister is praised for 'producing the texts he read', even though they may have been 'repressive, authoritarian, dogmatic, patriarchal in the extreme'. On the other hand, Stowe is condemned for allowing readers to become 'absorbed' in her thrilling novel (i.e. to consume it) despite the fact that she was presenting them with an ideology based upon a feminine mode of production and intended 'to effect a radical transformation of ... society'.[4] Such a view exposes the masculinist bias of much politically-oriented criticism that adopts metaphors of production and consumption in order to differentiate between progressive and regressive activities of reading (or viewing, as the case may be).

Tompkins' strategy is to correct this masculinist bias by expanding the definition of 'production' to include the kind of work that women do. An alternative strategy might consist of deconstructing the hierarchical relation that exists in the oppositions production/consumption and writerly/readerly in order to search out the radical potential of the subordinate terms, each of which, as we have seen, is typically associated with the feminine. Indeed, as one might expect in our postmodern age, such a project has already been initiated by artists and theorists alike.

Manuel Puig's acclaimed novel *Kiss of the Spider Woman* provides an excellent example of such a deconstructive text. The novel takes place in an Argentinian prison where the homosexual 'queen' Molina helps pass the time by relating film plots to his cellmate, a Marxist revolutionary named Valentin. The setting of the novel obviously gives new meaning to the usually pejorative designation of mass-produced art as 'escapist'. The novel draws on the conventions of the prison film, only here the films themselves function as 'the great escape'. [...]

At the beginning of the novel, although Valentin very much enjoys indulging in the 'escapist' pleasures offered him by Molina, he deeply distrusts this enjoyment and insists on restricting the storytelling to bedtime, for he adopts the standard leftist view of popular culture. Not unlike Douglas's Calvinist minister, Valentin forces himself to struggle with his difficult political science tracts, repudiating the attractions of the film stories. 'It can become a vice, always trying to escape from reality like that, it's like taking drugs or something ... If you read something, if you study something, you transcend any cell you're inside of, do you understand what I'm saying?'[5] At one point, Valentin condemns himself for his 'weakness' in becoming attached to the characters in one of the stories and feeling sad that the 'film' has ended (41). It becomes clear that Valentin associates this 'weakness' with femininity and fears the passivity involved in the processes of identification and empathy – those *bêtes noires* of Marxist literary and film criticism. Surrendering oneself *to* the texts is to assume an uncomfortable resemblance to the women *in* the texts [...].

It is to assume, as well, an uncomfortable resemblance to Molina, who, as the consumer *par excellence,* yields himself to the films with utter abandon, resents Valentin's attempts to analyse the stories, and weeps when Valentin criticises his favourite film, which is, significantly, a Nazi propaganda film that he admires for its aesthetic beauty and for the love story. Furthermore, Molina's attitude towards men, like his attitude towards films, is one of complete surrender of self. For example, he tells Valentin of a fantasy he has of living with a waiter with whom he is infatuated. He dreams of helping him study and arranging things so that the man will never have to work again. 'And I'd pass along whatever small amount of money was needed to give the wife for child support, and make him not worry about anything at all, nothing except himself, until he got what he wanted and lost all that sadness of his for good, wouldn't that be marvelous?' (69).

Having set up the traditional polarities that we saw were operative in Douglas's work (masculine = production and work; feminity = consumption and passivity), Puig proceeds to effect a transvaluation of the terms. The project of the novel is to get Valentin to accept the otherness that Molina represents – femininity, homosexuality, and mass culture – and, ultimately to allow himself to be sexually and textually seduced by Molina, whom he calls 'the spider woman'. The spider woman is featured in the drug-induced dream Valentin has at the end of the book: at first she appears to Valentin to be trapped in a spider's web, but then it becomes clear that the spider's web is growing out of her own body, 'the threads are coming out of her waist and hips, they're part of her body, so many threads that look like hairy ropes and disgust me, even though if I were to touch them they might feel as smooth as who knows what, but it makes me queasy to touch them ...' (280). The description of the spider woman, an image of femininity and of homosexuality taken from mass culture, suggests what is at stake in Valentin's attitude toward his others: the fear of entrapment and absorption, which is simultaneously desired and dreaded.

Throughout the novel Puig is satirising traditional Marxism in the figure of Valentin, and in both the narrative and the accompanying footnotes, the book indicates that a revolution must occur in the personal realm as well as the political and must be concerned with sex and gender as well as class. For Marxism, which is classically preoccupied with production, this sexual revolution would involve a new and more positive attitude towards consumption. [...] Valentin at first resists being nurtured by Molina, as he resists the film stories. Finally, however, he comes to accept the various consumer pleasures offered and embodied by Molina and changes his mind about the importance of 'sensory gratification' which he earlier repudiated. At the beginning, for example, he protests that Molina's cooking and storytelling is getting him into 'bad habits':

There's no way I can live for the moment because my life is dedicated to political struggle ... Social revolution, that's what's important, and gratifying the senses is only secondary. The great pleasure's something else, it's knowing I've put myself in the service of a noble ... ideology ... Marxism ... And I can get that pleasure anywhere, right here in this cell and even in torture. (27–8)

One of the ironies of Valentin's manifesto is his lack of awareness that his machismo contains strong elements of passivity and even masochism (pleasure in torture). Thus the traits that Valentin rejects as feminine are revealed early in the novel to be important parts of his character. By the end, Valentin has been reduced to helplessness at the hands of Molina, who feeds him, wipes and bathes him after he has been incontinent, and continues to tell him films at bedtime 'like lullabies' (279). He learns to view his 'weaknesses' as less shameful and, at least to a certain extent, comes to enjoy being submissive.

As for Molina, his identification with the passive and often masochistic heroines of his films, his swooning rapture over the films he describes, would appear to make him the ideal manipulated consumer. On the contrary, however, it becomes increasingly apparent as the novel progresses that Molina uses the films in order to do his own manipulating. On occasion he admits to resorting to strategy, as when he confesses that he likes to leave Valentin 'hanging' so he will enjoy the film more. [...] Molina uses the techniques of manipulation he has learned from his adored mass culture in order to seduce Valentin into his web. Mass culture becomes not the enemy, as it is for the Marxist, but the very agency through which Molina accomplishes his coup and conquers Valentin. The triumph that Molina achieves precisely through his utter devotion both to men and to the films, as well as by his apparent submission to the law represented by the warden, is attributable to what Jean Baudrillard, quoting Hegel, calls 'the eternal irony of femininity' that supposedly characterises the masses – 'the irony of a false fidelity to the law, an ultimately impenetrable simulation of passivity and obedience ... which in return annuls the law governing them'.[6] Molina's exaggeration of the feminine – his simulation of womanhood, derived from emulating film heroines, realises an ideal of femininity as mas(s)querade: the homosexual 'queen' as exemplar of the hyperreal.

In the above passage, taken from *In the Shadow of the Silent Majorities or the End of the Social,* Baudrillard himself is justifying the masses, rather than condemning them on account of their putative femininity. This is the only reference to the feminisation of culture in the entire work, and yet it is crucial, for the essay builds upon this Hegelian notion of feminine seduction, which is really a synonym for that very fashionable term introduced by Baudrillard: 'simulation'. [...] Thus, the word 'simulation' itself dissimulates, masking the extent to which Baudrillard's theorisation of the masses and mass culture duplicates the theorisation of the feminine in much contemporary thought.

Just as Molina refuses to accept Valentin's analyses of the films ('why break the illusion for me, and for yourself too?' (17)), Baudrillard's masses resist the intellectual's attempts to impose on them 'the imperative of rational communication' (10). Instead, they demand spectacle; they prefer to be fascinated rather than provoked to thought. Thus far, of course, Baudrillard is in complete agreement with most critics of mass culture. He differs from them crucially, however, in placing a positive value on the masses' refusal of meaning. Again like Molina, whose ingenuousness continually exposes Valentin's Marxist principles as narrow and inflexible, the masses, according to Baudrillard, 'scent the simplifying terror which is behind the ideal hegemony of meaning' (10). Baudrillard here aligns himself with various contemporary thinkers, like Roland Barthes, who implicitly denounces the terrorism of the 'hegemony of meaning' when he speaks of 'regime of meaning'.[7] Barthes, however, considers this regime to be in the service of mass culture and repeatedly calls on high art to challenge and overthrow it. For Baudrillard, on the contrary, the *masses* are in the best position to answer Barthes' call; they 'realise here and now everything which the most radical critics have been able to envisage', as they 'wander through meaning, the political, representation history, ideology, with a somnambulant strength of denial' (49). They annihilate everything that seeks to control them, not by their strength of will but by their very will-less-ness and passivity.

The masses function as a 'gigantic black hole', a simile ostensibly taken from physics, but perhaps owing something to (feminine) anatomy as well: 'an implosive sphere', a 'sphere of potential engulfment' (9). According to Baudrillard, the rabid consumerism suggested by the term 'engulfment' is truly radical in its potential. For 'a system is abolished only by pushing it into hyperlogic ... You want us to consume – O.K. let's consume always more, and anything whatsoever; for any useless and absurd purpose' (46). Here the values espoused by Ann Douglas and other traditional leftist thinkers are completely reversed. Meaning, regardless of who 'produces' it or how, is explosive and terroristic; consumption is implosive and revolutionary. [...]

And, as we have seen, Baudrillard, unlike Douglas, is far from denigrating the putative femininity of mass culture. The masses who push the system into a hyper-logic are engaging in the same 'excessive fidelity to the law' that characterises Hegel's eternal feminine, the same 'simulation of passivity and obedience' that 'annuls the law governing them'. It is the mute acquiescence of the masses to the system – the silence of the majority – that renders them most feminine. The masses, outside of meaning, are outside of language and of representation: hence the end of politics as we know it. 'Withdrawn into their silence ... they can no longer be spoken for, articulated, represented, nor pass through the political "mirror" stage, and the cycle of imaginary identifications' (22). Baudrillard here is extending contemporary psychoanalytic definitions of woman to a political analy-sis of the masses. For in current theory it is *woman* who has been consigned to silence because of her inability to pass through the mirror stage, to enter language, the symbolic and the social. Thus she had been called 'the ruin of representation'. In her 'formlessness' she can only, paradoxically, represent lack – that is, the hor-rible possibility of *un*representability, the 'abyss' or 'void' of meaning, to use Baudrillard's term. Declaring the masses to be the ruin of (political) representation, Baudrillard gleefully and apocalyptically proclaims the death of the social. [...]

It is important for feminists to draw out and scrutinise the implications of Baudrillard's conceptualisation of the masses and mass culture, and in particular to question its significance for feminism. Feminists disturbed by contemporary theory's relegation of women to the realm of the pre-social might be tempted to rejoice pre-maturely in the end of the social and the consignment of almost *everyone* to the place hitherto reserved for women. But that would be to gloss over crucial distinctions. [...]

The death of the social is another of phallocentrism's masks, likewise authoris-ing the 'end of woman' without consulting her: 'the social itself no longer has any name. Anonymous. THE MASS. THE MASSES' (19). Only those who have had privi-leged access to the social can gleefully announce its demise. For women, who throughout most of history have not been given political representation or a polit-ical voice – a state of affairs that has made them the *true* silent majority – there is little reason to be sanguine about the possibilities of a revolution based on the mute tactics of the eternal 'feminine'.

Not the least of the problems involved in equating the masses and mass culture with the feminine is that it becomes much more difficult for women to interro-gate their role within that culture. As Freud put it in his essay on 'Femininity' (employing patriarchal strategies of deviousness), if women *are* the question, they cannot *ask* the questions. And yet it is crucial for us to ask them, because, as feminist critics have begun to show, women are victimised in many and complex ways in mass culture. Valentin was undoubtedly right the first time: the spider woman *was* in fact entrapped in that web, as almost all the women in the movies Molina discusses are ensnared in various patriarchal traps, and as Molina himself is destroyed at the end, letting 'himself be killed because that way he could die like some heroine in a movie' (279).

Despite the suggestion in *Kiss of the Spider Woman* of a role reversal and a shift in power dynamics – with Molina temporarily in the ascendency as a result of his feminine strategies, which are also the strategies of the consumer – nothing much ever really changes. Throughout, Molina remains in the feminine role of nurturer and caretaker, while Valentin reaps all the benefits of consumerism (nobody feeds Molina or tells him stories). And despite Baudrillard's implicit denial of the contemporary relevance of sexual difference, as all difference and all politics – including feminist politics – are supposedly absorbed into a feminised mass, women daily experience a sense of oppression in a social order that is at least alive enough to ensure the continuance of that oppression. A feminist approach to mass culture might begin, then, by recognising and challenging the dubious sexual analogies that pervade a wide variety of discourses, however seductive they may at first appear. And this is especially important when, as in the case of Baudrillard, such discourses masquerade as theories of liberation.

## Notes

1. Fredric Jameson, 'Reification and utopia in mass culture', *Social Text* I, 1979, p. 148.
2. Ann Douglas, *The Feminization of American Culture* (New York: Avon, 1977), p. 13. All further references are to this edition.
3. Jane P. Tompkins, 'Sentimental power: *Uncle Tom's Cabin* and the politics of literary history', *Glyph* 8, 1981, p. 98. Tompkins is directly responding to Douglas's book.
4. Ibid.
5. Manuel Puig, *Kiss of the Spider Woman*, trans. Thomas Colchie (New York: Vintage, 1980), p. 78. All further references are to this edition.
6. Jean Baudrillard, *In the Shadow of the Silent Majorities or the End of the Social and Other Essays*, trans. Paul Foss, Paul Patton and John Johnston (New York: *Semiotexte*, 1983), p. 33. All further references are to this edition.
7. Roland Barthes, *Image, Music Text*, trans. Stephen Heath (New York: Hill and Wang, 1977), p. 167.

# Chapter 5

# Morag Shiach

# The Popular

The first use which the *OED* [Oxford English Dictionary] cites of the word 'popular' is as a legal term. Here it denotes an action open to all people living under a particular government. J. Rastell says of an 'action popular' in 1579: 'This action is not given to one man specially but generally to any of the Queene's people as will sue'.[1] [...]

William Lambard discusses the nature and implications of such actions in *Eirenarcha,* in 1581. Here he draws a distinction between two forms of social control: Suertie of the Peace, and Suertie of the Good Abearing. The former refers to the financial bond which a Justice of the Peace may force an individual to pay as a guarantee of peaceable behaviour. This bond may either be requested by another individual, or deemed appropriate by the Justice of the Peace. Suertie of the Good Abearing is also a financial guarantee of peaceable behaviour, but one that can be contravened without necessarily causing a disturbance. It refers to potentially disruptive meetings, or to the carrying of arms. It can be used against those disturbing a preacher, against poachers, against non-church-attenders, or those going to brothels.

Thus, Lambard argues, 'it seemeth more popular than the Suertie of the Peace'.[2] By this, he means that general social disruption is, by definition, detrimental to all those living within a particular state, whereas civil disturbance is more commonly aimed at particular individuals. Thus, 'the popular' seems to be identified with the interests of the state, that which disturbs social harmony being conceived as an offence against the people, although this identification is troubled by the complex mechanisms of social control which Lambard describes.

Rastell's example of the sort of event which might occasion an 'action popular' is also concerned with the stability of apparatuses of government. He cites the

From: Morag Shiach, *Discourse on Popular Culture: Class, Gender and History in Cultural Analysis, 1730 to the Present.* London: Polity Press, 1989.

case of a corrupt jury member, who may, within one year of his offence, be sued by 'every man that will'.[3] The disruption of legal processes is construed as an offence to every person, or at least every man, living within a particular state, and thus necessitates an 'action popular'.

This legal definition of the concept 'popular' is thus seen to rest upon an equation of the interests of the people with the interests of the state, at least in some of its formulations. The resonances of this equation are picked up in the uses which the *OED* defines as: 'of, pertaining to, or consisting of the common people, or the people as a whole as distinguished from any particular class'.[4] The slipperiness of the term here becomes apparent. The common people can surely be distinguished from the people as a whole. The people as a whole might perhaps be seen as constituted by different classes, rather than as distinguished from any class. [...]

In Strype's *Ecclesiastical Memorials* of 1721, we find considerable discussion of the relation between the people and the sovereign power, particularly in the appendix containing William Thomas's discourses to Edward VI (then aged eleven) entitled 'Whether it be better for a Commonwealth that the power be in the Nobility or in the Commonalty': the fundamental question of political legitimacy.

Strype himself seems caught between two different representations of the people. One is basically paternalist, as he argues against the social disruption caused by the enclosure of common lands. Criticizing the greed of the rich, he insists that the increased misery of the people is bad for the whole state. [...]

The instability of this political structure is apparent, however, as he introduces 'the Ignorant People, refusing to obey'.[5] This is the fickle multitude, with idle insinuations buzzing about in their heads. Here, the people emerges as a separate entity, dangerously in need of control.

It is to this dilemma that William Thomas addresses himself. He structures his discourse around several questions, including

1   Whether a Multitude without Head may prosper?
2   Whether is wiser and most constant, the Multitude or the Prince?
3   Whether it is better for the Commonwealth, that the Power be in the Nobility, or in the People?[6]

He ventures several answers, moral, practical and political, and the relations between these depend to a large extent on slippages in the notion of 'the people' or 'popular government'. At one moment 'the people' refers to all those ruled by a particular monarch, both nobility and commonalty, and the question becomes in which of these groups political power should rest. Thomas argues that stability and prosperity can only be achieved when power remains in the hands of the nobility. The nobility emerges through diligence, and must thus be maintained in ease, while those who lack material wealth must be constrained to work. [...]

Any popularly constituted government will fall apart, destroying both the nobility and the people themselves: 'what Popular Estate can be read that hath thirty years together eschewed Sects, Sedition and Commotions'.[7]

Both the people and popular government, then, take on a meaning that can only be seen as threatening. Despite his insistence that no popular government could survive its internal contradictions, Thomas devotes considerable energy to policies of social control. [...] He criticizes the nobility for excessive ambition and tyranny, not because these represent an assault on individual liberty, as Rousseau and Locke would later argue, but because they threaten the practical maintenance of power. [...]

In North's translation of Plutarch's *Lives* (1579) we find the concept of benevolent interdependency brought into play once more in representations of the people. Popular government is here contrasted with the excesses of tyrannical power, and equated with liberty: 'Such ... as misliked popular Government and liberty, and always followed the Nobility'.[8]

The term 'popular government' remains troubled, sometimes referring to government with the consent of the people, sometimes government in the interests of the people, and sometimes, though always with fear, to government by the people. Since 'the people' refers variously, and often within the same text, to all the inhabitants of a particular nation, the multitude, the commonalty, or the ignorant, the problem is compounded.

In Archibald Alison's *History of Europe from the Commencement of the French Revolution to the Restoration of the Bourbons in 1815* we find reference to 'completely popular' elections to the Legislative Assembly of revolutionary France.[9] It turns out, however, that by this he means that the vote was given to 'every labouring man of the better sort'.[10] 'The people' is thus both male and securely placed within dominant social and economic relations. [...]

A popular government thus cannot include, or represent 'the least informed and most dangerous, but at the same time most numerous portions of the people', since 'the equal division of property ... will, in every age, be the wish of the unthinking multitude'.[11] When this latter remark is contrasted with the claim 'Universal suffrage, or a low qualification for electors, has, in every age of democratic excitement, been the favourite object of the people', it becomes clear that at least one distinction between 'the people' and 'the multitude' lies in their perceived relation of threat to the social order.[12] [...]

All of these examples represent attempts to utilize the apparent universality of 'the people' while simultaneously demarcating the boundaries of 'the people' in relation to political power. At other moments, however, 'popular' refers quite explicitly to one part of the social formation: those 'of lowly birth; belonging to the commonalty or populace; plebeian'.[13] [...]

'Popular' thus becomes associated with a cluster of themes attributed to those of low social standing, as when Montaigne, in Florio's translation, talks of 'popular or base men', who are to be distinguished from men of taste, understanding and education.[14] Naunton, in *Fragmenta Regalia*, written in the early seventeenth century, having praised Queen Elizabeth as 'a most gracious and popular Prince', by which he means that she acted in the interests of, and with the support of, her people, then goes on to criticize James's Parliament as being full of 'popular and discontented persons'.[15] Here, 'popular' seems to indicate lacking in discretion, reckless and opportunist. It is interesting to note the link made between this term and the youthful nature of the Parliament: 'forty Gentlemen, not above twenty, and some not exceeding sixteen of Age'.[16] This theme is echoed later in Alison's attention to the extreme youth of the members of the Legislative Assembly. This relationship between 'the popular' and 'youthfulness' or immaturity will re-emerge later in relation to the concept of popular culture. [...]

In *Every Man out of His Humour* (1600) 'the popular' is clearly what every aspiring gentleman must avoid. Sogliardo is given the following advice: 'be sure you mix your selfe still, with such as flourish in the spring of the fashion, and are least popular; studie their cariage and behavior in all'.[17] The advice is satirical, but the resonances of 'popular' are, at least in this particular social vocabulary, extremely negative. The negative connotations of 'popular' are picked up again in Milton's *Samson Agonistes* (1671). Samson is subjected to the disturbance of a festival: '... with leave/Retiring from the popular noise, I seek/This unfrequented place to find some ease'.[18] Here the 'popular' is associated with chaos and vulgarity, with the multitude from whom Samson must absent himself.

'Popular' has, at certain moments, come to mean simply 'full of people'. [...] In a text such as *The Hermit: Or the Unparalleled Sufferings and Surprising Adventures of Mr Philip Quarll, an Englishman* (1727) the resonances of this use of the term 'popular' become clear. This text purports to be an account by an English merchant of the discovery of a hermit living alone on an island: '... a second Garden of Eden, only here's no forbidden Fruit, nor Women to tempt a Man'.[19] The hermit is described as uniquely fortunate, having escaped the superficiality and hypocrisy that characterize 'busy Worlds and Trading-Peopled Towns'.[20] Quarll visits the island, sees the lifestyle of the hermit, eats with him, meets his monkey-servant ... and concludes thus: 'Oh! may I once more see that dear old Man, whose Habitation is 'free from all anxious Cares, from Oppression and Usury and all the Evils that attend this popular World'.[21] Thus the sense of 'popular' as meaning 'full of people' is stretched to include the notion of corruption and evil.

Thus far, we have seen the word 'popular' applied to governments, legal actions and social structures, but there is still another set of meanings of the word which refer to texts, language, argument and forms of knowledge: to what we might now call 'cultural forms'. Here, 'popular' refers to a cultural form which is 'intended for ordinary people', whether in terms of accessibility, of mode of address, or of the facts of reception.[22]

The earliest cited use of popular, meaning generally accessible, is from 1573, when Gabriel Harvey protests against the dilution of philosophical debate into 'popular and plausible theams'.[23] Later, we find 'popular language' and 'popular style'. The latter is Macaulay in 1849, who defines a popular style as one 'which boys and women could comprehend'.[24] Thus 'popular' is related to those excluded from the institutions of knowledge production.

The term begins to be applied specifically to certain forms of literature and to ephemeral publications generally in the early nineteenth century. In 1835, John Stuart Mill refers to the 'popular press'.[25] In 1841, T. Wright produces *Popular Treatises on Science*. By 1901, the concept of 'popular romance' is well established, and by the mid-twentieth century, phrases such as 'popular newspapers' no longer seem to demand any explanation.

At one level, the reason for this increasing confidence in designating certain publications as 'popular' is not hard to understand. Increases in general literacy throughout the nineteenth century, developments in communications technology allowing for the cheap reproduction of texts, and changes in patterns of ownership and distribution of printed texts brought about a distinctive shift in patterns of cultural production and consumption [...].

In relation to cultural forms, however the term 'popular' commonly refers to a particular mode of address identified within the text as presumed to appeal to the 'common people'. This usage refers back to earlier meanings of 'popular' as 'studious of, or designed to gain the favour of the common people'.[26] Earlier uses of the word in this sense do not refer to texts, but rather to political strategies. Thus,

POPULAR C

60

It is not si
makes the
when h
Cham
172

in 1622, Francis Bacon describes Lord Audley as 'unq
that he is manipulative and untrustworthy in his pol
the relations between Nobles and Commons in Athen
'popular and ambitious Men who will, in the end,
more, 'popular' is associated with dishonesty and op
actions are those which address the apparent desires
long term, ill-conceived and dangerous. This carrie
that popular political leaders practise some form of
people as to their true interests. [...]

From a notion of 'popular' as being a function of t
ical discourse or strategy we move to a definition of popular in terms
'finding favour with, or approved by, the people'.[29] This refers initially to individuals. Cockeram's dictionary of 1623 defines 'popular' as 'in great favour with the common people'. [...]

By the mid-nineteenth century, we find the term increasingly applied to aspects of cultural forms which appeal to, or are favoured by, people generally. Thus, Samuel Bamford, in 1841, observes that 'A hundred or two of our handsomest girls ... danced to the music, or sang snatches of popular songs.'[30] Carl Engel, in 1866, discusses 'the peculiar character of the popular music of a nation'.[31]

In these cases, however, it is very difficult to specify the meaning of 'popular'. Reference is being made to its use in a number of different discourses. Thus Engel, in relating 'popular music' to nationalism is calling on a notion of 'the people' as a more or less self-conscious political and cultural unit. Aldous Huxley makes a similar connection when he argues that 'where popular art is vulgar, there the life of the people is essentially vulgar in its emotional quality'.[32] A claim about the specificity of popular culture is being made here which involves more than the facts of consumption. In these texts, popular culture is the expression of the spirit of a nation or a people. [...]

At other times, the distinguishing feature of 'popular music' seems to be neither the authenticity of its production, nor its general consumption, but rather its exclusion from the institutions of cultural validation. In 1911, H.F. Chorley warns that, 'the large share ... which popular ... music has taken and takes in mourning for the dead in Ireland is a characteristic not to be overlooked'.[33] This takes us back to the notion of the 'popular' as common, lowly, or founded in ignorance.

Finally, the notion of hypocrisy and manipulation returns in the following description of popular art: 'By popular art we mean creative work that measures its success by the size of its audience and the profit it brings to its maker.'[34] 'Popular' is here a matter of debasing the product in order to maintain the audience. The increasing dominance of this definition is, however, challenged by the following claim made in 1966, 'popular culture ... which is to be sharply distinguished from ... commercialized 'pop culture' ... is the style of life of the majority of the members of a community'.[35] Here a definite attempt is being made to reinstate some of the reverberations of 'the popular' as an expression of national cultural identity, against an increasing tendency to dismiss popular forms as commercial and trivial. [...]

'The popular' can also be understood as that which is prevalent among, or accepted by, the people. Florio's translation of Montaigne mentions a 'popular sicknesse, which some yeares since, greatly troubled the townes about mee'.[36] The *Medical Journal* of 1803 talks of 'popular diseases'.[37] Here the emphasis is on the non-selective and uncontrollable element of the diseases concerned.

mply diseases, however, which rage among the people. Ben Jonson
correlation between general acceptance and lack of discrimination
writes, 'Sir, that's a popular error, deceives many'.[38] Again, in Ephraim
bers's *Cyclopaedia, or an Universal Dictionary of Arts and Sciences* of
7–41, popular errors are 'such as people imbibe from one another, by custom,
ucation, and tradition'. Here, 'popular' seems to be equated with exclusion from
the institutions of knowledge production. It signals a form of knowledge supported
by tradition and superstition, rather than by reason, and thus one particularly
prone to error. 'Accepted by the people' means non-legitimate and crude.

The *OED* lists another meaning of 'the popular' which is now obsolete.
'Popular' functioned in the sixteenth and seventeenth centuries as a noun referring either to the populace as a whole, or to the common people. […] In the late
sixteenth century, Sir Thomas Smith condemns the instability of democracy as
'the rule or the usurping of the popular', who are the 'rascall or viler sort'.[39] Smith is
capable of giving within his text a very detailed social hierarchy. He is untroubled
by notions of 'the people' as a unit of political legitimation, starting instead with
the facts of existing political power and then reconstituting them structurally.
Social distinctions thus appear both marked and natural: '… such as be exempted
out of the number of the rascabilitie of the popular, bee called and written yeoman'.[40]

This obsolete usage returns us once more to the importance of 'the popular' as
a term in political discourses of quite different historical moments and ideological positions. There is, however, a marked continuity in the uses we have cited
so far. Basically, 'the popular' has always been 'the other'. The use of the term
seems to imply a certain distance, a position from which 'the popular' can be
evaluated, analysed, and perhaps dismissed. Writing from within the dominant
culture, observations are produced about popular errors or beliefs. Thus, for
example, in the nineteenth century, writers and critics condemn the evil and the
excesses of popular fiction, while today, television critics write off large segments
of television as popular, trivial, and addictive: an addiction from which they presume themselves to be immune. With the security of a legitimate culture, excursions can be made into the realms of popular culture. Folks songs can be collected
and popular taste evaluated, without ever involving those who have preserved and
transmitted such songs. From a position of political authority the instability and
danger of popular government can be pointed out: something which the people
could never be relied upon to understand.

All this, of course, is what we mean by a dominant discourse. We can, however,
find uses of 'the popular' which trouble this consensus, which speak from a different position. One such use is cited by the *OED*, although, interestingly, attention is
drawn to the surprising point of view. The *Saturday Review of Politics, Literature,
Science and Art* of 8 November 1884 reports a remark overheard in a New York
restaurant, 'I don't call this very popular pie', but quickly points out that 'they have
come … to take popular quite gravely and sincerely as a synonym for good'.[41]
Clearly an intolerable slippage. To find other examples of attempts to reappropriate
the concept of 'the popular' we would have to look in other sorts of institutional
sites. For example, in the Chartist *People's Paper,* we find 'popular action' as a form
of collective strength against oppression. In 'Popular Front' politics, 'the popular' is
the location of political legitimacy against fascism. It is the possibility of such oppositional meanings that is at stake in contemporary debates about the politics of
popular culture. Such attempts to re-evaluate the concept of 'popular' are also clear

in the popular theatre movement of the 1920s and 1930s, and in recent debates about the analysis of popular television.

This history of changing definitions of 'popular' as offered by the *OED* is now complete. It might, however, be useful to review the major historical shifts which we have detected in its use and significance. The earliest uses of 'popular' are as a term of legal or political thought. These depend on a notion of 'the people' as a constituted political unit. Popular government is the expression of the collective will, or alternatively a manifestation of the multitudinous confusion, of this unit. Popular legal actions are those that are accessible to all persons living within a particular state. They are applicable only in relation to offences judged dangerous to the fabric of the state. Later uses of 'popular' to mean 'accepted by the people', or 'favoured by the people' also refer initially to political strategies, with implications of manipulation and distortion, and only later to cultural texts.

Ambiguity as to who, or what, constitutes 'the people' is echoed in the shifting significance of 'popular'. It is generally applicable only to actions, or individuals, excluded from power, to the common, the lowly, the plebeian. It thus acquires a cluster of negative connotations: of crudity, ignorance, chaos and tyranny.

By the time that Johnson produced his dictionary in 1755, the relationship between 'the popular' and the legitimation of political power seems to have been diminished. He lists five meanings of 'popular':

1   vulgar, plebeian
2   suitable to the common people
3   beloved by the people, pleasing to the people
4   studious of the favour of the people
5   prevailing or raging among the populace

A tantalizing selection of definitions, whose conceptual relations are far from clear. Again, we see slippages from 'the vulgar' to 'the common people', to 'the people' and finally to 'the populace'. There is no notion here of 'popular' indicating generally accessible, except in the very patronizing sense of an action or text rendered 'suitable to' the common people. [...]

From the late eighteenth century, we find 'popular' applied to cultural texts: to music, the press, art, science and fiction. These uses depend partially on the relationship between popular consciousness and national identity. They also reproduce notions of 'the popular' as that which is excluded from institutions of legitimation, either because of the material conditions of its production, or because its general accessibility lays it open to charges of debasement or simplicity.

When we look at definitions of 'popular' in recently published dictionaries, we can detect further shifts in its signification. Longman's *New Universal Dictionary*, published in 1982, lists four meanings for 'popular':

1   of the general public
2   suited to the needs, means, tastes or understanding of the general public
3   having general currency
4   commonly liked or approved

As we can see, the idea of 'the people' has completely disappeared, to be replaced by that of 'the general public'. Similarly, there is no indication of social hierarchy in these definitions, of differential power, of the lowly or plebeian. The notion of a calculated manipulation (studious of the favour of the people) gives way to personal choice. *Collins Concise Dictionary,* also published in 1982, gives a similar range of definitions. 'The popular' is that which is well liked by a number of individuals, or that which is accessible to the lay man.

All of this serves to evacuate the relations between social power, political democracy and cultural production which are so inescapable in the history of 'popular' constituted by the *OED. A* seemingly egalitarian discourse merely serves to shift the emphasis from social power to individual choice and taste. There is no reference to institutions, or to the facts of cultural production. The general public, a collection of discriminating consumers, linked only through opinion polls, designates 'the popular' according to individual tastes and needs. [...]

## Notes

1. J. Rastell, *An Exposition of Certaine Difficult and Obscure Words, and Termes of the Lawes of this Realme* (1592), p. 8.
2. William Lambard, *Eirenarcha,* 1st edn 1581 (London, 1599), p. 126.
3. Rastell, *An Exposition,* p. 8.
4. OED, 'popular', definition 2.
5. W. Strype, *Ecclesiastical Memorials,* 3 vols (London, 1721), II, 91.
6. Ibid., p. 100.
7. Ibid., p. 66.
8. Plutarch, *Lives,* trans. by Sir Thomas North (London, 1676), p. 223.
9. Archibald Alison, *History of Europe from the Commencement of the French Revolution to the Restoration of the Bourbons in 1815,* 14 vols (London, 1849–50), II, 110.
10. Ibid., p. 110.
11. Ibid., pp. 112 and 111.
12. Ibid., p. 110.
13. *OED,* 'popular', definition 2/b.
14. Michel de Montaigne, *The Essayes,* trans. John Florio, 1st edn 1603 (London, 1632), p. 624.
15. Sir Robert Naunton, *Fragmenta Regalia* (1641), pp. 3 and 9.
16. Ibid., p. 9.
17. B. Jonson, *Every Man out of His Humour,* reprinted from the Holmes Quarto of 1600 (London, 1907), Act 1, sc. i, p. 19.
18. J. Milton, *Paradise Regain'd and Samson Agonistes* (London, 1671), *Samson Agonistes,* lines 15–17.
19. E. Dorrington, *The Hermit: Or the Unparalleled Sufferings and Surprising Adventures of Mr Philip Quarll, An Englishman* (London, 1727), p. 16.
20. Ibid., p. ix.
21. Ibid., p. 47.
22. *OED,* 'popular', definition 4.
23. *Letter Book of Gabriel Harvey,* ed. Edward John Long Scott, Camden Society (London, 1884), pp. 10–11.
24. Thomas Babington Macaulay, *The History of England,* 5th edn, 2 vols (London, 1849), II, 108.
25. J.S. Mill in *London Review,* 2 (1835), p. 273.
26. *OED,* 'popular', definition 5/a.

27. Francis Bacon, *The Historie of the Raigne of King Henry the Seventh* (London, 1622), p. 165.

28. J. Swift, *A Discourse on the Contests and Dissensions between the Nobles and the Commons in Athens and Rome, with the Consequences they had upon both those States* (London, 1701), p. 25.

29. *OED*, 'popular', definition 6.

30. Samuel Bamford, *Passages in the Life of a Radical*, 2 vols (London, 1844), I, 200.

31. Carl Engel, *Introduction to the Study of National Music* (London, 1866), p. 168.

32. Aldous Huxley, *Beyond the Mexique Bay* (London, 1934), p. 267.

33. H.F. Chorley, *The National Music of the World* (London, 1911), p. 201.

34. *Saturday Review of Literature,* 10 May 1947, p. 9.

35. David Jenkins, *The Educated Society* (London, 1966), p. 58.

36. Montaigne, *The Essayes,* p. 432.

37. *Medical and Physical Journal, 9,* (1803), 422.

38. B. Jonson, *The Divell is an Asse* (London, 1631), Act 1, sc. ii. p. 101.

39. Sir Thomas Smith, *The Commonwealth of England* (London, 1633), p. 5.

40. Ibid., p. 64.

41. *Saturday Review of Politics, Literature, Science and Art,* 8 November 1884, p. 590.

# Chapter 6

# Stuart Hall

# Notes on Deconstructing 'the Popular'

[...] 'Cultural change' is a polite euphemism for the process by which some cultural forms and practices are driven out of the centre of popular life, actively marginalised. Rather than simply 'falling into disuse' through the Long March to modernisation, things are actively pushed aside, so that something else can take their place. The magistrate and the evangelical police have, or ought to have, a more 'honoured' place in the history of popular culture than they have usually been accorded. Even more important than ban and proscription is that subtle and slippery customer – 'reform' [...]. One way or another, 'the people' are frequently the object of 'reform': often, for their own good, of course – 'in their best interests'. We understand struggle and resistance, nowadays, rather better than we do reform and transformation. Yet 'transformations' are at the heart of the study of popular culture. I mean the active work on existing traditions and activities, their active re-working, so that they come out a different way: they appear to 'persist' – yet, from one period to another, they come to stand in a different relation to the ways working people live and the ways they define their relations to each other, to 'the others' and to their conditions of life. Transformation is the key to the long and protracted process of the 'moralisation' of the labouring classes, and the 'demoralisation' of the poor, and the 're-education' of the people. Popular culture is neither, in a 'pure' sense, the popular traditions of resistance to these processes; nor is it the forms which are superimposed on and over them. It is the ground on which the transformations are worked.

From: *People's History and Socialist Theory*: Ed. Raphael Samuel. London: Routledge & Kegan Paul, 1981.

In the study of popular culture, we should always start here: with the double-stake in popular culture, the double movement of containment and resistance, which is always inevitably inside it.

The study of popular culture has tended to oscillate wildly between the two alternative poles of that dialectic – containment/resistance. We have had some striking and marvellous reversals. Think of the really major revolution in historical understanding which has followed as the history of 'polite society' and the Whig aristocracy in eighteenth-century England has been upturned by the addition of the history of the turbulent and ungovernable people. The popular traditions of the eighteenth-century labouring poor, the popular classes and the 'loose and disorderly sort' often, now, appear as virtually independent formations: tolerated in a state of permanently unstable equilibrium in relatively peaceful and prosperous times; subject to arbitrary excursions and expeditions in times of panic and crisis. Yet, though formally these were the cultures of the people 'outside the walls', beyond political society and the triangle of power, they were never, in fact, outside of the larger field of social forces and cultural relations. [...] From these cultural bases, often far removed from the dispositions of law, power and authority, 'the people' threatened constantly to erupt: and, when they did so, they break on to the stage of patronage and power with a threatening din and clamour – with fife and drum, cockade and effigy, proclamation and ritual – and, often, with a striking, popular, ritual discipline. Yet never quite overturning the delicate strands of paternalism, deference and terror within which they were constantly if insecurely constrained. In the following century, where the 'labouring' and the 'dangerous' classes lived without benefit of that fine distinction the reformers were so anxious to draw (this was a *cultural* distinction as well as a moral and economic one: and a great deal of legislation and regulation was devised to operate directly on it), some areas preserved for long periods a virtually impenetrable enclave character. It took virtually the whole length of the century before the representatives of 'law and order' – the new police – could acquire anything like a regular and customary foothold within them. Yet, at the same time, the penetration of the cultures of the labouring masses and the urban poor was deeper, more continuous – and more continuously 'educative' and reformatory – in that period than at any time since.

One of the main difficulties standing in the way of a proper periodisation of popular culture is the profound transformation in the culture of the popular classes which occurs between the 1880s and the 1920s. [...] It was a period of deep structural change. The more we look at it, the more convinced we become that somewhere in this period lies the matrix of factors and problems from which *our* history – and our peculiar dilemmas – arise. Everything changes – not just a shift in the relations of forces but a reconstitution of the terrain of political struggle itself. It isn't just by chance that so many of the characteristic forms of what we now think of as 'traditional' popular culture either emerge from or emerge in their distinctive modern form, in that period. What has been done for the 1790s and for the 1840s, and is being done for the eighteenth-century, now radically needs to be done for the period of what we might call the 'social imperialist' crisis.

The general point made earlier is true, without qualification, for this period, so far as popular culture is concerned. There is no separate, autonomous, 'authentic' layer of working-class culture to be found. Much of the most immediate forms of popular recreation, for example, are saturated by popular imperialism. Could we expect otherwise? How could we explain, and what would we *do* with the idea of, the culture of a dominated class which, despite its complex interior formations and differentiations, stood in a very particular relation to a major restructuring of capital; which itself stood in a peculiar relation to the rest of the world; a people bound by the most complex ties to a changing set of material relations and conditions; who managed somehow to construct 'a culture' which remained untouched by the most powerful dominant ideology – popular imperialism? Especially when that ideology – belying its name – was directed as much at them as it was at Britain's changing position in a world capitalist expansion?

Think, in relation to the question of popular imperialism, of the history and relations between the people and one of the major means of cultural expression: the press. To go back to displacement and superimposition – we can see clearly how the liberal middle-class press of the mid-nineteenth century was constructed on the back of the active destruction and marginalisation of the indigenous radical and working-class press. But, on top of that process, something qualitatively new occurs towards the end of the nineteenth century and the beginning of the twentieth century in this area: the active, mass insertion of a developed and mature working-class audience into a new kind of *popular*, commercial press. This has had profound cultural consequences: though it isn't in any narrow sense exclusively a 'cultural' question at all. It required the whole reorganisation of the capital basis and structure of the cultural industry; a harnessing of new forms of technology and of labour processes; the establishment of new types of distribution, operating through the new cultural mass markets. But one of its effects was indeed a reconstituting of the cultural and political relations between the dominant and the dominated classes: a change intimately connected with that containment of popular democracy on which 'our democratic way of life' today, appears to be so securely based. Its results are all too palpably with us still, today: a popular press, the more strident and virulent as it gradually shrinks; organised by capital 'for' the working classes; with, nevertheless, deep and influential roots in the culture and language of the 'underdog', of 'Us': with the power to represent the class to itself in its most traditionalist form. This is a slice of the history of 'popular culture' well worth unravelling. [...]

Next, I want to say something about 'popular'. The term can have a number of different meanings: not all of them useful. Take the most common-sense meaning: the things which are said to be 'popular' because masses of people listen to them, buy them, read them, consume them, and seem to enjoy them to the full. This is the 'market' or commercial definition of the term: the one which brings socialists out in spots. It is quite rightly associated with the manipulation and debasement of the culture of the people. In one sense, it is the direct opposite of the way I have been using the word earlier. I have, though, two reservations about entirely dispensing with this meaning, unsatisfactory as it is.

First, if it is true that, in the twentieth century, vast numbers of people *do* consume and even indeed enjoy the cultural products of our modern cultural industry, then it follows that very substantial numbers of working people must be included within the audiences for such products. Now, if the forms and relationships, on which participation in this sort of commercially provided 'culture' depend, are purely manipulative and debased, then the people who consume and enjoy them must either be themselves debased by these activities or else living in a permanent state of 'false consciousness'. They must be 'cultural dopes' who can't tell that what they are being fed is an up-dated form of the opium of the people. That judgment may make us feel right, decent and self-satisfied about our denunciations of the agents of mass manipulation and deception – the capitalist cultural industries: but I don't know that it is a view which can survive for long as an adequate account of cultural relationships; and even less as a socialist perspective on the culture and nature of the working class. Ultimately, the notion of the people as a purely *passive*, outline force is a deeply unsocialist perspective.

Second, then: can we get around this problem without dropping the inevitable and necessary attention to the manipulative aspect of a great deal of commercial popular culture? There are a number of strategies for doing so, adopted by radical critics and theorists of popular culture, which, I think, are highly dubious. One is to counterpose to it another, whole, 'alternative' culture – the authentic 'popular culture'; and to suggest that the 'real' working class (whatever that is) isn't taken in by the commercial substitutes. This is a heroic alternative; but not a very convincing one. Basically what is wrong with it is that it neglects the absolutely essential relations of cultural power – of domination and subordination – which is an intrinsic feature of cultural relations. I want to assert on the contrary that there is *no* whole, authentic, autonomous 'popular culture' which lies outside the field of force of the relations of cultural power and domination. Second, it greatly underestimates the power of cultural implantation. This is a tricky point to make, for, as soon as it *is* made, one opens oneself to the charge that one is subscribing to the thesis of cultural incorporation. The study of popular culture keeps shifting between these two, quite unacceptable, poles: pure 'autonomy' or total incapsulation.

Actually, I don't think it is necessary or right to subscribe to either. Since ordinary people are not cultural dopes, they are perfectly capable of recognising the way the realities of working-class life are reorganised, reconstructed and reshaped by the way they are represented (i.e. re-presented) [...]. The cultural industries do have the power constantly to rework and reshape what they represent; and, by repetition and selection, to impose and implant such definitions of ourselves as fit more easily the descriptions of the dominant or preferred culture. That is what the concentration of cultural power – the means of culture-making in the heads of the few – actually means. These definitions don't have the power to occupy our minds; they don't function on us as if we are blank screens. But they do occupy and rework the interior contradictions of feeling and perception in the dominated classes; they *do* find or clear a space of recognition in those who respond to them. Cultural domination has real effects – even if these are neither all-powerful nor all-inclusive. If we were to argue that these imposed forms have no influence, it would be tantamount to arguing that the culture of the people can exist as a separate enclave, outside the distribution of cultural power and the relations of cultural force. I do not believe that. Rather, I think there is a continuous and necessarily uneven and unequal struggle, by the dominant culture, constantly to disorganise and reorganise popular culture; to enclose and confine its definitions and forms within a more inclusive range of dominant forms. There are points of resistance; there are also moments of supersession. This is the dialectic of cultural struggle. In our times, it goes on continuously, in the complex lines of resistance and acceptance, refusal and capitulation, which make the field of culture a sort of constant battlefield. A battlefield where no once-for-all victories are obtained but where there are always strategic positions to be won and lost.

This first definition, then, is not a useful one for our purposes; but it might force us to think more deeply about the complexity of cultural relations, about the reality of cultural power and about the nature of cultural implantation. If the forms of provided commercial popular culture are not purely manipulative, then it is because, alongside the false appeals, the foreshortenings, the trivialisation and shortcircuits, there are also elements of recognition and identification, something approaching a recreation of recognisable experiences and attitudes, to which people are responding. The danger arises because we tend to think of cultural forms as whole ahd coherent: either wholly corrupt or wholly authentic. Whereas, they are deeply contradictory; they play on contradictions, especially when they function in the domain of the 'popular'. [...]

The second definition of 'popular' is easier to live with. This is the descriptive one. Popular culture is all those things that 'the people' do or have done. This is close to an 'anthropological' definition of the term: the culture, mores, customs and folkways of 'the people'. What defines their 'distinctive way of life'. I have two difficulties with this definition, too.

First, I am suspicious of it precisely because it is too descriptive. This is putting it mildly. Actually, it is based on an infinitely expanding inventory. Virtually *anything* which 'the people' have ever done can fall into the list. Pigeon-fancying and stamp-collecting, flying ducks on the wall and garden gnomes. The problem is how to distinguish this infinite list, in any but a descriptive way, from what popular culture is *not*.

But the second difficulty is more important – and relates to a point made earlier. We can't simply collect into one category all the things which 'the people' do, without observing that the real analytic distinction arises, not from the list itself – an inert category of things and activities – but from the key opposition: the people/not of the people. That is to say, the structuring principle of 'the popular' in this sense is the tensions and oppositions between what belongs to the central domain of elite or dominant culture, and the culture of the 'periphery'. It is this opposition which constantly structures the domain of culture into the 'popular' and the 'non-popular'. But you cannot construct these oppositions in a purely descriptive way. For, from period to period, the *contents* of each category changes. Popular forms become enhanced in cultural value, go up the cultural escalator – and find themselves on the opposite side. Others things cease to have high cultural value, and are appropriated into the popular, becoming transformed in the process. The structuring principle does not consist of the contents of each category – which, I insist, will alter from one period to another. Rather it consists of the forces and relations which sustain the distinction, the difference: roughly, between what, at any time, counts as an elite cultural activity or form, and what does not. These categories remain, though the inventories change. What is more, a whole set of institutions and institutional processes are required to sustain each – and to continually mark the difference between them. The school and the education system is one such institution – distinguishing the valued part of the culture, the cultural heritage, the history to be transmitted, from the 'valueless' part. The literary and scholarly apparatus is another – marking-off certain kinds of valued knowledge from others. The important fact, then, is not a mere descriptive inventory – which may have the negative effect of freezing popular culture into some timeless descriptive mould – but the relations of power which are constantly punctuating and dividing the domain of culture into its preferred and its residual categories.

So I settle for a third definition of 'popular', though it is a rather uneasy one. This looks, in any particular period, at those forms and activities which have their roots in the social and material conditions of particular classes; which have been embodied in popular traditions and practices. In this sense, it retains what is valuable in the descriptive definition. But it goes on to insist that what is essential to the definition of popular culture is the relations which define 'popular culture' in a continuing tension (relationship, influence and antagonism) to the dominant culture. It is a conception of culture which is polarised around this cultural dialectic. It treats the domain of cultural forms and activities as a constantly changing field. Then it looks at the relations which constantly structure this field into dominant and subordinate formations. It looks at the *process* by which these relations of dominance and subordination are articulated. It treats them as a process: the process by means of which some things are actively preferred so that others can be dethroned. It has at its centre the changing and uneven relations of force which define the field of culture – that is, the question of cultural struggle and its many forms. Its main focus of attention is the relation between culture and questions of hegemony.

What we have to be concerned with, in this definition, is not the question of the 'authenticity' or organic wholeness of popular culture. Actually, it recognises that almost *all* cultural forms will be contradictory in this sense, composed of antagonistic and unstable elements. The meaning of a cultural form and its place or position in the cultural field is *not* inscribed inside its form. Nor is its position fixed once and forever. This year's radical symbol or slogan will be neutralised into next year's fashion; the year after, it will be the object of a profound cultural nostalgia. Today's rebel folksinger ends up, tomorrow, on the cover of *The Observer* colour magazine. The meaning of a cultural symbol is given in part by the social field into which it is incorporated, the practices with which it articulates and is made to resonate. What matters is *not* the intrinsic or historically fixed objects of culture, but the state of play in cultural relations: to put it bluntly and in an over-simplified form – what counts is the class struggle in and over culture. [...]

Cultural struggle, of course, takes many forms: incorporation, distortion, resistance, negotiation, recuperation. Raymond Williams has done us a great deal of service by outlining some of these processes, with his distinction between emergent, residual and incorporated moments. We need to expand and develop this rudimentary schema. The important thing is to look at it dynamically: as an historical process. Emergent forces reappear in ancient historical disguise; emergent forces, pointing to the future, lose their anticipatory power, and become merely backward looking; today's cultural breaks can be recuperated as a support to tomorrow's dominant system of values and meanings. The struggle continues: but it is almost never in the same place, over the same meaning or value. It seems to me that the cultural process – cultural power – in our society depends, in the first instance, on this drawing of the line, always in each period in a different place, as to what is to be incorporated into 'the great tradition' and what is not. Educational and cultural institutions, along with the many positive things they do, also help to discipline and police this boundary.

This should make us think again about that tricky term in popular culture, 'tradition'. Tradition is a vital element in culture; but it has little to do with the mere persistence of old forms. It has much more to do with the way elements have been linked together or articulated. These arrangements in a national-popular culture have no fixed or inscribed position, and certainly no meaning which is carried along, so to speak, in the stream of historical tradition, unchanged. Not only can the elements of 'tradition' be rearranged, so that they articulate with different practices and positions, and take on a new meaning and relevance. It is also often the case that cultural struggle arises in its sharpest form just at the point where different, opposed traditions meet, intersect. They seek to detach a cultural form from its implantation in one tradition, and to give it a new cultural resonance or accent. Traditions are not fixed forever: certainly not in any universal position in relation to a single class. Cultures, conceived not as separate 'ways of life' but as 'ways of struggle' constantly intersect: the pertinent cultural struggles arise at the points of intersection. [...]

This provides us with a warning against those self-enclosed approaches to popular culture which, valuing 'tradition' for its own sake, and treating it in an a-historical manner, analyse popular cultural forms as if they contained within themselves, from their moment of origin, some fixed and unchanging meaning or value. The relationship between historical position and aesthetic value is an important and difficult question in popular culture. But the attempt to develop some universal popular aesthetic, founded on the moment of origin of cultural forms and practices, is almost certainly profoundly mistaken. What could be more eclectic and random than that assemblage of dead symbols and bric-a-brac, ransacked from yesterday's dressing-up box, in which, just now, many young people have chosen to adorn themselves? These symbols and bits and pieces are profoundly ambiguous. A thousand lost cultural causes could be summoned up through them. Every now and then, amongst the other trinkets, we find that sign which, above all other signs, ought to be fixed – solidified – in its cultural meaning and connotation forever: the swastika. And yet there it dangles, partly – but not entirely – cut loose from its profound cultural reference in twentieth-century history. What does it mean? What is it signifying? Its signification is rich, and richly ambiguous: certainly unstable. This terrifying sign may delimit a range of meanings but it carries no guarantee of a single meaning within itself. The streets are full of kids who are not 'fascist' because they may wear a swastika on a chain. On the other hand, perhaps they could be. ... What this sign means will ultimately depend, in the politics of youth culture, less on the intrinsic cultural symbolism of the thing in itself, and more on the balance of forces between, say, the National Front and the Anti-Nazi League, between White Rock and the Two Tone Sound.

Not only is there no intrinsic guarantee within the cultural sign or form itself. There is no guarantee that, because at one time it was linked with a pertinent struggle, that it will always be the living expression of a class: so that every time you give it an airing it will 'speak the language of socialism'. If cultural expressions register for socialism, it is because they have been linked as the practices, the forms and organisation of a living struggle, which has succeeded in appropriating those symbols and giving them a socialist connotation. Culture is not already permanently inscribed with the conditions of a class before that struggle begins. The struggle consists in the success or failure to give 'the cultural' a socialist accent.

The term 'popular' has very complex relations to the term 'class'. We know this, but are often at pains to forget it. We speak of particular forms of working-class culture; but we use the more inclusive term, 'popular culture' to refer to the general field of enquiry. It's perfectly clear that what I've been saying would make little sense without reference to a class perspective and to class struggle. But it is also clear that there is no one-to-one relationship between a class and a particular cultural form or practice. The terms 'class' and 'popular' are deeply related but they are not absolutely interchangeable. The reason for that is obvious. There are no wholly separate 'cultures' paradigmatically attached, in a relation of historical fixity, to specific 'whole' classes – although there are clearly distinct and variable class-cultural formations. Class cultures tend to intersect and overlap in the same field of struggle. The term 'popular' indicates this somewhat displaced relationship of culture to classes. More accurately, it refers to that alliance of classes and forces which constitute the 'popular classes'. The culture of the oppressed, the excluded classes: this is the area to which the term 'popular' refers us. And the opposite side to that – the side with the cultural power to decide what belongs and what does not – is, by definition, not another 'whole' class, but that other alliance of classes, strata and social forces which constitute what is not 'the people' and not the 'popular classes': the culture of the power-bloc.

The people versus the power-bloc: this, rather than 'class-against-class', is the central line of contradiction around which the terrain of culture is polarised. Popular culture, especially, is organised around the contradiction: the popular forces versus the power-bloc. This gives to the terrain of cultural struggle its own kind of specificity. But the term 'popular', and even more, the collective subject to which it must refer – 'the people' – is highly problematic. It is made problematic by, say, the ability of Mrs Thatcher to pronounce a sentence like, 'We have to limit the power of the trade unions because that is what the people want.' That suggests to me that, just as there is no fixed content to the category of 'popular culture', so there is no fixed subject to attach to it – 'the people'. 'The people' are not always back there, where they have always been, their culture untouched, their liberties and their instincts intact, still struggling on against the Norman yoke or whatever: as if, if only we can 'discover' them and bring them back on stage, they will always stand up in the right, appointed place and be counted. The capacity to *constitute* classes and individuals as a popular force – that is the nature of political and cultural struggle: to *make* the divided classes and the separated peoples – divided and separated by culture as much as by other factors – *into* a popular-democratic cultural force.

We can be certain that *other* forces also have a stake in defining 'the people' as something else: 'the people' who need to be disciplined more, ruled better, more effectively policed, whose way of life needs to be protected from 'alien cultures', and so on. There is some part of both those alternatives inside each of us. Sometimes we can be constituted as a force against the power-bloc: that is the historical opening in which it is possible to construct a culture which is genuinely popular. But, in our society, if we are not constituted like that, we will be constituted into its opposite: an effective populist force, saying 'Yes' to power. Popular culture is one of the sites where this struggle for and against a culture of the powerful is engaged: it is also the stake to be won or lost *in* that struggle. It is the arena of consent and resistance. It is partly where hegemony arises, and where it is secured. It is not a sphere where socialism, a socialist culture – already fully formed – might be simply 'expressed'. But it is one of the places where socialism might be constituted. That is why 'popular culture' matters. Otherwise, to tell you the truth, I don't give a damn about it.

# Chapter 7

# Juan Flores

# 'Pueblo Pueblo': Popular Culture in Time

## 1

Popular culture is energized in 'moments of freedom,' specific, local plays of power and flashes of collective imagination. It is 'popular' because it is the culture of 'the people,' the common folk, the poor and the powerless who make up the majority of society. The creative subject of popular culture is the 'popular classes,' and its content the traditions and everyday life of communities and their resistance to social domination. It is typically referred to as 'low' culture, or 'subculture,' and marked off from the 'high' culture of the elite. In another familiar image, it is 'marginal' culture or the culture of marginality, thus sidelined from the core 'mainstream' cultural life and values of society. It is this topography of top and bottom, center and periphery, that is upset and radically unsettled in the 'moments of freedom,' those pregnant conjunctures and contexts when it becomes clear, however fleetingly, that the top is 'frequently dependent on the low-Other ... [and even] *includes* that low symbolically.' This dependence and this secret desire for what is excluded and disdained go to account for the deepest irony of popular culture, that 'what is socially peripheral is so frequently *symbolically* central.'[1]

Midway through its two-hundred-year life since the late eighteenth century, the idea of popular culture began a gradual shift of focus from this traditional, collective creativity, commonly called 'folklore,' to the domain of the mass media,

From: Juan Flores, *From Bomba to Hip-Hop: Puerto Rican Culture and Latino Identity*. New York: Columbia University Press, 2000.

the 'mass culture' of technical reproduction and industrial commercialization.[2] This shift has intensified over the course of the twentieth century, as new means of reproduction and diffusion came into place in the cultural sphere, such that by the 1940s and 1950s, especially with the advent of television, the mediated culture *for* the people came to eclipse and replace, in most theoretical assessments, the expressive culture *of the* people which had been the object of knowledge of popular culture and folklore studies in earlier generations. While the critical theorists Theodor Adorno and Walter Benjamin in their writings of the 1930s were the first to describe and analyze this change, in the United States it can be traced with some precision to the 'mass culture debate' of the 1950s as exemplified in the thinking of critics and commentators like Dwight MacDonald, Oscar Handlin, and Clement Greenberg. MacDonald, for example, went so far as to revise the title of his most influential essay, from 'Theory of Popular Culture' in its original 1944 version to 'Theory of Mass Culture' for the publication of 1953. Even more explicitly, Handlin in the same years so much as pronounced a requiem for traditional popular culture with the advent of the mass media; the dean of American immigration historians bemoaned the demise of regionally and ethnically differentiated popular cultures as a result of the leveling effects of mediated mass culture. In subsequent decades this narrative of the effective replacement of popular cultures by mass culture became common sense, such that by our times any discussion of traditional, community-based cultural experience has come to be regarded as a sign of romantic nostalgia which flies in the face of contemporary realities. In most recent work, including much of that conducted in the name of 'cultural studies,' the concept of popular culture is directly equated with the offerings of the 'culture industry' and their consumption; any productive agency or oppositionality on the part of 'the people' is effectively reduced to its ability to consume in a differential and critical way.[3]

Another basis for the generalized skepticism as to the persistence and theoretical utility of popular culture in its traditional sense has been the ideological manipulation of the concept of 'the people' in the hands of populism in its various twentieth-century guises. The recurrent appeal to 'the people' in opportunistic political mobilizations of left, right, and center, whether in the name of democracy, national liberation, the free world, or the cause of labor, has so perverted that slogan as to empty it of all meaning, contestatory or otherwise. The work of Ernesto Laclau is often cited as the most rigorous critical exposé of the vagaries of populism as rhetoric and ideology; it has served recent cultural theorists like Stuart Hall and John Frow to rethink notions of 'the people' and 'the popular' in radically skeptical terms as constructs deployed for the purpose of deflecting political and cultural movements from more solidly verifiable realities of class as well as racial and sexual contestation, particularly in view of the conservative hegemonies of the 1980s.[4] Latin American social theorists like Nestor García Canclini have also propounded a trenchant critique of populism, in this case even more squarely associated with the remnants of retrogressive folklorism in the social sciences.[5] Reeling from the horrors of the dictatorship period, García Canclini and other contemporary scholars of 'popular cultures' are concluding that it has become necessary to dispense with that category altogether, in favor of what are considered less misleading concepts like citizenship and civil society.[6] Along similar lines, the idea of 'public culture' has been advanced, and has gained favor, as an alternative to 'popular culture' in its diverse significations.[7]

Thus discredited by the compelling forces of global and regional modernity, the ideas of vernacular popular culture and 'the people' have been reduced to a tenuous status at best, with the interventions of some postmodernist thinking only adding to the general skepticism by casting it as still another of the spurious master narratives that go to obscure the multiplicity and heterogeneity of cultural subjects and perspectives in present-day social experience. In a characteristic move, both of the component terms – *the people* and *culture* – are taken to be salvageable only when pluralized – *peoples* and *cultures* – and beyond that, only when employed in their adjectival form, as in the opting for 'the cultural' rather than 'culture' or 'cultures' in the suggestive work of Arjun Appadurai.[8] The shift away from a sense of popular culture as products and traditions to a complex idea of signifying 'practice,' performance, and institutional process, as in the writings of Michel de Certeau and Pierre Bourdieu, has given the field new life and sophistication, but has by no means gone to counteract the near consensual reluctance to sustain the tenability of the concept in contemporary social analysis. The word *folklore*, the only terminological recourse to differentiate popular cultural expression from the engulfing phenomenon of popular culture qua mass cultural consumption, is so patently outmoded and laden with ideological baggage that its use only sets up the intellectual endeavor for further ridicule. Even the notion of 'traditional' as distinguished from 'modern' popular culture explicitly projects the community-based, expressive variant into a past tense, and cedes to the mass-mediated experience the crucial space of contemporaneity.

Is there any life left in 'the people' as a social concept after the deadening impact of industrial mediation and ideological manipulation? Does the household term *popular culture* still bear any substantive content, or has it become so replete with referents to every aspect and detail of social experience as to have been depleted of any and all specificity? Even if it is acknowledged that such cultural agency does exist, is there any way of talking about it without falling into some kind or other of essentialism or reductive simplification, and without minimizing the omnipresent role of the media and the active reelaboration of cultural meanings on the part of the public? Put another way, is it possible to engage this direct, expressive cultural practice of everyday life – those 'moments of freedom' which Johannes Fabian sees at the core of popular culture – without positing some space outside of and unaffected by the industrial, ideological, and mobile demographic conditions that so obviously prevail in contemporary society on a world scale?

# 2

'It takes moments of freedom to catch moments of freedom,' Fabian writes in a phrase whose insistently temporal imagery suggests an alternative way of conceptualizing popular culture.[9] He invites us to think of popular culture not so much as an entity comprised of products and processes, or as a bounded social space such as low or marginal, but as a relation or system of relations. Rather than marking off boundaries and defining separate spheres of cultural practice, perhaps popular culture is about the traversing and transgressing of them, and characterized by a dialogic among classes and social sectors, such as the popular and non-popular, high and low, restricted and mass. As for thinking popular culture and developing a concept of the popular, the main correlation has to do with the 'catching,' the interplay between practice and theory, the 'people' as subject and as object of knowledge, between lived social reality and the observer.

The familiar old ethnographic dilemma is at the heart of popular culture as an idea, but it is important to see – with Fabian – the relation between the people and the writer in terms of time, temporally, and as a historical relationship. For only in this way can the concept of popular culture address the need for contemporaneity and be rescued from its relegation to archaic and residual roles in today's global modernity and mass culture. Fabian concludes: 'Observations on the privileging, in received culture theory, of shape over movement and of space over time made me consider the problem of contemporaneity as it poses itself specifically in the study of popular culture: as the coexistence of tradition and modernity. Such coexistence must be assumed and understood if our ambition is to recognize popular culture as contemporary practice, that is, as neither derivative epiphenomenon nor something that, in some evolutionary perspective on history, inevitably follows tradition when the latter disappears under the onslaught of modernity.'[10]

There needs to be a correspondence, or a congruence of some kind, between the energized 'moments of freedom' of popular cultural practice and the disposition of the writer at the moment and in the act of 'catching.' That symbiosis is temporal, an accordance in time and history, and conditioned by the 'coexistence of tradition and modernity.' If popular cultural practices are 'arts of timing,' in de Certeau's phrase, then the ethnographic intervention is a corresponding 'art of timing,' and the relative accuracy of our interpretation of those practices will depend on the quality of that correspondence. By historicizing the ethnographic relation, the reflexive presence of the writer may help contextualize cultural practice and dramatize the coexistence and interpenetration of historical periods, stages, and generations. While crossing multiple social spaces, the writer ignites associations across time not immediately visible at the site of cultural activity, yet latent as meanings and indispensable to its conceptualization.

'It should already be becoming clear,' says the writer at the beginning of Edgardo Rodríguez Juliá's memoir *El entierro de Cortijo* (1983), 'that this chronicle will be the encounter of many historical crossings.'[11] Like many works of recent Puerto Rican writing, *El entierro de Cortijo* is a 'chronicle' of contemporary popular culture and aims to 'catch' the styles and language of everyday life in the colony in the wake of its aborted – or at least contorted – modernization process under the refurbished imperial arrangement of commonwealth status. And Rodríguez Juliá's chronicler goes straight to 'the people': moved by the occasion of the funeral for his favorite popular musician Rafael Cortijo, the conspicuously middle-class intellectual ventures into the notoriously 'underclass' housing projects called Lloréns Torres, after the laureled national poet Luis Lloréns Torres, in the heart of Cortijo's home neighborhood and where the deceased musician's body lay in wake. Amidst the family, friends, and local folk who have come to pay their respects, mostly poor and uneducated black women, men, and children, the bespectacled writer of visibly Mallorcan stock is nervously self-conscious of being himself 'othered' by the 'Other,' and sets to thinking about the meaning of it all. He notices that, with all the solemnity of the occasion, there is a sense of playfulness and even festivity in the air, and he himself seems to let his guard down so as to make the most of this 'moment of freedom,' this fortunate 'art of timing.'

Surveying the scene, he sees people, regular Puerto Rican people, paying tribute to an emblem of their culture, Cortijo, whose music stands as a supreme example of popular culture and of the 'coexistence of tradition and modernity.' Yet the event itself, marking the popular artist's passing, is also an act of popular culture, and it includes the writer himself and his complex, paradoxical relation to it. The sparks of historical associations fly, and he waxes philosophical about the meaning of death, the question of immortality, and how 'the people,' *those* people yet at the same time *his* people, might be defined. 'How to define this people?' he asks, and responds with an explanation which points to a novel way to get beneath the representational and ideological constructions of popular culture that prevail in the public mind. 'To define it is easy,' he says, 'but how difficult it is to describe it! It is people people [pueblo pueblo], my Puerto Rican people in all its contradictory diversity: ...'[12] The distinction drawn between 'definition' and 'description' is an important one, as it signals the need to go beyond a facile naming or labeling based on political rhetoric or sociological categorizing ('definir'), and to somehow account for the variety, richness, and the complexity of the phenomenon ('describir'), that is, to retain a sense of concreteness and specificity while generalizing. The doubling of the noun 'pueblo' has to do, first of all, with emphasis; perhaps the English equivalent would be 'real people,' or 'down-home people.' But from the context it is clear that the reiterated 'pueblo pueblo' is the term appropriate to 'description' rather than 'definition,' that in order to make it clear that he is talking about living human beings and not the abstract slogan and category 'the people' used to objectify them, it is necessary to say it twice, 'people people.'

Yet the writer is also wary of the pitfall of essentialism implicit in the claim to unmediated experience and authenticity. His version of 'the people' is itself mediated through his own perceptions and explicitly stated social position. Nevertheless, Rodríguez Juliá – and Johannes Fabian – would insist that, without positing some 'popular' experience outside the dominant ideological field or mass media culture, there is a difference between mediation as a creative and intellectual activity and that of the media with their commercial and political overdeterminations. The Colombian cultural theorist Jesús Martín Barbero titled his important book 'From the media to mediations' (*De los medios a las mediaciones*),[13] and argues for the value of keeping the historical sense of popular culture as 'folklore' alive even while recognizing the encompassing role of the media in twentieth-century culture.

The medium of the literary ethnographer or chronicler of popular culture, which allows for the closest possible approximation to the perspective of that culture, is the imagination, a faculty referred to emphatically by Rodríguez Juliá along with other contemporary theorists like Fabian and Appadurai.[14] The work of the imagination in this sense is historical memory, that is, the association of social experiences through and in time by means of interpretive recognition and recollection. Immediately after his programmatic reference to 'pueblo pueblo,' the phrase 'in all its contradictory diversity' is followed by a colon, and the chronicler offers an example: 'the sickly-looking woman with her hair in a bun and wearing sneakers because of her bunions, you know, like the bunions in the plena song "Los juanetes de Juana"' ('la *jipata* señora de moño calza tenis para los *juanetes* de Juana'). The ethnographic mediation continues when this succinct but culturally rich description is brought into association with similar class and cultural experiences as awakened in the author's own recollection; the 'little beads of greasy sweat' he notices on the woman's brow 'remind me of those self-sacrificing ironing-women and domestic cooks who used to pass by on Saturdays along the streets of my childhood and head off to their proletarian places of evangelical worship [al proletario culto evangélico].'[15] The black working-class woman he sees there at the wake for Cortijo takes on emblematic significance as an embodiment of 'pueblo pueblo' not for some hidden essence or archetypicality, but by force of the historical parallels and richly contradictory mnemonic associations her presence evokes. It is important to understand that along with the obvious continuities between the woman before him and those of his memories, there is also a sharp contrast because of the historical lapse resulting from the colonial modernization process and its so-called 'lumpenizing' or de-proletarianizing consequences. Both are 'pueblo pueblo,' their visage and beads of sweat may be identifiable, but intervening historical change has brought alterations in their everyday social practices and beliefs. In both cases, though, their concreteness and specificity are maintained, and imaginative memory allows for the study of popular culture in time.

# 3

More than merely emphasis, the effect of the doubling in the term 'pueblo pueblo' is to provide a necessary marker of specification or qualification. It is a sign of internal difference and contradiction, and of the abiding need to address the questions, 'Which people?' and 'Which popular culture?' With the hegemonic meaning of the term *popular culture* so identified with global media culture and communication, some specification of the time or site of the popular becomes indispensable. It is this need for specification that Stuart Hall stresses when he takes up, in cautiously nonessentialist terms, the thorny question, 'What Is This 'Black' in Black Popular Culture?'[16] He recognizes bluntly that popular culture has become 'the scene, par excellence, of commodification,' 'the space of homogenization where stereotyping and the formulaic mercilessly process the material and experiences it draws into its web, where control over narratives and representations passes into the hands of the established cultural bureaucracies, sometimes without a murmur.'[17] Though openly 'available for expropriation,' however, popular culture may signal alternative spaces, temporalities, and practices when the marker 'Black' is added – that is, when there is a qualifying reference to the experiences of a historically specified people. Accounting for these two distinct levels of meaning, Hall demonstrates how this doubling of the term through social markers helps in establishing a more dynamic understanding of contemporary popular culture: 'However deformed, incorporated, and inauthentic are the forms in which black people and black communities and traditions appear and are represented in popular culture,' he writes, 'we continue to see, in the figures and repertoires on which popular culture draws, the experiences that stand behind them. In its expressivity, its musicality, its orality, in its rich, deep, and varied attention to speech, in its inflections toward the vernacular and the local, in its rich production of counternarratives, and above all, in its metaphorical use of the musical vocabulary, black popular culture has enabled the surfacing, inside the mixed and contradictory modes even of some mainstream popular culture, of elements of a discourse that is different – other forms of life, other traditions of representation.'[18]

'It is this mark of difference *inside* forms of popular culture,' Hall concludes, 'that is carried by the signifier "black",' and he sees what is called 'American popular culture' as a prime example of this internal differentiation: 'the fact of American popular culture itself, which has always contained within it, whether silenced or not, black American popular vernacular traditions.'[19] To further underscore his strictly historical intentions, Hall is emphatic in stating that the 'difference' marked off has to do not only with race but with other forms of marginality and difference as well, and that 'blackness' has preeminently to do with unifying experiences of colonization, enslavement, and diasporic displacement. The point of the signifier, and the value of such seeming tautologies as 'popular vernacular' and 'pueblo pueblo,' is specification in historical time and social position, which is why Hall speaks so affirmatively of Gramsci's concept of 'the national-popular.' Though some contemporary theorists, like the Brazilian Renato Ortiz, claim that the 'national-popular' is by now fully eclipsed by what he calls 'uma cultura internacional popular,'[20] Hall argues that this national qualification remains cogent and continues to alter the meaning of the 'popular' in our times: 'The role of the "popular" in popular culture is to fix the authenticity of popular forms, rooting them in the experiences of popular communities from which they draw their strength, allowing us to see them as expressive of a particular subordinate social life that resists its being constantly made over as low and outside.'[21] Inside and behind the surface of commonality and the homogenizing pressure of 'popular culture' in its hegemonic appearance, there is the popular culture defined by historical experiences of exclusion and subordination, of 'difference' along the axes of social power.

It is important to recall that this dimension of national and colonial particularity has intersected the sense of popular culture as a 'common,' class-unified culture since the earliest conceptualization of the term. Long before Gramsci, Herder and the Grimm brothers along with other 'discoverers' of the popular had in mind this differentiation along lines of national and center-periphery contrast in their quest for some alternative to the cultural hegemony of France and England.[22] The history of the term, in fact, has witnessed this tension between the popular as 'low' or 'common' within a given society and that of some variant of what Gramsci then came to call the 'national-popular,' the national marker always indicating a colonial or peripheralizing relation of power. As engulfing as the 'international-popular' may have become, the vector of national and regional hierarchies has by no evidence been effaced, and thus continues to point up contexts of popular cultural expression of a local and community-based kind.[23]

Rather than among advertently isolated and disconnected groups, in our time these 'national-popular' contexts are particularly alive in diasporic settings, and under conditions, not of purity or boundedness, but of what García Canclini refers to, in his influential book, as 'hybrid cultures.'[24] The preservation and reenergizing of national traditions is most active at the seams of contemporary transnational formations, at the point of rupture and refashioning characteristic of diasporic conditions and migratory peoples, where an appeal to those traditions helps to provide a sense of grounding in place and time. The particularity characteristic of popular culture practice is now present not so much in some presumed untampered lineage of native heritage as in the very hybridization itself, in the blending and juxtaposition of seemingly disparate elements of divergent traditions and practices.

# 4

But cultural hybridity in García Canclini's sense
cultural traditions resulting from the mutua
groups, a phenomenon which he studies closely
Mexican-U.S. border culture.[25] He is also referri
tration of the cultural domains themselves, the bl
between high and low, and between elite, folklor
ing conceptual term is 'reconversion,' by which
supposedly 'high' culture features by the 'low' (v
versa, such that as a result of multidirectional 'r
becomes in our time – in 'postmodernity,' he woul
interactions unified by transnational demographi(

POPULAR CULTUR

80

Disney's quest for
'reconversion,' t
the heart of
references t
states th
expl
ar

practices. Such an interpretation of cultural relations has its obvious appeal
among contemporary readers in Latin America and elsewhere (which accounts
for the book's huge influence), for it helps free the conceptualization of popular
culture from the usual binarisms of high and low, inside or outside. It also allows
for a more careful reading of Bakhtin's idea of cultural inversion and the topsy-
turvy creativity of the carnivalesque. As Hall points out, 'The carnivalesque is not
simply an upturning of two things which remain locked within their oppositional
frameworks; it is also crosscut by what Bakhtin calls the dialogic.'[26]

An especially rich example of cultural reconversion and the dialogic interplay of
high and low may be seen in the current strategies of the Walt Disney Company.[27] The
entertainment colossus, long the world's supreme purveyor of mass culture, is resolutely going upscale, dedicating a surprisingly large share of its $22.5 billion in rev-
enues (for 1998) to the patronage of high culture. Disney chairman and CEO Michael
Eisner, described as 'a man who can shape culture on a global basis like perhaps no
other person in history,' is now 'the Medici behind Disney's high art.' Currently, he is
commissioning two choral symphonies to mark the millennium, an idea that came to
him while attending a performance of Mahler's Eighth Symphony, the 'Symphony of
a Thousand,' at Carnegie Hall in 1996. Similar ventures in sophistication are afoot in
the areas of theater and architecture, and the pretensions of elite cultural status are
most evident and serious, as might be expected, in France and in the vast endeavors
of EuroDisney. In 1989 Eisner hired Jean-Luc Choplin, of indubitable high-culture
pedigree as the former managing director of the Paris Opera Ballet, to program the
entertainment at Disneyland Paris. In a move that would leave Theodor Adorno and
the Frankfurt School theorists aghast, the quintessential 'culture industry' is on a mission to 'help new culture flower,' as one of the commissioned composers has it, 'when
what we're seeing is this overwhelming junk culture.'

And, of course, neither patron Eisner nor ambassador Choplin sees any contradiction between their 'serious culture' endeavors and what Disney has done all
along. As always, it is about the marriage, or symbiosis, between culture and business; as Eisner responds to the many attacks on his entertainment corporation, 'To
be broadly commercial, you have to be broadly talented, so nothing we do now is
inconsistent with what Walt did with his early pioneering work in animation, or
with 'Fantasia' or with working with Westinghouse to adapt the technology of his
day to his theme parks.' Choplin in turn, more at ease with his imbued cultural
capital than with marketing projections, is expansive in his justification of

cultural sophistication; in his view, it is the long history of the age-old interdependence of the high and the low, that lies at the Disney mission and points to the vision for the future. With ranging widely to Botticelli, Mahler, Sibelius, and Charles Ives, he at 'they were all inspired by popular traditions, by roots. I think we have red a lot of one-way streets at the end of the twentieth century, and I think needs to go back to more popular roots. And roots are not in the ether; they're in popular culture.' The process of reconversion is thus multidirectional, and in this case may be seen to come full circle: what starts as commercial mass culture turning to elite culture becomes the recognition by the newfound purveyors of high culture of the need for 'roots' in popular culture traditions.

# 5

The playing field of contemporary culture may be new but it is still not level; lines have been redrawn but not erased. García Canclini is careful to distinguish between 'reconversión hegemónica' and 'reconversión popular,' and thereby to lodge his theory of cultural hybridizations in structures of corporate and state power. Homogenizing tendencies engendered by global consumer culture are met by countervailing moves of reappropriation and reindigenization. Diasporic experiences demonstrate that the global encounters opposition not only at the local but at the translocal level as well, and thus belie the logic of a narrowly territorial geopolitics of cultural relations. The persistence of structures of social domination in general involves their persistence in the cultural field as well, though the relational lines between them, between social and cultural power, are shifting and oblique. That is, the socially dominant is also the culturally dominant, but the Bakhtinian paradox has it that the exercise of cultural domination inherently entails a 'dependency on the low-Other,' and further that 'the top *includes* that low symbolically, as a primary eroticized constituent of its own fantasy life.'[28]

No matter how the field of cultural practices is reconfigured in line with political and economic changes, popular culture of the vernacular, community-based kind will continue to be present as a mode of social relations, not to be wished away or analyzed out of existence in response to the pervasiveness of media consumption. The need for 'roots' is unrelenting, if not intensifying, in our times, and because of the carnivalesque inversion – that 'what is socially peripheral is so frequently *symbolically* central' – the roots of popular culture traditions are strongest among colonized nationalities and racialized communities and peoples. Here is where those 'moments of freedom' are most visible, the 'arts of timing' characteristic of popular culture in refusing incorporation and retaining what Hall calls 'the cutting edge of difference and transgression.'[29] But to 'capture' such moments, as Fabian continues his temporal imagery, requires an acute and perhaps redefined sense of time and temporal relations: it in turns calls for 'moments of freedom' and 'arts of timing' as well. This means, most obviously, historical awareness in order to counteract the excessively spatial conception of cultural relations that prevails in popular culture theory; the primacy of context in history over the usual privileging of an ahistorically constructed 'location' in social space. The imperative is temporality not just historicity, though, because too often history, and historical contexts, are confused with a teleology of progress and 'development,' and the puzzling over 'modernity' with the sense that modernity (and postmodernity) are somehow the goal or end-result of cultural experience on an individual and collective level.

Popular culture 'in time' calls for historical rather than preponderantly spatial contexts, but above all it refers to the enactment and the 'capturing' of popular culture as the establishing of temporal relations, associations fashioned by acts of memory and imagination. Relations in space and time, of course, interactions and intersections among social classes, racialized groups, diasporic locations, periods in history, generations – all are at work, and revealed, through popular cultural practice and interpretation. But what is particular about popular culture is its particularity, and as 'moments of freedom' the particularity of time in popular culture is that it is momentary, that with all its embeddedness in tradition and the historical past, it is present, it is contemporary, it is always *now.*

The concept of *popularity* itself is not particularly popular. It is not realistic to believe that it is. There is a whole series of abstract nouns in 'ity' which must be viewed with caution. Think of *utility, sovereignty, sanctity;* and we know that the concept of *nationality* has a quite particular, sacramental, pompous and suspicious connotation, which we dare not overlook. We must not ignore this connotation, just because we so urgently need the concept *popular.*

—BERTOLT BRECHT

## Notes

1. Peter Stallybrass and Allon White, *The Politics and Poetics of Transgression* (Ithaca: Cornell Univesity Press, 1986), 3. This process of 'symbolic inversion,' developed by Stallybrass and White, is actually taken from Barbara Babcock, *The Reversible World: Symbolic Inversion in Art and Society* (Ithaca: Cornell University Press, 1978), 3. The concept of 'moments of freedom' forms the title of the book by Johannes Fabian, *Moments of Freedom: Anthropology and Popular Culture* (Charlottesville: University Press of Virginia, 1998).

2. See Stuart Hall, 'Notes on Deconstructing 'the Popular',' in Raphael Samuel, ed., *People's History and Socialist Theory* (London: Routledge, 1981), 227–40. See also note 22, this chapter.

3. Such, for example, is the perspective of John Fiske in his frequently cited primer *Understanding Popular Culture* (London: Routledge, 1989), as well as that of the thoughtful critical response by John Frow, *Cultural Studies and Cultural Value* (Oxford: Oxford University Press, 1995). For an extended discussion of this theoretical shift, see my 'Reinstating Popular Culture: Responses to Christopher Lasch,' *Social Text* 12 (1985): 113–23.

4. See John Frow, *Cultural Studies and Cultural Value,* esp. 75–79, where frequent reference is made to the relevant writings of Hall and others.

5. See García Canclini, *Culturas híbridas: estrategias para entrar y salir de la modernidad* (Mexico City: Grijalbo, 1989), and *Consumidores y ciudadanos: conflictos multiculturales de la globalización* (Mexico City: Grijalbo, 1995).

6. See García Canclini, *Consumidores y ciudadanos,* 27–30.

7. See Arjun Appadurai and Carol A. Breckenridge, 'Why Public Culture?' *Public Culture Bulletin* 1.1 (Fall 1988): 5–9.

8. See Arjun Appadurai, *Modernity at Large: Cultural Dimensions of Globalization* (Minneapolis: University of Minnesota Press, 1996), 12 passim.

9. Fabian, *Moments of Freedom,* 133.

10. Ibid., 133–34.

11. Edgardo Rodríguez Juliá, *El entierro de Cortijo* (Río Piedras, P.R.: Ediciones Huracán, 1983), 12 ('... ya se perfila que esta crónica será el encuentro de muchas cruces históricas').

12. Ibid., 18. ('¿Cómo definir este pueblo? Definirlo es fácil, pero iqué difícil es describirlo! Es pueblo pueblo, mi pueblo puertorriqueño en toda su diversidad más contradictoria.')

13. Jesús Martín Barbero, *De los medios a las mediaciones* (Barcelona: Grijalbo, 1987).

14. On the role of the 'imagination' in the study of contemporary popular culture, see especially Appadurai, *Modernity at Large,* 3ff.

15. Rodríguez Juliá, *El entierro de Cortijo,* 18 ('las perlitas de su grasoso sudor me recuerdan aquellas abnegadas planchadoras y cocineras que pasaban los sábados por la calle de mi infancia, allá dirigiéndose al proletario culto evangélico').

16. Stuart Hall, 'What Is This "Black" in Black Popular Culture?' in Gina Dent, ed., *Black Popular Culture* (Seattle: Bay Press, 1992), 21–33.

17. Hall, 'What Is This "Black"... ,' 26.

18. Ibid., 27.

19. Ibid., 22.

20. See Renato Ortiz, *Mundializaçáo e Cultura* (São Paulo: Braziliense, 1994), 105–45.

21. Hall, 'What Is This "Black"...,' 26.

22. See Peter Burke, *Popular Culture in Early Modern Europe* (New York: New York University Press, 1978), esp. 3–22. See also William A. Wilson, 'Herder, Folklore, and Romantic Nationalism,' *Journal of Popular Culture* 6:4 (Spring 1973): 819–35; and Renato Ortiz, *Románticos e Folcloristas: Cultura Popular* (São Paulo: Editora Olho d'Agua, n.d.). On the history of the concept, see Morag Shiach, *Discourse on Popular Culture: Class, Gender, and History in Cultural Analysis, 1730 to the Present* (Stanford, Calif.: Stanford University Press, 1989).

23. George Yúdice has pointed out the need to differentiate further between the 'national' and the regional or local dimensions. Speaking of the situation of popular culture in Latin America, Yúdice states: 'Historically, national cultures have entailed the priorization of some local cultures above others, and at least since the early 20th century, through mass culture, especially radio. ... I would argue that those forms of culture identified with the national in Latin America tend to have gotten that valence through mass culture, since the twenties. And a controlled mass culture has prioritized one local culture as the national culture' (letter to author, March 7, 1999).

24. See García Canclini, *Culturas híbridas.*

25. See García Canclini et al., *Tijuana, la casa de toda la gente* (Iztapalapa [Mexico]: INAH-ENAH, 1989).

26. Hall, 'What Is This "Black"...,' 32.

27. For the following, see Peter Applebome, 'The Medici Behind Disney's High Art,' *New York Times,* October 4,1998, sec. 2, pp. i, 38.

28. Stallybrass and White, *The Politics and Poetics of Transgression,* 5.

29. Hall, 'What Is This "Black"...,' 24.

# Reference

Edgardo Rodríguez Juliá (1983) *El entierro de Cortijo.* Río Piedras, P. R.: Ediciones Huracán.

# PART TWO

# COMMODIFYING:

# THE COMMODITY, CULTURE AND SOCIAL LIFE

Immediately succeeding the issue of terminology in the study of popular culture is the significance of the term commodity, for to understand popular culture it is necessary to contend with the interconnection of both its material and ideological capacities. Because the commodity, or the modern unit of exchange, is the site where value and meaning cohere and are contested, it bears upon how we understand the objects that surround us and through which we negotiate our relationship to the culture that surrounds us. As Michael T. Taussig makes plain in *The Devil and Commodity Fetishism in South America* (1980), a study of 'the cultural reactions of peasants to industrial capitalism' (3):

> the market system of modern capitalism engenders a marketing mentality in which people tend to be seen as commodities and commodities tend to be seen as animated entities that can dominate persons. This socially instituted paradox arises because, unlike earlier forms of organization which joined persons into direct relationships for production and exchange ... the market interposes itself between persons, mediating direct awareness of social relations by the abstract laws of relationships between commodities. (25)

For better or for worse, the commodification of culture is an incontestable outgrowth of the processes of industrialization that have shaped the modern world. With the advent of mass production came the basis for widespread transformations in social and political life. New forms of distribution dependent on shifts in the organization of international power structures, for example via colonization as well as through expanded trade, supported the circulation of the commodities being produced by industrialized nations. This interconnectedness, one that hinges on the emergence of the commodity-form's centrality within modern life, is powerfully encapsulated in the opening pages of *The Communist Manifesto* (orig., 1848; London: International Publishers Co., 1948): 'Modern industry has established the world market, for which the discovery of America paved the way. This market has given an immense development to commerce, to navigation, to communication by land. This development has, in its turn, reacted on the extension of industry' (10). The spread of modern industry simultaneously involves the spread of bourgeois ideology, and its concomitant social and political consequences. As Marx and Engels later insist:

> The cheap prices of its commodities are the heavy artillery with which it batters down all Chinese walls, with which it forces the barbarians' intensely obstinate hatred of foreigners to capitulate. It compels all nations, on pain of extinction, to adopt the bourgeois mode of production; it compels them to introduce what it calls civilization into their midst, i.e., to become bourgeois themselves. In a word, it creates the world after its own image. (13)

The commodity thus exercises considerable influence over the establishment and maintenance of hegemony, a concept that is central to numerous considerations of the exercise of style and identity through popular practice.

Beginning with Karl Marx's elaboration of the commodity as fetish, the articles collected in this section treat the nature of the commodity in general as well as what happens to commodities in the arena of popular culture. The commodity is situated within a variety of contexts. In that sense, the section is very much concerned with how objects are understood and circulate within the particular political economy that marks culture and the influences that have been exerted on it over a long historical period of immense economic, social and political change. Because of this focus, the section shares much common ground with this volume's focus on marketing and practicing, although it is inarguably relevant to many of this book's themes.

In his development of nineteenth-century philosopher G. W. F. Hegel's theory of history, Karl Marx engaged the relationship of culture to political economy. Arguing for historical materialism (as opposed to Hegelian idealism), Marx paved the way for much of the most influential work in the study of popular culture, from the Frankfurt School's development of critical theory in 1930's Germany to its relocation in the USA in the 1940s–50s and the Birmingham Centre's contributions to cultural studies in Britain during the 1960s. In addition, Marx's work resonates within Antonio Gramsci's theorizations of hegemony, Louis Althusser's considerations of ideology, and Immanuel Wallerstein's contributions to world-systems analysis, as well as numerous other interventions. Marx's major works include: *The German Ideology* with Friedrich Engels (1845), *The Communist Manifesto* with Friedrich Engels (1848), and *Capital, Volume One* (1867), from which the present article is excerpted. In **'The Fetishism of Commodities and the Secret Thereof'** Marx undertakes a massive, yet cleverly understated project of demystification. How is it, he asks, that value is attributed to the inanimate world in a manner that resembles that of social relations? The subject of his inquiry is a basic unit of exchange within capitalism: the commodity. 'A commodity', he describes as, 'a mysterious thing [...] because the relation of the producers to the sum total of their own labor is presented to them as a social relation, existing not between themselves, but between the products of their labor'. As an example, Marx turns readers' attention to a common object: a table. Neither the raw materials of which it is comprised nor the labor that transforms this raw material into a commodity, adequately reflect the value of wood and labor in the table as a commodity. As a result, he suggests that the commodity must be understood in its capacity as 'social thing'. For Marx, the very category of 'social thing' is fetishistic because it attributes special social, otherwise human qualities, to inanimate objects. Through a process of occultation, both exchange-value and use-value, necessarily human creations, are assumed to be inherent to, rather than projected on, objects and their circulation within bourgeois political economy. In brief, Marx's theorization of the commodity merits significant attention because of the valuable insights that it engenders with respect to our relationship to the social world of things that come under the category of popular.

'That which withers in the age of mechanical reproduction is the aura of the work of art.' These famous words written by Walter Benjamin in his forever influential essay, **'The Work of Art in the Age of Mechanical Reproduction'** (1992 [1936]), speak to the effects of mass production, modes of consumption, and modern technology upon the status of art as well as their implications for contemporary forms of popular culture. Benjamin's essay examines how mechanical reproduction redefines and restructures the work of art's claims to 'authenticity', 'authority', and its 'unique' existence in time and space. The 'decay of aura', on account of modern technology, removes the work of art from its authorial status: 'By making many reproductions it substitutes a plurality of copies for a unique existence. And in permitting the reproduction to meet the beholder or listener in his own particular situation, it reactivates the object reproduced.' This absence is not mourned by Benjamin; for the absence of authority (based upon ritual and tradition) opens the object to a plurality of interpretations. It frees the object to be placed in unlimited and different contexts. Unlike his contemporaries, members of the Frankfurt School, Benjamin's thesis is not antagonistic toward mass culture: mechanical reproduction makes art, if not all culture that is reproducible, more accessible, democratic, and available, while opening up the ways in which art can be experienced and received. Major works (most of which were collected into book form after his untimely death) include: *Charles Baudelaire: A Lyric Poet in the Era of High Capitalism* (trans., H. Zohn. London: Verso, 1973), *Illuminations* (trans., 1992 [1936], London: Fontana), *Origin of German Tragic Drama* (trans., J. Osborne. London: Verso, 1977), *Reflections: Aphorisms, Essays and Autobiographical Writings* (trans., E. Jephcott. New York and London: Harcourt Brace Jovanovich, 1978), and *One-Way Street and Other Writings* (trans., E. Jephcott and K. Shorter. London: Verso, 1979). More recently, four volumes of his *Selected Writings* (Cambridge, MA: The Belknap Press), as well as his monumental *The Arcades Project* (trans., H. Eiland and K. McLaughline, Cambridge, MA: Harvard University Press, 1999), have been published in English. Benjamin's work is returned to again and again for the richness of its analysis. He was hopeful about culture, change, and about the possibilities of transforming capitalism in an era within which the majority of scholars were not. It is not surprising that many scholars during the world wars' upheaval and turn to fascism found it difficult, if not impossible, to discern any possible good emerging from the changes underway. Benjamin did.

Seminal to the study of culture in all of its complex and disputed meanings is Max Horkheimer and Theodor W. Adorno's neologism, 'the culture industry'. According to Martin Jay's excellent book, *The Dialectical Imagination* (Boston: Little, Brown and Co., 1973), members of the University of Frankfurt's Institut für *Sozialforschung* (best known in the Anglo-American academy simply as the Frankfurt School) became 'a major force in the revitalization of Western European Marxism in the postwar years'. Rather than lead their readers to attribute agency on the part of the masses, Horkheimer and Adorno opt for the term 'culture industry' to explain the hegemony of mass culture, as well as its standardizing, commodifying, and controlling effects in *Dialectic of Enlightenment* (English trans., 1973). Included here in a later essay enti- tled **'Culture Industry Reconsidered'** (1991) are Adorno's reflections on the culture industry thesis, not least of which is that: 'The power of the culture industry's ideol- ogy is such that conformity has replaced consciousness'. Despite its harsh condem- nation of what has come to be known as popular culture, Adorno's work has greatly influenced the development of critical theory and expresses the complex relationship of culture and political economy that has become a generative site of cultural theo- rization for subsequent scholars.

Guy Debord wrote little as 'Guy Debord'. His accredited texts include the remark- able *The Society of the Spectacle* (1967, English trans. 1973), *Comments on The Society of the Spectacle* (1988, English trans. M. Imrie. London: Verso, 1991) (an even more pessimistic account of the condition of culture and everyday life than its predecessor), and the first volume of his autobiography, *Panegyric* (1989, English trans. J. Brook. London: Verso, 1991). As a filmmaker he is known, albeit in select cir- cles, for his *Screams in Favor of De Sade* (1952), *In girum imus nocte et consumimur igni* (1978), and *La société du spectacle* (1973) to name a few. Debord's writings are commonly experienced through his anonymous (and sometimes acknowledged) con- tributions to the French journal, *Internationale Situationniste* – the mouthpiece of the radical group/movement known as the Situationist International. For the situationists and implicit throughout Debord's writing, everyday life has become commodified and, drawing from Marx, the commodity form signifies alienation in contemporary society. The commodity is recast as 'the spectacle': the social thing has become a spectacu- lar event. 'Spectacle' captures the hegemonic power of capitalism whereby culture – even in its most mundane forms – becomes repressive, alienating; life and experience are rendered passive, known only through relational subordination to the spectacle. 'The spectacle is the moment when the commodity has attained the total occupation of social life', claims Debord in the excerpt **'The Commodity as Spectacle'**. Com- menting on modern life Debord writes in an earlier section of his *the Society of the Spectacle* that: 'The promise of self-fulfillment and expression, pleasure and inde- pendence which adorn every billboard are realizable only through consumption, and the only possible relation to the social world and one's own life is that of the observer, the contemplative and passive spectator.'

Fredric Jameson, Marxist literary theorist and cultural critic, has been a major voice in contemporary debates over the relationship of political economy to cultural produc- tion. His major works, which engage developments in structuralist, poststructuralist and postmodern theory, include: *Marxism and Form* (Princeton, NJ: Princeton University Press, 1971), *The Political Unconscious* (Ithaca, NY: Cornell University Press, 1981), *Postmodernism, or the Cultural Logic of Late Capitalism* (Durham, NC:

Duke University Press, 1991), and *The Geopolitical Aesthetic* (Bloomington, IN: Indiana University Press, 1992). Through the concepts of pastiche, parody and the 'death of the subject', as well as through an analysis of nostalgia in film, artistic and literary production, Jameson's influential work on postmodernism characterizes the relationship of cultural production and social life. The work presented in this collection, **'Reification and Utopia in Mass Culture'**, excerpted from his *Signatures of the Visible* (New York: Routledge, 1990, orig. 1979), considers the impact of commodification on aesthetics and the debates that the latter generates. Jameson begins with an examination of the tension between populist and elitist conceptualizations of culture, a tension that he considers to be counter-productive. Criticism of mass culture from populist radicals carries an anti-intellectual thrust that belies such critics' own (disavowed) position as intellectuals and overlooks the critical function of modern art. Elitist criticism, as represented by the Frankfurt School, premises its critical apparatus on the valorization of high culture, a move that fails to recognize that high culture is also fully implicated in the capitalist scheme that it is used to criticize. In place of the binary between populist and elitist cultural criticism, Jameson suggests that: 'we must rethink the opposition high culture/mass culture in such a way that the emphasis on evaluation to which it has traditionally given rise … is replaced by a genuinely historical and dialectical approach to these phenomena'. In other words, Jameson calls for a new area of study that can contend with the interrelationship of mass culture and modernism (reification and repetition are, for example, a 'key structural feature of both') that characterizes the present. In the succeeding portion of the essay, which we have not reproduced in this collection, Jameson works through the implications of his theory by applying it to three commercial films: Steven Spielberg's *Jaws* (1975) and the first two installments of Francis Ford Coppola's *The Godfather* (1972, 1974).

In *The Politics of Culture in the Shadow of Late Capital* (1997) Lisa Lowe, the author of *Immigrant Acts: On Asian American Cultural Politics* (Durham, NC: Duke University Press, 1996), and David Lloyd, author of *Anomalous States: Irish Writing in the Post-colonial Moment* (Durham, NC: Duke University Press, 1993), draw together an influential array of essays that demonstrate contemporary scholars' revision and upending of received knowledge about the role of culture in light of recent developments in the economic and political spheres. Their **'Introduction'** radically extends the definition of culture as well as the relationship of politics to culture, and frames the book's contents as a powerful response to the fiercely relentless climate of contemporary neocolonial capitalism, all of which carry clear implications for an understanding of popular culture. Lowe and Lloyd tap Walter Benjamin's theory of history, Antonio Gramsci's articulation of hegemony, and a variety of interventions from scholars of postcoloniality, such as Franz Fanon, to make the case that social practices, including though not limited to anticolonial and antiracist struggles, feminist struggles, labor organizing, and cultural movements, 'challenge contemporary neocolonial capitalism as a highly differentiated mode of production'. They also critique theorizations of culture that assume either a homogeneous globalizing tendency or the facile reduction of culture to the hopelessly commodified. In brief, culture emerges as 'a terrain in which politics, culture, and the economic form an inseparable dynamic'. It produces its own politics, a politics of contradiction that results from the relationship of cultural formations to 'economic or political logics that try to refunction it for exploitation or domination'.

# Play List

Appadurai, Arjun (ed.) (1986) *The Social Life of Things: Commodities in Cultural Perspective.* Cambridge: Cambridge University Press.

Baudrillard, Jean (1975) *The Mirror of Production.* Trans. Mark Poster. St. Louis: Telos Press.

Baudrillard, Jean (1981) *For A Critique of the Political Economy of the Sign.* Trans. C. Levin. St. Louis: Telos Press.

Baudrillard, Jean (1996) *The System of Objects.* Trans. James Benedict. London: Verso.

Buck-Morss, Susan (1989) *The Dialectics of Seeing: Walter Benjamin and the Arcades Project.* Cambridge, MA: MIT University Press.

Debord, Guy (1973) *La société du spectacle.* videocassette.

Defoe, Daniel (1983 [1719]) *The Life and Strange and Surprising Adventures of Robinson Crusoe.* New York: Atheneum.

Du Bois, W. E. B. (1962 [1935]) *Black Reconstruction in America: An Essay Toward A History of the Part Which Black Folk Played in the Attempt to Reconstruct Democracy in America, 1860–1880.* Cleveland, OH: World Pub. Co.

Franklin, Benjamin (1964) *The Autobiography of Benjamin Franklin.* New Haven: Yale UP.

Harvey, David (1990) *The Condition of Postmodernity.* Oxford: Blackwell.

Horkheimer, Max and Adorno, Theodor W. (1973) *Dialectic of Enlightenment.* Trans. J. Cumming. New York: Herder and Herder, Inc.

Huyssen, Andreas (1986) *After the Great Divide: Modernism, Mass Culture, Postmodernism.* Bloomington, IN: Indiana University Press.

Kracauer, Siegfried (1995) *The Mass Ornament: Weimar Essays.* Trans. Thomas Y. Levin. Cambridge, MA: Harvard University Press.

Lee, Martyn L. (1993) *Consumer Culture Reborn: The Cultural Politics of Consumption.* London: Routledge.

Linebaugh, Peter and Rediker, Marcus (2000) *The Many-Headed Hydra: Sailors, Slaves, Commoners, and the Hidden History of the Revolutionary Atlantic.* Boston, MA: Beacon Press.

Lukács, Georg (1971) *History and Class Consciousness.* London: Merlin Press.

Mauss, Marcel (1976) *The Gift.* New York: Norton.

Plant, Sadie (1992) *The Most Radical Gesture: The Situationist International in a Postmodern Age.* London: Routledge.

Ross, Kristin (1995) *Fast Cars, Clean Bodies: Decolonization and the Reordering of French Culture.* Cambridge, MA: MIT Press.

Taussig, Michael T. (1980) *The Devil and Commodity Fetishism in South America.* Chapel Hill, NC: University of North Carolina Press.

Williams, Raymond (1977) *Marxism and Literature.* Oxford: Oxford University Press.

# Chapter 8

# Karl Marx

# The Fetishism of Commodities and the Secret Thereof

A commodity appears, at first sight, a very trivial thing, and easily understood. Its analysis shows that it is, in reality, a very queer thing, abounding in metaphysical subtleties and theological niceties. So far as it is a value in use, there is nothing mysterious about it, whether we consider it from the point of view that by its properties it is capable of satisfying human wants, or from the point that those properties are the product of human labour. It is as clear as noon-day, that man, by his industry, changes the forms of the materials furnished by Nature, in such a way as to make them useful to him. The form of wood, for instance, is altered, by making a table out of it. Yet, for all that, the table continues to be that common, every-day thing, wood. But, so soon as it steps forth as a commodity, it is changed into something transcendent. It not only stands with its feet on the ground, but, in relation to all other commodities, it stands on its head, and evolves out of its wooden brain grotesque ideas, far more wonderful than 'table-turning' ever was.

The mystical character of commodities does not originate, therefore, in their use-value. Just as little does it proceed from the nature of the determining factors of value. For, in the first place, however varied the useful kinds of labour, or productive activities, may be, it is a physiological fact, that they are functions of the human organism, and that each such function, whatever may be its nature or form, is essentially the expenditure of human brain, nerves, muscles, &c. Secondly, with regard to that which forms the groundwork for the quantitative determination of value, namely, the duration of that expenditure, or the quantity of labour, it is quite clear that there is a palpable difference between its quantity and quality. In all states of

From: Karl Marx, *Capital: Volume One*. (Orig. 1867). Reprinted in *The Marx-Engels Reader*. R. Tucker (ed.) London: W.W. Norton & Co., 1972.

society, the labour-time that it costs to produce the means of subsistence, must necessarily be an object of interest to mankind, though not of equal interest in different stages of development. And lastly, from the moment that men in any way work for one another, their labour assumes a social form.

Whence, then, arises the enigmatical character of the product of labour, so soon as it assumes the form of commodities? Clearly from this form itself. The equality of all sorts of human labour is expressed objectively by their products all being equally values; the measure of the expenditure of labour-power by the duration of that expenditure, takes the form of the quantity of value of the products of labour; and finally, the mutual relations of the producers, within which the social character of their labour affirms itself, take the form of a social relation between the products.

A commodity is therefore a mysterious thing, simply because in it the social character of men's labour appears to them as an objective character stamped upon the product of that labour; because the relation of the producers to the sum total of their own labour is presented to them as a social relation, existing not between themselves, but between the products of their labour. This is the reason why the products of labour become commodities, social things whose qualities are at the same time perceptible and imperceptible by the senses. In the same way the light from an object is perceived by us not as the subjective excitation of our optic nerve, but as the objective form of something outside the eye itself. But, in the act of see-ing, there is at all events, an actual passage of light from one thing to another, from the external object to the eye. There is a physical relation between physical things. But it is different with commodities. There, the existence of the things *qua* com-modities, and the value-relation between the products of labour which stamps them as commodities, have absolutely no connexion with their physical properties and with the material relations arising therefrom. There it is a definite social rela-tion between men, that assumes, in their eyes, the fantastic form of a relation between things. In order, therefore, to find an analogy, we must have recourse to the mist-enveloped regions of the religious world. In that world the productions of the human brain appear as independent beings endowed with life, and entering into relation both with one another and the human race. So it is in the world of commodities with the products of men's hands. This I call the Fetishism which attaches itself to the products of labour, so soon as they are produced as com-modities, and which is therefore inseparable from the production of commodities.

This Fetishism of commodities has its origin, as the foregoing analysis has already shown, in the peculiar social character of the labour that produces them.

As a general rule, articles of utility become commodities, only because they are products of the labour of private individuals or groups of individuals who carry on their work independently of each other. The sum total of the labour of all these pri-vate individuals forms the aggregate labour of society. Since the producers do not come into social contact with each other until they exchange their products, the specific social character of each producer's labour does not show itself except in the act of exchange. In other words, the labour of the individual asserts itself as a part of the labour of society, only by means of the relations which the act of exchange establishes directly between the products, and indirectly, through them, between the producers. To the latter, therefore, the relations connecting the labour of one individual with that of the rest appear, not as direct social relations between indi-viduals at work, but as what they really are, material relations between persons and social relations between things. It is only by being exchanged that the products of labour acquire, as values, one uniform social status, distinct from their varied forms of existence as objects of utility. This division of a product into a useful thing and a value becomes practically important, only when exchange has acquired such an extension that useful articles are produced for the purpose of being exchanged, and their character as values has therefore to be taken into account, beforehand, during production. From this moment the labour of the individual producer acquires socially a two-fold character. On the one hand, it must, as a definite useful kind of labour, satisfy a definite social want, and thus hold its place as part and parcel of the collective labour of all, as a branch of a social division of labour that has sprung up spontaneously. On the other hand, it can satisfy the manifold wants of the individual producer himself, only in so far as the mutual exchangeability of all kinds of useful private labour is an established social fact, and therefore the private useful labour of each producer ranks on an equality with that of all others. The equalisation of the most different kinds of labour can be the result only of an abstraction from their inequalities, or of reducing them to their common denominator, viz., expenditure of human labour-power or human labour in the abstract. The two-fold social character of the labour of the individual appears to him, when reflected in his brain, only under those forms which are impressed upon that labour in everyday practice by the exchange of products. In this way, the character that his own labour possesses of being socially useful takes the form of the condition, that the product must be not only useful, but useful for others, and the social character that his particular labour has of being the equal of all other particular kinds of labour, takes the form that all the physically different articles that are the products of labour, have one common quality, viz., that of having value.

Hence, when we bring the products of our labour into relation with each other as values, it is not because we see in these articles the material receptacles of homogeneous human labour. Quite the contrary: whenever, by an exchange, we equate as values our different products, by that very act, we also equate, as human labour, the different kinds of labour expended upon them. We are not aware of this, nevertheless we do it. Value, therefore, does not stalk about with a label describing what it is. It is value, rather, that converts every product into a social hieroglyphic. Later on, we try to decipher the hieroglyphic, to get behind the secret of our own social products; for to stamp an object of utility as a value, is just as much a social product as language. The recent scientific discovery, that the products of labour, so far as they are values, are but material expressions of the human labour spent in their production, marks, indeed, an epoch in the history of the development of the human race, but, by no means, dissipates the mist through which the social character of labour appears to us to be an objective character of the products themselves. The fact, that in the particular form of production with which we are dealing, viz., the production of commodities, the specific social character of private labour carried on independently, consists in the equality of every kind of that labour, by virtue of its being human labour, which character, therefore, assumes in the product the form of value—this fact appears to the producers, notwithstanding the discovery above referred to, to be just as real and final, as the fact, that, after the discovery by science of the component gases of air, the atmosphere itself remained unaltered.

What, first of all, practically concerns producers when they make an exchange, is the question, how much of some other product they get for their own? in what proportions the products are exchangeable? When these proportions have, by custom, attained a certain stability, they appear to result from the nature of the products, so that, for instance, one ton of iron and two ounces of gold appear as naturally to be of equal value as a pound of gold and a pound of iron in spite of their different physical and chemical qualities appear to be of equal weight. The character of having value, when once impressed upon products, obtains fixity only by reason of their acting and re-acting upon each other as quantities of value. These quantities vary continually, independently of the will, foresight and action of the producers. To them, their own social action takes the form of the action of objects, which rule the producers instead of being ruled by them. It requires a fully developed production of commodities before, from accumulated experience alone, the scientific conviction springs up, that all the different kinds of private labour, which are carried on independently of each other, and yet as spontaneously developed branches of the social division of labour, are continually being reduced to the quantitative proportions in which society requires them. And why? Because, in the midst of all the accidental and ever fluctuating exchange-relations between the products, the labour-time socially necessary for their production forcibly asserts itself like an over-riding law of Nature. The law of gravity thus asserts itself when a house falls about our ears. The determination of the magnitude of value by labour-time is therefore a secret, hidden under the apparent fluctuations in the relative values of commodities. Its discovery, while removing all appearance of mere accidentality from the determination of the magnitude of the values of products, yet in no way alters the mode in which that determination takes place.

Man's reflections on the forms of social life, and consequently, also, his scientific analysis of those forms, take a course directly opposite to that of their actual historical development. He begins, post festum, with the results of the process of development ready to hand before him. The characters that stamp products as commodities, and whose establishment is a necessary preliminary to the circulation of commodities, have already acquired the stability of natural, self-understood forms of social life, before man seeks to decipher, not their historical character, for in his eyes they are immutable, but their meaning. Consequently it was the analysis of the prices of commodities that alone led to the determination of the magnitude of value, and it was the common expression of all commodities in money that alone led to the establishment of their characters as values. It is, however, just this ultimate money-form of the world of commodities that actually conceals, instead of disclosing, the social character of private labour, and the social relations between the individual producers. When I state that coats or boots stand in a relation to linen, because it is the universal incarnation of abstract human labour, the absurdity of the statement is self-evident. Nevertheless, when the producers of coats and boots compare those articles with linen, or, what is the same thing, with gold or silver, as the universal equivalent, they express the relation between their own private labour and the collective labour of society in the same absurd form.

The categories of bourgeois economy consist of such like forms. They are forms of thought expressing with social validity the conditions and relations of a definite, historically determined mode of production, viz., the production of commodities. The whole mystery of commodities, all the magic and necromancy that surrounds the products of labour as long as they take the form of commodities, vanishes therefore, so soon as we come to other forms of production.

Since Robinson Crusoe's experiences are a favourite theme with political economists, let us take a look at him on his island. Moderate though he be, yet some few wants he has to satisfy, and must therefore do a little useful work of various sorts, such as making tools and furniture, taming goats, fishing and hunting. Of his prayers and the like we take no account, since they are a source of pleasure to him, and he looks upon them as so much recreation. In spite of the variety of his work, he knows that his labour, whatever its form, is but the activity of one and the same Robinson, and consequently, that it consists of nothing but different modes of human labour. Necessity itself compels him to apportion his time accurately between his different kinds of work. Whether one kind occupies a greater space in his general activity than another, depends on the difficulties, greater or less as the case may be, to be overcome in attaining the useful effect aimed at. This our friend Robinson soon learns by experience, and having rescued a watch, ledger, and pen and ink from the wreck, commences, like a true-born Briton, to keep a set of books. His stock-book contains a list of the objects of utility that belong to him, of the oper-ations necessary for their production; and lastly, of the labour-time that definite quantities of those objects have, on an average, cost him. All the relations between Robinson and the objects that form this wealth of his own creation, are here so sim-ple and clear as to be intelligible without exertion, even to Mr. Sedley Taylor. And yet those relations contain all that is essential to the determination of value.

Let us now transport ourselves from Robinson's island bathed in light to the European middle ages shrouded in darkness. Here, instead of the independent man, we find everyone dependent, serfs and lords, vassals and suzerains, laymen and clergy. Personal dependence here characterises the social relations of produc-tion just as much as it does the other spheres of life organised on the basis of that production. But for the very reason that personal dependence forms the ground-work of society, there is no necessity for labour and its products to assume a fan-tastic form different from their reality. They take the shape, in the transactions of society, of services in kind and payments in kind. Here the particular and natural form of labour, and not, as in a society based on production of commodities, its general abstract form is the immediate social form of labour. Compulsory labour is just as properly measured by time, as commodity-producing labour, but every serf knows that what he expends in the service of his lord, is a definite quantity of his own personal labour-power. The tithe to be rendered to the priest is more matter of fact than his blessing. No matter, then, what we may think of the parts played by the different classes of people themselves in this society, the social relations between individuals in the performance of their labour, appear at all events as their own mutual personal relations, and are not disguised under the shape of social relations between the products of labour.

For an example of labour in common or directly associated labour, we have no occasion to go back to that spontaneously developed form which we find on the threshold of the history of all civilised races. We have one close at hand in the patriarchal industries of a peasant family, that produces corn, cattle, yarn, linen, and clothing for home use. These different articles are, as regards the family, so many products of its labour, but as between themselves, they are not commodi-ties. The different kinds of labour, such as tillage, cattle tending, spinning, weav-ing and making clothes, which result in the various products, are in themselves, and such as they are, direct social functions, because functions of the family, which, just as much as a society based on the production of commodities, pos-sesses a spontaneously developed system of division of labour. The distribution of the work within the family, and the regulation of the labour-time of the several members, depend as well upon differences of age and sex as upon natural conditions varying with the seasons. The labour-power of each individual, by its very nature, operates in this case merely as a definite portion of the whole labour-power of the family, and therefore, the measure of the expenditure of individual labour-power by its duration, appears here by its very nature as a social character of their labour.

Let us now picture to ourselves, by way of change, a community of free individuals, carrying on their work with the means of production in common, in which the labour-power of all the different individuals is consciously applied as the combined labour-power of the community. All the characteristics of Robinson's labour are here repeated, but with this difference, that they are social, instead of individual. Everything produced by him was exclusively the result of his own personal labour, and therefore simply an object of use for himself. The total product of our community is a social product. One portion serves as fresh means of production and remains social. But another portion is consumed by the members as means of subsistence. A distribution of this portion amongst them is consequently necessary. The mode of this distribution will vary with the productive organisation of the community, and the degree of historical development attained by the producers. We will assume, but merely for the sake of a parallel with the production of commodities, that the share of each individual producer in the means of subsistence is determined by his labour-time. Labour-time would, in that case, play a double part. Its apportionment in accordance with a definite social plan maintains the proper proportion between the different kinds of work to be done and the various wants of the community. On the other hand, it also serves as a measure of the portion of the common labour borne by each individual, and of his share in the part of the total product destined for individual consumption. The social relations of the individual producers, with regard both to their labour and to its products, are in this case perfectly simple and intelligible, and that with regard not only to production but also to distribution. [...]

To what extent some economists are misled by the Fetishism inherent in commodities, or by the objective appearance of the social characteristics of labour, is shown, amongst other ways, by the dull and tedious quarrel over the part played by Nature in the formation of exchange-value. Since exchange-value is a definite social manner of expressing the amount of labour bestowed upon object, Nature has no more to do with it, than it has in fixing the course of exchange.

The mode of production in which the product takes the form of a commodity, or is produced directly for exchange, is the most general and most embryonic form of bourgeois production. It therefore makes its appearance at an early date in history, though not in the same predominating and characteristic manner as now-a-days. Hence its Fetish character is comparatively easy to be seen through. But when we come to more concrete forms, even this appearance of simplicity vanishes. Whence arose the illusions of the monetary system? To it gold and silver, when serving as money, did not represent a social relation between producers but were natural objects with strange social properties. And modern economy, which looks down with such disdain on the monetary system, does not its superstition come out as clear as noon-day, whenever it treats of capital? How long is it since economy discarded the physiocratic illusion, that rents grow out of the soil and not out of society?

But not to anticipate, we will content ourselves with yet another example relating to the commodity-form. Could commodities themselves speak, they would say: Our use-value may be a thing that interests men. It is no part of us as objects. What, however, does belong to us as objects, is our value. Our natural intercourse as commodities proves it. In the eyes of each other we are nothing but exchange-values. Now listen how those commodities speak through the mouth of the economist. 'Value' – (i.e., exchange-value) 'is a property of things, riches' – (i.e., use-value) 'of man. Value, in this sense, necessarily implies exchanges, riches do not.' 'Riches' (use-value) 'are the attribute of men, value is the attribute of commodities. A man or a community is rich, a pearl or a diamond is valuable. ... A pearl or a diamond is valuable' as a pearl or diamond. So far no chemist has ever discovered exchange-value either in a pearl or a diamond. The economic discoverers of this chemical element, who by-the-by lay special claim to critical acumen, find however that the use-value of objects belongs to them independently of their material properties, while their value, on the other hand, forms a part of them as objects. What confirms them in this view, is the peculiar circumstance that the use-value of objects is realised without exchange, by means of a direct relation between the objects and man, while, on the other hand, their value is realised only by exchange, that is, by means of a social process. Who fails here to call to mind our good friend, Dogberry, who informs neighbour Seacoal, that, 'To be a well-favoured man is the gift of fortune; but reading and writing comes by Nature.'

# Chapter 9

# Walter Benjamin

## The Work of Art in the Age of Mechanical Reproduction

'Our fine arts were developed, their types and uses were established, in times very different from the present, by men whose power of action upon things was insignificant in comparison with ours. But the amazing growth of our techniques, the adaptability and precision they have attained, the ideas and habits they are creating, make it a certainty that profound changes are impending in the ancient craft of the Beautiful. In all the arts there is a physical component which can no longer be considered or treated as it used to be, which cannot remain unaffected by our modern knowledge and power. For the last twenty years neither matter nor space nor time has been what it was from time immemorial. We must expect great innovations to transform the entire technique of the arts, thereby affecting artistic invention itself and perhaps even bringing about an amazing change in our very notion of art.'[1]

—Paul Valéry, PIÈCES SUR L'ART,
'La Conquète de l'ubiquité,' Paris.

## Preface

When Marx undertook his critique of the capitalistic mode of production, this mode was in its infancy. Marx directed his efforts in such a way as to give them prognostic value. He went back to the basic conditions underlying capitalistic production and through his presentation showed what could be expected of capitalism in the

From: Walter Benjamin, *Illuminations*. Ed. H. Arendt and trans. H. Zohn. London: Fontana, 1992 (orig. 1936).

future. The result was that one could expect it not only to exploit the proletariat with increasing intensity, but ultimately to create conditions which would make it possible to abolish capitalism itself.

The transformation of the superstructure, which takes place far more slowly than that of the substructure, has taken more than half a century to manifest in all areas of culture the change in the conditions of production. Only today can it be indicated what form this has taken. Certain prognostic requirements should be met by these statements. However, theses about the art of the proletariat after its assumption of power or about the art of a classless society would have less bearing on these demands than theses about the developmental tendencies of art under present conditions of production. Their dialectic is no less noticeable in the superstructure than in the economy. It would therefore be wrong to underestimate the value of such theses as a weapon. They brush aside a number of outmoded concepts, such as creativity and genius, eternal value and mystery – concepts whose uncontrolled (and at present almost uncontrollable) application would lead to a processing of data in the Fascist sense. The concepts which are introduced into the theory of art in what follows differ from the more familiar terms in that they are completely useless for the purposes of Fascism. They are, on the other hand, useful for the formulation of revolutionary demands in the politics of art.

# I

In principle a work of art has always been reproducible. Manmade artifacts could always be imitated by men. Replicas were made by pupils in practice of their craft, by masters for diffusing their works, and, finally, by third parties in the pursuit of gain. Mechanical reproduction of a work of art, however, represents something new. Historically, it advanced intermittently and in leaps at long intervals, but with accelerated intensity. The Greeks knew only two procedures of technically reproducing works of art: founding and stamping. Bronzes, terra cottas, and coins were the only art works which they could produce in quantity. All others were unique and could not be mechanically reproduced. With the woodcut graphic art became mechanically reproducible for the first time, long before script became reproducible by print. The enormous changes which printing, the mechanical reproduction of writing, has brought about in literature are a familiar story. However, within the phenomenon which we are here examining from the perspective of world history, print is merely a special, though particularly important, case. During the Middle Ages engraving and etching were added to the woodcut; at the beginning of the nineteenth century lithography made its appearance.

With lithography the technique of reproduction reached an essentially new stage. This much more direct process was distinguished by the tracing of the design on a stone rather than its incision on a block of wood or its etching on a copperplate and permitted graphic art for the first time to put its products on the market, not only in large numbers as hitherto, but also in daily changing forms. Lithography enabled graphic art to illustrate everyday life, and it began to keep pace with printing. But only a few decades after its invention, lithography was surpassed by photography. For the first time in the process of pictorial reproduction, photography freed the hand of the most important artistic functions which henceforth devolved only upon the eye looking into a lens. Since the eye perceives more swiftly than the hand can draw, the process of pictorial reproduction was accelerated so enormously that it could keep pace with speech. A film operator shooting a scene in the studio captures the images at the speed of an actor's speech. Just as lithography virtually implied the illustrated newspaper, so did photography foreshadow the sound film. The technical reproduction of sound was tackled at the end of the last century. These convergent endeavors made predictable a situation which Paul Valéry pointed up in this sentence: 'Just as water, gas, and electricity are brought into our houses from far off to satisfy our needs in response to a minimal effort, so we shall be supplied with visual or auditory images, which will appear and disappear at a simple movement of the hand, hardly more than a sign' (*op. cit.,* p. 226). Around 1900 technical reproduction had reached a standard that not only permitted it to reproduce all transmitted works of art and thus to cause the most profound change in their impact upon the public; it also had captured a place of its own among the artistic processes. For the study of this standard nothing is more revealing than the nature of the repercussions that these two different manifestations – the reproduction of works of art and the art of the film–have had on art in its traditional form.

# II

Even the most perfect reproduction of a work of art is lacking in one element: its presence in time and space, its unique existence at the place where it happens to be. This unique existence of the work of art determined the history to which it was subject throughout the time of its existence. This includes the changes which it may have suffered in physical condition over the years as well as the various changes in its ownership.[2] The traces of the first can be revealed only by chemical or physical analyses which it is impossible to perform on a reproduction; changes of ownership are subject to a tradition which must be traced from the situation of the original.

The presence of the original is the prerequisite to the concept of authenticity. Chemical analyses of the patina of a bronze can help to establish this, as does the proof that a given manuscript of the Middle Ages stems from an archive of the fifteenth century. The whole sphere of authenticity is outside technical–and, of course, not only technical–reproducibility.[3] Confronted with its manual reproduction, which was usually branded as a forgery, the original preserved all its authority; not so *vis à vis* technical reproduction. The reason is twofold. First, process reproduction is more independent of the original than manual reproduction. For example, in photography, process reproduction can bring out those aspects of the original that are unattainable to the naked eye yet accessible to the lens, which is adjustable and chooses its angle at will. And photographic reproduction, with the aid of certain processes, such as enlargement or slow motion, can capture images which escape natural vision. Secondly, technical reproduction can put the copy of the original into situations which would be out of reach for the original itself. Above all, it enables the original to meet the beholder halfway, be it in the form of a photograph or a phonograph record. The cathedral leaves its locale to be received in the studio of a lover of art; the choral production, performed in an auditorium or in the open air, resounds in the drawing room.

The situations into which the product of mechanical reproduction can be brought may not touch the actual work of art, yet the quality of its presence is always depreciated. This holds not only for the art work but also, for instance, for a landscape which passes in review before the spectator in a movie. In the case of the art object, a most sensitive nucleus–namely, its authenticity–is interfered with whereas no natural object is vulnerable on that score. The authenticity of a thing is the essence of all that is transmissible from its beginning, ranging from its substantive duration to its testimony to the history which it has experienced. Since the historical testimony rests on the authenticity, the former, too, is jeopardized by reproduction when substantive duration ceases to matter. And what is really jeopardized when the historical testimony is affected is the authority of the object.[4]

One might subsume the eliminated element in the term 'aura' and go on to say: that which withers in the age of mechanical reproduction is the aura of the work of art. This is a symptomatic process whose significance points beyond the realm of art. One might generalize by saying: the technique of reproduction detaches the reproduced object from the domain of tradition. By making many reproductions it substitutes a plurality of copies for a unique existence. And in permitting the reproduction to meet the beholder or listener in his own particular situation, it reactivates the object reproduced. These two processes lead to a tremendous shattering of tradition which is the obverse of the contemporary crisis and renewal of mankind. Both processes are intimately connected with the contemporary mass movements. Their most powerful agent is the film. Its social significance, particularly in its most positive form, is inconceivable without its destructive, cathartic aspect, that is, the liquidation of the traditional value of the cultural heritage. This phenomenon is most palpable in the great historical films. It extends to ever new positions. In 1927 Abel Gance exclaimed enthusiastically: 'Shakespeare, Rembrandt, Beethoven will make films ... all legends, all mythologies and all myths, all founders of religion, and the very religions ... await their exposed resurrection, and the heroes crowd each other at the gate.'[5] Presumably without intending it, he issued an invitation to a far-reaching liquidation.

# III

During long periods of history, the mode of human sense perception changes with humanity's entire mode of existence. The manner in which human sense perception is organized, the medium in which it is accomplished, is determined not only by nature but by historical circumstances as well. The fifth century, with its great shifts of population, saw the birth of the late Roman art industry and the Vienna Genesis, and there developed not only an art different from that of antiquity but also a new kind of perception. The scholars of the Viennese school, Riegl and Wickhoff, who resisted the weight of classical tradition under which these later art forms had been buried, were the first to draw conclusions from them concerning the organization of perception at the time. However far-reaching their insight, these scholars limited themselves to showing the significant, formal hallmark which characterized perception in late Roman times. They did not attempt – and, perhaps, saw no way–to show the social transformations expressed by these changes of perception. The conditions for an analogous insight are more favorable in the present. And if changes in the medium of contemporary perception can be comprehended as decay of the aura, it is possible to show its social causes.

The concept of aura which was proposed above with reference to historical objects may usefully be illustrated with reference to the aura of natural ones. We define the aura of the latter as the unique phenomenon of a distance, however close it may be. If, while resting on a summer afternoon, you follow with your eyes a mountain range on the horizon or a branch which casts its shadow over you, you experience the aura of those mountains, of that branch. This image makes it easy to comprehend the social bases of the contemporary decay of the aura. It rests on two circumstances, both of which are related to the increasing significance of the masses in contemporary life. Namely, the desire of contemporary masses to bring things 'closer' spatially and humanly, which is just as ardent as their bent toward overcoming the uniqueness of every reality by accepting its reproduction.[6] Every day the urge grows stronger to get hold of an object at very close range by way of its likeness, its reproduction. Unmistakably, reproduction as offered by picture magazines and newsreels differs from the image seen by the unarmed eye. Uniqueness and permanence are as closely linked in the latter as are transitoriness and reproducibility in the former. To pry an object from its shell, to destroy its aura, is the mark of a perception whose 'sense of the universal equality of things' has increased to such a degree that it extracts it even from a unique object by means of reproduction. Thus is manifested in the field of perception what in the theoretical sphere is noticeable in the increasing importance of statistics. The adjustment of reality to the masses and of the masses to reality is a process of unlimited scope, as much for thinking as for perception.

# IV

The uniqueness of a work of art is inseparable from its being imbedded in the fabric of tradition. This tradition itself is thoroughly alive and extremely changeable. An ancient statue of Venus, for example, stood in a different traditional context with the Greeks, who made it an object of veneration, than with the clerics of the Middle Ages, who viewed it as an ominous idol. Both of them, however, were equally confronted with its uniqueness, that is, its aura. Originally the contextual integration of art in tradition found its expression in the cult. We know that the earliest art works originated in the service of a ritual–first the magical, then the religious kind. It is significant that the existence of the work of art with reference to its aura is never entirely separated from its ritual function.[7] In other words, the unique value of the 'authentic' work of art has its basis in ritual, the location of its original use value. This ritualistic basis, however remote, is still recognizable as secularized ritual even in the most profane forms of the cult of beauty.[8] The secular cult of beauty, developed during the Renaissance and prevailing for three centuries, clearly showed that ritualistic basis in its decline and the first deep crisis which befell it. With the advent of the first truly revolutionary means of reproduction, photography, simultaneously with the rise of socialism, art sensed the approaching crisis which has become evident a century later. At the time, art reacted with the doctrine of *l'art pour l'art,* that is, with a theology of art. This gave rise to what might be called a negative theology in the form of the idea of 'pure' art, which not only denied any social function of art but also any categorizing by subject matter. (In poetry, Mallarmé was the first to take this position.)

An analysis of art in the age of mechanical reproduction must do justice to these relationships, for they lead us to an all-important insight: for the first time in world history, mechanical reproduction emancipates the work of art from its parasitical dependence on ritual. To an ever greater degree the work of art reproduced becomes the work of art designed for reproducibility.[9] From a photographic negative, for example, one can make any number of prints; to ask for the 'authentic' print makes no sense. But the instant the criterion of authenticity ceases to be applicable to artistic production, the total function of art is reversed. Instead of being based on ritual, it begins to be based on another practice–politics.

[...]

## Notes

1. Quoted from Paul Valéry, *Aesthetics,* 'The Conquest of Ubiquity,' translated by Ralph Manheim, p. 225. Pantheon Books, Bollingen Series, New York, 1964.

2. Of course, the history of a work of art encompasses more than this. The history of the 'Mona Lisa,' for instance, encompasses the kind and number of its copies made in the 17th, 18th, and 19th centuries.

3. Precisely because authenticity is not reproducible, the intensive penetration of certain (mechanical) processes of reproduction was instrumental in differentiating and grading authenticity. To develop such differentiations was an important function of the trade in works of art. The invention of the woodcut may be said to have struck at the root of the quality of authenticity even before its late flowering. To be sure, at the time of its origin a medieval picture of the Madonna could not yet be said to be 'authentic.' It became 'authentic' only during the succeeding centuries and perhaps most strikingly so during the last one.

4. The poorest provincial staging of *Faust* is superior to a Faust film in that, ideally, it competes with the first performance at Weimar. Before the screen it is unprofitable to remember traditional contents which might come to mind before the stage–for instance, that Goethe's friend Johann Heinrich Merck is hidden in Mephisto, and the like.

5. Abel Gance, 'Le Temps de l'image est venu,' *L'Art cinématographique,* Vol. 2, pp. 94 f, Paris, 1927.

6. To satisfy the human interest of the masses may mean to have one's social function removed from the field of vision. Nothing guarantees that a portraitist of today, when painting a famous surgeon at the breakfast table in the midst of his family, depicts his social function more precisely than a painter of the 17th century who portrayed his medical doctors as representing this profession, like Rembrandt in his 'Anatomy Lesson.'

7. The definition of the aura as a 'unique phenomenon of a distance however close it may be' represents nothing but the formulation of the cult value of the work of art in categories of space and time perception. Distance is the opposite of closeness. The essentially distant object is the unapproachable one. Unapproachability is indeed a major quality of the cult image. True to its nature, it remains 'distant, however close it may be.' The closeness which one may gain from its subject matter does not impair the distance which it retains in its appearance.

8. To the extent to which the cult value of the painting is secularized the ideas of its fundamental uniqueness lose distinctness. In the imagination of the beholder the uniqueness

of the phenomena which hold sway in the cult image is more and more displaced by the empirical uniqueness of the creator or of his creative achievement. To be sure, never completely so; the concept of authenticity always transcends mere genuineness. (This is particularly apparent in the collector who always retains some traces of the fetishist and who, by owning the work of art, shares in its ritual power.) Nevertheless, the function of the concept of authenticity remains determinate in the evaluation of art; with the secularization of art, authenticity displaces the cult value of the work.

9. In the case of films, mechanical reproduction is not, as with literature and painting, an external condition for mass distribution. Mechanical reproduction is inherent in the very technique of film production. This technique not only permits in the most direct way but virtually causes mass distribution. It enforces distribution because the production of a film is so expensive that an individual who, for instance, might afford to buy a painting no longer can afford to buy a film. In 1927 it was calculated that a major film, in order to pay its way, had to reach an audience of nine million. With the sound film, to be sure, a setback in its international distribution occurred at first: audiences became limited by language barriers. This coincided with the Fascist emphasis on national interests. It is more important to focus on this connection with Fascism than on this setback, which was soon minimized by synchronization. The simultaneity of both phenomena is attributable to the depression. The same disturbances which, on a larger scale, led to an attempt to maintain the existing property structure by sheer force led the endangered film capital to speed up the development of the sound film. The introduction of the sound film brought about a temporary relief, not only because it again brought the masses into the theaters but also because it merged new capital from the electrical industry with that of the film industry. Thus, viewed from the outside, the sound film promoted national interests, but seen from the inside it helped to internationalize film production even more than previously.

# Chapter 10

# Theodor W. Adorno

## Culture Industry Reconsidered

The term culture industry was perhaps used for the first time in the book *Dialectic of Enlightenment,* which Horkheimer and I published in Amsterdam in 1947. In our drafts we spoke of 'mass culture'. We replaced that expression with 'culture industry' in order to exclude from the outset the interpretation agreeable to its advocates: that it is a matter of something like a culture that arises spontaneously from the masses themselves, the contemporary form of popular art. From the latter the culture industry must be distinguished in the extreme. The culture industry fuses the old and familiar into a new quality. In all its branches, products which are tailored for consumption by masses, and which to a great extent determine the nature of that consumption, are manufactured more or less according to plan. The individual branches are similar in structure or at least fit into each other, ordering themselves into a system almost without a gap. This is made possible by contemporary technical capabilities as well as by economic and administrative concentration. The culture industry intentionally integrates its consumers from above. To the detriment of both it forces together the spheres of high and low art, separated for thousands of years. The seriousness of high art is destroyed in speculation about its efficacy; the seriousness of the lower perishes with the civilizational constraints imposed on the rebellious resistance inherent within it as long as social control was not yet total. Thus, although the culture industry undeniably speculates on the conscious and unconscious state of the millions towards which it is directed, the masses are not primary, but secondary, they are an object of calculation; an appendage of the machinery. The customer is not king, as the culture industry would have us believe, not its subject but its object. The very word mass-media, specially honed for the culture industry,

From: Theodor W. Adorno, *The Culture Industry: Selected Essays on Mass Culture.* London: Routledge, 1991 (orig. English trans., 1975).

already shifts the accent onto harmless terrain. Neither is it a question of primary concern for the masses, nor of the techniques of communication as such, but of the spirit which sufflates them, their master's voice. The culture industry misuses its concern for the masses in order to duplicate, reinforce and strengthen their mentality, which it presumes is given and unchangeable. How this mentality might be changed is excluded throughout. The masses are not the measure but the ideology of the culture industry, even though the culture industry itself could scarcely exist without adapting to the masses.

The cultural commodities of the industry are governed, as Brecht and Suhrkamp expressed it thirty years ago, by the principle of their realization as value, and not by their own specific content and harmonious formation. The entire practice of the culture industry transfers the profit motive naked onto cultural forms. Ever since these cultural forms first began to earn a living for their creators as commodities in the market-place they had already possessed something of this quality. But then they sought after profit only indirectly, over and above their autonomous essence. New on the part of the culture industry is the direct and undisguised primacy of a precisely and thoroughly calculated efficacy in its most typical products. The autonomy of works of art, which of course rarely ever predominated in an entirely pure form, and was always permeated by a constellation of effects, is tendentially eliminated by the culture industry, with or without the conscious will of those in control. The latter include both those who carry out directives as well as those who hold the power. In economic terms they are or were in search of new opportunities for the realization of capital in the most economically developed countries. The old opportunities became increasingly more precarious as a result of the same concentration process which alone makes the culture industry possible as an omnipresent phenomenon. Culture, in the true sense, did not simply accommodate itself to human beings; but it always simultaneously raised a protest against the petrified relations under which they lived, thereby honouring them. In so far as culture becomes wholly assimilated to and integrated in those petrified relations, human beings are once more debased. Cultural entities typical of the culture industry are no longer *also* commodities, they are commodities through and through. This quantitative shift is so great that it calls forth entirely new phenomena. Ultimately, the culture industry no longer even needs to directly pursue everywhere the profit interests from which it originated. These interests have become objectified in its ideology and have even made themselves independent of the compulsion to sell the cultural commodities which must be swallowed anyway. The culture industry turns into public relations, the manufacturing of 'goodwill' per se, without regard for particular firms or saleable objects. Brought to bear is a general uncritical consensus, advertisements produced for the world, so that each product of the culture industry becomes its own advertisement.

Nevertheless, those characteristics which originally stamped the transformation of literature into a commodity are maintained in this process. More than anything in the world, the culture industry has its ontology, a scaffolding of rigidly conservative basic categories which can be gleaned, for example, from the commercial English novels of the late seventeenth and early eighteenth centuries. What parades as progress in the culture industry, as the incessantly new which it offers up, remains the disguise for an eternal sameness; everywhere the changes mask a skeleton which has changed just as little as the profit motive itself since the time it first gained its predominance over culture.

Thus, the expression 'industry' is not to be taken too literally. It refers to the standardization of the thing itself – such as that of the Western, familiar to every movie-goer – and to the rationalization of distribution techniques, but not strictly to the production process. Although in film, the central sector of the culture industry, the production process resembles technical modes of operation in the extensive division of labour, the employment of machines and the separation of the labourers from the means of production – expressed in the perennial conflict between artists active in the culture industry and those who control it – individual forms of production are nevertheless maintained. Each product affects an individual air; individuality itself serves to reinforce ideology, in so far as the illusion is conjured up that the completely reified and mediated is a sanctuary from immediacy and life. Now, as ever, the culture industry exists in the 'service' of third persons, maintaining its affinity to the declining circulation process of capital, to the commerce from which it came into being. Its ideology above all makes use of the star system, borrowed from individualistic art and its commercial exploitation. The more dehumanized its methods of operation and content, the more diligently and successfully the culture industry propagates supposedly great personalities and operates with heart-throbs. It is industrial more in a sociological sense, in the incorporation of industrial forms of organization even when nothing is manufactured – as in the rationalization of office work – rather than in the sense of anything really and actually produced by technological rationality. Accordingly, the misinvestments of the culture industry are considerable, throwing those branches rendered obsolete by new techniques into crises, which seldom lead to changes for the better.

The concept of technique in the culture industry is only in name identical with technique in works of art. In the latter, technique is concerned with the internal organization of the object itself, with its inner logic. In contrast, the technique of the culture industry is, from the beginning, one of distribution and mechanical reproduction, and therefore always remains external to its object. The culture industry finds ideological support precisely in so far as it carefully shields itself from the full potential of the techniques contained in its products. It lives parasitically from the extra-artistic technique of the material production of goods, without regard for the obligation to the internal artistic whole implied by its functionality (*Sachlichkeit*), but also without concern for the laws of form demanded by aesthetic autonomy. The result for the physiognomy of the culture industry is essentially a mixture of streamlining, photographic hardness and precision on the one hand, and individualistic residues, sentimentality and an already rationally disposed and adapted romanticism on ,the other. Adopting Benjamin's designation of the traditional work of art by the concept of aura, the presence of that which is not present, the culture industry is defined by the fact that it does not strictly counterpose another principle to that of aura, but rather by the fact that it conserves the decaying aura as a foggy mist. By this means the culture industry betrays its own ideological abuses.

It has recently become customary among cultural officials as well as sociologists to warn against underestimating the culture industry while pointing to its great importance for the development of the consciousness of its consumers. It is to be taken seriously, without cultured snobbism. In actuality the culture industry is important as a moment of the spirit which dominates today. Whoever ignores its influence out of scepticism for what it stuffs into people would be naive. Yet there is a deceptive glitter about the admonition to take it seriously. Because of its social role, disturbing questions about its quality, about truth or untruth, and about the aesthetic niveau of the culture industry's emissions are repressed, or at least excluded from the so-called sociology of communications. The critic is accused of taking refuge in arrogant esoterica. It would be advisable first to indicate the double meaning of importance that slowly worms its way in unnoticed. Even if it touches the lives of innumerable people, the function of something is no guarantee of its particular quality. The blending of aesthetics with its residual communicative aspects leads art, as a social phenomenon, not to its rightful position in opposition to alleged artistic snobbism, but rather in a variety of ways to the defence of its baneful social consequences. The importance of the culture industry in the spiritual constitution of the masses is no dispensation for reflection on its objective legitimation, its essential being, least of all by a science which thinks itself pragmatic. On the contrary: such reflection becomes necessary precisely for this reason. To take the culture industry as seriously as its unquestioned role demands, means to take it seriously critically, and not to cower in the face of its monopolistic character.

Among those intellectuals anxious to reconcile themselves with the phenomenon and eager to find a common formula to express both their reservations against it and their respect for its power, a tone of ironic toleration prevails unless they have already created a new mythos of the twentieth century from the imposed regression. After all, those intellectuals maintain, everyone knows what pocket novels, films off the rack, family television shows rolled out into serials and hit parades, advice to the lovelorn and horoscope columns are all about. All of this, however, is harmless and, according to them, even democratic since it responds to a demand, albeit a stimulated one. It also bestows all kinds of blessings, they point out, for example, through the dissemination of information, advice and stress reducing patterns of behaviour. Of course, as every sociological study measuring something as elementary as how politically informed the public is has proven, the information is meagre or indifferent. Moreover, the advice to be gained from manifestations of the culture industry is vacuous, banal or worse, and the behaviour patterns are shamelessly conformist.

The two-faced irony in the relationship of servile intellectuals to the culture industry is not restricted to them alone. It may also be supposed that the consciousness of the consumers themselves is split between the prescribed fun which is supplied to them by the culture industry and a not particularly well-hidden doubt about its blessings. The phrase, the world wants to be deceived, has become truer than had ever been intended. People are not only, as the saying goes, falling for the swindle; if it guarantees them even the most fleeting gratification they desire a deception which is nonetheless transparent to them. They force their eyes shut and voice approval, in a kind of self-loathing, for what is meted out to them, knowing fully the purpose for which it is manufactured. Without admitting it they sense that their lives would be completely intolerable as soon as they no longer clung to satisfactions which are none at all.

The most ambitious defence of the culture industry today celebrates its spirit, which might be safely called ideology, as an ordering factor. In a supposedly chaotic world it provides human beings with something like standards for orientation, and that alone seems worthy of approval. However, what its defenders imagine is preserved by the culture industry is in fact all the more thoroughly destroyed by it. The colour film demolishes the genial old tavern to a greater extent than bombs ever could: the film exterminates its imago. No homeland can survive being processed by the films which celebrate it, and which thereby turn the unique character on which it thrives into an interchangeable sameness.

That which legitimately could be called culture attempted, as an expression of suffering and contradiction, to maintain a grasp on the idea of the good life. Culture cannot represent either that which merely exists or the conventional and no longer binding categories of order which the culture industry drapes over the idea of the good life as if existing reality were the good life, and as if those categories were its true measure. If the response of the culture industry's representatives is that it does not deliver art at all, this is itself the ideology with which they evade responsibility for that from which the business lives. No misdeed is ever righted by explaining it as such.

The appeal to order alone, without concrete specificity, is futile; the appeal to the dissemination of norms, without these ever proving themselves in reality or before consciousness, is equally futile. The idea of an objectively binding order, huckstered to people because it is so lacking for them, has no claims if it does not prove itself internally and in confrontation with human beings. But this is precisely what no product of the culture industry would engage in. The concepts of order which it hammers into human beings are always those of the status quo. They remain unquestioned, unanalysed and undialectically presupposed, even if they no longer have any substance for those who accept them. In contrast to the Kantian, the categorical imperative of the culture industry no longer has anything in common with freedom. It proclaims: you shall conform, without instruction as to what; conform to that which exists anyway, and to that which everyone thinks anyway as a reflex of its power and omnipresence. The power of the culture industry's ideology is such that conformity has replaced consciousness. The order that springs from it is never confronted with what it claims to be or with the real interests of human beings. Order, however, is not good in itself. It would be so only as a good order. The fact that the culture industry is oblivious to this and extols order *in abstracto,* bears witness to the impotence and untruth of the messages it conveys. While it claims to lead the perplexed, it deludes them with false conflicts which they are to exchange for their own. It solves conflicts for them only in appearance, in a way that they can hardly be solved in their real lives. In the products of the culture industry human beings get into trouble only so that they can be rescued unharmed, usually by representatives of a benevolent collective; and then in empty harmony, they are reconciled with the general, whose demands they had experienced at the outset as irreconcileable with their interests. For this purpose the culture industry has developed formulas which even reach into such non-conceptual areas as light musical entertainment. Here too one gets into a 'jam', into rhythmic problems, which can be instantly disentangled by the triumph of the basic beat.

Even its defenders, however, would hardly contradict Plato openly who maintained that what is objectively and intrinsically untrue cannot also be subjectively good and true for human beings. The concoctions of the culture industry are neither guides for a blissful life, nor a new art of moral responsibility, but rather exhortations to toe the line, behind which stand the most powerful interests. The consensus which it propagates strengthens blind, opaque authority. If the culture industry is measured not by its own substance and logic, but by its efficacy, by its position in reality and its explicit pretensions; if the focus of serious concern is with the efficacy to which it always appeals, the potential of its effect becomes twice as weighty. This potential, however, lies in the promotion and exploitation of the ego-weakness to which the powerless members of contemporary society, with its concentration of power, are condemned. Their consciousness is further developed retrogressively. It is no coincidence that cynical American film producers are heard to say that their pictures must take into consideration the level of eleven-year-olds. In doing so they would very much like to make adults into eleven-year-olds.

It is true that thorough research has not, for the time being, produced an airtight case proving the regressive effects of particular products of the culture industry. No doubt an imaginatively designed experiment could achieve this more successfully than the powerful financial interests concerned would find comfortable. In any case, it can be assumed without hesitation that steady drops hollow the stone, especially since the system of the culture industry that surrounds the masses tolerates hardly any deviation and incessantly drills the same formulas on behaviour. Only their deep unconscious mistrust, the last residue of the difference between art and empirical reality in the spiritual make-up of the masses explains why they have not, to a person, long since perceived and accepted the world as it is constructed for them by the culture industry. Even if its messages were as harmless as they are made out to be – on countless occasions they are obviously not harmless, like the movies which chime in with currently popular hate campaigns against intellectuals by portraying them with the usual stereotypes – the attitudes which the culture industry calls forth are anything but harmless. [...]

Human dependence and servitude, the vanishing point of the culture industry, could scarcely be more faithfully described than by the American interviewee who was of the opinion that the dilemmas of the contemporary epoch would end if people would simply follow the lead of prominent personalities. In so far as the culture industry arouses a feeling of well-being that the world is precisely in that order suggested by the culture industry, the substitute gratification which it prepares for human beings cheats them out of the same happiness which it deceitfully projects. The total effect of the culture industry is one of anti-enlightenment, in which, as Horkheimer and I have noted, enlightenment, that is the progressive technical domination of nature, becomes mass deception and is turned into a means for fettering consciousness. It impedes the development of autonomous, independent individuals who judge and decide consciously for themselves. These, however, would be the precondition for a democratic society which needs adults who have come of age in order to sustain itself and develop. If the masses have been unjustly reviled from above as masses, the culture industry is not among the least responsible for making them into masses and then despising them, while obstructing the emancipation for which human beings are as ripe as the productive forces of the epoch permit.

# Chapter 11

# Guy Debord

## The Commodity as Spectacle

For it is only as the universal category of total social being that the commodity can be understood in its authentic essence. It is only in this context that reification which arises from the commodity relation acquires a decisive meaning, as much for the objective evolution of society as for the attitude of met towards it, for the submission of their consciousness to the forms in which this reification is expressed. ... This submission also grows because of the fact that the more the rationalization and mechanization of the work process increases, the more the activity of the worker loses its character as activity and becomes a *contemplative* attitude.

Lukács,
*History and Class Consciousness.*

## 35

In the essential movement of the spectacle, which consists of taking up within itself all that existed in human activity *in a fluid state*, in order to possess it in a coagulated state, as things which have become the exclusive value by their *formulation in negative* of lived value, we recognize our old enemy, *the commodity*, who knows so well how to seem at first glance something trivial and obvious, while on the contrary it is so complex and so full of metaphysical subtleties.

---

From: Guy Debord, *Society of the Spectacle*. Detroit: Black and Red, 1970.

# 36

This is the principle of commodity fetishism, the domination of society by 'intangible as well as tangible things,' which reaches its absolute fulfillment in the spectacle, where the tangible world is replaced by a selection of images which exist above it, and which at the same time are recognized as the tangible par *excellence*.

# 37

The world at once present and absent which the spectacle *makes visible* is the world of the commodity dominating all that is lived. And the world of the commodity is thus shown *as it is*, because its movement is identical to the *estrangement* of men among themselves and vis-à-vis their global product.

# 38

The loss of quality so evident at all levels of spectacular language, of the objects it praises and the behavior it regulates, merely translates the fundamental traits of the real production which brushes reality aside: the commodity-form is through and through equal to itself, the category of the quantitative. It is the quantitative which the commodity-form develops, and it can only develop within the quantitative.

# 39

This development which excludes the qualitative is, as development, itself subject to a passage into the qualitative: the spectacle signifies that it has crossed the threshold of its own abundance; this is as yet true only locally at some points, but is already true on the universal scale which is the original context of the commodity, a context which its practical movement, encompassing the Earth as a world market, has verified.

# 40

The development of productive forces has been the real unconscious history which built and modified the conditions of existence of human groups as conditions of survival, and extended these conditions: the economic basis of all their enterprises. Within a natural economy, the commodity sector represented a surplus of survival. The production of commodities, which implies the exchange of varied products among independent producers, could for a long time remain craft production, contained within a marginal economic function where its quantitative truth was still masked. However, when commodity production met the social conditions of large scale commerce and of the accumulation of capitals, it seized the total domination of the economy. The entire economy then became what the commodity had shown itself to be during the course of this conquest: a process of quantitative development. This incessant deployment of economic power in the form of the commodity, which transformed human labor into commodity-labor, into *wage-labor*, cummulatively led to an abundance in which the primary question of survival is undoubtedly resolved, but in such a way that it is constantly rediscovered; it is posed over again each time at a higher level. Economic growth frees societies from the natural pressure which demanded their direct struggle for survival, but at that point it is from their liberator that they are not liberated. The *independence* of the commodity was extended to the entire economy over which it rules. The economy transforms the world, but transforms it only into a world of economy. The pseudo-nature within which human labor is alienated demands that it be *served* ad infinitum, and this service, being judged and absolved only by itself, in fact acquires the totality of socially permissible efforts and projects as its servants. The abundance of commodities, that is, the commodity relation, can be no more than augmented survival.

# 41

The domination of the commodity was at first exerted over the economy in an obscure manner; the economy itself, the material basis of social life, remained unperceived and not understood, like the familiar which remains unknown. In a society where the concrete commodity is rare or unusual, it is the apparent domination of money which presents itself as an emissary armed with full powers which speaks in the name of an unknown force. With the industrial revolution, the division of labor in manufactures, and mass production for the world market, the commodity appears in fact as a power which comes really to *occupy* social life. It is then that political economy takes shape, as the dominant science and as the science of domination.

# 42

The spectacle is the moment when the commodity has attained the *total occupation* of social life. The relation to the commodity is not only visible, but one no longer sees anything but it: the world one sees is its world. Modern economic production extends its dictatorship extensively and intensively. In the least industrialized places, its domination is already present with a few star commodities and as imperialist domination by zones which are ahead in the development of productivity. In these advanced zones, social space is invaded by a continuous superimposition of geological layers of commodities. At this point in the 'second industrial revolution,' alienated consumption becomes for the masses a supplementary duty to alienated production. It is *all the sold labor* of a society which globally becomes the *total commodity* for which the cycle must be continued. For this to be done, it is necessary for this total commodity to return as a fragment to the fragmented individual, absolutely separated from the productive forces operating as an ensemble.

Thus it is here that the specialized science of domination must in turn specialize: it fragments itself into sociology, psychotechnics, cybernetics, semiology, etc., watching over the self-regulation of all the levels of the process.

# 43

Whereas in the primitive phase of capitalist accumulation, 'political economy sees in the *proletarian* only the *worker*,' who must receive the minimum indispensable for the conservation of his labor power without ever considering him 'in his leisure, in his humanity,' this position of the ideas of the dominant class is reversed as soon as the degree of abundance attained in the production of commodities demands a surplus of collaboration from the worker. This worker suddenly washed of the total scorn which is clearly shown to him by all the modalities of organization and surveillance of production, finds himself each day, outside of production, seemingly treated as a grown up, with a zealous politeness under the mask of a consumer. *Then the humanism of the commodity* takes charge of the 'leisure and humanity' of the worker, simply because political economy can and must now dominate these spheres *as political economy*. Thus the 'perfected denial of man' has taken charge of the totality of human existence.

# 44

The spectacle is a permanent opium war whose aim is to make acceptable the identification of goods with commodities, and of satisfaction with survival augmenting according to its own laws. But if consumable survival is something which must always increase, this is because it never ceases *to contain privation*. If there is nothing beyond augmented survival, no point where it might stop its growth, this is because it is not beyond privation, but is privation become enriched.

# 45

With automation, which is both the most advanced sector of modern industry and the model where its practice is perfectly summed up, the world of the commodity must surmount the following contradiction: the technical instrumentation which objectively eliminates labor must at the same time *conserve labor as a commodity* and as the only source of the commodity. In order for automation (or any other less extreme form of increasing the productivity of labor) not to diminish the actual social labor necessary for the entire society, new jobs must be created. The tertiary sector, services, represents an immense extension of continuous rows of the army of distribution, and a eulogy of present-day commodities: the tertiary sector is thus a mobilization of supplementary forces which opportunely encounters the necessity for such an organization of rear-guard labor in the very artificiality of the needs for such commodities.

# 46

Exchange value could originate only as an agent of use value, but its victory by means of its own weapons created the conditions for its autonomous domination. Mobilizing all human use and seizing the monopoly of its satisfaction, exchange value has ended up by *directing use.* The process of exchange became identified with all possible use and reduced use to the mercy of exchange. Exchange value is the condottiere of use value, which ends up carrying on the war for itself.

# 47

*The tendency of use value to fall*, this constant of capitalist economy, develops a new form of privation within augmented survival. The new privation is not liberated to any extent from the old penury since it requires the participation of most men as wage workers in the endless pursuit of its attainment, and since everyone knows he must submit or die. The reality of this blackmail lies in the fact that use in its most impoverished form (eating, inhabiting) exists only to the extent that it is imprisoned within the illusory wealth of augmented survival, the real basis for the acceptance of illusion in general in the consumption of modern commodities. The real consumer becomes a consumer of illusions. The commodity is this factually real illusion, and the spectacle is its general manifestation.

# 48

Use value, which was implicitly contained in exchange value, must now be explicitly proclaimed, in the inverted reality of the spectacle, precisely because its factual reality is eroded by the overdeveloped commodity economy; and because a pseudo-justification becomes necessary for counterfeit life.

# 49

The spectacle is the other side of money: it is the general abstract equivalent of all commodities. But if money has dominated society as the representation of the central equivalence, namely as the exchangeable property of the various goods whose uses remained incomparable, the spectacle is its developed modern complement, in which the totality of the commodity world appears as a whole, as a general equivalence for what the totality of the society can be and do. The spectacle is the money which *one only looks at*, because in the spectacle the totality of use is already exchanged for the totality of abstract representation. The spectacle is not only the servant of *pseudo-use*, it is already in itself the pseudo-use of life.

# 50

At the moment of *economic* abundance, the concentrated result of social labor becomes visible and subjugates all reality to appearance, which is now its product. Capital is no longer the invisible center which directs the mode of production: accumulation spreads it to the periphery in the form of tangible objects. The entire expanse of society is its portrait.

# 51

The victory of the autonomous economy must at the same time be its defeat. The forces which it has unleashed eliminate the *economic necessity* which was the immutable basis of earlier societies. When economic necessity is replaced by the necessity for boundless economic development, the satisfaction of primary human needs is replaced by an uninterrupted fabrication of pseudo-needs which are reduced to the single pseudo-need of maintaining the reign of the autonomous economy. But the autonomous economy separates itself forever from basic need to the extent that it emerges from the *social unconscious* which depended on it without knowing it. 'All that is conscious is used up. That which is unconscious remains unalterable. But once freed, does it not fall to ruins in its turn?' (Freud)

# 52

When society discovers that it depends on the economy, the economy, in effect, depends on it. This subterranean power, which has grown to the point of seeming to be sovereign, has lost its power. That which was the economic *it* must become the *I*. The subject can only emerge from society, namely from the struggle within it. The subject's possible existence hangs on the outcome of the class struggle which shows itself to be the product and the producer of the economic foundation of history.

# 53

The consciousness of desire and the desire for consciousness are identically the project which, in its negative form, seeks the abolition of classes, that is, the direct possession by the workers over all the moments of their activity. Its *opposite* is the society of the spectacle, where the commodity contemplates itself in a world which it has created.

# Chapter 12

# Fredric Jameson

## Reification and Utopia in Mass Culture

The theory of mass culture – or mass audience culture, commercial culture, 'popular' culture, the culture industry, as it is variously known – has always tended to define its object against so-called high culture without reflecting on the objective status of this opposition. As so often, positions in this field reduce themselves to two mirror images, which are essentially staged in terms of value. Thus the familiar motif of *elitism* argues for the priority of mass culture on the grounds of the sheer numbers of people exposed to it; the pursuit of high or hermetic culture is then stigmatized as a status hobby of small groups of intellectuals. As its anti-intellectual thrust suggests, this essentially negative position has little theoretical content but clearly responds to a deeply rooted conviction in American populism and articulates a widely based sense that high culture is an establishment phenomenon, irredeemably tainted by its association with institutions, in particular with the university. The value invoked is therefore a social one: it would be preferable to deal with tv programs, *The Godfather,* or *Jaws*, rather than with Wallace Stevens or Henry James, because the former clearly speak a cultural language meaningful to far wider strata of the population than what is socially represented by intellectuals. Populist radicals are however also intellectuals, so that this position has suspicious overtones of the guilt trip; meanwhile it overlooks the anti-social and critical, negative (although generally not revolutionary) stance of much of the most important forms of modern art; finally, it offers no method for reading even those cultural objects it valorizes and has had little of interest to say about their content.

From: Fredric Jameson, *Signatures of the Visible*. London: Routledge, 1990.

This position is then reversed in the theory of culture worked out by the Frankfurt School; as is appropriate for this exact antithesis of the populist position, the work of Adorno, Horkheimer, Marcuse, and others is an intensely theoretical one and provides a working methodology for the close analysis of precisely those products of the culture industry which it stigmatizes and which the radical view exalted. Briefly, this view can be characterized as the extension and application of Marxist theories of commodity reification to the works of mass culture. The theory of reification (here strongly overlaid with Max Weber's analysis of rationalization) describes the way in which, under capitalism, the older traditional forms of human activity are instrumentally reorganized and 'taylorized,' analytically fragmented and reconstructed according to various rational models of efficiency, and essentially restructured along the lines of a differentiation between means and ends. This is a paradoxical idea: it cannot be properly appreciated until it is understood to what degree the means/ends split effectively brackets or suspends ends themselves, hence the strategic value of the Frankfurt School term 'instrumentalization' which usefully foregrounds the organization of the means themselves over against any particular end or value which is assigned to their practice.[1] In traditional activity, in other words, the value of the activity is immanent to it, and qualitatively distinct from other ends or values articulated in other forms of human work or play. Socially, this meant that various kinds of work in such communities were properly incomparable; in ancient Greece, for instance, the familiar Aristotelian schema of the fourfold causes at work in handicraft or *poeisis* (material, formal, efficient, and final) were applicable only to artisanal labor, and not to agriculture or war which had a quite different 'natural' – which is to say supernatural or divine – basis.[2] It is only with the universal commodification of labor power, which Marx's *Capital* designates as the fundamental precondition of capitalism, that all forms of human labor can be separated out from their unique qualitative differentiation as distinct types of activity (mining as opposed to farming, opera composition as distinct from textile manufacture), and all universally ranged under the common denominator of the quantitative, that is, under the universal exchange value of money.[3] At this point, then, the quality of the various forms of human activity, their unique and distinct 'ends' or values, has effectively been bracketed or suspended by the market system, leaving all these activities free to be ruthlessly reorganized in efficiency terms, as sheer means or instrumentality.

The force of the application of this notion to works of art can be measured against the definition of art by traditional aesthetic philosophy (in particular by Kant) as a 'finality without an end,' that is, as a goal-oriented activity which nonetheless has no practical purpose or end in the 'real world' of business or politics or concrete human praxis generally. This traditional definition surely holds for all art that works as such: not for stories that fall flat or home movies or inept poetic scribblings, but rather for the successful works of mass and high culture alike. We suspend our real lives and our immediate practical preoccupations just as completely when we watch *The Godfather* as when we read *The Wings of the Dove* or hear a Beethoven sonata.

At this point, however, the concept of the commodity introduces the possibility of structural and historical differentiation into what was conceived as the universal description of the aesthetic experience as such and in whatever form. The concept of the commodity cuts across the phenomenon of reification – described above in terms of activity or production – from a different angle, that of consumption. In a world in which everything, including labor power, has become a commodity, ends remain no less undifferentiated than in the production schema – they are all rigorously quantified, and have become abstractly comparable through the medium of money, their respective price or wage – yet we can now formulate their instrumentalization, their reorganization along the means/ends split, in a new way by saying that, by its transformation into a commodity, a thing of whatever type has been reduced to a means for its own consumption. It no longer has any qualitative value in itself, but only insofar as it can be 'used': the various forms of activity lose their immanent intrinsic satisfactions as activity and become means to an end.

The objects of the commodity world of capitalism also shed their independent 'being' and intrinsic qualities and come to be so many instruments of commodity satisfaction: the familiar example is that of tourism – the American tourist no longer lets the landscape 'be in its being' as Heidegger would have said, but takes a snapshot of it, thereby graphically transforming space into its own material image. The concrete activity of looking at a landscape – including, no doubt, the disquieting bewilderment with the activity itself, the anxiety that must arise when human beings, confronting the non-human, wonder what they are doing there and what the point or purpose of such a confrontation might be in the first place[4] – is thus comfortably replaced by the act of taking possession of it and converting it into a form of personal property. This is the meaning of the great scene in Godard's *Les Carabiniers* (1962–63) when the new world conquerors exhibit their spoils: unlike Alexander, 'Michel-Ange' and 'Ulysse' merely own images of everything, and triumphantly display their postcards of the Coliseum, the pyramids, Wall Street, Angkor Wat, like so many dirty pictures. This is also the sense of Guy Debord's assertion, in an important book, *The Society of The Spectacle,* that the ultimate form of commodity reification in contemporary consumer society is precisely the image itself.[5] With this universal commodification of our object world, the familiar accounts of the other-directedness of contemporary conspicuous consumption and of the sexualization of our objects and activities are also given: the new model car is essentially an image for other people to have of us, and we consume, less the thing itself, than its abstract idea, open to all the libidinal investments ingeniously arrayed for us by advertising.

It is clear that such an account of commodification has immediate relevance to aesthetics, if only because it implies that everything in consumer society has taken on an aesthetic dimension. The force of the Adorno-Horkheimer analysis of the culture industry, however, lies in its demonstration of the unexpected and imperceptible introduction of commodity structure into the very form and content of the work of art itself. Yet this is something like the ultimate squaring of the circle, the triumph of instrumentalization over that 'finality without an end' which is art itself, the steady conquest and colonization of the ultimate realm of non-practicality, of sheer play and anti-use, by the logic of the world of means and ends. But how can the sheer materiality of a poetic sentence be 'used' in that sense? And while it is clear how we can buy the idea of an automobile or smoke for the sheer libidinal image of actors, writers, and models with cigarettes in their hands, it is much less clear how a narrative could be 'consumed' for the benefit of its own idea.

In its simplest form, this view of instrumentalized culture [...] suggests that the reading process is itself restructured along a means/ends differentiation. It is instructive here to juxtapose Auerbach's discussion of the *Odyssey* in *Mimesis,* and his description of the way in which at every point the poem is as it were vertical to itself, self-contained, each verse paragraph and tableau somehow timeless and immanent, bereft of any necessary or indispensable links with what precedes it and what follows; in this light it becomes possible to appreciate the strangeness, the historical unnaturality (in a Brechtian sense) of contemporary books which, like detective stories, you read 'for the end' – the bulk of the pages becoming sheer devalued means to an end – in this case, the 'solution' which is itself utterly insignificant insofar as we are not thereby in the real world and by the latter's practical standards the identity of an imaginary murderer is supremely trivial.

The detective story is to be sure an extremely specialized form: still, the essential commodification of which it may serve as an emblem can be detected everywhere in the sub-genres of contemporary commercial art, in the way in which the materialization of this or that sector or zone of such forms comes to constitute an end and a consumption-satisfaction around which the rest of the work is then 'degraded' to the status of sheer means. Thus, in the older adventure tale, not only does the *dénouement* (victory of hero or villains, discovery of the treasure, rescue of the heroine or the imprisoned comrades, foiling of a monstrous plot, or arrival in time to reveal an urgent message or a secret) stand as the reified end in view of which the rest of the narrative is consumed – this reifying structure also reaches down into the very page-by-page detail of the book's composition. Each chapter recapitulates a smaller consumption process in its own right, ending with the frozen image of a new and catastrophic reversal of the situation, constructing the smaller gratifications of a flat character who actualizes his single potentiality (the 'choleric' Ned Land finally exploding in anger), organizing its sentences into paragraphs each of which is a sub-plot in its own right, or around the object-like stasis of the 'fateful' sentence or the 'dramatic' tableau, the whole tempo of such reading meanwhile overprogrammed by its intermittent illustrations which, either before or after the fact, reconfirm our readerly business, which is to transform the transparent flow of language as much as possible into material images and objects we can consume.[6]

Yet this is still a relatively primitive stage in the commodification of narrative. More subtle and more interesting is the way in which, since naturalism, the bestseller has tended to produce a quasi-material 'feeling tone' which floats about the narrative but is only intermittently realized by it: the sense of destiny in family novels, for instance or the 'epic' rhythms of the earth or of great movements of 'history' in the various sagas can be seen as so many commodities towards whose consumption the narratives are little more than means, their essential materiality then being confirmed and embodied in the movie music that accompanies their screen versions.[7] This structural differentiation of narrative and consumable feeling tone is a broader and historically and formally more significant manifestation of the kind of 'fetishism of hearing' which Adorno denounced when he spoke about the way the contemporary listener restructures a classical symphony so that the sonata form itself becomes an instrumental means toward the consumption of the isolatable tune or melody.

It will be clear, then, that I consider the Frankfurt School's analysis of the commodity structure of mass culture of the greatest interest; if, below, I propose a somewhat different way of looking at the same phenomena, it is not because I feel that their approach has been exhausted. On the contrary, we have scarcely begun to work out all the consequences of such descriptions, let alone to make an exhaustive inventory of variant models and of other features besides commodity reification in terms of which such artifacts might be analyzed.

What is unsatisfactory about the Frankfurt School's position is not its negative and critical apparatus, but rather the positive value on which the latter depends, namely the valorization of traditional modernist high art as the locus of some genuinely critical and subversive, 'autonomous' aesthetic production. Here Adorno's later work (as well as Marcuse's *The Aesthetic Dimension*) mark a retreat over the former's dialectically ambivalent assessment, in *The Philosophy of Modern Music*, of Arnold Schoenberg's achievement: what has been omitted from the later judgments is precisely Adorno's fundamental discovery of the historicity, and in particular, the irreversible aging process, of the greatest modernist forms. But if this is so, then the great work of modern high culture – whether it be Schoenberg, Beckett, or even Brecht himself – cannot serve as a fixed point or eternal standard against which to measure the 'degraded' status of mass culture: indeed, fragmentary and as yet undeveloped tendencies[8] in recent art production – hyper- or photorealism in visual art; 'new music' of the type of Lamonte Young, Terry Riley, or Philip Glass; post-modernist literary texts like those of Pynchon – suggest an increasing interpenetration of high and mass cultures.

For all these reasons, it seems to me that we must rethink the opposition high culture/mass culture in such a way that the emphasis on evaluation to which it has traditionally given rise – and which however the binary system of value operates (mass culture is popular and thus more authentic than high culture, high culture is autonomous and, therefore, utterly incomparable to a degraded mass culture) tends to function in some timeless realm of absolute aesthetic judgment – is replaced by a genuinely historical and dialectical approach to these phenomena. Such an approach demands that we read high and mass culture as objectively related and dialectically interdependent phenomena, as twin and inseparable forms of the fission of aesthetic production under capitalism. In this, capitalism's third or multinational stage, however, the dilemma of the double standard of high and mass culture remains, but it has become – not the subjective problem of our own standards of judgment – but rather an objective contradiction which has its own social grounding.

Indeed, this view of the emergence of mass culture obliges us historically to respecify the nature of the 'high culture' to which it has conventionally been opposed: the older culture critics indeed tended loosely to raise comparative issues about the 'popular culture' of the past. Thus, if you see Greek tragedy, Shakespeare, *Don Quijote*, still widely read romantic lyrics of the type of Hugo, and best-selling realistic novels like those of Balzac or Dickens, as uniting a wide 'popular' audience with high aesthetic quality, then you are fatally locked into such false problems as the relative value – weighed against Shakespeare or even Dickens – of such popular contemporary auteurs of high quality as Chaplin, John Ford, Hitchcock, or even Robert Frost, Andrew Wyeth, Simenon, or John O'Hara. The utter senselessness of this interesting subject of conversation becomes clear when it is understood that from a historical point of view the only form of 'high culture' which can be said to constitute the dialectical opposite of mass culture is that high culture production contemporaneous with the latter, which is to say that artistic production generally designated as *modernism*. The other term would then be Wallace Stevens, or Joyce, or Schoenberg, or Jackson Pollock, but surely not cultural artifacts such as the novels of Balzac or the plays of Molière which essentially antedate the historical separation between high and mass culture.

But such specification clearly obliges us to rethink our definitions of mass culture as well: the commercial products of the latter can surely not without intellectual dishonesty be assimilated to so-called popular, let alone folk, art of the past, which reflected and were dependent for their production on quite different social realities, and were in fact the 'organic' expression of so many distinct social communities or castes, such as the peasant village, the court, the medieval town, the polis, and even the classical bourgeoisie when it was still a unified social group with its own cultural specificity. The historically unique tendential effect of late capitalism on all such groups has been to dissolve and to fragment or atomize them into agglomerations (*Gesellschaften*) of isolated and equivalent private individuals, by way of the corrosive action of universal commodification and the market system. Thus, the 'popular' as such no longer exists, except under very specific and marginalized conditions (internal and external pockets of so-called underdevelopment within the capitalist world system); the commodity production of contemporary or industrial mass culture has nothing whatsoever to do, and nothing in common, with older forms of popular or folk art.

Thus understood, the dialectical opposition and profound structural interrelatedness of modernism and contemporary mass culture opens up a whole new field for cultural study, which promises to be more intelligible historically and socially than research or disciplines which have strategically conceived their missions as a specialization in this or that branch (e.g., in the university, English departments vs. Popular Culture programs). Now the emphasis must lie squarely on the social and aesthetic situation – the dilemma of form and of a public – shared and faced by both modernism and mass culture, but 'solved' in antithetical ways. Modernism also can only be adequately understood in terms of that commodity production whose all-informing structural influence on mass culture I have described above: only for modernism, the omnipresence of the commodity form, *not* to be a commodity, to devise an aesthetic language incapable of offering commodity satisfaction, and resistant to instrumentalization. The difference between this position and the valorization of modernism by the Frankfurt School [...] lies in my designation of modernism as reactive, that is, as a symptom and as a result of cultural crises, rather than a new 'solution' in its own right: not only is the commodity the prior form in terms of which alone modernism can be structurally grasped, but the very terms of its solution – the conception of the modernist text as the production and the protest of an isolated individual, and the logic of its sign systems as so many private languages ('styles') and private religions – are contradictory and made the social or collective realization of its aesthetic project (Mallarmé's ideal of *Le Livre* can be taken as the latter's fundamental formulation[9]) an impossible one (a judgment which, it ought not to be necessary to add, is not a judgment of value about the 'greatness' of the modernist texts).

Yet there are other aspects of the situation of art under monopoly and late capitalism which have remained unexplored and offer equally rich perspectives in which to examine modernism and mass culture and their structural dependency. Another such issue, for example, is that of *materialization* in contemporary art – a phenomenon woefully misunderstood by much contemporary Marxist theory (for obvious reasons, it is not an issue that has attracted academic formalism). Here the misunderstanding is dramatized by the pejorative emphasis of the Hegelian tradition (Lukács as well as the Frankfurt School) on phenomena of aesthetic reification – which furnishes the term of a negative value judgment – in juxtaposition to the celebration of the 'material signifier' and the 'materiality of the text' or of 'textual production' by the French tradition which appeals for its authority to Althusser and Lacan. If you are willing to entertain the possibility that 'reification' and the emergence of increasingly materialized signifiers are one and the same phenomenon – both historically and culturally – then this ideological great debate turns out to be based on a fundamental misunderstanding. Once again, the confusion stems from the introduction of the false problem of value (which fatally programs every binary opposition into its good and bad, positive and negative, essential and inessential terms) into a more properly ambivalent dialectical and historical situation in which reification or materialization is a key structural feature of both modernism and mass culture.

The task of defining this new area of study would then initially involve making an inventory of other such problematic themes or phenomena in terms of which the interrelationship of mass culture and modernism can usefully be explored, something it is too early to do here. At this point, I will merely note one further such theme, which has seemed to me to be of the greatest significance in specifying the antithetical formal reactions of modernism and mass culture to their common social situation, and that is the notion of *repetition.* This concept, which in its modern form we owe to Kierkegaard, has known rich and interesting new elaborations in recent post-structuralism: for Jean Baudrillard, for example, the repetitive structure of what he calls the simulacrum (that is, the reproduction of 'copies' which have no original) characterizes the commodity production of consumer capitalism and marks our object world with an unreality and a free-floating absence of 'the referent' (e.g., the place hitherto taken by nature, by raw materials and primary production, or by the 'originals' of artisanal production or handicraft) utterly unlike anything experienced in any earlier social formation.

If this is the case, then we would expect repetition to constitute yet another feature of the contradictory situation of contemporary aesthetic production to which both modernism and mass culture in one way or another cannot but react. This is in fact the case, and one need only invoke the traditional ideological stance of all modernizing theory and practice from the romantics to the *Tel Quel* group, and passing through the hegemonic formulations of classical Anglo-American modernism, to observe the strategic emphasis on innovation and novelty, the obligatory break with previous styles, the pressure – geometrically increasing with the ever swifter temporality of consumer society, with its yearly or quarterly style and fashion changes – to 'make it new,' to produce something which resists and breaks through the force of gravity of repetition as a universal feature of commodity equivalence. Such aesthetic ideologies have, to be sure, no critical or theoretical value – for one thing, they are purely formal, and by abstracting some empty concept of innovation from the concrete content of stylistic change in any given period end up flattening out even the history of forms, let alone social history, and projecting a kind of cyclical view of change – yet they are useful symptoms for detecting the ways in which the various modernisms have been forced, in spite of themselves, and in the very flesh and bone of their form, to respond to the objective reality of repetition itself. In our own time, the post-modernist conception of a 'text' and the ideal of schizophrenic writing openly demonstrate this vocation of the modernist aesthetic to produce sentences which are radically discontinuous, and which defy repetition not merely on the level of the break with older forms or older formal models but now within the microcosm of the text itself. Meanwhile, the kinds of repetition which, from Gertrude Stein to Robbe-Grillet, the modernist project has appropriated and made its own, can be seen as a kind of homeopathic strategy whereby the scandalous and intolerable external irritant is drawn into the aesthetic process itself and thereby systematically worked over, 'acted out,' and symbolically neutralized.

But it is clear that the influence of repetition on mass culture has been no less decisive. Indeed, it has frequently been observed that the older generic discourses – stigmatized by the various modernist revolutions, which have successively repudiated the older fixed forms of lyric, tragedy, and comedy, and at length even 'the novel' itself, now replaced by the unclassifiable 'livre' or 'text' – retain a powerful afterlife in the realm of mass culture. Paperback drugstore or airport displays reinforce all of the now sub-generic distinctions between gothic, best-seller, mysteries, science fiction, biography, or pornography, as do the conventional classification of weekly tv series, and the production and marketing of Hollywood films (to be sure, the generic system at work in contemporary commercial film is utterly distinct from the traditional pattern of the 1930s and 1940s production, and has had to respond to television competition by devising new metageneric or omnibus forms, which, however, at once become new 'genres' in their own right, and fold back into the usual generic stereotyping and reproduction – as, recently, with disaster film or occult film).

But we must specify this development historically: the older pre-capitalist genres were signs of something like an aesthetic 'contract' between a cultural producer and a certain homogeneous class or group public; they drew their vitality from the social and collective status (which, to be sure, varied widely according to the mode of production in question) of the situation of aesthetic production and consumption – that is to say, from the fact that the relationship between artist and public was still in one way or another a social institution and a concrete social and interpersonal relationship with its own validation and specificity. With the coming of the market, this institutional status of artistic consumption and production vanishes: art becomes one more branch of commodity production, the artist loses all social status and faces the options of becoming a *poète maudit* or a journalist, the relationship to the public is problematized, and the latter becomes a virtual 'public introuvable' (the appeals to posterity, Stendhal's dedication 'To the Happy Few,' or Gertrude Stein's remark, 'I write for myself and for strangers,' are revealing testimony to this intolerable new state of affairs).

The survival of genre in emergent mass culture can thus in no way be taken as a return to the stability of the publics of pre-capitalist societies: on the contrary, the generic forms and signals of mass culture are very specifically to be understood as the historical reappropriation and displacement of older structures in the service of the qualitatively very different situation of repetition. The atomized or serial 'public' of mass culture wants to see the same thing over and over again, hence the urgency of the generic structure and the generic signal: if you doubt this, think of your own consternation at finding that the paperback you selected from the mystery shelf turns out to be a romance or a science fiction novel; think of the exasperation of people in the row next to you who bought their tickets imagining that they were about to see a thriller or a political mystery instead of the horror or occult film actually underway. Think also of the much misunderstood 'aesthetic bankruptcy' of television: the structural reason for the inability of the various television series to produce episodes

which are either socially 'realistic' or have an aesthetic and fu
transcends mere variation has little enough to do with the ta
involved (although it is certainly exacerbated by the increasing 'ex.
rial and the ever-increasing tempo of the production of new ep.
precisely in our 'set' towards repetition. Even if you are a read
Dostoyevsky, when you watch a cop show or a detective series, you do
tation of the stereotyped format and would be annoyed to find the vid
making 'high cultural' demands on you. Much the same situation obtain         .t,
where it has however been institutionalized as the distinction between A .erican
(now multinational) film – determining the expectation of generic repetition – and
foreign films, which determine a shifting of gears of the 'horizon of expectations' to
the reception of high cultural discourse or so-called art films.

This situation has important consequences for the analysis of mass culture which
have not yet been fully appreciated. The philosophical paradox of repetition –
formulated by Kierkegaard, Freud, and others – can be grasped in this, that it can
as it were only take place 'a second time.' The first-time event is by definition not
a repetition of anything; it is then reconverted into repetition the second time
round, by the peculiar action of what Freud called 'retroactivity' [*Nachträglichkeit*].
But this means that, as with the simulacrum, there is no 'first time' of repetition, no
'original' of which succeeding repetitions are mere copies; and here too, modernism
furnishes a curious echo in its production of books which, like Hegel's *Phenomenology*
or Proust or *Finnegan's Wake*, you can only *reread.* Still, in modernism, the hermetic text remains, not only as an Everest to assault, but also as a book to whose
stable reality you can return over and over again. In mass culture, repetition effectively volatilizes the original object – the 'test,' the 'work of art' – so that the student
of mass culture has no primary object of study.

The most striking demonstration of this process can be witnessed in our reception of contemporary pop music of whatever type – the various kinds of rock,
blues, country western, or disco. I will argue that we never hear any of the singles
produced in these genres 'for the first time'; instead, we live a constant exposure
to them in all kinds of different situations, from the steady beat of the car radio
through the sounds at lunch, or in the work place, or in shopping centers, all the
way to those apparently full-dress performances of the 'work' in a nightclub or
stadium concert or on the records you buy and take home to hear. This is a very
different situation from the first bewildered audition of a complicated classical
piece, which you hear again in the concert hall or listen to at home. The passionate attachment one can form to this or that pop single, the rich personal
investment of all kinds of private associations and existential symbolism which
is the feature of such attachment, are fully as much a function of our own familiarity as of the work itself: the pop single, by means of repetition, insensibly
becomes part of the existential fabric of our own lives, so that what we listen to
is ourselves, our own previous auditions.[10]

Under these circumstances, it would make no sense to try to recover a feeling for
the 'original' musical text, as it really was, or as it might have been heard 'for the first
time.' Whatever the results of such a scholarly or analytical project, its object of
study would be quite distinct, quite differently constituted, from the same 'musical
text' grasped as mass culture, or in other works, as sheer repetition. The dilemma
of the student of mass culture therefore lies in the structural absence, or repetitive
volatilization, of the 'primary texts'; nor is anything to be gained by reconstituting

orpus' of texts after the fashion of, say, the medievalists who work with pre-capitalist generic and repetitive structures only superficially similar to those of contemporary mass or commercial culture. Nor, to my mind, is anything explained by recourse to the currently fashionable term of 'intertextuality,' which seems to me at best to designate a problem rather than a solution. Mass culture presents us with a methodological dilemma which the conventional habit of positing a stable object of commentary or exegesis in the form of a primary text or work is disturbingly unable to focus, let alone to resolve; in this sense, also, a dialectical conception of this field of study in which modernism and mass culture are grasped as a single historical and aesthetic phenomenon has the advantage of positing the survival of the primary text at one of its poles, and thus providing a guide-rail for the bewildering exploration of the aesthetic universe which lies at the other, a message or semiotic bombardment from which the textual referent has disappeared.

The above reflections by no means raise, let alone address, all the most urgent issues which confront an approach to mass culture today. In particular, we have neglected a somewhat different judgment on mass culture, which also loosely derives from the Frankfurt School position on the subject, but whose adherents number 'radicals' as well as 'elitists' on the Left today. This is the conception of mass culture as sheer manipulation, sheer commercial brainwashing and empty distraction by the multinational corporations who obviously control every feature of the production and distribution of mass culture today. If this were the case, then it is clear that the study of mass culture would at best be assimilated to the anatomy of the techniques of ideological marketing and be subsumed under the analysis of advertising texts and materials. Roland Barthes's seminal investigation of the latter, however, in his *Mythologies*, opened them up to the whole realm of the operations and functions of culture in everyday life; but since the sociologists of manipulation (with the exception, of course, of the Frankfurt School itself) have, almost by definition, no interest in the hermetic or 'high' art production whose dialectical interdependency with mass culture we have argued above, the general effect of their position is to suppress considerations of culture altogether, save as a kind of sandbox affair on the most epiphenomenal level of the superstructure.

The implication is thus to suggest that real social life – the only features of social life worth addressing or taking into consideration when political theory and strategy are at stake – is what the Marxian tradition designates as the political, the ideological, and the juridical levels of superstructural reality. Not only is this repression of the cultural moment determined by the university structure and by the ideologies of the various disciplines – thus, political science and sociology at best consign cultural issues to that ghettoizing rubric and marginalized field of specialization called the 'sociology of culture' – it is also and in a more general way the unwitting perpetuation of the most fundamental ideological stance of American business society itself, for which 'culture' – reduced to plays and poems and highbrow concerts – is par excellence the most trivial and non-serious activity in the 'real life' of the rat race of daily existence.

Yet even the vocation of the esthete (last sighted in the U.S. during the pre-political heyday of the 1950s) and of his successor, the university literature professor acknowledging uniquely high cultural 'values,' had a socially symbolic content and expressed (generally unconsciously) the anxiety aroused by market competition and the repudiation of the primacy of business pursuits and business values: these are then, to be sure, as thoroughly repressed from academic formalism as culture is from the work of the sociologists of manipulation, a repression which goes a long way towards accounting for the resistance and defensiveness of contemporary literary study towards anything which smacks of the painful reintroduction of just that 'real life' – the socio-economic, the historical context – which it was the function of aesthetic vocation to deny or to mask out in the first place.

What we must ask the sociologists of manipulation, however, is whether culture, far from being an occasional matter of the reading of a monthly good book or a trip to the drive-in, is not the very element of consumer society itself. No society, indeed, has ever been saturated with signs and messages like this one. If we follow Debord's argument about the omnipresence and the omnipotence of the image in consumer capitalism today, then if anything the priorities of the real become reversed, and everything is mediated by culture, to the point where even the political and the ideological 'levels' have initially to be disentangled from their primary mode of representation which is cultural. Howard Jarvis, Jimmy Carter, even Castro, the Red Brigade, B.J. Vorster, the Communist 'penetration' of Africa, the war in Vietnam, strikes, inflation itself – all are images, all come before us with the immediacy of cultural representations about which one can be fairly certain that they are by a long shot not historical reality itself. If we want to go on believing in categories like social class, then we are going to have to dig for them in the insubstantial bottomless realm of cultural and collective fantasy. Even ideology has in our society lost its clarity as prejudice, false consciousness, readily identifiable opinion: our racism gets all mixed up with clean-cut black actors on tv and in commercials, our sexism has to make a detour through new stereotypes of the 'women's libber' on the network series. After that, if one wants to stress the primacy of the political, so be it: until the omnipresence of culture in this society is even dimly sensed, realistic conceptions of the nature and function of political praxis today can scarcely be framed.

It is true that manipulation theory sometimes finds a special place in its scheme for those rare cultural objects which can be said to have overt political and social content: sixties protest songs, *The Salt of the Earth* (Biberman, 1954), Clancy Sigal's novels or Sol Yurick's, Chicano murals, the San Francisco Mime Troop. This is not the place to raise the complicated problem of political art today, except to say that our business as culture critics requires us to raise it, and to rethink what are still essentially thirties categories in some new and more satisfactory contemporary way. But the problem of political art – and we have nothing worth saying about it if we do not realize that it is a problem, rather than a choice or a ready-made option – suggests an important qualification to the scheme outlined in the first part of the present essay. The implied presupposition of those earlier remarks was that authentic cultural creation is dependent for its existence on authentic collective life, on the vitality of the 'organic' social group in whatever form (and such groups can range from the classical polis to the peasant village, from the commonality of the ghetto to the shared values of an embattled pre-revolutionary bourgeoisie). Capitalism systematically dissolves the fabric of all cohesive social groups without exception, including its own ruling class, and thereby problematizes aesthetic production and linguistic invention which have their source in group life. The result, discussed above, is the dialectical fission of older aesthetic expression into two modes, modernism and mass culture, equally dissociated from group praxis. Both of these modes have attained an admirable level of technical virtuosity; but it is a daydream to expect that either of these semiotic structures could be retransformed, by fiat, miracle, or sheer talent, into what could be called, in its strong form, political art, or in a more general way, that living and authentic culture of which we have virtually lost the memory, so rare an experience it has become. This is to say that of the two most influential recent Left aesthetics – the Brecht-Benjamin position, which hoped for the transformation of the nascent mass-cultural techniques and channels of communication of the 1930s into an openly political art, and the *Tel Quel* position which reaffirms the 'subversive' and revolutionary efficacy of language revolution and modernist and post-modernist formal innovation – we must reluctantly conclude that neither addresses the specific conditions of our own time.

The only authentic cultural production today has seemed to be that which can draw on the collective experience of marginal pockets of the social life of the world system: black literature and blues, British working-class rock, women's literature, gay literature, the *roman québécois*, the literature of the Third World; and this production is possible only to the degree to which these forms of collective life or collective solidarity have not yet been fully penetrated by the market and by the commodity system. This is not necessarily a negative prognosis, unless you believe in an increasingly windless and all-embracing total system; what shatters such a system – it has unquestionably been falling into place all around us since the development of industrial capitalism – is however very precisely collective praxis or, to pronounce its traditional unmentionable name, class struggle. Yet the relationship between class struggle and cultural production is not an immediate one; you do not reinvent an access onto political art and authentic cultural production by studding your individual artistic discourse with class and political signals. Rather, class struggle, and the slow and intermittent development of genuine class consciousness, are themselves the process whereby a new and organic group constitutes itself, whereby the collective breaks through the reified atomization (Sartre calls it the seriality) of capitalist social life. At that point, to say that the group exists and that it generates its own specific cultural life and expression, are one and the same. That is, if you like, the third term missing from my initial picture of the fate of the aesthetic and the cultural under capitalism; yet no useful purpose is served by speculation on the forms such a third and authentic type of cultural language might take in situations which do not yet exist. As for the artists, for them too 'the owl of Minerva takes its flight at dusk,' for them too, as with Lenin in April, the test of historical inevitability is always after the fact, and they cannot be told any more than the rest of us what is historically possible until after it has been tried.

This said, we can now return to the question of mass culture and manipulation. Brecht taught us that under the right circumstances you could remake anybody over into anything you liked (*Mann ist Mann*), only he insisted on the situation and the raw materials fully as much or more than on the techniques stressed by manipulation theory. Perhaps the key problem about the concept, or pseudo-concept, of manipulation can be dramatized by juxtaposing it to the Freudian notion of repression. The Freudian mechanism, indeed, comes into play only after its object – trauma, charged memory, guilty or threatening desire, anxiety – has in some way been aroused, and risks emerging into the subject's consciousness. Freudian repression is therefore determinate, it has specific content, and may even be said to be something like a 'recognition' of that content which expresses itself in the form of denial, forgetfulness, slip, *mauvaise foi,* displacement or substitution.

But of course the classical Freudian model of the work of art (as of the dream or the joke) was that of the symbolic fulfillment of the repressed wish, of a complex structure of indirection whereby desire could elude the repressive censor and achieve some measure of a, to be sure, purely symbolic satisfaction. A more recent 'revision' of the Freudian model, however – Norman Holland's *The Dynamics of Literary Response* – proposes a scheme more useful for our present problem, which is to conceive how (commercial) works of art can possibly be said to 'manipulate' their publics. For Holland, the psychic function of the work of art must be described in such a way that these two inconsistent and even incompatible features of aesthetic gratification – on the one hand, its wish-fulfilling function, but on the other the necessity that its symbolic structure protect the psyche against the frightening and potentially damaging eruption of powerful archaic desires and wish-material – be somehow harmonized and assigned their place as twin drives of a single structure. Hence Holland's suggestive conception of the vocation of the work of art to *manage* this raw material of the drives and the archaic wish or fantasy material. To rewrite the concept of a management of desire in social terms now allows us to think repression and wish-fulfillment together within the unity of a single mechanism, which gives and takes alike in a kind of psychic compromise or horse-trading; which strategically arouses fantasy content within careful symbolic containment structures which defuse it, gratifying intolerable, unrealizable, properly imperishable desires only to the degree to which they can be momentarily stilled.

This model seems to me to permit a far more adequate account of the mechanisms of manipulation, diversion, and degradation, which are undeniably at work in mass culture and in the media. In particular it allows us to grasp mass culture not as empty distraction or 'mere' false consciousness, but rather as a transformational work on social and political anxieties and fantasies which must then have some effective presence in the mass cultural text in order subsequently to be 'managed' or repressed. Indeed, the initial reflections of the present essay suggest that such a thesis ought to be extended to modernism as well, even though I will not here be able to develop this part of the argument further.[11] I will therefore argue that both mass culture and modernism have as much content, in the loose sense of the word, as the older social realisms; but that this content is processed in all three in very different ways. Both modernism and mass culture entertain relations of repression with the fundamental social anxieties and concerns, hopes and blind spots, ideological antinomies and fantasies of disaster, which are their raw material; only where modernism tends to handle this material by producing compensatory structures of various kinds, mass culture represses them by the narrative construction of imaginary resolutions and by the projection of an optical illusion of social harmony.

## Notes

1. See for the theoretical sources of this opposition my essay on Max Weber, 'The Vanishing Mediator,' in *The Ideologies of Theory*, Vol. II (Minneapolis: University of Minnesota Press, 1988), pp. 3–34.

2. The classical study remains that of J.-P. Vernant; see his 'Travail et nature dans la Gréce ancienne' and 'Aspects psychologiques du travail,' in *Mythe et pensée chez les grecs* (Paris: Maspéro, 1965).

3. Besides Marx, see Georg Simmel, *Philosophy of Money* (London: Routledge, 1978) and also his classic 'Metropolis and Mental Life,' translated in Simmel, *On Individuality and Social Forms* (Chicago: University of Chicago Press, 1971), pp. 324–39.

4. '[Bourgeois city-dwellers] wander through the woods as through the moist tender soil of the child they once were; they stare at the poplars and plane trees planted along the road, they have nothing to say about them because they are doing nothing with them, and they marvel at the wondrous quality of this silence,' etc. J.-P. Sartre, *Saint Genêt* (Paris: Gallimard, 1952), pp. 249–250.

5. Guy Debord, *The Society of the Spectacle* (Detroit: Black and Red Press, 1973).

6. Reification by way of the *tableau* was already an eighteenth-century theatrical device (reproduced in Buñuel's *Viridiana*), but the significance of the book illustration was anticipated by Sartre's description of 'perfect moments' and 'privileged situations' in *Nausea* (the illustrations in Annie's childhood edition of Michelet's *History of France*).

7. In my opinion, this 'feeling tone' (or secondary libidinal investment) is essentially an invention of Zola and part of the new technology of the naturalist novel (one of the most successful French exports of its period).

8. Written in 1976. A passage like this one cannot be properly evaluated unless it is understood that they were written before the elaboration of a theory of what we now call the postmodern (whose emergence can also be observed in these essays).

9. See Jacques Scherer, *Le 'Livre' de Mallarmé* (Paris: Gallimard, 1957).

10. My own fieldwork has thus been seriously impeded by the demise some years ago of both car radios: so much the greater is my amazement when rental cars today (which are probably not time machines) fill up with exactly the same hit songs I used to listen to in the early seventies, repeated over and over again!

11. Written before a preliminary attempt to do so in *The Political Unconscious* (Ithaca: Cornell University Press, 1981); see in particular chapter three, 'Realism and Desire.'

# Chapter 13

## Lisa Lowe and David Lloyd

## Introduction to the Politics of Culture in the Shadow of Late Capital

*The Politics of Culture in the Shadow of Capital* is a collection of essays that, in their combination, advance a critical approach to the 'international,' the 'global,' or the 'transnational' as theoretical frameworks within which intersecting sets of social practices can be grasped. These practices include anticolonial and antiracist struggles, feminist struggles, labor organizing, cultural movements – all of which challenge contemporary neocolonial capitalism as a highly differentiated mode of production. While such practices are ubiquitous, they generally take place in local and heterogeneous sites, and rarely make the claim to be 'global' models in scope or ambition. Accordingly, the kind of intervention that *The Politics of Culture* makes has become necessary insofar as neither the postmodern conception of the transnational nor the liberal assumption of the congruence of capitalism, democracy, and freedom are currently adequate to address the ubiquity and variety of alternatives.

We understand the transnational to denote the stage of globalized capitalism characterized by David Harvey, Fredric Jameson, and others as the universal extension of a differentiated mode of production that relies on flexible accumulation and mixed production to incorporate all sectors of the global economy into its logic of commodification.[1] It is the tendency of such understandings of transnationalism to assume a homogenization of global culture that radically reduces possibilities for the creation of alternatives, in confining them either to the domain of commodified

From: *The Politics of Culture in the Shadow of Late Capital.* Ed. Lisa Lowe and David Lloyd Durham. NC: Duke University Press, 1997.

culture itself or to spaces that, for reasons of mere historical contingency, have seemed unincorporated into globalization.[2] It will be our contention, to the contrary, that transnational or *neocolonial* capitalism, like colonialist capitalism before it, continues to produce sites of contradiction that are effects of its always uneven expansion but that cannot be subsumed by the logic of commodification itself. We suggest that 'culture' obtains a 'political' force when a cultural formation comes into contradiction with economic or political logics that try to refunction it for exploitation or domination. Rather than adopting the understanding of culture as one sphere in a set of differentiated spheres and practices, we discuss 'culture' as a terrain in which politics, culture, and the economic form an inseparable dynamic. This entails not simply a critique of liberal cultural, political, and legal theories that are the social correlative of capitalist economics, but an affirmative inventory of the survival of alternatives in many locations worldwide. Our interest is not in identifying what lies 'outside' capitalism, but in what arises historically, in contestation, and 'in difference' to it. [...]

## Nationalism, Marxism, Feminism, and the Question of Alternatives

As Arturo Escobar has argued, in the period following World War II the domination by the West through direct colonialisms is transformed into a global project of domination by way of modernization and development.[3] For this period, the state is the principal form demanded of postcolonial nations in order that they can provide the body of institutions through which modernization is imposed. Etienne Balibar argues that, practically speaking, the state is the form through which nations enter the modern world system.[4] But the state form entails more than a pragmatic adjustment to that world system; it implies not only an assimilation to a hierarchized system of global power, but compliance with a normative distribution of social spaces within that state's definitions. The entry of the nation through the medium of the modern state into the global world system requires the massive conversion of populations and their cultural forms into conformity with the post-World War II project of universal modernization. Civil society must be reshaped to produce subjects who might function in terms of modern definitions of social spaces, as the political subject of the state, the economic subject of capitalism, and the cultural subject of the nation, however much the discreteness of these spaces is contradicted by conditions that are lived as racialized and gendered labor stratification, apartheid, and poverty. The state form's importance extends beyond the immediate post-World War II geopolitical system; we would wish to maintain that even in the post-Fordist, postmodern transnational economy, the modern state form and its contradictions persist within the mobility of global capital as the primary set of institutions for regulating resources, investments, and populations. Hence the state becomes the site of contradictions and the object of contestation for political projects such as bourgeois nationalism, Marxism, and feminism.[5] To a large extent, the state defines the terms and stakes of these projects: the continuing extension and redefinition of popular democracy or citizenship and the promotion of national culture; the antagonism to regulation of labor on behalf of national and international capital; the contestation of the legal and social subordination of racialized populations and women within the context of a discourse on 'rights.' In different ways, bourgeois nationalist, Marxist, and feminist movements confront the limits of state-oriented definitions both in the form of the direct antagonism of the state and in the form of the alternative spheres and practices that emerge in the very formation of modernity itself. The contradictions of modernity are not new, though they may take new forms at any given historical moment; they are embedded in the history of colonization and of global capitalism and have been constitutive in the emergence of contemporary social formations. It will be our contention here that productive rethinkings of the categories of these movements take place through the alternative formations that emerge in the space of contradictions.

## Nationalism

The nationalism articulated in Western state formations posits a historical continuity between the emergence of a people and the development of the state that represents its political sovereignty.[6] But even contemporary Western theorists of nations and nationalism, such as Gellner, Hobsbawm, Nairn, and Breuilly, do not fundamentally challenge this assumption. The emergence of the nation-state is largely understood in contemporary history as a Western development and as a more or less organic emergence of European civilizations. Even where contemporary historians are skeptical of the nineteenth-century backward projection of the 'spirit of the nation' into primordial origins, and prefer the concept of the 'invented tradition' by which the people is constituted retrospectively by the modern political imagination, the territorial boundaries and historical claims to legitimacy of modern European nations are accepted as givens of Western modernity. Correspondingly, the European nation-state remains the template of proper political formations globally despite the singularity, from a genuinely world-historical perspective, of its formation. The historical or temporal dimension of the nation, the development and maturation of civil and political society and the formation of their proper subjects, and the spatial dimension, what Akhil Gupta and James Ferguson call 'the isomorphism of place, culture, nation, and state,' provide the terms to which the political formations of other societies are required to conform or approximate.[7]

Following such theories of the nation-state and of nationalism as a political force, the emergence of the European nation-state and its political ideology is distinct from the forms of anticolonial or 'belated' nationalism. Not all thinkers demarcate European from non-European nationalisms as strictly as Hans Kohn in his seminal distinction of 'Western' from 'non-Western' forms, but the tendency to make such distinctions is virtually ubiquitous.[8] What is being marked in this kind of formulation is a certain incommensurability between the cultural forms of non-Western societies and the political forms they have sought or been obliged to adopt in the course of decolonization. From the perspective of Western modernity, this incommensurability is perceived as a lack, and the remedy is generally held to be the state-directed development of a mature civil society with its corresponding ethical civil subjects. This prescription is the political correlative of capitalist economic development as imposed by Western-dominated international organizations.

Both prescriptions preclude the emergence of alternatives out of contradictions with equal force and constitute the leading edge of neocolonialism as powerfully in the era of transnational capital as at any previous moment.

Contradiction is virtually constitutive of the practices of anticolonial nationalism. On the one hand, the ends of anticolonial nationalism are defined by the goal of the capture of the state, and its ideology is in large part structured in terms of liberal discourses and for liberal state institutions: it speaks of rights and the citizen, of equality, fraternity, and liberty, makes its claims to self-determination on the basis of enlightenment universality, and asserts the cultural if not economic and military equivalence of its nation-people to that of the imperial power. At the same time, within the terms of an anticolonial struggle, it is rare for a nationalist movement not to draw on conceptions of 'tradition,' of cultural antimodernity, and indeed, of alternatives to capitalist development in order to mobilize the antagonism of the populace against the colonial power and to mark the differences that transform that populace into a people with a legitimate right to separate and sovereign statehood. In this, nationalism repeats the very distinction between tradition and modernity that colonialism institutes to legitimate domination. In the first place, this demands the transformation of the colonial model that largely assumes that tradition must be reformed by modernization. Instead nationalism invokes tradition in order to assert the antagonism between irreconcilable social and cultural values. For this reason, in fact, the moment of anticolonial struggle is generally very productive of 'emancipatory' possibilities far in excess of nationalism's own projects, a point to which we shall return. But the ultimate fixation of anticolonial nationalism on the state form tends to reproduce the articulation of tradition and modernity by which traditional society requires to be modernized – even if the forms of postcolonial modernity are modified to accommodate a fetishized version of tradition through which a distinct people is to be interpellated by the nation-state. State nationalism then seeks to mask the contradictions that reemerge between formal political independence and economic dependence (the contradictions of neocolonialism) and to contain the excess of alternatives released by the decolonizing forces of which it was a part.

We would want, therefore, to distinguish, but not separate out, state-oriented nationalism from a larger and potentially more productive decolonizing process that emerges and persists in the very contradictions of colonialism in all its stages. As a range of anticolonial intellectuals from Fanon to Cabral argue, racialization of the colonized population is fundamental to the dynamics of colonial society, constituting the principal impetus that brings nationalist movements into being.[9] The racialization of all colonized subjects permits what Bipan Chandra analyzes as the nationalist 'vertical integration' of the caste- and class-stratified colonial society, and enables the nationalist movement to cut across such distinctions.[10] Bourgeois nationalism tends to reshape its antiracist practices and ideologies around a notion of the nation's capacity to develop and assimilate European cultural and political forms. Popular movements, on the contrary, organize around antagonisms to colonialism that are founded on an understanding of racialized exploitation under colonialism that leads to modes of decolonization aimed at creating new and radically democratic forms of social organization. This latter decolonizing process is what Fanon terms, in his broad sense, 'national culture,' as opposed to bourgeois nationalism's fetishization of selected and canonized 'traditions,' which artificially freeze cultural difference, reintroducing or reinforcing lines of ethnic or 'tribal' stratification within the new nation. With regard to the new nation's external relations to global capitalism and neocolonial powers, the fixing of popular culture into artificial national forms and the racial stratification of society help to reproduce the concept of a specific 'underdevelopment' that facilitates and legitimates neocolonialist exploitation.

Although nationalism seeks, in the Gramscian sense, to direct popular forces, and thereby to gain hegemony over them, it is in fact constituted within a rich site of intersections among simultaneous social processes and modes of organization, which include not only antiracism but linked practices such as subaltern agitation and women's movements, to which nationalism contributes in often unpredictable ways and by which it is inflected at every moment. [...] Focus on nationalism accordingly not only obscures the ways in which alternative social processes, both within the anticolonial struggle and across the longer duration of what we conceive of as decolonization, work concomitantly with and through nationalism; this focus also renders invisible the fact that such struggle occupies another terrain constituted by its externality to the state and shaped by the rhythms of different temporalities. This is at once a historiographical question and suggestive regarding contemporary contradictions. [...] When the antagonism between colonialism and nationalism is considered the only legitimate site for the political, it relegates alternatives to the domain 'outside of history,' and obscures the ongoing constitution of other social formations through contemporary antagonisms. For the antagonism between nationalism and imperialism also unleashed other contradictions than those addressed by decolonizing or nationalist movements specifically. [...] The retrieval of such spaces and struggles that are by definition at odds with state projects and elite nationalism has been the characteristic work of subaltern and feminist historiographies, though we will take up later the different emphases of both projects.

## Marxism

[...] Marxist theory and practice have been crucial correctives to bourgeois nationalism. For although Marxism has tended to share with nationalism the political frame of the nation-state, it has consistently critiqued forms of bourgeois and cultural nationalism that ignore class difference. The classical Marxist understanding of contradiction asserts that the contradiction between capital and labor takes place within the totality of nationalist capitalist relations, and that the exacerbation of contradiction is part of a progressive development that includes the emergence of proletarian consciousness within that totality. For Western Marxism, the proletarian subject emerges primarily in relation to the goal of the capture of the state: in an earlier form in Leninism, dictatorship of the proletariat, in a later form in Gramsci, the construction of working-class hegemony through institutions Gramsci describes as institutions of the ethical state. Gramsci's refinement of the Leninist position for less autocratic states than czarist Russia suggests that the emergence of working-class hegemony necessitates a detour through 'culture' by means of working-class consciousness and concomitant cultural forms. It is further assumed that the territorial basis of this culture is national, and that there is a correspondence between a national popular culture and political hegemony; the state that is to be captured is ultimately the expression of that correspondence. Whereas Gramsci would seem to be the Western theorist of Marxism who, through the discussion of the Southern Question, links analysis of the democratic industrial state with the different issues and conditions that affect colonized regions, what he in fact marks are problems of uneven cultural and political, as well as economic, development. We observe that 'third world' Marxisms emerge not only from what Western Marxism would designate as such unevennesses, but from entirely different conditions and social formations. In particular, the condition of these Marxisms is that the forms of state and the forms of culture are incompatible. [...]

Our critique of Western Marxism, then, is at one with our critique of the developmental narratives of Western modernity, but does not extend to the materialism that founds Marx's method. Rather, 'third world' Marxisms, we would emphasize, already diverge from the classical Western Marxist formulation, having sought to come to terms with the intersection of colonization of largely agrarian societies with capitalist exploitation. The differences of Leninism in Bolshevik Russia or Maoism in revolutionary China are precisely an effect of their analyses of different material and historical conditions. Donald Lowe has argued that while the orientalist construction of the 'Asiatic mode of production' within Western Marxism had fixed understandings of 'China' and other peasant societies in a static, unchanging concept of 'underdevelopment,' the 'later' Lenin and Mao rethought Marxism for Russia and China not in relation to 'underdevelopment' but through the understanding that peasant societies are materially different and contain different historical possibilities for transformation.[11]

The rethinking of Marxism by Lenin and Mao for their societies is echoed in the rethinking of Marxism in other contexts. For example, Dipesh Chakrabarty has demonstrated in his study of the Calcutta jute mill workers between 1890 and 1940 that the reproduction of capitalist social relations did not necessarily pass through European-style proletarianization but through cultural forms quite incompatible with that model of development [...].[12] Aihwa Ong has similarly argued that Malaysian factory women protest capitalist discipline not through Western class consciousness or feminist consciousness but by stopping production on the factory floor through local cultural forms like spirit possession.[13] Both arguments are materialist in their modes of investigation, yet clearly demand a rethinking of classic Marxist formulations. In our critical engagement with Marxist theory, there are two axes of analysis that concern us: one is the emergence of new forms of political subjectivity, the other is the domain of race and culture in relation to the transformation of capitalist social relations; both, of course, are closely related.

Western Marxism assumes that conflicts that fall 'outside' the development of class consciousness are politically subordinate, or constitute 'false consciousness': antagonisms articulated, for example, around gender or race, are seen as effects of a more fundamental contradiction. According to the same logic, it also assumes the necessity of a globalization of capitalist proletarianization that would privilege the locations of greatest modernization and development in ways that obscure the historical expansion of capital through uneven differentiation of geographies, sectors, and labor forces. Thus far, we agree with the postmodern critiques of Western Marxism that argue that, contrary to its classical formulation by Marx, capitalism has proceeded not through global homogenization but through differentiation of labor markets, material resources, consumer markets, and production operations. But we wish to add that it is not simply that there has not been an even, homogeneous spread of development, but that, in what Bipan Chandra has called the 'colonial mode of production,' different problems emerge in the encounter between 'indigenous' forms of work and cultural practices and the modern capitalist economic modes imposed upon them.[14] Whereas the relations of production of nineteenth-century industrial capitalism were characterized by the management of the urban workers by the urban bourgeoisie, colonialism was built on the racialized split between colonial metropolis and agrarian colony, organizing the agrarian society into a social formation in which a foreign class functioned as the capitalist class. In order to maximize the extraction of surplus, the necessary reproduction of the relations of production in the colonial mode was not limited to the reproduction of class relations, but emphasized also that of hierarchical relations of region, culture, language, and, especially, race. In *Reading Capital,* Louis Althusser and Etienne Balibar extend Marx's original formulation of the relationship between the 'mode of production' and the 'social formation' by defining a social formation as the complex structure in which more than one mode of production, or set of economic relations, may be combined.[15] Their elaboration suggests not only that the situations of uneven development, colonialist incorporation, and global restructuring and immigration are each characterized by the combination of several simultaneous modes of production, but that each constitutes a specific, historically distinct social formation (that includes economic, political, and ideological levels of articulation). The need to understand the differentiated forms through which capital profits through mixing and combining different modes of production suggests, too, that the complex structures of a new social formation may indeed require interventions and modes of opposition specific to those structures. Whereas Western Marxism assumes to a greater or lesser extent the correspondence of the institutions of civil society to the needs of the reproduction of capitalist social relations, in colonial and neocolonial social formations there arise what we might term 'discoordinated' structures of civil society, which in themselves mediate a disjunction between existing cultural practices and the modernizing forces embodied in the rationalizing forms of civil society put in place by the nation-state.

That 'discoordination,' although it is not always theorized as such, can be understood as requiring us to think the existence of different historical temporalities that are simultaneously active within a given social formation. At the level of political analysis, 'third world' or national Marxisms, as in the work of Fanon and Cabral, have always understood the necessity for mobilizing anticolonial resistance around the antagonism between indigenous social forms and the colonial state; class relations themselves in the colonial state are always already predicated upon racialization, and thus the dynamic of nationalist revolution is seen by them to involve race and class inseparably. However, in the formation of postindependence policy, national states with quite various political agendas have tended to contain popular movements, and have by and large attempted to resolve the peculiar contradictions of the 'colonial mode of production' by adapting Western modernization models. [...]

It is our intention to intervene in discourses on transnational capitalism whose tendency is to totalize the world system, to view capitalist penetration as complete and pervasive, so that the site of intervention is restricted to commodification; or, more insidiously, with the result that all manifestations of difference appear as just further signs of commodification. To pose the argument about transnationalism at the level of commodification not only obscures the practices of exploitation that lead to antagonism, but also ignores the ways in which transnational capital's exploitation of cultural differentiation produces its own contradictions. Our critique of the assumption of absolute globalization or universal commodification does not lead us to fetishize imaginary spaces that are not yet under the sway of capitalism. Rather, what we focus on is the intersection of commodification and labor exploitation under postmodern transnational modes of production with the historical emergence of social formations in time with but also in antagonism to modernity; these social formations are not residues of the 'premodern,' but are *differential* formations that mediate the processes through which capital profits through the mixing and combination of exploitative modes. What we are concerned with is the multiplicity of significant contradictions rooted in the longer histories of antagonism and adaptation. All of these are obscured by either a totality governed by globalization of capitalism or the superordination of the proletarian subject.

The work of Aihwa Ong, Swasti Mitter, and Maria Mies, for example, suggests that flexible accumulation depends precisely on capitalism's laying hold of 'traditional' social formations that have not been leveled by modernity either in terms of labor relations or the political nation; in these encounters, capitalism 'respects' those forms even if for exploitative aims.[16] In these analyses, questions of gender, within the racialized consolidation of social forms into traditions that takes place under colonization, are inseparable from the exploitation of labor. As Dipesh Chakrabarty has argued in his study of the Bengali working class, capitalism under colonialism is not reproduced through the formation of abstract political subjects but rather through the formation of subjects embedded in pre-capitalist social relations. To the extent that the formation of these subjects belies the homogenization of capitalist social relations according to the Western model, it also contradicts the assumption of a correspondence between the cultural and political domains and their reproduction for economic exploitation. Yet at the same time, the 'culture' that emerges from this encounter mediates in complex ways the contradiction between contemporary global capitalist development and the culture whose social relations have an extended history that is always in part determined by encounters with emergent modernity. Accordingly, these encounters do not erase contradiction; neither do they produce the resolution of contradictions. Against theoretical prediction, cultural forms that might seem incompatible with capitalist social relations both permit their reproduction and provide for oppositional modes. In other words, it is neither that capitalist modernity expands and commodifies the 'traditional,' nor that it simply destroys it, making it necessary for one to look for 'pure' sites that have not yet been incorporated in order to find 'resistance' (as in the as-yet-undiscovered primitive tribe in the Amazon), but rather that both antagonism and adaptation have been part of the process of the emergence of modernity over time. That is, what we are calling the alternative is not the 'other' outside, but the 'what-has-been-formed' in the conjunction with and in differentiation from modernity over time. The alternative takes place in the contradictions that emerge when the cultural forms of one mode of production are taken up and exploited by an apparently incommensurable mode of production.

## Feminism

There is from the outset a dissymmetry between our discussion of 'feminism' and the preceding discussions of nationalism and Marxism: it is less possible to discuss a singular 'feminism,' since its emergence both inside and outside of national contexts, not only in the West but globally, has given rise to a wide variety of theories and practices. Even in the West, given that versions of modern liberal feminism have sought enfranchisement for female subjects within national political spheres articulated through the concept of 'rights,' no feminist movement has sought a 'capture' of the state in the manner proposed by nationalism or Marxism, and feminist projects must be distinguished as nonanalogous to nationalist and Marxist ones.

To the extent that the dominant strands of Western feminism have been articulated within the terms of liberal modernity, the limits of that feminism have been discussed by Chandra Talpade Mohanty, Angela Davis, Chela Sandoval, and others as being marked by their historical articulation with both imperial projects and state racisms.[17] Indeed, where neither nationalism nor Marxism has fully critiqued the 'nationalist subject' or the 'class subject,' international and antiracist feminisms, as well as Anglo-American feminism, have interrogated the subject of feminism – 'woman' – as embodying an implicit universalism that obscures unequal power relations that are the consequence of colonialism and capitalism.[18] Therefore, it will not be our task here to write generally about all feminisms, but to look specifically at women's struggles within the racialized structures of colonial modernity and transnational capitalism. The women's struggles we are foregrounding demand neither a homogeneous subject nor a conception of a fixed social totality; rather, they are practices antagonistic to the distinct modes of subjectivity disciplined by divisions of the modern state – the political, economic, or cultural (and its attendant separation into 'public' and 'private'). To frame the contemporary situation of women, we begin by situating the historical contradictions of women in their encounter with modernity, contradictions that remain active in and continue to determine the dynamics of transnationalism. By the encounter with modernity, we mean with the racialized and gendered regimes of the colonial state and the modern nation-state, which extend not only to the formation and reproduction of gender in the family and in other social spaces and institutions such as schooling, religion, law, the workplace, and cultural and popular media, but to ideological and epistemological suppositions of the particular and universal, constructions of interiority and exteriority, and evaluations of purity and impurity. While the modern state has in theory offered women emancipation in the economic and political spheres, and even participation in anticolonial nationalist struggles, the regulation and consolidation of national identity has generally led to women's political/juridical exclusion, their educational subordination, economic exploitation, and ideological suppression.[19] Within this history, it is often in the violent contestations over the meaning and place of cultural practices that women's contradictory status in relation to the state becomes evident. At the same time, the subordination of women in contradiction with modernity allows transnational capital access to women's labor as a site of hyperextraction. In turn, the contestatory sites of contradiction within modern national forms can provide the very opportunities and tools for practices that challenge transnational exploitation. This is why we need to understand that new subjects operate not exclusively through the 'political' or 'economic' categories of nationalism and Marxism, but through the politics of culture as well.

It has been the tendency of nationalism and Marxism to consider gender a secondary formation, which has subordinated women's activism to anticolonial nationalist struggle or proletarian labor struggles, respectively. This tendency has symptomatized the most serious limit of these political projects, that is, the insistence on totality and unity to the exclusion of different axes of determination and struggle, other axes whose intersections may be the sites of the most aggravated contradictions. We've argued that the political subject of modernity has been conceived as either the citizen of the nation or the proletarian class subject. Both forms of political subjectivity depend on a gendered ideology of separate spheres; the political and economic subject is presumed to be male and must be differentiated from realms cast as 'feminine': the domestic sphere of the 'home,' the 'spiritual' cultural antecedents of modernity, and labors situated as 'reproductive.' The counter-spheres marked 'feminine' are seen as sites of *reproduction* rather than *production,* and in that respect correspond to sites of culture. Along with the antinomy 'private' and 'public,' women have been subject to the construction of 'tradition' and 'modernity,' which perpetually locates 'third world women' as the 'other' of modernity, the symbol of premodern 'tradition' to be 'modernized.' We contend, to the contrary, that women have always been agents in the dialectical production of the heterogeneous, differentiated forms of modernity itself.[20] Even before the currently gendered international division of labor, women under colonialisms and in so-called developing nations composed the primary labor force exploited in the production of economic modernity.

Extending materialist theory in ways adequate to the present moment requires an understanding of the gendered division of labor that not only interprets the era of transnationalism but allows us to grasp retrospectively the historical occlusion of women's struggle. Feminist historiography sheds light on formerly undocumented and unanalyzed histories of women's contradictory engagement with modernity. As much as feminist historiography that recaptures the agencies of women as makers of history shares some of the impulse of subaltern historiography, its methods and purposes are not identical. Subaltern historiography in general seeks to recover practices from domains that are defined as external to the state or public sphere; consequently, the reference point of subaltern study has continued to be the relation of subaltern struggles and practices to elite nationalist or colonialist formations. In contradistinction, feminist historiography that regards women's activities and gendered social relations as central is concerned with sets of cultural and political practices that cut across all domains of the social and require a different periodization and temporality.[21] Though nationalist narratives have subordinated the ubiquity of women's participation in social struggles to the terms of a national model, it is not a matter now of simply inserting 'women' into the nationalist narrative. As Kumkum Sangari and Sudesh Vaid state, 'A feminist historiography rethinks historiography as a whole and discards the idea of women as something to be *framed* by a context, in order to be able to think of gender difference as both structuring and structured by the wide set of social relations.'[22] Radha Radhakrishnan has put it this way: 'feminist historiography secedes from the structure [of nationalist totality] not to set up a different and oppositional form of totality, but to establish a different relation to totality.'[23] In a way that nationalism cannot, and Marxism has not yet, this feminism rethinks historical periodization and agency, reconceptualizes the division of social spheres, and ultimately advances a new conception of the political subject itself. [...]

Feminist historiography thus reveals that women's practices are only partially grasped when reduced to the horizon of the national state, and that implicitly those practices demand alternatives to the formations prescribed by the modern state, whose emancipatory promise is contradicted by the persistent subordinations. In the transnational era, the 'modern' forms in which the nation mediates capital come into contradiction with the 'postmodern' forces and movements of the global economy; yet we maintain that even in the postmodern transnational economy, the modern patriarchal state form persists within the mobility of global capital as the primary set of institutions for regulating women's labor and sexuality and for dictating spheres of gendered social practice. Furthermore, the globalization of capitalism reorganizes the operations of production exploiting women precisely in ways permitted by their subordination by national patriarchal states. Patriarchal definitions of gender are continuously reproduced throughout a genealogy of social formations: patriarchy is consistently dominant, though not identically so, under colonial rule, in nationalist regimes, and in postcolonial and neocolonial state formations. There is a perpetual dialectic between 'traditional' patriarchy and its 'modern' rearticulations, whereby the selective redefinition of the 'traditional' woman through which modernity rearticulates patriarchy serves both to intensify the constraints upon and to extract differentiated labor from female subjects. The hyperexploitation of women under transnationalism brings women's cultural practices to the fore as incommensurable with capitalist rationality. Since the 1970s and 1980s, the deindustrialization of the United States and Europe has been accomplished by a shifting of production to Asia and Latin America, particularly making use of female labor in overseas export assembly and manufacturing zones.[24] [...] One of the distinct features of global restructuring is capital's ability to profit not through a homogenization of the mode of production, but through the differentiation of specific resources and markets that permits the exploitation of gendered labor within regional and national sites. Part of this differentiation involves transactions between national states and transnational capital, which formalize new capital accumulation and production techniques that exploit by specifically targeting female labor markets. This occurs where women are disciplined by state-instituted traditional patriarchy, whether in Malaysia or Guatemala, or by racialized immigration laws that target female immigrants in particular, such as in California, These conditions, produced by the differentiating mode of transnational capital, counter a center–periphery model of spatial or developmental logic, and hence point to the timeliness, which we will take up later, of conceptualizing linkages between and across varied sites of contradiction. Such linkages recognize the dispersed forms of transnational operations of capital accumulation and exploitation as an opportunity for, rather than a limit on, new political practices.

While it is the understanding of some analysts of transnationalism that global capitalism has penetrated and saturated all social terrains, exhausting the possibilities for challenges or resistance, the situations of women workers suggest that transnational capitalism, like colonial capitalism before it, continues to produce sites of contradiction and the dynamics of its own negation and critique. These contradictions produce new possibilities precisely because they have led to a breakdown and a reformulation of the categories of nation, race, class, and gender, and in doing so have led to a need to reconceptualize the oppositional narratives of nationalism, Marxism, and feminism. The latest shift toward the transnationalization of capital is not exclusively manifested in the 'denationalization' of corporate power or the nation-state, but, perhaps more importantly, it is expressed in the reorganization of oppositional interventions against capital that articulate themselves in terms and relations other than the 'national' or the 'international proletariat' – notably feminist activism among U.S. women of color, cross-border labor organizing, and neocolonized and immigrant women's struggles [...].

In its intensification of exploitation, transnational capitalism has exacerbated the gendered political and economic contradictions that were active in modern state capitalisms; paradoxically, this takes place in part through an erosion of the legal and social regulations that underwrite the ideology of separate spheres. Making use of the structures of patriarchal societies and their modes of gender discipline to maximize its exploitation of 'docile' female labor, transnational capital simultaneously undermines the reproduction of patriarchies by moving women from one sphere of gendered social control to another. Yet the reconstitution of patriarchy within the transnational capitalist system, we argue, produces different and more varied practices of resistance to that system, practices that do not turn exclusively on the opposition of abstract labor to capital. Where this 'feminized' domain of culture is in contradiction with capitalist production we find a convergence of struggles generated by different axes of domination: capitalism, patriarchy, and the processes of racialization that take place through colonialism and immigration. The specific modes of discipline that apply to women as gendered subjects necessarily give rise to different modes of organization and politicization; for example, *maquiladora* workers in Mexico protesting the factory's regular requirement of 'beauty pageants' that rearticulate patriarchal domination of women in the workplace have generated cross-border workers' organizations that have targeted more generally the gendered nature of both U.S. and transnational industry's exploitation of *maquiladora* workers in Mexico and Central America.[25] With the feminization and racialization of work that more and more relies on immigrant women and women in the neocolonized world, different strategies for organizing emerge; for example, the variety of strategies for addressing the international garment industry's abuse of immigrant women workers includes actions in the realms of both national and international law, consumer boycotts, and national and cross-border labor organizing modes.[26] These mixed strategies do not imply the dispersal of struggle, we contend, but they recognize a 'new' laboring subject impacted at once by axes of domination previously distinguished within an ideology of separate spheres.

It must be emphasized that the differentiated nature of globalization also produces contradictions that give rise to feminist activism in the site of 'culture,' precisely because the globalization of capitalism depends on the patriarchal cultural regulation of women, and because transnational capitalism reproduces those cultural regulations in the workplace itself. Maria Mies's discussion of the 'housewifization' of women's labor in the transnational economy, for example, demonstrates the ways in which global restructuring is both transgressive of and parasitic on the material culture of gendered 'public' and 'private' spheres as they have distributed and organized social relations.[27] A culturally practiced division of labor that directed women toward atomized, isolated 'domestic' work is extended and rearticulated in what Swasti Mitter has termed a newly 'spatialized' gendered division of labor that moves women from 'domestic' spaces to the international workspaces of casual, ill paid, insecure work.[28] As Aihwa Ong argues, the 'cultural' formation of women, which often appears to run counter to modernization, becomes a specific resource and mode of 'capitalist discipline' for forming workers who will fit into the current needs of transnational capital.[29] By the same token, women's resistance on the level of culture has ramifications for every other sphere of social life. [...]

## Cultural Politics as Alternative Rationalities

Transnational capitalism has reconfigured the mode of production in ways that are parasitic on the nation-state and its institutions, but rely on a disempowered citizenry; it continues to exploit labor, but redefines and differentiates who that labor is in terms of gender, race, and nation, and thus seeks to preclude the formation of a univocal international proletarian subject. It seeks to extend universal commodification, but by conditions that so impoverish the mass of the global workforce that unrestricted access to those commodities is limited to a few elites within a few nations. This unevenness in the processes of commodification generates contradictions across the globe: the deindustrialization of the United States and Europe and the shift of manufacturing operations to Asia and Latin America result not only in a relatively diminished base of consumers in relation to the expanded exploitation of labor power, but also in an intensification of the monopolization of resources by some and the immiseration of an ever increasing proportion of the world's population. Furthermore, as the base of consumers fails to expand in keeping with the expansion of the mode of production, the capitalist transformation of culture by way of universal commodification falls short of the exaggerated completion claimed by some theorists of globalization. Therefore, contradictions emerge along the fault lines between the exigencies of capitalist production and the cultural forms directly and indirectly engaged by those disciplines of production.

Within modernity, the sphere of culture is defined by its separation from the economic and political, within the general differentiation of spheres that constitute 'society.' Against this model, 'premodern cultures' are defined as lacking such differentiation or complexity. [...] Orientalist definitions of modernity suggest that modern societies 'have' culture, while nonmodern societies 'are' culture. Against either of these notions – culture specialized as the aesthetic, or culture defined in anthropological terms – we have sought to elaborate a conception of culture as emerging in the economic and political processes of modernization. This is not to say that culture is the space in which capital as commodification reigns; rather, as we have been arguing, it is the space through which both the reproduction of capitalist social relations and antagonism to that reproduction are articulated. If the tendency of transnational capitalism is to commodify everything and therefore to collapse the cultural into the economic, it is precisely where labor, differentiated rather than 'abstract,' is being commodified that the cultural becomes political again.[30] Insofar as transnational or neocolonial capitalism has shown itself able to proliferate through the seizure of multiple cultural forms, at the same time it brings to light more clearly than earlier capital regimes the volatility of the cultural space as a site of contradictions. To repeat our earlier formulation, culture becomes politically important where a cultural formation comes into contradiction with an economic or political logic that tries to refunction it for exploitation or domination.

One classic instance of such a contradiction between cultural formations and a dominant logic has been analyzed in relation to anticolonial nationalism that seeks to use 'traditional' cultural forms in a modernizing project. It is no less true for the political function of culture in postmodern capitalism. As we have seen, under colonialism the correspondence between the modern differentiation of spheres and the reproduction of capitalism did not hold. Postmodern capitalism, in new ways, dispenses with the differentiation of spheres as part of its logic of exploitation; rather than passing by way of a fully articulated civil society, postmodern transnational capitalism exacerbates and intensifies the unevennesses of various national states' transformations of colonial societies. In some cases, it passes by way of state-sponsored modernization, as in some authoritarian states in Asia and Latin America, where it produces the economic forms of capital without the corresponding civil society; the effects of these contradictions have already become manifest in the antagonism between 'indigenous' movements and the state, and in liberalizing movements. Where transnational capital comes into contradiction with the autonomy of the nation-state, national struggles against global capitalism, such as in Cuba, China, and Nicaragua, attest to the difficulties and successes of such struggles that often are forced by international pressures into their own forms of state modernization. But where transnational capital grasps hold of forms it might regard as 'backward,' brutally seizing on existent social forms rather than awaiting their transformation through the nation-state's modernizing projects, it precisely produces conditions for alternative practices that have not been homogenized by economic and political modernity within the postcolonial nation-state.

While it should be clear that we are making use of the Marxist concept of contradiction, we are revising it away from the classical notions of the primary antagonism between capital and labor and the emergence of proletarian consciousness in order to reconceptualize its sites and effects. Multiple sites of contradiction emerge where heterogeneous social formations that are the differential counter-formations of modernity are impacted by and brought into contradiction with postmodern modes of global capitalism. [...] These contradictions give rise to cross-race and cross-national projects, feminist movements, anticolonial struggles, and politicized cultural practices.

Linkages between such differentiated movements are of paramount importance. Transnational capitalism no longer needs to operate within the nation as a legal, political, cultural entity, but instead needs the nation as a means of regulating labor, materials, and capital. As we have argued, transnational capitalism exacerbates contradiction and antagonism between the 'local' or regional sites of exploitation and the nation-state. It is the differentiation of the mode of production that permits the exploitation of localities and makes them, rather than the national, the principal nodes of contradiction and therefore the sites of emergent political practices. Indeed, it may be that resistances are more and more articulated through linkings of localities that take place across and below the level of the nation-state, and not by way of a politics that moves at the level of the national or modern institutions. [...]

Antiracism, feminism, and anticolonialism must constantly address national economic exploitation and political disenfranchisements, and in doing so deploy countercultural forms and create alternative public spheres. *The Politics of Culture in the Shadow of Capital* emphasizes that the linking of such forms 'below' the level of the nation, and across national sites, has had a long and inadequately documented history, the recovery of which is equally if not more important in the present conjuncture.

[...] We hope not only to document but to stimulate the pursuit of further possibilities for linking through a differently conceived 'politics of culture.' In doing so, we argue that returning to political economy as the master narrative and the foundational rationale for 'political' transformation, by both left and conservative thinkers, is itself an aftereffect of modernity that would overlook the work of culture, regarding it as universally commodified. To relegate culture to commodification is to replay older arguments about the autonomy of the cultural sphere; neither conception of culture, as commodified or as aesthetic culture, admits culture's imbrication in political and economic relations. The essays here specify instead cultural formations that have emerged, over time, in contradiction to the modern division of spheres and its rationalizing modes; described here, culture involves simultaneously work, pleasure, consumption, spirituality, 'aesthetic' production, and reproduction, within an ongoing process of historical transformation in contradiction with colonial and neocolonial capitalism. Culture, understood in this way, constitutes a site in which the reproduction of contemporary capitalist social relations may be continually contested. In such cultural struggles, we find no less a redefinition of 'the political,' for in contradistinction to abstract modern divisions of society, the political has never been a discrete sphere of practice within the nation-state; [...] 'politics' must be grasped instead as always braided within 'culture' and cultural practices. The politics of culture exists as the very survival of alternative practices to those of globalized capital, the very survival of alternatives to the incessant violence of the new transnational order with its reconstituted patriarchies and racisms. Violence is manifest wherever capital generates its contradictions. The unimaginable violence of the past years – in Indonesia, Korea, Taiwan, the Philippines, South Africa, Chile, Guatemala, and Nicaragua, to name only a few spaces – is the sign not only of capital's now unrestricted brutality, but also of the insistence of alternatives and the refusal to submit to homogenization. Our moment is not one of fatalistic despair; faces turned toward the past, we do not seek to make whole what has been smashed, but to move athwart the storm into a future in which the debris is more than just a residue: it holds the alternative.

## Notes

1. David Harvey, *The Condition of Postmodernity: An Enquiry into the Origins of Cultural Change* (Oxford: Basil Blackwell, 1990); Fredric Jameson, *Postmodernism, or the Cultural Logic of Late Capitalism* (Durham: Duke University Press, 1992); Masao Miyoshi, 'A Borderless World? From Colonialism to Transnationalism and the Decline of the Nation-State,' *Critical Inquiry* 19 (summer 1993): 726–751.

2. This is, for example, Jameson's conclusion to *The Geopolitical Aesthetic* (Bloomington: Indiana University Press, 1992). He writes: 'those doctrines of reification and commodification which played a secondary role in the traditional or classical Marxian heritage, are now likely to come into their own and become the dominant instruments of analysis and

struggle ... today as never before, we must focus on a reification and a commodification that have become so universalized as to seem well-nigh natural and organic entities and forms' (212).

3. Arturo Escobar, *Encountering Development* (Princeton: Princeton University Press, 1995).

4. Etienne Balibar, Preface to *Race, Nation, Class: Ambiguous Identities* (London: Verso, 1991).

5. When they emphasize 'civil rights,' antiracist movements may be said to encounter some of the same kinds of contradictions that face the state-centered projects of bourgeois nationalism and liberal feminism. However, we argue that in relation to decolonization movements worldwide, antiracist anticolonial struggles have produced a profound crisis in the legitimation of the state and in its institutions themselves. As we go on to discuss in the nationalism section, antiracist anticolonialisms have gone beyond the notion of civil rights within the nation-state to a critique of the state form itself. Within the U.S. context, civil rights struggles for racialized peoples always had ramifications beyond enfranchisement within the nation-state; these struggles were met with state violence precisely because mobilizations by racialized peoples not only named the contradiction between the promise of political emancipation and the conditions of racialized segregation and economic exploitation, but they revealed the racial exclusions upon which U.S. liberal capitalism and U.S. neocolonialism are founded. Civil rights struggles in the United States have revealed that the granting of rights does not abolish the economic system that profits from racism; see Melvin L. Oliver and Thomas M. Shapiro, *Black Wealth, White Wealth: A New Perspective on Racial Inequality* (New York: Routledge, 1995); and Cheryl Harris, 'Whiteness as Property,' *Harvard Law Review* 106, no. 8 (June 1993): 1707–1791. On the extended critique waged by civil rights struggles, see Angela Davis in this volume; Michael Omi and Howard Winant, *Racial Formation in the United States, from the 1960s to the 1990s* (New York: Routledge, 1994); and Robert Allen, *Black Awakening in Capitalist America: An Analytic History* (Trenton, NJ: Africa World Press, 1990). For a social history of the civil rights movement and organizing tradition, see Charles M. Payne, *I've Got the Light of Freedom: The Organizing Tradition and the Mississippi Freedom Struggle* (Berkeley: University of California Press, 1995). At our present moment, it is an understanding of *race* not as a fixed singular essence, but as the locus in which economic, gender, sex, and race contradictions converge that organizes current struggles for immigrant rights, prisoner's rights, affirmative action, racialized women's labor, and AIDS and HIV patients in communities of color. Both the 'successes' and the 'failures' of struggles over the past thirty years demonstrate the degree to which *race* remains, after civil rights, the material trace of history, and thus the site of struggle through which contradictions are heightened and brought into relief.

6. This founding equivalence between the history of a people and the history of its political institutions is common to nineteenth-century thinkers as various as Coleridge in England, Fichte in Germany, Michelet and Renan in France, and Mazzini in Italy.

7. Akhil Gupta and James Ferguson, 'Beyond "Culture": Space, Identity, and the Politics of Difference,' *Cultural Anthropology* 7, no. 1 (February 1992): 6–22.

8. Cited in Partha Chatterjee, *Nationalist Thought and the Colonial World: A Derivative Discourse?* (Minneapolis: University of Minnesota Press, 1993), 3. _

9. Frantz Fanon, *The Wretched of the Earth*, trans. Constance Farrington (New York: Grove Press, 1968); Amílcar Cabral, *Unity and Struggle: Speeches and Writings of Amílcar Cabral*, trans. Michael Wolfers (New York: Monthly Review Press, 1979). See also Bipan Chandra, 'Colonialism, Stages of Colonialism and the Colonial State,' *Journal of Contemporary Asia* 10, no. 3 (1980): 272–285; Benedict Anderson, *Imagined Communities* (London: Verso, 1991).

10. Bipan Chandra, 'Colonialism, Stages of Colonialism and the Colonial State,' *Journal of Contemporary Asia* 10, no. 3 (1980): 272–285.

11. See Donald Lowe, *The Function of 'China' in Marx, Lenin, and Mao* (Berkeley: University of California Press, 1966).

12. Dipesh Chakrabarty, *Rethinking Working-Class History: Bengal 1890–1940* (Princeton: Princeton University Press, 1989).

13. Aihwa Ong, *Spirits of Resistance and Capitalist Discipline: Factory Women in Malaysia* (Albany: State University of New York Press, 1987).

14. Chandra, 'Colonialism, Stages of Colonialism and the Colonial State.'

15. Louis Althusser and Etienne Balibar, 'On the Basic Concepts of Historical Materialism,' in *Reading Capital* (London: Verso, 1968).

16. Aihwa Ong, *Spirits of Resistance and Capitalist Discipline;* Swasti Mitter, *Common Fate, Common Bond: Women in the Global Economy* (London: Pluto, 1986); Maria Mies, *Patriarchy and Accumulation on a World Scale: Women in the International Division of Labor* (London: Zed Press, 1986).

17. As we have suggested concerning 'Western Marxism,' it is the case for 'Western feminism' that its existence is not limited to the geographical West. See Chandra Talpade Mohanty, 'Under Western Eyes: Feminist Scholarship and Colonialist Discourse,' in *Third World Women and the Politics of Feminism*, ed. Chandra Talpade Mohanty, Ann Russo, and Lourdes Torres (Bloomington: Indiana University Press, 1991), 52. For discussions of white liberal feminism and antiracist feminism in the United States, see Angela Davis, *Women, Race, and Class* (New York: Random House, 1981); and Chela Sandoval, 'U.S. Third World Feminism: The Theory and Method of Oppositional Consciousness in the Postmodern World,' *Genders* 10 (spring 1991): 1–24.

18. Anglo-American and European feminist interrogations of 'woman' include Parveen Adams and Elizabeth Cowie, *The Woman in Question* (Cambridge, MA: MIT Press, 1990); Donna Haraway, *Simians, Cyborgs, and Women* (New York: Routledge, 1991); and Judith Butler, *Bodies That Matter: On the Discursive Limits of Sex* (New York: Routledge, 1993).

19. For a greater elaboration of this argument, see Deniz Kandiyoti, 'Identity and Its Discontents,' in *Colonial Discourse and Post-Colonial Theory: A Reader,* ed. Patrick Williams and Laura Chrisman (New York: Columbia University Press, 1994).

20. For accounts of women's roles in anticolonial political and labor struggles, see Kumari Jayawardena, *Feminism and Nationalism in the Third World* (London: Zed Books, 1986); and Nanneke Redclift and M. Thea Sinclair, eds., *Working Women: International Perspectives on Labour and Gender Ideology* (London: Routledge, 1991). On women's survival within formal and informal economies, see Homa Hoodfar, *Between Marriage and the Market: Intimate Politics and Survival in Cairo* (Berkeley: University of California Press, 1997).

On women's activities in labor struggles in the United States, see for example Ruth Milkman, *Gender at Work: The Dynamics of Job Segregation by Sex during World War II* (Urbana: University of Illinois Press, 1987); Jacqueline Jones, *Labor of Love, Labor of Sorrow: Black Women, Work, and the Family from Slavery to the Present* (New York: Basic Books, 1985); Vicki Ruiz, *Cannery Women, Cannery Lives: Mexican Women, Unionization, and the California Food Processing Industry, 1930–1950* (Albuquerque: University of New Mexico, 1987).

Our consideration of non-Western and antiracist feminism as the site for the convergence of feminist, labor, anticolonial, and antiracist work is sympathetically allied with a variety of feminist projects represented by, for example, Kumkum Sangari and Sudesh Vaid, eds., *Recasting Women: Essays in Indian Colonial History* (New Brunswick, NJ: Rutgers University Press, 1990); Mohanty, Russo, and Torres, eds., *Third World Women and the Politics of Feminism;* Inderpal Grewal and Caren Kaplan, eds., *Scattered Hegemonies: Postmodernity and Transnational Feminist Practices* (Minneapolis: University of Minnesota, 1994); and M. Jacqui Alexander and Chandra Talpade Mohanty, eds., *Feminist Genealogies, Colonial Legacies, Democratic Futures* (New York: Routledge, 1996).

21. Kapil Kumar's essay 'Rural Women in Oudh 1917–1947: Baba Ram Chandra and the Women's Question' in Sangari and Vaid, *Recasting women,* is exemplary in this respect. Rather than focusing on the punctual moment of a specific peasant revolt in Oudh, or on the genderless 'peasant' subject, the essay not only explores the roles of women in the

revolt, but suggests how the refiguration of the cultural forms of womanhood in relation to particular economic and social issues necessitates a rethinking of the nature, temporality, and periodization of the struggle.

22. Sangari and Vaid, *Recasting Women,* 3.

23. Radha Radhakrishnan, 'Nationalism, Gender and the Narrative of Identity,' in *Nationalisms and Sexualities,* ed. Andrew Parker et al. (New York: Routledge, 1992.), 81.

24. Committee for Asian Women, *Many Paths, One Goal: Organizing Women Workers in Asia* (Hong Kong: CAW, 1991); June Nash and Maria Patricia Fernandez-Kelly, eds., *Women in the International Division of Labor* (Albany: State University of New York Press, 1983); Vicki Ruiz and Susan Tiano, eds., *Women on the U.S.-Mexican Border* (Boston: Allen & Unwin, 1987); Paul Ong, Edna Bonacich, and Lucie Cheng, eds., *New Asian Immigration in Los Angeles and Global Restructuring* (Philadelphia: Temple University Press, 1994); Richard P. Appelbaum, 'Multiculturalism and Flexibility: Some New Directions in Global Capitalism,' in *Mapping Multiculturalism,* ed. Avery Gordon and Christopher Newfield (Minneapolis: University of Minnesota, 1996).

25. See Kyungwon Hong and Mary Tong, 'Aguirre v. AUG: A Case Study,' in *Multinational Human Resource Management: Cases and Exercises,* ed. P.C. Smith (Tulsa, OK: Dame Publishing Company, forthcoming).

26. See Laura Ho, Catherine Powell, and Leti Volpp, '(Dis)Assembling Rights of Women Workers along the Global Assemblyline: Human Rights and the Garment Industry,' *Harvard Civil Rights–Civil Liberties Law Review* 31, no. 2 (summer 1996): 383–414.

27. Mies, *Patriarchy and Accumulation on a World Scale.*

28. Mitter, *Common Fate, Common Bond.*

29. See also Aihwa Ong's study of Malaysian factory women's practices, *Spirits of Resistance and Capitalist Discipline,*

30. Marx theorized that it is the tendency of capital to use 'abstract labor,' or labor as 'use value' unencumbered by specific human qualities. In the *Grundrisse,* Marx describes abstract labor: 'as *the* use value which confronts money posited as capital, labour is not this or another labour, but *labour pure and simple,* abstract labour; absolutely indifferent to its particular specificity. ... but since capital *as such* is indifferent to every particularity of its substance, and exists not only as the totality of the same but also as the abstraction from all its particularities, the labour which confronts it likewise subjectively has the same totality and abstraction in itself' (Karl Marx, *Grundrisse: Foundations of the Critique of Political Economy [rough draft],* trans. Martin Nicolaus [Harmondsworth: Penguin, 1993], 296). However, in most capitalist situations, capital lays hold of labor that is precisely not abstract but differentiated by race, gender, and nationality. In the development of racialized U.S. capitalism, in colonial capitalism, and now in transnational capitalism, it is through differentiating, rather than homogenizing, labor forces that capital expands and profits. For further discussion of Marx's concepts of 'abstract' and 'real' labor, see Dipesh Chakrabarty's 'The Time of History and the Times of Gods' in this volume; and Lisa Lowe, *Immigrant Acts: On Asian American Cultural Politics* (Durham: Duke University Press, 1996), chap. 1

Our argument throughout this introduction, and that of the papers in this volume, is that within the logic of capital, neither the economic nor the political subject have ever emerged as pure abstractions. To grasp the implications of this demands a rethinking of Marxism, right at the core of the labor theory of value, and prompts a new understanding of the continual production of cultural differences in the history of modernity. Culture is, over and again, the field on which economic and political contradictions are articulated.

# PART THREE

# MARKETING:

## SOCIO-ECONOMIC CONSIDERATIONS OF POPULAR CULTURE

'Obey your thirst'. Sprite issues its well-known marketing slogan as a no-nonsense command. The television commercials that present this command ask their viewers to see beyond celebrity endorsements for Sprite and to 'obey' not the corporate hand behind the image, but their own instincts and judgment. Thirst. Easily and satisfactorily quenched by sugary-water Coca-Cola products. Obeisance is positioned within recognizable codes of hip-hop culture: dance, style, music, sports, and young African-American and Latino consumers happily endorsing Sprite as a 'real' and 'authentic' soft-drink for today's street stylist. This enduring ad and its plundering of popular culture to promote its products is neither alone in its targeting of niche lifestyles for marketing purposes, nor an isolated corporation dependent upon cultural capital to promote its products for a global mass market. What it brings to light, and the significance of which cannot be overstated, is the complicated energies that corporations employ to produce meaning through popular culture. Cultural theorists have long debated the tension between commodification and agency. However, their interventions have frequently taken place at the level of abstraction. Terms like 'culture industry' and 'mass culture' have tended to reference the products of such industries rather than the specific industries themselves. The essays in this section effect an essential reorientation toward analysis of specific corporate practices to produce critical perspectives on the complex and always negotiated character of popular culture as both about commodification *and* the indispensability of social actors.

The study of fashion in popular culture is often preoccupied with how clothing, hairstyles, make-up, and accessories, are brought into systems of meanings generated through use and reappropriation. Companies and globally recognized brands such as Nike, Puma, Adidas, Levi-Strauss, Abercrombie and Fitch, and the Gap, as well as the more 'up-scale' yet mass-designed styles introduced into the marketplace by designers like Ralph Lauren, Tommy Hilfiger, Hugo Boss, and their manufacturing practices within global capitalism cannot go unaddressed in the study of popular culture. Having appeared in *No Sweat: Fashion, Free Trade, and the Rights of Garment Workers* (1997), a much-needed collection on garment workers and the fashion industry, Paul Smith's **'Tommy Hilfiger in the Age of Mass Customization'** examines new marketing 'relationships' being established through the process of 'mass customization'. Tommy Hilfiger's clothing company is a fascinating case study as its marketing campaigns force us to consider how ideas of race (white 'preppy' and African-American hip hop), gender (the invention of 'Tommy Girl'), and nation (the American flag as brand identity) are intricately woven into both cultural and economic processes.

Setting out to study the difficult question of whether or not a genuine black culture exists within the USA, sociologist Ellis Cashmore's *The Black Culture Industry* (1997) considers concepts such as 'black authenticity' and 'black ownership' within practices of black popular culture and the formation of a black culture industry. The book carefully works its academic address through a skeptical engagement with popular music culture and the industry of popular music production via attention to the stardom of Michael Jackson, Prince's conflicted relationship to Warner Brothers, and in-depth consideration of record labels ranging from Berry Gordy's Motown to Death Row Records. Excerpted here is the final chapter, **'America's Paradox'**, a reflection on the conditionality of black artists and entrepreneurs' positions with mainstream culture: 'White culture has enforced a definition of its normality by admitting only black interlopers who lived up or down to its images: others, who possessed exotic or peculiar gifts but at a cost to their full humanity.'

Barbie is many things: an icon the world over, a plastic toy that commands its own aisle in US toy stores, an object that sparks intense debates over representation and gender. Academics, such as Erica Rand, Lynn Spigel, Frances Negrón-Muntaner, and Ann Ducille, have constructed critiques of Barbie from a number of critical positions that implicate the doll into debates centered on feminism, queer theory, ethnicity, nation, and race. Here, as Inderpal Grewal's **'Traveling Barbie: Indian Transnationality and New Consumer Subjects'** (1999) makes possible, Barbie is studied as a global commodity that perpetuates ideas of gender, class, and capitalism across national boundaries. Grewal, whose books include *Scattered Hegemonies: Postmodernity and Transnational Feminist Practices* (edited with Caren Kaplan, Minneapolis, MN: University of Minnesota Press, 1994) and *Home and Harem: Nation, Gender, Empire, and the Cultures of Travel* (Durham, NC: Duke University Press, 1996), discusses the marketing of Barbie in India and the formation of new consumer subjects: 'In a context of localization through transnational formations, it is important to note that Barbie in a sari being sold in India is not an Indian or South Asian Barbie. She is what Mattel calls the traditional Barbie, a white, American Barbie, but one who travels; she has, in one version, blond hair, the standard face, the ideal female Euro-American body, a shiny sari, and a red *bindi* on her forehead.'

Disney, like Mattel's Barbie, produces globally recognized products, and its well-known cast of characters are perhaps the most visible brands around the globe. At the same time, the Disney Corporation is also a place of employment for thousands. 'The Disney name is an attraction for potential employees, who may have dreamed all their lives about working at the studio or one of the theme parks. Still, the allure of the Magic Kingdom can be deceptive.' In **'Corporate Disney in Action'**, excerpted from her book *Understanding Disney: The Manufacture of Fantasy* (2001), Janet Wasko dissolves the 'magic' of Disney in her study of the Disney corporation and its international business practices. Wasko's tour behind the mouse's façade reveals a lobbying campaign that helped to pass the Copyright Extension Act of 1998, as well as the use of subcontracted animation work, a highly regulated and controlled labor force, and a below average pay scale for its theme park employees. What Wasko's work indicates is that there is no easy way to settle the contradiction between idealizations of popular culture as pleasure, fantasy, and entertainment, and the decidedly profit-driven exploits through which it is frequently generated.

Henry Yu, author of *Thinking Oriental: Migration, Contact and Exoticism in Modern America* (Oxford: Oxford University Press, 2002), explores the limitations as well as the promise of post-nationalist American studies for generating engaged cultural criticism that takes into account the transnational dimension of labor and markets. Specifically, Yu considers the international marketing of multiculturalism through the traditionally white world of professional golf in **'How Tiger Woods Lost His Stripes: Post-Nationalist American Studies as a History of Race, Migration, and the Commodification of Culture'** from John Carlos Rowe (ed.) (2000) *Postnationalist American Studies.* Berkeley, CA: University of California Press. A key proposition of the essay is that Woods' commercial debut presents a means of 'examining how race, ethnicity, and the mass market in the United States can no longer be understood (and perhaps were never properly understood) without the context of global capitalism that frames definitions of cultural and national difference', and this is precisely what Yu goes on to explore through close attention to how Woods' diverse ethnic and racial designations have figured in public representations of his celebrity both in the USA and abroad. The concept of culture figures largely in this analysis, functioning as both a theory and an historical and social concept that connects with the impact of the state, racial experience and population migration. On the basis of this configuration, Yu asserts that 'Tiger Woods' story exemplifies the crossroads between the commercialization of sport in the United States and the production of racial and cultural difference'; within this story multicultural narratives serve as shorthand histories for international migration and the 'perceived international appeal of Tiger's mixed ethnicity'.

# Play List

Bank, Jack (1996) *Monopoly Television: MTV's Quest to Control the Music.* Boulder, CO: Westview Press.

Boyd, Todd (2003) *Young Black Rich and Famous: The Rise of the NBA, The Hip Hop Invasion and the Transformation of American Culture.* New York: Doubleday.

Dávila, Arelene (2001) *Latinos INC.:The Marketing and Making of a People.* Berkeley, CA: University of California Press.

Davis, Susan G. (1997) *Spectacular Nature: Corporate Culture and the Sea World Experience.* Berkeley, CA: University of California Press.

Goodman, Barak (dir.) (2001) *Merchants of Cool.* Videocassette. PBS Frontline.

Hendershot, Heather (1998) *Saturday Morning Censors: Television Regulation before the V-Chip.* Durham, NC: Duke University Press.

Jameson, Fredric and Miyoshi, Masao (eds) (1998) *Cultures Of Globalization.* Durham, NC: Duke University Press.

Kempadoo, Kamala and Doezema, Jo (eds) (1998) *Global Sex Workers: Rights, Resistance, And Redefinitions.* New York: Routledge.

Lee, Spike (dir.) (2000) *Bamboozled.* DVD. New Line Entertainment.

Lessig, Lawrence (2004) *Free Culture: How Big Media Uses Technology and the Law to Lock Down Culture and Control Creativity.* New York: Penguin Books .

Martin, Randy and Miller, Toby (eds) (1999) *Sportcult.* Minneapolis, MN: University of Minnesota Press.

Miller, Toby, Govil, Nitlin, McMurria, John, and Maxwell, Richard (eds) (2001) *Global Hollywood.* London: British Film Institute.

Negus, Keith (1999) *Music Genres and Corporate Cultures.* London: Routledge.

Project on Disney (1995) *Inside the Mouse: Work and Play at Disney World.* Durham, NC: Duke University Press.

Quart, Alissa (2003) *Branded: The Buying and Selling of Teenagers.* Cambridge, MA: Perseus Publishing.

Rand, Erica (1995) *Barbie's Queer Accessories.* Durham, NC: Duke University Press.

Rhines, Jesse Algeron (1996) *Black Film/White Money.* New Brunswick, NJ: Rutgers University Press.

Ross, Andrew (ed.) (1997) *No Sweat: Fashion, Free Trade, and the Rights of Garment Workers.* New York: Verso.

Savidge, Lee and Roberts, Darryl (dirs) (2001) *Welcome to Death Row.* DVD. Xenon Studios.

Shohat, Ella (2004) "Corruption in Corporate Culture" Themed Issue. *Social Text,* 77.

Simmons, Russell (2001) *Life and Def: Sex, Drugs, Money, and God.* New York: Crown Publishers Group.

Steinberg, Shirley R. and Kincheloe, Joe L. (eds) (1997) *Kinderculture: The Corporate Construction of Childhood.* Boulder, Co: Westview Press.

Tate, Greg (ed.) (2003) *Everything But The Burden: What White* People *Are Taking From Black Culture.* New York: Harlem Moon.

Wagnleitner, Reinhold and May, Elaine Tyler (eds) (2000) *'Here, There and Everywhere': The Foreign Politics of American Popular Culture.* Hanover, CT: University Press of New England.

Wasko, Janet (1994) *Hollywood in the Information Age: Beyond the Silver Screen.* Cambridge: Polity Press.

Weitzer, Ronald (ed.) (1999) *Sex for Sale: Prostitution, Pornography, and the Sex Industry.* New York: Routledge.

# Chapter 14

# Paul Smith

## Tommy Hilfiger in the Age of Mass Customization

The June 1995 issue of *Bobbin*, a garment industry trade journal, contained interviews with a number of high-ranking executives from the top forty apparel companies in the U.S. Each was asked to make some predictions about the industry and the challenges facing it in the run-up to the millennium. Of the primary concerns these industry leaders expressed, the first related to the organization of labor: they were clear about the need for continued downsizing, particularly within the domestic side of manufacturing. The second related to product development – they saw the need, in essence, to speed up the industry's process of product design, manufacture, and distribution in order to satisfy the ever changing and accelerating demands of retail outlets and their customers.[1]

These two areas of concern reflect the bipolar nature of the industry in the 1990s and in the era of the so-called globalization of economic processes. On the one hand, the 'global' economy, dominated by Northern nations, is in the process of shifting the place of production to the South or the Third World, with the aim of reducing the costs of variable capital; in other words, core labor is being located on the periphery. On the other hand, or simultaneously, the place of consumption – and, of course, capital concentration – becomes ever more centralized in the North itself, opening up new channels of product distribution, marketing, and retailing.

In terms of the disposition of world labor power, then, this is a moment of redefinition, or of the search for a renewed vitality in capitalist rates of profit, and it is coincident with the tendency to abandon the old liberal productivist economic order and move toward the ideal, or the fantasy, of global capitalism. For the

From: *No Sweat: Fashion, Free Trade, and the Rights of Garment Workers*. Ed. Andrew Ross. New York: Verso, 1997.

Northern 'developed' nations, this shift has already subvented the rapid expansion and intensification of the means of consumption in the 1980s and '90s, provoking cultural changes and challenges as well as political and economic ones. The economic shape of the last two decades, especially here in the U.S., has been relatively clear in that respect: a downward turn in productive capital and a rise in the importance of financial capital have had the cultural effect of installing what can only be called a revolution in consumerism. For the garment industry, this revolution has had special relevance. The industry has responded by developing mass designer fashion, extending and expanding the role of mass-produced clothing, affecting all kinds of cultural arenas and encouraging the construction of cultural identities by way of apparel choices. However, it is open to question whether the industry is in fact responding to cultural demand or whether it is producing that demand as a way of itself responding to the changing conditions of global capitalism. Much of the pressure on apparel companies to refunction their production, to contract it out and offshore it, or simply to sweat it in the domestic workplace, derives from a perceived functioning of the domestic market which is said to be more highly competitive than ever and to be driven by the demands of retail companies – especially department stores – which are themselves responding to straitened domestic circumstances.

Apparel manufacturers have argued that this cranking up is driven by retailers alone. The fact that the tendency is equally bound up with the manufacturers' own continual offshoring of labor, in response to globalization trends, is too often downplayed. Northern apparel producers have to compete with Southern labor, but they can scarcely do so in terms of simple cost – the social conditions and the consumerist nature of Northern societies cannot countenance a drop in wages sufficient to compete. Thus, other modes or areas of competitive advantage have to be found, and these tend to concentrate around the acceleration of sales and, therefore, the speeding up of product development and change. [...] The possibility of such accelerated turnaround and delivery, provoked by the international labor conditions of the industry, has its effect then in the consumer markets of the North. The retail industry and the apparel companies themselves adjust to this acceleration with speedier fashion cycles and merchandise availability. In any case, apparel companies find themselves in a position where they have to create a demand for the ever more transient commodities in the retail space.

The companies themselves call this process 'mass customization,' according to a recent lengthy survey of industry practice in the *Daily News Record*.[2] Mass customization entails a number of components that are, if not relatively new for the industry, at least of increasingly central importance. The imperatives of mass customization boil down to three essentials: greater product variety in stores, higher turnover, and lower and better managed inventories. Success in each area depends upon increased cooperation between apparel companies and their retailing outlets. As one executive notes, 'Retail partnership is more critical than ever before. We have to share information about the consumer.' Such sharing is by now heavily dependent on the use of new information technologies, or what the industry calls 'data mining.' 'We're heavily into Electronic Data Interchange,' another executive explains. EDI helps increase the speed and flexibility of merchandise sourcing, the flow and distribution of goods, and their replenishment and inventorization. In general the industry is now seeking to cut down the time between retailers' orders and warehouse shipment. Some manufacturers now accelerate these processes even more by shipping pre-priced goods, which can be put on display with minimal checking by in-store workers.

EDI has a second essential function, that of enabling research into the habits of consumers – both groups and individuals. One company claims that, as a result of data mining, 'On a daily basis, we know 75 percent of what is sold, down to the lot and size.' Such statistics are used to 'anticipate' consumer trends and to fine-tune inventory control, but also to contribute to what the industry euphemistically calls 'consumer communications,' a term that exceeds the traditional sense of advertising. Companies now expect to engage in 'an ongoing dialog with the consumer' – a 'dialog' encouraged by means of a whole array of mechanisms, from 800 phonelines, Internet communications and Web sites, to in-store surveys and special event sponsorship (both in and out of stores), in addition to the more familiar use of visual and print media advertising.

Tommy Hilfiger's clothing company, TOM Inc., has been among the leading exponents in this intensified process of mass customization over the last few years. Indeed, Hilfiger clothing can be seen as an extreme case of how the idea of mass designer fashion operates. Mass designer fashion is a specific formation within the industry; it is not equivalent to traditional haute couture [...]. Nor is mass designer fashion equivalent to standard garment production [...]. Mass designer fashion is that peculiar formation which occurs within this nexus of the globalizing economy and the concomitant expansion of the means of consumption. Almost by definition it demands the capture of ever wider segments of the mass market at the same time as it needs to maintain familiar standards of product differentiation between brands, and offer frequent variation. Thus Hilfiger's relative importance and visibility in this context is in part a result of an ongoing strategy which has put his company in a position to cover just about all segments of the clothing market, but which also marks the products as identifiable and unique (the familiar Hilfiger logo and red-white-and-blue designs), offering appreciably variable 'looks' or themes from season to season and year to year. While older companies like Levi Strauss, Timberland, or even Ralph Lauren have been slow in entering the mass designer fashion stakes – some being particularly wary of attempting to enter ethnically or racially identified areas of consumer culture – and while many other companies have been content with their long established market niches and hierarchies of market segmentation, the story of Hilfiger's company is just the opposite.

Beginning with a line of preppie-looking, clean-cut, and conservative sportswear [...] Hilfiger set out in the early 1990s to compete against department store staple lines like Ralph Lauren and Liz Claiborne with essentially Young Republican clothing. In the course of only a few years, this basically khaki, crew, and button-down WASP style, while remaining a constant theme in Hilfiger collections, has been submitted to variations which were intended to bring the product closer to hip hop style: bolder colors, bigger and baggier styles, more hoods and cords, and more prominence for logos and the Hilfiger name. These variations on a house-in-the-Hamptons theme opened up the doorway to black consumers, and Hilfiger's status is often closely linked to his popularity among African Americans. But at the same time, that market has clearly been only one focus for Hilfiger's ambitions, set on maintaining and expanding markets among nonblack consumers, and continually multiplying the range of products offered. In addition to hip hop styles, Hilfiger now sells golf wear, casual sportswear, jeans, sleepwear, underwear, spectacles, fragrances, and even telephone beepers. Tommy has recently moved into women's wear, and offers a women's cologne to go with the popular men's line. [...]

Hilfiger's success has been quite astounding since the initial public offering of TOM in 1992. The company now has over 850 in-store department store sales points in the U.S. In addition, there are now almost fifty Hilfiger specialty stores across the country, a figure that has almost doubled in the course of two years. [...] The sound financial health of the company ensures its regular appearance on stockbrokers' to-buy lists, even though share prices keep rising. Early in 1995, the small consortium of TOM's original investors – which had bought the company from Mohan Murjani in the late 1980s – sold their remaining TOM stock for over $50 million, after a year in which the value of the stock had increased by 106 percent. Hilfiger himself was one of this small group, of course, and after his profit-taking he remained as an employee of the company, drawing more than $6 million a year in salary.

The economic success of TOM is explicable largely because the company has led the way in many aspects of mass customization. [...] TOM's corporate strategies have been ahead of those of many of its competitors, stressing the acceleration of product delivery, new forms of retailing partnership, innovative EDI usage for inventories and customer tracking, and of course, the speedy and timely introduction of new lines and redesigned goods, assuring consumers a wide range of product choices [...].

TOM has been especially willing – again, leading the field – to engage in what is now the standard industry practice of licensing. TOM has licensing agreements with some of the world's major clothing companies. [...] While licensing agreements probably have little impact on consumer consciousness, one advantage they have for a company like TOM is that they offer the borrowed cachet of known and respected manufacturers. This is all-important in negotiating sales points with department stores and generally in testifying to the quality of TOM products. [...] Added to TOM's strategies for speeding up product design, delivery, and turnover, licensing helps ensure access to what is still the principal channel for clothing sales in the U.S., where 65 percent of all clothing is sold by only thirty-five companies, the majority of which are chain retailers with department stores in malls and urban spaces all across the country.

One reason why the department stores are crucial for mass designer fashion is that many of them are located in the very malls where teenagers proverbially hang out. But perhaps a more important reason is that most big department stores offer their own credit cards which are relatively easy to obtain even if the consumer has low income or a bad credit rating. The industry standard is to offer such cards on the spot with only minimal credit checking and with an initial credit line [...] that would encourage the purchase of, say, one complete outfit which would then be paid off over a period of about a year. Naturally, consumers pay heavily for this privilege, since interest rates on department store cards are typically about 21 percent per annum, almost 5 percent higher than the average U.S. credit card rate. However, this cost does not seem to deter those who can access these credit lines. In both Britain and the U.S., clothing purchases constitute a huge part of consumer credit spending. [...]

Where the nexus of consumer-retailer-manufacturer is always most apparent, however, is in the area of advertising. Although TOM [...] has not explored the area of 'consumer communications' quite so thoroughly as companies like Levi Strauss or retailers like Carson Pirie Scott, Hilfiger's exploitation of advertising media has been both thorough and path-breaking. Perhaps the most prominent feature of Hilfiger's strategy in this realm has been the use of high-visibility consumers. In a way that has still not been copied by many other apparel companies [...], Hilfiger has always ensured that his clothing is found on celebrity bodies. In the last few years his clothing has been publicly displayed by sports figures like Don Nelson, coach of the New York Knicks, popular musicians such as Michael Jackson and the women of TLC, and by black male models like Tyson Beckford. In a series of 1994 spots on the music cable channel, VH1, Hilfiger tried to keep tabs on a more mainstream audience too, featuring performers like Tori Amos and Phil Collins. Any of these celebrities is, of course, a trendsetter, whose mostly urban image is intended to then become desirable in the shopping meccas of suburban malls.

Most important, Hilfiger clothes have been sported by a whole succession of African-American rap musicians. The story of Hilfiger seeing Grand Puba in the street wearing his clothes and inviting him to wear Hilfiger in public appearances is perhaps apocryphal, but it does speak to the general strategy that Hilfiger has adopted in relation to garnering a huge clientele among African Americans. Frequently donated Hilfiger outfits for use in performances and music videos, rappers have functioned as conduits of approval and authorization – authenticity, perhaps – for this white business attempting to sell what are essentially white styles to black consumers. In that sense, Hilfiger has used prominent African Americans in ways that, while they are often less formalized and contractual than the relationship between, say, Nike and Michael Jordan or PepsiCo and Michael Jackson, essentially serve the same purpose.

A certain rank of black sportspeople and entertainment figures (usually men) act as what I call a 'regulatory elite' in U.S. black culture. These are people who, earning millions of dollars a year in the face of the chronic and systematic immiseration and devastation of black communities in the U.S., are elevated to the status of cultural icons and are taken to bear virtually the whole burden of representing blackness in the culture. Even though the bill for the rewards collected by this regulatory elite are footed by predominantly white capital, their cultural significance stems from being venerated as bearers of black identity [...].

And yet it is no simple matter in U.S. culture to criticize this black regulatory elite, since it carries such a burden of African-American identity. It does, of course, become easier to criticize when someone so prominent as Michael Jordan shrugs off the ethical and political problems in his sponsorship relation with Nike and its Third World labor practices. Called to answer for the contradiction of his position, Jordan simply suggested that he could trust Nike 'to do the right thing.'[3] But for the most part, and as Jordan in fact demonstrates, the system does its work, and the African-American stars can count on there being little concern about the cultural and financial gap between them and the African Americans who are called upon to be their loyal and admiring audience.

For Hilfiger's company, the deployment of rappers like Grand Puba and Snoop Doggy Dogg in extended 'consumer communications' has constituted a crucial part of the process of mass customization and has enabled a deliberate and thoroughgoing entry into the black youth market. It is, however, just one such component, and its efficacy depends absolutely on Hilfiger's coordinated effort in other areas of mass customization. The effectiveness of TOM's assault on this particular segment of the market is a function of the successful implementation of industry-wide strategies which have to be seen in conjunction with capital's tendency to outsource labor, to cut the costs of variable capital, and to expand the means of consumption in Northern markets. According to TOM's 1995 annual report, the five places where most Hilfiger clothing is made are Hong Kong, Sri Lanka, Macao, Indonesia, and Montebello, California. In that light, when Hilfiger gives away clothes to rappers, or establishes a loose professional alliance with African Americans like Def Jam boss Russell Simmons (also the owner of Phat Farm clothing company), or hires Kidada Jones (daughter of record tycoon Quincey Jones) to appear in his ads, these are in a sense epiphenomenal activities. What is crucial is the political and economic circuits in which they have their effects. Similarly, when black kids wear TOM merchandise, adopting the clothes and accessories and the Tommy logo as signs not just of fashionability but even of racial authenticity, they are doing more than just establishing a cultural identity and communality. Equally, they are placing themselves in a particular relation to political-economic circuits for which the possibility of their consuming in this way is one of capitalism's central desiderata or imperatives at this juncture when capital is dreaming of globalizing itself.

Of course, not all of Hilfiger's desired consumer audience and clientele is necessarily content with the spectacle of so many black males devotedly sporting Hilfiger clothing and willy-nilly directing African-American dollars into the Hilfiger coffers. One of the most vibrant forums on the Internet where the issues of fashion consumption are discussed is the 'chat-room' of Streetsound,[4] a wildly energetic and mind-boggling torrent of opinion, most of which seems to be submitted by African-American men. Hilfiger's clothing and the operations of his company are perennial topics – a testament in itself to the central role his fashions play right now in black culture. But even though Hilfiger merchandise appears to enjoy support and patronage in towns from coast to coast, there are some dissenting voices.

The most common opposition to Hilfiger on this site appears to be an objection to the very principle of black patronage of white business. One such posting will give the flavor of many similar ones:

> Y'all are nothing but Tommy's wench. Some of you do not even have enough money to support the people who put on the jams (the place where you show how real you are and get your new bitch). Yet you spend your last fucking dollar to support some yout' in New York who doesn't give a fuck about give a flying fuck about you. Y'all are real stupid!!!

Such objections are both common and powerful – especially when seen as versions of how black identity might be safeguarded while rejecting the regulatory means put into place by white capitalism, and they echo longstanding debates within black culture. But obviously, they fall short of making connections between cultural and economic processes in the era of global capitalism and the age of mass customization.

This can be seen in an even starker light if we consider the nature of many of the advertisements for Hilfiger merchandise that appear in popular magazines. The principal motif in nearly all of them is the American flag. For instance, in Hilfiger's 1996 campaign for his new line of jeans, the American flag is spread out behind the figure of Kidada Jones, or is apparently the pillow for Ivanka Trump's pouting face. The American theme is even more overt – in the sense that it is verbal as much as visual – in ads for Hilfiger fragrances. The men's fragrance, Tommy, is now advertised under the slogan, 'the real american fragrance' [...], while the ads for the women's perfume, Tommy Girl, call it 'a declaration of independence.'

In the double context of, on the one hand, increasingly internationalized economic processes (where core labor is zoned to the periphery), and on the other hand, rampant mass customization (with its production of regulated subcultural identities in the North), TOM's use of this American-national motif is utterly symptomatic. The display of the U.S. flag and the appeal to American identity obscure both the international and the subnational processes that are at stake in the political-economic and cultural formations of this our new world order. Another way of putting this is to say that the U.S. national motif precisely names the power which presides over a division between the zoned labor of the South and massified consumption in the North and confirms that division as an opposition of interests.

These U.S. nationalist emblems in TOM do have the unintended consequence of highlighting some of the complexities and difficult issues that are involved in thinking through the politics of the present situation. What we might call 'production activists' in the North sometimes have a limited view of the way labor issues relate to the processes of consumption in the North, and often seem reluctant to address the fact that capitalism deliberately sets off the Northern consumer's 'right' to forge cultural identity through consumption against the economic and social rights of core labor. But it is in everyone's interest to challenge such an imposed opposition between the interests of core labor and the interests of massified consumers.

There are, that is, potential benefits in stressing the fact that international labor issues are inextricably tied to the current expansion of the means of consumption in the North. A sharper understanding of the cultural consequences of mass customization might allow production activists to more effectively address those cultural constituencies whose interests are routinely represented as disjunct from the interests of laborers in the periphery. By the same token, cultural activists and organizers, especially within minority communities in the North, might perhaps be able to intensify their opposition to the international aspect of economic processes in the recognition that these are what underpin – indeed, regulate – contemporary forms of cultural identity.

Not that anyone would claim that such recognitions would immediately bring to a halt capital's double-headed movement – the international reorganization of labor power and the expansion of the means of consumption. But they might help produce a bit more anger.

## Notes

1. 'Top 40 Focus,' *Bobbin* (June 1996).

2. All the quotes in this and the following paragraph are from the various executives interviewed, and all information has been 'mined' from the account of the interviews in 'Views from the Top,' *Daily News Record,* May 29, 1996.

3. Quoted from CNN Headline News Channel, July 17, 1996.

4. Streetsound's board can be accessed on <<http://streetsound.clever.net/style/ fashhiphop.html>>. It is worth keeping in mind here that the Internet itself, however much its advocates (myself included) want to think of it as a means toward a certain cultural freedom and even resistance, is also at the same time part of the expansion of the means of consumption that I've been referring to.

# Chapter 15

# Ellis Cashmore

## America's Paradox

Is there such a thing as genuine black culture? The black culture industry has an interest in promoting the idea that there is. Its products are created by blacks in concert with whites and consumed, in the main, by whites. The industry that started with the rough recording of blues players now recycles itself into cassettes, laserdiscs and cd-roms; it begets baseball caps and other apparel, it becomes a movie, [and] novelization [...].

Meanwhile, many Afrocentrists posit Africa as the site of the origins of a distinct and unique culture that has mutated, but continues to animate the street life of first world metropolises: an expression of a distinct and still-vital spirit, a set of values that embodies an essential Africanness. 'Black culture is the product of an ongoing struggle between the extremes of defiance and assimilation, of resistance and complacency,' writes Ada Gay Griffin in *Black Popular Culture,* adding that: 'Those aspects of our culture and history that come most often to our attention, usually because they have been popularized by or expropriated by the dominant society, tend to line up along the side of assimilation and, as a consequence, are available as vehicles for our oppression' (1992: 231).

On this view, much of what passes for black culture today would be dismissed as assimilated and potentially oppressive. Real black culture, presumably, lies somewhere in an alternative space: 'Black films, Black videos, and Black media are those productions directed by Black artists on subjects and forms that reference the Black experience and imagination.' This somewhat preachy approach suffers when we realize that, in the 1990s, the black culture industry has actually been run by black artists and producers, who have had more control over their product than ever. Are they the genuine article, or have they been coopted and assimilated by the 'dominant society'?

From: Ellis Cashmore, *The Black Culture Industry.* London: Routledge, 1997.

The kind of argument advanced by Griffin is a perfect complement to those who profit from the black culture. Idealizing it sells it. Exactly who does profit? It is easy to be a cynic and answer: whites. In fact, since 1990, an even greater number of African Americans have maneuvered their way into the kind of positions historically reserved for whites. Berry Gordy was an exception in his day; but in the early 1990s dozens of black entrepreneurs listed themselves as company directors and sat on boards where they could wield power over their products.

By the mid-1990s, the music industry was carved up between six big corporations. Biggest was Warner, which claimed 22.65 percent of an industry worth about $11–12 billion per year; it formed part of Time Warner, the world's largest media company after the mega-merger with Turner Broadcasting in 1996. Its nearest rivals were PolyGram and Sony, which held 14.37 and 13.19 shares respectively. The other three were BMG (owned by Bertelsmann) with 12.12 percent, MCA (owned by Seagram, the Canadian liquor company) with 10.42 percent, and EMI (de-mergered from Thorn-EMI, of Britain, in 1996) with 8.64 percent. The remainder was splintered among independents. In a typical year, Warner would expect to generate earnings before interest, tax, depreciation and amortization of around $800 million on $4.1 billion worth of sales through its various labels, including Atlantic, Elektra and Warner Bros. Thanks to its Island Records, A & M and Motown, PolyGram – 75 percent owned by Philips of Holland – was able to close the gap.

Bestselling artists were the corporations' principal assets. For example, up to 1996 Madonna sold some 180 million cassettes, cds and music videos, generating $1.5 billion for Warner Bros, which secured her services for $60 million. More than 30 million copies of Janet Jackson's three albums had been bought up to 1996, enabling Virgin Records, owned by EMI, to pay out $80 million for her next four albums, while brother Michael had to limp by with his $60 million from Sony. Yet, in the 1990s, the shape of the market altered in such a way as to make it impossible for corporations simply to bank on their safe stars. They needed to diffuse; and the manner in which they did this created a new tier of the black culture industry.

David Samuels recounts how, in the summer of 1991, Soundscan, a computerized system for tracking music sales, changed *Billboard* magazine's method of counting record sales in the USA. Soundscan accumulated its data from the barcodes scanned at chain store cash registers in malls across the country. Previously, the magazine had relied on a more haphazard and less accurate method, logging the sales of big city stores and from the subjective accounts of radio programmers. The change to a much more complete and accurate collection system yielded enlightening results. 'So it was that America awoke on June 22, 1991, to find that its favorite record was not *Out of Time,* by aging college-boy rockers REM, but *Niggaz4life,* a musical celebration of gang rape and other violence by NWA' observes Samuels (1991: 24). [...]

It was bracing news and one of its effects was to alert the major corporations to the need to stay closer than they had to rapidly changing tastes. Most of the big six had already set up divisions or semi-independent units specializing in music by black artists. [...]

The other option available to the corporations was predatory: to wait until a smaller independent outfit threatened to become a force, then buy it. Every label of note specializing in black music, whether owned by blacks or whites, has eventually been bought by white-controlled organizations. This was workable, if expensive. The black music division was a leaner and more controlled way of keeping abreast of changing trends, though, as the Soundscan system revealed, far from guaranteed. A suspicion grew that, with the rise of rap and associated forms of street music – garage, house, jungle, newjack and so on – the sands were shifting. The corporations needed to find a way of staying in touch without sacrificing control of their product.

In 1992, MCA closed what proved to be a landmark deal with Andre Harrell, former colleague of Russell Simmons and, later, head of his own Uptown Records. MCA had, in the 1980s, risen to the position of market leader in black music, squeezing Motown from the top spot and acquiring a reputation, principally through its head, Jheryl Busby. [...] After creating a black music division at A & M Records in the early 1980s, Busby moved to MCA where he was given authority to set up a black music division that would sign its own artists and handle its own promotion, marketing and advertising. Under Busby, MCA signed, developed and worked with New Edition, Bobby Brown and Gladys Knight, among others. Virtually every album by these artists sold more than a million copies.

MCA had done well out of the popularity of black music. *Black Enterprise* writers Rhonda Reynolds and Ann Brown estimated that, collectively, the black genres (including rap, r'n'b, gospel and reggae) accounted for 24 percent of all music sales (1994). Even if we deduct the 3.3 percent contribution of jazz, which has never been an exclusively black musical form, this still leaves a significant 20.7 percent. In its efforts to stay ahead of the field, MCA focused on Uptown Records, a small independent label that boasted then up-and-coming artists, like Mary J. Blige and Heavy D and the Boyz. The seven-year deal was worth a shocking $50 million to Harrell. [...]

Two years later, one of Harrell's producers at Uptown, Sean 'Puffy' Combs, repeated the trick. He struck a deal with Arista and BMG worth $10 million over three years that committed him to deliver three albums a year from his Bad Boy Entertainment. Combs, then 24 years old, had recently left Harrell's company. In the first year of the deal, Bad Boy launched two million-selling acts, Craig Mack and Notorious BIG. [...]

All this signalled a willingness on behalf of the big corporations to invest money in smaller labels in the expectation of medium-term rewards. The corporations risked money; the labels risked autonomy. After Harrell's move to Motown, MCA retained the master tapes, the roster of artists and, perhaps most importantly, the Uptown name. Harrell, reflecting on his period as the Uptown boss, announced to *Newsweek's* Johnnie Roberts: 'I had fake control' (1995: 48). [...]

Typically, a 1990s-style deal with an independent label would implicate the major corporation in a time-specific arrangement: the bigger company would demand product at a certain rate from the smaller company, which it would undertake to distribute and, under some agreements, to market. In return, it paid out a lump sum or an annual allowance. Let us say, a working allowance of a million dollars was provided to the label. An additional recording fund of, say, $300,000 was allowed for each artist on the roster. Promotion and marketing would add more cost. [...]

None of this money was given out of the goodness of the corporation's heart: it was strictly investment and every nickel was expected to be paid back out of sales. By the estimates of Reynolds and Brown: 'On a basic low-end deal, the black label wants to make 16% to 20% of the retail music sales. The label signs an artist and forks over 10% to 14%, then keeps the remaining 4% to 6% as profit' (1994: 89). The label, or 'sub-label,' existed on the slim profit margin. When all this is considered, the deals do not look so fabulous: of the $15–17 a consumer paid for a cd, the artist got a little more than $1.50 and the label got about 50 cents, but only after all the front money received from the major corporation had been paid off. [...]

The benefits to the label are obvious: exposure to a wider market, better distribution and promotion, and the possibility of big money should sales stay up. [...] Independent labels in the 1990s were hard pressed to manufacture, distribute, market, sell and collect on a record beyond the level of a 100,000 units or so. So, the prospect of a bigger organization handling the noncreative aspects of this was clearly attractive.

More generally, the trend encouraged entrepreneurship among African Americans and created at least some millionaires and many more others who could boast the title 'President and CEO.' It also offered a low-risk strategy for would-be music moguls: the capital put up by the corporations was effectively an interest-free loan. [...]

'But not everyone can achieve a high level of success,' according to Tariq K. Muhammad, who writes for *Black Enterprise*. 'Thus, for every successful sub-label that has generated enough sales to renegotiate their deal into a more favorable joint venture arrangement, there are probably 10 or more sub-labels in 'plantation-like' situations' (1995: 76). The same writer also speculates on the wider implications of making more money available in this way to black entrepreneurs: 'It has exacerbated an existing problem – the lack of cooperation and unity among African Americans in the industry.' Like crabs in a barrel trying to escape, black entrepreneurs were prepared to crawl over each other as the major corporations dangled money before them. Muhammad refers to 'a new system of exploitation' in which a few spectacularly successful music entrepreneurs obscured the real struggle that lay beneath them.

The black culture industry operates just as any other industry in advanced capitalist societies. In the 1990s the major music corporations' acquisition strategy is but one part of a wider process of aggressive globalization that takes place between a variety of entertainment and electronics conglomerates. As Stephen Lee writes in his informative article 'Re-examining the concept of the 'independent' record label': 'The consolidation of film, television, recording, publishing, electronics, computers, advertising and talent brokering has resulted in a group of powerful oligopolies that broker cultural materials in much the same way any other commodity would be sold' (1995: 16).

Lee's case study of the independent Wax Trax label shows how small labels in the early 1990s were increasingly unable to maintain independence in the face of market pressures. Their fate is often to operate independently for a short period before collapsing, or to sell to a bigger company. Sometimes, the limit of the owner's aspirations is to sell out at a profit and become a titular CEO but an effective employee of a major corporation. So it is with the new heads of the black culture industry: media moguls by name, millionaires by bank balance, but paid staff nevertheless. And, for every Andre Harrell or Puffy Combs, there are countless other failed or failing record label owners who will never come close to touching the hem of greatness.

In his essay on the African American film-maker Oscar Micheaux, J. Ronald Green writes: 'Black musicians, preachers and writers showed there were different ways to make improvisational music, oral jeremiad, and narratives that could both be understood by their own cultures and later be celebrated by Eurocentric cultures' (1993: 35). He adds that: 'The contribution of these forms to art and to pleasure has been the greater for their ethnic authenticity.' There seems to be a contradiction here. In the process of reaching the stage at which they were appreciated by 'Eurocentric cultures' – by which I take Green to mean whites – the music at least has lost whatever 'ethnic authenticity' it once had.

One of the arguments of *The Black Culture Industry* is that what we popularly accept to be black culture is, on closer inspection, a product of blacks' and whites' collaborative efforts. [...] Black culture is not devalued because it is a hybrid. But we should not neglect the conditions under which the hybridity is allowed to occur. Historically, those conditions have been more conducive to the prosperity of white entrepreneurs than that of black artists; though black capitalists have emerged since the 1960s.

There is great commercial value in promoting a product as if it were 'authentic,' but it is difficult to demarcate between authentic and inauthentic. Deborah Root argues: 'Authenticity is a tricky concept because of the way the term can be manipulated and used to convince people they are getting something profound when they are just getting merchandise' (1996: 78). So effective has it been as a selling point that Root, in her revelational *Cannibal Culture,* refers to a 'commodification of authenticity.' In this case, the purported authenticity attributed to so much of what is received as black culture might be regarded as a definition imposed by those who profit most from it. The ethnic authenticity about which Green enthuses may not exist outside of the industry that promotes and exploits it.

On the account presented here, its primary role has been in assuaging white guilt. The paradox or 'dilemma' is addressed, if not solved. There is an almost addictive remuneration from integrating black culture into the mainstream. Not only to whites: in a context in which many of the rewards are not readily available to blacks, there is atonement of sorts in seeing one's culture represented in mainstream media. Shohat and Stam, in discussing identifications with films, use the term 'compensatory outlet' and suggest there is a process like transferring 'allegiance to another sports team after one's own has been eliminated from the competition' (1994: 351). If you do not believe your group is getting enough breaks, it is at least some recompense to see representations of that group in the popular media. [...]

Whether they like it or not, whites are parties in a certain kind of discourse that has rendered black people subalterns, lowly ranked groups without any meaningful voice. African Americans have been virtually silenced, their political views and artistic endeavors made irrelevant or smirked at. Even now, we might argue that concessions need to be made before African Americans are allowed to make their imprint. In a memorably vulgar epigram from a May 1995 interview with Kevin Powell, bell hooks reminded *Vibe* magazine readers of the continuing presence of the racial hierarchy: 'Black people get to the top and stay on top only by sucking the dicks of white culture.'

Black artists' admission into the cultural mainstream is conditional. Historically, artists have either conformed to whites' preconceptions of what blacks were or should be like, or they have been denied commercial success. In some cases, properties have been imputed to black performers that at least made them seem to fit whites' expectations. The case of Michael Jackson shows that these are not either/or alternatives. White culture has enforced a definition of its normality by admitting only black interlopers who lived up or down to its images: others, who possessed exotic or peculiar gifts but at a cost to their full humanity. The symbolic eunuch has been welcomed by white culture, as has the exotic temptress. Despite their testosterone-pumped posturing and scornful dismissal of all things feminine, the gangsta rap artists of the 1990s were emasculated players in a white psychodrama. Like other members of the black entertainment elite, their role was a tightly defined one: amuse, play music, kill each other, if you will; make like you hate whites and enjoy scaring them. 'The successful black people zoo' is hooks' term for this state of representational captivity.

[...] Many a black actor or singer, male and female, has managed to resist the pressures to conform, though [...] the likes of Dorothy Dandridge and Lena Horne were eventually squeezed into marginal roles. It is also interesting that Dandridge's co-star in *Porgy and Bess,* Sidney Poitier, avoided stereotypes in search of more nuanced roles and was, in the late 1960s, rebuked by many blacks for assimilating. [...] In the late 1990s, any number of black overachievers in the entertainment business shun two-dimensional images in favor of more complex parts. Yet, there are always counterweights. For every Denzel Washington, Whitney Houston or Luther Vandross, there is an Eddie Murphy, Whoopie Goldberg or Snoop Doggy Dogg. This kind of ambivalence is actually functional: it is a reminder that a minority of 'nice ones' can always make it.

[...] Black people have served as a kind of mirror to whites, but not one that gives a true image: more like a warped, polished surface that provides a distorted representation. Much of whites' self-image has been constructed as a response to what they believe blacks are not. If whites understand themselves to be superior, intellectually and culturally, then images of blacks have signified ignorance and barbarity. It has been vital to maintain those reflections, no matter how hideously inaccurate. One way has been to create a context in which blacks have had little choice but to act up to whites' expectations. [...] Black people, especially those conspicuously engaged in entertainment, have been reminders to whites of what they are *not*. The very category of whiteness was invented in counterposition to blackness. In simple terms, without black people, there were no whites; no 'others,' no 'us.'

[...] What people define as difference and how they interpret that difference changes from context to context, from one historical epoch to another, depending on the specific calculus of power and knowledge that holds sway. Today, we live in a market: the scope of commodification is now so wide that everything, including difference, can be reshaped into a package that can be bought and sold. [...] This has been facilitated by the emergence of what Michael Read calls *Super Media,* 'the apex of development of media and culture' (1989: 19).

No sooner is a film released than we are invited to buy the soundtrack, visit the web site, take the downloads, enter the competitions, read the books, study production notes, wear the apparel; when we see the movie, we are tempted by popcorn, soda pop and trailers of upcoming films. We return home to watch television, where a complementary process begins and we become captivated by a new set of invitations, all of which involve parting with money. Our days are spent, our lives are lived buying products; and the advent of digitization means that we have no need to leave our homes.

When we do, we clothe and accessorize ourselves in products bearing the names and logos of the companies that exploit our weakness for commodities: T-shirts plastered with DKNY, Armani motif'd eyeglasses, personal stereos with Sony's insignia, knockoff Rolexes that look 'authentic.' These are not just products: they are commodified values. And we do not just buy them: we collude with the manufacturers to become ambulant advertisements. It is as if we are proud to exhibit our own exploitation. [...]

It is not only romantic, but foolish to believe that African American culture exists outside this process. Nor should we imagine that this is a new phenomenon: the appropriation of cultures associated with blacks began in the early years of the nineteenth century, as soon as whites realized the commercial possibilities in them. Now, the heirs to the industry crudely inaugurated by the promoters of minstrel shows own record labels or chairs in corporation boardrooms. Like W. C. Handy, who operated in the early 1900s, some are African Americans themselves. But, there are equally permanent features of the black culture industry: it is still owned by whites, has a predominantly white market and, if the argument advanced here is accepted, has functions that are rarely, if ever, discussed. I will close with a résumé of its principal one.

I have often thought that *An American Dilemma* [1944/1996] was a misnomer. After all, a dilemma suggests a choice between two equally unacceptable alternatives and what Gunnar Myrdal was really trying to convey was that no choice was necessary. The practical reality of contemporary America, with its obdurate racial hierarchy, is at odds with its official commitment to democratic egalitarianism in which basic rights are inviolable. There is never any doubt about America's option. What Myrdal was actually describing was 'An American Paradox': a contradiction between rhetorical freedom and actual oppression.

More than fifty years after Myrdal disclosed the paradox in 1944 and assembled copious data to support his finding, America still struggles unavailingly with its most intractable and embarrassing problem. The unemployment rate for black males is more than twice that of their white counterparts. Even black men with jobs and higher education do not, for the most part, receive the same pay as white men. Among recent college graduates with one to five years on the job, black men earned less than 88 percent of the amount earned by white men. The leading cause of death among black males between the ages of 15 and 24 was homicide. [...]

No nation has been as tortured by racism as the United States. In the late 1950s, its civil rights movement brought both agony and redemption as previously undisturbed institutions were challenged, then broken. The attempt to bring together ideal and reality took the form of legislation guaranteeing the rights stipulated in the US constitution – that hallowed document designed in the spirit of revolutionary France and Tom Paine's vision of a federalist-republican England.

Whatever flights of fancy whites may have about the advances made over the past three decades, they are brought to earth with a bump when the views of black Americans are solicited. As Eddy Harris writes, in his *South of Haunted Dreams*: 'To be black is always to be reminded that you are a stranger in your native land. To be black is to be surrounded by those who would remind you' (1993: 102).

The integration of what passes as African American culture may be a type of resolution; one that affords whites the benefits of identifying with blacks and welcoming them without actually doing much about the fundamental inequalities that remain. Cornel West uses the term 'redemptive culturalism,' to describe the view that culture can yield political redemption for black people (1993: 66). There is appeal in the idea that cultural change can be an agent of more wide-reaching social changes. But, we should at least allow the possibility that black culture is, to borrow from chemistry's lexicon, amphoteric – capable of acting both ways. The spread and acceptance of African American inspired music, particularly over the past thirty years, may have come not as an agent, but *instead* of social change.

If there is black culture, it is more likely to be discovered in the kinds of attitudes, customs, values and language uncovered by John Langston Gwaltney in his study *Drylongso: A self-portrait of black America.* The 'core black culture' documented by anthropologist Gwaltney bears no resemblance to the genres that have been industrialized and reach us via the channels of the corporation-owned media. Black culture in his conception is nourished by the minor everyday thoughts and practices of people, their mishaps and achievements; the disarray and organization that characterizes any living culture. Cultures cannot be force-grown, but spring seemingly unaided from tiny seeds of experience.

Culture is a dangerous and, in some ways, daunting subject. Offending someone's mother is often dealt with less severely than offending that person's culture. Yet, we often seem to forgive the commodified versions. I recall sitting in a cinema in Kingston, Jamaica, watching the movie *Marked for Death* in which Jamaicans were depicted as belief-beggaring stereotypes. The crowd roared approvingly with laughter, while I cringed. As an Englishman, I should be insulted by fluffy notions of my countryfolk as silly-asses with 'Golly gosh' and 'Oh, rather!' accents. Still, I can endure the likes of *Four Weddings and a Funeral* without getting upset and reminding all around me that this is the same culture that brought the world Sade and Seal. It is as if we accept the distortions as long as they are perpetrated in celluloid, particularly in the pursuit of mammon.

The iconography of black culture is full of Gangstas, Shafts, and Black Venuses. As black people make headway socially, as they have since days of civil rights, the culture attributed to them has attracted interest from all quarters. Elements have been picked up and changed into products, which have in turn stimulated greater interest. The dynamic that keeps the cycle going is likely to continue. As a consequence, black culture, or at least a commodified version of it, will be sought after, acquired and appreciated by a widening audience. But, there are other consequences. One of them is an alleviation of the white guilt that Malcolm X once recognized as the bitterly relentless force that drives racism.

While we may enjoy black culture in all its saleable forms, we should remind ourselves of the misanthropic opportunism that brought it to our ears and eyes. In black culture, we can find a history of American perfidy, American violence, American oppression and American racism, all captured for our delectation in a way that provokes reflection without spurring us to action. For all the resistance promised by those who valorize 'cultural redemption,' black culture provides more comfort than challenge and, for this reason, must be approached with the same kind of skepticism that once greeted the minstrels, themselves empowered by the money they earned yet constrained by the very environment in which they prospered. The same might be said of all those associated with the black culture industry.

## References

Green, J.R. (1993) '"Twoness" in the style of Oscar Micheaux', pp. 26–48 in M. Diawara (ed.) *Black American Cinema,* New York: Routledge.

Griffin, A.G. (1992) 'Seizing the moving image', pp. 228–233 in M. Wallace and G. Dent (eds) *Black Popular Culture,* Seattle, WA: Bay Press.

Gwaltney, J.L. (1993) *Drylongso: A self-portrait of black America.* New York: The New Press.

Harrell is cited in Roberts, J. (1995) 'A piece of the action', *Newsweek,* vol. 125, no. 25 (December 18), pp. 48–53.

Harris, E. (1993) *South of Haunted Dreams: A ride through slavery's old back yard.* London: Viking.

Lee, S. (1995) 'Re-examining the concept of the "independent" record label: The case of Wax Trax records', *Popular Music,* vol. 14, no. 1, pp. 13–31.

Muhammad, T.K. (1995) 'The real lowdown on labels', *Black Enterprise,* vol. 26, no. 5 (December) pp. 74–78 .

Read, M. (1989) *Super Media: A Cultural Studies Approach.* Newbury Park, CA: Sage.

Reynolds, R. and Brown, A. (1994) 'A new rhythm takes hold', *Black Enterprise,* vol. 25, no. 5, pp. 82–89.

Root, D. (1996) *Cannibal Culture: Art, appropriation and the commodification of difference.* Boulder, CO: Westview Press.

Samuels, D. (1991) 'The rap on rap', *The New Republic,* November 11, pp. 24–29.

Shohat, E. and Stam, R. (1994) *Unthinking Eurocentrism: Multiculturalism and the media.* New York: Routledge.

West, C. (1993) *Keeping Faith: Philosophy and race in America.* New York: Routledge.

# Chapter 16

# Iderpal Grewal

# Traveling Barbie: Indian Transnationality and New Consumer Subjects

In the extensive field of cultural studies of Barbie, there are only some cursory references to international dimensions.[1] Mostly written from the feminist viewpoint, scholarly work on Barbie continues to grow in the direction of U.S.-based race and queer studies. However, very little in this area of U.S. feminist and cultural studies concerns the matter of Barbie in the world. This essay examines the globalization of Barbie and her limited marketing success in India through the theoretical perspective of transnational feminist cultural studies. By focusing on consumers as active participants in the construction of national, gendered, and classed subjectivities through consumption, this essay analyzes the new subjects of consumption created as a result of economic liberalization policies in India and their transnational contexts.

These subjects may not be wholly resistant to the spread of global brands such as Barbie but may certainly subvert the project because they are not hailed by it. The failure of new products on the market certainly suggests such possibilities; people do not buy indiscriminately. Why some products sell and some do not suggests important issues of culture, identity, and subjectivity. Resistance to multinationals in India comes from different locations and cannot be seen as always subversive to dominant formations; such resistances are also recuperated by the multinational companies. Whereas parties on the left have been organizing opposition to multinationals, so that it is clear that the Indian central government's support of open markets is opposed at many levels, resistance also comes from

From: Inderpal Grewal, 'Traveling Barbie: Indian Transnationality and New Consumer Subjects', *positions* 7.3: 799–826, 1999.

religious fundamentalist groups such as the RSS (the Rashtriya Swayamsevak Sangh, the Hindu right-wing party), who in the struggle for political power use the example of multinationals as the 'American' threat to national sovereignty. Other kinds of resistance appear in the obsession with ethnic chic,[2] for instance, or the recuperations of 'tradition' by various entities. My analysis of the marketing of Barbie in India suggests both the subversions and the recuperations that occur in the formation of new consumer subjects.

In a context of localization through transnational formations, it is important to note that Barbie in a sari being sold in India is not an Indian or South Asian Barbie. She is what Mattel calls the traditional Barbie, a white, American Barbie, but one who travels; she has, in one version, blond hair, the standard face, the ideal female Euro-American body, a shiny sari, and a red *bindi* on her forehead. The side panel on the box reads, 'Dressing in an all-seasons classic saree with exotic borders, Barbie is totally at home in India.' This reconfiguration of Euro-American fashion discourse uses the term *all-seasons* to differentiate the sari from the fashion industry in the West, which is organized around seasonal clothes. The term *exotic* resonates in reference to colonialism, tourism, and the eroticization of the female Asian body that depends on the misrecognition of socioeconomic realities and changes. Barbie in a sari is material evidence of the movements of transnational capital to India. The doll suggests that difference, as homogenized national stereotype, could be recovered by multinational corporations, that the national could exist in this global economy.

The impact of India's process of economic liberalization, which began in the 1980s with increased incentives for foreign investment and multinationals and a more open market policy, has been important not only in changing the nature of consumption and new consumer subjects in India, but also in connecting such subjects to patterns of globalized consumption, production, and circulation. One aspect of the economic liberalization process has been the Indian government's focus on Indian diasporics' as potential investors, such that tax breaks and special investment incentives for the category of persons termed *nonresident Indian* (NRI) have been created. This incorporation of the diaspora has turned the national imaginary into a transnational imaginary, in which diasporic cultural formations create new forms of community under conditions of globalization. Diaspora and home have become connected in new ways in this new economic climate, such that NRIs have become integrated into the political, cultural, and economic practices of the Indian nation-state.

An important aspect of this transnationalism can be understood not only in terms of the movements of migrant labor and bodies of various kinds, but also in how goods, media, and information get 'transcoded,' as Stuart Hall has termed this process of localization, at different sites, sometimes in terms of nationalism and at other times for localized agendas related to gender and class hegemonies.[3] Within India's economic liberalization, diasporic lifestyles of South Asian immigrants in the United States have become utilized to market consumer lifestyles. While diaspora culture is being theorized in many contexts, mostly in Europe and North America, as a subcultural resistance to white, Eurocentric culture, it is quite differently incorporated within India in consumer contexts as a marketing tool to imagine a transnational nation. Such a nation proposes new practices of nationalism and new national identities that connect people through ties of consumption to home as nation-state.

As a result, the study of migration has to be rethought in relation to transnationality. Transnational theories not only account for bicultural rather than unicultural perspectives of the immigrant, but they also include how, for instance, the consumer lifestyles of those within one nation-state become transnationalized across many national boundaries. In the wake of economic liberalization policies and NRI investment incentives, the increased travel by elites and migrants has created a new Indian transnational imaginary, in which new elites and new subalterns are emerging, not only in the so-called diaspora but also in India. Since not only elite classes participate in globalized consumption, given that one important aspect of new subjects of consumption is their highly segmented nature, the identities produced are also segmented in terms of gender, sexuality, class, caste, and religion while also being nationalist in various ways. Barbie, as the doll is being marketed in India, participates in the gendered segmentation of these new consumer subjects as global brands become localized in specific ways.[4]

Since market segmentation in the United States has used ethnicity and multiculturalism to sell products that have participated in the construction of gendered subjects, the notion of multiculturalism has also become transnationalized through global marketing practices by U.S.-based transnational corporations. Here it is useful to examine how the Indian NRIs in the United States have become valuable as multicultural experts for U.S. multinationals. Multiculturalism, as it has been understood in the context of the United States, is no longer solely a claim on civil rights but also circulates globally as consumer culture in which ethnic immigrants create negotiated lifestyles from the American lifestyle that is so much a part of late twentieth-century U.S. capitalism. The impact of market segmentation and the emergence of target markets mean that differentiated cultural formations, existing under the sign of multiculturalism, can travel to different sites, and become used in other localized contexts.

While Rob Wilson and Wimal Dissanayake think of the transnational imaginary as a way to understand uneven globalization in terms of the global/local assemblage that is a 'sublated agent of the "world system"' and as an undoing of the nation-state, I argue that the nation-state remains important, since new forms of globalization emerge from or in conjunction with and often extend beyond the boundaries of the nation-state.[5] Global capital may resuscitate the nation-state in many ways, at the same time reducing its compass.[6] Nationalism, given its cultural, ethnic, religious, or nation-state manifestations at present, can neither be ignored nor seen as the localized form of resistance to the global; the local itself is also reconfigured just as Indian nationalism has become reconfigured by including those noncitizens who claim diasporic relation to the nation. Our task, then, is to examine how transnational localisms produce multiple subjects, who may not be in opposition to either globalization or nationalism.

## The Global Consumer and the National Consumer

Consumer subjects, seen by the marketing industry in India as predominantly urban but that in North India exist in most towns and cities, depending on class and caste status, are gendered and classed in ways that have continuities and discontinuities with colonial and nationalist subjects. Contemporary business magazines articulate these subjects through a notion of a global consumer, one who is able to recognize global brand names, even if this consumer might be incorporating this recognition into particular localisms that are quite different from cultural practices in the United States or the West.

Recent surveys by Indian and global marketing agencies have started to examine consumer attitudes globally, categorizing and constructing consuming subjects by nationality. Differentiations between surveyed subjects by local specificities suggest the localization of transnational consumption. One particular survey, undertaken by the Marketing and Research Group based in India in conjunction with other such groups internationally, polled Indian consumers by location in 'metro' areas (suggesting global metropolitan subjects), by class (minimum income of Rs. 1,500 a month), and by age (18–55)[7] The survey showed that while multinational corporations are gaining strength, national and local brands also are seen as superior or second best. [...]

According to this survey, the subject of transnational consumption is a national Indian consumer, gendered masculine, sexuality unclear, who is a 'brand loyalist' and a 'luxury innovator' who feels his consumer confidence is not high because of the state of the economy and because 'money is a problem.' His social beliefs are quite conservative in regard to poverty but more liberal regarding the environment. His opinions on women's issues, which are quite often discussed in the popular media in India, are not surveyed. This new profile of the Indian consumer suggests a change from the older version of media marketing in which women were seen as primary purchasers. This consumer has the knowledge about global brand names and brand loyalty that outstrips his ability to purchase. The Indian consumer is nationalist but also cosmopolitan, an urban man who would like to work more but often does not get the chance.[8] Apparently, to be a global consumer is not seen as contradictory to being a national consumer. The survey reveals class differences are being constructed in such marketing research through consumption of global and national branded goods rather than being based simply on ownership of property, education, family status or connections, or job opportunities, although these are, of course, connected to ability to consume. The connection between the global and the national becomes part of the new transnational arena of consumption that produces these classed and gendered subjects in new ways.

Mattel needs this global/national consumer in order to sell its goods. In the case of India, the specificities of the Indian consumer lie in how the national and the global are mediated. In the case of Barbie, the lack of such mediations has meant that Barbie has not taken the Indian market by storm. Furthermore, as many might believe, Barbie does not sell simply because it is an American product; 'America' as a marketing tool has to be mediated. Initially its sales were quite unremarkable. [...] Only when Barbie appeared in a sari and advertising practices utilized a transnational context specific to India did sales improve. Thus the Americanness of Barbie and the standard of its white femininity had to be mediated by various other factors that were localized, diasporic, and transnational.

In fact, Mattel has had to rely on specificities of cultural practices in urban India in order to create successful advertising campaigns so that Barbie achieves greater brand-name recognition. Thus it is not Americanization as simple cultural imperialism that can be seen as a theoretical explanation of global consumer culture, but a very mediated notion of America, which is used to sell goods. Leslie Sklair has written at length about the centrality of the American Dream as a lifestyle in the functioning of global capitalism.[9] This notion of America, though quite different from an older notion of the cosmopolitan West of colonial moderniy that was created under U.S. Cold War imperialism, is also not dissociated from it. U.S. corporations still use U.S. imperial power to create markets by utilizing neoimperial inequities and practices. Yet by expanding the notion of the American lifestyle of consumption to incorporate the emergence of a heterogeneous and multicultural America of conflicting ethnicities, transnational corporations such as Mattel can create new kinds of gendered, age-differentiated, and classed consumers in different regions. [...]

Since American goods and geopolitics circulate globally, transnational localisms absorb, utilize, and rework the notion of America into particular agendas and strategies, within which states and nations play uneven and heterogeneous roles. As various market segments rework and re-create the American lifestyle, the emergence of global/national consumers with both national and ethnic specificities indicates a very selective and changing incorporation of Americanness.

## Mattel and its Corporate Practices: Constructing Difference and Universality

In 1985 Mattel had affiliates and plants in South Korea, Japan, Hong Kong, the Philippines, Australia, Chile, Venezuela, Puerto Rico, the United Kingdom, France, Spain, Switzerland, and Canada. Today Mattel is a multinational corporation with factories, offices, and affiliates in Tijuana, Monterey, Guangdong China (1991), Jakarta, Japan, Berlin, Budapest, Prague, Kuala Lumpur, and Bombay, in addition to those already in the United Kingdom, France, Switzerland, Spain, Puerto Rico, Chile, and Venezuela. A new plant opened in Thailand in 1985 after applying for an eight-year tax holiday, a common practice to invite not only worldwide but also U.S. investors.[10] Mattel closed two plants in the Philippines in 1988 after conflicts with what the corporation called 'militant labor unions.'[11] Most Barbies sold in the United States are made in China, Malaysia, and Indonesia with plastics made in Taiwan from oil bought from Saudi Arabia, hair from Japan, and packaging from the United States. Making Barbie is extremely labor-intensive work, requiring at least fifteen separate paint stations and, thus, an enormous supply of cheap labor. Labor expenses are about 35 cents for a Barbie costing about $10 (of which almost $8 goes to shipping, marketing, and wholesale and retail profits; Mattel keeps about $1 of this amount).[12] Mattel continues to seek lower costs and to increase its visibility globally. While it espouses a discourse of universality of children's play alongside American values of heteronormative, gendered racism as marketing strategy, its practices in India suggest that it relies on localized gendered formations to succeed. In their transnational localism, American values remain but become modified.

After increasing sales from 1985 that showed steady U.S. sales but big jumps in international sales of almost 40 percent every year, sales declined in 1987, necessitating layoffs in the Hawthorne, California, headquarters of 22 percent, almost five hundred jobs. The Bombay office opened in 1988 in the midst of 30 percent declining sales, a fact not surprising when the corporate view was, according to the chief executive officer, that 'the future of the toy industry lies in international markets.'[13] By 1992 Mattel had come out of its economic slump with a net sales increase of 25 percent. By 1993 Barbie sales worldwide had hit $1 billion but have fluctuated since then. That year Mattel donated $1 million to children's health programs in the United States.

Mattel sees the whole world as open to buying the company's products. The annual reports reveal a belief that every child naturally wants these toys and that their desirability is transparent. [...] To pursue this children's market, Mattel linked up with Disney, another iconic name in the U.S. 'children's global culture,' as I call it. Mattel now makes all the Disney brand toys, and the awareness of Disney as a nationalist signifier of Americanness has been well documented.[14] In 1992, after the deal with Disney, Mattel called Barbie and Disney its 'global power brands.'[15]

How does Mattel explain its belief in Barbie's continued power and fascination? It is clear that the corporation does not connect Barbie with U.S. histories of imperialism and global power. However, these histories are marketed implicitly by U.S. corporations as an attractive and powerful Americanness in so many ways by so many U.S. entities, from the notion of democracy and freedom to Hollywood cinema and TV to its imperial and military power. [...] Mattel attributes its success to its understanding of little girls' fantasies, all of which Mattel universalizes in its discourse of play. These fantasies, as Erica Rand argues, are a form of hegemonic discourse such that the language of 'infinite possibility' that Mattel deploys is used to 'camouflage what is actually being promoted: a very limited set of products, ideas, and actions.'[16] According to Rand, even if subversive uses of Barbie are rampant, these do not change the fact that the ideological effects that Mattel promotes are compulsory heterosexuality, ageism, sexism, white superiority, capitalism, and the unequal distribution of resources.

According to Mattel, if boys need high-tech toys, such as BraveStarr, girls grow through imagination and play with dolls. I do not suggest that such play is not powerful or complex or subversive of gendered stereotypes.[17] Yet the corporate focus on fantasy for girls suggests that the play that they enact is typical of the symbolic and virtual nature of consumer culture. Such play participates in the construction of consuming subjects. In a global framework of consumption, as Arjun Appadurai's work suggests, fantasy links translocal practices that are connected through the imagination.[18] The transnational imaginary of new nationalisms seems most easily available through consumption, given that one aspect of modernity and postmodernity has been the emergence of the citizen as consumer. For instance, Lauren Berlant and Elizabeth Freeman argue that even for subversive groups such as Queer Nation, consumer pleasure becomes part of activist reformulations of public culture, linking 'the Utopian pleasures of the commodity with those of the nation.'[19]

Yet these modalities depend on very specific economic and social understandings and negotiations of global inequalities, utilizing complex socio-economic and cultural differences to sell products, establish markets, and make profits. Universality is, once again, a means to create differences. The notion of a universal play pattern may operate only superficially to suggest merely that girls play with dolls all around the world; however, how and what girls play may be highly specific to region, history, and culture. It seems that Mattel's goal is that the girl-child, the global subject of U.N. discourse,[20] becomes a subject of consumption.

In its statements to its stockholders, Mattel tries to emphasize universality through a liberal discourse of claims of concern for the global welfare of children. In 1990 Barbie 'hosted' an international summit where forty children from twenty-eight countries discussed issues relevant to themselves. Mattel's 1990 annual report used this event to state that 'their deliberations identified world peace as a principal concern.' The summit seems to be on the order of deliberations by contestants at beauty pageants, where the most commonplace clichés are spoken by contestants, so that there is a connection here to the kinds of discourses that may be voiced at such occasions. Rand suggests that these are 'popular but largely uncontroversial forms of political consciousness' that Mattel uses to reach more consumers.[21] Yet in a transnational frame, such practices suggest Barbie's big-sister benevolence to those less fortunate, a benevolence that relies on inequities and differences in production, consumption, and circulation within late capitalism.[22]

An example of the recuperation of inequalities as diversity is Mattel's multicultural Barbies. Ann Ducille has critiqued Mattel's use of multiculturalism as the commodification of race and gender difference.[23] Using the work of anthropologists Jackie Urla and Alan Swedlund on the anthropometry of Barbie, which shows that the African American Barbie has the same body as the 'regular' Barbie, but its back is angled differently, Ducille points out that difference is merely a matter of costume (sometimes skin color is changed, but not in every case).[24] Though wishing to retain the notion of a genuinely transformative multiculturalism, Ducille suggests that the practices of Mattel and other corporate multiculturalism are 'an easy and immensely profitable way off the hook of Eurocentrism that gives us the face of cultural diversity without the particulars of racial difference.'[25]

Such target marketing increasingly uses U.S. ethnic and sexual identities to sell products and to seek new markets through diversified products, just as consumption practices may be used by groups to differentiate themselves from one another. Transnational corporations rely on the work of multicultural experts to mediate and to produce difference. Ducille's essay emphasizes the place of experts consulting with Mattel about culture, such as the African American experts on children's play who came to believe in the value of a black Barbie as a role model. [...]

Yet in Mattel's story of diversity in the U.S. market, the international as a plurality of homogenized stereotypic national forms also has an important place. This international form is suggested as a market for the fashion and beauty industries, both of which are internationalized in important ways and which support the selling of Barbie. Caricatures of national and international stereotypes include an Elke signifying Sweden, a Mimi from France, a Zizi from Kenya, a Chelsea from England, and a Stacey from the United States. Yet this diversity is framed by an imperial discourse in which, as Ducille points out, English Barbie is dressed as a lady but Jamaican Barbie is dressed as a maid.[26] All of the names can be easily pronounced by people in all parts of the world. This collection is also supposedly educational, since Mattel's annual report mentions that 'little girls can have tons of fun learning to become fashion models.[27] The links of Barbie to the fashion industry and international beauty pageants where racial, ethnic, and national differences are managed in complex ways are visible.[28] This internationalizing of the fashion industry, so that clothes are made in many parts of Asia, has made European and U.S. fashion brands household names in terms of goods both to be made in the garment industry and to be seen in department stores not only in the First World but also in the Third. Such an awareness becomes part of a cultural context in which Barbie is marketed globally.

## Mattel in India: The Production of New Consumer Subjects

In any toy store in India's urban centers catering to the children of the middle and upper classes, one can find not only the whole array of Masters of the Universe dolls […], but also a large range of Barbie dolls. This range includes the blonde Barbie, the brunette, and the bride ('standard,' of course) as well as one refinement for the South Asian market: the Barbie in a sari.

When Mattel began manufacturing for the Indian market in 1986–1987, Barbie was only known to the affluent section of the urban population, to those who traveled to the United States for various reasons, or to Indian immigrants living in the West. In 1991, after the standard Barbie did not sell very well, Barbie emerged with an Indian look, complete with sari, bangles, *bindi*, and black hair. While the Indian affiliate, Leo Mattel, based in Nagpur, produces the dolls, the marketing also is now done by an Indian company, Blowplast Inc., presumably to find more locally specific ways to sell the product by using the services of a company that knows the Indian market. […] Since then, five categories of Barbies have emerged: (1) the penetration Barbie, which is a marketing term denoting that this is the low-end, most accessible Barbie, with shoulder-length hair and Western clothes; (2) Activity Barbie, which includes both black-haired and blonde, long-haired Barbies in a sari; (3) Theme Barbie, such as Best Friend Barbie and Birthday Barbie; (4) Glamour Barbie, such as Happy Holidays Barbie; and (5) Collector Barbie, or Limited Edition Barbie, such as the Expressions of India series, which includes Barbie in Indian costumes from various states (Rajasthan, Panjab, etc.). This array presents diversity in an Indian context. Though Ken does appear in Indian clothes, sales of Ken are small compared with those of Barbie.

Mattel targets the middle and upper classes in India as well as the overseas and diaspora markets, as it creates Barbie in a sari and the new series of Barbies in various authentic and ethnic costumes. While the bottom-line, Western-dress Barbie sells for about Rs. 99 (approx. $2), the traveling Barbie in Indian dress (which did penetrate the market) sells for about Rs. 250 (approx. $6), and the Expressions of India Barbie sells for Rs. 600 (approx. $15). The availability of different Barbies varies with location. The most expensive Barbies, the Collector and Glamour dolls, are available only in the big cities. These expensive Barbies, with depictions of ethnic and regional diversity, are targeted to NRIs and tourists from the West, and Mattel has started to sell these in five-star hotels, airports, and other tourist areas. These versions are priced far above what most people would spend in India and are targeted at the very rich and buyers with dollars, pounds, currrency more powerful than the rupee. […]

Yet gaining a market for Barbie has been difficult for Mattel. There are about two hundred toy stores in all of India; their size ranges from two hundred to about twelve hundred feet. Except for major multinational brands such as Mattel and Funskool, no other manufacturer advertises, and it is left to these two companies to create a new market.[29] The unorganized sector, which used to make most toys, is not able to compete with Mattel and Hasbro, corporations that can afford to buy the molds for these toys, unlike the local manufacturers without transnational links. Whereas Indian versions of many toys popular in the West were available in relatively inexpensive models made from sometimes obsolete molds that were bought in East Asia, at present there is a lack of available molds. Most of the molds are now going to China, where a huge number of toys are being manufactured for the global market. [...]

The Indian government's decision to put toys in the small-scale industry sector (which gets special lower interest rates for loans and other advantages that the manufacturers wish to retain) is also seen as a problem for local manufacturers who do not want to lose their status but wish to expand for the export market. These manufacturers feel that the toy industry could be a large export industry, as in China, but given the government's toy policy, they do not have the support or the incentives to export.[30] Local quality also does not enable them to export, as the government has little interest in toys or their safety. [...]

The localized small-business community considers the toy business a risky investment. Even Lego in India has not done as well as could be supposed, given that it is marketed as an educational toy. This is primarily because until now, children were not the consumer subjects that they are in other parts of the world. The advertising and marketing practices of Mattel and Hasbro are now aimed at turning children into consumers, and gendered ones, within the context of a more transnational media and culture. But as yet, this process has some obstacles. The marketing community itself does not see children as consumers. [...] Economic issues are also key here, since as yet consumption of toys and products designed especially for children is not possible for any except the wealthy. Leo Mattel is trying to advertise toys as an impulse buy in the urban markets, thus attempting to promote shopping as a pastime and as part of a lifestyle motivated by needs spontaneously created from shop windows and displays, and it is taking the lead in developing the toy market in India.

Highly specific, middle-class cultural practices, such as preparing children for an intensely competitive academic arena that determines the future for many, dictate consumption. Board games are best-sellers since they are seen as educational for both boys and girls and they amuse children within the confines of the house, a key element for middle-class girls in an unequal society. Stuffed toys have also been marketed successfully, primarily because they are inexpensive and are made by the unorganized sector. One industry expert told me that in his opinion, toys are primarily sold to the middle classes as birthday gifts, and it is believed that the larger the gift, the better it appears.[31] [...]

Turning many classes of children into active consumers of global brands requires changing the nature of familial aspirations and goals, interactions between parents and children, the segmentation of children's identities in to age groups through consumption, and gender relations within the family. Market segmentation by age and gender as it is slowly emerging in liberalized India means that not only women and men but, increasingly, children are targets of media advertising on TV. The process of incorporating these children into a globalized economy and giving them a sense of themselves within a national as well as a transnational sphere seems now to have begun. The lack of an age-defined children's culture, as it has developed in the West and Japan, however, prevents the formation of the child as consumer, and children remain unindividuated as members of families.

Given the mixed success of Mattel and Hasbro, the emergence of the child-consumer has multiple obstacles, but with changes already occurring in cultural practices in response to the new economic conditions and to NRIs, some consumer segments are emerging. The influence of global media, made possible by the presence of media conglomerates and their local affiliates, has also been key here. The Masters of the Universe toys produced by Mattel were quite a success in the Indian market because they were based on a TV show that was shown frequently and became quite popular. These toys sold well partly because they were targeted at boys, who, I assume, would get more of the discretionary income of families than would girls.[32] [...]

There are some signs, however, that the production of a youth consumer market analogous but not similar to that in the West and in Japan, defined by age, ethnicity, gender, and class, is emerging not only through the media advertising of Hasbro or Mattel, but also through diasporic music culture such as that of *bhangra*, for instance. Historically, no specific market has existed for youth and children in the areas of movies, magazines, and fashion, or even the book industry (which is small except for textbooks and other consumer items related to schoolwork), so that there were few media representations of youth culture outside the productions of transnational media (especially British publications for children, a legacy of colonialism).

In recent years, and given these differences, the marketing of Barbie has been utilizing the emerging modeling, fashion culture that is targeting ever younger age groups among the middle and upper classes and the burgeoning garment industry. Mattel participates in the production of consuming subjects who would buy its products by tapping into the gendered and classed forms that multinational culture in India has created. Thus not only is Mattel's Indian affiliate working to use the gender and class formations that emerged in the 1980s and 1990s, but all of its advertising is geared toward this new Indian global consumer. This new consumer culture includes a pop feminist ideology that sees itself as transnational in that it includes women living in India as well as in its diasporas. Advertising appears in women's general and movie magazines such as *Stardust*, *Savvy*, and *Filmfare*, since women are still seen as primary consumers on behalf of children. These magazines are much more diverse and are renewing themselves through liberalization. Their direction is toward a specific form of patriarchal quasi-feminism that keeps a dominant patriarchy in place just as it does in the United States, where Mattel sells huge numbers of astronaut and doctor Barbies.

With a boom in what is called the vanity industry in urban, middle-class India, it is clear that the nature of urban consumption participates in and constructs new gender relations. The emergence of advertising in many realms means that appearance as symbolic capital has much more currency than it did in the area of middle-class employment, especially if women are to participate as workers in multinational corporations and their affiliates. This Indian pop feminism, denoting a participation in a globalized economy not only as consumers but also as professionals (models, advertising executives, marketing experts, and small-business owners, especially in garment manufacturing), is influencing the career goals of more Indian urban women of the middle and upper classes, just as the role of working-class and poor urban women as factory workers and garment industry workers is also increasing. [...]

Leo Mattel's recent campaign utilized the burgeoning transnational modeling and fashion industry to increase interest in Barbie. Mattel sponsored a fashion design competition in the urban schools in Bombay. A model dressed in Barbie clothes was sent to the schools to give away Barbies and to initiate a design competition among the schoolgirls. All entries were exhibited at two huge exhibition halls, and the entrants and their parents were invited to this event. Movie star Hema Malini was brought in to inaugurate the marketing campaign, which was conducted in urban schools in Calcutta, New Delhi, and Bangalore as well. Interschool competitions were also encouraged, and the winning designs were put together and featured in a fashion show. Two famous models were brought in as judges. The winners from the Bombay show will be used in a limited-edition Barbie with the schoolgirl designer's name and school on the package. Mattel's 'Fun and Learn' concept is being used to encourage young schoolgirls to become fashion designers in a transnational garment industry in which the *salwar-kameez* is now a widespread item of clothing in South Asia as well as its diasporas. It is clear that Mattel's advertising utilizes the existing children's culture in which preparation for a career remains the dominant motivator for consumption.

Participation in localized gendering practices, in which economic liberalization has led to the promotion of fashion design and fashion modeling as new career opportunities for middle- and upper-class girls and women, fosters the proliferation of new body images (thinner and taller) and new fashions (hybrids of European and Indian clothing acceptable in diaspora and urban India). Transnationalization incorporates diaspora fashion to present successful role models and opportunities, promoting ethnic looks and encouraging darker, Asian models in the West to participate in the transnational garment industry much more than they used to. Gendered consumers, constructed by an Indian pop-cosmopolitan feminism formed as much by Bollywood's as by Hollywood's circulating productions, are participating as producers and workers as well as consumers in the transnational garment/fashion/beauty industry, to which Mattel is allying its products. Ethnic and Asian looks will sell not only as exotica but also because of the large diasporic Asian markets in multiple locations.

## Diasporic Subjects and Transnational Contexts

During the 1980s the youth and transnational market had not yet emerged, so Barbie sales did not fulfill expectations. But the changing context of the 1990s indicates that sales might improve. Two contexts are important here: the transnational market for Indian goods, which includes the diaspora, and the alteration of the Barbie image and marketing that tapped into and hailed new consumer subjects. Given the ways in which diasporic and national formations are intertwined in the socioeconomic practices of economic liberalization in India, the Barbie in a sari could enable, for instance, children of South Asian immigrants in the United States to give their children what they want, the standard Barbie, but with a difference that reminds them of their traditional culture – an important aspect of the formation of multicultural identity in America. Since national icons of female beauty have been transnational for decades because of the reach and circulation of Bombay cinema, the incorporation of diasporic female bodies into these productions has brought new representations back home. In the context of a national culture where unity and diversity were seen as typical of India, the creation of ethnic types moves both from India to diasporic communities and back to India as well.

As I mentioned before, the Barbie in a sari is very popular among Indian immigrants in the United States, but the interplay between the diaspora culture in the United States, the multinationals, and the production and circulation of gendered subjects is taking place in complex ways. The traditional female icons of the Bombay cinema, with their images based on Bollywood versions of Ajanta and Ellora figures, remain powerful but conflict with the diaspora cultures of the United Kingdom and the United States.[33] These two diasporas have influenced cultural productions such as music and fashion more than other South Asian diaspora cultures from East Asia or Africa, which emerged at very different periods of history and through different economic conditions.[34]

In recent years the Indian diasporas have been targeted as investors in the Indian liberalization program and as consumers of Indian products. For many decades the dominance of Bombay cinema, for one, has been in a complex relation with national and transnational culture, since its audience has not been solely within India. In the earlier decades of the industry, the Middle East was a big market for Bombay cinema, and at the present time the video market overseas amongst the South Asian diasporas competes with the video market in India. Bombay cinema is also the main attraction on many TV channels shown in India, as well as in the Hong Kong-based Star TV network. [...]

The Indian fashion industry, using the *salwar-kameez* as the primary new South Asian costume, spans the globe, selling to native South Asians and women of South Asian descent around the world, as well as to many Middle Easterners. The emergence of the ready-to-wear *salwar-kameez* as the dress for women of Indian origin living elsewhere as well as for the many women entering the professionalized workforce in multinational corporations within India has changed the Indian garment industry.[35] This industry is located not only in India or Pakistan but also in London, from whence fashion catalogs printed on glossy paper sell expensive garments. The interest in tradition and ethnicity has emerged among cosmopolitans in India as well as its diaspora.

That such a nationalism has to negotiate transnational contexts is apparent in the many beauty contests proliferating among South Asian communities in the United States. The Miss India Los Angeles pageant presents the American female body ideal in a very different style inspired as much by Bollywood and an urban Indian culture as by the U.S.-European fashion industry. [...]

These diasporic subjects, even those seen as Westernized according to Indian nationalists, are crucial for the global economy and for the nation-states. The creation of the NRI as a financial category indicates this imperative. In addition to the practices of the nation-state that creates the NRI category, media productions from India also maintain relations between the South Asian diaspora and its home. Newsmagazines such as *India Today*, an India-based publication, have created North American special editions to actively promote such investments and keep up NRI interest. [...]

Many South Asian professionals are discovering that multinationals allow them a return to home in the form of positions within Indian branches and affiliates. Since these professionals are often paid in dollars, their economic status is far above that of Indians who are paid in rupees. Multinationals are finding it useful to employ the expertise of immigrants who have worked in the West but who speak the language of and have grown up in India. Their affiliations, loyalties, and conflicts within the local and the global economies become contingent and flexible. It can certainly be said, however, that real estate and other price levels in India might rise with the creation of this transnational class that will include not only certain NRIs but also Indian residents who are able to insert themselves into the multinational corporate culture.

This upper-class, transnational NRI, or the international Indian, is being targeted by the Indian state not only to invest but also to buy Indian goods. This NRI is separated by class position from persons of Indian origin who live within the country or outside it and who do not directly benefit from the new investment climate in India. One new and recent publication was created just for this transnational, upper-class NRI by a group called Media Transasia in New Delhi. Titled *Elite: For the International Indian*, the two first issues feature 'successful Indians' on the cover: Zubin Mehta with his wife, Nancy, and Arjun Waney, a garment entrepreneur with his wife, Judy.[36] In this context, success denotes marrying a white, American woman. This glossy magazine not only sells India as a place for investment; it also sells the lifestyle of the transnational NRI in America, with ads for carpets, expensive clothes, jewelry, furniture, and of course, five-star tourism. [...]

This international Indian is not the only cosmopolitan subject within India. The category also includes professionals of Indian origin who have lived in the West and who move to India for corporate assignments. Whereas many professionals in India have European or U.S. training, these people were not the corporate heads, who were mostly white males stationed in what were seen as distant locations. In the 1990s, however, multinational corporations increasingly utilized the local knowledge of some executives to send them home. AT&T, Motorola, Digital International, and PepsiCo are some companies with Indian expatriates at their head. Companies run advertisements in Indian newspapers such as *India Today* in the United States to recruit engineers and financial executives. [...]

For the transnational NRI who lives in the West, concern for Indian tradition and culture and, by extension, for daughters and sons growing up in the United States, is crucial here. The control of women's sexuality, done very differently in the United States and in India, is negotiated in terms of an imagined India where female sexuality is believed to be safeguarded and an impure United States where it is thought to be constantly in jeopardy. Control of sons is done both through sexuality and through their ability to earn and to become part of the professional class. Diasporic masculinity is policed rigorously through notions of a modern heteromasculinity in which, for the middle classes, professions such as the sciences, technology, or medicine count for success. With an increasing homophobia among U.S.-based South Asian communities in light of more visible gay and lesbian communities of color, the policing of male sexuality is also taking new forms. [...]

Magazines such as *India Today* are directed at the professional immigrants who fit both the model-minority notion of ethnicity in the United States and the image of the NRI as investor in the nation-state. Neglected both as audiences and as subjects are the two-thirds of the immigrants of Indian origin who are neither professionals nor from the upper classes, such as various groups who migrated from Fiji, Malaysia, the Caribbean, or Africa. Although about 12 percent of immigrants from India live below the poverty line in the United States, these are not people at whom the Indian government directs its advertisements for investment.

## Transnational Subjects of Consumption: Barbie, Diaspora, and Home

The presence of the national in the multicultural and of the American lifestyle in the ethnic and in the global reveals that nationalisms are crucial in this global economy. Indeed many of the subjects of nationalism and multiculturalism are produced through transnational consumption practices. An examination of such practices reveals that America as symbol of consumption style is both powerful and heterogeneous. As Stuart Hall puts it, the new cultural forms in the global mass culture are recognizable in their ability to 'recognize and absorb ... differences within the larger overarching framework of what is essentially an American conception of the world' in which capital has had 'to negotiate, ... to incorporate and partly to reflect the differences it was trying to overcome.'[37] The conjunction of modernity and consumption with identity has indeed come to be hegemonic. To be Indian or Pakistani or Bangladeshi in the United States means shopping at particular stores, be they Pakistani or Indian, wearing and buying *salwar-kameez* and saris, and living in relation to an ethnic style, where style, as Stuart Ewen suggests, has emerged as the 'predominant expression of meaning.'[38] For some diasporics, looking toward home for the latest style becomes an important aspect of constructing a multicultural identity, even as the denial of the diaspora as a site of cultural production can be used for new nationalisms.

The problem of a hyphenated identity becomes highlighted here. For many immigrant groups ethnicized in particular ways in the United States, a hyphenated identity may only be part of the story of subjects in transnationality. The NRI is a subject produced by the discourses of the Indian nation-state in conjunction with diasporic nationalisms and global finance capital. The American subject figures prominently in metropolitan discourses of the global consumer in India and within many formations of Indian nationalist anxieties in different sites. Consumption practices are thus a crucial part of the formation of subjects in transnationality. Barbie  in a sari enables the localization of these subjects.

## Notes

My thanks and deep appreciation to all who encouraged and supported me in writing this essay. In particular, I'd like to thank Caren Kaplan, Parama Roy, Tani Barlow, Eric Smoodin, Minoo Moallem, Arvind Rajagopal, and Jasbir Puar. I'd also like to thank the Center for South Asia Studies, University of California, Berkeley, and the Center for South Asia, University of Wisconsin, Madison, for inviting me to present this paper and for the feedback from the audiences.

1. See, for instance, Erica Rand, *Barbie's Queer Accessories* (Durham, N.C.: Duke University Press, 1995); Ann Ducille, 'Dyes and Dolls: Multicultural Barbie and the Merchandising of Difference,' *differences* 6 (spring 1994): 46–68.

2. See the chapter titled 'Fashion Fables of an Urban Village,' in Emma Tarlo's *Clothing Matters: Dress and Identity in India* (Chicago: University of Chicago Press, 1996), 284–317.

3. For a good explanation of this concept see Stuart Hall's chapter 'The Spectacle of the "Other,"' in *Representation: Cultural Representations and Signifying Practices,* ed. Stuart Hall, (London: Sage, 1997), 270.

4. A parallel issue of the role of cultural studies and the intersection of diaspora studies, feminist studies, and area studies in a transnational perspective is raised by my choice of topic: Barbie.

5. Rob Wilson and Wimal Dissanayake, 'Introduction: Tracking the Global/Local,' in *Global/Local: Cultural Production and the Transnational Imaginary,* ed. Wilson and Dissanayake (Durham, N.C.: Duke University Press, 1996), 1–19.

6. See, for instance, Roger Rouse's discussion of 'America' as marketing tool in 'Thinking through Transnationalism: Notes on the Cultural Politics of Class Relations in the Contemporary United States,' *Public Culture* 7 (winter 1995): 353–402.

7. *BusinessWorld,* 1–14 November 1995, 42–49.

8. Ibid.

9. Leslie Sklair, *Sociology of the Global System* (Baltimore, Md.: Johns Hopkins University Press, 1991).

10. *Asian Wall Street Journal,* 6 October 1985.

11. *Asian Wall Street Journal,* 1 January 1988.

12. *Los Angeles Times,* 22 September 1996.

13. *Mattel Corporation Annual Report,* 1989.

14. See Eric Smoodin's *Disney Discourse* (New York: Routledge, 1994), and Smoodin, *Animating Culture* (New Brunswick, N.J.: Rutgers University Press, 1993), for the connections between U.S. nationalism, imperialism, and the Cold War.

15. *Mattel Corporation Annual Report,* 1992.

16. Rand, *Barbie's Queer Accessories,* 28–29.

17. See Rand, *Barbie's Queer Accessories,* for more on this topic.

18. Arjun Appadurai, *Modernity at Large: Cultural Dimensions of Globalization* (Minneapolis, MN: University of Minnesota Press, 1996), 54–55.

19. Lauren Berlant, *The Queen of America Goes to Washington, D.C.* (Durham, N.C.: Duke University Press, 1997), 158. The chapter quoted is coauthored with Elizabeth Freeman.

20. I am indebted to Liisa Malkki for this idea about the girl-child as an international subject.

21. Rand, *Barbie's Queer Accessories,* 87.

22. Caren Kaplan, 'A World without Boundaries: The Body Shop's Trans/national Geographies,' *Social Text* 13 (fall 1995): 45–66.

23. Ducille, 'Dyes and Dolls,' 46–68.

24. Jacquiline Urla and Alan Swedlund, 'The Anthropometry of Barbie: Unsettling Ideals of the Feminine Body in Popular Culture,' in *Deviant Bodies: Critical Perspectives on Difference in Science and Popular Culture,* ed. Jennifer Terry and Jacquiline Urla (Bloomington, IN: Indiana University Press, 1995).

25. Ducille, 'Dyes and Dolls,' 52.

26. Ibid.

27. *Mattel Corporation Annual Report,* 1986.

28. Colleen B. Cohen, Richard Wilk, and Beverly Stoeltje, eds., *Beauty Queens on the Global Stage* (New York: Routledge, 1996).

29. *BusinessWorld,* 18 September–1 October 1996, 74–78.

30. *BusinessWorld,* 11–24 March 1996, 131–132.

31. Conversation with Bharat Ponga, an entrepreneur in Ludhiana, January 1997.

32. I am making this point contrary to industry experts and parents with whom I spoke in India who assured me that there was gender parity in how income was spent on boys and girls. Much feminist research indicates otherwise.

33. It is worthy of note that the Miss World contest sponsored by the Indian consumer-goods manufacturer Godrej and movie star Amitabh Bachchan's new corporation, ABCL, used an image from the Ajanta caves in its publicity campaign.

34. An earlier and quite different example is M. K. Gandhi's experiences in Africa and their impact on the trajectory of Indian nationalism.

35. Naseem Khan, 'Asian Women's Dress: From Burqah to Bloggs – Changing Clothes for Changing Times,' in *Chic Thrills*, ed. Juliet Ash and Elizabeth Wilson (Berkeley and Los Angeles: University of California Press, 1993): 61–74.

36. *Elite* 1, no. 1 (February–March 1994), and no. 2 (April–May 1994).

37. Stuart Hall, 'The Local and the Global: Globalization and Ethnicity,' in *Dangerous Liaisons: Gender, Nation, and Postcolonial Perspectives*, ed. Anne McClintock, Aamir Mufti, and Ella Shohat (Minneapolis, MN: University of Minnesota Press, 1997), 173–187.

38. Stuart Ewen, *All Consuming Images: The Politics of Style in Contemporary Culture* (New York: Basic Books, 1988), 271.

# Chapter 17

## Janet Wasko

# Corporate Disney in Action

[...] The enforcement of intellectual property rights has become a vital issue for media and entertainment companies, especially in light of the proliferation of branded products, as well as the increased global marketing of products. For instance, American film companies have elicited the assistance of an army of lawyers and the FBI to enforce their property rights in the USA, as well as the State Department and Interpol in foreign markets. Piracy remains a thorn in the side of the Hollywood majors, which claim that billions of dollars are lost each year from unauthorized use and sale of their products.[1]

Disney has long been known for its tough enforcement of intellectual property rights and has a rich history of litigation against and/or harassment of potential copyright violators. When Team Disney took command, the campaign accelerated to the point that the company declared a 'war on merchandise pirates' in 1988. 'This anti-piracy program continues as one of our top priorities,' said Paul Pressler, vice-president of Disney's merchandise licensing. 'Our characters are the foundation of our business and project the image of our company, so it's imperative that we control who uses them and how they are used.'[2] Between 1986 and 1991, the company filed 28 suits against more than 1,322 defendants. One of the largest actions was in 1991, when Disney filed against 123 California companies and 99 Oregon companies for unauthorized use of characters in various types of merchandise. [3]

While the company regularly pursues a large number of copyright cases, some incidents have received more attention than others. For instance, in 1989, Disney threatened to sue three Florida day-care centers for unauthorized use of their characters in murals. The day-care centers removed the figures and replaced them with

From: Janet Wasko, *Understanding Disney: The Manufacture of Fantasy*. Cambridge: Polity Press, 2001.

characters from Universal and Hanna-Barbera cartoons, which were provided at no expense. The incident was widely reported and is often used as a classic example of Disney's obsession with controlling its characters.

Also in 1989, Disney sued the Academy of Motion Pictures Arts and Sciences when performers dressed as *Snow White* characters were used in the Academy Awards presentation without Disney's permission. The case was withdrawn, but many in Hollywood were amazed at Disney's pettiness.

More recently, the Disney company was able to force a French AIDS association to withdraw a campaign featuring provocative versions of *Snow White* and *Cinderella* characters. While French law allows for parodies of copyrighted cartoon characters, the president of the advertising agency handling the campaign admitted that the campaign was withdrawn because of pressure from the Disney company.

While the corporation may be within its rights in protecting its properties, the company's public responses are often brash and arrogant. To cite an instance, British papers reported early in 1998 that the Disney company was closely watching the development of the Millennium Dome in Greenwich after visits to Orlando, Florida, by British Secretary of State for Trade and Industry Peter Mandelson. One journalist pointed out that the Disney company is 'famously protective of its copyright' and cited a Disney executive: 'He [Mandelson] may be a minister of the British Government, but we are the Walt Disney Corporation and we don't roll over for anyone.'[4]

Yet another case was the refusal of the company to provide free use of Disney characters for US postage stamps celebrating American animation. We have seen Bugs Bunny, Daffy Duck, Tweetie Pie, and Sylvester (Warner Brothers' characters) adorning US mail. As one reporter says:

> But don't expect to see such other cartoon favorites as Mickey Mouse, Donald Duck or Goofy on stamps any time soon. At least not as long as the money-hungry executives at Walt Disney Studios demand that the Postal Service pay royalties for the right to depict their stable of characters on stamps.
>
> Ironically, it was Disney that first suggested a series of stamps depicting the studio's cartoon characters. After securing tentative agreement from Washington, Disney's minions asked how much the quasi-governmental agency would pay for the right to issue a Minnie Mouse or Pluto stamp.
>
> [Postmaster General Marvin] Runyon is reported to have said 'not one red cent,' and Disney replied 'no deal.' It was a good ruling on the Postal Service's part.
>
> Warner Brothers immediately stepped in and agreed to allow use of its trademark characters without requiring royalty payments. That's why we saw thousands of bunnies instead of mice on stamps this year.[5]

## Copyright Extension Act, 1998

The company's concern with intellectual property rights became crystal clear when Congress faced the issue of extending copyright protection in 1998. Michael Eisner and the Disney company led a successful lobbying campaign to convince Congress to pass legislation extending copyrights, representing a classic example of how Hollywood clout can influence the legislative process.

The bill, initially introduced by singer/actor turned Congressman Sonny Bono, proposed changes in the copyright law to allow corporations to have exclusive rights over their copyrighted properties for 95 years rather than the 75 years allowed in the existing law. Also, copyrights held by individuals were to be extended to a total of 70 years after death, rather than 50 years.

While proponents argued that the extension was necessary to match the European Union's recent copyright extension, some legal experts pointed out that the bill represented a 'wealth transfer' benefiting large entertainment and publishing corporations. While supporters of the bill who held that it was noncontroversial were able to keep it out of public debate, opponents argued that the bill was not in the public's interest. 'Making money isn't what copyright law is about,' said Adam Eisgrau of the American Libraries Association. 'The purpose of the law is to provide a sufficient incentive to authors and inventors to create information, not because there is a constitutional entitlement to compensation but because the information created was regarded as a public good.'[6]

Corporate copyright holders, such as Disney, lobbied Congress directly, as well as calling on their pals at the Motion Picture Association of America (MPAA), which used 'its own heavyweight lobbyist: its president, Jack Valenti, who called on his own decades-long contacts with legislators to move the bill.'[7] But the legislation was apparently too important to rely only on face-to-face lobbying tactics. Disney provided campaign contributions to ten of the 13 initial sponsors of the House bill and eight of the 12 sponsors of the Senate bill.

The significance of the legislation was revealed in press coverage of the eventual success of the campaign, which pointed out that Disney's copyright on Mickey Mouse was scheduled to expire in 2003, on Pluto in 2005, on Goofy in 2007, and on Donald Duck in 2009.[8]

While Disney plays tough when it comes to protecting its own properties, the same treatment is not accorded for those bold enough to offer their ideas to the Mouse House. The Disney website explains that the company's policy prohibits the acceptance of creative ideas or materials, other than those requested. However, if someone does submit such material, the policy is clear:

> the Submissions shall be deemed, and shall remain, the property of DISNEY(sic). ... DISNEY shall exclusively own all now known or hereafter existing rights to the Submissions of every kind and nature throughout the universe and shall be entitled to unrestricted use of the Submissions for any purpose whatsoever, commercial or otherwise, without compensation to the provider of the Submissions.[9]

[...]

## Controlling Labor: Working for the Mouse House

Another element in Disney's exercise of control is its relationship with its workers. According to the 1998 10-K report, the company employed approximately 117,000 people, including a wide assortment of workers in its diverse businesses. The Disney name is an attraction for potential employees, who may have dreamed all their lives about working at the studio or one of the theme parks. Still, the allure of the Magic Kingdom can be deceptive.

It appears that many Disney employees are quite pleased with their work environment, as reported in a 'company snapshot' from VaultReports.com, a website that includes information on corporations for prospective employees. Based on interviews and surveys, the report noted that employees feel that working for Disney is a boost to their career, and that the perks offered them are seldom matched by other companies (theme park admission, merchandise discounts, etc.).

Yet, the study also found that salaries are typically below industry standards and that the company's bureaucracy can be discouraging if employee expectations are too high. The report warns prospective workers, 'Despite the warm and fuzzy material it produces, at its core Disney is a rigid corporate bureaucracy.' As a seasoned Disney worker explained, new employees become 'disillusioned because they envision The Walt Disney Company as a Magic Kingdom kind of place which is a fairytale land devoid of bureaucracy, politics, and other unsavory things like financial analysis. No such place exists.'[10]

The company promotes itself as a 'community,' in which employees share in decision making, and promotions are made from within the company. The informal familiarity at Disney is well known, symbolized by everyone being addressed by their first name. However, within different sectors of the company, there are specific ways that employees are controlled. The next two sections discuss workers at the studio and at the theme parks.

## Studio Workers/Animation

Historically, the employees who have attracted the most attention at Disney have been those involved with animation. As John Lent explains, American animation was founded on labor exploitation, not only at Disney, but at most of the Hollywood animation companies, where 'talented animators worked extremely long hours at grueling, tedious jobs for low wages and with virtually no credit.'[11]

[...] the labor strife in the early 1940s was not at all surprising considering the low pay and lack of recognition at the Disney studio. Salaries were reported to be the lowest in the film industry, with inkers and in-betweeners at Disney receiving between $17 and $26 a week in the 1930s into the 1940s. Long hours and quotas were common, and animators were sometimes forced to take work home. But the loss of control over their work also frustrated Disney employees. Whatever was produced by employees while at the studio belonged to the company, and [...] Walt Disney controlled virtually the entire animation process. Consequently, the Disney style of animation that developed left little room for experimentation and individual creative touches.

During the 1960s, Disney joined other companies in sending work overseas, where it could be done more cheaply. The 1990s renaissance in animation has been due in part to Team Disney's revival of the Classic Disney animated features, but also to new television and cable channels featuring cartoons and animated series. This has meant more work for animators in Hollywood, but also more animation work abroad, especially in the growing offshore animation centers in Japan, Taiwan, South Korea, Canada, and Australia. Typically, pre-production activities are done in the USA, while cel drawing, coloring (by hand), inking, painting, and camera work are done abroad. Post-production is still typically done in the USA.[12]

Although it is claimed that there has been a shortage of animators in the USA during this animation boom, there is ample evidence that producers have looked to offshore animation workers to save money. As one producer explains, 'If we had to do animation here, it would cost a million dollars instead of $100,000 to $150,000 to produce a half hour, and nobody could afford to do it except for Disney.'[13]

Yet Disney also sends a good deal of its animation work overseas, either to its own companies or as the sole client of other companies. When Disney accelerated its animation production for both film and television in the mid-1980s, it turned to Japanese animation companies. In 1989, Walt Disney Animation Japan was created, where drawing, inking, coloring, and shooting were done. Disney also purchased the Hanna-Barbera Australia studio in 1989, where work on the company's series, specials, and made-for-video movies has been done. Additional work on Disney animated productions is subcontracted to companies in South Korea and China. Closer to home, Disney opened studios in Toronto and Vancouver in 1996, creating about 225 jobs for animators, directors, designers, storyboard and layout artists, as well as a digital ink and paint production team.

While wages at the Asian animation factories are reported to be relatively high for animators and managers, conditions for other workers who perform the 'drudge work' of inking, coloring, etc., are less than impressive. As Lent points out, 'Of course, that is what attracts the foreign companies in the first place: large numbers of individuals willing to work hard for low wages in a stable setting.'[14] How these pools of trained animators contribute to building domestic animation in these countries is still an open question.

Meanwhile, it is also unclear what this offshore activity means for US animators, especially when and if the animation boom slows. Previously, American animators have protested runaway production, specifically in 1979, when the Motion Picture Screen Cartoonists IATSE Local 839 walked out and demanded a restriction on the export of work from Los Angeles studios unless qualified union members were hired first. Nevertheless, the studios continue to use foreign labor, even when high unemployment rates are experienced by union workers. Consequently, it seems likely that the historical tension between animators and management may continue.

## Theme Park Workers

The 'happiest places on earth' are renowned for their happy and helpful employees. But this doesn't happen automatically, and, by some accounts, working at the Magic Kingdom is not always magical.[15] After a two-year study of Walt Disney World, Kuenz concluded that 'Disney's control of its labor force is apparently near total; the workers themselves certainly perceive it as such.' Despite the company policy requiring employees to waive their right to write about their work experiences, Kuenz found employees who were more than anxious to talk about their jobs at the Magic Kingdom.

As noted above, the chance of working at one of the Disney parks is an alluring fantasy for some people. Thus, the Disney company seems to have no problem in finding plenty of interested workers for its parks and resorts. It's a question of whether these potential employees fit (or are willing to fit) the Disney mold.

One of the ways that Disney actively recruits young, eager workers is through the Walt Disney World College Program, which attracts over 3,000 students from the USA and other countries each year. The program includes seminars that encompass work and classroom experiences. While a job at the park may not necessarily follow, students who complete the program are awarded mock degrees, a Mousters or a Ductorate.

Employee training is a common practice for many American corporations, but Disney's training of theme park employees is legendary. With the opening of Disneyland in the 1950s, the company created its own training program called 'The Disney University,' which now operates 'campuses' at each of the theme parks and at the Disney studio in Burbank. The training program includes teaching future employees ('cast members') the company history and philosophy in a two-day course called 'Traditions,' which has been cited by management experts as one of the 'best indoctrination programs' in the world.[16] It is here that new employees learn to accept the control of the company. Zibart explains it as 'a mix of company legend, behavioral guidelines, and psycho-social bonding. 'You come out totally believing in "The Disney Way",' said a five-year veteran. 'It's almost like Walt is alive and well … . We call it getting doused with pixie dust. It lasts about a year – and of course some people have to go through it again."[17]

During the course, new employees learn about 'The Disney Culture' – defined in company literature as 'the values, myths, heroes and symbols that have a significant meaning to the employees … Ours is a culture that is so strong it has withstood the test of time and is recognized all over the world.'

Most importantly, park workers learn about the Disney approach to serving the public and 'preserving the integrity of the show.' Employees are required to smile, to make eye contact, to display appropriate body language, and to seek out guests. Some analysts have referred to this as 'emotional labor,' defined as 'expressing socially desired emotions during service transactions.'[18] There is also a long list of taboos, including: never embarrass a guest, never be out of character, never improvise with scripts, never fraternize with other workers, never wear costumes anywhere but in the assigned area, etc. Those employees who learn well and exhibit exemplary service are called Guest Service Fanatics, as outlined in Box 17.1.

## BOX 17.1 GUIDELINES FOR A GUEST SERVICE FANATIC

### Service

- Always makes eye contact and smiles
- Exceeds guest expectations and seeks out guest contact
- Always gives outstanding quality service
- Greets and welcomes each and every guest
- Maintains a high personal standard of quality in their work

### Teamwork

- Goes 'beyond the call of duty'
- Demonstrates strong team initiative
- Communicates aggressively with guests and fellow Cast Members
- Preserves the 'magical' guest experience

*(Continued)*

**BOX 17.1 (Continued)**

**Attitude**

- 100% Performance
- Extremely courteous and friendly
- Displays appropriate body language at all times
- Exemplifies the Disney Look
- Says 'Thank You' to each and every guest

**Recovery**

- Provides immediate service recovery
- Aggressively seeks opportunities to fully satisfy our guests
- Solves guest problems before they become dissatisfied
- Demonstrates patience and honesty in handling complaints
- Always preserves the integrity of our show

Emphasizes safety, courtesy, show quality, and efficiency!

*Source*: Material distributed by the Walt Disney Company

Training also includes specific guidelines on what to do in emergency situations, as the Disney company is notorious for keeping these situations under their control. For instance, safety guidelines instruct workers never to use 'panic words' – fire, car accident, ambulance, and evacuation – but to use 'Disney terminology' – Signal 25, Signal 4, Alpha Unit, and Exiting. Employees are carefully instructed on how to deal with these situations to avoid upsetting guests, as well as to control the potentially damaging publicity that may follow. [19]

After the Disney indoctrination, all 'cast members' are on probationary status for a specific period of time, while their 'leader' (or just 'lead') monitors their performance. Seasonal cast members are on continuous probationary status and are thus advised by the company to 'pay particular attention to our policies and procedures.'[20]

In addition to wearing specific 'costumes,' 'cast members' must also adhere to a strict grooming code. In other words, the uniform, 'squeaky-clean' look of employees at the parks is not automatic or natural, but the result of strict enforcement of 'The Disney Look.' Some of the specifications of the code, drawn from a company brochure entitled 'The Disney Look,' include the following:

For hosts – neat, natural haircuts 'tapered so that it does not extend beyond or cover any part of your ears.' [Illustrations in the 'Disney Look' manual provide examples of acceptable and unacceptable haircuts.] No mustaches or beards are allowed, however, deodorant is required.

For hostesses – no 'extremes' in hair styles; confinement of long hair by acceptable accessories, ... a plain barrette, comb or headband in gold, silver, or tortoise shell without ornamentation of any kind including bows. No more than two barrettes or combs; only natural makeup is permitted, and only clear or flesh toned fingernail polish. Polishes that are dark red, frosted, gold or silver toned are not considered part of the 'Disney Look.' Finger nails should not exceed one-fourth of an inch beyond the fingertip.

More recently, the restrictions have been expanded to include no shaved heads, no visible tattoos, no nose or other piercing, except the ear lobe, where two are allowed for women only. The Disney Look is serious business. According to the employee (or 'cast member') handbook, 'continued violation' of the appearance policy is grounds for dismissal.

There are lots of other reasons why theme park employees may be 'fired on the spot' – especially those workers who wear the famed Disney character costumes around the park and hotels and for special appearances. Most importantly, they are never, ever, ever allowed to remove their character's head in front of park guests, even if they are ill or unconscious, which apparently is quite often. With no peripheral vision, navigating in the awkward and sometimes dangerous outfits can be tricky, although the workers inside them must always stay in character. The costumes are so hot and heavy that those inside them often become sick to their stomachs or pass out.[21] It seems obvious that preserving the 'magical' guest experience is more important than workers' welfare. [...]

In addition to staying in character, maintaining the show, and serving guests, park employees must also be aware that they are being watched or monitored. Employees report an obsession with getting people through the rides as quickly as possible, with time-motion experts monitoring the 'hourly operational ride capacity.' A former employee explains, 'At Big Thunder Mountain, I'm supposed to handle 2,000 visitors an hour. It's just like a factory with assembly-line production, only this is a fun factory.'[22]

Furthermore, the workers who Kuenz interviewed suggested that everyone is spying on everyone else at the theme parks. 'Foxes' are disguised employees (dressed as tourists with cameras) who spy on guests, attempting to prevent various kinds of mischief, including shoplifting and theft in the park. Meanwhile, 'shoppers' – also disguised as tourists – monitor and test employees to make sure they are adhering to the Disney rules of behavior. Kuenz concludes:

> The collective paranoia inculcated in Disney workers from the get go – manifested in the suspicion that there is always another rule one can be found breaking – and which results in their feeling that they are always expected to perform the frequently irritating role of 'Disney cast member,' is a function of both the tight control that the company exercises over its dominions and a segmented and hierarchical system of relations between management and labor and within labor itself.[23]

## The rewards: salaries, promotions, perks

Although the workers at the parks are subject to a particular kind of control, other policies apply to all employees of the company. The VaultReport cited earlier notes that 'The Disney pay scale, unfortunately, doesn't match the high sheen of the Disney name.' Prospective employees are warned that the company's pay scale is 10–15 percent below the market, and raises are slow and erratic. Another employee explains that 'in a way, you're paid just with the Disney name.' The report concludes that 'This works to Disney's advantage, but can be a trap [for employees].[24]

Moreover, Disney workers are certainly well aware of the 'exorbitant executive salaries' discussed in chapter 3. Recall that the Chief Mouse, Michael Eisner, receives a $750,000 salary with stock options that regularly place him in the top

Table 17.1  *Salary compensation comparisons*

|  | Annual | Weekly | Daily | Hourly | Per minute |
|---|---|---|---|---|---|
| Eisner | $204,236,801 | $3,927,631 | $785,526 | $98,191 | $1,637 |
| Minimum wage earner | $9,880 | $190 | $38 | $4.75 | $0.08 |
| Average Worker | $24,700 | $475 | $95 | $11.88 | $0.20 |
| President of the USA | $200,000 | $3,846 | $769 | $96 | $1.60 |

*Source*: 'Paywatch Fact Sheet,' NABET-CWA website, http://pw2.netcom.com/-nabet16/page24.html (using 1997 AFL-CIO data)

brackets of executive compensation. Meanwhile, the lowliest of Worker Mice at the Disney theme parks typically work for minimum wage.[25] A comparison of these different salaries is presented in Table 17.1. As a union representative explains:

> The fact of the matter is that real wages and benefits for most rank-and-file workers at Disney have gone down significantly since Eisner and his top crew came aboard. And, to be sure, this sacrifice on their part is a major reason why corporate profit and executive salaries have gone up at Disney. But what about the sacrifice on the part of Eisner and his senior executives. Where is it? I guess leadership by example doesn't count for much these days.[26]

The company also appears to be inflexible in negotiations with prospective employees. The VaultReport quotes an employee who explains that 'Disney is an 800-pound gorilla in the marketplace. They know it and aren't afraid to use it, which can be frustrating.'

Despite the rhetoric of equal opportunity and promotion from within, employees claim that 'to move into a higher position, they had to be favored by someone above them, which usually requires them to be obsequious, not make problems, not complain.'[27] For instance, promotions at the theme parks are often made to the position of 'lead' – a sub-management job that is not actually considered that of a supervisor or a manager. However, leads are still the 'first line of supervision,' although they have little power and, contrary to company rhetoric, do not often move subsequently into actual supervisory positions.[28] The hierarchical system at the parks divides the work force into specialized units with separate managers, who are 'all working earnestly at their one task, the left hand oblivious to the right.' As Kuenz notes, it's the model for work in the new world order: 'This is a world in which all social planning has been replaced – as every attraction at EPCOT's Future World predicts and hopes it will be – by corporate planning, every advance in social coordination conforming to and confirming the logic of the company's needs.'[29]

Contributing to this Brave New World scenario, many employees are exceptionally devoted to the Disney company, which is claimed to have an unusually low employee turnover rate (although there are contradictory claims of a relatively high worker turnover).[30] One explanation is that the company 'fosters both a sense of responsibility and a sense of fun.'[31] It's a company where the lowliest worker calls the CEO 'Michael,' where 'cast members' make people from all over the world happy, where employees receive free passes to the parks, where apparently there is an endless supply of pixie dust.

## Mickey as teamster

Disney deals with a number of trade union organizations, as do other Hollywood corporations.[32] Generally, union representation for the film and entertainment industries has become increasingly more diversified, as the different types of businesses incorporated by Hollywood companies have involved further differentiation of labor, making it difficult for workers to form a united front against one corporation. For instance, workers employed by Disney include animators at the Disney Studio, hockey players on the Mighty Ducks hockey team, and Jungle Cruise operators at Disneyland.

The differentiation of labor is especially apparent at the theme parks, where workers are represented by a wide array of labor organizations, many unrelated to those active in the film industry. For instance, over a dozen labor organizations have contracts with Disney World, where unions have formed trade councils to negotiate contracts.[33] Over 30 unions have been represented by eight contracts, with 14 unions negotiating under two trade council agreements.[34] Meanwhile, at Disneyland, five unions usually negotiate a master agreement for about 3,000 employees. The trade unions include the United Food and Commercial Workers; Service Employees International Union; Hotel Employees and Restaurant Employees; Bakery, Tobacco and Confectionery Workers; and the International Brotherhood of Teamsters (who represent workers who wear the Disney character costumes at the park). Although the notion of Mickey Mouse and Donald Duck as Teamsters may be jolting to many Disney aficionados, at least they are represented by an employee association, which is sometimes not the case at other theme parks.

Generally, the trend towards diversification has contributed to a weakening of trade unions' power as well as to a lack of unity among workers. As *Los Angeles Times* labor reporter Harry Bernstein has observed, 'These days, corporate tycoons own conglomerates that include businesses other than studios and networks. They may enjoy movie-making, but money seems to be their primary goal. So if production is stopped by a film industry strike, their income may be slowed, but money can still roll in from other sources.'[35]

Thus, the Disney company attempts in various ways to maintain control over its workers throughout its diverse business endeavors. And, despite the techniques that some employees use to find their own pleasures and satisfaction in their work, the company usually gets what it wants. As a Disney insider quoted in the VaultReport advises those considering working for The Mouse, 'It's important not to lose sight of the fact that Disney is a huge company which is in business for the sake of our stockholders—owners who want to make money by growing the company's value.'[36]

## Control Through Tough Tactics

The 800-pound gorilla analogy used above is fitting for Disney's tactics beyond the labor market, for the company has become notorious for its tough and sometimes unscrupulous style of dealing with other companies, as well as its employees.

Since Team Disney took over, the company's 'formula for success' has been 'talk tough, talk cheap, and keep total control.'[37] In addition to the cost-cutting measures discussed in chapter 3, the company has stepped on numerous toes in the industry to get what it wants. Examples abound, but one of the most often cited is the lucrative licensing arrangement for the Disney–MGM Studios, which Disney was able to negotiate for a pittance with MGM's lawyers and refused to reconsider. The park's construction also became controversial when Disney's supporters helped convince the Florida legislature not to support a similar plan by MCA/Universal. To add to the drama, the very idea of a studio theme park in Florida was claimed to have been lifted by Eisner, while he was at Paramount, during a meeting with the head of Universal.[38]

Disney's tactics have led to a plethora of lawsuits, not only over copyright issues, as discussed previously, but over a wide range of other business deals. One lawyer observed that tangling with the Disney company was 'like suing God in the Vatican.'[39] The company is known for not paying bills, withholding royalty payments, insisting on its own terms with theater owners, etc. Lewis notes that in 1987 Disney was involved in 17 major lawsuits involving 700 defendants in the USA and 78 others overseas.[40] As one industry observer noted, 'Disney's critics say doing business with the company means facing teams of lawyers who will stake out extreme positions on virtually every negotiating point and often return to try to reargue issues later if Disney isn't pleased. Mickey Mouse may be the soul of this company, but you'll find the heart somewhere over in the legal department.'[41] It is no wonder, then, that the Disney studio is known around Hollywood as Mousewitz, and Team Disney as the Rat Pack.

## Notes

1. See Ronald V. Bettig, *Copyrighting Culture: The Political Economy of Intellectual Property* (Boulder, Colo.: Westview Press, 1996), for a thorough analysis of these issues.
2. Cited in 'Disney Sues 200 People for Copyright Infringement,' UPI Regional News release, 6 Oct. 1988.
3. 'Disney Files Suit against 123 California Cos., 99 Oregon Cos.,' *The Entertainment Litigation Reporter*, 22 July 1991.
4. Tom Baldwin, 'Mandelson Mustn't Take Mickey,' *Sunday Telegraph*, 18 Jan. 1998.
5. 'Cartoon Character Controversy,' *Asbury Park Press* (Neptune, N.J.), 21 Dec. 1997.
6. Jonathan D. Salant, 'Copyright Extended for Mickey Mouse,' AP story, 16 Oct. 1998.
7. Ibid.
8. Sabra Chartrand, 'Congress Has Extended its Protection for Goofy, Gershwin and Some Moguls of the Internet,' *New York Times*, 19 Oct. 1998.
9. http://www. disney.com/Legal/conditions_of_use.html.
10. 'Disney Employees Report on Work Culture at VaultReports.com,' *Business Wire*, 25 Aug. 1999.
11. John Lent, 'The Animation Industry and its Offshore Factories,' in *Global Productions: Labor in the Making of the 'Information Society,'* ed. Gerald Sussman and John Lent (Cresskill, N.J.: Hampton Press, 1998), pp. 239–54, at p. 241. See also N. M. Klein, *7 Minutes: The Life and Death of the American Animated Cartoon* (London: Verso, 1993).
12. Lent, 'Animation Industry,' p. 245.

13. Cited, ibid.

14. Ibid., p. 252.

15. The discussion in this section is drawn from material distributed during the summer internship program at Walt Disney World, plus Jane Kuenz, 'Working at the Rat,' in *Inside the Mouse: Work and Play at Disney World,* ed. Project on Disney (Durham, N.C.: Duke University Press, 1995), pp. 110–62. Other sources on working at the parks include David Koenig and Art Linkletter, *Mouse Tales: A Behind-the-Ears Look at Disneyland* (Irvine, Calif.: Bonaventure Press, 1995); David Koenig and Van Arsdale France, *More Mouse Tales: A Closer Peek Backstage at Disneyland* (Irvine, Calif.: Bonaventure Press, 1999); and Thomas Connelan, *Inside the Magic Kingdom: Seven Keys to Disney's Success* (Austin, TX.: Bard Press, 1997).

16. The company has developed seminars and courses based on the Traditions model for managers and educators. More discussion of these courses is included in chapter 6.

17. Eve Zibart, *The Unofficial® Disney Companion* (New York: Macmillan, 1997), p. 177.

18. Cited and discussed in Alan Bryman, 'The Disneyization of Society,' *Sociological Review,* 47, 1 (1999), p. 28.

19. Apparently, there are numerous stories of accidents and other incidents, whether true or not, that 'cast members' are forbidden to discuss, on pain of being 'fired on the spot.' Kuenz (pp. 115–16) discusses some examples; others are included on the Los Disneys website (www.losdisneys.com) discussed further in chapter 7.

20. *Cast Member's Handbook,* Walt Disney Company publication.

21. Kuenz talked to one worker who spends much of his time during the summer driving around the park, picking up passed-out characters. See Kuenz, 'Working at the Rat,' pp. 134–7; Zibart, *Unofficial® Disney Companion,* p. 182.

22. Wayne Ellwood, 'Service with a Smile,' *New Internationalist,* Dec. 1998, p. 17.

23. Kuenz, 'Working at the Rat,' p. 117.

24. http://www.VaultReports.com/links/Disney.

25. Ellwood, 'Service with a Smile,' p. 18, claims that two-thirds of the workers at the park make $6.57 an hour or less.

26. 'Top Dogs Should Toss their Workers a Bone,' *Los Angeles Times,* 10 Mar. 1996, p. D–2.

27. Kuenz, 'Working at the Rat,' p. 122.

28. Ibid., pp. 119–20.

29. Ibid., p. 117.

30. Jon Lewis, 'Disney after Disney: Family Business and the Business of Family,' in *Disney Discourse: Producing the Magic Kingdom,* ed. Eric Smoodin (New York: Routledge, 1994), p. 94, reports that turnover at the lower management level is encouraged, to bring in fresh and enthusiastic new employees.

31. Zibart, *Unofficial® Disney Companion,* p. 177.

32. In addition, Hollywood film companies such as Disney have taken advantage of non-union production, although there are differing reports as to its prevalence. According to IATSE reports, 65 percent of films produced in Southern California in 1989 were made with non-union crews. More recently, IATSE claimed that only 31 percent (121 out of 400) of the pictures released in the USA in 1993 were made with union labor; in 1992, 109 out of 390 films (27.9 percent) released were produced by union workers. See Janet Wasko, 'Challenges to Hollywood's Labor Force in the 1990s,' in *Global Productions,* ed. Sussman and Lent, p. 178–9.

33. See 'Actors' Equity Concludes Initial Accord Covering Performers at Walt Disney World,' *Daily Labor Report,* no. 166 (1990), p. A–7.

34. Walt Disney World College Program material, 'Human Resources,' p. 5.

35. Harry Bernstein, 'Hollywood May Take the Drama Out of Settling Disputes,' *Los Angeles Times,* 11 Apr. 1989, p. 1.

36. http://www.VaultReports.com/links/Disney.

37. Lewis, 'Disney after Disney,' p. 94.

38. More examples are discussed by Lewis, 'Disney after Disney,' pp. 87–94, and Ronald Grover, *The Disney Touch* (Homewood, Ill.: Business One Irwin, 1991), pp. 237–54.

39. Quote from 'Suing Disney is Like Suing God in the Vatican,' *San Diego Union Tribune, 5* Mar. 1985, p. D–1.

40. Lewis, 'Disney after Disney,' pp. 89–90.

41. Paul Richter, 'Disney's Tough Tactics,' *Los Angeles Times,* 8 July 1990, p. D–1.

# Chapter 18

## Henry Yu

# How Tiger Woods Lost his Stripes: Post-Nationalist American Studies as a History of Race, Migration, and the Commodification of Culture

As the summer waned in 1996, the world was treated to the coronation of a new public hero. Eldrick 'Tiger' Woods, the twenty-year-old golf prodigy, captured his third straight amateur championship and then promptly declared his intention to turn professional. The story became a media sensation, transferring the material of sports page headlines to the front page of newspapers in a way usually reserved for World Series championships or athletes involved in sex and drug scandals. Television coverage chronicled every step of Tiger's life, debating his impact upon the sport, and wondering if he was worth the reported $40 million which Nike was going to pay him for an endorsement contract. The strange career of Tiger Woods said much about the current situation of race, ethnicity, and capitalism in the United States. It also spoke to the still relatively unexamined ways in which definitions of racial and cultural difference in the United States connect to the global market of consumption and production.

Woods's eagerly anticipated professional debut was hailed in August 1996 as a multicultural godsend to the sport of golf. As a child of multiracial heritage, Woods added color to a sport that traditionally appealed to those who were white

From: Henry Yu, *Post-nationalist American Studies*. Ed. J.C. Rowe. Berkeley, CA: University of California Press, 2000.

and rich. A multicolored Tiger in hues of black and yellow would forever change the complexion of golf, attracting inner-city children to the game in the same way that Michael Jordan had for basketball. Nike's initial T.V. ad campaign emphasized the racial exclusivity that has marked golf in the United States, stating that there were golf courses at which Tiger Woods still could not play. A Tiger burning bright would change all of that, of course, with a blend of power, grace, skill, and sheer confidence that could not be denied. 'Hello World,' Tiger Woods announced in another T.V. spot, asking America and the world whether they were ready for the new partnership of Tiger and Nike. The answer to the challenge seemed to be a resounding yes. A year later, in October of 1997, a poll published in *USA Today* reported that Nike's campaign featuring Tiger Woods was by far the most popular advertising campaign of the year.[1]

In this essay, I would like to discuss Tiger Woods' commercial debut as a way of examining how race, ethnicity, and the mass market in the United States can no longer be understood (and perhaps was never properly understood) without the context of global capitalism that frames definitions of cultural and national difference. Notions of ethnic and cultural difference in the United States have always depended upon transnational connections and comparisons. The increasing awareness recently among scholars and the mass media of global perspectives has been marked by a hope that globalization will lead to a decrease in tribalism and ethnicity. Consequently, the practice of a 'post-nationalist American Studies' might be construed as an act of self-immolation, erasing national identity formation by pointing towards a future without nations. For me, such a vision would be misguided and dangerously deluded. National formation, and the concurrent practices of cultural and racial differentiation, have always been transnational in character, and they have always called for a perspective that can link ethnic formation with processes that transcend national borders. A post-nationalist American Studies, therefore, should strive to place nation formation within transnational contexts of racial and cultural differentiation.

Tiger Woods's story exemplifies the crossroads between the commercialization of sport in the United States and the production of racial and cultural difference. Golf is perhaps the epitome of a commodification of leisure that characterizes the current global success of American capitalism, and like many of the multibillion dollar sports and entertainment industries (cultural productions such as movies, television, music, etc.), golf is marked by representations of racial and cultural hierarchies. Perhaps more than any other sport, golf stands for white male privilege and racial exclusion. Some of the fascination with Tiger Woods can be explained by how acts of conspicuous leisure and consumption have become essential to both racial and class distinction in the United States. For its very significance as a bastion of hierarchy, golf has also become a marker of the opposition to racial and class exclusion. Similar to how Jackie Robinson's entry into baseball symbolized for Americans more than just the eventual desegregation of baseball but also that of American society, Tiger Wood's entry into golf was heralded as the entry of multiculturalism into the highest reaches of country-club America.

The manner in which observers initially explained Tiger's potential appeal was very revealing. A *Los Angeles Times* article on Tuesday, August 27, 1996, the day after Woods turned pro, declared that Tiger had a 'rich ethnic background,' calculating that his father was 'a quarter Native American, a quarter Chinese, and half African American,' and that his mother was 'half Thai, a quarter Chinese, and a quarter white.' How did we arrive at these fractions of cultural identity? Did they mean that he practiced his multicultural heritage in such a fractured manner, eating chow mein one day out of four, soul food on one of the other days, and Thai barbecue chicken once a week? Obviously not. The exactness of the ethnic breakdown referred to the purported biological ancestry of Woods' parents and grandparents.

The awkward attempts to explain Tiger's racial classification showed the continuing bankruptcy of languages of race in the United States. The racial calculus employed by both print and television reporters to explain Tiger's heritage reminds us uncomfortably of the biological classifications used in the Old South. The law courts of Louisiana tried for much of the nineteenth and twentieth centuries to calculate a person's racial makeup in the same precise manner, classifying people as mulatto if they were half white and half black, a quadroon if they were a quarter black, an octoroon if an eighth, and so on. The assumption was that blood and race could be broken down into precise fractions, tying a person's present existence in a racially segregated society with a person's purported biological ancestry. The upshot was that a single drop of black blood made a person colored, and no amount of white blood could overwhelm that single drop to make a person pure again.[2]

What was disturbing about the reception of Tiger Woods is how little we have changed from that conception of biological identity. Within American conceptions of race, Tiger Woods is an African American. The intricate racial calculus that broke Tiger into all manner of stripes and hues was a farce not only in terms of its facile exactitude, but also in its false complexity. According to the calculations, Tiger Woods is more Asian American than African American (a quarter Chinese on the father's side, plus a quarter Chinese and a half Thai on the mother's side, for a total of one-half Asian in Tiger, versus only half African American on the father's side, for a total of one-quarter black in Tiger ...).[3] But this is an empty equation because social usage, and the major market appeal of Tiger, classifies him as black. 'How Tiger Woods lost his stripes' describes the process by which the complexities of human migration and intermingling in this country become understood in the simplifying classifications of race.[4]

In his trek from the sports page to the front page, Tiger Woods quickly became another example of a black man making it in America because of his athletic skill. Woods earned his success through his prodigious accomplishments, but his popular apotheosis as black male hero fits him into generic modes of understanding African American masculinity. The strange way in which multinational sports corporations value minority sports stars is indicative of the more general American craving for individual black heroes to redeem its ugly history. Whether it is Jackie Robinson, Michael Jordan, Colin Powell, or Tiger Woods, we constantly fantasize that a single person will save us from racial problems which are endemic and built into the structure of U.S. society. [...]

The attempt to see within Tiger Woods the embodiment of multiculturalism was a valiant attempt to contain within a single body all of the ethnic diversity in the social body that multiculturalism claims to represent. The awkwardness of description, and its inevitable failure, resulted both from a flawed conception of ethnic origins and from our inability to leave behind an obsession with the idea that race is a biological category represented by individuals. It is possible to describe a person's racial history in terms of fractions, because each of those fractions was supposedly a whole person one or two generations before. Tiger Woods as a single body, however, cannot express the fractions within – like almost all children of supposed mixed heritage in this country, his whole quickly becomes his darkest part.

Woods himself, as a child, attempting to rebut his reduction by others to a state of blackness, came up with the term 'Cablinasian' (CAucasian + BLack + INdian + ASIAN) to encapsulate his mixed makeup. Mentioned briefly by the press, the term achieved no currency or usage. Since the power of racial categories comes from their work of tying a number of people together under a single description, a label such as Cablinasian that serves only to describe Woods' own individual admixture has little use. Indeed, though Woods had found a name for his own unique brand of pain, he might as well have used his own name 'Tiger' to label what was in the end a virtually singular racial description.

The confusion of tongues regarding how to name Tiger's complex heritage is a direct result of the confusion over race that continues to bedevil this country. Multiculturalism in the form embraced by corporate America is no more than this tired language with an added commodification of ethnicity. We want racial and cultural categories to be neatly represented by individuals, so that a multicultural Benetton or Calvin Klein advertisement will have a number of visible people of color – an African American, an Asian American, a Latino or Latina – and an assortment of generic white people. Multiculturalism is about different individuals getting along, and this is the version which is being sold by multinational corporations like Nike, in the hopes that all of these differing people will buy the same objects in a shared market of goods.[5] Nike's ad campaign showing young children of various visible minorities chanting the mantra of 'I am Tiger Woods' ostensibly offered Tiger as the role model for multicultural America, but it also managed to call forth a world market ready to consume Nike's products. Like Nike's earlier slogan for basketball icon Michael Jordan, 'I want to be like Mike,' the phrase 'I am Tiger Woods' could be translated by consumers as 'My body is black and I am up and coming just like him,' but more likely it meant 'I want to wear what Tiger wears.'

Tiger Woods serves as an example to introduce some issues concerning race and culture in an international perspective, particularly in terms of the interaction among ethnicity, national definition, and global capitalism. There has been a great deal of exciting scholarship in recent years exploring transnational perspectives, and my account is not meant to survey these works, but to sketch some suggestive issues which I see arising out of them. I want first to think about multicultural narratives as shorthand histories for international migration, and then to tie this to the perceived international appeal of Tiger's mixed ethnicity.

The awkward attempts to describe Woods's heritage bear the legacy of Old South notions of race, but they also arise from the late-nineteenth-century context of massive international labor migration.[6] Culture as a theory describing human difference can be linked to two particular historical developments of the nineteenth century: national formation and the rise of migrant labor to satisfy the expanding production that resulted from expanding capitalist development. The rise and triumph of the concept of culture at the beginning of the twentieth century supposedly eclipsed earlier biological definitions of race, but in some ways the idea of culture, and of multiculturalism, is little more than the grafting of nonbiological claims onto preexisting categories of race. Moreover, like the category of biological race, the culture concept erases history, suppressing into static categories the historical origins of how some people become defined as different.

Theories of biological race that arose in the nineteenth century emphasized belonging to some fictive category (for instance, Negroid, Mongoloid, Caucasoid) that collapsed racial type and geographical location. This mythic tie between race and spatial location called forth an epic history stretching back to prehistoric ancestors, tying racial difference to origins deep in time. We still operate with a version of this classificatory scheme when we identify some physical features as 'Asian' (straight black hair) and others as 'African' (brown skin) or 'European' (light skin).[7] American Studies has acquired a central awareness of how racial theories that attributed variations in behavior and in physical and mental abilities to differences in racial type have for centuries served as justification for social oppression and hierarchy.

An anthropological conception of culture that came to the fore in the early twentieth century redefined variety in human behavior and practice as a consequence of social processes. Meant to eliminate any association of mental capacity with biological race, the theory of culture proved relatively successful as a way of attacking biological justifications for social hierarchy. The culture concept as it has been used in theories of multiculturalism, however, has mirrored the suppositions of racial theories about the centrality of biological ties to the past. Particularly in the way differences in behavior between people whose ancestors have come from Africa, Asia, or Europe have been explained as cultural in origin, cultural difference has paralleled the boundaries of earlier definitions of racial difference.

Created by anthropologists visiting exotic locales, culture as an intellectual concept has always been riven by the contradiction that it has come to be an *object* of description (the actual practices of various 'cultures') at the same time that it has really only been the description of practices. Culture, as it was defined by early theorists such as Franz Boas, is transferred among physical human bodies through social means of communication. Embodied in social rituals and practices, culture was a way of life, reproduced by social groups that were bound together by such acts. As a set of descriptions, ethnographies were claimed by anthropologists to describe actual 'cultures,' but the differentiation between what was unique to one culture versus another always depended upon the perspective of Europeans or Americans implicitly comparing their objects of study to other ways of life (often, unwittingly, their own). Arising out of a systematic awareness of differences, the concept of culture is undermined when users forget its origin as a description. *Culture* as a word is continually used as if it were an object with causal powers ('Franz did that because his culture is German'), rather than a product of the very act of describing that is the way of life of anthropologists and those who see the world anthropologically ('Franz, in comparison with other people I have known, does things differently, and I make sense of that difference by describing those acts and linking them to my awareness that he and other people I have known who do things that way all come from Germany'). Unfortunately, in popular language such as that of multiculturalism, the word *culture* has come to have universal significance at the same time that it signifies less and less. [...]

Cultural differentiations, like the biological notions of race that they purportedly replace, rely upon an historical narrative of population migration. No matter how much even the most astute observers believe that culture is a purely social phenomenon, divorced from biology, there are presumed links to histories of the physical migration of human bodies that lead to generalizations based upon physical type. On the whole, these links have practical functions, connecting individual human bodies to histories of population migration. Seeing a body, and being trained to perceive that it shares particular physical characteristics with those descended from individuals who live in Asia, allows fairly accurate suppositions about biological ancestors from somewhere in Asia.

But almost inevitably false assumptions are made concerning the cultural knowledge and practices of such a person, and the relation of culture to the body's biological origin. So children of American missionaries in China, never having set foot in the United States until the age of eighteen or nineteen, can get off a boat in San Francisco and instantly be American in the legal and cultural senses. The norm of American identity has been so equated historically with whiteness that the very term *white American* in most situations is repetitive and redundant. Americans of color require a modifying term such as African or Asian or Hispanic. The term *European American* has been invented to extend the logic of geographic origins for differnt races, but in the absence of any color modifier, the term *American* means white.

The children, grandchildren, and great-grandchildren of Chinese immigrants to the United States will always be seen as possessing Chinese culture, no matter how inept they are at what it means to be Chinese in China (and in America) – they will be asked whether they know how to translate Chinese characters, how to cook chow mein, and to discuss the takeover of Hong Kong. Orphans from Korea who grew up in Minneapolis with Scandinavian American parents, no matter how young they were when they were transported from South Korea, will always be linked to Korean culture [...]. At worst, and in a manner reminiscent of the internment of Japanese Americans, airport security officers or the FBI will suspect Arab Americans of being terrorists because of the way they spell their names, the clothes they wear, or the color of their skin. At the heart of all of these distinctions is not race as a biological category or culture as a nonbiological category, but a presumed history of population migrations.

Multiculturalism in the United States has had a long history of making transnational connections. If it really is because someone's grandfather came from Croatia and someone else's came from Canada that one is different from the other, then present cultural differences echo past national differences. Since there is an assumption that what makes someone different here in the United States is their link to some other place in the world, origins and biological heritage are all-important. Even when the differences are supposedly racial, they still presume a difference today arising from a difference in origin yesterday. Tiger Woods's formula of admixture, for instance, reveals a foundation in national, racial, and cultural difference. His Thai portion is national and/or cultural in origin. The Chinese would presumably be the same, with a hint of racial determinism (his Chinese grandparents were probably legally Thai in a national sense, with an indeterminately long history of living in Thailand). His African and Native American parts most certainly fixate on (some notion of) biological race with an assumption that there would be some accompanying cultural differences. His Caucasian (or white) heritage is racial and cultural in the same sense as his blackness, presuming an illusory tie to some mountains in Eastern Europe.

As an historical narrative defining the origins of difference, multiculturalism has linked the politics of the present to a biological genealogy of the individual body's past. This narrative has been a program for political empowerment, because it opposes the racial descriptions it mirrors, but in overturning the exclusion of those previously left out by promising their inclusion, multiculturalism as a political ideology has curiously reiterated the very 'foreign' nature of those left out. Multiculturalism has valued those who were previously excluded by turning the terms of their exclusion into the terms of their inclusion. Embracing the foreign nature of ethnicity rather than sending foreigners packing, cultural pluralists have replaced nativism with exoticism.

Multiculturalism, like the narrative of biological race that it opposes, reveals the defining power of imperialism, when Europeans surveyed populations of the world and marked the boundaries between them. Long histories of continual population migration and movement were erased as bodies were given the attribute of 'native' – mapping them into a 'local' origin that was assigned to them by European knowledge.[8] Categorized by abstract identities such as race, nation, and culture, individuals and social groups all over the globe were defined and came to define themselves through such identifications.[9] The power of these identities for the last two centuries in creating imagined social and institutional ties is undeniable, but there is always the danger of missing the underlying demographic changes that lay at the base of such arbitrary ties.

There are myriad ways in which people are similar and different – male or female, position in a family, age, sexuality, height, shoe size, on and on. One of these ways is where one's grandparents came from, but if the reason someone has been treated differently in the United States is that their grandfather came from China, this tie is important less because of what was unique and native to China (both in the nineteenth century and now) and more because of how racial difference and animosity have been defined in North America; how, in other words, people in the United States have come to define 'whiteness' by European origin and linked otherness in racial and cultural terms with non-European origin. Racial, cultural, and national categorization therefore have been inextricably linked in history, and in the most foundational sense these linkages have depended upon an awareness of population migration. Ultimately, however, these definitions of race and culture have not actually been about the migration histories of biological bodies; the definition of whiteness in opposition to other racial types, at its core, has been about the social privileges of not being considered colored. The strange conundrum of culture as a theory is that it assumes and then hides the same links between physical bodies and migration that biological theories of race did. In attempting to define more fairly in this way, we may end up reproducing the logic of justifying white privilege in the United States.

## I Sing the Body Eclectic? Transnational Fractions and National Wholes

The fractional nature of the racial and cultural categories in Tiger Woods was as arbitrary as the classification of him as African American. The key factor that undermines Tiger Woods's racial formula is the fiction that somehow his ancestors were racially or culturally whole. When he was broken up into one-fourth Chinese, one-fourth Thai, one-fourth African American, one-eighth American Indian, and one-eighth Caucasian, the lowest common denominator of one-eighth leads to a three-generation history. Tracing a three-step genealogy of descent back to an original stage of pure individuals places us at the end of the nineteenth century. If we were to consider other striped, Tiger Woods–like bodies in a similar manner, they might be described as containing fractions like a sixteenth or even a thirty-second. But in any case the individuals who are imagined to live at the beginning point of the calculations are whole only because they have been assumed to originally exist in a shared moment of purity.

The timing of this moment of imagined purity is partly founded upon the coincidence of migration with national identity. The illusion of ethnic and racial wholeness of a grandparent's generation marks the importance of nineteenth-century nationalism in defining bodies. Emigrating from established or emergent nations, migrants during the nineteenth and early twentieth centuries had their bodies marked by nationality – Irish, Chinese, Japanese, Italian, German. That their bodies were whole in a national sense allowed for a consequent holistic definition of their racial and cultural origin.

Both race and culture as categories of belonging have often presupposed a biological genealogy of national origin. This view was legally enshrined in the 1924 National Origins legislation, when each nation was given a maximum quota for migrants to the United States. Every immigrant entering and every body already in the United States was defined by a national past. A migrant body was marked as a member of a single nation, and thus a national purity was conveyed regardless of a person's heterogeneous or complicated origins. Immigrants may have come from a place that did not exist as a political and legal nation, or they may have gone through numerous national entities before entering the United States, any of which could come to be defined as their 'national origin.' For instance, migrants from the area now known as South Korea were in the early part of the twentieth century counted as Japanese nationals. Virtually all Koreans understood that as a colonized and subject people they were not Japanese in a cultural or biological sense, but their legal status according to the National Origins Act meant that they had to have a national origin, and like other members of the nation of Japan, they were to be excluded from the United States on the basis of national categories.

Even with the supposed eclipse of biological notions of race in the twentieth century, we cling to definitions of national and cultural origin as a shorthand for describing biological origin. If you are a descendent of Asian immigrants to this country, for instance, you are forever being asked where you are originally from, regardless of whether you were born in Los Angeles, Denver, or New York. The confusion is not over whether an individual is American-born or not, since those asking are inevitably not satisfied with the answer of Los Angeles, Denver, or New York. What they are looking for is national origin, and therefore biological origin, even if the moment of origination is an act of migration undertaken by a grandparent. What they want to know is whether you are Japanese, Korean, Chinese, or Vietnamese (I suppose that they believe they can tell if you are from the Philippines, Polynesia, or India and therefore do not have to ask).[10]

The three-generation history of intermarriage that the one-eighth fractions ostensibly revealed actually described a family tree arbitrarily truncated. The hypothetically whole grandparents, given their own family genealogies of ancestry, would have themselves pointed to a past of intermingling population migrations. Further and further back in time, these genealogies would reveal that there has never been a set of racially whole individuals from which we have all descended. Whether in purportedly mixed or pure fashion, biological descent that invokes racially whole individuals in the past is an illusion. [...]

## National Diversity and International Marketing

The processes of national and racial differentiation have contemporary resonance in a time when claims of a new globalism resound. The tying of what is ethnic here in the United States to what is native there in some other nation in the world is what makes Tiger Woods so appealing as a marketing force for corporations looking for global sales. Multinational corporations have already disaggregated every step of production and farmed each out to whatever specific locations in the world offer the cheapest production and labor costs. If the production side is no longer linked to singular nation-states, the consumption side perhaps never has been. The desire for international markets for goods is not a recent dream for capitalists – mercantilists three hundred years ago looked to national exports as a way of creating favorable balances of trade, and European and American manufacturers in the late nineteenth century fantasized about the vast China market long before companies like Nike dreamed about a billion pairs of Air Jordans being purchased by Chinese.

Understanding the perception of so many people that Tiger Woods had the potential for foreign marketing involves connecting international sales with an American-born, mixed racial or cultural body, and the narrative that allows that connection is a multicultural ideology that identifies the origins of his ethnic fractions with foreign nations. The potential of developing Asian markets for golf wear and athletic products is tied to the international appeal of Tiger's partial Asian heritage. Lost in the blackness of America's perception of Tiger, his Asian stripes can be earned on the global market, parlayed into increased sales for Nike in Southeast Asia and other growth markets for Nike's leisure products. If Michael Jordan has been the best ambassador for the international growth of basketball as a marketing vehicle, then Tiger Woods can be golf's equivalent, instantiating such global possibilities in his body. The image of Woods also serves to hide the idealization in golf of white male hierarchy by providing a nonwhite, multiracial body as a fantasy pinnacle.

There is a perverse irony in selling products back to the places where capital has gone to find cheap labor. Marketing golf in Thailand, Indonesia, and other Southeast Asian nations, such as Vietnam, evokes the ultimate capitalist dream of pouring relatively little capital into a location in order to produce products for export to places that will pay a healthy mark-up on production costs, and also recouping as much as possible from those very sites of production. Of course, it's not the women and children being paid thirteen cents an hour in Indonesia who will be able to play golf and buy Nike shoes. But even if it is local elites who make their portion of the profit from managing the cheap labor and creating the professional services and infrastructure for production, the dream remains of new markets springing up alongside labor sites.

Initial indications are that Nike's fantasy of Tiger Woods creating global markets is achieving mixed results. Jan Weisman's work on Thai perceptions of Tiger Woods suggests that the attempt to market Woods as a Thai hero was eagerly embraced by a number of sectors of Thai society. Upon his initial visit as a professional golfer in 1997, newspapers hailed him as native son, and the Thai prime minister met his entourage. Unfortunately, racial hierarchies in Thailand cut against Tiger's inclusion into an imagined Thai social body, and in particular his blackness made constructions of him as Thai difficult.

As in the United States, Tiger's African American military father became the defining characteristic of Tiger's mixed heritage, but within the historical context of U.S. military presence in Thailand during the Vietnam war, Tiger's blackness also painted his mother with questionable moral stripes. Despite widespread efforts to portray Tiger's father as an elite Green Beret and thus different from the morally suspect GIs who had created a flourishing sex-trade industry in Thailand, Kultida Woods was trapped by the prejudices against Thai women who had sex with American soldiers, in particular black GIs. Though Woods's father was an elite officer, his mother was still marked with a low social status by such an association. Tiger Woods also did not act like a Thai national, neither speaking the language nor expressing the proper humility and devoutness of Thai Buddhism. In the end, Woods's triumphant visit to Thailand succeeded in publicizing him as a sports superstar and marketing icon, but it failed to establish him as a native Thai.

More important than his inability (or unwillingness, since Tiger went out of his way to mark himself as American) to perform culture in a manner that would allow his inclusion, categories of color hierarchy threatened the extinction of Tiger's value as Thai. In a society which mirrored an American fetishization of white purity, Wood's Thai heritage was lost in his father's blackness. The globalization of American leisure products has also exported the commodity of whiteness. Weisman's fascinating research contains an analysis of how partial 'white' heritage has been commodified in Thai beauty pageants. A recent Miss Universe from Thailand, for instance, was originally recruited to be a Miss Thailand contestant because of her perceived 'white' physical features.[11]

The spreading awareness of global perspectives as somehow explaining changes in contemporary society has led to interesting narrative variations. In the recent book *Jihad vs. McWorld,* Benjamin R. Barber argues that the twin forces of global homogenization and ethnic tribalism are tearing the world apart.[12] Enabled by technological advances in communications and transportation, the bland plasticity and homogenization of capital is embodied in the international spread of McDonald's. Combined with the mass production of superficial images that conflate culture with advertising, a world has been created in which leisure, consumption, and happiness all fall within the range between sports and MTV.[13] Opposed to such globalization, but often partaking in the spread of capital, has been the politics of identity, fragmenting nations and fomenting fratricide and genocide. Globalism and tribalism, both destructive in their own way, each threaten to end democracy and free citizenship as we know it.

Of course, if racial differentiation is seen as a foundational element in the formation of national citizenship, then it is clear that democracy and free citizenship are, contrary to Barber's view, future goals that history teaches us have always been ideals built on racial and gender oppression. It might seem a trite point that American democracy, the globe's shining example of egalitarian society, was built upon the self-evident freedom of white men to rule everyone else,[14] but it points out how such narratives of nostalgic longing for a golden age of democracy are empty gestures. Barber may fancy himself a Cassandra warning of the decline of democracy in the face of globalism and ethnic fragmentation, but he resembles Chicken Little decrying a falling firmament that was never that heavenly.

Decline, however, might be preferable to narratives of progress and modernity that assume global capitalism is bringing a better and brighter world. Each and every day we are all becoming better people, closer to and more like each other, or so the story goes. The resistance to global tendencies from ethnic tribalism thus easily produces the idea that identities based on difference are somehow impeding the progress of global humanity. Whether racial, cultural, or national, an awareness of difference seems to buck the trend towards world peace and togetherness. The dream of Tiger Woods as the future thus resides in his embodiment of racial, cultural and national fusion, allowing for the equation of 'We are Tiger Woods' and 'We are the world.'

The classic tale of Western progress, with its concurrent descriptions of development and underdevelopment, has been almost the sole narrative of global history. There have also been a number of powerful explanations for the global connections of capitalist production and consumption that critique the dominance of the West – world systems theory and dependency theory being the foremost.[15] In the end, however, all of them are united in a shared belief that capitalism has become a global phenomenon, disagreeing only on when exactly this happened, and whether it is a desirable development. Whether the global spread of capitalism signals the progress of universal modernity or whether it encapsulates an oppressive Western system foisted upon the world, it is a global phenomenon nonetheless.[16] Whether we chase the spirit of capitalism, or decry the specter of commodification, we live in a world that has structured its life around production and consumption. [...]

## Notes

Thanks to the members of the UCHRI research group and Hazel Carby, Michael Denning, Patricia Pessar, Andrés Resendez, Jace Weaver, and Bryan Wolf of the Race, Ethnicity, and Migration Program brown-bag colloquium at Yale for their helpful comments. Walter Johnson of NYU showed me an unpublished paper. Special acknowledgment to Kariann Yokota for her multiple, careful readings and large-scale additions to the subject matter and body of this essay, as well as numerous suggestions on the applicability of postcolonial theory to U.S. history.

1. 'Money' section report on popularity of Tiger Woods advertising campaign, *USA Today* (October 20, 1997); James K. Glassman, 'A Dishonest Ad Campaign,' *Washington Post* (Sept. 17, 1996); Larry Dorman, 'We'll Be Right Back, after This Hip and Distorted Commercial Break,' *New York Times*, 145, sec. 8 (Sept. 1, 1996; hype surrounding entrance into professional golfing world of twenty-year-old Tiger Woods); Robert Lipsyte, 'Woods Suits Golf's Needs Perfectly,' *New York Times*, 145, sec. 1 (Sept. 8, 1996); David Segal, 'Golfs $60 Million Question: Can Tiger Woods Bring Riches to Sponsors, Minorities to Game?' *Washington Post* (August 31, 1996); Ellen Goodman, 'Black (and White, Asian, Indian) like Me,' *Washington Post* (April 15, 1995; golfer Tiger Woods is multiracial); Ellen Goodman, 'Being More Than the Sum of Parts: When Tiger Woods Speaks of His Background as Multiracial, He Speaks for a Generation That Shuns Labels,' *Los Angeles Times*, 114 (April 14, 1995); 'Tiger, Tiger,

Burning Bright,' *Los Angeles Times,* 113 (Sept. 1, 1994; Tiger Woods wins U.S. Amateur Golf Championship).

2. Virginia Domínguez, *White by Definition: Social Classification in Creole Louisiana* (New Brunswick, NJ: Rutgers University Press, 1986).

3. Somewhat in jest, but further revealing the absurdity of such calculations, this is not even counting as Asian American the one-eighth American Indian coursing through his veins, a legacy of the original immigrants from Asia crossing over the Bering land bridge.

4. The phrase "how Tiger lost his stripes' was suggested to me by George Sánchez.

5. On different types of multiculturalism, see David Palumbo-Liu's 'Introduction,' in *The Ethnic Canon: Histories, Institutions, and Interventions* (Minneapolis: University of Minnesota Press, 1995). The marketing of diversity has been the subject of numerous newspaper articles, including the following: Patrick Lee, 'As California's Ethnic Makeup Changes, Companies Are Facing New Challenges in Serving Diverse Customers,' *Los Angeles Times,* 113 (Oct. 23, 1994); 'So Long, Betty,' *Christian Science Monitor,* 87 (Sept. 21, 1995); George White, 'The Ethnic Side of Sears: Retailer Leads in Effort to Reach Diverse Markets,' *Los Angeles Times,* 114 (Jan. 29, 1996); Walter C. Farrell, Jr., and James H. Johnson, Jr., 'Toward Diversity, and Profits,' *New York Times,* 146, sec. 3 (Jan. 12, 1997; workplace diversity makes both moral and economic sense).

6. There has been a good deal of interesting literature already on transnational movements of labor and how these diasporic movements have been at the heart of ethnic identity within the nation-states which arose at the same time. The United States was like many nations in the nineteenth century that derived part of their sense of national homogeneity from racializing and excluding diasporic labor from definitions of the national body.

7. Ashley Montagu, *Man's Most Dangerous Myth: The Fallacy of Race,* 5th ed. (New York: Oxford University Press, 1974).

8. Mary Louise Pratt, *Imperial Eyes: Travel Writing and Transculturation* (New York: Routledge, 1992); Margaret Hunt, 'Racism, Imperialism, and the Traveler's Gaze in Eighteenth-Century England,' *Journal of British Studies* 32 (October 1993): 333–57.

9. Postcolonial scholarship, such as that of South Asian scholars on India and partition, has described how nations arose in the wake of decolonization, and the problems of ethnicity within states which were abstract entities created by colonial map-makers' fantasies of geographic and administrative order. A well-known example of this scholarship is Benedict Anderson's *Imagined Communities,* 2nd ed. (London: Verso, 1991), which includes an interpretation of the end of Dutch rule in the islands of the East Indies and the creation of the nation of Indonesia out of a myriad of diverse peoples, united by armed and political struggle, but also by an imagined unity that came out of a shared history of domination by Dutch colonizers. See also Jan Nederveen Pieterse and Bhikhu Parekh, eds., *The Decolonization of Imagination: Culture, Knowledge, and Power* (Atlantic Highlands, NJ: Zed Books, 1995); Arif Dirlik, ed., *The Postcolonial Aura: Third World Criticism in the Age of Global Capitalism* (Boulder: Westview Press, 1997), in particular the essay by Ann Stoler, '"Mixed-bloods" and the Cultural Politics of European Identity in Colonial Southeast Asia,' pp. 128–48; Arif Dirlik, *What's in a Rim? Critical Perspectives on the Pacific Region Idea* (Boulder: Westview Press, 1993), in particular the introduction, 'Introducing the Pacific,' and the essays by Alexander Woodside, 'The Asia-Pacific Idea as a Mobilization Myth,' pp. 13–28; Bruce Cumings, 'Rimspeak: Or, the Discourse of the "Pacific Rim,"' ' pp. 29–49; Neferti Xina M. Tadiar, 'Sexual Economies in the Asia-Pacific Community,' pp. 183–210; and Meredith Woo-Cumings, 'Market Dependency in U.S.-East Asian Relations,' pp. 135–57.

10. If a shared Asian American identity is formed for the most part from the experience of being treated as 'Orientals' in a similar manner by other Americans, including being mistaken for each other, perhaps one of the largest reasons for the continued practice of excluding South Asians and most Filipinos and Pacific Islanders from a sense of identity with Asian Americans is that they are not mistaken for migrants from East Asia.

11. Jan Weisman, 'Multiracial Amerasia Abroad: Thai Perceptions and Constructions of Tiger Woods,' a paper given at the 1998 Association for Asian American Studies, Fifteenth Annual Conference, Honolulu, Hawaii. Weisman's research can be found in her 1998 doctoral dissertation in anthropology at the University of Washington.

12. Benjamin R. Barber, *Jihad vs. McWorld: How the Planet Is Both Falling Apart and Coming Together – and What This Means for Democracy* (New York: Times Books, 1995).

13. Fredric Jameson, *Postmodernism: Or, the Cultural Logic of Late Capitalism* (Durham, NC: Duke University Press, 1991).

14. For histories of the role of race in early American and Jacksonian democracy, see Edmund Morgan, *American Slavery, American Freedom: The Ordeal of Colonial Virginia* (New York: Norton, 1975); Alexander Saxton, *The Rise and Fall of the White Republic: Class Politics and Mass Culture in Nineteenth-Century America* (London: Verso, 1990); David Roediger, *The Wages of Whiteness: Race and the Making of the American Working Class* (London: Verso, 1991).

15. Patrick Wolfe, 'Review Essay: History and Imperialism: A Century of Theory, from Marx to Postcolonialism,' *American Historical Review* 102, no. 2 (April 1997): 388–420; Amy Kaplan and Donald Pease, eds., *Cultures of United States Imperialism* (Durham, NC: Duke University Press, 1993); John Tomlinson, *Cultural Imperialism: A Critical Introduction* (Baltimore: Johns Hopkins University Press, 1991); 'Imperialism – A Useful Category of Historical Analysis?' Forum in *Radical History Review* 57 (1993). On modernization theory, see Walter W. Rostow, *The Stages of Economic Growth: A Non-Communist Manifesto* (Cambridge: Cambridge University Press, 1960); Partha Chatterjee, *Nationalist Thought and the Colonial World: A Derivative Discourse?* (Minneapolis: University of Minnesota Press, 1993), and *The Nation and Its Fragments: Colonial and Postcolonial Histories* (Princeton: Princeton University Press, 1993); Immanuel Wallerstein, *The Modern World-System,* vol. 1, *Capitalist Agriculture and the Origins of the European World-Economy in the Sixteenth Century* (New York: Academic Press, 1974), and vol. 2, *Mercantilism and the Consolidation of the European World-Economy, 1600–1750* (New York: Academic Press, 1980); see also his *The Capitalist World-Economy* (New York: Academic Press, 1989).

16. See Francis Fukuyama, *End of History and the Last Man* (New York: Free Press, 1992), for a prominent example of such a universal narrative of history and capitalism; on the foisting of capitalism on other societies, see Reinhold Wagnleitner, *Coca-Colonization and the Cold War,* trans. Diana Wolf (Chapel Hill: University of North Carolina Press, 1994). For a trenchant critique of the narratives of progress, see Dipesh Chakrabarty, 'Postcoloniality and the Artifice of History: Who Speaks for 'Indian' Pasts?' *Representations* 37 (1992): 1–26.

# PART FOUR

# PRACTICING:

# POPULAR TASTES AND
# WAYS OF CONSUMING

In Nick Hornby's *High Fidelity* (London: Victor Gollancz, 1995) the disgruntled record store owner Rob (played by John Cusack in Stephen Frears' film adaptation (2000)) reflects upon how he and his record-collecting cohort have come to determine the suitability of prospective partners: 'what really matters is *what* you like, not what you *are* like …'. Rob goes on to explain that this decision, reached in unanimous agreement by the three men, is not trivial: 'the truth was that these things matter, and it's no good pretending that any relationship has a future if your record collections disagree violently, or if your favourite films wouldn't even speak to each other if they met at a party'. Not wanting to spoil the narrative for readers who have not read Hornby's book, all we will say is that Rob changes his tune. Nevertheless, the notion of 'what you like', perhaps less clumsily articulated as 'taste', is paramount for the study of popular culture. What do people make of their daily encounters with media and commodities – the artifacts of mass culture? Do people consume blindly, or are discriminating practices employed? How is meaning created and recreated through diverse modes of consumption posited not on a passive model of consumption, but on a model within which people are regarded as active in the production of meaning? How is taste expressed – created, maintained, defended – within popular culture? How is one's identity tied to one's practices of consumption and knowledge of popular culture? After all, in terms of this last question, the character Rob, after suffering a bad break-up, consoles himself by reorganizing his record collection autobiographically. This section concentrates on diverse practices, experiences, reading protocols, and social relations to popular culture. Renegotiations of the binaries between high and low culture and the significance in shifts in value and to taste hierarchies located in different subjectivities (classed, gendered, raced) demonstrate a complex relation between fans and audiences of popular culture and the commodities they claim, consume/produce, use, assign value to, identify with/through, and make 'meaning' with in everyday life.

John Fiske's work synthesizes aspects of Bakhtin, Barthes, Bourdieu, de Certeau and Foucault's thought to provide students and scholars with a means of considering semiotics and the function of pleasure in diverse popular practices. Examples of his approach include: *Reading Television* (New York: Methuen, 1978, co-authored with John Hartley) and *Television Culture* (London: Methuen, 1987), as well as *Understanding Popular Culture* (Boston, MA: Unwin Hyman, 1989) and *Reading the Popular* (Boston, MA: Unwin Hyman, 1989), companion texts that attempt to distinguish between 'mass' and 'popular' culture to engage popular practices of negotiating meaning. '**Popular Discrimination**', the article included here, is taken from James Naremore and Patrick Brantlinger's edited collection, *Modernity and Mass Culture* (1991). Popular discrimination, as Fiske argues, 'begins with the choices of which products to use in the production of popular culture and then passes on the imaginative linking of the meanings and pleasure produced from them with the conditions of everyday life'. Drawing from Barthes' concepts of 'readerly' and 'writerly' texts, Fiske develops his notion of 'the producerly' to explain how people (often audiences and fans) make sense of and use the commodities of mass culture in popular practices understood as productive and active processes.

Having appeared in the Grossberg et al. reader, *Cultural Studies* (1992), Laura Kipnis' '**(Male) Desire and (Female) Disgust: Reading *Hustler*'** is one of the most important essays of the early 1990s to consider questions of sexuality and sex as popular culture. Kipnis, whose books include *Ecstasy Unlimited: On Sex, Capital, Gender, and Aesthetics* (Minneapolis, MN: University of Minnesota Press, 1993), *Bound and Gagged: Pornography and the Politics of Fantasy in America* (New York: Grove Press, 1996) and *Against Love: A Polemic* (New York: Pantheon Books, 2003), turns to infamous *Hustler* magazine and performs a textual analysis that inquires after the type of body produced through *Hustler*'s discourses of excess and explicitness. In doing so, Kipnis chooses to strategically extract herself from the accepted accusations of misogyny, exploitation, and dehumanization leveled against Larry Flynt's magazine, to reveal a classed (transgressive) body constructed in possible opposition to bourgeois ideas of the normative body and taste. 'What this seems to imply', and it is an observation that might well be applied to the study of popular culture in general, 'is that there is no guarantee that counter-hegemonic or even specifically anti-bourgeois cultural forms are necessarily also going to be progressive'.

Best known for his instrumental ethnographic studies on British working-class culture, *Learning to Labour: How Working Class Kids Get Working Class Jobs* (London: Saxon House, 1977) and *Profane Culture* (London: Routledge and Kegan Paul, 1978), Paul Willis was a member of the University of Birmingham's Centre for Contemporary Cultural Studies. His more recent *Common Culture: Symbolic Work at Play in the Everyday Cultures of the Young* (1990) is a collaborative research project. '**Symbolic Creativity**', the excerpt presented here, highlights the concept of 'grounded aesthetics' as the 'creative element in a process whereby meanings are attributed to symbols and practices and where symbols and practices are selected, reselected, highlighted and recomposed to resonate further appropriated and particularized meanings'. Through its incorporation of interviews, the excerpt examines the concept of 'symbolic creativity' – a necessary part of everyday life and a major factor in the construction of self – as practiced by young people. Examples include how youth differentiate watching a film at home on videocassette versus in the cinema, as well as how they understand popular magazines directed at their taste and imagined social lives, consumption/ production practices of music, and uses of fashion.

The study of fans – whether adherents to particular television shows, film, music or sports – is pertinent to understanding popular culture. Lisa A. Lewis's edited collection, *The Adoring Audience: Fan Culture and Popular Media* (London: Routledge, 1992), Constance Penley's *Nasa/Trek: Popular Science and Sex in America* (London: Verso, 1997), and Henry Jenkins' influential, *Textual Poachers: Television Fans and Participatory Culture* (New York and London: Routledge, 1992) are a few of the key texts that explore the importance of fandom and fan practices for the function of taste, value, and social identity within popular culture. Jenkins' **'Star Trek: Rerun, Reread, Rewritten: Fan Writing as Textual Poaching'**, taken from *Close Encounters: Film, Feminism, and Science Fiction* (1991), founds its analysis of *Star Trek* fans on Michel de Certeau's notion of popular reading as a practice of 'poaching' ('readers are like travelers; they move across lands belonging to someone else, like nomads poaching their way across fields they did not write...'). According to Jenkins, readers (fans) actively repossess the text in question. Here Trekkers' devotion to commercial culture is sundered from its frequently derogatory connotations and recast in de Certeauian terms of poaching. Consumption is regarded as a potentially complex process, rather than tyrannical exploitation of a supposed 'cultural dupe'.

How fans attempt to build social communities around taste is addressed in Joan Hawkins' **'Sleaze Mania, Euro-Trash, and High Art: The Place of European Art Films in American Low Culture'** (2000). Examining the fanzine cultures of cult film fans, Hawkins works through recent arguments on popular film cultures (most notably, Jeffrey Sconce's 'Trashing the Academy: Taste, Excess, and an Emerging Politics of Cinematic Style', *Screen* 36(4): 371–393 (Winter, 1995)) to explain how cult fandom – expressed by 'paracinema' catalogs and fanzines – reworks, if not dismantles, existing boundaries between 'high' and 'low' film cultures.

# Play List

Bourdieu, Pierre (1984) *Distinction: A Social Critique of the Judgment of Taste*. London: Routledge.

Cartmell, D., Hunter, I.Q., Kaye, H. and Whelehan, I. (eds) (1997) *Trash Aesthetics: Popular Culture and its Audience*. London: Pluto Press.

Clerc, Susan (1996) 'Estrogen brigades and "big tits" threads: media fandom online and off', in Cherny, L. and Weise, E.R. (eds) *Wired_Women: Gender and New Realities in Cyberspace*, Seattle: Seal Press

Coats, Paul (1994) *Film at the Intersection of High and Low Culture*. Cambridge: Cambridge University Press.

DeAngelis, Michael (2001) *Gay Fandom and Crossover Stardom: James Dean, Mel Gibson, and Keanu Reeves*. Durham, NC: Duke University Press.

de Certeau, Michel (1984) *The Practices of Everyday Life*. Berkeley: University of California Press.

Evans, David II (dir.) (1997) *Fever Pitch*. DVD. Vidmark/Trimark.

Frears, Stephen (dir.) (2000) *High Fidelity*. DVD. Walt Disney Home Video.

Forman, Milos (dir.) (1996) *People Vs Larry Flynt*. DVD. Columbia Pictures.

Glynn, Kevin (2000) *Tabloid Culture: Trash Taste, Popular Power, and the Transformation of American Television*. Durham, NC: Duke University Press.

Gwenllian-Jones, Sara and Pearson, Roberta E. (eds) (2004) *Cult Television*. Minneapolis, MN: University of Minnesota Press.

Hawkins, Joan (2000) *Cutting Edge: Art-Horror and the Horrific Avant-garde*. Minneapolis, MN: University of Minnesota Press.

Hills, Matt (2002) *Fan Cultures*. London: Routledge.

Hoberman, James and Rosenbaum, Jonathan (1983) *Midnight Movies*. New York: Harper and Row.

Nelson, Alondra and Thuy Linh N. Tu (2001) *Technicolor: Race, Technology, and Everyday Life*. New York: New York University Press.

Nygard, Roger (dir.) (1997) *Trekkies*. DVD. Paramount Studio.

Redhead, Steve (ed.) (1993) *The Passion and the Fashion: Football Fandom in The New Europe*. Aldershot: Avebury.

Sanjek, David. (1990) 'Fans' notes: the horror film fanzine', *Literature/Film Quarterly* Vol. 18 No. 3: 150–159.

Sprinkle, Annie (1998) *Post-Porn Modernist: Annie Sprinkle, My 25 Years as a Multimedia Whore*. San Francisco, CA: Cleis Press.

Stabile, Carol A. and Harrison, Mark (eds) (2003) *Prime Time Animation: Television Animation and American Culture*. London: Routledge.

Telotte, J.P. (ed.) (1991) *The Cult Film Experience: Beyond All Reason*. Austin, TX: University of Texas.

Tulloch, John and Jenkins, Henry (1995) *Science Fiction Audiences: Watching Doctor Who and Star Trek*. London: Routledge.

Vale, V. and Juno, Andrea (eds) (1994) *Incredibly Strange Music Volume II*. San Francisco, CA: Re/Search Publications.

Williams, Linda (ed.) (2004) *Porn Studies*. Durham, NC: Duke University Press.

Zwigoff, Terry (dir.) (2001) *Ghost World*. DVD. MGM/UA Studio.

# Chapter 19

# John Fiske

## Popular Discrimination

Films such as *Ishtar* with major stars, huge budgets, and expensive marketing still fail at the box office. Four out of five new prime time TV shows, carefully researched and expensively produced, will be axed before the end of the season, despite their so-called captive audience. Eight or nine out of ten new products, however heavily advertised, fail in the marketplace in their first year, and twelve out of thirteen pop records fail to make a profit. The ability of the people to discriminate between the products of capitalism, particularly those of its culture industries, should never be underestimated.

Yet academia has, until comparatively recently, consistently underestimated and ignored this complex process that plays so central a role in our contemporary society and its culture. Indeed, implicitly if not directly, popular culture has been denied discriminatory ability, for the concept of critical discrimination has been applied exclusively to high culture in its constant effort to establish its superiority over and difference from mass or popular culture. In the line of thought that can be traced from Coleridge through Matthew Arnold to T.S. Eliot, F.R. Leavis, and most recently Alan Bloom, the ability to discriminate is the one quality that best distinguishes 'the cultured' from the 'uncultured' – whether these be, in Arnold's terms, the Philistines (the new materialist middle class of tradespeople and industrialists) or the Barbarians (the decaying, degenerate aristocracy) or the Populace – the new working class who had *no* culture and were thus a potential source of anarchy and social disintegration. The concept of critical discrimination has always contained, however repressed, a dimension of social discrimination.

What I wish to do in this essay is sketch in some of the criteria and processes by which discrimination operates in popular culture. Popular culture in our society

From: *Modernity and Mass Culture*. ed. James Naremore and Patrick Brantlinger. Bloomington, IN: Indiana University Press, 1991.

is made by the various formations of the people at the interface between the products of capitalism and everyday life. But the products of capitalism always exceed the needs of the people, so popular discrimination begins with the choice of which products to use in the production of popular culture and then passes on to the imaginative linking of the meanings and pleasure produced from them with the conditions of everyday life. The two key characteristics of popular discrimination are, therefore, those of relevance and productivity and, even though we may separate them for analytical purposes, in practice they are almost indistinguishable.

Popular discrimination is thus quite different from the critical discrimination valued so highly by the educated bourgeoisie and institutionalized so effectively in the academic critical industry. The major difference is that between productivity and relevance on the one hand and quality and aesthetics on the other. Raymond Williams relates the increasing importance of aesthetics in the nineteenth century to the growth of industrialism with both its materialist values and its new, and potentially terrifying, urban working class.[1] Aestheticism, therefore, became a weapon in the class struggle, for it functioned to distinguish the cultured, fine sensibility from the rest. These cultured sensibilities were found almost exclusively among the educated fractions of the high bourgeoisie and the 'culture' they enabled their owners to appreciate was that of their class and gender, particularly the Graeco-Roman and European 'great tradition' in literature, music, and the visual arts. What aestheticism did was to universalize these social tastes into ahistorical, asocial values of beauty and harmony, and to construct from them an artificial set of universals that claimed to express the finest, best, and most moral elements of the human condition: the taste of the high bourgeois white male was universalized into the essence of humanity – a major ideological prize for any class to win! The function of critical discrimination, then, was to mask the social under the aesthetic, so that aesthetic 'quality' became a hidden marker of the social quality of those who could appreciate it.

Popular discrimination's concern with relevance, then, separates it clearly from the universals of critical discrimination, for relevance is the interconnections between a text and the immediate social situation of its readers – it is therefore socially and historically specific and will change as a text moves through the social structure or through history. [...]

A friend of mine returning from South America told me of the popularity of *Miami Vice* there because of the pleasures of its representations of Hispanics enjoying wealth and power in the United States. These pleasures far outweighed the narrative positioning of those Hispanics as villainous drug dealers who ultimately fall to the heroes Crockett and Tubbs. Indeed, it is quite possible that their status of villains enhanced their relevance, insofar as it could function as a concrete metaphor for Latin America's sense of how its nations are regarded by the United States. In popular culture, social relevance is far more powerful than textual structure.

This points to another difference between the aesthetic and the popular – the popular is functional. Aestheticism distances art from necessity in a way that parallels the freedom of the monied classes from economic necessity. The antimaterialism of aesthetics means that the artwork it appreciates is seen as self-contained. It is completed, finished, and contains within itself all that is necessary to appreciate it: the work of art awaits only the cultured sensibility that has the key to unlock its intricate secrets. So, as Pierre Bourdieu argues, to ask of an aesthetic object 'What is it *for*?' or 'What use is it?' amounts almost to sacrilege, for this suggests that it needs to be *used* in order to be completed.[2] But proletarian tastes are for artworks that are functional – they serve as reminders of holidays, or family histories, or they help one make sense of, and thus cope with, one's subordination in society. [...] David Halle's study of the paintings hanging in the homes of different classes in and around New York gives us further examples of popular functionalism and bourgeois aesthetic distance.[3] In both upper-middle- and working-class (mainly Polish and Italian) homes, the most common genre was landscape. But the landscapes in the working-class homes were either painted by family members or friends, or were of the homeland – they were relevantly connected to people's lives and served as reminders of family membership and histories. The landscapes in the upper-middle-class homes, however, bore no relationship to family origin: they were, in order of frequency, of Japan, England, and Europe and were chosen by aesthetic criteria rather than those of relevance or function.

This functionalism of art, like its relevance, works to pluralize the meanings, pleasures, and uses of the text, for it must serve different functions for different socially situated readers. Indeed, functionalism and relevance are directly related – for an artwork can only be useful if it is relevant, and one of the criteria of its relevance is its potential function. Popular taste, then, is for polysemic texts that are open to a variety of readings. This polysemy is different from that of aestheticism, for it is not organized into a textured, multilayered organic unity of meaningfulness, but is rather a resource bank from which different, possibly widely divergent, readings can be made. This means that there can be no hierarchy of readings, for there is no universal set of criteria by which to judge that one reading is better (i.e., more insightful, richer, closer to the artist's intention, or ultimately more correct) than another. [...]

The role of the academic critic of popular culture is social as much as, if not more than, textual. As well as tracing the play of meanings within the text, he or she also traces which meanings are generated and put into circulation in which social formation, and how this social play of meaning relates to the social structure at large, in particular its differential distribution of power.

Texts that meet the criteria of popular discrimination are cultural resources rather than art objects. Michel de Certeau uses the metaphor of the text as a supermarket from which readers select the items that they want, combine them with those already in their cultural 'pantry' at home, and cook up new meals or new readings according to their own needs and creativities.[4] This sort of text is the product of a completely different reading practice. The reader of the aesthetic text attempts to read it on *its* terms, to subjugate him- or herself to its aesthetic discipline. The reader reveres the text. The popular reader, on the other hand, holds no such reverence for the text but views it as a resource to be used at will. Aesthetic appreciation of a text requires the understanding of how its elements relate and contribute to its overall unity, and an appreciation of this final, completed unity is its ultimate goal. Popular readers, on the other hand, are concerned less with the final unity of a text than with the pleasures and meanings that its elements can provoke. They are undisciplined, dipping into and out of a text at will. Television detective shows, for instance, can be watched quite differently, which means that different elements are selected as significant by different viewers. [...]

Many soap opera viewers watch only those storylines that interest them, or are relevant to them, and ignore the rest. Children, too, 'frequently' show no respect for any unity of the television text, but pay only sporadic attention to it, focusing often on moments of high spectacle or comedy rather than narrative sequence or unity.[5]

This disrespect for the integrity of the text frequently accompanies a disregard for the artist in popular culture that again differentiates it from the aesthetic. The working-class woman who, when asked who painted Van Gogh's sunflowers hanging on her wall, peered at the reproduction and read out, 'Vincent' is typical,[6] for popular discrimination focuses on the conditions of consumption of art rather than those of its production. In aesthetics, however, the uniqueness of the text leaks into the uniqueness of the artistic imagination that produced it. The former is displaced onto the individuality of the artist and its highly prized emblem – the signature (whether literal or stylistic) that authentically ties the unique text to its unique producer. Of course, such authenticity is as highly valued financially as it is aesthetically, for in the world of bourgeois culture, the two value systems underwrite and guarantee each other so that the functions of the critic and the insurance assessor become almost indistinguishable. [...]

Popular films, novels, and TV narratives such as soap opera are frequently dismissed by highbrow critics for three main sets of reasons: One set clusters around their conventionality, their conforming to generic patterns and their conditions of mass production. Another set centers on criteria such as superficiality, sensationalism, obviousness, and predictability, while the third is concerned with their easiness, their failure to offer any challenge. Yet these qualities, which in aesthetic or critical discrimination are negative, are, in the realm of the popular, precisely those which enable the text to be taken up and used in the culture of the people.

Popular taste tends to ignore traces of authorial signature and focuses rather on generic convention, for genres are the result of a three-way contract between audience, producer, and text. A generic text meets not only the current tastes of its audiences but also the production needs of its producers. But this is a loose contract which leaves plenty of space for different readers to produce different forms of popular culture from it. [...]

This necessary openness of the popular text is due not only to its conventionality, but also to its superficiality, its lack of depth. Its appeal is all on the surface, so the 'meanings' of that surface have to be supplied by the reader. *Dallas's* rich interior decorations and costumings are indicative of a generalized class and national lifestyle rather than of the individuality of their characters, which has to be supplied, if it is wanted, by a productive reading. So, too, the acting style does not project individually held feelings and reactions, but relies on the viewer to 'read' a raised eyebrow or a downturn of the corner of the mouth. The camera, in *Dallas* as in soap opera in general, dwells on such conventional expressions and offers them up for viewer interpretation. And different readers read them differently. By contrast, a literary novel or Broadway play will attempt to express the inner feelings and thoughts of its characters as precisely and sensitively as possible and will thus require its readers to 'decipher' its meanings rather than produce their meanings of and from it. Conventionality and superficiality not only keep production costs down, they also open the text up to productive reading strategies.

The conventionality of plot lines, too, enables readers to write ahead, to predict what will happen and then to find pleasure (or sometimes frustration) in comparing their own projected 'scripts' with those actually broadcast. They frequently feel that their 'scripts' are superior to the script-writers', that they 'know' the characters better and are thus better able to say how they should behave or react.

The 'authored' text does not allow its readers such an empowered or productive reading position. Generic readers know the conventions and are thus situated in a far more democratic relationship with the text than are the readers of highbrow literature, with its authoritative authors.

Because authors and their texts are not seen as 'superior' to their popular readers there is no requirement, in the popular domain, for a text to be difficult, challenging, or complex. In fact, just the reverse is the case. The popular text must align itself with the tastes and concerns of its readers, not its author, if the readers are to choose it from the wide repertoire of other texts available: it must offer inviting access to the pleasures and meanings it may provoke. But the accessibility of the text does not mean the passivity of the reader, for all the studies of popular reading show how active that process is, though the activity is not necessarily laborious. The 'difficulty' of highbrow texts functions less to ensure or measure the 'quality' of the text itself and more as a social turnstile: it works to exclude those who have not the cultural competence (or the motivation) to decode it on its own terms. 'Difficulty' is finally a measure of social exclusivity rather than of textual quality, and, of course, it is much prized by the criticism industry because it guarantees the role of the critic.

The idea that a text should be 'challenging' is an important and paradoxical one to explore. Popular texts can be and are challenging; but they offer a different sort of challenge to that of highbrow texts, and the difference lies mainly in *who* is challenged, that is, in what social conflicts are activated. The challenge of the highbrow however, is aesthetic, and occurs in two main arenas – the individual and the social. The individualized challenge is that between the reader and the decoding of the text and involves the development of a finer hermeneutic sensibility that Leavis, for instance, believed would lead to a finer understanding of human life in general. These abilities would then produce a superior individual who would, in company with his [sic] fellows produce an elite who would ensure a high-quality society. What Leavis did not point out, of course, was that the individuals who were most likely to develop these fine sensibilities were already members of the dominant class, so that aesthetic discrimination worked socially as a self-confirming conservatism. Textual challenge still had social distinction built into it, but the distinction worked not only to maintain, but actually to increase, social difference and to defend current power relations. The social dimension is thus not challenging but confirming: the challenge occurs on the level of the individual's self-development through aesthetic discrimination.

The more socially inflected challenge of the aesthetic is that offered by the avant-garde to the more traditional art forms, but although the avant-garde may be radical aesthetically, Roland Barthes doubts if the challenge it offers can ever be social, for it is comfortably confined not only within the bourgeoisie, but within that fraction of the bourgeoisie which Arnold called the cultured (against the Philistines)[7] and which Bourdieu has characterized as possessing more cultural than economic capital (the Philistines, of course, possess more economic than cultural): Bourdieu calls them, in a provocative phrase, 'the dominated dominant.'[8]

The challenge of highbrow texts, then, is always offered primarily within the realm of the aesthetic and any social dimension never crosses class barriers and thus never challenges the economic base of society, nor its differential distribution of power. Recently, feminists have produced a wide variety of avant-garde art with a powerful social dimension that offers a direct challenge to patriarchal power. But this challenge still fails to cross class barriers and even to reach out to other fractions of the middle class, such as Arnold's Philistines.

The challenge of popular art, however, is not aesthetic but social. The various formations of the people who experience various forms of subordination are challenged constantly by the conditions of their social experience: they do not need challenge in their art as well. What they do need is that their art should be functional and thus should be of use in meeting the challenges of which their daily lives are comprised. [...] The meanings, complexities, and challenges of popular art are to be found in the ways in which its potential is mobilized socially, not in its texts alone. The reader who becomes intensely involved in popular culture will often become a fan, and when this occurs some interesting changes begin to take place. Fandom is poised between popular culture and high culture, so the fan works with features of both popular and aesthetic discrimination.

In its relations with popular culture, fandom is marked by excess: fans are frequently not content to produce their own readings from the texts of the culture industry, but turn these readings into full-blown fan texts which in many cases they will circulate among themselves through a distribution network that is almost as well organized as that of the industry. [...]

If many of the practices of fandom are exaggerations of those of the more popular reader, there are others which align themselves with those of critical discrimination. Some fans, for example, become acute at recognizing an individual artist's stylistic signature – whether of a musician who may play or have played in a number of bands, or of a visual artist who illustrated particular issues of a comic. This fan knowledge or expertise, which may at times be both voluminous and esoteric, constitutes a fan cultural capital that is the equivalent of the official cultural capital of the educated bourgeoisie. It brings with it similar social benefits – prestige, the sense of belonging to an elite minority that is sharply distinguished from those who lack it, and a feeling of self-worth – but it also differs from official cultural capital in that it cannot be so readily converted into economic capital. Official cultural capital, produced and promoted by the educational system, can become economically profitable because of its convertibility, via 'qualifications,' into careers, salaries, and pensions. Fan cultural capital, however, is part of the world of popular discrimination and thus is excluded from the social (and therefore economic) rewards of critical or aesthetic discrimination.

But there is one area of fandom where its cultural capital is convertible into economic capital. Some fan memorabilia and industrial texts can become economically valuable according to criteria similar to those operating in high art. So first issues of comics or first releases of records are now economically valuable, as are first editions of books, and fans often speak of, and I suspect exaggerate, the economic value of their collections. The value attached to the 'first' edition/issue/release is the equivalent, in the world of the mass reproduction of cultural objects, of the unique original artwork: a value that in the economic domain is a function of its scarcity, in the social of its distinctiveness, and in the cultural of its authenticity. The final step in this 'gentrifying' of the popular artwork occurs when its value is enhanced still further if it is in 'mint' condition – that is, if it is unread, unused – for this signals its final shift from a popular cultural resource to be used to an art object to be revered and preserved. So, too, autographed photographs, bats, balls, posters, etc. in fandom are of higher value than their otherwise identical counterparts because of their cultural authenticity, their social distinctiveness, and their material scarcity. The 'signature' guarantees the convertibility of cultural into economic capital in the world of fandom just as much as in the Manhattan art gallery.

It must be said, too, that the (generally welcome) inclusion of popular culture into academia allows for its conversion into economic rewards and social status for academics, at least. My professional status and its rewards, to take a personal example, come at least as much from my enjoyment of television and popular culture, from my wholehearted participation in its pleasures, as from the official cultural capital I acquired through my education and my reproduction of much that it stands for in my teaching and writing. So too, other academics who are well endowed with official cultural capital are increasing their 'investment' by bringing to it their popular cultural capital and its knowledge and competencies: they not only enjoy and experience rock music, soap opera, or sport in their alignment with 'the popular,' but also theorize, write, and teach about the objects of their enthusiasm in their alignment with institutional power. It requires a developed political sensitivity on the part of these academics to prevent their insertion of the popular into the academic canon from becoming an act of incorporation, for in some ways, the academic and the popular must remain in conflict.

'The people' is a remarkably difficult concept to define: it consists of a shifting set of allegiances that is mapped onto, but can cross, the structures of social power and subordination – class, gender, race, region, education, religion, and so on. But, as Stuart Hall argues, the people must always be conceived of as antagonistic in some way to the interests of the power-bloc.[9] I have situated the cultural arena for this struggle in the interface between the textual and the social. In the last instance it is not the text or art object itself which determines whether or not it is part of high or popular culture, but its social circulation within which criticism, academia, and other cultural institutions play such crucial roles. [...] It is the social use of texts rather than their essential qualities that determines their 'brow' level.

Having said this, however, we must recognize that some texts are less likely to move between levels than others and that there are textual characteristics that facilitate such movement.[10] The presence of such characteristics, however, does not guarantee a text's social mobility, though their absence makes it less likely. It also appears that in twentieth-century capitalist societies, few texts or art objects appeal to different class tastes simultaneously – the social mobility of a text occurs only with historical change. This again supports the thesis that difference in cultural taste is a reenactment of social difference, and that cultural and social discrimination are part and parcel of the same process. Popular discrimination, then, is necessarily opposed to aesthetic or critical discrimination. [...]

## Notes

1. Raymond Williams, *Keywords* (London: Fontana, 1976).

2. Pierre Bourdieu, *Distinction: A Social Critique of the Judgement of Taste* (Cambridge: Harvard University Press, 1984).

3. David Halle, 'Deconstructing Taste: Class and Culture in Modern America,' presented at the American Sociological Association Conference, San Francisco, August 1989.

4. Michel de Certeau, *The Practice of Everyday Life* (Berkeley, CA: University of California Press, 1984).

5. Henry Jenkins, 'Star Trek: Rerun, Reread, Rewritten: Fan Writing as Textual Poaching,' *Critical Studies in Mass Communication* 5, no. 2 (1989): 85–107; Patricia Palmer, *The Lively Audience: A Study of Children around the TV Set* (Sydney: Allen and Unwin, 1986).

6. Halle, 'Deconstructing Taste.'

7. Roland Barthes, *Mythologies* (London: Cape, 1970).

8. Bourdieu, *Distinction.*

9. Stuart Hall, 'Notes on Deconstructing the Popular,' in *People's History and Socialist Theory*, ed. Raphael Samuel (London: Routledge and Kegan Paul, 1981).

10. John Fiske, *Understanding Popular Culture* (Boston: Unwin Hyman, 1989).

# Chapter 20

# Laura Kipnis

# (Male) Desire and (Female) Disgust: Reading *Hustler*

Let's begin with two images. The first is of feminist author–poet Robin Morgan as she appears in the anti–pornography documentary *Not a Love Story*. Posed in her large book–lined living room, poet–husband Kenneth Pitchford at her side, she inveighs against a number of sexualities and sexual practices: masturbation–on the grounds that it promotes political quietism–as well as 'superficial sex, kinky sex, appurtenances and [sex] toys' for benumbing 'normal human sensuality.' She then breaks into tears as she describes the experience of living in a society where porno-graphic media thrives.[1] The second image is the one conjured by a recent letter to *Hustler* magazine from E.C., a reader who introduces an account of an erotic expe-rience involving a cruel–eyed, high–heeled dominatrix with this vivid vocational self–description: 'One night, trudging home from work–I gut chickens, put their guts in a plastic bag and stuff them back in the chicken's asshole–I varied my rou-tine by stopping at a small pub ... .'[2] Let's say that these two images, however hyperbolically [...], however inadvertently, offer a route toward a consideration of the relation between discourses on sexuality and the social division of labor, between sexual representation and class. On one side we have Morgan, laboring for the filmmakers and audience as a feminist intellectual, who constructs, from a particular social locus, a normative theory of sexuality. And while 'feminist intel-lectual' is not necessarily the highest paying job category, it is a markedly differ-ent class location – and one definitively up the social hierarchy–from that of E.C., whose work is of a character which tends to be relegated to the lower rungs within a social division of labor that categorizes jobs dealing with things that smell, or

From: *Cultural Studies*. Ed. Lawrence Grossberg et al. London: Routledge,1992.

that for other reasons we prefer to hide from view – garbage, sewerage, dirt, animal corpses–as of low status, both monetarily and socially. E.C.'s letter, carefully (certainly more carefully than Morgan) framing his sexuality in relation to his material circumstances and to actual conditions of production, is fairly typical of the discourse of *Hustler* – in its vulgarity, its explicitness about 'kinky' sex, and in its imbrication of sexuality and class. So as opposed to the set of norms Morgan attempts to put into circulation [...], *Hustler* also offers a theory of sexuality–a 'low theory.' Like Morgan's radical feminism, it too offers an explicitly political and counter-hegemonic analysis of power and the body; unlike Morgan it is also explicit about its own class location.

The feminist anti-porn movement has achieved at least temporary hegemony over the terms in which debates on pornography take place: current discourses on porn on the left and within feminism are faced with the task of framing themselves in relation to a set of arguments now firmly established as discursive landmarks: pornography is defined as a discourse about male domination, is theorized as the determining instance in gender oppression – if not a direct cause of rape – and its pleasures, to the extent that pleasure is not simply conflated with misogyny, are confined to the male sphere of activity. 'Pro-sex' feminists have developed arguments against these positions on a number of grounds, but invariably in response to the terms set by their opponents: those classed by the discourse as sexual deviants (or worse, as 'not feminists') – S/M lesbians,women who enjoy porn – have countered on the basis of experience, often in first person, asserting both that women *do* 'look' and arguing the compatibility of feminism and alternative sexual practices – while condemning anti-porn forces for their universalizing abandon in claiming to speak for all women. There have been numerous arguments about the use and misuse of data from media effects research by the anti-porn movement and charges of misinterpretation and misrepresentation of data made by pro-porn feminists (as well as some of the researchers). On the gendered pleasure front, psychoanalytic feminists have argued that identification and pleasure don't necessarily immediately follow assigned gender: for instance, straight women may get turned on by gay male porn or may identify with the male in a heterosexual coupling. Others have protested the abrogation of hard-won sexual liberties implicit in any restrictions on sexual expression, further questioning the politics of the alliance of the anti–porn movement and the radical right.[3] Gayle Rubin (1984) has come closest to undermining the terms of the anti-porn discourse itself: she points out, heretically, that feminism, a discourse whose object is the organization of gendered oppression, may in fact not be the most appropriate or adequate discourse to analyze sexuality, in relation to which it becomes 'irrelevant and often misleading.' Rubin paves the way for a re–examination of received truths about porn: is pornography, in fact, so obviously and so simply a discourse about gender? Has feminism, in arrogating porn as its own privileged object, foreclosed on other questions? If feminism, as Rubin goes on, 'lacks angles of vision which can encompass the social organization of sexuality,' it seems clear that at least one of these angles of vision is a theory of class, which has been routinely undertheorized and undetermined within the anti-porn movement in favor of a totalizing theory of misogyny. While class stratification, and the economic and profit motives of those in the porn industry have been exhaustively covered, we have no theory of how class plays itself out in nuances of representation. [...]

*Hustler* is certainly the most reviled instance of mass circulation porn, and at the same time probably one of the most explicitly class-antagonistic mass circulation periodicals of any genre. Although it's been the tendency among writers on porn to lump it together into an unholy triad with *Penthouse* and *Playboy*, the other two top circulating men's magazines, *Hustler* is a different beast in any number of respects, even in conventional men's magazine terms. *Hustler* set itself apart from its inception through its explicitness, and its crusade *for* explicitness, accusing *Playboy* and *Penthouse* of hypocrisy, veiling the body, and basically not delivering the goods. The strategy paid off – *Hustler* captured a third of the men's market with its entree into the field in 1974 by being the first to reveal pubic hair – with *Penthouse* swiftly following suit (in response to which a *Hustler* pictorial presented its model shaved),[4] then upping the explicitness ante and creating a publishing scandal by displaying a glimpse of pubic hair on its cover in July 1976 [...]. Throughout these early years *Hustler's* pictorials persisted in showing more and more of the forbidden zone (the 'pink' in *Hustler*-speak) with *Penthouse* struggling to keep up and *Playboy* – whose focus was always above the waist anyway – keeping a discreet distance. *Hustler* then introduced penises, first limp ones, currently hefty erect–appearing ones, a sight verboten in traditional men's magazines where the strict prohibition on the erect male sexual organ impels the question of what traumas it might provoke in the male viewer. *Hustler*, from its inception, made it its mission to disturb and unsettle its readers, both psycho-sexually and socio-sexually, interrogating, as it were, the typical men's magazine codes and conventions of sexual representation: *Hustler's* early pictorials included pregnant women, middle-aged women [...], overweight women, hermaphrodites, amputees, and in a moment of true frisson for your typical heterosexual male, a photo spread of a pre-operative transsexual, doubly well-endowed. *Hustler* continued to provoke reader outrage with a 1975 interracial pictorial (black male, white female) which according to *Hustler* was protested by both the KKK and the NAACP. It's been known to picture explicit photo spreads on the consequences of venereal disease, the most graphic war carnage ... None of these your typical, unproblematic turn-on.

And even more so than in its explicitness, *Hustler's* difference from *Playboy* and *Penthouse* is in the sort of body it produces. Its pictorials, far more than other magazines, emphasize gaping orifices, as well as a consistent sharp-focus on *other* orifices. *Hustler* sexuality is far from normative. It speaks openly of sexual preferences as 'fetishes' and its letters and columns are full of the most specific and wide-ranging practices and sexualities, which don't appear to be hierarchized, and many of which have little to do with the standard heterosexual telos of penetration. [...] The *Hustler* body is an unromanticized body – no vaselined lenses or soft focus: this is neither the airbrushed top-heavy fantasy body of *Playboy*, nor the ersatz opulence, the lingeried and sensitive crotch shots of *Penthouse,* transforming female genitals into *objets d'art*. It's a body, not a surface or a suntan: insistently material, defiantly vulgar, corporeal. In fact, the *Hustler* body is often a gaseous, fluid-emitting, *embarrassing* body, one continually defying the strictures of bourgeois manners and mores and instead governed by its lower intestinal tract – a body threatening to erupt at any moment. *Hustler's* favorite joke is someone accidentally defecating in church.

Particularly in its cartoons, but also in its editorials and political humor, *Hustler* devotes itself to what tends to be called 'grossness': an obsessive focus on the lower stratum, humor animated by a downward movement, representational techniques of exaggeration and inversion. *Hustler's* bodily topography is straight out of Rabelais, as even a partial inventory of the subjects it finds of interest indicates: fat women, assholes, monstrous and gigantic sexual organs, body odors (the notorious Scratch and Sniff centerfold, which due to 'the limits of the technology,' publisher Larry Flynt apologized, smelled definitively ot lilacs); and anything that exudes from the body: piss, shit, semen, menstrual blood, particularly when it sullies a sanitary or public site; and most especially, farts: farting in public, farting loudly, Barbara Bush farting, priests and nuns farting, politicians farting, the professional classes farting, the rich farting ... (see Bakhtin, 1984). Certainly a far remove from your sleek, overlaminated *Playboy/Penthouse* body. As *Newsweek* complained, 'The contents of an average issue read like something Krafft-Ebing might have whispered to the Marquis de Sade ... *Hustler* is into erotic fantasies involving excrement, dismemberment, and the sexual longings of rodents ... where other skin slicks are merely kinky, *Hustler* can be downright frightful ... The net effect is to transform the erotic into the emetic.'[5]

It's not clear if what sets *Newsweek* to crabbing is that *Hustler* transgresses bourgeois mores of the proper or that *Hustler* violates men's magazine conventions of sexuality. On both fronts its discourse is transgressive – in fact on *every* front *Hustler* devotes itself to producing generalized transgression. Given that control over the body has long been associated with the bourgeois political project, with both the 'ability and the right to control and dominate others' (Davidoff, 1979, p. 97), *Hustler*'s insistent and repetitive return to the iconography of the body out of control, rampantly transgressing bourgeois norms and sullying bourgeois property and proprieties, raises certain political questions. On the politics of such social transgressions, for example, Peter Stallybrass and Allon White (1986), following Bakhtin, write of a transcoding between bodily and social topography, a transcoding which sets up an homology between the lower bodily stratum and the lower social classes – the reference to the body being invariably a reference to the social.

Here perhaps is a clue to *Newsweek*'s pique, as well as a way to think about why it is that the repressive apparatuses of the dominant social order return so invariably to the body and to somatic symbols. (And I should say that I write this during the Cincinnati Mapplethorpe obscenity trial, so this tactic is excessively visible at this particular conjuncture.) It's not only because these bodily symbols 'are the ultimate elements of social classification itself' but because the transcoding between the body and the social sets up the mechanisms through which the body is a privileged political trope of lower social classes, and through which bodily grossness operates as a critique of dominant ideology. The power of grossness is predicated on its opposition from *and to* high discourses, themselves prophylactic against the debasements of the low (the lower classes, vernacular discourses, low culture, shit ... ). And it is dominant ideology itself that works to enforce and reproduce this opposition – whether in producing class differences, somatic symbols, or culture. The very highness of high culture is structured through the obsessive banishment of the low, and through the labor of suppressing the grotesque body (which is, in fact, simply the material body, gross as that can be) in favor of what Bakhtin refers to as 'the classical body.' This classical body – a refined, orifice-less, laminated surface – is homologous to the forms of official high culture which legitimate their authority by reference to the values – the highness – inherent in this classical body. According to low-theoretician Larry Flynt: 'Tastelessness is a necessary tool in challenging preconceived notions in an uptight world where people are afraid to discuss their attitudes, prejudices and misconceptions.' This is not so far from Bakhtin on Rabelais:

Things are tested and reevaluated in the dimensions of laughter, which has defeated fear and all gloomy seriousness. This is why the material bodily lower stratum is needed, for it gaily and simultaneously materializes and unburdens. It liberates objects from the snares of false seriousness, from illusions and sublimations inspired by fear. (p. 376)

So in mapping social topography against bodily topography, it becomes apparent how the unsettling effects of grossness and erupting bodies condense all the unsettling effects (to those in power) of a class hierarchy tenuously held in place through symbolic (and less symbolic) policing of the threats posed by bodies, by lower classes, by angry mobs. [...]

So we can see, returning to our two opening images, how Morgan's tears, her sentiment, might be constructed *against* E.C.'s vulgarity, how her desire to distance herself from and if possible banish from existence the cause of her distress – the sexual expression of people unlike herself – has a sort of structural imperative: as Stallybrass and White (1986) put it, the bourgeois subject has 'continuously defined and redefined itself through the exclusion of what it marked out as low–as dirty, repulsive, noisy, contaminating ... [the] very act of exclusion was constitutive of its identity' (p. 191). So disgust has a long and complicated history, the context within which should be placed the increasingly strong tendency of the bourgeois to want to remove the distasteful from the sight of society [...]. These gestures of disgust are crucial in the production of the bourgeois body, now so rigidly split into higher and lower stratum that tears will become the only publicly permissible display of bodily fluid. So the bodies and bodily effluences start to stack up into neat oppositions: on the one side upper bodily productions, a heightened sense of delicacy, and the project of removing the distasteful from sight (and sight, of course, at the top of the hierarchization of the senses central to bourgeois identity and rationality); and on the other hand, the lower body and *its* productions, the insistence on vulgarity and violations of the bourgeois body. To the extent that, in Morgan's project, discourse and tears are devoted to concealing the counter-bourgeois body from view by regulating its representation and reforming its pleasures into ones more consequent with refined sensibilities, they can be understood, at least in part, as the product of a centuries–long socio–historical process, a process that has been a primary mechanism of class distinction, and one that has played an important role as an as ongoing tool in class hegemony. So perhaps it becomes a bit more difficult to see feminist disgust in isolation, and disgust at pornography as strictly a gender issue, for any gesture of disgust is not without a history and not without a class character. And whatever else we may say about feminist arguments about the proper or improper representation of women's bodies – and I don't intend to imply that my discussion is exhaustive of the issue – bourgeois disgust, even as mobilized against a sense of violation and violence to the female body, is not without a function in relation to class hegemony, and more than problematic in the context of what purports to be a radical social movement.

Perhaps this is the moment to say that a large part of what impels me to write this essay is my own disgust in reading *Hustler*. In fact, I have wanted to write this essay for several years, but every time I trudge out and buy the latest issue, open it and begin to try to bring analytical powers to bear upon it, I'm just so disgusted that I give up, never quite sure whether this almost automatic response is one of feminist disgust or bourgeois disgust. Of course, whether as feminist, bourgeois, or academic, I and most likely you, are what could be called *Hustler*'s implied target, rather than its implied reader. The discourse of *Hustler* is quite specifically *constructed against* – not only the classical body, a bourgeois hold-over of the aristocracy, but against all the paraphernalia of petit-bourgeoisiehood as well. At the most manifest level *Hustler* is simply against any form of social or intellectual pretension: it is against the pretensions (and the social power) of the professional classes – doctors, optometrists, dentists are favored targets; it is against liberals, and particularly cruel to academics who are invariably prissy and uptight. (An academic to his wife: 'Eat your pussy? You forget Gladys, I have a Ph.D.') It is against the power of government – which is by definition corrupt, as are elected officials, the permanent government, even foreign governments. Of course, it is against the rich, particularly rich women, down on the Chicago Cubs, and devotes many pages to the hypocrisy of organized religion – with a multiplication of jokes on the sexual instincts of the clergy, the sexual possibilities of the crucifixion, the scam of the virgin birth – and, as mentioned previously, the plethora of jokes involving farting/shitting/fucking in church and the bodily functions of nuns, priests, and ministers. In *Hustler* any form of social power is fundamentally crooked and illegitimate.

These are just *Hustler*'s more manifest targets. Reading a bit deeper, its offenses provide a detailed road map of a cultural psyche. Its favored tactic is to zero in on a subject, an issue, which the bourgeois imagination prefers to be unknowing about, which a culture has founded itself upon suppressing, and prohibits irreverent speech about. Things we would call 'tasteless' at best, or might even become physically revulsed by: the materiality of aborted fetuses,[6] where homeless people go to the bathroom, cancer, the proximity of sexual organs to those of elimination – any aspect of the material body, in fact. A case in point, one which again subjected *Hustler* to national outrage: its two cartoons about Betty Ford's mastectomy. If one can distance oneself from one's automatic indignation for a moment, *Hustler* might be seen as posing, through the strategy of transgression, an interesting metadiscursive question: which are the subjects that are taboo ones for even sick humor? Consider for a moment that while, for example, it was not uncommon, following the Challenger explosion, to hear the sickest jokes about scattered body parts, while jokes about amputees and paraplegics are not entirely unknown even on broadcast TV (and, of course, abound on the pages of *Hustler*), while jokes about blindness are considered so benign that one involving Ray Charles features in a current 'blind taste test' soda pop commercial, mastectomy is one subject that appears to be completely off limits as a humorous topic. But back to amputees for a moment, perhaps a better comparison: apparently a man without a limb is considered less tragic by the culture at large, less mutilated, and less of a cultural problem it seems, than a woman without a breast. A mastectomy more of a tragedy than the deaths of the seven astronauts. This, as I say, provides some clues into the deep structure of a cultural psyche – as does our outrage. After all, what *is* a woman without a breast in a culture that measures breasts as the measure of the woman? Not a fit subject for comment. It's a subject so veiled that it's not even available to the 'working through' of the joke. (And again a case where *Hustler* seems to be deconstructing the codes of the men's magazine: where *Playboy* creates a fetish of the breast, and whose *raison d'être* is, in fact, very much the cultural obsession with them, *Hustler* perversely points out that they are, after all, materially, merely tissue – another limb.)[7]

*Hustler's* uncanny knack for finding and attacking the jugular of a culture's sensitivity might more aptly be regarded as intellectual work on the order of the classic anthropological studies which translate a culture into a set of structural oppositions (obsession with the breast/prohibition of mastectomy jokes), laying bare the structure of its taboos and arcane superstitions. [...] *Hustler,* in fact, performs a similar cultural mapping to that of anthropologist Mary Douglas, whose study *Purity and Danger* (1966) produces a very similar social blueprint. The vast majority of *Hustler* humor seems to be animated by the desire to violate what Douglas describes as 'pollution' taboos and rituals – these being a society's set of beliefs, rituals, and practices having to do with dirt, order, and hygiene (and by extension, the pornographic). As to the pleasure produced by such cultural violations as *Hustler's*, Douglas cheerily informs us, 'It is not always an unpleasant experience to confront ambiguity,' and while it is clearly more tolerable in some areas than in others, 'there is a whole gradient on which laughter, revulsion and shock belong at different points and intensities' (p. 37).

The sense of both pleasure and danger that violation of pollution taboos can invoke is clearly dependent on the existence of symbolic codes, codes that are for the most part only semi-conscious. Defilement can't be an isolated event, it can only engage our interest or provoke our anxiety to the extent that our ideas about such things are systematically ordered and that this ordering matters deeply – in our culture, in our subjectivity. As Freud (1963) notes, 'Only jokes that have a purpose run the risk of meeting with people who do not want to listen to them.'

Of course, a confrontation with ambiguity and violation can be profoundly displeasurable as well, as the many opponents of *Hustler* might attest. And for Freud this displeasure has to do with both gender and class (p. 9a).[8] One of the most interesting things about Freud's discussion of jokes is the theory of humor and gender he elaborates in the course of his discussion of them, with class almost inadvertently intervening as a third term. He first endeavors to produce a typology of jokes according to their gender effects. For example, in regard to excremental jokes (a staple of *Hustler* humor) Freud tells us that this is material *common to both sexes*, as both experience a common sense of shame surrounding bodily functions. And it's true that *Hustler's* numerous jokes on the proximity of the sexual organs to elimination functions, the confusion of assholes and vaginas, turds and penises, shit and sex – i.e., a couple fucking in a hospital room while someone in the next bed is getting an enema, all get covered with shit – can't really be said to have a gender basis or target (unless, that is, we women put ourselves, more so than men, in the position of upholders of 'good taste').

But obscene humor, whose purpose is to expose sexual facts and relations verbally, is, for Freud, a consequence of male and female sexual incommensurability, and the dirty joke is something like a seduction gone awry. The motive for (men's) dirty jokes is 'in reality nothing more than women's incapacity to tolerate undisguised sexuality, an incapacity correspondingly increased with a rise in the educational and social level.' Whereas both men and women are subject to sexual inhibition or repression, apparently upper-class women are the more seriously afflicted in the Freudian world, and dirty jokes thus function as a sign for both sexual difference [...], and class difference. So apparently, if it weren't for women's lack of sexual willingness and class refinement the joke would be not a joke, but a proposition: 'If the woman's readiness emerges quickly the obscene speech has a short life; it yields at once to a sexual action,' hypothesizes Freud. While there are some fairly crude gender and class stereotypes in circulation here – the figure of the lusty barmaid standing in for the lower-class woman – it's also true that obscene jokes and pornographic images *are* perceived by *some* women as an act of aggression against women. But these images and jokes are aggressive only insofar as they're capable of causing the woman discomfort, and they're capable of causing discomfort *only* insofar as there *are* differing levels of sexual inhibition between at least some men and some women. So Freud's view would seem to hold out: the obscene joke is directed originally toward women; it presupposes not only the presence of a woman, but that women are sexually constituted differently than men; and upper classness or upper-class identification – as Morgan's discourse also indicates – exacerbates this difference.

But if there are differing levels of inhibition, displeasure, or interest between some men and some women (although *Hustler*'s readership is primarily male, it's not exclusively male), the origins of this pleasure/displeasure disjunction are also a site of controversy in the porn debates. For Freud it's part of the process of *differentiation* between the sexes, not originative – little girls are just as 'interested' as little boys. Anti-porn forces tend to reject a constructionist argument such as Freud's in favor of a description of female sexuality as inborn and biologically based – something akin to the 'normal human sensuality' Morgan refers to.[9] Women's discomfiture at the dirty joke, from this vantage point, would appear to be twofold. There is the discomfort at the intended violation – at being assailed 'with the part of the body or the procedure in question.' But there is the further discomfort at being addressed as a subject of repression – as a subject with a history – and the rejection of porn can be seen as a defense erected against representations which mean to unsettle her in her subjectivity. In other words, there is a violation of the *idea* of the 'naturalness' of female sexuality and subjectivity, which is exacerbated by the social fact that not all women *do* experience male pornography in the same way. That 'pro-sex' feminists, who tend to follow some version of a constructionist position on female sexuality, seem to feel less violated by porn is some indication that these questions of subjectivity are central to porn's address, misaddress, and violations. To the extent that pornography's discourse engages in setting up disturbances around questions of subjectivity and sexual difference – after all, what does *Hustler*-variety porn consist of but the male fantasy of women whose sexual desires are in concert with men's – and that this fantasy of undifferentiation is perceived as doing violence to female subjectivity by some women but not others, the perception of this violence is an issue of difference between women.[10] But the violence here is that of misaddress, of having one's desire misfigured as the male's desire. It is the violence of being absent from the scene. The differentiation between female spectators as to how this address or misaddress is perceived appears to be bound up with the degree to which a certain version of female sexuality is hypostatized as natural, versus a sense of mobility of sexuality, at least at the level of fantasy. But hypostatizing female sexuality and assigning it to all women involves universalizing an historically specific class position as well, not as something acquired and constructed through difference, privilege, and hierarchy, but as also somehow inborn – as identical to this natural female sexuality. Insisting that all women are violated by pornography insists that class or class identification doesn't figure as a difference between women, that 'normal human sensuality' erases all difference between women.

For Freud, even the form of the joke is classed, with a focus on joke technique associated with higher social classes and education levels. In this light it's interesting to note how little *Hustler* actually engages in the technique of the joke – even to find a pun is rare. But then as far as obscene humor, we're subject to glaring errors of judgment about the 'goodness' of jokes insofar as we judge them on formal terms, according to Freud – the technique of these jokes is often 'quite wretched, but they have immense success in provoking laughter.' Particularly in regard to obscene jokes, we aren't 'in a position to distinguish by our feelings what part of the pleasure arises from the sources of their technique and what part from those of their purpose. Thus, strictly speaking, we do not know what we are laughing at' (p. 102). And so too with displeasure – it would seem we can't be entirely sure what we're *not* laughing at either, and this would be particularly true of both the bourgeois and the anti-pornography feminist, to the extent that both seem likely to displace or disavow pleasure or interest in smut, one in favor of technique – like disgust, a mechanism of class distinction – and the other against perceived violations against female subjectivity. So for both, the act of rejection takes on far more significance than the terrains of pleasure; for both, the nuances and micro-logics of *displeasure* are defining practices.

Yet at the same time, there does seem to be an awful lot of interest in porn among both, albeit a negative sort of interest. It's something of a Freudian cliché that shame, disgust, and morality are reaction-formations to an original interest in what is not 'clean.' One defining characteristic of a classic reaction-formation is that the subject actually comes close to 'satisfying the demands of the opposing instinct while actually engaged in the pursuit of the virtue which he affects,' the classic example being the housewife obsessed with cleanliness who ends up 'concentrating her whole existence on dust and dirt (Laplanche and Pontalis, 1973, pp. 376–278). And it does seem to be the case that a crusader against porn will end up making pornography the center of her existence. Theorizing it as central to women's oppression means, in practical terms, devoting one's time to reading it, thinking about it, and talking about it. It also means simultaneously conferring this *interest*, this subject-effect, onto others – predicting tragic consequences arising from such dirty pursuits, unvaryingly dire and uniform effects, as if the will and individuality of consumers of porn are suddenly seized by some (projected) all-controlling force, a force which becomes – or already is – the substance of a monotonic male sexuality. Thusly summing up male sexuality, Andrea Dworkin (1987) writes: Any violation of a woman's body can become sex for men; this is the essential truth of pornography' (p. 138).

The belief in these sorts of essential truths seems close to what Mary Douglas (1966) calls 'danger-beliefs' –

[A] strong language of mutual exhortation. At this level the laws of nature are dragged in to sanction the moral code: this kind of disease is caused by adultery, that by incest ... the whole universe is harnessed to men's attempts to force one another into good citizenship. Thus we find that certain moral values are upheld and certain social rules defined by beliefs in dangerous contagion. (p. 3)

And Douglas, like Freud, also speaks directly about the relation of gender to the 'gradient' where laughter, revulsion, and shock collide: her discussion of danger beliefs also opens onto questions of class and hierarchy as well. For her, gender is something of a trope in the realm of purity rituals and pollution violations: it functions as a displacement from issues of social hierarchy.

I believe that some pollutions are used as analogies for expressing a general view of the social order. For example, there are beliefs that each sex is a danger to the other ... Such patterns of sexual danger can be seen to express symmetry or hierarchy. It is implausible to interpret them as expressing something about the actual relation of the sexes. I suggest that many ideas about sexual dangers are better interpreted as symbols of the relation between parts of society, as mirroring designs of hierarchy or symmetry which apply in the larger social system. (p. 3)[11]

To put a feminist spin on Douglas's pre-feminist passage, while men do certainly pose actual sexual danger to women, the content of pollution beliefs expresses that danger symbolically at best: it would be implausible to take the content of these beliefs literally. So while, for Douglas, gender is a trope for social hierarchy, a feminist might interpret the above passage to mean that *danger* is a trope for gender hierarchy. Douglas's observations on the series of displacements between defilement, danger, gender, and class puts an interesting cast on female displeasure in pornography in relation to class hierarchies and 'the larger social system' – in relation to *Hustler*'s low-class tendentiousness and its production of bourgeois displeasure, and why it might happen that the feminist response to pornography ends up reinscribing the feminist into the position of enforcer of class distinctions.

But historically, female reformism aimed at bettering the position of women has often had an unfortunately conservative social thrust, as in the case of the temperance movement. The local interests of women in reforming male behavior can easily dovetail with the interests of capital in producing and reproducing an orderly, obedient, and sober workforce. In social history terms we might note that *Hustler* galumphs onto the social stage at the height of the feminist second wave, and while the usual way to phrase this relation would be the term 'backlash,' it can also be seen as a retort – even a political response – to feminist calls for reform of the male imagination. There's no doubt that *Hustler* sees itself as doing battle with feminists: ur-feminist Gloria Steinem makes frequent appearances in the pages of the magazine as an uptight, and predictably, upper-class, bitch. It's fairly clear that from *Hustler*'s point of view, feminism is a class-based discourse. So *Hustler*'s production of sexual differences are also the production of a form of class consciousness – to accede to feminist reforms would be to identify upward on the social hierarchy.

But any automatic assumptions about *Hustler*-variety porn aiding and abetting the entrenchment of male power might be put into question by actually reading the magazine. Whereas Freud's observations on dirty jokes are phallocentric in the precise sense of the word – phallic sexuality is made central – *Hustler* itself seems much less certain about the place of the phallus, much more wry and often troubled about male and female sexual incommensurability. On the one hand it offers the standard men's magazine fantasy babe – always ready, always horny, willing to do anything, and who finds the *Hustler* male inexplicably irresistible. But just as often there is her flip side: the woman who is disgusted by the *Hustler* male's desires and sexuality, a superior, rejecting, often upper-class woman. It becomes clear how class resentment is modulated through resentment of what is seen as the power of women to humiliate and reject: 'Beauty isn't everything, except to the bitch who's got it. You see her stalking the aisles of Cartier, stuffing her perfect face at exorbitant cuisineries, tooling her Jag along private-access coastline roads....' Doesn't this reek of a sense of disenfranchisement rather than any sort of certainty about male power over women? The fantasy life here is animated by cultural disempowerment in relation to a sexual caste system and a social class system. This magazine is tinged with frustrated desire and rejection: *Hustler* gives vent to a vision of sex in which sex is an arena for failure and humiliation rather than domination and power. There are numerous ads addressed to male anxieties and sense of inadequacy: various sorts of penis enlargers [...], penis extenders, and erection aids [...]. One of the problems with most porn from even a pro-porn feminist point of view is that men seize the power and privilege to have public fantasies about women's bodies, to imagine and represent women's bodies without any risk, without any concomitant problematization of the male body – which is invariably produced as powerful and inviolable. But *Hustler* does put the male body at risk, representing and never completely alleviating male anxiety (and for what it's worth, there is a surprising amount of castration humor in *Hustler* as well). Rejecting the sort of compensatory fantasy life mobilized by *Playboy* and *Penthouse* in which all women are willing and all men are studs – as long as its readers fantasize and identify upward, with money, power, good looks, and consumer durables – *Hustler* pulls the window dressing off the market/exchange nature of sexual romance: the market in attractiveness, the exchange basis of male-female relations in patriarchy. Sexual exchange is a frequent subject of humor: women students are coerced into having sex with professors for grades, women are fooled into having sex by various ruses, lies, or barters usually engineered by males in power positions: bosses, doctors, and the like. All this is probably truer than not true, but problematic from the standpoint of male fantasy: power, money, and prestige are represented as essential to sexual success, but the magazine works to disparage and counter identification with these sorts of class attributes on every other front. The intersections of sex, gender, class, and power here are complex, contradictory, and political.

Much of *Hustler*'s humor *is,* in fact, manifestly political, and much of it would even get a warm welcome in left-leaning circles, although its strategies of conveying those sentiments might give some of the flock pause. A 1989 satirical photo feature titled 'Farewell to Reagan: Ronnie's Last Bash' demonstrates how the magazine's standard repertoire of aesthetic techniques – nudity, grossness, and offensiveness – can be directly translated into scathingly effective political language. It further shows how the pornographic idiom can work as a form of political speech that refuses to buy into the pompously serious and highminded language in which official culture conducts its political discourse: *Hustler* refuses the language of high culture along with its political forms. The photospread, laid out like a series of black and white surveillance photos, begins with this no-words-minced introduction:

It's been a great eight years – for the power elite, that is. You can bet Nancy planned long and hard how to celebrate Ron Reagan's successful term of filling special-interest coffers while fucking John Q. Citizen right up the yazoo. A radical tax plan that more than halved taxes for the rich while doubling the working man's load; detaxation of industries, who trickled down their windfalls into mergers, takeovers, and investments in foreign lands; crooked deals with enemies of U.S. allies in return for dirty money for right wing killers to reclaim former U.S. business territories overseas; more than 100 appointees who resigned in disgrace over ethics or outright criminal charges ... are all the legacies of the Reagan years ... and we'll still get whiffs of bullyboy Ed Meese's sexual intimidation policies for years to come, particularly with conservative whores posing as Supreme Court justices.

The photos that follow are of an elaborately staged orgiastic White House farewell party as imagined by the *Hustler* editors, with the appropriate motley faces of the political elite photomontaged onto naked and semi-naked bodies doing fairly obscene and polymorphously perverse things to each other. [...] That more of the naked bodies are female and that many are in what could be described as a service relation to male bodies clearly opens up the possibility of a reading limited to its misogynistic tendencies. But what becomes problematic for such a singular reading is that within these parodic representations, this staging of the rituals of male hegemony also works in favor of an overtly counter-hegemonic political treatise. [...]

While the anti-establishment politics of the photospread are fairly clear, *Hustler* can also be maddeningly incoherent, all over what we usually think of as the political spectrum. Its incoherence as well as its low-rent tendentiousness can be laid at the door of publisher Larry Flynt as much as anywhere, as Flynt, in the early days of the magazine, maintained such iron control over the day-to-day operations that he had to approve even the pull quotes. Flynt is a man apparently both determined and destined to play out the content of his obsessions as psychodrama on our public stage; if he weren't so widely considered such a disgusting pariah, his life could probably supply the material for many epic dramas. The very public nature of Flynt's blazing trail through the civil and criminal justice system and his one-man campaign for the first amendment justify a brief descent into the murkiness of the biographical, not to make a case for singular authorship, but because Flynt himself has had a decisive historical and political impact in the realpolitik of state power. In the end it has been porn king Larry Flynt − not the left, not the avantgarde − who has decisively expanded the perimeters of political speech.

Larry Flynt is very much of the class he appears to address − his story is like a pornographic Horatio Alger. He was born in Magoffin County, Kentucky, in the Appalachians − the poorest county in America. The son of a pipe welder, he quit school in the eighth grade, joined the Navy at fourteen with a forged birth certificate, got out, worked in a G.M. auto assembly plant, and turned $1,500 in savings into a chain of go-go bars in Ohio named the Hustler Clubs. The magazine originated as a 2-page newsletter for the bars, and the rest was rags to riches: Flynt's income was as high as $30 million a year when *Hustler* was at its peak circulation of over 2 million [...].

[...] All proceeded as normal (for Flynt) until his well-publicized 1978 conversion to evangelical Christianity at the hands of presidential sister Ruth Carter Stapleton. The two were pictured chastely hand in hand as Flynt announced plans to turn *Hustler* into a *religious* skin magazine and told a Pentecostal congregation in Houston (where he was attending the National Women's Conference) 'I owe every woman in America an apology.' Ironically, it was this religious conversion that led to the notorious *Hustler* cover of a woman being ground up in a meat grinder, which was, in fact, another sheepish and flat-footed attempt at apologia by Flynt. 'We will no longer hang women up as pieces of meat,' was actually the widely ignored caption to the photo. [...]

In 1978, shortly after the religious conversion, during another of his obscenity trials in Lawrenceville, Georgia, Flynt was shot three times by an unknown assassin with a 44 magnum. His spinal nerves were severed, leaving him paralyzed from the waist down and in constant pain. He became a recluse, barricading himself in his Bel Air mansion, surrounded by bodyguards. His wife Althea, then 27, a former go-go dancer in the Hustler clubs, took over control of the corporation and the magazine, and returned the magazine to its former focus. Flynt became addicted to morphine and Dilaudid, finally detoxing to methadone. (He repudiated the religious conversion after the shooting.) Now confined to a wheelchair, he continued to be hauled into court by the government for obscenity and in various civil suits. He was sued by *Penthouse* publisher Bob Guccione and a female *Penthouse* executive who claimed *Hustler* had libeled her by printing that she had contracted VD from Guccione. He was sued by author Jackie Collins after the magazine published nude photos it incorrectly identified as the nude author. He was fined $10,000 a day – increased to $20,000 a day – when he refused to turn over to the feds tapes he claimed he possessed documenting a government frame of DeLorean. Flynt's public behavior was becoming increasingly bizarre. He appeared in court wearing an American flag as a diaper and was arrested. At another 1984 Los Angeles trial, described by a local paper as 'legal surrealism,' his own attorney asked for permission to gag his client and after an 'obscene outburst' Flynt, like Black Panther Bobby Seale, was bound and gagged at his own trial.

The same year the FCC was forced to issue an opinion on Flynt's threat to force television stations to show his X-rated presidential campaign commercials. Flynt, whose compulsion it was to find loopholes in the nation's obscenity laws, vowed to use his presidential campaign(!) to test those laws by insisting that TV stations show his campaign commercials featuring hard core sex acts. [...] In 1986 a federal judge ruled that the U.S. Postal Service could not constitutionally prohibit *Hustler* and Flynt from sending free copies of the magazine to members of Congress, a ruling stemming from Flynt's decision to mail free copies of *Hustler* to members of Congress, so they could be 'well informed on all social issues and trends.' Flynt's next appearance, ensconced in a gold-plated wheelchair, was at the $45 million federal libel suit brought by the Reverend Jerry Falwell over the notorious Campari ad parody, in which the head of the Moral Majority describes his 'first time' as having occurred with his mother behind an outhouse. A Virginia jury dismissed the libel charge but awarded Falwell $200,000 for intentional infliction of emotional distress. A federal district court upheld the verdict, but when it landed in the Rehnquist Supreme Court the judgment was reversed by a unanimous Rehnquist-written decision that the Falwell parody was not reasonably believable, and thus fell into category of satire – an art form often 'slashing and one-sided.' This Supreme Court decision significantly extended the freedom of the press won in the 1964 New York Times vs. Sullivan ruling (which mandated that libel could only be founded in cases of 'reckless disregard'), and 'handed the press one of its most significant legal triumphs in recent years,' was 'an endorsement of robust political debate,' and ended the influx of 'pseudo-libel suits' by celebrities with hurt feelings, crowed the grateful national press, amidst stories generally concluding that the existence of excrescences like *Hustler* are the price of freedom of the press.

Flynt and wife Althea had over the years elaborated various charges and conspiracy theories about the shooting, including charges of a CIA-sponsored plot (Flynt claimed to have been about to publish the names of JFK's assassins – conspiracy theories being another repeating feature of the *Hustler mentalité*). Further speculation about the shooting focused on the mob, magazine distribution wars, and even various disgruntled family members. The shooting was finally acknowledged by white supremacist Joseph Paul Franklin, currently serving two life sentences for racially motivated killings. No charges were ever brought in the

Flynt shooting. That Flynt, who has been regularly accused of racism, should be shot by a white supremacist is only one of the many ironies of his story. In another – one which would seem absurd in the most hackneyed morality tale – this man who made millions on the fantasy of endlessly available fucking is now left impotent. And in 1982, after four years of constant and reportedly unbearable pain, the nerves leading to his legs were cauterized to stop all sensation – Flynt, who built an empire on offending bourgeois sensibilities with their horror of errant bodily functions, is now left with no bowel or urinary control.

Flynt, in his obsessional one-man war against state power's viselike grip on the body of its citizenry, seized as his *matériel* the very pornographic idioms from which he had constructed his *Hustler* empire. The exhibitionism, the desire to shock, the deployment of the body – these are the very affronts that have made him the personification of evil to both the state and anti-porn feminists. Yet willingly or not, Flynt's own body has been very much on the line as well – the pornographer's body has borne the violence of the political and private enforcement of the norms of the bourgeois body. If *Hustler's* development of the pornographic idiom as a political form seems – as with other new cultural political forms – politically incoherent to traditional political readings based on traditional political alliances and political oppositions – right-left, misogynist-feminist – then it is those very political meanings that *Hustler* throws into question. It is *Hustler's* very political incoherence – in conventional political terms – that makes it so available to counter-hegemonic readings, to opening up new political alliances and strategies. And this is where I want to return to the question of *Hustler's* misogyny, another political category *Hustler* puts into question. Do I feel assaulted and affronted by *Hustler's* images, as do so many other women? Yes. Is that a necessary and sufficient condition on which to base the charge of its misogyny? Given my own gender and class position I'm not sure that I'm exactly in a position to trust my immediate response.

Take, for example, *Hustler's* clearly political use of nudity. It's unmistakable from the 'Reagan's Farewell Party' photospread that *Hustler* uses nudity as a leveling device, a deflating technique following in a long tradition of political satire. And perhaps this is the subversive force behind another of *Hustler's* scandals (or publishing coups from its point of view), its notorious nude photospread of Jackie Onassis, captured sunbathing on her Greek island, Skorpios. Was this simply another case of misogyny? The strategic uses of nudity we've seen elsewhere in the magazine might provoke a conceptual transition in thinking through the Onassis photos: from Onassis as unwilling sexual object to Onassis as political target. Given that nudity is used throughout the magazine as an offensive against the rich and powerful – Reagan, North, Falwell, Abrams, as well as Kirkpatrick, and in another feature, Thatcher, all, unfortunately for the squeamish, through the magic of photomontage, nude – it would be difficult to argue that the nudity of Onassis functions strictly in relation to her sex, exploiting women's vulnerability as a class, or that its message can be reduced to a genericizing one like 'you may be rich but you're just a cunt like any other cunt.' Onassis's appearance on the pages of *Hustler* does raise questions of sex and gender insofar as we're willing to recognize what might be referred to as a sexual caste system, and the ways in which the imbrication of sex and caste make it difficult to come to any easy moral conclusions about *Hustler's* violation of Onassis and her right to control and restrict how her body is portrayed. [...] This is not so entirely dissimilar from *Hustler's* quotidian and consenting models, who while engaged in a similar activity are confined to very different social sites. Such social sites as those pictured in a regular *Hustler* feature, 'The Beaver Hunt,' a photo gallery of snapshots of non-professional models sent in by readers.[12] Posed in paneled rec rooms, on plaid Sears sofas or chenille bedspreads, amidst the kind of matching bedroom suites seen on late night easy credit furniture ads, nude or in polyester lingerie, they are identified as secretaries, waitresses, housewives, nurses, bank tellers, cosmetology students, cashiers, factory workers, saleswomen, data processors, nurse's aides. ... Without generalizing from this insufficiency of data about any kind of *typical* class-based notions about the body and its appropriate display,[13] we can simply ask, where are the doctors, lawyers, corporate execs, and college professors? Or moving up the hierarchy, where are the socialites, the jet-setters, the wives of the chairmen of the board? Absent because of their fervent feminism? Or merely because they've struck a better deal? Simply placing the snapshots of Onassis in the place of the cashier, the secretary, the waitress, violates the rigid social distinctions of place and hardened spatial boundaries (boundaries most often purchased precisely as protection from the hordes) intrinsic to class hierarchy. These are precisely the distinctions that would make us code differently the deployment of femininity that achieves marriage to a billionaire shipping magnate from those that land you a spot in this month's Beaver Hunt. These political implications of the Onassis photospread indicate, I believe, the necessity of a more nuanced theory of misogyny than those currently in circulation. If any symbolic exposure or violation of *any* woman's body is automatically aggregated to the transhistorical misogyny machine that is the male imagination, it overlooks the fact that *all* women, simply by virtue of being women, are not necessarily political allies, that women can both symbolize and exercise class power and privilege, not to mention oppressive political power.

Feminist anti-pornography arguments, attempting to reify the feminine as an a priori privileged vantage point against pornographic male desires work on two fronts: apotropaic against the reality of male violence they simultaneously work to construct a singular version of (a politically correct) femininity against other 'unreconstructed' versions. Their reification of femininity defends against any position that might suggest that femininity is not an inherent virtue, an inborn condition, or in itself a moral position from which to speak – positions such as those held by pro-sex feminists, psychoanalytic theory, and the discourse of pornography itself. But among the myriad theoretical problems which the reification of femininity gives rise to,[14] there are the contradictions of utilizing class disgust as a vehicle of the truly feminine. A theory of representation that automatically conflates bodily representations with real women's bodies, and symbolic or staged sex or violence as equivalent to real sex or violence, clearly acts to restrict political expression and narrow the forms of political struggle by ignoring differences between women – and the class nature of feminist reformism. The fact that real violence against women is so pervasive as to be almost unlocalizable may lead us to want to localize it within something so easily at hand as representation; but the political consequences for feminism – to reduce it to another variety of bourgeois reformism – make this not a sufficient tactic.

However, having said this, I must add that *Hustler* is certainly not politically unproblematic. If *Hustler* is counter-hegemonic in its refusal of bourgeois proprieties, its transgressiveness has real limits. It is often only incoherent and banal where it means to be alarming and confrontational. Its banality can be seen in its politics of race, an area where its refusal of polite speech has little countercultural force. *Hustler* has been frequently accused of racism, but *Hustler* basically just wants to offend – anyone, of any race, any ethnic group. Not content merely to offend the right, it makes doubly sure to offend liberal and left sensibilities too, not content merely to taunt whites, it hectors blacks. Its favored tactic in regard to race is to simply reproduce the stupidest stereotype it can think of – the subject of any *Hustler* cartoon featuring blacks will invariably be huge sexual organs which every woman lusts after, or alternately, black watermelon-eating lawbreakers. *Hustler's* letter columns carry out a raging debate on the subject of race, with black readers writing both that they find *Hustler's* irreverence funny or resent its stereotypes, whites both applauding and protesting. It should also be noted that in the area of ugly stereotypes *Hustler* is hardly alone these days. The most explicitly political forms of popular culture recently are ones which also refuse to have proper representations – as any number of examples from the world of rap, which has also been widely accused of misogyny, as well as anti-Semitism, would attest. What this seems to imply is that there is no guarantee that counter-hegemonic or even specifically anti-bourgeois cultural forms are necessarily also going to be progressive. And as one of the suppositions in recent American cultural studies seems to have been that there is something hopeful to find in popular culture this might demand some rethinking.[15] *Hustler* is against government, against authority, against the bourgeoisie, diffident on male power – but its anti-liberalism, anti-feminism, anti-communism, and anti-progressivism leave little space for envisioning any alternative kind of political organization.

*Hustler* does powerfully articulate class resentment, and to the extent that anti-porn feminism lapses into bourgeois reformism, and that we devote ourselves to sanitizing representation, we are legitimately a target of that resentment. Leninism is on the wane around the world. The model of a vanguard party who will lead the rest of us to true consciousness holds little appeal these days. The policing of popular representation seems like only a path to more domination, and I despair for the future of a feminist politics that seems dedicated to following other vanguard parties into dogma and domination.

## Notes

I'd like to thank Lauren Berlant for her extensive and exhaustive aid and comfort on this paper, and Lynn Spigel for many helpful suggestions.

1. For an interesting and far more extensive analysis of the politics of *Not a Love Story* see B. Ruby Rich (1986), 'Anti-Porn: Soft Issue, Hard World' in *Films For Women,* ed. Charlotte Brunsdon, London: British Film Institute, pp. 31–43.

2. Several writers who have visited the *Hustler* offices testify that to their surprise these letters *are* sent by actual readers, and *Hustler* receives well over 1000 letters a month. As to whether this particular letter is genuine in its authorship I have no way of knowing, but I'm happy enough to simply consider it as part of the overall discourse of *Hustler.*

3. Central anti-anti-porn texts are *Pleasure and Danger,* ed. Carole S. Vance (1984), London: Routledge & Kegan Paul; *Caught Looking: Feminism, Pornography and Censorship,* ed. Kate Ellis, et al. (1988), Seattle: Real Comet Press; *Powers of Desire: The Politics of Sexuality,* ed. Ann Snitow, Christine Stansell, and Sharon Thompson (1983), New York: Monthly Review Press, especially section VI on 'Current Controversies.' Also see Linda Williams (1989), *Hard Core: Power, Pleasure and the Frenzy of the Visible,* Berkeley, CA: University of California Press, and Andrew Ross (1989), 'The Popularity of Pornography' in *No Respect: Intellectuals and Popular Culture* (1989), New York, London: Routledge, pp. 171–208 for a thorough summation of anti-pornography arguments.

4. This corresponds to Linda Williams's analysis of pornography as a 'machine of the visible' devoted to intensifying the visibility of all aspects of sexuality, but most particularly, to conducting detailed investigations of female bodies. Williams (1989), pp. 34–57.

5. *Newsweek* (February 16, 1976), p. 69.

6. And there are ongoing attempts to regulate this sort of imagery. In the current NEA controversies, a Republican representative plans to introduce amendments that would prohibit funding of art that depicts aborted fetuses, the *New York Times* reports (October 10, 1990, p. B6). This would seem to be something of a shortsighted strategy for anti-abortion forces, as the aborted fetus has been the favored incendiary image of anti-abortion forces, including anti-abortion artists. See Laura Kipnis (1986), 'Refunctioning Reconsidered: Toward a Left Popular Culture,' *High Culture/Low Theory,* ed. Colin MacCabe, New York: St Martins Press, pp. 29–31.

7. Of course, the counter-argument could be made that such a cartoon really indicates the murderous male desire to see a woman mutilated, and that the cartoon thus stands in for the actual male desire to do violence to women. This was, of course, a widespread interpretation of the infamous *Hustler* 'woman in the meat grinder' cover, about which more later. This sort of interpretation would hinge on essentializing the male imagination and male sexuality as, a priori, violent and murderous, and on a fairly literal view of humor and representation, one that envisions a straight leap from the image to the social practice rather than the series of mediations between the two I'm describing here.

8. Freud's observations on jokes, particularly on obscene humor, might be extended to the entirety of *Hustler* as so much of its discourse, even aside from its cartoons and humor, is couched in the joke form.

9. For an interesting deconstruction of the essentialist/anti-essentialism debate see Diana Fuss (1989), *Essentially Speaking: Feminism, Nature and Difference,* New York: Routledge, Chapman and Hall.

10. By violence here I mean specifically violence to subjectivity. On the issue of representations of actual physical violence to women's bodies that is represented as non-consensual – as opposed to the sort of tame consensual S/M occasionally found in *Hustler* – my view is that this sort of representation should be analyzed as a subgenre of mainstream violent imagery, not only in relation to pornography. I find the continual conflation of sexual pornography and violence a deliberate roadblock to thinking through issues of porn – only abetted by a theorist like Andrea Dworkin for whom *all* heterosexuality is violence. The vast majority of porn represents sex, not physical violence, and while sexuality generally undoubtedly contains elements of aggression and violence, it's important to make these distinctions.

11. The passage in the ellipsis reads 'For example, there are beliefs that each sex is a danger to the other through contact with sexual fluids.' Compare Douglas to this passage by Andrea Dworkin, '... in literary pornography, to ejaculate is to *pollute* the woman' [her emphasis]. Dworkin goes on to discuss, in a lengthy excursus on semen, the collaboration of women-hating women's magazines, which 'sometimes recommend spreading semen on the face to enhance the complexion' and pornography, where ejaculation often occurs on the woman's body or face [see Linda Williams, pp. 93–119, on another reading of the 'money shot'], to accept semen and eroticize it. Her point seems to be that men prefer that semen be a violation of the woman by the man, as the only way they can get sexual pleasure is through violation. Thus semen is 'driven into [the woman] to dirty her or make her more dirty or make her dirty by him.' But at the same time semen has to be eroticized to get the woman to comply in her own violation. Andrea Dworkin (1987), p. 187. In any case, that Dworkin sees contact with male 'sexual fluids' as harmful to women seems clear, as does the relation of this pollution (Dworkin's word) danger to Douglas's analysis.

12. Recently *Hustler,* after yet another legal entanglement, began threatening in its model release form to prosecute anyone who sent in a photo without the model's release. They now demand photocopies of two forms of ID for both age and identity purposes; they

also stopped paying the photographer and began paying only the model (currently $250 and the promise of consideration for higher paying photospreads).

13. Throughout this essay, my intent has not been to associate a particular class with particular or typical standards of the body, but rather to discuss how *Hustler* opposes hegemonic, historically bourgeois, conceptions of the body. Whether the *Hustler* bodily idiom represents a particular class or class fraction is not readily ascertainable without extensive audience studies of the sort difficult to carry out with a privatized form like porn magazines. The demographics that are available aren't current (because the magazine doesn't subsist on advertising, its demographics aren't made public, and *Hustler* is notoriously unwilling to release even circulation figures). The only readership demographics I've been able to find were published in *Mother Jones* magazine in 1976, and were made available to them because publisher Larry Flynt desired, for some reason, to add *Mother Jones* to his distribution roster. Jeffrey Klein (1978) writes: 'Originally it was thought that *Hustler* appealed to a blue collar audience yet ... demographics indicate that except for their gender (85 percent male), *Hustler* readers can't be so easily categorized. About 40 percent attended college; 23 percent are professionals; 59 percent have household incomes of $15,000 or more a year [about $29,000 in 1989 dollars], which is above the national mean, given the median reader age of 30.' His analysis of these figures is: 'Probably it's more accurate to say that *Hustler* appeals to what people would like to label a blue-collar urge, an urge most American men seem to share.'

14. For an analysis of the structuring contradictions in the discourse of Catharine MacKinnon, who along with Dworkin, is the leading theorist of the anti-pornography movement, see William Beatty Warner (1989), 'Treating Me Like an Object: Reading Catharine MacKinnon's Feminism.'

15. For a critique of this tendency see Mike Budd, Robert M. Entman, and Clay Steinman (1990), 'The Affirmative Character of U.S. Cultural Studies.'

# References

Bakhtin, Mikhail (1984) *Rabelais and His World.* Trans. Hélène Iswolsky. Bloomington, IN: Indiana University Press.

Budd, Mike, Entman, Robert and Steinman, Clay (1990) 'The affirmative character of U.S. cultural studies.' *Critical Studies in Mass Communication,* 7, pp. 169–184.

Davidoff, Leonore (1979) 'Class and gender in Victorian England.' *Feminist Studies,* 5.

Douglas, Mary (1966) *Purity and Danger: An Analysis of the Concepts of Pollution and Taboo.* London: Routledge.

Dworkin, Andrea (1987) *Intercourse.* New York: Macmillan.

Freud, Sigmund (1963) *Jokes and Their Relation to the Unconscious.* Trans. James Strachey. New York: W. W. Norton and Company, Inc.

Klein, Jeffrey (1978) 'Born against porn.' *Mother Jones,* Feb./Mar., p. 18.

Laplanche, J. and Pontalis, J.B. (1973) *The Language of Psychoanalysis.* New York: W. W. Norton and Company, Inc.

Rubin, Gayle (1984) 'Thinking Sex: Notes for a radical theory of the politics of sexuality', in Carole Vance (ed.) *Pleasure and Danger.* Boston: Routledge. pp. 267–319.

Stallybrass, Peter and White, Allon (1986) *The Politics of Transgression.* Ithaca, NY: Cornell University Press.

Warner, William (1989) 'Treating me like an object: Reading Catharine MacKinnon's Feminism.' In L. Kaufmann (ed.) *Feminism and Institutions: Dialogues on Feminist Theory.* Cambridge: Basil Blackwell.

# Chapter 21

# Paul Willis

## Symbolic Creativity

## Commodities and Consumerism

The main cultural materials and resources used in the symbolic work of leisure are cultural commodities. They are supplied to the market overwhelmingly by the commercial cultural industries and media for profit. Indeed it was the market discovery, exploitation and development in the 1950s and 60s of a newly defined affluent and expanding consumer group of young people which produced the popular conception of 'the teenager'.[1] We're currently experiencing a renewed and it seems even less caring emphasis on market forces in cultural matters. The rise of leisure we've referred to is really the rise of commercialized leisure. Does this matter? Does their production in a commercial nexus devalue cultural commodities and the contents of the cultural media?

There is a strange unanimity – and ghostly embrace of their opposites – between left and right when it comes to a condemnation of consumerism and especially of the penetration of the market into cultural matters. It is the profane in the Temple for the artistic establishment. For some left cultural analysts it constitutes a widened field of exploitation which is in and for itself unwelcome; now workers are exploited in their leisure as well as in their work. The circuit of domination is complete with no escape from market relations.

We disagree with both assessments, especially with their shared underlying pessimism. They both ignore the dynamic and living qualities of everyday culture and especially their necessary work and symbolic creativity. These things have always been in existence, though usually ignored or marginalized. They continue to be ignored

From: Paul Willis, *Common Culture: Symbolic Work at Play in the Everyday Cultures of the Young.* Milton Keynes: Open University Press, 1990.

even when an extraordinary development and transformation of them are in progress. For symbolic work and creativity mediate, and are simultaneously expanded and developed *by,* the uses, meanings and 'effects' of cultural commodities. Cultural commodities are catalyst, not product; a stage in, not the destination of, cultural affairs. Consumerism now has to be understood as an active, not a passive, process. Its play includes work.

If it ever existed at all, the old 'mass' has been culturally emancipated into popularly differentiated cultural citizens through exposure to a widened circle of commodity relations. These things have supplied a much widened range of usable symbolic resources for the development and emancipation of everyday culture. Certainly this emancipation has been partial and contradictory because the consumer industries have sought to provide some of the contents and certainly the forms as well as the possibilities for cultural activity. Consumerism continuously reproduces an image of, and therefore helps to encourage, selfishness and narcissism in individualized consumption and hedonism. But those tendencies are now given features of our cultural existence. It is the so far undervalued balance of development and emancipation which has to be grasped. As we shall see, the images and offers of consumerism are not always taken at face value, nor are 'individualized' forms of consciousness as socially isolated and self-regarding as the pessimists suppose. Meanwhile a whole continent of informal, everyday culture has been recognized, opened up and developed.

Capitalism and its images speak directly to desire for its own profit. But in that very process it breaks down or short-circuits limiting customs and taboos. It will do anything and supply any profane material in order to keep the cash tills ringing. But, in this, commerce discovered, *by exploiting,* the realm of necessary symbolic production within the undiscovered continent of the informal. No other agency has recognized this realm or supplied it with usable symbolic materials. And commercial entrepreneurship of the cultural field has discovered something real. For whatever self-serving reasons it was accomplished, we believe that this is an historical *recognition.* It counts and is irreversible. Commercial cultural forms have helped to produce an historical present from which we cannot now escape and in which there are many more materials – no matter what we think of them – available for necessary symbolic work than ever there were in the past.[2] Out of these come forms not dreamt of in the commercial imagination and certainly not in the official one – forms which make up common culture.

The hitherto hidden continent of the informal (including resources and practices drawn from traditional folk and working-class culture) produces, therefore, from cultural commodities much expounded, unprefigured and exciting effects – and this is why, of course, commerce keeps returning to the streets and common culture to find its next commodities. There is a fundamental and unstable contradictoriness in commercial rationality and instrumentality when it comes to consumer cultural goods. Blanket condemnations of market capitalism will never find room for it or understand it.

For our argument perhaps the basic complexity to be unravelled is this. Whereas it may be said that work relations and the drive for efficiency now hinge upon *the suppression* of informal symbolic work in most workers, the logic of the cultural and leisure industries hinges on the opposite tendency: a form of *their enablement and release.* Whereas the ideal model for the worker is the good time kept, the disciplined and empty head, the model for the good consumer is the converse – a head full of unbounded appetites for symbolic things.

Oddly and ironically, it is from capitalism's own order of priorities, roles, rules and instrumentalities *in production* (ironically, of leisure goods and services too) that informal cultures seek escape and alternatives in capitalist leisure *consumption*. Commerce appears twice in the cultural argument, as that which is to be escaped from and that which provides the means and materials for alternatives. Modern capitalism is now not only parasitic upon the puritan ethic, but also upon its instability and even its subversion.

There is a widespread view that these means and materials, the cultural media and cultural commodities, must appeal to the lowest common denominators of taste. Not only do they have no intrinsic value but, more disturbingly, they may have coded-in negative values which manipulate, cheapen, degrade and even brutalize the sensibilities of 'the masses'.

In contradiction we argue that there is no such thing as an autonomous artefact capable of printing its own intrinsic values, one way, on human sensibility. This is to put a ludicrous (actually crude Marxist) emphasis on *production* and what is held to be initially coded into artefacts.

What has been forgotten is that circumstances change cases, contexts change texts. The received view of aesthetics suggests that the aesthetic effect is internal to the text, and a universal property of its form. This places the creative impulse squarely on the material productions of the 'creative' artist, with the reception or consumption of art wholly determined by its aesthetic form, palely reflecting what is timelessly coded within the text. Against this we want to rehabilitate consumption, creative consumption, to see creative potentials in it for itself, rather than see it as the dying fall of the usual triplet: production, reproduction, reception. We are interested to explore how far 'meanings' and 'effects' can change quite decisively according to the social contexts of 'consumption', to different kinds of 'de-coding' and worked on by different forms of symbolic work and creativity. We want to explore how far *grounded* aesthetics are part, not of things, but of processes involving consumption, processes which make consumption pleasurable and vital. Viewers, listeners and readers do their own symbolic work on a text and create their own relationships to technical means of reproduction and transfer. There is a kind of cultural production all within consumption.

Young TV viewers, for instance, have become highly critical and literate in visual forms, plot conventions and cutting techniques. They listen, often highly selectively, to pop music now within a whole shared history of pop styles and genres. These knowledges clearly mediate the meanings of texts. The fact that many texts may be classified as intrinsically banal, contrived and formalistic must be put against the possibility that their living reception is the opposite of these things.

The 'productive' reception of and work on texts and artefacts can also be the start of a social process which results in its own more concrete productions, either of new forms or of recombined existing ones. Perhaps we should see the 'raw materials' of cultural life, of communications and expressions, as always intermediate. They are the products of one process as well as the raw materials for another, whose results can be, in turn, raw materials for successive groups. Why shouldn't bedroom decoration and personal styles, combinations of others' 'productions', be viewed along with creative writing or song and music composition as fields of aesthetic realization? Furthermore the grounded appropriation of new technology and new hardware may open new possibilities for expression, or recombinations of old ones, which the dominant culture misses because it does not share the same conditions and contradictory pressures of that which is to be explained or come to terms with.

Our basic point is that human consumption does not simply repeat the relations of production – and whatever cynical motives lie behind them. Interpretation, symbolic action and creativity are *part* of consumption. They're involved in the whole realm of necessary symbolic work. This work is at least as important as whatever might originally be encoded in commodities and can often produce their opposites. Indeed some aspects of 'profanity' in commercial artefacts may be liberating and progressive, introducing the possibility of the new and the socially dynamic.

It is pointless and limiting to judge artefacts *alone,* outside their social relations of consumption, with only the tutored critic's opinion of an internal aesthetic allowed to count. This is what limits the 'Official Arts' in their institutions. People bring living identities to commerce and the consumption of cultural commodities as well as being formed there. They bring experiences, feelings, social position and social memberships to their encounter with commerce. Hence they bring a necessary creative symbolic pressure, not only to make sense of cultural commodities, but partly through them also to make sense of contradiction and structure as they experience them in school, college, production, neighbourhood, and as members of certain genders, races, classes and ages. The results of this necessary symbolic work may be quite different from anything initially coded into cultural commodities.

## Grounded Aesthetics

As we have used the term so far, 'symbolic creativity' is an abstract concept designating a human capacity almost in general. It only exists, however, in contexts and, in particular, sensuous living processes. To identify the particular dynamic of symbolic activity and transformation in concrete named situations we propose the term 'grounded aesthetic'. This is the creative element in a process whereby meanings are attributed to symbols and practices and where symbols and practices are selected, reselected, highlighted and recomposed to resonate further appropriated and particularized meanings. Such dynamics are emotional as well as cognitive. There are as many aesthetics as there are grounds for them to operate in. Grounded aesthetics are the yeast of common culture.

We have deliberately used the term 'aesthetic' to show both the differences and the continuities of what we are trying to say with respect to the culture and arts debate. We are certainly concerned with what might be called principles of beauty, but as qualities of living symbolic activities rather than as qualities of things; as ordinary aspects of common culture, rather than as extraordinary aspects of uncommon culture. This is the sense of our clumsy but strictly accurate use of 'grounded'.

Our 'groundedness' for some will seem simply no more than the reckless destruction of flight, potting birds of paradise with sociological lead. For others the strange search for archaic aesthetics in grounded, everyday social relations will seem perverse, un-material and even mystical. We're happy to work on the assumption that 'the truth' lies somewhere, always provisionally, in between, that human be-ing-ness needs both air and earth and, in turn, makes possible our very idea of both.

Within the process of creating meanings from and within the use of symbols there may be a privileged role for texts and artefacts, but a grounded aesthetic can also be an element and a quality of everyday social relations. For instance, there is a dramaturgy and poetics of everyday life, of social presence, encounter and event. It may have become invisible in the routinized roles of adult life, but the young have much more time and they face each other with fewer or more fragile masks. They are the practical existentialists. They sometimes have no choice but to be, often too, absorbed in the moment and to ransack immediate experience for grounded aesthetics. For them some features of social life may not be about the regulation and containment of tension, but about its creation and increase. The 'aimless' life of groups and gangs may be about producing something from nothing, from 'doing nothing'. It may be about building tensions, shaping grounded aesthetics, orchestrating and shaping their release and further build-ups, so that a final 'catharsis' takes with it or changes other tensions and stresses inherent in the difficulties of their condition. Making a pattern in an induced swirl of events can produce strangely still centres of heightened awareness where time is held and unusual control and insight are possible. Grounded aesthetics are what lift and mark such moments.

Grounded aesthetics are the specifically creative and dynamic moments of a whole process of cultural life, of cultural birth and rebirth. To know the cultural world, our relationship to it, and ultimately to know ourselves, it is necessary not merely to be in it but to change – however minutely – that cultural world. This is a making specific – in relation to the social group or individual and its conditions of life – of the ways in which the received natural and social world is made human *to them* and made, to however small a degree (even if finally symbolic), controllable by them.

The possibility of such control is, of course, a collective principle for the possibility of political action on the largest scale. But it also has importance in the individual and collective awareness of the ability to control symbols and their cultural work. Grounded aesthetics produce an edge of meaning which not only reflects or repeats what exists, but transforms what exists – received expressions and appropriated symbols as well as what they represent or are made to represent in some identifiable way.

In so called 'primitive art' and culture, for instance, a central theme is the naming of fundamental forces as gods and demons, thereby to reveal them, make them somehow knowable and therefore subject to human persuasion or placation. Of course, the urban industrial world is much more complex in its organization than are 'primitive' societies, and our apparent technical control over the threatening forces of nature seems greater and different in kind from theirs. What we seek to control, persuade or humanize through grounded aesthetics may be, in part, the force and expression of other human beings rather than forces emanating directly from nature – if you like the work of culture on culture.

A sense of or desire for timelessness and universality may be part of the impulse of a grounded aesthetic. The natural, obvious and immutable become particular historical constructions capable of variation. Subjectivity, taken to some degree out of the particular, is the force which can change it. But we may equally focus on the particular extracted from its context to make sense of the universal (Blake's grain of sand). Such psychic separation may be part of and/or a condition for some grounded aesthetics.

This is not to say that 'universals' really exist, certainly not internally in 'art-objects'. It is extraordinary how many universals – and contradictory ones – are claimed. Nevertheless, experienced universalism, as a movement out of or reperception of the particular, may well be a universal feature of heightened human awareness. This universalism is also a kind of awareness of the future in terms of what it is possible to become. This is part of heightened aspiration and the quest for wider significance and expanded identity. Universalism also gives some vision of the kind of socialness and human mutuality which might locate better and more expanded identities. Grounded aesthetics provide a motivation towards realizing different futures, and for being in touch with the self as a dynamic and creative force for bringing them about.

The received sense of the 'aesthetic' emphasizes the cerebral, abstract or sublimated quality of beauty. At times it seems to verge on the 'an-aesthetic' – the suppression of all senses. By contrast we see grounded aesthetics as working through the senses, through sensual heightening, through joy, pleasure and desire, through 'fun' and the 'festive'.

Concrete skills, concretely acquired rather than given through natural distinction or gift, are involved in the exercise of grounded aesthetics. 'Economy', and 'skill', for instance, enter into the grounded aesthetics of how the body is used as a medium of expression. A bodily grounded aesthetic enters into personal style and presence, dance and large areas of music and performance.

Although they are not things, grounded aesthetics certainly have uses. Such uses concern the energizing, developing and focusing of vital human powers on to the world in concrete and practical ways, but also in lived connected cognitive ways. This is in producing meanings, explanations and pay-offs in relation to concrete conditions and situations which seem more efficient or adequate than other proffered official or conventional meanings. Such 'useful' meanings may well have moral dimensions in providing collective and personal principles of action, co-operation, solidarity, distinction or resistance.

But 'useful' meanings can also be very private. There are perhaps especially private, symbolic and expressive therapies for the injuries of life. They 'work', not through their direct musical, literary or philosophical forms, but through the ways in which a grounded aesthetic produces meanings and understandings which were not there before. This may involve internal, imaginative and spiritual life. It may be in the realm of dream and fantasy, in the realm of heightened awareness of the constructedness and constructiveness of the self: alienation from obvious givens and values; the sense of a future made in the present changing the present; the fear of and fascination for the 'terra incognita' of the self. The usefulness of grounded aesthetics here may be in the holding and repairing, through some meaning creation and human control even in desperate seas, of the precariousness and fragmentedness of identity whose source of disturbance is outside, structural and beyond the practical scope of individuals to influence.

The crucial failure and danger of most cultural analysis are that dynamic, living grounded aesthetics are transformed and transferred into ontological properties of things, objects and artefacts which may represent and sustain aesthetics but which are, in fact, separate. The aesthetic effect is not *in* the text or artefact. It is part of the sensuous/emotive/cognitive creativities of human receivers, especially as they produce a stronger sense of emotional and cognitive identity as expanded capacity and power – even if only in the possibility of *future* recognitions of a similar kind. These creativities are not dependent on texts, but might be enabled by them.[3]

Surprising meanings and creativities can be generated from unpromising materials through grounded aesthetics. But texts and artefacts can also fail to mediate symbolic meanings for many reasons. Many supply only a narrow or inappropriate (for particular audiences) range of symbolic resources. Others encourage *reification* (literally, making into a thing) rather than the *mediation* and enablement of the possibility of grounded aesthetics. They move too quickly to supply a putative aesthetic. The receivers are simply sent a 'message', the meaning of which is pre-formed and pre-given. Signs are pinned succinctly and securely to their meanings. Human receivers are allowed no creative life of their own. The attempt to encapsulate directly an aesthetic militates against the possibility of its realization through a grounded aesthetic because the space for symbolic work of reception has been written out.

There are many ways in which the 'official arts' are removed from the possibility of a living symbolic *mediation,* even despite their possible symbolic richness and range. Most of them are out of their time and, even though this should enforce no veto on current *mediation,* the possibilities of a relevant structuring of symbolic interest are obviously limited. The institutions and practices which support 'art', however, seem designed to break any living links or possibilities of inducing a grounded aesthetic appropriation. 'Official' art equates aesthetics with artefacts. In literature, for instance, all of our current social sense is read *into* the text as its 'close reading' – the legacy of deadness left by I.A. Richards and F.R. Leavis. Art objects are put into the quietness and stillness of separate institutions – which might preserve them, but not their relation to the exigencies of current necessary symbolic work. The past as museum, Art as objects! The reverence and distance encouraged by formality, by institutions, and by the rites of liberal-humanist education as 'learning the code', kill dead, for the vast majority, what the internal life of signs might offer through grounded aesthetics to current sensibility and social practice. It is as hard for the 'official arts' to offer themselves to grounded aesthetics, as it is for grounded aesthetics to find recognition in the formal canons.

Commercial cultural commodities, conversely, offer no such impediments. At least cultural commodities – for their own bad reasons – are aimed at exchange and therefore at the possibility of use. In responding to, and attempting to exploit, current desires and needs, they are virtually guaranteed to offer some relevance to the tasks of current socially necessary symbolic work. In crucial senses, too, the modern media precisely 'mediate' in passing back to audiences, at least in the first instance, symbolic wholes they've taken from the streets, dance-halls and everyday life. Along with this they may also take, however imperfectly and crudely, a field of aesthetic tensions from daily life and from the play of grounded aesthetics there.

Of course, part of the same restless process is that cultural commodities, especially style and fashion 'top end down', may become subject overwhelmingly to reification, symbolic rationalization and the drastic reduction of the symbolic resources on offer. But consumers move too. When cultural commodities no longer offer symbolic mediation to grounded aesthetics, they fall 'out of fashion'. And in the cumulative symbolic landscape of consumer capitalism, dead packaged, reified grounded aesthetics are turned back into primary raw material for other processes of inevitable necessary symbolic work, with only the cultural theorists paranoically labouring back along their 'meta-symbolic' routes to 'golden age' symbolic homologies. This commercial process may, to say the least, be flawed, but it offers much more to grounded aesthetics than do the dead 'offical arts'.

There may well be a better way, a better way to cultural emancipation than through this continuous instability and trust in the hidden – selfish, blind, grabbing – hand of the market. But 'official art' has not shown it yet. Commercial cultural commodities are all most people have. History may be progressing through its bad side. But it progresses. For all its manifest absurdities, the cultural market may open up the way *to* a better way. We have to make our conditions of life before we can dominate and use them. Cultural pessimism offers us only road-blocks. [...]

## Notes

1. See the first major study of youth culture in Britain, Mark Abrams, *The Teenage Consumer,* London Press Exchange, 1959.

2. We're bending the stick of argument here to emphasize how cultural products are creatively *used,* rather than passively *consumed.* We should not, of course, ignore the continuing ubiquity of forms of direct cultural production such as writing, photography and 'storying' (c.f. D. Morley and K. Worpole, *The Republic of Letters,* Comedia, 1981; S. Beszceret and P. Corrigan, *Towards a Different Image,* Comedia/Methuen, 1986; S. Yeo, *Whose Story?,* Blackwell, 1990). Equally, against élitism, we should recall activities like knitting and gardening as combining both production and use. Our general argument here should not obscure that varieties of such 'home produce' are important fields for symbolic work and creativity.

3. It is possible to get into a fine and tautological argument about the distinctions and relationships between 'invisible' internal subjective meanings and external 'visible' signs, symbols and practices. Though we insist that grounded aesthetics are a quality of living processes of meaning-making, not of things, this is not necessarily a wholly invisible internal process, though it can be. Words, signs, symbols and practices as 'things' in the world can certainly be part of the operation of particular grounded aesthetics for particular people. They are also taken in by and made sense of in the meaning-making of others. Also we recognize and, in what follows, give many examples of the possibility of grounded aesthetics becoming properly externalized: formalized, made concrete and public in some way. We argue for this as a process which decisively blurs and questions the conventional distinctions between consumption and production. What's crucial here, though, is not the 'thing-like' qualities of such externalizations, but their capacity both to reflect *and promote* the grounded aesthetics of their producers and of others, individuals and collectivities.

Our internal subjective meanings will never transcend or make redundant the 'givenness' of textuality, of things, of forms, of symbols. Indeed these latter are intrinsic to the possibility and creativity of human meanings, but they should always be seen transitively for their role in the mediation of human meaning. They're humble, malleable things, not the kings and queens of expression and experience. In particular, we should understand that processes of human meaning-making and creativity are stopped dead when aesthetics are attached to things instead of to human activities.

# Chapter 22

# Henry Jenkins III

## *Star Trek* Rerun, Reread, Rewritten: Fan Writing as Textual Poaching

> Suppose we were to ask the question: what became of the Sphinx after the encounter with Oedipus on his way to Thebes? Or, how did Medusa feel seeing herself in Perseus' mirror just before being slain?
>
> Teresa de Lauretis, *Alice Doesn't* (1982)

> How does Uhura feel about her lack of promotion, what does she try to do about it, how would she handle an emergency, or a case of sexual harassment? What were Chapel's experiences in medical school, what is her job at Starfleet headquarters, what is her relationship with Sarek and Amanda now ...?
>
> E. Osbourne, *Star Trek fan* (1987)

In late December 1986, *Newsweek* marked the twentieth anniversary of *Star Trek* with a cover story on the program's fans, 'the Trekkies, who love nothing more than to watch the same 79 episodes over and over.'[1] The *Newsweek* article, with its relentless focus on conspicuous consumption and 'infantile' behavior and its patronizing language and smug superiority to all fan activity, is a textbook example of the stereotyped representation of fandom found in both popular writing and academic criticism. [...] Illustrated with photographs of a sixty-six-year-old bookstore worker who goes by the name of 'Grandma Trek' and who loves to play

From: *Close Encounters: Film, Feminism, and Science Fiction.* Ed. Constance Penley, Elisabeth Lyon, Lynn Spigel, and Janet Bergstrom. Minneapolis, MN: University of Minnesota Press, 1991.

with toy spaceships, of a balding and paunchy man in a snug Federation uniform, and of an overweight, middle-aged woman with heavy eyeshadow and rubber 'Spock Ears,' the article offers a lurid account of the program's loyal followers. Fans are characterized as 'kooks' (p. 68) obsessed with trivia, celebrity, and collectibles; as social inepts, cultural misfits, and crazies; as 'a lot of overweight women, a lot of divorced and single women' (p. 68). Borrowing heavily from pop Freud, ersatz Adorno, and pulp paperback sociology, *Newsweek* explains the 'Trekkie' phenomenon in terms of repetition compulsion, infantile regression, commodity fetishism, nostalgic complacency, and future shock. [...] Perhaps most telling, *Newsweek* consistently treats *Trek* fans as a problem to be solved, a mystery to be understood, rather than as a kind of cultural activity that many find satisfying and pleasurable.

Academic writers depict 'Trekkers' in essentially the same terms. For Robin Wood, the fantasy film fan is 'reconstructed as a child, surrendering to the reactivation of a set of values and structures [the] adult self has long since repudiated.'[2] The fan is trapped within a repetition compulsion similar to that which an infant experiences through the fort/da game. A return to such 'banal' texts could not possibly be warranted by their intellectual content but can only be motivated by a return to 'the lost breast,' by the need for reassurance provided by the passive reexperience of familiar pleasures: 'The pleasure offered by the *Star Wars* films corresponds very closely to our basic conditioning; it is extremely reactionary, as all mindless and automatic pleasure tends to be. The finer pleasures are those we have to work for' (p. 164). Wood valorizes academically respectable texts and reading practices at the expense of popular works and their fans. 'It is possible to read a film like *Letter from an Unknown Woman or Late Spring* twenty times and still discover new meanings, new complexities, ambiguities, possibilities of interpretation. It seems unlikely, however, that this is what takes people back, again and again, to *Star Wars*' (p. 163). Academic rereading produces new insights; fan rereading rehashes old experiences.[3]

As these two articles illustrate, the fan constitutes a scandalous category in contemporary American culture, one that calls into question the logic by which others order their aesthetic experiences, one that provokes an excessive response from those committed to the interests of textual producers. Fans appear to be frighteningly 'out of control,' undisciplined and unrepentant, rogue readers. Rejecting 'aesthetic distance,' fans passionately embrace favored texts and attempt to integrate media representations within their own social experience. Like cultural scavengers, fans reclaim works that others regard as 'worthless' trash, finding them a source of popular capital. Like rebellious children, fans refuse to read by the rules imposed upon them by the schoolmasters. For the fan, reading becomes a kind of play, responsive only to its own loosely-structured rules and generating its own kinds of pleasure.

Michel de Certeau has characterized this type of reading as 'poaching,' an impertinent 'raid' on the literary 'preserve' that takes away only those things that seem useful or pleasurable to the reader: 'Far from being writers ... readers are travellers; they move across lands belonging to someone else, like nomads poaching their way across fields they did not write, despoiling the wealth of Egypt to enjoy it themselves.'[4] De Certeau perceives popular reading as a series of 'advances and retreats, tactics and games played with the text' (p. 175), as a kind of cultural bricolage through which readers fragment texts and reassemble the broken shards according to their own blueprint, salvaging bits and pieces of found material in making sense of their own social experience. Far from viewing consumption as imposing meanings upon the public, de Certeau suggests, consumption involves reclaiming textual material, 'making it one's own, appropriating or reappropriating it' (p. 166).

But such conduct cannot be sanctioned; it must be contained, through ridicule if necessary, since it challenges the very notion of literature as a kind of private property to be controlled by textual producers and their academic interpreters. Public attacks on media fans keep other viewers in line, making it uncomfortable for readers to adapt such 'inappropriate' strategies of making sense of popular texts. [...] These same stereotypes reassure academic writers of the validity of their own interpretations of the program content, readings made in conformity with established critical protocols, and free them of any need to come into direct contact with the program's 'crazed' followers.[5]

In this essay, I propose an alternative approach to fandom, one that perceives 'Trekkers' (as they prefer to be called) not as cultural dupes, social misfits, or mindless consumers, but rather as, in de Certeau's terms, 'poachers' of textual meanings. [...] Fandom is a vehicle for marginalized subcultural groups (women, the young, gays, and so on) to pry open space for their cultural concerns within dominant representations; fandom is a way of appropriating media texts and rereading them in a fashion that serves different interests, a way of transforming mass culture into popular culture.

[...] My primary concern will be with what happens when these fans produce their own texts, texts that inflect program content with their own social experience and displace commercially-produced commodities for a kind of popular economy. For these fans, *Star Trek* is not simply something that can be reread; it is something that can and must be rewritten to make it more responsive to their needs, to make it a better producer of personal meanings and pleasures. [...]

## Fan Readers/Fan Writers

The popularity of *Star Trek* has motivated a wide range of cultural productions, creative reworkings of program materials from children's backyard play to adult interaction games, from needlework to elaborate costumes, from private fantasies to computer programing and home video production. This ability to transform personal reaction into social interaction, spectatorial culture into participatory culture, is one of the central characteristics of fandom. One becomes a 'fan' not by being a regular viewer of a particular program but by translating that viewing into some kind of cultural activity, by sharing feelings and thoughts about the program content with friends, by joining a 'community' of other fans who share common interests. For fans, consumption naturally sparks production, reading generates writing, until the terms seem logically inseparable. In fan writer Jean Lorrah's words.

> Trekfandom ... is friends and letters and crafts and fanzines and trivia and costumes and artwork and filksongs and buttons and film clips and conventions–something for everybody who has in common the inspiration of a television show which grew far beyond its TV and film incarnations to become a living part of world culture.[6]

Lorrah's description of fandom blurs all boundaries between producers and consumers, spectators and participants, the commercial and the home crafted, to construct an image of fandom as a cultural and social network that spans the globe.

Many fans characterize their entry into fandom in terms of a movement from the social and cultural isolation doubly imposed upon them as women within a patriarchal society and as seekers after alternative pleasures within dominant media representations, toward more and more active participation in a 'community' receptive to their cultural productions, a 'community' within which they may feel a sense of 'belonging'.

> I met one girl who liked some of the TV shows I liked ... but I was otherwise a bookworm, no friends, working in the school library. Then my friend and I met some other girls a grade ahead of us but ga-ga over *ST*. From the beginning, we met each Friday night at one of the two homes that had a color TV to watch *Star Trek* together ... Silence was mandatory except during commercials, and, afterwards, we 'discussed' each episode. We re-wrote each story and corrected the wrongs done to 'Our Guys' by the writers. We memorized bits of dialog. We even started to write our own adventures.[7]

Some fans are drawn gradually from intimate interactions with others who live near them toward participation in a broader network of fans who attend regional, national, and even international science fiction conventions. One fan writes of her first convention: 'I have been to so many conventions since those days, but this one was the ultimate experience. I walked into that Lunacon and felt like I had come home without ever realizing I had been lost.'[8] Another remarks simply 'I met folks who were just as nuts as I was, I had a wonderful time.'[9]

For some women, trapped in low-paying jobs or within the socially-isolated sphere of the housewife, participation within an (inter)national network of fans grants a degree of dignity and respect otherwise lacking. For others, fandom offers a training ground for the development of professional skills and an outlet for creative impulses constrained by their workday lives. Fan slang draws a sharp contrast between the 'mundane' – the realm of everyday experience and/or those who dwell exclusively within that space – and fandom – an alternative sphere of cultural experience that restores the excitement and freedom that must be repressed to function in ordinary life. One fan writes, 'Not only does 'mundane' mean 'everyday life,' it is also a term used to describe narrow-minded, pettiness, judgmental, conformity, and a shallow and silly nature. It is used by people who feel very alienated from society.'[10] To enter fandom is to 'escape' from the 'mundane' into the marvelous.

The need to maintain contact with these new friends, often scattered across a broad geographic area, can require speculations and fantasies about the program content to take written form, first as personal letters, later as more public newsletters, 'letterzines,' or fan fiction magazines. Fan viewers become fan writers. [...]

## Gendered Readers/Gendered Writers

Media fan writing is an almost exclusively feminine response to mass media texts.[11] Men actively participate in a wide range of fan-related activities, notably interactive games and conference-planning committees, roles consistent with patriarchal norms that typically relegate combat – even combat fantasies – and organizational authority to the 'masculine' sphere. Media fan writers and fanzine readers, however, are almost always female. Camille Bacon-Smith has estimated that more than 90 percent of all media fan writers are female.[12] The greatest percentage of male participation is found in the 'letterzines,' like *Comlink* and *Treklink*, and in 'nonfiction' magazines, like *Trek,* that publish speculative essays on aspects of the program's 'universe'; men may feel comfortable joining discussions of future technologies or military lifestyle, but not in pondering Vulcan sexuality, McCoy's childhood, or Kirk's love life.

Why this predominance of women within the media fan-writing community? Research suggests that men and women have been socialized to read for different purposes and in different ways. David Bleich asked a mixed group of college students to comment, in free-association fashion, on a body of canonized literary works. His analysis of their responses suggested that men focused primarily on narrative organization and authorial intent, while women devoted more energy to reconstructing the textual world and understanding the characters. He writes, 'Women enter the world of the novel, take it as something "there" for that purpose; men see the novel as a result of someone's action and construe its meaning or logic in those terms.'[13] [...] Bleich also found that women were more willing to enjoy free play with the story content, making inferences about character relationships that took them well beyond the information explicitly contained within the text. Such data strongly suggest that the practice of fan writing, the compulsion to expand speculations about characters and story events beyond textual boundaries, draws more heavily upon the types of interpretive strategies common to the 'feminine' than to the 'masculine.'

Bleich's observations provide only a partial explanation as they do not fully account for why many women find it necessary to go beyond the narrative information while most men do not. As Teresa de Lauretis has noted, female characters often exist only in the margins of male-centered narratives:

> Medusa and the Sphinx, like the other ancient monsters, have survived inscribed in hero narratives, in someone else's story, not their own; so they are figures or markers of positions – places and topoi – through which the hero and his story move to their destination and through which they accomplish meaning.[14]

Texts written by and for men yield easy pleasures to their male readers yet may resist feminine pleasure. To fully enjoy the text, women are often forced to perform a kind of intellectual transvestitism – identifying with male characters in opposition to their own cultural experiences, or constructing unwritten countertexts through their daydreams or through their oral interaction with other women – that allows them to explore their own narrative concerns. This need to reclaim feminine interests from the margins of 'masculine' texts produces endless speculation, speculation that draws the reader well beyond textual boundaries into the domain of the intertextual. Mary Ellen Brown and Linda Barwick have shown how women's gossip about soap opera inserts program content into an existing feminine oral culture.[15] Fan writing represents the logical next step in this cultural process: the transformation of oral countertexts into a more tangible form, the translation of verbal speculations into written works that can be shared with a broader circle of women. To do so, their status must change; no longer simply spectators, these women become textual producers. [...]

## Why *Star Trek?*

While most texts within a male-dominated culture potentially spark some sort of feminine countertext, only certain programs have generated the kind of extended written responses characteristic of media fandom. Why, then, has the bulk of fan writing centered on science fiction, which Judith Spector has characterized as a 'genre which ... [has been until recently] hostile toward women,' a genre 'by, for and about men of action'?[16] Or around others like it (the cop show, the detective drama, or the western) that have represented the traditional domain of male readers? Why do these women struggle to reclaim such seemingly unfertile soil when there are so many other texts that more traditionally reflect 'feminine' interests, and which feminist media critics are now trying to reclaim for their cause? In short, why *Star Trek?*

Obviously, no single factor can adequately account for all fanzines, a literary form that necessarily involves the translation of homogeneous media texts into a plurality of personal and subcultural responses. One partial explanation, however, might be that traditionally 'feminine' texts – the soap opera, the popular romance, the 'woman's picture' – do not need as much reworking as science fiction and westerns do in order to accommodate the social experience of women. The resistance of such texts to feminist reconstruction may require a greater expenditure of creative effort and therefore may push women toward a more thorough reworking of program materials than so-called feminine texts that can be more easily assimilated or negated.

Another explanation would be that these 'feminine' texts satisfy, at least partially, the desires of traditional women yet fail to meet the needs of more professionally-oriented women. Indeed, a particular fascination of *Star Trek* for these women appears to be rooted in the way that the program seems to hold out a suggestion of nontraditional feminine pleasures, of greater and more active involvement for women within the adventure of professional space travel, while finally reneging on those promises. Sexual equality was an essential component of producer Gene Roddenberry's optimistic vision of the future. A woman, Number One (Majel Barrett), was originally slated to be the Enterprise's second-in-command. Network executives, however, consistently fought efforts to break with traditional 'feminine' stereotypes, fearing the alienation of more conservative audience members.[17] 'Number One' was scratched after the program pilot, but throughout the run of the series, women were often cast in nontraditional jobs, everything from Romulan commanders to weapons specialists. The networks, however reluctantly, were offering women a future, a 'final frontier,' that included them.

Fan writers, though, frequently express dissatisfaction with these women's characterizations within the episodes. In the words of fan writer Pamela Rose (1977), 'When a woman is a guest star on *Star Trek,* nine out of ten times there is something wrong with her.'[18] Rose notes that these female characters have been granted positions of power within the program only to demonstrate through their erratic emotion-driven conduct that women are unfit to fill such roles. Another fan writer, Toni Lay, expressed her mixed feelings about *Star Trek's* social vision:

> It was ahead of its time in some ways, like showing that a Caucasian, all-American, all-male crew was not the only possibility for space travel. Still, the show was sadly deficient in other ways, in particular, its treatment of women. Most of the time, women were referred to as 'girls.' And women were never shown in a position of authority unless they were aliens, i.e., Deela, T'Pau, Natira, Sylvia, etc. It was like the show was saying 'Equal opportunity is OK for their women but not for our girls.'[19]

Lay states that she felt 'devastated' over the repeated failure of the series and the later feature films to give Lieutenant Uhura command duties commensurate with her rank: 'When the going gets tough, the tough leave the womenfolk behind' (p. 15). She contends that Uhura and the other women characters should have been given a chance to demonstrate what they could do confronted by the same kinds of problems that their male counterparts so heroically overcome. The constant availability of the original episodes through re-runs and shifts in the status of women within American society throughout the past two decades have only made these unfulfilled promises more difficult to accept, requiring progressively greater efforts to restructure the program in order to allow it to produce pleasures appropriate to the current reception context.

Indeed, many fan writers characterize themselves as 'repairing the damage' caused by the program's inconsistent and often demeaning treatment of its female characters. Jane Land, for instance, characterizes her fan novel, *Kista,* as 'an attempt to rescue one of *Star Trek's* female characters [Christine Chapel] from an artificially imposed case of foolishness.'[20] Promising to show 'the way the future never was,' *The Woman's List*, a recently established fanzine with an explicitly feminist orientation, has called for 'material dealing with all range of possibilities for women, including: women of color, lesbians, women of alien cultures and women of all ages and backgrounds.' [...]

Telling such stories requires the stripping away of stereotypically feminine traits. The series characters must be reconceptualized in ways that suggest hidden motivations and interests heretofore unsuspected. They must be reshaped into full-blooded feminist role models. While in the series Chapel is defined almost exclusively in terms of her unrequited passion for Spock and her professional subservience to Dr. McCoy, Jane Land represents her as a fiercely independent woman, capable of accepting love only on her own terms, prepared to pursue her own ambitions wherever they take her, outspoken in response to the patronizing attitudes of the command crew. [...]

Fan writers like Jane Land and Karen Bates (whose novels explore the progression of a Chapel-Spock marriage through many of the problems encountered by contemporary couples trying to juggle the conflicting demands of career and family)[21] speak directly to the concerns of professional women in a way which more traditionally 'feminine' works fail to do.[22] These writers create situations in which Chapel [...] must heroically overcome the same kinds of obstacles that challenge [her] male counterparts within the primary texts and often discuss directly the types of personal and professional problems particular to working women. Land's fan novel, *Demeter,* is exemplary in its treatment of the professional life of its central character, Nurse Chapel.[23] Land deftly melds action sequences with debates about gender relations and professional discrimination, images of command decisions with intimate glimpses of a Spock-Chapel marriage. An all-woman crew, headed by Uhura and Chapel, is dispatched on a mission to a feminist separatist space colony under siege from a pack of intergalactic drug smugglers who regard rape as a 'manly' sport. In helping the colonists to overpower their would-be assailants, the women are at last given a chance to demonstrate their professional competence under fire, forcing Captain Kirk to reevaluate some of his command policies. *Demeter* raises significant questions about the possibilities of male-female interaction outside of patriarchal dominance. The meeting of a variety of different planetary cultures that represent alternative social philosophies and organizations, alternative ways of coping with the same essential debates surrounding sexual difference, allows for a far-reaching exploration of contemporary gender relations. [...]

## 'The Right Way': The 'Moral Economy' of Fan Fiction

Their underground status allows fan writers the creative freedom to promote a range of different interpretations of the basic program material and a variety of reconstructions of marginalized characters and interests, to explore a diversity of different solutions to the dilemma of contemporary gender relations. Fandom's IDIC philosophy ('Infinite Diversity in Infinite Combinations,' a cornerstone of Vulcan thought) actively encourages its participants to explore and find pleasure within their different and often contradictory responses to the program text. It should not be forgotten, however, that fan writing involves a translation of personal response into a social expression and that fans, like any other interpretive community, generate their own norms, which work to ensure a reasonable degree of conformity among readings of the primary text. The economic risk of fanzine publishing and the desire for personal popularity ensure some responsiveness to audience demand, discouraging totally idiosyncratic versions of the program content. Fans try to write stories to please other fans; lines of development that do not find popular support usually cannot achieve financial viability.

Moreover, the strange mixture of fascination and frustration characteristic of fannish response means that fans continue to respect the creators of the original series, even as they wish to rework some program materials to better satisfy their personal interests. Their desire to revise the program material is often counterbalanced by their desire to remain faithful to those aspects of the show that first captured their interests. E.P. Thompson has employed the term 'moral economy' to describe the way that eighteenth-century peasant leaders and street rioters legitimized their revolts through an appeal to 'traditional rights and customs' and 'the wider consensus of the community,' asserting that their actions worked to protect existing property rights against those who sought to abuse them for their own gain.[24] The peasants' conception of a 'moral economy' allowed them to claim for themselves the right to judge the legitimacy both of their own actions and those of the landowners and property holders: 'Consensus was so strong that it overrode motives of fear or deference' (pp. 78–79).

An analogous situation exists in fandom: the fans respect the original texts yet fear that their conceptions of the characters and concepts may be jeopardized by those who wish to exploit them for easy profits, a category that typically includes Paramount and the network but excludes Roddenberry and many of the show's writers. The ideology of fandom involves both a commitment to some degree of conformity to the original program materials, as well as a perceived right to evaluate the legitimacy of any use of those materials, either by textual producers or by textual consumers. The fans perceive themselves as rescuing the show from its producers, who have manhandled its characters and then allowed it to die. In one fan's words, 'I think we have made *ST* uniquely our own, so we do have all the right in the world (universe) to try to change it for the better when the gang at Paramount start worshipping the almighty dollar, as they are wont to do.'[25] Rather than rewriting the series content, the fans claim to be keeping *Star Trek* 'alive' in the face of network indifference and studio incompetence, of remaining 'true' to the text that first captured their interest some twenty years before: 'This relationship came into being because the fan writers loved the characters and cared about the ideas that are *Star Trek* and they refused to let it fade away into oblivion.'[26] Such a relationship obliges fans to preserve a certain degree of 'fidelity' to program materials, even as they seek to rework them toward their own ends. *Trek* magazine contributor Kendra Hunter writes, '*Trek* is a format for expressing rights, opinions, and ideals. Most every imaginable idea can be expressed through *Trek* … . But there is a right way.'[27] Gross 'infidelity' to the series' concepts constitutes what fans call 'character rape' and falls outside of the community's norms. In Hunter's words:

> A writer, either professional or amateur, must realize that she … is not omnipotent. She cannot force her characters to do as she pleases. … The writer must have respect for her characters or those created by others that she is using, and have a full working knowledge of each before committing her words to paper. (p. 75)

Hunter's conception of 'character rape,' one widely shared within the fan community, rejects abuses by the original series writers as well as by the most novice fan and implies that the fans themselves, not program producers, are best qualified to arbitrate conflicting claims about character psychology because they care about the characters in a way that more commercially motivated parties frequently do not. In practice, the concept of 'character rape' frees fans to reject large chunks of the aired material, including entire episodes, and even to radically restructure the concerns of the show in the name of defending the purity of the original series concept. What determines the range of permissible fan narratives is finally not fidelity to the original texts but consensus within the fan community itself. The text they so lovingly preserve is the *Star Trek* they created through their own speculations, not the one that Gene Roddenberry produced for network airplay.

Consequently, the fan community continually debates what constitutes a legitimate reworking of program materials and what represents a violation of the special reader-text relationship that the fans hope to foster. The earliest *Trek* fan writers were careful to work within the framework of the information explicitly included within the broadcast episodes and to minimize their breaks with series conventions. In fan writer Jean Lorrah's words, 'Anyone creating a *Star Trek* universe is bound by what was seen in the aired episodes; however, he is free to extrapolate from those episodes to explain what was seen in them.'[28] Leslie Thompson explains, 'If the reasoning [of fan speculations] doesn't fit into the framework of the events as given [on the program], then it cannot apply no matter how logical or detailed it may be.'[29] As *Star Trek* fan writing has come to assume an institutional status in its own right and therefore to require less legitimization through appeals to textual 'fidelity,' a new conception of fan fiction has emerged, one that perceives the stories not as a necessary expansion of the original series text but rather as chronicles of 'alternate universes,' similar to the program world in some ways and different in others:

> The 'alternate universe' is a handy concept wherein you take the basic *Star Trek* concept and spin it off into all kinds of ideas that could never be aired. One reason Paramount may be so liberal about fanzines is that by their very nature most fanzine stories could never be sold professionally. (L. Slusher, personal communication, August 1987)

Such an approach frees the writers to engage in much broader play with the program concepts and characterizations, to produce stories that reflect more diverse visions of human interrelationships and future worlds, to overwrite elements within the primary texts that hinder fan interests. But even 'alternate universe' stories struggle to maintain some consistency with the original broadcast material and to establish some point of contact with existing fan interests, just as more 'faithful' fan writers feel compelled to rewrite and revise the program material in order to keep it alive in a new cultural context.

## Borrowed Terms: Kirk/Spock Stories

The debate in fan circles surrounding Kirk/Spock (K/S) fiction, stories that posit a homoerotic relationship between the show's two primary characters and frequently offer detailed accounts of their sexual couplings, illustrates these differing conceptions of the relationship between fan fiction and the primary series text.[30] Over the past decade, K/S stories have emerged from the margins of fandom toward numerical dominance over *Star Trek* fan fiction, a movement that has been met with considerable opposition from more traditional fans. For many, such stories constitute the worst form of character rape, a total violation of the established characterizations. Kendra Hunter argues that 'it is out of character for both men, and as such, comes across in the stories as bad writing … . A relationship as complex and deep as Kirk/Spock does not climax with a sexual relationship' (p. 81). Other fans agree but for other reasons. 'I do not accept the K/S homosexual precept as plausible,' writes one fan. 'The notion that two men that are as close as Kirk and Spock are cannot be 'just friends' is indefensible to me.'[31] Others struggle to reconcile the information provided on the show with their own assumptions about the nature of human sexuality: 'It is just as possible for their friendship to progress into a love affair, for that is what it is, than to remain status quo … . Most of us see Kirk and Spock simply as two people who love each other and just happen to be of the same gender.'[32]

Some K/S fans frankly acknowledge the gap between the series characterizations and their own representations but refuse to allow their fantasy life to be governed by the limitations of what was actually aired. One fan writes, 'While I read K/S and enjoy it, when you stop to review the two main characters of *Star Trek* as extrapolated from the TV series, a sexual relationship between them is absurd.'[33] Another argues somewhat differently:

> We actually saw a very small portion of the lives of the Enterprise crew through 79 episodes and some six hours of movies. ... How can we possibly define the entire personalities of Kirk, Spock, etc., if we only go by what we've seen on screen? Surely there is more to them than that! ... Since I doubt any two of us would agree on a definition of what is 'in character,' I leave it to the skill of the writer to make the reader believe in the story she is trying to tell. There isn't any limit to what could be depicted as accurate behavior for our heroes.[34]

Many fans find this bold rejection of program limitations on creative activity, this open appropriation of characters, to be unacceptable since it violates the moral economy of fan writing and threatens fan fiction's privileged relationship to the primary text:

> [If] 'there isn't any limit to what could be depicted as accurate behavior of our heroes,' we might well have been treated to the sight of Spock shooting up heroin or Kirk raping a yeoman on the bridge (or vice-versa). ... The writer whose characters don't have clearly defined personalities, thus limits and idiosyncrasies and definite characteristics, is the writer who is either very inexperienced or who doesn't have any respect for his characters, not to mention his audience.[35]

But as I have shown, all fan writing necessarily involves an appropriation of series characters and a reworking of program concepts as the text is forced to respond to the fan's own social agenda and interpretive strategies. What K/S does openly, all fans do covertly. In constructing the feminine countertext that lurks in the margins of the primary text, these readers necessarily redefine the text in the process of rereading and rewriting it. As one fan acknowledges, 'If K/S has 'created new characters and called them by old names,' then all fandom is guilty of the same.'[36] Jane Land agrees: 'All writers alter and transform the basic *Trek* universe to some extent, choosing some things to emphasize and others to play down, filtering the characters and concepts through their own perceptions.'[37] If these fans have rewritten *Star Trek* in their own terms, however, many of them are reluctant to break all ties to the primary text that sparked their creative activity and, hence, feel the necessity to legitimate their activity through appeals to textual fidelity. The fans are uncertain how far they can push against the limitations of the original material without violating and finally destroying a relationship that has given them great pleasure. Some feel stifled by those constraints; others find comfort within them. Some claim the program as their personal property, 'treating the series episodes like silly putty,' as one fan put it.[38] Others seek compromises with the textual producers, treating the original program as something shared between them.

What should be remembered is that whether they cast themselves as rebels or loyalists, it is the fans themselves who are determining what aspects of the original series concept are binding on their play with the program material and to what degree. The fans have embraced *Star Trek* because they found its vision somehow compatible with their own, and they have assimilated only those textual materials that feel comfortable to them. Whenever a choice must be made between fidelity to their program and fidelity to their own social norms, it is almost inevitably made in favor of lived experience. The women's conception of the *Star Trek* realm as inhabited by psychologically rounded and realistic characters ensures that no characterization that violated their own social perceptions could be satisfactory. The reason some fans reject K/S fiction has, in the end, less to do with the stated reason that it violates established characterization than with unstated beliefs about the nature of human sexuality that determine what kinds of character conduct can be viewed as plausible. When push comes to shove, as Hodge and Tripp suggest, 'Non-televisual meanings can swamp televisual meanings' and usually do.[39] [...]

## Notes

1. Charles Leerhsen, '*Star Trek's* Nine Lives.' *Newsweek* (Dec. 22, 1986), p. 66.
2. For representative examples of other scholarly treatments of *Star Trek* and its fans, see Karin Blair, 'Sex and *Star Trek,' Science Fiction Studies* 10 (1983), pp. 292–297; Harvey Greenberg, 'In Search of Spock: A Psychoanalytic Inquiry,' *Journal of Popular Film and Television* 12 (1984), pp. 53–65; Robert Jewett and John S. Lawrence, *The American Monomyth* (Garden City, NY: Anchor Press, 1977); and William B. Tyre, '*Star Trek* as Myth and Television as Myth Maker,' *Journal of Popular Culture* 10 (1977), pp. 711–719. Attitudes range from the generally sympathetic Blair to the openly hostile Jewett and Lawrence.
3. Robin Wood, *Hollywood: From Vietnam to Reagan* (New York: Columbia University Press, 1986), p. 164.
4. Michel de Certeau, *The Practice of Everyday Life* (Berkeley, CA: University of California Press, 1984), p. 174.
5. No scholarly treatment of *Star Trek* fan culture can avoid these pitfalls, if only because making such a work accessible to an academic audience requires a translation of fan discourse into other terms, terms that may never be fully adequate to the original. I come to both *Star Trek* and fan fiction as a fan first and a scholar second. My participation as a fan long precedes my academic interest in it. I have sought, where possible, to employ fan terms and to quote fans directly in discussing their goals and orientation toward the program and their own writing. I have shared drafts of this essay with fans and have incorporated their comments into the revision process. I have allowed them the dignity of being quoted from their carefully crafted, well-considered published work rather than from a spontaneous interview that would be more controlled by the researcher than by the informant. I leave it to my readers to determine whether this approach allows for a less mediated reflection of fan culture than previous academic treatments of this subject.
6. Jean Lorrah, Foreword to *The Vulcan Academy Murders* (New York: Pocket, 1984).
7. P.L. Caruthers Montgomery, letter to *Comlink* 28 (1987), p. 8.
8. Linda Deneroff, 'A Reflection on the Early Days of *Star Trek* Fandom,' *Comlink* 28 (1987), p. 3.
9. Toni Lay, letter to *Comlink* 28 (1986), p. 15.
10. Elizabeth Ocbourne, letter to *Treklink* 9 (1987), pp. 3–4.
11. Media fan writing builds upon a much older tradition of 'zine' publication within literary science fiction culture, dating back to the mid-1930s. For discussions of this earlier

tradition, see Lester Del Rey, *The World of Science Fiction* (New York: Ballantine, 1979); Harry Warner, *All Our Yesterdays* (New York: Advent, 1969); and Sam Moskowitz, *The Immortal Storm* (New York: ASFO Press, 1954). These earlier fanzines differ from media fanzines in a number of significant ways: they were dominated by male fans; they published primarily essays or original fiction that borrowed generic elements of science fiction but not specific characters and situations; they were focused upon literary rather than media science fiction; they were far fewer in number and enjoyed smaller circulation than media zines. Media fans borrow traditional formats from these earlier zines, but give them a new focus and a new function; they were met with considerable hostility by the older literary science fiction community, though a number of media fans participate in traditional zine publishing as well as media-oriented ventures. Roberta Pearson has suggested to me that an interesting parallel to media fanzine publication may be the fan writings surrounding Sherlock Holmes, which date back to the beginning of this century. I do not at this time know enough about these publications to assess their possible relationship to *Trek* fan publishing.

12. Camille Bacon-Smith, 'Spock Among the Women,' *The New York Times Book Review* (Nov. 16, 1986), pp. 1, 26, 28.

13. David Bleich, 'Gender Interests in Reading and Language,' *Gender and Reading: Essays on Readers, Texts and Contexts,* eds. Elizabeth A. Flynn and P.P. Schweickart (Baltimore: Johns Hopkins University Press, 1986), p. 239.

14. Teresa de Lauretis, *Alice Doesn't: Feminism, Semiotics, Cinema* (Bloomington: Indiana University Press, 1982), p. 109.

15. Mary Ellen Brown and Linda Barwick, 'Fables and Endless Generations: Soap Opera and Women's Culture.' Paper presented at a meeting of the Society for Cinema Studies, Montreal (May 1987).

16. Judith Spector, 'Science Fiction and the Sex War: A Womb of One's Own,' *Gender Studies: New Directions in Feminist Criticism,* ed. Judith Spector (Bowling Green, OH: Bowling Green State University Press, 1986), p. 163.

17. S.E. Whitfield and Gene Roddenberry, *The Making of Star Trek* (New York: Ballantine Books, 1968).

18. Pamela Rose, 'Women in the Federation.' In *The Best of Trek 2,* eds. W. Irwin and G.B. Love (New York: New American Library, 1977).

19. Lay, letter to *Comlink*, p. 15.

20. Jane Land, *Kista* (Larchmont, NY: Author), p. 1.

21. Karen Bates, *Starweaver Two* (Missouri Valley, IA: Ankar Press, 1982); *Nuages One* and *Nuages Two* (Tucson, AZ: Checkmate Press, 1982 and 1984).

22. Although a wide range of fanzines were considered in researching this essay, I have decided, for the purposes of clarity, to draw my examples largely from the work of a limited number of fan writers. While no selection could accurately reflect the full range of fan writing, I felt that Bates, Land [and] Lorrah [...] had all achieved some success within the fan community, suggesting that they exemplified, at least to some fans, the types of writing that were desirable and reflected basic tendencies within the form. Further, these writers have produced a large enough body of work to allow some commentary about their overall project rather than localized discussions of individual stories. I have also, wherever possible, focused my discussion around works still currently in circulation and therefore available to other researchers interested in exploring this topic. No slight is intended to the large number of other fan writers who also met these criteria and who, in some cases, are even better known within the fan community.

23. Jane Land, *Demeter* (Larchmont, NY: Author, 1987).

24. Thompson, E.P. (1971) 'The moral economy of the English crowd in the 18th century', *Past and Present*, 50 (February): 76–136.

25. Shari Schnuelle, letter to *Sociotrek* 4 (1987), p. 9.

26. Kendra, Hunter (1977) 'Characterization of rape', in *The Best of Trek 2*. eds Walter Irwin and G.B. Love. New York: New American Library.

27. Hunter, p. 83.

28. Lorrah, introduction to *The Vulcan Academy Murders.*

29. Leslie Thompson, '*Star Trek* Mysteries – Solved!,' *The Best of Trek,* eds. Walter Irwin and G.B. Love (New York: New American Library, 1974), p. 208.

30. The area of Kirk/Spock fiction falls beyond the project of this particular paper, raising issues similar yet more complex than those posed here. My reason for discussing it here is because of the light its controversial reception sheds on the norms of fan fiction and the various ways fan readers and writers situate themselves toward the primary text. For a more detailed discussion of this particular type of fan writing, see Patricia Frazer Lamb and Diana Veith, ' Romantic Myth, Transcendence, and *Star Trek* Zines,' Donald Palumbo (ed.), *Erotic Universe: Sexuality and Fantastic Literature* (New York: Greenwood Press, 1986), pp. 235–256, who argue that K/S stories, far from representing a cultural expression of the gay community, constitute another way of feminizing the original series text and of addressing feminist concerns within the domain of a popular culture that offers little space for heroic action by women.

31. Randal Landers, letter to *Treklink* 7 (1986), p. 10.

32. T'hera Snaider, letter to *Treklink* 8 (1987), p. 10.

33. M. Chandler, letter to *Treklink* 8 (1987), p. 10.

34. Regina Moore, letter to *Treklink* 4 (1986), p. 7.

35. Slusher, personal communication, p. 11.

36. Moore, p. 7.

37. Land, *Demeter*, p. ii.

38. Blaes, Tim, Letter to *Treklink* 9 (1987), p. 6.

39. Robert Hodge and David Tripp, *Children and Television: A Semiotic Approach* (Cambridge, England: Polity Press, 1986), p. 144.

# Chapter 23

# Joan Hawkins

## Sleaze Mania, Euro-Trash and High Art: the Place of European Art Films in American Low Culture

Open the pages of any U.S. horror fanzine – *Outré, Fangoria. Cinefantastique* – and you will find listings for mail order video companies which cater to aficionados of what Jeffrey Sconce has called 'paracinema' and trash aesthetics.[1] Not only do these mail order companies represent one of the fastest-growing segments of the video market,[2] their catalogues challenge many of our continuing assumptions about the binary opposition of prestige cinema (European art and avant-garde/experimental films) and popular culture.[3] Certainly, they highlight an aspect of art cinema which is generally overlooked or repressed in cultural analysis, namely, the degree to which high culture trades on the same images, tropes, and themes which character-ize low culture.

In the world of horror and cult film fanzines and mail order catalogues, what Carol J. Clover calls 'the high end' of the horror genre[4] mingles indiscriminately with the 'low end'. Here, Murnau's *Nosferatu* (1921) and Dreyer's *Vampyr* (1931) appear alongside such drive-in favorites as *Tower of Screaming Virgins* (1971) and *Jail Bait* (1955). Even more interesting, European art films which have little to do with horror – Antonioni's *L'avventura* (1960), for example – are listed alongside movies which Video Vamp labels 'Eurociné-trash.' European art films are not

From: Joan Hawkins, 'Sleaze Mania, Euro-Trash and High Art: The Place of European Art Films in American Low Culture', *Film Quarterly* 53.2, 2000.

easily located through separate catalogue subheadings or listings. Many catalogues simply list film titles alphabetically, making no attempt to differentiate among genres or subgenres, high or low art. In *Luminous Film and Video Wurks Catalogue 2.0*, for example, Jean-Luc Godard's edgy *Weekend* (1968) is sandwiched between *The Washing Machine* (1993) and *The Werewolf and the Yeti* (1975). Sinister Cinema's 1996–97 catalogue, which organizes titles chronologically, lists Godard's *Alphaville* (1965) between *Lightning Bolt* (1965) and *Zontar, the Thing from Venus* (1966).[5]

Where separate genre and subgenre headings are given, the only labels which apply are the labels important to the fans who purchase tapes. European art and experimental film titles are woven throughout catalogue listings, and may be found under the headings 'Science Fiction,' 'Horror,' 'Barbara Steele,' 'Christopher Lee,' 'Exploitation,' 'Weird Westerns,' and 'Juvenile Schlock.'[6] Where art films are bracketed off, they are often described in terms that most film historians would take pains to avoid. Instead of presenting Pier Paolo Pasolini's *Salò* (1975) as a work which explicitly links 'fascism and sadism, sexual licence [sic] and oppression,'[7] as the *Encyclopedia of European Cinema* does, Mondo simply notes that the film 'left audiences gagging.'[8]

The operative criterion here is affect; the ability of a film to thrill, frighten, gross out, arouse, or otherwise directly engage the spectator's body. And it is this emphasis on affect which characterizes paracinema as a low cinematic culture. Paracinema catalogues are dominated by what Clover terms 'body genre' films, films which, Linda Williams notes, 'privilege the sensational.'[9] Most of the titles are horror, porn,[10] exploitation, horrific sci-fi, or thrillers; and other, non-body genre films – art films, Nixon's infamous Checkers speech, sword-and-sandal epics, etc. – tend to be collapsed into categories dictated by the body genres which are the main focus. [...]

Williams identifies three pertinent features shared by body genres (which she defines as porn, horror, and melodrama). 'First,' she writes, 'there is the spectacle of a body caught in the grips of intense sensation or emotion' (142): the spectacle of orgasm in porn; of terror and violence in horror; of weeping in melodrama. Second, there is the related focus on ecstasy, 'a direct or indirect sexual excitement and rapture,' which borders on what the Greeks termed insanity or bewilderment (142–3). Visually this is signalled in films through what Williams calls the 'involuntary convulsion or spasm – of the body "beside itself" in the grips of sexual pleasure, fear and terror, and overpowering sadness' (143). Aurally, ecstasy is marked by the inarticulate cry – of pleasure in porn, of terror in horror, and of grief or anguish in melodrama (143).

Finally, body genres directly address the spectator's body. And it is this last feature which, Williams argues, most noticeably characterizes body genres as degraded cultural forms. 'What seems to bracket these particular genres from others,' she writes, 'is an apparent lack of proper aesthetic distance, a sense of over-involvement in sensation and emotion ... viewers feel too directly, too viscerally, manipulated by the text' (144). The body of the spectator involuntarily mimics 'the emotion or sensation of the body onscreen' (143). The spectator cringes, becomes tense, screams, weeps, becomes aroused. [...]

While Williams' assessment of the way body genres work – particularly the way they work in 'specifically gendered ways' (144) – is excellent, the distinction between high and low, properly distanced and improperly involved audience response is not as neat as Williams suggests. Consider, for example, Amos Vogel's description of *The War Game* (Peter Watkins, 1965), a British art film which is frequently listed in paracinema catalogues. 'A terrifying, fabricated documentary records the horrors of a future atomic war in the most painstaking, sickening detail. Photographed in London, it shows the flash burns and firestorms, the impossibility of defence [sic], the destruction of all life. Produced by the BBC, the film was promptly banned and became world-famous and rarely seen.'[11] Similarly, Stan Brakhage's *The Act of Seeing with One's Own Eyes* (1972), which is hard to find outside experimental and avant-garde film venues, encourages an uncomfortably visceral reaction in the spectator. The chronicle of a real autopsy, the film is, Amos Vogel writes, 'an appalling, haunting work of great purity and truth. It dispassionately records whatever transpires in front of the lens: bodies sliced length-wise, organs removed, skulls and scalp cut open with electric tools' (267)[12] While such descriptive terms as 'haunting work of great purity and truth' are seldom found in paracinema catalogues, *The War Game* and *The Act of Seeing with One's Own Eyes* do address the spectator in ways that paracinema fans would appreciate. Clearly designed to break the audience's aesthetic distance, the films encourage the kind of excessive physical response which we would generally attribute to horror. Furthermore, their excessive visual force and what paracinema catalogues like to term 'powerful subject matter' mark them as subversive. Banned, marginalized through being screened exclusively in museums and classrooms, these are films which most mainstream film patrons never see.

Of course *The War Game* and *The Act of Seeing with One's Own Eyes* use sensational material differently than many body genre movies do. Seeking to instruct or challenge the spectator, not simply titillate her, films like Watkins' and Brakhage's are deemed to have a higher cultural purpose, and certainly a different artistic intent, from low-genre blood and gore fests. That is, high culture – even when it engages the body in the same way that low genres do – supposedly evokes a different kind of spectatorial pleasure/response than the one evoked by low genres.

Supposedly. But that doesn't mean that it always does. Consider the works of the Marquis de Sade, whose books are sold in mainstream bookstores and adult bookstores, and housed in university libraries. De Sade's works, which the intellectual elite views as masterful analyses of the mechanisms of power and economics,[13] are also – at least if we are to take their presence in adult bookstores and magazines seriously – still regarded as sexually arousing, as masturbatory aids. Furthermore, as Jane Gallop's powerful admission that she masturbated while reading de Sade demonstrates, one set of cultural uses – one kind of audience pleasure – doesn't necessarily preclude the other.[14] It is possible for someone to be simultaneously intellectually challenged *and* physically titillated: and it is possible for someone to simultaneously *enjoy* both the intellectual and the physical stimulation.

Finally, it is not so clear that low genres seek *only* to titillate. As Laura Kipnis remarks in her famous article on *Hustler* magazine, low genres, too, can be analyzed for serious content and purpose. Using a vocabulary similar to the one generally used to analyze the powerful cultural critique mounted by the high pornography of pre-Revolutionary France, Kipnis writes that '*Hustler* also offers a theory of sexuality – a 'low theory.' Like [Robin] Morgan's radical feminism, it too offers an explicitly political and counterhegemonic analysis of power and the body.' The fact that it does so in a way that middle-class readers – Kipnis included – find disgusting is evidence that 'it is explicit about its own class location.'[15]

In a similar fashion, low cinematic genres – as Clover, Williams, Robin Wood, and others have pointed out[16] – often handle explosive social material which mainstream cinema is reluctant to touch. Carlos Clarens notes in *An Illustrated History of the Horror Film* that the B thrillers that Roger Corman's studios quickly cranked out depicted – for all their fabulous premises – a resolutely contemporary world, a world 'usually ignored by Hollywood or blown up beyond recognition.'[17] And Eric Schaefer has demonstrated that, historically, art films which failed to get the Hays Office's coveted seal of approval were screened in bump-and-grind houses, marketed to patrons of body genre pictures as well as to European art film connoisseurs.[18] [...]

If the operative criterion in paracinema culture is affect, the most frequently expressed patron desire is to see something 'different' something unlike contemporary Hollywood cinema. As A.S. Hamrah and Joshua Glenn put it, 'Let's face it: Hollywood films are cautious, uninventive. and bland, and young filmgoers are increasingly uninterested.[19] Paracinema fans, like the cineaste elite, 'explicitly situate themselves in opposition to Hollywood cinema' (Sconce, 381); and they do so in a way which academics would recognize as highly sophisticated. [...] Paracinema consumption can be understood, then, as American art cinema consumption has often been understood, as a reaction against the hegemonic and normalizing practices of mainstream, dominant, Hollywood production.

Providing for the demand for affective products and the demand for 'something different' – something unlike contemporary Hollywood movies – often takes a company's list in what appear to be wildly different directions. Paracinema catalogues not only list classic films by Godard, Antonioni, and Bergman, they are often the only places where European cinema fans can find video titles which are otherwise not available for sale in the U.S. These include everything from the uncut horror films of Jess Franco to Peter Greenaway's *The Baby of Macon* (1993) to Jean-Luc Godard's historically important *Tout va bien* (1972). If 'entertainment is one of the purest marketplaces in the world,' as Robert Shayé, Director of New Line Cinema, maintained during the 1993 GATT controversy,[20] then the alternative mail-order video industry is one of the purest (i.e., uncontaminated by any prejudice) entertainment marketplaces around. Certainly, its mail order catalogues encourage a reading strategy much like the one which Fredric Jameson proposes in *Signatures of the Visible.* That is, they invite us to 'read high and mass culture as objectively related and dialectically interdependent phenomena, as twin and inseparable forms of the fission of aesthetic production under capitalism.'[21]

Historically speaking, paracinema catalogues, with their levelling of cultural hierarchies and abolition of binary categories, are reminiscent of an earlier age – an age preceding what Lawrence W. Levine has called the 'sacralization' of high art, when the mingling of high and low culture was commonplace[22]. In his book *Highbrow Lowbrow,* Levine describes the historical emergence of a cultural hierarchy in the United States during the late nineteenth century. Prior to that time there was little cultural stratification – be it of cultural products or of audiences. This was a time when opera could exist *simultaneously* as a popular and an elite art form;[23] a time when American audiences might hear a soliloquy from *Hamlet* and a popular song in the course of one evening's entertainment at a local venue. In the early nineteenth century, Levine tells us, no art form – opera, painting, theater – was 'elevated above other forms of expressive culture ...; they were part of the general culture and were experienced in the midst of a broad range of other cultural genres by a catholic audience that cut through class and social lines. This situation began to change after mid-century' (149).

The change, which Levine calls 'the sacralization of culture,' involved the establishment of a hierarchy of cultural products and spaces. Shakespeare's works were increasingly played 'straight,' without the accompaniment of farce (a form of entertainment usually scheduled between acts) or popular music; and gradually they acquired the patina of high art. They were seen as more culturally valuable or sophisticated than the travelling road shows which catered to 'popular taste.' The emergence of a growing differentiation of cultural products brought with it a nearly simultaneous differentiation of performance space and audience. Since tickets to the opera house, an edifice of high culture, commanded a much higher price than tickets to the music hall, audiences who attended performances at the opera house tended to be a much tonier crew than audiences who attended the newly devalued variety shows. More importantly, however, as certain cultural products picked up elite status, they also acquired a certain restrictive class inflection. Shakespeare not only moved into theaters, he moved off the board. He was transformed, as Levine tells us, 'from a playwright for the general public into one for a specific audience' (56). Shakespeare became high class and highbrow.

The reasons for the sacralization of high culture in the nineteenth century are, as Levine argues, complicated. Then as now, 'culture' – as a concept – had politico-economic as well as aesthetic and social resonance, and 'aesthetics by themselves cannot account for the nature of the mores and the institutions' that accompanied the historical development of high culture (228). As Levine writes, 'these were shaped by the entire [historic] context – social, cultural, and economic – in which that development took place' (228). Certainly, the categorization and stratification of cultural products seems, at this remove at least, to be the logical aesthetic extension of the stratification, compartmentalization, and commodification that accompanied most cultural production during industrialization and the rise of capitalism. [...]

But while Levine stresses the need for a holistic paradigm to explain the cultural shift which occurred in the United States during industrialization, he also emphasizes the degree to which the sacralization of culture served particular partisan political goals. For Levine, cultural stratification was one logical outcome of a conservative political reformation. 'It should not really surprise us,' he writes,

> that the thrust of the Mugwumps – those independent Republicans whose devotion to the cause of orderly and efficient civil service reform led them to desert their own party in the election of 1884 – was not confined to the political sphere. Once we understand that the drive for political order was paralleled by a drive for cultural order, that the push to organize the economic sphere was paralleled by a push to organize the cultural sphere, that the quest for social authority ('the control of action through the giving of commands') was paralleled by a quest for cultural authority ('the construction of reality through definitions of fact and value'), we can begin to place the cultural dynamics of the turn of the century in clearer perspective (228).

Certainly, we can see the way that the impetus to sacralize specific cultural products, spaces, and historic artifacts as 'culture' had the same sociopolitical and economic implications in the nineteenth century that it has today. The recent debates surrounding the educational curriculum (particularly regarding the canon and which books may or may not be considered 'literature' by the public schools), the concern over the free circulation of both information and images on the Internet, the disputes over continued funding for the National Endowment for the Arts and the Public Broadcasting Service, and the public lambasting of violent and sexual content in rap music, popular Hollywood cinema, and commercial television by both politicians and intellectuals all demonstrate the degree to which culture, economics, and politics continue to be interrelated terms in a society very much concerned with issues of social control. Now, as in the late nineteenth century, 'there is ... the same sense that culture [in the sacralized sense of the word] is something created by the few for the few, threatened by the many, and imperiled by democracy: the conviction that culture cannot come from the young, the inexperienced, the untutored, the marginal' (252). And it is largely in opposition to this sense that 'culture' is exclusionary and elitist that paracinema consumption must be understood. As Michael Weldon notes in the foreword to the *Psychotronic Video Guide,* 'unlike other movie guides, nothing is omitted [here] because it's in bad taste. All of this stuff is out there. You should know about it' (vii).

Exploitation companies are not the only places which cater to European art film fans. Other – more upscale – video companies pick up most of the art film business, and while they don't carry some of the truly obscure titles that characterize Mondo or Cinemacabre's lists, they have a broader range of European art selections than the paracinema companies do (and their tapes are usually much better quality). Interestingly, like Mondo, they do attempt to cater to the horror tastes, as well as the art tastes of their clients. Facets Multimedia, one of the most complete mail-order video services in the country, has listings for cult and horror films, as well as for hard-to-find avant-garde and European art titles. Even Home Film Festival, whose slogan, 'the best films you never saw,' specifically targets a middle-class art and independent film audience, has begun carrying some horror titles – *Night of the Living Dead* (1968), *Spanish Dracula* (1931)[24] *Eyes Without a Face (Les Yeux sans visage,* 1959), *Nadja* (1995), and *Mute Witness* (1995), to name just a few. The fact that 'art' companies as well as 'sleaze' companies market both high art and low culture titles[25] suggests that the sacralization of performance culture (its division into high and low art) never completely took root among art and horror/sleaze/exploitation film fans.[26] [...]

While the European *horror* film listings in exploitation publications include recent films as well as films of historical interest,[27] the European art films which show up in these catalogues tend to date from the height of the art cinema movement, the period which Susan Sontag elegized in her *New York Times* article, 'The Decay of Cinema.'[28] The post-1970 auteurs mentioned by Timothy Corrigan, Thomas Elsaesser, and Jill Forbes in their studies of postwar European and postmodern cinema[29] are largely passed over in favor of the 'classic' auteurs[30] – Godard, Fellini, Antonioni, Buñuel. The most frequently represented American auteur is Orson Welles. Exploitation catalogues feature, then, art film titles which don't sell well in other venues: films of historical interest or titles which haven't been officially released. In that sense, it's not clear to what degree they actually compete with more upscale specialty video companies. What is clear is that the catalogue companies themselves comprise and address what Dick Hebdige might recognize as a true video subculture,[31] a subculture identified less by a specific style than by a certain strategy of reading.[32]

In addition to art, horror, and science fiction films, 'paracinema' catalogues 'include entries from such seemingly disparate genres' as badfilm, splatterpunk, mondo films, sword-and-sandal epics, Elvis flicks, government hygiene films, Japanese monster movies, beach party musicals, and 'just about every other historical manifestation of exploitation cinema from juvenile delinquency documentaries to … pornography' (Sconce, 372). As Sconce explains, this is an 'extremely elastic textual category,' and comprises 'less a distinct group of films than a particular reading protocol, a counter-aesthetic turned subcultural sensibility devoted to all manner of cultural detritus. In short, the explicit manifesto of paracinematic culture is to valorize all forms of cinematic 'trash' whether such films have been either explicitly rejected or simply ignored by legitimate film culture' (372).

This valorization is achieved, he argues, largely through heavily ironized strategies of cinematic reading. Connoisseurs of trash cinema are always on the lookout for movies that are so awful they're good. But they also consume films which are recognized by 'legitimate' film culture as masterpieces. And catalogue descriptions do attempt to alert the consumer that such films might require a different reading strategy – less heavily ironized – than other films listed in the catalogue.[33] Sinister Cinema's description of *Vampyr* is a good example: 'If you're looking for a fast-paced horror film with lots of action go to another movie in our listings. If you like mood and atmosphere this is probably the greatest horror movie ever made. The use of light, shadow, and camera angles is translated into a pureness of horror seldom equaled, in this chilling vampire-in-a-castle tale. One of the best.'[34]

Clearly, the description serves an important economic purpose. Customers are less likely to be disappointed, to return tapes, if they understand clearly what they're getting. But the delineation of important stylistic elements is instructional as well as cautionary. It tells the collector what to look for, how to read a film which might seem lugubrious or boring. The fact that the catalogue lists two versions of the film – a longer, foreign-language version and a shorter version with English subtitles – marks the company's economic stake in serious collectors and completionists (people who collect many versions of the same title – the U.S. theatrical release, the director's cut or uncut European version, the rough cut, etc.). But it also gives the catalogue a curiously academic or scholarly air, which links Sinister Cinema to more upscale 'serious' video companies like Facets.

While paracinema catalogues often tag art films as films which require a different reading strategy than *Reefer Madness* (1939) or *Glen and Glenda* (1953), they also tag certain B movies as films which can be openly appreciated on pure aesthetic grounds. In the same catalogue which characterizes *Vampyr* as 'one of the best,' for example, the reader can also find a listing for *Carnival of Souls* (1962), a B-grade American horror film which *The Encyclopedia of Horror Movies* calls 'insufferably portentous.' The script, the *Encyclopedia* tells us 'harks back to those expressionistic dramas which solemnly debated this life and the next with heavy-breathing dialogue.'[35] For Sinister Cinema catalogue patrons, however, the film is described in terms not unlike the ones used to describe *Vampyr*: 'A riveting pipe organ music score. Seldom have the elements of sight and sound come together in such a horrifying way. A haunting film that you'll never forget. Original uncut 80-minute version.'[36] Although this description does not praise *Carnival of Souls*' use of 'light, shadow, and camera angles,' its observation that 'sight and sound come together in a ... horrifying way' is a tribute to the film's formal style. And the use of the word 'haunting' in the next-to-last line reminds the reader that schlock, too, can be beautiful. [...]

Negotiating paracinema catalogues often calls, then, for a more complicated set of textual reading strategies than is commonly assumed. Viewing/reading the films themselves – even the trashiest films – demands a set of sophisticated strategies which, Sconce argues, are remarkably similar to the strategies employed by the cultural elite.

> Paracinematic taste involves a reading strategy that renders the bad into the sublime, the deviant into the defamiliarized and in so doing, calls attention to the aesthetic aberrance and stylistic variety evident but routinely dismissed in the many subgenres of trash cinema. By concentrating on a film's formal bizarreness and stylish eccentricity, the paracinematic audience, *much like the viewer attuned to the innovations of Godard* ... foregrounds structures of cinematic discourse and artifice so that the material identity of the film ceases to be a structure made invisible in service of the diegesis, but becomes instead the primary focus of textual attention (388, emphasis mine).

Since Sconce is mainly interested in theorizing trash aesthetics, he doesn't take the 'high' art aspects of the catalogues' video lists into account. So he does not thoroughly discuss the way in which the companies' listing practices erase the difference between what's considered trash and what's considered art through a deliberate levelling of hierarchies and recasting of categories. But his comments about 'the viewer attuned to the innovations of Godard' help to explain the heavy representation of Godard's films in these catalogues. As Godard himself repeatedly demonstrated, there is a very fine line between the reading strategies demanded by trash and the reading strategies demanded by high culture.

Earlier I mentioned that the design of paracinema mail order catalogues – which list titles alphabetically or chronologically, and make no attempt to differentiate between high and low genres – encourages a kind of dialectical cultural reading. Certainly, it highlights an aspect of art cinema generally overlooked or repressed in cultural analysis, namely, the degree to which high culture trades on the same images, tropes, and themes that characterize low culture. 'Film is a vivid medium,' as Steven Shaviro notes.[37] And there is something vividly scandalous and transgressive about the films of Peter Greenaway, Derek Jarman, Luis Buñuel, Jean-Luc Godard, and the other European filmmakers mentioned above. In fact, European art cinema has followed a trajectory in the United States not unlike that of pure exploitation cinema, in that historically it has been seen as delving 'unashamedly into often disreputable content,' often 'promoting it in ... [a] disreputable manner.'[38] [...]

While Michael Mayer gives a long list of reasons for the rise in popularity of foreign films in the U.S. after the war – the Paramount decision, which had the effect of decreasing the number of films produced in the U.S., the increased American interest in all things foreign, the end of political isolationism, more travel opportunities, the increased sophistication of the viewing public ('the public no longer requires complete clarity on film') – most interesting for our purposes is the importance he places on the 'violent' change in Americans' sexual mores.[39] Certainly, this is the 'lesson' which Hollywood learned from the rise of art cinema. As Kristin Thompson and David Bordwell note in *Film History*, 'one way of competing with television, which had extremely strict censorship,' as well as with European art films, 'was to make films with more daring subject matter. As a result, producers and distributors pushed the code further and further.'[40]

For many Americans, however, throughout the late 50s and early 60s, European art cinema retained a scandalous reputation which marked its difference from Hollywood cinema (even a Hollywood cinema dedicated to 'push[ing] the code further and further'). In 1960, the residents of Fort Lee, New Jersey, protested the opening of a 'film art house' in their community. 'It is a known fact that many of the foreign films are without doubt detrimental to the morals of the young and old,' one pastor maintained. Apparently, the president of the Borough Council, agreed. 'I would not hesitate to pass an ordinance barring all future theatres from Fort Lee,' he claimed, 'if that's the only way to keep this one out.'[41] And both Janet Staiger and Douglas Gomery stress the degree to which the audience for art films in the U.S. has always been a 'special interest group.'[42] Hollywood's need to compete for art film audiences, then, should be seen more as an indication of changing audience demographics (mainstream audiences were going less and less frequently to the movies; special interest groups were going more and more) than as an index of changing mainstream tastes. The moviegoing audience was not only becoming segmented, as Janet Staiger claims,[43] it was becoming polarized (into mainstream and 'alternative' or 'fringe' audiences). Interestingly, the majority of historical titles on horror and exploitation video mail order lists are drawn from films made during the era when this polarization became pronounced. Agreeing with Richard Kadrey that 'everything interesting is out at the edges,'[44] the catalogues celebrate the two extreme tastes of the postwar, youthful filmgoing public: low-budget horror, sci-fi, and exploitation films on the one hand; art-film 'classics,' on the other.

In addition to these, there is an interesting array of films which, put quite simply, are difficult to categorize. Films with high production values, European art-film cachet, and enough sex and violence to thrill all but the most jaded horror fan: Roger Vadim's *Blood and Roses* (1960), Stanley Kubrick's *Clockwork Orange* (1971), Harry Kuemel's *Daughters of Darkness* (1971), Georges Franju's *Eyes Without a Face* (1959), Roman Polanski's *Repulsion* (1965) and *The Tenant* (1976), to name just a few. There are films, like Tod Browning's *Freaks* (1932), which began their career as horror or exploitation films and were later revived as art films; films, like Paul Morrissey's *Andy Warhol's Frankenstein* (1973) and *Andy Warhol's Dracula* (1974), which belong to New York avant-garde culture as well as to horror; and experimental films, like the Surrealist classic *Un Chien andalou* (1929), which contain sequences as shocking as those in any contemporary splatter film.[45] These are films which promise *both* affect and 'something different'; films which defy the traditional genre labels by which we try to make sense of cinematic history and cultures, films which seem to have a stake in both high and low art.

Unlike *Nosferatu* or *Vampyr* – films which I earlier designated 'the high end of horror' – these films still directly engage the viewer's body. Like the slasher films which Clover analyzes, many of them are 'drenched in taboo' and encroach 'vigorously on the pornographic.'[46] All of them meet both Linda Williams' and William Paul's criteria for lower cinematic forms. In *Laughing Screaming*, Paul writes:

From the high perch of an elitist view, the negative definition of the lower works would have it that they are less subtle than higher genres. More positively, it could be said they are more direct. Where lower forms are explicit, higher forms tend to operate more by indirection. Because of this indirection the higher forms are often regarded as being more metaphorical and consequently, more resonant, more open to the exegetical analyses of the academic industry.[47]

This concurs with Williams' characterization of body genres as physically excessive, viscerally manipulative genres. For both Williams and Paul, so-called 'low' genres lack 'proper aesthetic distance' (Williams, 144). In fact, the title of Paul's book, *Laughing Screaming*, specifically foregrounds the kind of undistanced involuntary response – what Williams might call the ecstatic response – which direct, body-genre films evoke from the audience. As Williams notes, 'aurally, excess is marked by recourse not to the coded articulations of language but to inarticulate cries' (143) – laughing, screaming – both onscreen and in the audience.

The films listed above are nothing if not direct. There may be a 'metaphorical' significance to the slashing of a woman's eye in *Un Chien andalou* – in fact, feminist film theory would argue that there's a profound metaphorical significance to such an act – but that significance is very much bound up with the immediate physical jolt experienced by the spectator. Similarly, when Dracula vomits blood in *Andy Warhol's Dracula*, when Dr. Génessier peels the skin from a woman's face in *Eyes Without a Face*, and when Stephan, in *Daughters of Darkness*, whips his wife in an excess of sadistic sexual frenzy, the directness of the image, as Paul points out, 'makes metaphoric significance seem secondary to the primary power' of the image itself (32).

Which is not to say these films don't simultaneously operate at the high end of the horror spectrum. They do. The pacing, the blatant disregard for the cause-effect logic of classical Hollywood cinema, the strategic use of discontinuous editing, the painterly composition of certain scenes all serve to mark these films as art cinema.[48] The fact that the films seem to operate at both ends of the horror spectrum is at least partly responsible for the fact that the best of them were so poorly received at the time of their release. [...]

In a way, hybrid genres like art-horror films simply point up the problems which have historically characterized all attempts at genre definition. As S.S. Prawer notes,

(i) Every worthwhile work modifies the genre [horror] to some extent, brings something new to it, and therefore forces us to rethink definitions and delimitations.
(ii) There are borderline cases, works that belong to more than one genre – the overlap between the 'fantastic terror' film and the 'science fiction' film is particularly large.
(iii) Wide variations in quality are possible within a given genre.
(iv) There are works which as a whole clearly do not belong to the genre in question but which embody references to that genre, or contain sequences that derive from, allude to, or influence it. The first dream sequence in Bergman's *Wild Strawberries* ... clearly ... [belongs] in that category.[49]

While Prawer is speaking here mainly of horror films, his remarks – as he himself points out – can be adapted to fit 'genre studies in any medium' (37). Certainly, they can be adapted to fit other film genres. Film noir, the thriller, and melodrama have a great deal of overlap with other genres. Avant-garde cinema is just as divergent in scope and quality as horror cinema. The European art film is so diverse that it is generally not represented as a genre at all. And, as Jim Collins maintains in *Architectures of Excess*, the 80s and 90s have been marked by the increasing number of 'eclectic, hybrid genre films': films such as *Road Warrior* (1981), *Blade Runner* (1982), *Blue Velvet* (1986), *Near Dark* (1988), and *Thelma and Louise* (1991), which 'engage in specific tranformations across genres.'[50] In fact, genre overlap and instability is so common, Robin Wood maintains, that the tendency to treat genres as discrete has been one of the major obstacles to developing what he calls a synthetic definition of the term.[51] [...]

As I've suggested, horror is not the only genre/category which is hard to pin down and it's not the only genre/category which continually flirts with the possibility of existing simultaneously as high and low art.[52] To some degree, as William Paul asserts, all film still has something disreputable about it,[53] all film still has to struggle to be seen as art at all. And yet, we do, as he also notes, consistently make distinctions between good cinema and bad, between artistic films and films that are 'just entertainment.' Even within as democratic a medium as film, we worry about 'taste,' 'a phenomenon which, social critics from Pierre Bourdieu to V. Vale and Andrea Juno maintain, is always already bound up with questions of class.[54]

But while it is not the only popular genre which continually flirts with a kind of high-art double – in this case, the European art film or prestige import cinema – horror is perhaps the best vantage point from which to study the cracks that seem to exist everywhere in late twentieth-century 'sacralized' film culture. Precisely because it plays so relentlessly on the body, horror's 'low' elements are easy to see. As Joe Bob Briggs is fond of reminding us, fans of low horror are drawn by the body count ('We're talking two breasts, four quarts of blood, five dead bodies ... Joe Bob says check it out').[55] And as catalogues from mail order video companies remind us, prestigious films, too, can play relentlessly on the public's desire – or at least its willingness – to be physically affronted. Like the lowest of low horror, European art films can 'leave audiences gagging.'

## Notes

A shorter version of this article was presented at the 1997 Society for Cinema Studies Conference. I would like to thank Chris Anderson, Carol J. Clover, Skip Hawkins, Eric Schaefer, Ann Martin, and the Editorial Board of *Film Quarterly*, all of whom read earlier versions of the essay and made helpful suggestions. Also, a special thanks to Eric Schaefer for his sensitive reading of the piece and the references he gave me.

1. See Jeffrey Sconce, ' "Trashing" the Academy: Taste, Excess, and an Emerging Politics of Cinematic Style,' *Screen* 36: 4 (Winter 1995), 372. Michael Weldon calls this cinema 'psychotronic.' See Michael Weldon, *The Psychotronic Encyclopedia* (New York: Ballantine Books, 1983): Michael Weldon, *The Psychotronic Video Guide* (New York: St. Martin's Griffin, 1996). Subsequent references to these three works will be given in the text. See also Michael Weldon, ed. *Psychotronic Video* (serial, Narrowsburg, New York).

2. Remarkably little has been written on the low end of the mail order video business. Fanzines and mass-market horror publications periodically publish addresses and lists. But, since they're preaching to the converted, they provide very little analysis of the

phenomenon. At the time of this writing, Sconce's '"Trashing" the Academy' remains the only article which attempts to theorize the phenomenon and the aesthetic it represents. The best general interest articles on mail order video were published in the July–August 1991 issue of *Film Comment*. See Elliot Forbes, 'The "Lost" World'; Maitland McDonagh, 'The House by the Cemetery'; and Peter Hogue. 'Riders of the Dawn,' *Film Comment* 27 (July–Aug. 1991), 41–49. See also Richard Kadrey, 'Director's Cuts' *World Art* 3/1996, 64–68, which discusses the aesthetic of bootlegs. Tony Williams' 'Resource Guide: Video Sales and Rentals,' *Jump Cut* 37 (1992), 99–109, and 'Mail Order and Video Companies II, *Jump Cut* 41 (1994), 110–118, mainly list companies. It's interesting, though, that in an article geared mainly toward teachers and film professionals, Williams mentions paracinema companies as well as more upscale, traditional sources.

3. For years, scholars have been challenging the binary opposition of high art and popular culture, and have been problematizing the uninflected use of the two terms. But the 1993 General Agreement on Tariffs and Trade (GATT) discussions over audiovisual products illustrated the degree to which the North American mainstream press continues to reproduce and valorize a dichotomy which cultural scholars and fans of paracinema find problematic. See Matthew Fraser, 'A Question of Culture: The Canadian Solution Resolves a GATT Standoff,' *MacLean's* v. 106 n. 52 (Canada, Dec. 27, 1993), 50; David Lawday, 'France Guns for Clint Eastwood,' *U.S. News and World Report* v. 115 n. 23 (Dec. 13, 1993), 72; and Daniel Singer, 'GATT and the Shape of Our Dreams.' *The Nation* v. 258 n. 2 (Jan. 17, 1994), 54.

4. Carol J. Clover, 'Her Body, Himself: Gender in the Slasher Film.' *Representations* 20 (Fall, 1987), 187.

5. While most art-cinema mail order companies separate films into generic categories, Home Film Festival simply lists titles alphabetically – to similarly startling effect. In *Program Guide* #12, for example, George Romero's *Night of the Living Dead (*1968) comes between Charles Laughton's *Night of the Hunter* (1955) and Paolo and Vittorio Taviani's *Night of Shooting Stars* (1982). *Home Film Festival Program Guide* #12, 140.

6. The 1996–97 Sinister Cinema catalogue does list 'Mexican Horr/Sci-fi' and 'Spaghetti Westerns' as separate categories.

7. Ginette Vincendeau, *Encyclopedia of European Cinema* (New York: Facts on File, 1995), 327.

8. *Mondo Video Catalogue*: Mondo Video. Cookeville. Tennessee, n.d., n.p. One scholarly treatment which does emphasize the horror in Pasolini's films, albeit not as brutally as Mondo's catalogue, is Leo Bersani and Ulysse Dutoit, 'Merde Alors: Pasolini's *Salo,'* *October* No. 13 (Summer 1980), 23–35.

9. See Carol J. Clover, *Men, Women and Chainsaws: Gender in the Modern Horror Film* (Princeton: Princeton University Press, 1992), and Linda J. Williams, 'Film Bodies: Gender, Genre and Excess,' in Barry Keith Grant, ed., *Film Genre Reader II* (Austin: University of Texas Press, 1995), 142. Subsequent references to the Williams article will be given in the text.

10. While most companies Carry only softcore and exploitation titles, an increasing number are stocking hardcore and XXX European and Asian videos. Luminous carries some XXX titles. Video Search of Miami and European Trash Cinema carry hardcore (including hardcore S & M) titles. The descriptions for these titles always include a warning so that consumers of softcore porn will not purchase titles that are more violent and sexually explicit than they expect.

11. Amos Vogel, *Film as a Subversive Art* (New York: Random House, 1974), 277. Subsequent citations will be given in the text.

12. It's interesting to note that there is a Eurotrash film with a similar theme to Brakhage's *The Act of Seeing with One's Own Eyes. Aftermath* (1994), by Spanish director Nacho Cerda, has created what *Luminous Film and Video Wurks Catalogue 3.0* calls 'the most disgusting 30 minutes ever.' Imagine that you have died, the catalogue invites, 'and ... you end

up in the Autopsy room. You see with your own dead eyes death after death and you feel the painful dissection of your innards ... . Very realistic fake (I hope) human corpses are dismembered and sexually assaulted in this beautifully shot short film. You must be 21 and over to order this sick piece of cinema.'

13. See for example, Angela Carter. *The Sadeian Woman and the Ideology of Pornography* (New York: Pantheon Books, 1978); Gilles Deleuze, 'Coldness and Cruelty,' in Deleuze, *Masochism,* trans. Jean McNeil (New York: Zone Books, 1989); and Jane Gallop. *Intersections: A Reading of Sade with Bataille, Blanchot and Klossowski* (Lincoln: University of Nebraska Press, 1981). For related discussions on the cultural meaning of sadistic representations, see Georges Bataille, *Visions of Excess: Selected Writings 1927–1939*, trans. Allan Stoekl with Carl R. Lovitt and Donald M. Leslie Jr. (Minneapolis: University of Minnesota Press, 1985), and Linda Williams, 'Power, Pleasure, and Perversion: Sadomasochistic Film Pornography,' in Williams, *Hardcore* (Berkeley: University of California Press, 1989), 184–229.

14. See Jane Gallop, 'The Bodily Enigma.' in Gallop, *Thinking Through the Body* (New York: Columbia University Press, 1988).

15. Laura Kipnis, '(Male) Desire and (Female) Disgust: Reading *Hustler*,' in Kipnis, *Ecstasy Unlimited: On Sex, Gender, Capital and Aesthetics* (Minneapolis: University of Minnesota Press, 1993), 220.

16. See Carol J. Clover, *Men, Women and Chainsaws*; Linda Williams, 'Film Bodies: Gender, Genre and Excess' and *Hardcore*; and Robin Wood, 'Return of the Repressed,' *Film Comment* (July–Aug. 1978), 25–32, 'Gods and Monsters,' *Film Comment* (Sept.–Oct. 1978), 19–25, and the horror chapters in *Hollywood from Vietnam to Reagan* (New York: Columbia University Press, 1986).

17. Carlos Clarens, *An Illustrated History of the Horror Film* (New York: Capricorn Books, 1967), 147–48.

18. Eric Schaefer, 'Resisting Refinement: The Exploitation Film and Self-Censorship,' *Film History* 6, no. 3 (1994), 293–313.

19. A.S. Hamrah and Joshua Glenn, 'Monsters, Sex, Sci-Fi, and Kung Fu,' *Utne Reader* no. 70 (July–Aug. 1995), 30.

20. Bernard Weinraub, 'Directors Fight for GATT's Final Cuts and Print,' *New York Times* (Sunday, Dec. 12, 1993), 14.

21. Fredric Jameson, *Signatures of the Visible* (New York: Routledge, 1992), 14. Subsequent citations will be given in the text.

22. As Jeffrey Sconce has noted, however, paracinema culture does construct itself in opposition to cineaste or high cinema culture. Thus it is often in the odd position of both challenging/destroying and upholding binary oppositions.

23. Lawrence W. Levine, *Highbrow Lowbrow: The Emergence of Cultural Hierarchy in America* (Cambridge, MA: Harvard University Press, 1988), 86. Subsequent citations given in the text.

24. This is the Spanish-language version of *Dracula* which Universal Studios made at the same time that Tod Browning was shooting *Dracula*. Directed by George Melford, the film utilizes essentially the same script and sets. The film stars Carlos Villarias in the role of the count; Lupita Tovar plays Eva.

25. The Home Film Festival (HFF) list doesn't carry many low-culture titles. Interestingly, *Texas Chainsaw Massacre* (1974), which is part of the Museum of Modern Art's film collection, is not part of the list, while *Night of the Living Dead* is. While HFF carries mainly art-horror titles, Facets handles an extensive list of slasher/cult/horror films.

26. Although upscale mail order video companies do tend to carry some low-genre titles, the sense that they are low-genre titles is clearly part of the marketing ploy. *Facets Multimedia Catalogue No. 14*, for example, contains a 'Guilty Pleasures' section.

27. Here I'm including the work of directors like Dario Argento. Jess Franco, Lucio Fulci, Jean Rollin, and Andrzej Zulawski.

28. Susan Sontag. 'The Decay of Cinema.' *New York Times Magazine* (Feb. 25, 1996), 60–61.

29. See Timothy Corrigan, *A Cinema Without Walls: Movies and Culture after Vietnam* (New Brunswick: Rutgers University Press, 1991); Thomas Elsaesser, *New German Cinema: A History* (New Brunswick: Rutgers University Press, 1989); and Jill Forbes, *The Cinema in France after the New Wave* (Bloomington: Indiana University Press, 1992).

30. Peter Greenaway, Rainer Werner Fassbinder, and Bertrand Blier are some notable exceptions to this. I should also mention that post-1970 films by the 'classic' directors are usually included – Godard's *Every Man for Himself* (1980), Fellini's *Intervista* (1988). It's also interesting to note that not all the films have subtitles. Luminous Film and Video Wurks provide a wider selection of contemporary European art films than most other companies do.

31. Dick Hebdige. *Subculture: The Meaning of Style* (New York: Routledge, 1987).

32. Richard Kadrey treats the paracinema subculture as part of a larger consumer (sub-culture) group which he identifies as 'covert' or 'fringe.' See Richard Kadrey, *Covert Culture Sourcebook* (New York: St. Martin's Press, 1993) and *Covert Culture Sourcebook 2.0* (New York: St. Martin's Press, 1994).

33. This is the only qualitative distinction which the catalogues make – films which require ironized strategies of reading and those which don't. It's important to note, however, that films which don't are not considered better (or worse) than the ones that do – just different.

34. *Sinister Cinema Catalogue*, 12.

35. The reviewer does admit that 'Harvey's direction has a weird flair, sometimes suggesting a throwback to the silent days and drawing a kind of awkward honesty out of the actors.' Phil Hardy, ed., *The Encyclopedia of Horror Movies* (New York: Harper and Row, 1986), 147. Subsequent references will be given in the text.

36. *Sinister Cinema Catalogue*, 21.

37. Steven Shaviro, *The Cinematic Body* (Minneapolis, MN: University of Minnesota Press, 1993), vii.

38. This is part of the 'exploitation' definition given by Thomas Doherty, in *Teenagers and Teenpics: The Juvenilization of American Movies in the 1950s* (Boston: Unwin Hyman, 1988), 8.

39. Michael F. Mayer, *Foreign Films on American Screens* (New York: Arco, 1965), 1–3.

40. Kristin Thompson and David Bordwell. *Film History: An Introduction* (New York: McGraw-Hill, 1994), 386.

41. 'Parochial Uproar in Ft. Lee: Panics, Before "Foreign Art Films,"' *Variety* (Wednesday, Feb. 24, 1960), 24, 3.

42. In fact, Hollywood's attempt to compete for art film audiences has much to do with the fact that the traditional movie-going base had been eroded. Staiger points out that younger, better-educated people were more likely to go to the movies than older, less-educated people. These people had very different tastes from the 'masses.' As Staiger notes, 'while the "masses" were not especially attracted to "realism" or "message" pictures, art-house audiences were typified as preferring those films.' Janet Staiger. *Interpreting Films: Studies in the Historical Reception of American Cinema* (Princeton: Princeton University Press, 1992), 185. For more information, see all of chapter 9. Douglas Gomery concurs, noting that audience studies 'found that art theatres attracted persons of above-average education, more men than women and many solitary movie-goers. This was the crowd who attended the opera, theatre, lectures and ballet.' Douglas Gomery, *Shared Pleasures: A History of Movie Presentation in the United States* (Madison: Wisconsin University Press, 1992), 189.

43. Staiger, *Interpreting Films,* 184.

44. Richard Kadrey, *Covert Culture Sourcebook*, 1.

45. A few minutes into *Un Chien andalou*, a man – played by Luis Buñuel – slices open a woman's eye with a razor. To gauge from student responses when I show the film in class,

the segment has lost none of its power to shock and horrify the spectator, to act directly on the spectator's body.

46. *Men, Women and Chainsaws*, 21.

47. William Paul, *Laughing Screaming: Modern Hollywood Horror and Comedy* (New York: Columbia University Press, 1994), 32. Subsequent citations will be given in the text.

48. Lack of cause and effect, and strategic use of discontinuous editing, also links these films with exploitation cinema, which, as Eric Schaefer points out, can utilize similar techniques because of their reliance on forbidden spectacle. And it's a key feature of almost all European horror films made during the 1956–84 period. As Cathal Tohill and Pete Tombs point out, 'Linear narrative and logic are always ignored in a *fantastique* (horror] film.' Cathal Tohill and Pete Tombs, *Immoral Tales: European Sex and Horror Movies 1956–1984* (New York: St. Martin's Griffin, 1994), 5.

49. S.S. Prawer, *Caligari's Children: The Film as Tale of Terror* (New York: Da Capo Press, 1980), 37–38.

50. Jim Collins, *Architectures of Excess: Cultural Life in the Information Age* (New York: Routledge, 1995), 131.

51. Robin Wood, 'Ideology, Genre, Auteur,' in Gerald Mast, Marshall Cohen, and Leo Braudy, eds., *Film Theory and Criticism*, fourth edition (New York: Oxford University Press, 1992), 478.

52. Comedy, thrillers, sci-fi, and melodrama all have this ability. Jim Collins has done an excellent job of analyzing the way 'the eclecticism of the contemporary genre films involves a hybridity of conventions that works at cross-purposes with the traditional notion of genre as a stable, integrated set of narrative and stylistic conventions.' *Architectures of Excess*, 126.

53. See Paul, *Laughing Screaming*.

54. See Pierre Bourdieu, *Distinction: A Social Critique of the Judgement of Taste*, trans. Richard Nice (Cambridge, MA: Harvard University Press, 1984); William Paul, *Laughing Screaming*; and V. Vale and Andrea Juno, 'Introduction.' in Jim Morton (guest editor), *Incredibly Strange Films*, RE/SEARCH #10 (San Francisco: RE/SEARCH, 1986), 4–6.

55. Quoted in *Men, Women and Chainsaws*, 21. See also note, 19.

# PART FIVE

# VOICING:

# IDENTITIES AND ARTICULATION

To voice, to articulate, is to speak, communicate and claim. From the grain of the voice posited by Roland Barthes to the question of whether the subaltern can speak posed by Gayatri Spivak and beyond, the tensions between identity, politics and culture have long contributed some of the most compelling cultural criticism in contemporary scholarship. In this section, the relationship between voicing and identity is further motivated by the sense of articulation, as advanced by Stuart Hall, that involves a dynamic between hegemonic and counter-hegemonic ideologies that neither reduces the socio-political sphere to the level of discourse nor subsumes everything to a banal conceptualization of economic overdetermination. Epistemologically, articulation diverges from the bias that privileges the lasting as somehow more important and more real than transitory or ephemeral unities. So to articulate identity, to give voice to its existence and transformations, is to enunciate the connections that it generates, with an eye toward the contingency that is both its condition of possibility and limitation as a shifting, and often contradictory, set of identifications and disidentifications motivated by diverse hopes, goals, and apprehensions. In their analysis of topics as diverse as diaspora and national mass cultural industries, the chapters presented in this section advance rigorously anti-essentialist interrogations of the relationship between identity and popular culture that remain sensitive to considerations of time and place as well as social and personal need. Movement, citizenship, racialization, sexuality, power and postcoloniality converge to productively critique modern modes of conceptualizing the self. Purposeful and creative revision of the ways that self may be understood ultimately divest structures of exclusion and political disempowerment of their commonality.

Stuart Hall, a scholar who constantly assesses his own position within the study of culture as well as within the discourses he engages, has been a major contributor to the formation of intellectual inquiry into popular culture. His work, initially associated with the British Culturalist tradition, was later influenced by Italian Marxist Antonio Gramsci. Hall's relationship to Gramsci contributed greatly to the influence of the concept of hegemony on the way that popular culture is studied today. In **'What is this "Black" in Black Popular Culture?'**, first presented at a 1991 conference on Black Popular Culture and published in 1992 in a volume of the same name, Hall begins by situating the question of black popular culture with respect to European models of high culture, the emergence of the USA as a global power – and center of global cultural production and circulation – and the decolonization of the third world. Against this backdrop, popular culture emerges as a significant site: 'What we are talking about is the struggle over cultural hegemony, which is these days waged as much in popular culture as anywhere else'; and to understand the term 'popular' as a site of struggle, we must acknowledge that it is always a contradictory space simultaneously rooted in popular experience and available for expropriation at any time. For these reasons, and in dialogue with considerations of gender and queer theory, Hall contends that the 'black' in black popular culture refers to 'a mark of difference *inside* forms of popular culture' that engages the politics of representation, rather than an essential quality of identity or experience.

Music, style, race, class, nation, and politics have served as the major points of entry into the study of popular culture in the UK. Paul Gilroy's *There Ain't No Black in the Union Jack: The Cultural Politics of Race and Nation* (Chicago: Chicago University Press, 1987) and Dick Hebdige's *Subculture: The Meaning of Style* (London: Routledge, 1979), just to cite two prominent texts, helped to set the debates along these parameters. The last decade of the twentieth century saw academic interest broaden these parameters in order to consider transnational and diasporic popular forms. The study of South Asian popular culture, especially the importance of bhangra style and music, has been considered in regards to Asian identity, Asian communities and cultural practices within Britain, the social/cultural construction of 'Asianness', a reconfiguration of the black/white binary, cultural hybridity, and diasporic ethnicities. Presented here is Gayatri Gopinath's '**"Bombay, UK, Yuba City": Bhangra Music and the Engendering of Diaspora'**. Gopinath's work is situated at the intersections of queer theory, South Asian diasporic culture, and popular culture. This article uses bhangra to question 'the potentialities and limits of diaspora as a theoretical framework'. 'Reading bhangra as a diasporic text allows for a far more complicated understanding of diaspora, in that it demands a radical reworking of the hierarchical relation between diaspora and the nation.' Gopinath turns to performance to examine how gender and sexuality are constructed within discourses of diaspora and provides a powerful critique of Paul Gilroy's inability to consider Asian cultural productions within the diasporic framework presented in *The Black Atlantic: Modernity and Double Consciousness* (Cambridge, MA: Harvard University Press, 1993).

Excerpted from Lauren Berlant's *The Queen of America Goes to Washington City: Essays on Sex and Citizenship* (1997), '**The Face of America and the State of Emergency'** interrogates the construction of what she calls 'normative citizenship' through the relationship of diverse popular texts such as Robert Zemeckis's *Forrest Gump* (1994) and the film adaptation of John Grisham's *The Pelican Brief* (London: Random House, 1992), as well as Michael Jackson's 'Black or White' (1991) music video to history, politics and national identity. The discussion included in this section focuses on an additional feature of the argument: a comparative analysis of *Time* magazine's modes of representing 'America'. Considerations of immigration, sexual mores, and racialization converge in a compelling invective of what Berlant refers to as the effect of hygienic governmentality:

> The expulsion of embodied public spheres from the national future/present involves a process I have been describing as an orchestrated politics of nostalgia and sentimentality marketed by the official national culture industry, a politics that perfumes its cruelty in its claims to loathe the culture war it is waging, blaming social divisions in the United States on the peoples against whom the war is being conducted.

In effect, Berlant offers a critical analysis of conservatism in popular national culture, a project extended by *Our Monica, Ourselves: The Clinton Affair and the National Interest* (New York: New York University Press, 2001) (co-edited with Lisa Duggan) and complicated by her work on the relationship between sexuality, discourses of privacy and the public sphere in her edited collection *Intimacy* (Chicago: University of Chicago Press, 2000).

In his introduction to *Disidentifications: Queers of Color and the Performance of Politics* (1999), José Esteban Muñoz explains that: 'Disidentification is about recycling and rethinking encoded meaning. The process of disidentification scrambles and reconstructs the encoded message of a cultural text in a fashion that both exposes the encoded message's universalizing and exclusionary machinations and recircuits its workings to account for, include, and empower minority identities and identification.' The volume conceptualizes identity and its relationships to culture and politics through performance from the perspective of radical women of color, psychoanalytic models, deconstruction, and Marxist theory. It considers an array of queer cultural practices – from visual, video and performance art – that speak to transformation of the world through performance. Existing as we do, immersed in culture/s that may or may not welcome or even acknowledge us, appropriation and transformation of fantasy, exoticism and otherness generated by culture industries enables communication of relationships to such cultural production as a textured and situated narrative of self, and of the self in history. The practice of 'disidentification', or a 'way of shuffling back and forth between reception and production', thus functions as a form of world-making in a frequently hostile environment. It explores the use of popular culture by minoritarian groups as much more than a simple dichotomy of unthinking acceptance or whole-hearted refusal. In the chapter excerpted here, '**Pedro Zamora's** *Real World* **of Counterpublicity: Performing an Ethics of the Self**', Muñoz also explores the ways that televisual dissemination of performances like Zamora's contribute to the '*possibility of counterpublics*' – or 'communities and relational chains of resistance that contest the dominant public sphere'. Employing the video confessional mode of MTV's *Real World* to promote AIDS awareness, Zamora both performs a Foucauldian ethics of self and accomplishes tasks that enable 'the enactment of queer and Latino identity practices in a phobic public sphere'.

Richard Fung runs the Centre for Independent Visual Media and Education at the University of Toronto's Ontario Institute for Studies in Education. He is a video artist whose work varies between experimental, documentary, and essay productions that explore the complexities and interconnected relations between queer sexualities, race and ethnicity. Fung's award-winning videos include: *Sea in the Blood* (2000), *Steam Clean* (1991), *Chinese Characters* (1986), *Dirty Laundry* (1996), *Fighting Chance* (1991), *School Fag* (1998), *My Mother's Place* (1990), and *Orientations: Lesbian and Gay Asians* (1984). In 2002 Fung's significance to the study of identity and representation was further concretized in the form of an edited collection dedicated to his *oeuvre: Like Mangoes in July: The Work of Richard Fung* (edited by Kerri Sakamoto and Helen Lee, Toronto Insomniac Press, 2002). Aside from being a video artist, Fung is also a teacher, AIDS activist, and writer. Included here is Fung's essay, '**Looking for My Penis: The Eroticized Asian in Gay Video Porn**'. Porn, like other forms of popular media, is a representational genre. Through an engagement with the concept of 'Orientalism' and a detailed discussion of Sum Yung Mahn's – 'perhaps the only Asian to qualify as a gay porn "star"' – placement and roles within gay porn. 'The barriers that impede pornography from providing representations of Asian men that are erotic and politically palatable (as opposed to correct) are similar to those that inhibit the Asian documentary, the Asian feature, the Asian experimental film and videotape. We are seen as too peripheral, not commercially viable – not the general audience.'

# Play List

Asian Dub Foundation (1995) *Facts and Fiction*. CD. Nation Records LTD.

Baker, Jr., Houston, A; Diawara, Manthia and Lindenborg, Ruth H. (1996) *Black British Cultural Studies: A Reader*. Chicago and London: University of Chicago Press.

Beatty, Paul (1996) *The White Boy Shuffle*. Boston: Houghton Mifflin.

*Bitch: Feminist Response to Pop Culture*. Magazine/www.bitchmagazine.com

Boyd, Todd (1997) *Am I Black Enough For You? Popular Culture From The 'Hood And Beyond*. Bloomington, IN: Indiana University Press.

*Bust: For Women With Something to Get Off Their Chest*. Magazine/www.bust.com

Butler, Judith (1993) *Bodies That Matter: On the Discursive Limits of 'Sex'*. London: Routledge.

Chow, Rey (1993) *Writing Diaspora: Tactics of Intervention in Contemporary Cultural Studies*. Bloomington, IN: Indiana University Press.

D, Chuck (1997) *Fight the Power: Rap, Race, and Reality*. New York: Dell Publishing.

Driscoll, Catherine (2002) *Girls: Feminine Adolescence in Popular Culture and Cultural Theory*. New York: Columbia University Press.

Dyer, Richard (1997) *White*. London: Routledge.

Ellison, Ralph (1952) *Invisible Man*. New York: Random House.

Fun-da-mental (1994) *Seize the Time*. CD. Beggars Banquet.

Gaspar de Alba, Alicia (ed.) (2003) *Velvet Barrios: Popular Culture & Chicana/o Sexualities*. New York: Palgrave Macmillan.

*Giant Robot: Asian Popular Culture and Beyond*. Magazine/www.giantrobot.com

Gurinder, Chadha (dir.) (2003) *Bend It Like Beckham*. DVD. Twentieth Century Fox Home Video.

Habell-Pallan, Michelle and Romero, Mary (2002) *Latino/a Popular Culture*. New York: New York University Press.

Harper, Phillip Brian (1996) *Are We Not Men? Masculine Anxiety and the Problem of African-American Identity*. New York: Oxford University Press.

Harper, Phillip Brian; McClintock, Anne; Munoz, José Esteban and Rosen, Trish (1997) 'Queer Transexions of Race, Nation, and Gender.' *Social Text*. 52–53 (Fall-Winter).

hooks, bell (1992) *Black Looks: Race and Representation*. Boston, MA: South End Press.

Kelley, Robin D.G. (1994) *Race Rebels: Culture, Politics, and the Black Working Class*. New York: The Free Press.

Kingston, Maxine Hong (1976) *The Woman Warrior: Memoirs of a Childhood Among Ghosts*. New York: Knopf.

Kolko, Beth E., Nakamura, Lisa and Rodman, Gilbert B. (2000) *Race in Cyberspace*. New York: Routledge.

Lee, Robert G. (1999) *Orientals: Asian Americans in Popular Culture*. Philadelphia, PA: Temple University Press.

Leguizamo, John (1993) *Mambo Mouth: A Savage Comedy*. New York: Bantam Books.

Linda Fregoso, Rosa (2003) *Mexicana Encounters: The Making of Social Identities on the Borderlands*. Berkeley, CA: University of California Press.

Maira, Sunaina Marr (2002) *Desis in the House: Indian American Youth Culture in New York*. Philadelphia, PA: Temple University Press.

Mayne, Judith (2000) *Framed: Lesbians, Feminists, and Media Culture*. Minneapolis, MN: University of Minnesota Press.

Moten, Fred (2003) *In the Break: The Aesthetics of the Black Radical Tradition*. Minneapolis, MN: University of Minnesota Press.

Nelson, Alondra (ed.) (2002) 'Afrofuturism'. *Social Text*. 71. Summer 2002.

Riggs, Marlon (1994) *Black Is … Black Ain't*. Videocassette. Independent Television Services.

Straayer, Chris (1996) *Deviant Eyes, Deviant Bodies: Sexual Re-Orientations in Film and Video*. New York: Columbia University Press.

O'Donnell, Damien (1999) *East is East*. Assassin Films, DVD. BBC and Channel Four.

Tatum, Charles M. (2001) *Chicano Popular Culture: Que Hable El Pueblo*. Tucson, AZ: University of Arizona Press.

Thomson, Rosemarie Garland (1997) *Extraordinary Bodies: Figuring Physical Disability in American Culture and Literature*. New York: Columbia University Press.

Turkle, Sherry (1995) *Life on the Screen: Identity in the Age of the Internet*. New York: Simon & Schuster.

Zemeckis, Robert (dir.) (1994) *Forrest Gump*. DVD. Paramount Pictures.

Zuberi, Nabeel (2001) *Sounds English: Transnational Popular Music*. Urbana and Chicago: University of Illinois Press.

# Chapter 24

# Stuart Hall

# What is this 'Black' in Black Popular Culture?

I begin with a question: what sort of moment is this in which to pose the question of black popular culture? These moments are always conjunctural. They have their historical specificity; and although they always exhibit similarities and continuities with the other moments in which we pose a question like this, they are never the same moment. And the combination of what is similar and what is different defines not only the specificity of the moment, but the specificity of the question, and therefore the strategies of cultural politics with which we attempt to intervene in popular culture, and the form and style of cultural theory and criticizing that has to go along with such an intermatch. In his important essay, 'The New Cultural Politics of Difference,'[1] Cornel West offers a genealogy of what this moment is, a genealogy of the present that I find brilliantly concise and insightful. His genealogy follows, to some extent, positions I tried to outline in an article that has become somewhat notorious,[2] but it also usefully maps the moment into an American context and in relation to the cognitive and intellectual philosophical traditions with which it engages.

According to Cornel, the moment, this moment, has three general coordinates. The first is the displacement of European models of high culture, of Europe as the universal subject of culture, and of culture itself in its old Arnoldian reading as the last refuge ... I nearly said of scoundrels, but I won't say who it is of. At least we know who it was against – culture against the barbarians, against the people rattling the gates as the deathless prose of anarchy flowed away from Arnold's pen. The second coordinate is the emergence of the United States as a world power and,

From: *Black Popular Culture*. Ed. Gina Dent. Seattle, WA: Bay Press, 1992.

consequently, as the center of global cultural production and circulation. This emergence is both a displacement and a hegemonic shift in the *definition* of culture – a movement from high culture to American mainstream popular culture and its mass-cultural, image-mediated, technological forms. The third coordinate is the decolonization of the third world, culturally marked by the emergence of the decolonized sensibilities. And I read the decolonization of the third world in Frantz Fanon's sense: I include in it the impact of civil rights and black struggles on the decolonization of the minds of the peoples of the black diaspora.

Let me add some qualifications to that general picture, qualifications that, in my view, make this present moment a very distinctive one in which to ask the question about black popular culture. First, I remind you of the ambiguities of that shift from Europe to America, since it includes America's ambivalent relationship to European high culture and the ambiguity of America's relationship to its own internal ethnic hierarchies. Western Europe did not have, until recently, any ethnicity at all. Or didn't recognize it had any. America has always had a series of ethnicities, and consequently, the construction of ethnic hierarchies has always defined its cultural politics. And, of course, silenced and unacknowledged, the fact of American popular culture itself, which has always contained within it, whether silenced or not, black American popular vernacular traditions. It may be hard to remember that, when viewed from outside of the United States, American mainstream popular culture has always involved certain traditions that could only be attributed to black cultural vernacular traditions.

The second qualification concerns the nature of the period of cultural globalization in progress now. I hate the term 'the global postmodern,' so empty and sliding a signifier that it can be taken to mean virtually anything you like. And, certainly, blacks are as ambiguously placed in relation to postmodernism as they were in relation to high modernism: even when denuded of its wide-European, disenchanted Marxist, French intellectual provenance and scaled down to a more modest descriptive status, postmodernism remains extremely unevenly developed as a phenomenon in which the old center/peripheries of high modernity consistently reappear. The only places where one can genuinely experience the postmodern ethnic cuisine are Manhattan and London, not Calcutta. And yet it is impossible to refuse 'the global postmodern' entirely, insofar as it registers certain stylistic shifts in what I want to call the cultural dominant. Even if postmodernism is not a new cultural epoch, but only modernism in the streets, that, in itself, represents an important shifting of the terrain of culture toward the popular – toward popular practices, toward everyday practices, toward local narratives, toward the decentering of old hierarchies and the grand narratives. This decentering or displacement opens up new spaces of contestation and affects a momentous shift in the high culture of popular culture relations, thus presenting us with a strategic and important opportunity for intervention in the popular cultural field.

Third, we must bear in mind postmodernism's deep and ambivalent fascination with difference – sexual difference, cultural difference, racial difference, and above all, ethnic difference. Quite in opposition to the blindness and hostility that European high culture evidenced on the whole toward ethnic difference – its inability even to speak ethnicity when it was so manifestly registering its effects – there's nothing that global postmodernism loves better than a certain kind of difference: a touch of ethnicity, a taste of the exotic, as we say in England, 'a bit of the other' (which in the United Kingdom has a sexual as well as an ethnic connotation). Michele Wallace was quite right, in her seminal easay 'Modernism, Postmodernism and the Problem of the Visual in Afro-American Culture,'[3] to ask whether this reappearance of a proliferation of difference, of a certain kind of ascent of the global postmodern, isn't a repeat of that 'now you see it, now you don't' game that modernism once played with primitivism, to ask whether it is not once again achieved at the expense of the vast silencing about the West's fascination with the bodies of black men and women of other ethnicities. And we must ask about that continuing silence within postmodernism's shifting terrain, about whether the forms of licensing of the gaze that this proliferation of difference invites and allows, at the same time as it disavows, is not really, along with Benetton and the mixed male models of the face, a kind of difference that doesn't make a difference of any kind.

Hal Foster writes – Wallace quotes him in her essay – 'the primitive is a modern problem, a crisis in cultural identity'[4] – hence, the modernist construction of primitivism, the fetishistic recognition and disavowal of the primitive difference. But this resolution is only a repression; delayed into our political unconscious, the primitive returns uncannily at the moment of its apparent political eclipse. This rupture of primitivism, managed by modernism, becomes another postmodern event. That managing is certainly evident in the difference that may not make a difference, which marks the ambiguous appearance of ethnicity at the heart of global postmodernism. But it cannot be only that. For we cannot forget how cultural life, above all in the West, but elsewhere as well, has been transformed in our lifetimes by the voicing of the margins.

Within culture, marginality, though it remains peripheral to the broader mainstream, has never been such a productive space as it is now. And that is not simply the opening within the dominant of spaces that those outside it can occupy. It is also the result of the cultural politics of difference, of the struggles around difference, of the production of new identities, of the appearance of new subjects on the political and cultural stage. This is true not only in regard to race, but also for other marginalized ethnicities, as well as around feminism and around sexual politics in the gay and lesbian movement, as a result of a new kind of cultural politics. Of course, I don't want to suggest that we can counterpose some easy sense of victories won to the eternal story of our own marginalization – I'm tired of those two continuous grand counternarratives. To remain within them is to become trapped in that endless either/or, either total victory or total incorporation, which almost never happens in cultural politics, but with which cultural critics always put themselves to bed.

What we are talking about is the struggle over cultural hegemony, which is these days waged as much in popular culture as anywhere else. That high/popular distinction is precisely what the global postmodern is displacing. Cultural hegemony is never about pure victory or pure domination (that's not what the term means); it is never a zero-sum cultural game; it is always about shifting the balance of power in the relations of culture; it is always about changing the dispositions and the configurations of cultural power, not getting out of it. There is a kind of 'nothing ever changes, the system always wins' attitude, which I read as the cynical protective shell that, I'm sorry to say, American cutural critics frequently wear, a shell that sometimes prevents them from developing cultural strategies that can make a difference. It is as if, in order to protect themselves against the occasional defeat, they have to pretend they can see right through everything – and it's just the same as it always was.

Now, cultural strategies that can make a difference, that's what I'm interested in – those that can make a difference and can shift the dispositions of power. I acknowledge that the spaces 'won' for difference are few and far between, that they are very carefully policed and regulated. I believe they are limited. I know, to my cost, that they are grossly underfunded, that there is always a price of incorporation to be paid when the cutting edge of difference and transgression is blunted into spectacularization. I know that what replaces invisibility is a kind of carefully regulated, segregated visibility. But it does not help simply to name-call it 'the same.' That name-calling merely reflects the particular model of cultural politics to which we remain attached, precisely, the zero-sum game – our model replacing their model, our identities in place of their identities – what Antonio Gramsci called culture as a once and for all 'war of maneuver,' when, in fact, the only game in town worth playing is the game of cultural 'wars of position.'

Lest you think, to paraphrase Gramsci, my optimism of the will has now completely outstripped my pessimism of the intellect, let me add a fourth element that comments on the moment. For, if the global postmodern represents an ambiguous opening to difference and to the margins and makes a certain kind of decentering of the Western narrative a likely possibility, it is matched, from the very heartland of cultural politics, by the backlash: the aggressive resistance to difference; the attempt to restore the canon of Western civilization; the assault, direct and indirect, on multiculturalism; the return to grand narratives of history, language, and literature (the three great supporting pillars of national identity and national culture); the defense of ethnic absolutism, of a cultural racism that has marked the Thatcher and the Reagan eras; and the new xenophobias that are about to overwhelm fortress Europe. The last thing to do is read me as saying the cultural dialectic is finished. Part of the problem is that we have forgotten what sort of space the space of popular culture is. And black popular culture is not exempt from that dialectic, which is historical, not a matter of bad faith. It is therefore necessary to deconstruct the popular once and for all. There is no going back to an innocent view of what it consists of.

Popular culture carries that affirmative ring because of the prominence of the word 'popular.' And, in one sense, popular culture always has its base in the experiences, the pleasures, the memories, the traditions of the people. It has connections with local hopes and local aspirations, local tragedies and local scenarios that are the everyday practices and the everyday experiences of ordinary folks. Hence, it links with what Mikhail Bakhtin calls 'the vulgar' – the popular, the informal, the underside, the grotesque. That is why it has always been counterposed to elite or high culture, and is thus a site of alternative traditions. And that is why the dominant tradition has always been deeply suspicious of it, quite rightly. They suspect that they are about to be overtaken by what Bakhtin calls 'the carnivalesque.' This fundamental mapping of culture between the high and the low has been charted into four symbolic domains by Peter Stallybrass and Allon White in their important book *The Politics and Poetics of Transgression.* They talk about the mapping of high and low in psychic forms, in the human body, in space, and in the social order.[5] And they discuss the high/low distinction as a fundamental basis to the mechanisms of ordering and of sense-making in European and other cultures despite the fact that the contents of what is high and what is low change from one historical moment to another.

The important point is the ordering of different aesthetic morals, social aesthetics, the orderings of culture that open up culture to the play of power, not an inventory of what is high versus what is low at any particular moment. That is why Gramsci, who has a side of common sense on which, above all, cultural hegemony is made, lost, and struggled over, gave the question of what he called 'the national popular' such strategic importance. The role of the 'popular' in popular culture is to fix the authenticity of popular forms, rooting them in the experiences of popular communities from which they draw their strength, allowing us to see them as expressive of a particular subordinate social life that resists its being constantly made over as low and outside.

However, as popular culture has historically become the dominant form of global culture, so it is at the same time the scene, par excellence, of commodification, of the industries where culture enters directly into the circuits of a dominant technology – the circuits of power and capital. It is the space of homogenization where stereotyping and the formulaic mercilessly process the material and experiences it draws into its web, where control over narratives and representations passes into the hands of the established cultural bureaucracies, sometimes without a murmur. It is rooted in popular experience and available for expropriation at one and the same time. I want to argue that this is necessarily and inevitably so. And this goes for black popular culture as well. Black popular culture, like all popular cultures in the modern world, is bound to be contradictory, and this is not because we haven't fought the cultural battle well enough.

By definition, black popular culture is a contradictory space. It is a sight of strategic contestation. But it can never be simplified or explained in terms of the simple binary oppositions that are still habitually used to map it out: high and low; resistance versus incorporation; authentic versus inauthentic; experiential versus formal; opposition versus homogenization. There are always positions to be won in popular culture, but no struggle can capture popular culture itself for our side or theirs. Why is that so? What consequences does this have for strategies of intervention in cultural politics? How does it shift the basis for black cultural criticism?

However deformed, incorporated, and inauthentic are the forms in which black people and black communities and traditions appear and are represented in popular culture, we continue to see, in the figures and the repertoires on which popular culture draws, the experiences that stand behind them. In its expressivity, its musicality, its orality, in its rich, deep, and varied attention to speech, in its inflections toward the vernacular and the local, in its rich production of counternarratives, and above all, in its metaphorical use of the musical vocabulary, black popular culture has enabled the surfacing, inside the mixed and contradictory modes even of some mainstream popular culture, of elements of a discourse that is different – other forms of life, other traditions of representation.

I do not propose to repeat the work of those who have devoted their scholarly, critical, and creative lives to identifying the distinctiveness of these diasporic traditions, to exploring their modes and the historical experiences and memories they encode. I say only three inadequate things about these traditions, since they are germane to the point I want to develop. First, I ask you to note how, within the black repertoire, *style* – which mainstream cultural critics often believe to be the mere husk, the wrapping, the sugar coating on the pill – has become *itself the* subject of what is going on. Second, mark how, displaced from a logocentric world – where the direct mastery of cultural modes meant the mastery of writing, and hence, both of the criticism of writing (logocentric criticism) and the deconstruction of writing – the people of the black diaspora have, in opposition to all of that, found the deep form, the deep structure of their cultural life in music. Third, think of how these cultures have used the body – as if it was, and it often was, the only cultural capital we had. We have worked on ourselves as the canvases of representation.

There are deep questions here of cultural transmission and inheritance, and of the complex relations between African origins and the irreversible scatterings of the diaspora, questions I cannot go into. But I do believe that these repertoires of black popular culture, which, since we were excluded from the cultural mainstream, were often the only performative spaces we had left, were overdetermined from at least two directions: they were partly determined from their inheritances; but they were also critically determined by the diasporic conditions in which the connections were forged. Selective appropriation, incorporation, and rearticulation of European ideologies, cultures, and institutions, alongside an African heritage – this is Cornel West again – led to linguistic innovations in rhetorical stylization of the body, forms of occupying an alien social space, heightened expressions, hairstyles, ways of walking, standing, and talking, and a means of constituting and sustaining camaraderie and community.

The point of underlying overdetermination – black cultural repertoires constituted from two directions at once – is perhaps more subversive than you think. It is to insist that in black popular culture, strictly speaking, ethnographically speaking, there are no pure forms at all. Always these forms are the product of partial synchronization, of engagement across cultural boundaries, of the confluence of more than one cultural tradition, of the negotiations of dominant and subordinate positions, of the subterranean strategies of recoding and transcoding, of critical signification, of signifying. Always these forms are impure, to some degree hybridized from a vernacular base. Thus, they must always be heard, not simply as the recovery of a lost dialogue bearing clues for the production of new musics (because there is never any going back to the old in a simple way), but as what they are – adaptations, molded to the mixed, contradictory, hybrid spaces of popular culture. They are not the recovery of something pure that we can, at last, live by. In what Kobena Mercer calls the necessity for a diaspora aesthetic, we are obliged to acknowledge they are what the modern is.

It is this mark of difference *inside* forms of popular culture – which are by definition contradictory and which therefore appear as impure, threatened by incorporation or exclusion – that is carried by the signifier 'black' in the term 'black popular culture.' It has come to signify the black community, where these traditions were kept, and whose struggles survive in the persistence of the black experience (the historical experience of black people in the diaspora), of the black aesthetic (the distinctive cultural repertoires out of which popular representations were made), and of the black counternarratives we have struggled to voice. Here, black popular culture returns to the ground I defined earlier. 'Good' black popular culture can pass the test of authenticity – the reference to black experience and to black expressivity. These serve as the guarantees in the determination of which black popular culture is right on, which is ours and which is not.

I have the feeling that, historically, nothing could have been done to intervene in the dominated field of mainstream popular culture, to try to win some space there, without the strategies through which those dimensions were condensed onto the signifier 'black.' Where would we be, as bell hooks once remarked, without a touch of essentialism? Or, what Gayatri Spivak calls strategic essentialism, a necessary moment? The question is whether we are any longer in that moment, whether that is still a sufficient basis for the strategies of new interventions. Let me try to set forth what seem to me to be the weaknesses of this essentializing moment and the strategies, creative and critical, that flow from it.

This moment essentializes differences in several senses. It sees difference as 'their traditions versus ours,' not in a positional way, but in a mutually exclusive, autonomous, and self-sufficient one. And it is therefore unable to grasp the dialogic strategies and hybrid forms essential to the diaspora aesthetic. A movement beyond this essentialism is not an aesthetic or critical strategy without a cultural politics, without a marking of difference. It is not simply rearticulation and reappropriation for the sake of it. What it evades is the essentializing of difference into two mutually opposed either/or's. What it does is to move us into a new kind of cultural positionality, a different logic of difference. To encapsulate what Paul Gilroy has so vividly put on the political and cultural agenda of black politics in the United Kingdom: blacks in the British diaspora must, at this historical moment, refuse the binary black *or* British. They must refuse it because the 'or' remains the sight of *constant contestation* when the aim of the struggle must be, instead, to replace the 'or' with the potentiality or the possibility of an 'and.' That is the logic of coupling rather than the logic of a binary opposition. You can be black *and* British, not only because that is a necessary position to take in 1992, but because even those two terms, joined now by the coupler 'and' instead of opposed to one another, do not exhaust all of our identities. Only some of our identities are sometimes caught in that particular struggle.

The essentializing moment is weak because it naturalizes and dehistoricizes difference, mistaking what is historical and cultural for what is natural, biological, and genetic. The moment the signifier 'black' is torn from its historical, cultural, and political embedding and lodged in a biologically constituted racial category, we valorize, by inversion, the very ground of the racism we are trying to deconstruct. In addition, as always happens when we naturalize historical categories (think about gender and sexuality), we fix that signifier outside of history, outside of change, outside of political intervention. And once it is fixed, we are tempted to use 'black' as sufficient in itself to guarantee the progressive character of the politics we fight under the banner – as if we don't have any other politics to argue about except whether something's black or not. We are tempted to display that signifier as a device which can purify the impure, bring the straying brothers and sisters who don't know what they ought to be doing into line, and police the boundaries – which are of course political, symbolic, and positional boundaries – as if they were genetic. For which, I'm sorry to say, read 'jungle fever' – as if we can translate from nature to politics using a racial category to warrant the politics of a cultural text and as a line against which to measure deviation.

Moreover, we tend to privilege experience itself, as if black life is lived experience outside of representation. We have only, as it were, to express what we already know we are. Instead, it is only through the way in which we represent and imagine ourselves that we come to know how we are constituted and who we are. There is no escape from the politics of representation, and we cannot wield 'how life really is out there' as a kind of test against which the political rightness or wrongness of a particular cultural strategy or text can be measured. It will not be a mystery to you that I think that 'black' is none of these things in reality. It is not a category of essence and, hence, this way of understanding the floating signifier in black popular culture now will not do.

There is, of course, a very profound set of distinctive, historically defined black experiences that contribute to those alternative repertoires I spoke about earlier. But it is to the diversity, not the homogeneity, of black experience that we must now give our undivided creative attention. This is not simply to appreciate the historical and experiential differences within and between communities, regions, country and city, across national cultures, between diasporas, but also to recognize the other kinds of difference that place, position, and locate black people. The point is not simply that, since our racial differences do not constitute all of us, we are always different, negotiating different kinds of differences – of gender, of sexuality, of class. It is also that these antagonisms refuse to be neatly aligned; they are simply not reducible to one another; they refuse to coalesce around a single axis of differentiation. We are always in negotiation, not with a single set of oppositions that place us always in the same relation to others, but with a series of different positionalities. Each has for us its point of profound subjective identification. And that is the most difficult thing about this proliferation of the field of identities and antagonisms: they are often dislocating in relation to one another.

Thus, to put it crudely, certain ways in which black men continue to live out their counter-identities as black masculinities and replay those fantasies of black masculinities in the theaters of popular culture are, when viewed from along other axes of difference, the very masculine identities that are oppressive to women, that claim visibility for their hardness only at the expense of the vulnerability of black women and the feminization of gay black men. The way in which a transgressive politics in one domain is constantly sutured and stabilized by reactionary or unexamined politics in another is only to be explained by this continuous cross-dislocation of one identity by another, one structure by another. Dominant ethnicities are always underpinned by a particular sexual economy, a particular figured masculinity, a particular class identity. There is no guarantee, in reaching for an essentialized racial identity of which we think we can be certain, that it will always turn out to be mutually liberating and progressive on all the other dimensions. It *can* be won. There *is* a politics there to be struggled for. But the invocation of a guaranteed black experience behind it will not produce that politics. Indeed, the plurality of antagonisms and differences that now seek to destroy the unity of black politics, given the complexities of the structures of subordination that have been formed by the way in which we were inserted into the black diaspora, is not at all surprising.

These are the thoughts that drove me to speak, in an unguarded moment, of the end of the innocence of the black subject or the end of the innocent notion of an essential black subject. And I want to end simply by reminding you that this end is also a beginning. As Isaac Julien said in an interview with bell hooks in which they discussed his new film *Young Soul Rebels*, his attempt in his own work to portray a number of different racial bodies, to constitute a range of different black subjectivities, and to engage with the positionalities of a number of different kinds of black masculinities:

> ... blackness as a sign is never enough. What does that black subject do, how does it act, how does it think politically ... being black isn't really good enough for me: I want to know what your cultural politics are.[6]

I want to end with two thoughts that take that point back to the subject of popular culture. The first is to remind you that popular culture, commodified and stereotyped as it often is, is not at all, as we sometimes think of it, the arena where we find who we really are, the truth of our experience. It is an arena that is *profoundly* mythic. It is a theater of popular desires, a theater of popular fantasies. It is where we discover and play with the identifications of ourselves, where we are imagined, where we are represented, not only to the audiences out there who do not get the message, but to ourselves for the first time. As Freud said, sex (and representation) mainly takes place in the head. Second, though the terrain of the popular looks as if it is constructed with single binaries, it is not. I reminded you about the importance of the structuring of cultural space in terms of high and low, and the threat of the Bakhtinian carnivalesque. I think Bakhtin has been profoundly misread. The carnivalesque is not simply an upturning of two things which remain locked within their oppositional frameworks; it is also crosscut by what Bakhtin calls the dialogic.

I simply want to end with an account of what is involved in understanding popular culture, in a dialogic rather than in a strictly oppositional way, from *The Politics and Poetics of Transgression* by Stallybrass and White:

> A recurrent pattern emerges: the 'top' attempts to reject and eliminate the 'bottom' for reasons of prestige and status, only to discover, not only that it is in some way frequently dependent upon the low-Other ... but also that the top *includes* that low symbolically, as a primary eroticized constituent of its own fantasy life. The result is a mobile, conflictual fusion of power, fear, and desire in the construction of subjectivity: a psychological dependence upon precisely those others which are being rigorously opposed and excluded at the social level. It is for this reason that what is socially peripheral is so frequently *symbolically* central ...[7]

## Notes

1. Cornel West, 'The New Cultural Politics of Difference,' in *Out There: Marginalization and Contemporary Cultures*, ed. Russell Ferguson, et al. (Cambridge: MIT Press in association with the New Museum of Contemporary Art, 1990), 19–36.

2. Stuart Hall, 'New Ethnicities,' *Black Film/British Cinema, ICA Document 7*, ed. Kobena Mercer (London: Institute of Contemporary Arts, 1988), 27–31.

3. Michele Wallace, 'Modernism, Postmodernism and the Problem of the Visual in Afro-American Culture,' in *Out There: Marginalization and Contemporary Cultures,* 39–50.

4. Hal Foster, *Recodings: Art, Spectacle, and Cultural Politics* (Port Townsend, Wash.: Bay Press, 1985), 204.

5. Peter Stallybrass and Allon White, *The Politics and Poetics of Transgression* (Ithaca: Cornell University Press, 1986), 3.

6. bell hooks. 'States of Desire' (interview with Issac Julien), *Transition* 1, no. 3, 175.

7. Stallybrass and White, *The Politics and Poetics of Transgression*, 5.

# Chapter 25

# Gayatri Gopinath

# 'Bombay, UK, Yuba City': Bhangra Music and the Engendering of Diaspora

> We must return to the point from which we started ... Not a return to the longing for origins, to some immutable state of Being, but a return to the point of entanglement from which we were forcefully turned away.
>
> Edouard Glissant, *Caribbean Discourse*

> [P]opular culture, commodified and stereotyped as it often is ... is an arena that is profoundly *mythic*. ... It is where we discover and play with the identifications of ourselves, where we are imagined, where we are represented, not only to the audiences out there who do not get the message, but to ourselves for the first time.
>
> Stuart Hall, 'What Is This "Black" in Black Popular Culture?'

In his 1992 song, 'Mera Laung Gawacha,' British Indian deejay and record producer Bally Sagoo mixes the voice of Rama, a female, British-based Indian folksinger, with that of Cheshire Cat, a male dance-hall rapper who (judging by his appearance on the compact-disc jacket) reads visually as white. Rama sings a traditional folk song from the North Western Indian state of Punjab, while Cheshire Cat provides the song with its raggamuffin beat, making it eminently danceable. The voices – one in Punjabi, the other in Jamaican patois – together narrate a multilingual, interracial tale of heterosexual desire. Yet the song eludes an easy reading as a utopian narrative of cultural, racial, and sexual harmony: it remains unclear

From: Gayatri Gopinath, '"Bombay, UK, Yuba City": Bhangra Music and the Engendering of Diaspora', *Diaspora* 4.3, 1995.

whether the male and female voices are actually singing to each other, an ambiguity underscored by the song's video, in which Rama and the rapper never share the same frame. Indeed, the video depicts Cheshire Cat as a black man with dread-locks, which suggests that it is not entirely acceptable for a (presumably) white man to do raggamuffin, particularly when it is a South Asian (Sagoo) who is employ-ing him. The separate framing of the two singers also implies that it is not entirely acceptable to have the black man explicitly address sexually suggestive lyrics to an older South Asian woman. In addition, Rama appears sedately dressed in tra-ditional Punjabi attire, while the Cheshire Cat stand-in provides all the movement in the video and acts as its visual focus.

I offer this cursory reading of 'Mera Laung Gawacha' here because the song seems to exemplify the complex negotiation of race, nation, gender, and sexual-ity undertaken by the South Asian popular music known as bhangra. Through a reading of bhangra as a particular diasporic cultural formation, I would like, in this essay, to examine both the potentialities and limits of diaspora as a theoreti-cal framework. What does diaspora reveal, hide, or privilege? What are the pos-sibilities it opens up or precludes? How do gender and sexuality play out in diasporic articulations of community, culture, and ethnicity? Tracing the dynamic and dialogic movement of bhangra between India and Britain (as well as North America and the Caribbean) enables a critical engagement with these questions, while simultaneously challenging the linear narrative of exile and return that has dominated conventional diasporic thinking.

Reading bhangra as a diasporic text allows for a far more complicated under-standing of diaspora, in that *it demands a radical reworking of the hierarchical relation between diaspora and the nation.* Bhangra, a transnational performance of culture and community, reveals the processes by which *multiple* diasporas inter-sect both with one another and with the national spaces that they are continuously negotiating and challenging. The diasporic web of 'affiliation and affect' (Gilroy, *Black Atlantic* 16) that bhangra calls into being within and across various national contexts displaces the 'home' country from its privileged position as originary site and redeploys it as but one of many diasporic locations. Similarly, bhangra's incor-poration into the nation in its transformed and transformative state refigures, to a certain extent, the very terms by which the nation is constituted. In this sense, an analysis of bhangra demands not only that diaspora be seen as part of the nation but that the nation be rethought as part of the diaspora as well.

Clearly, diasporic popular cultural forms such as bhangra are always many texts at once; they are never purely enabling, resistant, or celebratory, but are simulta-neously available to recuperation within hegemonic constructions of identity, cul-ture, and community. The instance at which bhangra most clearly reconsolidates such constructions is [...] in its deployment of gender and sexuality. It is here that the 'poetics of place' (Lipsitz 3) articulated by bhangra intersects, I suggest, with the gender ideologies constitutive of contemporary nationalist discourses. Of course, bhangra as a multivalenced text resists being read as purely patriarchal or sexist, yet it remains possible to identify certain dominant notions of gender and sexuality that surface in much of the music. As such, bhangra makes apparent the difficulty in thinking diaspora outside of a patrilineal, genealogical economy that even the most useful work in diasporic thinking (such as that of cultural theorist Paul Gilroy) tends to replicate.

## 1. Diaspora in Black and White

Any project that concerns itself with ethnicity, identity, and transnational cultural movements, as does this one, is necessarily informed by, and finds itself in dialogue with, the remarkably influential broad-ranging texts of Gilroy. Gilroy's intervention into theorizations of diaspora, particularly in his formulation of the 'black Atlantic,' has radically transformed the ways in which the transnational politics of culture, community, and place are understood. Yet the limits of diaspora as a theoretical framework also become apparent in Gilroy's work and are signaled by his inability to fully write Asians into his discourse of cultural production, as well as by his elision of gender at key instances in his argument. On the one hand, Gilroy is explicitly concerned with recuperating various histories and traditions left outside traditional narratives of race and cultural production, and in overcoming the ethnic absolutism and homogeneous, unitary conceptions of 'black' 'white' that he correctly identifies as characteristic of cultural studies models of race and cultural identity. Yet in so doing, he reinscribes within his own discourse the black/and white binary that he attempts to write against.[1]

One example of such binary logic is Gilroy's failure to engage with the implications of an Asian cultural presence in Britain and how such a presence impacts on his conceptualizations of 'race,' cultural production, and black Atlantic diaspora. Gilroy does mention in passing the ways in which an Asian youth culture in Britain has drawn upon black diasporic cultural forms such as hip hop (*There Ain't No Black* 217) and reggae (*Black Atlantic* 82) as a way of transforming and recreating 'Asian' identity. Yet he fails to address how this borrowing of Afro-Caribbean musical idioms not only refigures 'Asianness' but also, in the process, inevitably reconstitutes the black diasporic culture from which it draws. Gilroy's brief comments on Asian cultural production also ignore the ways in which Asian youth in Britain draw from their own constructed diaspora in their recreation of ethnic identity. Within such a framework, a dialogic relationship between the histories and cultural practices of Afro-Caribbean and Asian diasporic communities is not allowed for or recognized. While Gilroy is interested in exposing the untenability of black/white binary, he is unable, in his conflation of 'black' as nonwhite with 'black' as of African descent, to extricate himself from it; this is still the axis along and against which he works. Such a shoring up of the African diaspora as *the* paradigm for critiquing the nation-state, then, does not account for the simultaneous functionings and overlappings of multiple diasporas.[2]

I am not simply interested here in revealing the ways in which Gilroy's narrative is an exclusionary one; rather, I am suggesting that his elision of Asian diasporic cultural production is significant in that it points to a central limitation in dominant articulations of diaspora. If one critical flaw within these dominant models rests upon their reliance on a black/white binary, the other hinges upon the ways in which gender and sexuality are deployed within these formulations; inevitably, diaspora comes to be conceptualized in terms of patrilineality and organic heterosexuality. It may be helpful here to focus briefly on the roots of the term *diaspora,* in order to examine the naturalization of heterosexuality within diaspora. As Stefan Helmreich points out:

> The original meaning of diaspora summons up the image of scattered seeds and ...
> in Judeo-Christian ... cosmology, seeds are metaphorical for the male 'substance'

> that is traced in genealogical histories. The word 'sperm' is metaphorically linked to diaspora. It comes from the same stem [in Greek meaning to sow or scatter] and is defined by the OED as 'the generative substance or seed of male animals.' Diaspora, in its traditional sense, thus refers us to a system of kinship reckoned through men and suggests the questions of legitimacy in paternity that patriarchy generates. (245)

In light of these etymological roots of *diaspora*, Gilroy's notion of a 'residual inheritance' of Africa *(Black Atlantic* 81) upon which the 'common sensibilities' that constitute diaspora are in part based becomes a particularly troubling one, in that it seems to gesture toward a certain patrilineal system that effectively normalizes heterosexuality while erasing women or rendering them visible only as reproducers (rather than producers) of community. The dangers of positing certain notions of genealogy and patrilineality as the underlying logic of diaspora are particularly evident when considering the sites of cultural syncretism that are privileged in the production of diasporic culture. Gilroy, for instance, determines these sites to be the deejay's turntable and the ship,[3] both of which were and to a large extent still are spaces historically inaccessible to women (see Helmreich 245); access, or the lack of access, to these spaces of travel and cultural production constitutes diaspora in a deeply gendered way. This continued reliance on a genealogical model of diaspora is what in fact necessitates the elision of other genealogies. My project, conversely, attempts to foreground alternative notions of diaspora, while paying particular attention to the various forms of popular cultural practices by which they are produced.

## 2. 'Asian Music for Asians': Bhangra and the Performance of Community

It is precisely the effacement of 'other' genealogies that a consideration of bhangra music attempts to redress. Reading bhangra as a signifying practice of South Asian popular culture foregrounds the impossibility of thinking diaspora in the singular and instead demands that it be conceptualized as always multiply constituted, at the juncture of various cultural, racial, and political histories. Bhangra, as I shall discuss, offers a way out of a *scopic* economy of racial difference, one that relies on color as an easily intelligible signifier – and instead creates and works within a *spatial* economy, one that posits an alternative geography and relation to place. However, by reading diaspora through bhangra, I am not claiming the latter as a unitary subject around which a totalizing narrative can be constructed. Rather, 'bhangra' as such must be read as inhabiting multiple positions both *within* a particular local context and *across* local contexts and the diasporic web of identity it creates through the networks of transnational capital. I hope to focus, within the confines of this essay, on bhangra in a primarily British context, while referencing its multiple, simultaneous functionings elsewhere.

Bhangra, originally a male form of rural folk music and dance from the Punjab (where it is still performed), was brought to Britain by Punjabi immigrants in the 1950s and 1960s.[4] It became an important cultural marker of Punjabi communities in London, Manchester, Birmingham, and other cities with large numbers of Punjabi immigrants, where bhangra musicians were (and continue to be) a staple at weddings, religious celebrations (Hindu, Muslim, and Sikh), and other social functions.[5] Bhangra, until the late 1970s, was inaudible outside the confines of working-class South Asian communities in various British cities. At this time, bhangra groups began altering the music through their use of sampling, drum machines and synthesizers. By the mid-1980s, bhangra had become enormously popular among young, British-born South Asians and was the primary form of South Asian youth cultural production, one that was seen to cut across lines of religion, class, language, and nationality.[6] During its height in the late 1980s, bhangra concerts in London and other cities attracted thousands of young South Asians, often for day-long celebrations. More recently, bhangra has become increasingly syncretic through its incorporation of other genres, such as reggae, rap, techno, and house. Indeed, many younger South Asian performers are now foregrounding these other genres, singing in English instead of Punjabi, and referencing bhangra as just one out of many influences. In the past several years, bhangra has become the locus of a diasporic South Asian youth culture, with young South Asians outside of Britain adapting British bhangra to their own local contexts of Toronto, Vancouver, Port-of-Spain, New York, Delhi, and Bombay. Bhangra can be read within its multiple sites of production as a tremendously celebratory 'affirmation of particularity' (Gilroy's phrase) that, as I shall discuss below, always avows the constructedness of that particularity.

I would like to posit bhangra as functioning within and interpellating a South Asian diaspora in a way that both mimes and displaces dominant ideologies of community and identity, nation and homeland. Judith Butler's conceptualizations of performativity and parodic repetition are particularly helpful in looking at how bhangra, as both a literal and metaphorical performance of community, continually undermines a notion of a unitary subject even while asserting its existence. As Butler states:

> According to the understanding of identification as an enacted fantasy or incorporation ... it is clear that coherence is desired, wished for, idealized, and that this idealization is an effect of a corporeal signification. ... [A]cts, gestures, enactments generally construed, are *performative* in the sense that the essence or identity that they otherwise purport to express are *fabrications* manufactured and sustained through corporeal signs and other discursive means. (*Gender Trouble* 136)

Bhangra can be read in part as a response to the pressure to perform a coherent, stable, and essential ethnic identity in the face of white racism, as well as the elision of South Asians within a binary racial discourse of black and white. The early practitioners of bhangra in Britain in the late 1970s and early 1980s were mostly middle-aged, first-generation, male Punjabi immigrants from India, Pakistan, and the South Asian diasporic communities of East Africa, who very consciously saw the music as a means of constructing a shared notion of 'Asianness' that explicitly cut across lines of religion, caste, class, and nationality. Kuljit Bhamra, one of the first producers of bhangra in Britain, states:

> I think people maybe felt the need to identify themselves, and in order to do that a medium was needed, and that medium is bhangra. There is always this roots feeling, and people will always want to know where they came from: we are a different colour, we are from a different country originally, so where do we fit in? The Southall riots [of 1979 and 1981] made me aware of this as they did others. ... Prejudice exists

within societies, within cultures, but the whole of the Asian society is taking part in bhangra because there is always this need for a roots feeling. ... There is really a need to stay together and be amongst your own owing to racism, and bhangra music has provided [for] that need. (qtd. in Baumann 91)[7]

Komal, another early bhangra artist of the east London group Cobra, comments:

I can remember going to discos a long time ago, when all you heard was reggae, reggae, reggae. Asians were lost, they weren't accepted by whites, they drifted into the black culture, dressing like blacks, talking like them, and listening to reggae. But now bhangra has given them 'their' music and made them feel that they do have an identity. No matter if they are Gujarati, Punjabi, or whatever – Bhangra is Asian music for Asians. (qtd. in Baumann 91)[8]

What is striking in these statements by first-generation bhangra musicians is an overwhelming sense of 'being lost,' (dis)located within a scopic economy of black and white, in which as Asians they were rendered unintelligible. They could not be made sense of or read coherently as racially marked subjects, and were thus threatened with absolute effacement and erasure. Bhangra, to these early practitioners, while presenting a 'united front' in the face of a majority community through an assertion of ethnic particularity, was also seen as a strategic tool with which to transmit tradition and heritage to a younger generation. This is made explicit in the following comment by Channi, the lead singer of Alaap, the first group to popularize bhangra in South Asian British communities in the late 1970s: 'We noticed that young Punjabis in London knew little about their own culture and language and were immersed in the English disco scene. We started our bhangra songs to bring them back into their own culture. But for the music to appeal to them, we had to add the Western touch with a drum beat and synthesizers' (*Guardian Weekend Page* 13 Mar. 1993: 32). Bhangra, then, can be read as performing a certain notion of 'community' as one capable of being reproduced through the preservation of an essential and unmediated 'heritage' or 'culture.' Yet even while bhangra was being used as a way of positing a shared, essential identity, the radical impossibility of that identity was always being referenced by its very form: bhangra songs that 'add the Western touch,' for instance, inevitably involve an alteration of the 'culture' that they are supposedly only deploying strategically. In other words, these statements are enunciations of loss, of a yearning and longing to recover and recuperate that which is also simultaneously and implicitly acknowledged to be irrecoverable and irrecuperable.

## 3. Lost Homelands and the Fantasmatic Female

The figure of the woman is critical to the constitution of the 'heritage' or 'culture' to be transmitted through bhangra, as is evident in some of the lyrics and videos produced by first-generation bhangra musicians. Malkit Singh, for instance, one of the most established Punjabi folksingers in Britain, sings in his video 'My Golden Land':

Last night I had a dream about my homeland, my Punjab,
About the fields and the rivers,

the free play of a hybrid identity but rather as a creative response to the demand for coherence and stability within specific racial and cultural contexts, a means by which to 'work the trap that one is inevitably in' ('The Body You Want' 84).

Bhangra's functioning as a diasporic phenomenon further exposes 'origin' as performance, through which 'India' is radically displaced from its privileged position as mythic homeland and originary site. The tremendous popularity of British-Asian artists in India – Apache Indian in particular – demands that 'India' be written into the diaspora as yet another diasporic location, rather than remaining a signifier of an original, essentialized identity around which a diasporic network is constructed and to which it always refers. A reading of bhangra as a diasporic cultural practice, then, offers a new model of the place of the nation in diaspora: not only is the nation part of the diaspora, but the diaspora becomes (part of) the nation.

The displacement of 'India' as the point to which diaspora constantly refers is also brought about when bhangra is claimed by both its producers and consumers as a self-consciously British music. As such, bhangra acts as a means of asserting membership and locating a space within the national culture, thereby disrupting and redefining the very nature of that culture. In the elision of the boundaries of the nation-state that is allowed for through bhangra's referencing and construction of Asian and Afro-Caribbean diasporas, 'Britishness' as such is forced to resignify. Apache Indian, for instance, asserts that his own music 'happened effortlessly, because it's a combination of reggae from the streets, Indian music and the language at home, pop because of the country I grew up in. It's a very British music' (qtd. in McCann 18). The claiming of 'Britishness' through an assertion of difference and particularity again performs the move of categorically removing 'India' as a site of origination, redemptive return, or nostalgia, which again demands that the nation be read as part of the diaspora, rather than as separate from it. As one British-Asian music critic makes explicit: 'As more and more of this music is being made ... we are truly making Britain a home and not just a stop-over until we all go back to our grand-parents' villages' (Dhammi 28).

The processes by which bhangra allows for a refiguring of the relation of diaspora and nation can be traced in a video of Apache's concert in Delhi in June 1993. Apache opens his set by gazing out in amazement at an audience of several thousand Indian youths and shouting, 'I do not come to you as a pop star or a reggae star. I come to you as an Indian! [wild applause] I come to you as an Indian who loves his country and loves his people, all over the world!' Rather than 'Indianness' being figured as an essential quality located within the confines of the nation state, 'Indianness' here is being defined from outside the geographic boundaries of the nation while being consumed within it. The fact that this hybrid notion of 'Indianness' is produced within and deployed from the former colonial power, and is being consumed within the former colony, complicates a standard cultural imperialism argument, in which Britain could be seen as merely exporting another commodity – this time Indian identity – to India. Rather, the movement gestures toward a refashioning of what it means to be British through a refashioning of what it means to be Indian, and vice versa; it is a movement that disrupts the sanctity of the borders of the nation-state on all sides.

Yet the ways in which the alternative cultural and political geography generated by newer bhangra performers reasserts preeminent discourses of the nation at various critical instances must be critiqued. The move of claiming 'Britishness' that

I discussed earlier, for example, simultaneously brings to the surface bhangra's availability to recuperation, as a popular cultural form within hegemonic articulations of the nation.[13] This is evident in the explosion of interest in bhangra in mainstream British press accounts of the late 1980s, in which 'the bhangra scene' was heralded as indicative of a new, 'multicultural' Britain (Banerji 212). Such a media portrayal of the British-Asian youth culture that formed around bhangra allowed a way for 'Otherness,' transformed into 'multiculturalism,' to be recuperated into the national culture without changing the terms upon which it was predicated. Homi Bhabha, for instance, speaks of how the discourse of multiculturalism in Britain 'represented an attempt both to respond to and control the dynamic process of the articulation of cultural difference' ('The Third Space' 208), in that it seemed to recognize such difference only to disavow it. The multicultural rhetoric evident in the media coverage of bhangra allowed cultural difference to be contained and ultimately rendered transparent within the framework of cultural diversity. In fact, then, it is precisely bhangra's functioning as an assertion of Britishness – which on one level redefines nation and national culture – that also paradoxically allows for this recuperation into a dominant discourse of the nation.[14]

## 5. About Fathers and Sons

If bhangra's functioning within the multicultural rhetoric of 1980s Britain is one instance of its availability to recuperation into dominant national discourses, another such instance is in bhangra's deployment of gender within the dialogic relationship it negotiates between nation and diaspora. Bringing a gender critique to bear upon Apache's performance in Delhi foregrounds the uses to which gender and sexuality are put in the moment at which diaspora gets written into the nation, and the nation into the diaspora. Such a critique allows for an alternative reading of Apache's performance, one that brings to the surface and renders explicit the previously hidden traces of meaning in the concept of diaspora that I have already alluded to. Apache, for instance, makes his entrance on a horse, in the manner of a traditional Punjabi bridegroom. He goes on to bring his nine-year-old son – a miniature version of his father, sporting the same baggy shirt, jeans, and hair cut – onto the stage to accompany him in a song. Tho concert's final number is a staging of Apache's 1993 hit song, 'Arranged Marriage,' in which he sings:

> Me wan gal from Jullunder City, Me wan gal mon to look after me,
> Me wan gal dress up in a sari.
> Say the gal me like have the right figure
> And wear the chunee, kurtha pujamer,
> And talk the Indian with the patwa,
> Me wan gal respect Apache, Me wan gal go bring me sensi,
> Me wan gal to serva curee, Me wan gal respect me mum and daddy.

Butler's observation that not all parodic repetition displaces its conventions ('The Body You Want' 84) is appropriate here, as the song quite transparently reinserts women into a standard role as bearers of 'tradition,' even while, in his disruption of claims to origination or racial authenticity, Apache undermines the very notion of 'tradition' as a pure or recuperable space. The notion of 'Indianness' subscribed to here must be read within what Jacques Derrida terms the 'family scene,'[15] based as it is on a reified notion of paternity and inheritance where women are rendered barely discernible, unstable forms conspicuous only when they fulfill their assigned function as markers of male ethnic or communal affiliation, or as reproducers (both literally and metaphorically) of culture and community. It is only through this hegemonic articulation of gender difference that Apache is able to realize himself as a (male) diasporic subject; the celebratory, fluid, syncretic sense of 'Indianness' he proclaims at the beginning of the show is predicated, then, upon the maintenance of fixed and naturalized constructions of femininity and masculinity.

## 6. Diaspora(s) and the Hindu Nationalist Project

Diaspora, and the functioning of gender ideologies within it, must also be understood as a site of contestation, deployed by competing constituencies in often contradictory ways. Within the South Asian context, for instance, the Hindu nationalist movement in India utilizes the rhetoric of diaspora in order to mobilize an extensive network of donors, youth groups, religious groups, and others across the United States, Europe (particularly the United Kingdom) and Canada, funneling tremendous amounts of funds and other resources to various Hindu nationalist groups in India such as the Bharatiya Janata Party (BJP), Vishwa Hindu Parishad (VHP), and Rashtriya Swayamsevak Sangh (RSS). Various articles have documented the way in which Hindu nationalist groups create and dominate diasporic networks through the use of new technologies such as electronic bulletin boards, for instance, through which the class-based character of their project is explicitly articulated.[16] The diasporic consciousness espoused and disseminated by these groups is one based upon an ahistorical, essential notion of 'Indianness' that is seemingly at odds with the notion of diasporic identity put into play through bhangra – one that celebrates impurity and continuously references the performed and performative nature of 'India' and 'Indianness.' In this sense, bhangra can be read, to whatever limited extent, as resisting and subverting the dominant discourse of identity within various South Asian communities, as well as challenging the racist discourse of the broader society within which these communities are situated.

Yet the performance of diaspora through bhangra intersects, as I mentioned earlier, with nationalist discourse around the delineation of gender ideology. In its use of gendered imagery, current articulations of Hindu nationalist discourse draw heavily upon anticolonialist nationalist rhetoric, where women were central to a figuring of the nation. Replacing the British with the figure of the Muslim male, the Hindu Right utilizes images of victimized Hindu women and sexually predatory Muslim men, for instance, as a way of organizing men around the Hindu nationalist project (Pandey 13). Much of the rhetorical power of this project comes from using the language of kinship and 'brotherhood' to evoke notions of unity among various right-wing groups, where women function as liminal but necessary figures that allow for the metamorphosis of that brotherhood into family (see Basu). In their deployment of family metaphors, then, there is a striking similarity between Apache Indian's performance of diasporic identity that I have discussed above and the contemporary Hindu nationalist figuring of community and culture.

Bhangra as a performance of diaspora thus becomes complicit in these Hindu hegemonic projects to the extent that it reinforces dominant articulations of gender in its construction of a (male) diasporic subject. The fact that bhangra's exposing of the performative nature of ethnic or racial identity breaks down in its essentialized treatment of gender identity perhaps points to the limits of both bhangra and diaspora as enabling an alternative conceptualization of community and identity outside the masculinist logic of conventional nationalisms.

## 7. Coda: Toward a Post-Diaspora?

A reading of nation and diaspora through bhangra brings to the fore the necessity of thinking these terms together, given the inherent instabilities of both in their continuous overlappings and interpenetrations. I have suggested that the ways in which a diasporic sensibility is, at various instances, deployed and consumed within the nation calls for *diaspora to be seen as part of the nation itself.* 'The nation' as it is conventionally understood is thus forced to resignify, in that the constant underminings of its borders are brought to the surface. Of course, a reading of bhangra's functioning within the nation (both Britain and India) also demonstrates how such a movement can (sometimes simultaneously) act to reconsolidate the nation, which is able to incorporate a certain amount of Otherness in order to thereby renew itself.

As I hope I have made clear, a critique of bhangra also *allows the nation to be written into the diaspora,* with critical implications for the traditional hierarchical relationship between the two. Indeed, such a reading explodes this hierarchy, one that posits diaspora as, in some sense, the bastard child of the nation – disavowed, inauthentic, illegitimate, an impoverished imitation of the originary culture. In this light, Apache's performance in New Delhi, where he brings his son on stage, can be read as an attempt of a diasporic figure to claim legitimacy within the (originary) national culture by creating his own genealogy and patrimony. What is being inherited or passed on from father to son, then, is a certain diasporic sensibility or condition that draws from multiple sites within multiple diasporas, but bases its claim to legitimation upon a conventional deployment of women and masculinity. It is precisely at this moment that diasporic ideologies and those of the nation look increasingly alike.

However, as I mentioned earlier, such a theorization runs the risk of constructing a totalizing narrative around bhangra – an impossible project given that, as a popular cultural form, it is always in flux and under transformation. Indeed, the growing number of women becoming involved in the bhangra music industry – as both performers and deejays – poses a critical challenge to the dominant patriarchal structures through which the music has thus far been refracted, and instead opens up bhangra to yet another possible set of readings around gender and ethnic identity. I therefore want to close by stressing these multiple, simultaneous forms and meanings that bhangra encompasses. Apna Sangeet's 1991 hit, 'Soho Road,' for instance, can be read as setting forth potentially enabling constructions of gender in the diaspora, even if it remains within the confines of a heterosexual narrative. The song is a duet between a man and a woman, with the man singing about standing on Soho Road in Handsworth looking for his lover who had left him in India to come to England. He sings: 'I'm looking for you on Soho Road ... / We met in India, but after our fight you came to England where you forgot me. / To find you I went to London, to Coventry, to Scarborough, and in Midland I finally gave up.'[17] In a reversal of standard configurations of gender identities in the diaspora, here it is the woman who is portrayed not as a reified vision of lost homeland but as the diasporic subject capable of movement (and agency). The woman sings, for instance: 'I too thought of you/How can you know all the pain I've experienced/But I waited for you for seven years and then I did leave.' The repeated litany of names of various locations in the English Midlands maps out a translated geography, one that is claimed for new purposes. Such namings are in the vein of what Bhabha calls 'the tropic movement of cultural translation' through which, for instance, Salman Rushdie in *The Satanic Verses* is able to 'spectacularly rename London, in its Indo-Pakistani iteration, as 'Ellowen Deeowen'' (see *Location of Culture* 229). The song thus creates a specifically diasporic geography or spatial economy, but one whose very contours are here determined by a woman's journey within this landscape. Perhaps such an opening within bhangra offers a useful point of departure in gesturing toward some sort of post-diasporic position, one that takes into account the fluid and dialectical interplay between the nation and (multiple) diasporas, while simultaneously being locatable outside the family scene within which current articulations of nation and diaspora occur.

## Notes

I would like to thank Rob Nixon, John Archer, Qadri Ismail, George Lipsitz, and Judith Halberstam for their generous comments and suggestions, many of which I have incorporated here.

1. Here Judith Butler's observation that 'any consolidation of identity requires some set of differentiations and exclusions' comes to mind ('Imitation and Gender Insubordination' 19).

2. The only moment at which Gilroy does engage with other diasporic histories and the ways in which these might have impacted the black Atlantic is in his discussion of the Jewish diaspora (*Black Atlantic* 205–17). This is telling, in that the Jewish and African diasporas form two great narratives of Otherness against which other histories of dispersal and displacement are necessarily rendered marginal or irrelevant. As Indira Karamcheti points out, 'Indians in the diaspora have been defined as either irrelevant interlopers or as surrogates, stand-ins for an-Other's narrative,' continually displaced by 'the overwhelming, dominating presence of another people's displacement' (274).

3. Gilroy refers to the ship as 'the living means by which the points within the Atlantic world were joined' ('Cultural Studies' 193).

4. The majority of Punjabi immigrants during this time were Sikhs from Punjab, as well as East African Punjabis who were Sikh, Muslim, and Hindu.

5. See Baumann for a more detailed history of bhangra in Britain.

6. As Jitesh Gohil, a bhangra producer, explains: 'Bhangra is originally Punjabi music ... but that's not to say that only Punjabis buy the music. Whether they're Muslim, Hindu,

Sikh or whatever, they buy Bhangra and listen to it. Many don't understand it, but they call it their own music' (London *Times* 25 Jan. 1993: 35).

7. This 'need to stay together and be amongst your own' is specifically and directly a response to the state of British society in the late 1970s/early 1980s. The mid- to late 1970s saw an upsurge in support for the National Front and other far-right groups, as well as a concurrent rise of intense nationalistic fervor around the Royal Silver Jubilee of 1976. See Gilroy, *There Ain't No Black* ch. 3, for a trenchant discussion of the forms of antifascist and antiracist organizing of the time.

8. The term 'Asian' as deployed within these statements is hardly transparent or self-evident, particularly given that it seems to be synonymous with 'South Asian,' thereby shutting the Chinese British, for instance, out of its sphere of signification.

9. This is a rough translation from the Punjabi.

10. The names of many of the first-generation bhangra groups – such as Pardesi [foreign] Music Machine or the Safri [traveler or voyager] Boys – echo the sense of rootlessness, alienation, and separation from the nation-state expressed by Malkit.

11. Concurrent with the depiction of homeland as a female body is that of the nation as a virulently homosocial space or 'passionate brotherhood' (see Parker et al. 6). The diasporic community as imagined by first-generation bhangra artists can be seen to deploy masculinity to the same effect, that is, of creating and celebrating a community of men. For instance, Apna Sangeet, one of the most popular bhangra groups, sings: 'We are the tigers of Punjab/We dance on each others' shoulders/We put earrings in our ears and pendants around our necks.' Note here that it is a particularly Punjabi masculinity that is being asserted, one where the ornamentation of earrings and pendants is central to the constitution of a Punjabi male identity.

12. While there is a growing number of 'ragga' artists (those that blend bhangra with reggae), Apache in particular calls for a closer reading in that he remains the one most acceptable to mainstream labels such as Island Records (his current distributor) and is also one of the most commercially successful British-Asian musicians. As regards Apache's acceptability and 'cross-over' appeal, it most be noted that over the years much of his music has become increasingly devoid of bhangra rhythms or references in favor of straightforward dance-hall.

13. As Stuart Hall reminds us, '[Popular culture] is rooted in popular experience and is available for expropriation at one and the same time…. Black popular culture, like all popular cultures in the modern world, is bound to be contradictory' ('What is this "Black"' 16).

14. The scope of this chapter precludes an adequate exploration of the subject, but it must nevertheless be noted that bhangra's representation in the mainstream media was informed by the concurrent furor over Salman Rushdie's *The Satanic Verses* and forms part of the same discourse around Otherness and British national identity. The Rushdie debate enabled a construction of the figure of 'the Muslim' as irreducibly Other, its very alienness necessary for the constitution of the national body as naturally homogeneous, coherent, and stable. As images of 'Muslim fundamentalists' burning books in the streets of Bradford filled the media, 'the Muslim' was rendered the 'abject,' the 'not-me' (to use Julia Kristeva's terms) against and through which the boundaries of the national body and national subjectivity were defined. The 'bhangra scene,' then, allowed for an incorporation of Otherness into the national culture in a way resisted by the 'fundamentalists.'

15. Derrida speaks of 'the family scene' as 'all about fathers and sons, about bastards unaided by any public assistance, about glorious legitimate sons, about inheritance, sperm, sterility. Nothing is said of the mother …' (see *Dissemination* 143).

16. See, for example, S. Sudha's analysis of the religious/political discourses on 'India-net,' an electronic bulletin board (4).

17. The lyrics are roughly translated from the Punjabi.

## Works Cited

Anthias, Floya, and Yuval-Davis, Nira, eds. *Woman-Nation-State.* London: Women's, 1989.

Banerji, Sabita. 'Ghazals to Bhangra in Great Britain.' *Popular Music* 7.2 (1988): 207–13.

Basu, Amrita. 'Gender and the Hindu Nationalist Project.' Barbara Stoller Miller Lecture Series. Columbia University, 21 Mar. 1994.

Baumann, Gerd. 'The Re-invention of Bhangra.' *World of Music* 32.2 (1990): 81–95.

Bhabha, Homi. *The Location of Culture.* New York: Routledge, 1994.

————. 'The Third Space.' *Identity: Community, Culture and Difference.* ed. Jonathan Rutherford. London: Lawrence and Wishart, 1990: 207–21.

Butler, Judith. *Bodies That Matter: On the Discursive Limits of 'Sex.'* New York: Routledge, 1993.

————. 'The Body You Want.' *Artforum* Nov. 1992: 82–89.

————. *Gender Trouble: Feminism and the Subversion of Identity.* New York: Routledge, 1990.

————. 'Imitation and Gender Insubordination.' *Inside/Out: Lesbian Theories, Gay Theories.* Ed. Diana Fuss. New York: Routledge, 1991: 13–31.

Chatterjee, Partha. *The Nation and Its Fragments.* Princeton: Princeton UP, 1993.

Dent, Gina, ed. *Black Popular Culture.* Seattle: Bay, 1992.

Derrida, Jacques. *Dissemination.* Chicago: U of Chicago P, 1981.

Dhammi, O.S. 'Home is Where the House Is.' *Bazaar: South Asian Arts Magazine* 22 (Autumn 1992): 28.

Fuss, Diana. *Essentially Speaking: Feminism, Nature and Difference.* New York: Routledge, 1989.

Gilroy, Paul. *The Black Atlantic: Modernity and Double Consciousness.* Cambridge: Harvard UP, 1993.

————. 'Cultural Studies and Ethnic Absolutism.' *Cultural Studies.* ed. Lawrence Grossberg, Cary Nelson, and Paula Treichler. New York: Routledge, 1992: 187–98.

————. *There Ain't No Black in the Union Jack: The Cultural Politics of Race and Nation.* Chicago: U of Chicago P, 1987.

Goldberg, Jonathan. 'Bradford's "Ancient Members" and "A Case of Buggery ... Amongst Them."' *Nationalisms and Sexualities.* Ed. Andrew Parker et al. New York: Routledge, 1993: 60–76.

Hall, Stuart. 'What Is This 'Black' in Black Popular Culture?' *Black Popular Culture.* ed. Gina Dent. Seattle: Bay, 1992: 21–33.

Helmreich, Stefan. 'Kinship, Nation and Paul Gilroy's Concept of Diaspora.' *Diaspora* 2 (1992): 243–49.

Karamcheti, Indira. 'The Shrinking Himalayas.' *Diaspora* 2 (1992): 261–76.

Lipsitz, George. *Dangerous Crossings: Popular Culture, Postmodernism and the Poetics of Place.* London: Verso, 1994.

McCann, Ian. 'Bhangramuffin.' *ID: The Sound Issue* Fall 1993: 16–21.

McClintock, Anne (1995) *Imperial Leather: Race, Gender and Sexuality in the Colonial Contest.* New York: Routledge.

Pandey, Gyanendra, ed. *Hindus and Others.* New Delhi: Viking-Penguin India, 1993.

Parker, Andrew et al., ed. *Nationalisms and Sexualities.* New York: Routledge, 1993.

Sagoo, Bally. Interview. Radio Bandung. WBAI, New York. 2 Nov. 1993.

Spivak, Gayatri Chakravorty. 'Acting Bils/Identity Talk.' *Critical Inquiry* 18 (1992): 772–98.

Sudha, S. 'Compu-devata: Electronic Bulletin Boards and Communalism.' *Samar: South Asian Magazine for Action and Reflection* Summer 1993: 4–13.

# Chapter 26

# Lauren Berlant

## The Face of America and the State of Emergency

When can I go
into the supermarket
and buy what I
need with my good looks?

—Allen Ginsberg, 'America'

## The Political is the Personal

'The tradition of the oppressed teaches us that the 'state of emergency' in which we live is not the exception but the rule. We must attain to a conception of history that is in keeping with this insight. Then we shall clearly realize that it is our task to bring about a real state of emergency.'[1] When Walter Benjamin urges his cohort of critical intellectuals to foment a state of political counteremergency, he responds not only to the outrage of fascism in general, but to a particularly brutal mode of what we might call *hygienic governmentality:* this involves a ruling bloc's dramatic attempt to maintain its hegemony by asserting that an abject population threatens the common good and must be rigorously governed and monitored by all sectors of society.[2] Especially horrifying to Benjamin are the ways the ruling bloc solicits mass support for such 'governing': by using abjected populations as exemplary of all obstacles to national life; by wielding images and narratives of a

From: Lauren Berlant, *The Queen of America Goes to Washington City: Essays on Sex and Citizenship.* Durham, NC: Duke University Press, 1997.

threatened 'good life' that a putative 'we' have known; by promising relief from the struggles of the present through a felicitous image of a national future; and by claiming that, because the stability of the core image is the foundation of the narratives that characterize an intimate and secure national society, the nation must at all costs protect this image of a way of life, even against the happiness of some of its own citizens.

In the contemporary United States it is almost always the people at the bottom of the virtue/value scale – the adult poor, the nonwhite, the unmarried, the non-heterosexual, and the nonreproductive – who are said to be creating the crisis that is mobilizing the mainstream public sphere to fight the good fight on behalf of normal national culture, while those in power are left relatively immune. For example, while the public is incited to be scandalized by so-called welfare queens, the refusal of many employers to recompense their workers with a living wage and decent workplace conditions engenders no scandal at all. Indeed, the exploitation of workers is encouraged and supported, while it is poor people who are vilified for their ill-gotten gains. The manufactured emergency on behalf of 'core national values' advanced by people like William Bennett, magazines like the *National Review,* and organizations like FAIR (Federation for American Immigration Reform) masks a class war played out in ugly images and ridiculous stereotypes of racial and sexual identities and antinormative cultures.[3] As Stephanie Coontz has argued, this core U.S. culture has never actually existed, except as an ideal or a dogma.[4] But the cultural politics of this image of the normal has concrete effects, both on ordinary identity and the national life the state apparatus claims to be representing.

In this chapter I am going to tell another story about the transformation of the normative citizenship paradigm from a public form into the abstracted time and space of intimate privacy. [...] I will be engaging a [...] fictitious citizen: the new 'Face of America' who, gracing the covers of *Time, Mirabella,* and the *National Review,* has been cast as an imaginary solution to the problems of immigration, multiculturalism, sexuality, gender, and (trans)national identity that haunt the U.S. present tense.

This imaginary citizen or 'woman' was invented in 1993 by *Time* magazine. She is a nameless, computer-generated heterosexual immigrant, and the figure of a future core national population. In previous chapters, I have described the construction of modal citizenship into smaller and more powerless vehicles of human agency: fetuses and children. Joining this gallery of incipient citizens, the computer-generated female immigrant of our *Time* cannot act or speak on behalf of the citizenship she represents; she is more human than living Americans, yet less invested with qualities of personhood. With no capacity for agency, her value is also in her irrelevance to the concerns about achievement, intelligence, subjectivity, desire, demand, and courage that have recently sullied the image of the enfranchised American woman. Her pure isolation from lived history also responds to widespread debate about the value of working-class and proletarian immigrants to the American economy and American society. In the following pages I will show how sectors of the mainstream public sphere link whatever positive value immigration has to the current obsessive desire for a revitalized national heterosexuality and a white, normal national culture. [...]

## Making up Nations: 'A Melding of Cultures'[5]

In contrast to the zone of privacy where stars, white people, and citizens who don't make waves with their bodies can imagine they reside, the immigrant to the United States has no privacy, no power to incorporate automatically the linguistic and cultural practices of normal national culture that make life easier for those who can pass as members of the core society. This is the case whether or not the immigrant has 'papers': indeed, the emphasis placed on *cultural* citizenship by books like *The De-Valuing of America, Alien Nation,* and *In Defense of Elitism* confirms that acquiring the formal trappings of legitimate residence in the country is never sufficient to guarantee the diminution of xenophobic.[6]

These books argue that, where immigrants are concerned, the only viable model for nation-building is a process of 'Americanization.' I have suggested that, even for birthright citizens, the process of identifying with an 'American way of life' increasingly involves moral pressure to identify with a small cluster of privatized normal identities. But what kinds of special pressure does this process involve for immigrants? What kinds of self-erasure, self-transformation, and assimilation are being imagined by those who worry that even the successful 'naturalization' of immigrants will equal the denaturalization of the U.S. nation? What does the project of making this incipient citizen 'American' tell us about the ways national identity is being imagined and managed in the political public sphere?

When a periodical makes a 'special issue' out of a controversy, the controversy itself becomes a commodity whose value is in the intensity of identification and anxiety the journal can organize around it, and this is what is happening to immigration as a subject in the U.S. mainstream. Captioning *Time*'s first 'special issue' on immigration, *Immigrants: The Changing Face of America* (8 July 1985), is a passage that describes what kinds of boundaries get crossed and problems get raised when the immigrant enters the United States:

> Special Issue: Immigrants. They come from everywhere, for all kinds of reasons, and they are rapidly and permanently changing the face of America. They are altering the nation's racial makeup, its cities, its tastes, its entire perception of itself and its way of life.[7]

The emphasis on time and space in this framing passage – 'they' come from everywhere, 'they' incite rapid change – suggests that there is something 'special' about the contemporary immigrant to the United States that ought to create intensified anxieties about social change, even despite the widely held axiom that the United States is fundamentally 'a nation of immigrants.' The something that the force and velocity of immigrant cultural practices is radically changing is people's everyday lives in the nation, but that 'something' is underspecified. We see in particular a change in the default reference of the category 'race,' and concurrently the city and its dominant 'tastes.' These unsettlements, in turn, have forced alterations in what had ostensibly been a stable national self-concept, based on common affinities and ways of life.

Of course, every crisis of immigration in U.S. history has involved the claim that something essentially American is being threatened by alien cultural practices. In the 1985 *Time* magazine variant on this national anxiety, however, immigrants to the United States are made stereotypical in newly ambivalent ways. *Time* first represents their challenge to the 'us' and the 'our' of its readership – everywhere implicitly native-born, white, male salaried citizens – through a cover that shows a classic huddled mass made up mostly of Latinos and Asians of all ages, with lined or worried faces. Their faces are in various stages of profile facing the reader's right, as though the 'changing' face of America that the title declares is made visible in the dynamism of their rotation. In the present tense of a new national life, they are looking off toward the edge of the page at something unidentified: their future, America's future, the scene of their prospects contained in the magazine whose pages are about to be opened. The diverted gaze of the immigrants frees the reader from identification with them: the readers too, from their side of the border, are positioned to open the magazine and see their future prophesied and plotted.

I overread this cover story in part to set up a frame for thinking about the 1993 special issue of *Time* on immigration and national life, but also to look at how national publics are characterized and made in an age of mass mediation. *Time* presents its immigrants in segmented populations, which are defined in relation to the totality 'Americans': 'Hispanics,' 'Asians,' and 'Blacks' each get their own article. But *Time*'s task is not merely to document changes: to name a racial or ethnic population is to name for the public a difficult problem it faces. Specifically, the magazine responds to particular issues created by the 1965 Immigration and Nationality Act, which dissolved official preference given to European migration to the United States.[8] While some section headings confirm that immigrants like 'Asians' as a class and talented individuals like the Cuban poet Heberto Padilla contribute superbly to the core U.S. national culture, alien cultures are named mainly because they seem to pose threats. For 'Blacks' (said to be 'left behind' by the wave of new races), and the rest of the United States, 'Hispanics' are the new 'problem' population, so disturbing they get their own section and dominate several others, including 'Business,' 'Policy,' 'The Border,' 'Religion,' 'Video,' and 'Behavior.'

Yet the explicit rhetoric of the special issue is nothing if not optimistic: overall, the essays have a tinny and intense enthusiasm about immigration's effect on national life, and it is the ambivalent tone of voice they use to support optimism about the process of assimilation that is of interest here. An immigrant is defined by *Time* as a national alien who comes to America consciously willing to be exploited in exchange for an abstraction: 'opportunity.'[9] But in lived terms opportunity is not abstract. If the immigrant's value is in her/his willingness to be economically exploited for freedom, *Time* also argues that the intense labor or mass assimilation into cultural literacy itself will further enrich the already existing indigenous 'national culture.'[10]

The American schoolroom has traditionally provided a hopeful glimpse of the nation's future, and some people still imagine it to be a Rockwellian scene of mostly pink-cheeked children spelling out the adventures of Dick and Jane. But come for a moment to the playground of the Franklin elementary school in Oakland, where black girls like to chant their jump-rope numbers in Chinese. 'See you mañana,' one student shouts with a Vietnamese accent. 'Ciao!' cries another, who has never been anywhere near Italy. And let it be noted that the boy who won the National Spelling Bee in Washington last month was Balu Natarajan, 13, who was born in India, now lives in a suburb of Chicago, and speaks Tamil at home. 'Milieu' was the word with which he defeated 167 other competitors. Let it also be noted that Hung Vu and Jean Nguyen in May became the first Vietnamese-born Americans to graduate from West Point.[11]

Like their parents, these child immigrants are imagined as a heterogeneous population that lives mainly outside and on the streets of America. They compose a population whose tastes in food and art and whose creative knowledges ('Spanglish' is featured elsewhere)[12] are easily assimilable to the urges for commodity variation and self-improvement that already saturate the existing indigenous mass national 'milieu.' There are also *three* essays on elite immigrants who have freely brought 'wealth,' 'brain power,' and 'culture' to enrich the land of opportunity that is the United States. Children and the elite: these good immigrants are good, in *Time*'s view, because they are the gift that keeps giving, willing to assimilate and to contribute difference and variation to American culture.

Meanwhile, in separate articles on immigrant women and children, we see that worthy migration is determined not only by intercultural influence and economic activity, but also by its utility as symbolic evidence for the ongoing power of American democratic ideals. That is, immigration discourse is a central technology for the reproduction of patriotic nationalism: not just because the immigrant is seen as without a nation or resources and thus as deserving of pity or contempt, but because the immigrant is defined as *someone who desires America.*[13] Immigrant women especially are valued for having the courage to grasp freedom. But what is freedom for women? *Time* defines it not as liberation from oppressive states and economic systems, but as release from patriarchal family constraints, such that the free choice of love object is the pure image of freedom itself. Indeed, an explicit analogy is drawn between the intimacy form of consensual marriage and the value of American national culture:

> Women migrate for the same reasons that men do: to survive, because money has become worthless at home, to find schooling and jobs. But they also have reasons of their own. Single women may leave to escape the domination of their old-fashioned families, who want them to stay in the house and accept an arranged marriage.... [For] home, like parentage, must be legitimized through love; otherwise, it is only a fact of geography or biology. Most immigrants to America found their love of their old homes betrayed. Whether Ireland starved them, or Nazi Germany persecuted them, or Viet Nam drove them into the sea, they did not really abandon their countries; their countries abandoned them. In America, they found the possibility of a new love, the chance to nurture new selves.... [Americanization] occurs when the immigrant learns his ultimate lesson: above all countries, America, if loved, returns love.[14]

I will return to the utopian rhetoric of national love anon. Although *Time* admits that there are other reasons people come to the United States – for example, as part of the increasingly global proletarian workforce[15] – its optimism about immigration is most powerfully linked not to the economic and cultural *effects* of immigration on the United States or its current and incipient citizens, but to the symbolic implications immigration has on national vanity: it is proof that the United States is a country worthy of being loved. This is, after all, the only imaginable context in which the United States can be coded as antipatriarchal. Come to America and not only can you choose a lover and a specially personalized modern form of quotidian exploitation at work, but because you can and do choose them, they must be prima facie evidence that freedom and democracy exist in the United States.

Meanwhile, for all its optimism about immigrant-American nation formation, *The Changing Face of America* clearly emerges from a panic in national culture, and one motive for this issue is to substitute a new panic about change for an old one. Explicitly the issue responds to the kinds of nativist economic and cultural anxiety that helped shape the Immigration Reform and Control Act of 1986 and, more recently, California's Proposition 187. Three specific and self-contradictory worries predominate: the fear that immigrants, legal and illegal, absorb more resources than they produce, thus diverting the assets of national culture from legal citizens; the fear that immigrants, legal and illegal, are better capitalists than natal citizens, and thus extract more wealth and political prerogative than they by birthright should; and the fear that cities, once centers of cultural and economic capital, are becoming unlivable, as spatial boundaries between communities of the very poor, workers, and affluent residents have developed in a way that threatens the security of rich people and the authority of 'the family.'

The essay that most fully expresses this cluster of fears is the title essay, 'The Changing Face of America,' which provides a remarkable caption to the cover image. But what is striking about this essay, which equates 'face' with place of national origin ('That guy is Indian, next to him is a Greek, next to him is a Thai,' says one neighborhood tour guide*),*[16] is not the American xenophobia-style apprehension it expresses, acknowledges, and tries to manage. This panic of mistrust in the viability of a non-European-dominated 'America' almost goes without saying in any contemporary mainstream discussion of the immigrant effect: it is expressed in the chain of almost equivalent signs 'immigrant,' 'alien,' 'minority,' 'illegal'; it is expressed in the ordinary phrase 'wave of immigrants,' which never quite explicitly details the specter of erosion and drowning it contains, a specter that has long haunted American concerns about the solidity of national economic and cultural property.

Instead, what distinguishes this special issue on immigration is the way it characterizes birthright American citizenship, and particularly how it codes the relationship between the animated corporeality of immigrant desire and the enervation of the native or assimilated American. The essay about America's changing face is illustrated by photographs of immigrants who have just landed within the hour at New York's Kennedy Airport. The photographs are not meant to tell stories about the immigrants' histories. Rather, *Time* claims that the captured image of the face in the picture records an immigrant's true feeling at the threshold, the feeling of anticipation that history is about to begin again, in the context of the new nation: 'The moment of arrival stirs feelings of hope, anxiety, curiosity, pride. These emotions and many others show in the faces on the following pages.'[17] (These phrases caption a picture of a sleeping baby.) The immigrant portraits are like fetal sonograms or baby pictures. The specific bodies matter little. Their importance is in the ways they express how completely generic immigrant hopes and dreams might unfold from particular bodies, and they tell a secret story about a specific migrant's odds for survival – by which *Time* means successful Americanization.

The photographs of new immigrants are also made in an archaic style, often taking on the design of formal family daguerreotype portraits. Given *Time*'s explicit commitment, in this issue, to refurbishing Ellis Island, it is not surprising that these threshold images make the immigrants American ancestors before the process of living historically as an American has happened. What are the aims of this framing modality? First, to borrow the legitimating aura of American immigrants from past generations, with whom even Euro-Americans can still identify. Second, to signal without saying it that the 'wave' is no mob, but actually a series of families, bringing their portable privacy to a land where privacy is protected. Third, the structure of generationality provides a strong model of natural change, evolutionary reproduction being the most unrevolutionary structure of collective transformation imaginable, even while worries about burgeoning new-ethnic populations (of color) seem to threaten the future of (white) modern nationality. Fourth, as Roland Barthes argues, the portrait photograph is a figure of displacement and a performance of loss or death[18]; and as the immigrant has long been said to undergo a death and rebirth of identity in crossing the threshold to America, so too the picture might be said to record the 'changing' over of the face as the subjects change the register of their existence.

Yet if death (of identities, identifications, national cultures) is everywhere in this issue of *Time,* and if these processes are linked complexly to the production of America, it is not simply the kind of death one associates with the iconic symbolics of national rebirth; nor its opposite, in the privileged classes' typical construction of ghetto violence and its specters as the end of America as 'we' know it; nor in the standard depiction of an undervalued and exploited underclass with a false image of the *class's* undervaluation of 'life' – although the special issue periodically cues up this cruel translation in essays on the unlivable city. Mainly, *The Changing Face of America* deploys images of national death to say something extraordinary about the logics by which the American desire for property and privacy makes citizenship itself a death-driven machine.

The essay on America's changing face captions its photographs with a story about what happens to the immigrant's sensuous body in the process of becoming American.

> America is a country that endlessly reinvents itself, working the alchemy that turns 'them' into 'us.' That is the American secret: motion, new combinations, absorption. The process is wasteful, dangerous, messy, sometimes tragic. It is also inspiring.

'The story, in its ideal, is one of earthly redemption,' the magazine proclaims.[19] But the process of alchemy turns out to be virtually vampiric.

> It was America, really, that got the prize: the enormous energy unleashed by the immigrant dislocations. Being utterly at risk, moving into a new and dangerous land, makes the immigrant alert and quick to learn. It livens reflexes, pumps adrenaline. ... The immigrant who travels in both time and geographical space achieves a neat existential alertness. The dimensions of time and space collaborate. America, a place, becomes a time: the future. ... In this special issue, *Time* describes the newest Americans and addresses the myriad ways in which they are carrying on an honored tradition: contributing their bloodlines, their spirit and their energy to preserve the nation's vitality and uniqueness.[20]

The immigrant is full of vitality, and he/she provides an energy of desire and labor that perpetually turns America into itself. What then of the native citizen? Throughout the text the problem of immigration turns into the problem of abject America: we discover that to be an American citizen is to be anesthetized, complacent, unimaginative. 'There is nothing deadened or smug about immigrants,' the editors write. In contrast, U.S. citizenship is a form of annulment, for the attainment of safety and freedom from the anxiety for survival national capitalism promises turns out, again and again, to make old and new citizens enervated, passive in the expectation that at some point their constitutionally promised 'happiness' will be delivered to them. This passivity is central to America's economic and cultural decline, implies *Time;* the metaphysics of 'success' leads to the evacuation of ambition in the present tense, and threatens the national future.[21]

Thus along with the problem of cultural transformation that immigration presents to the anxious native public is a threatening, half-obscured question of national identification and identity: in 1985 *Time* proclaims the *new* immigrant as the only true American, while casting birthright and naturalized citizens as subject to enervation, decay, and dissolution. The very promise that lures persons to identify with their native or assumed U.S. national identity, the promise of freedom unearned and privacy enjoyed, is cast as an unmitigated economic disaster.

This is, perhaps, why *The Changing Face of America* emphasizes the difference between the economic and the ideal United States: if masses of immigrants are necessary to provide the proletarian and creative cultural energy for the nation's well-being, the essential nation itself must be untouched by the changing face of America, must be a theoretical nation where success is measured by civic abstractions and moral obligations.

'Love' of 'home' turns out to be *Time*'s foundation for democratic American morality; American morality turns out to be the reality effect of national culture. If America is constituted metaphysically, as an ethical space of faith or belief, then intimacy with the principles of American democratic culture – property, privacy, and individuality – is the only ground for the true practice of nationhood. There are no immigrants or citizens there, in that zone of abstraction: it is a dead space, dead to the fluctuations of change. All the rest is just history.

## Making up Nations: Another New Face of America

When in 1993 *Time* revised its earlier construction of the immigrant effect, the magazine felt compelled to do so not only because of the conflictual economic and cultural conditions of the present, but also because a new future was being assessed: it had just become common knowledge that 'sometime during the second half of the 21st century the descendants of white Europeans, the arbiters of the core national culture for most of its existence, are likely to slip into minority status ... [w]ithout fully realizing it,' writes Martha Farnsworth Riche, director of policy studies at Washington's Population Reference Bureau.'[22] The directionality of the earlier special issue on immigrants has reversed: whereas in the 1980s, the issue was immigration and the politics of assimilation (to Americanness), in the 1990s the issue seems to be the necessary adaptation all white Americans must make to the new multicultural citizenship norm, even the ones who don't live in New York, El Paso, and Los Angeles.

This special issue is thus a cultural memento mori for the white American statistical majority, but it is also a call to a mass action. What kind of mass action? At the moment of its statistical decline, it becomes necessary to reinvent the image archive of the nation in a way that turns the loss of white cultural prestige into a gain for white cultural prestige. To perform this process of transfiguration, the cover of this issue is both more and less than a death mask; it is a new commercial stereotype advertising the future of national culture: 'Take a good look at this woman. She was created by a computer from a mix of several races. What you see is a remarkable preview of The New Face of America.'

The changes this special issue rings on the citizen-energy crisis of the earlier issue is indicated in the facelift the newer version gives to the faciality of the earlier immigrant cover. Two particular domains of assimilation that have framed immigrant representation in the past are importantly altered here: in the threat and allure of the immigrant's body, and its relation to the ways assimilation is imagined, whether through generational change or the relation of labor and education to citizenship. What will count as full citizenship in the future which is also the now of the new? Whereas the earlier cover depicts multiple living ethnic-faced persons apparently involved with imagining their own future lives in America, the second cover foregrounds a single, beautiful woman looking directly out of the page, at the reader, who is, in turn, invited to 'Take a good look.' The earlier faces were lined – texts of history written on the body; the new face of America reveals only the labor of a faint smile on a generically youthful face. The earlier faces are clearly artificial, standing in for a 'wave' of face types that Americans, in their national anxiety, have difficulty seeing as human; the second image looks like a photograph of an actually existing human being who could come from anywhere, but she is actually a Frankenstein monster composed from other 'ethnic' human images, through a process of morphing. The new face of America involves a melding of different faces with the sutures erased and the proportions made perfect; she is a national fantasy from the present representing a posthistorical – that is, postwhite – future.

The 'new face of America,' then, has been manifestly individuated and gendered, specified and symbolized, in the eight years between *Time*'s special issues. Moreover, the contexts for the immigrant image have also changed in the interval. In the first issue immigrants are public, collective, constructed by the activity of changing nations and subjectivities on the way to becoming American; in the second, the background to the new girl in the polis is merely a phenotypic index, a subject effect. Behind her is a field of other immigrant faces, barely visible: the matrix of blurry faces, barely intelligible dots, is the dominant image of mass immigrant life in this *Time*, which is dedicated to disaggregating, categorizing, and managing the circulation and value of the contemporary immigrant population. The dots declare the immigrant a weak or faded sign, real only as an abstract racial type rather than as persons distinguished by movement through concrete and abstract spaces of any sort. As they recede behind the face of the future that is also called the 'new face of America' in a kind of whirl of temporalizing, the immigrant dots are also already being forgotten.

The new American face also has a body. In the first issue the changing faces sit atop clothed bodies, because these persons are figured as social agents, capable of making history; in the second issue, the bodies are still and naked, hidden demurely behind the screen of the text, but available for erotic fantasy and consumption. This again raises images of the national fetal person, but differently than in its first incarnation. In 1985, the immigrants photographed in situ of their transition into the status 'foreign national' were fetal-style because they were officially or wishfully caught as persons prior to their incorporation within the American national story: that is, the potential of their unfolding history was indistinguishable from their new identities as potential U.S. citizens. In 1993, the new face of America has the corporeality of a fetus, a body without history, an abstraction that mimes the abstraction of the American promise that retains power *because* it is unlived.

In short, the cover situates American posthistory in prelapsarian time. Appropriately, where the first issue describes the 'possibility of finding a new love' in the national context as a matter of collectively inhabiting lawful national spaces or 'homes,' the latter text proclaims, early on, a kind of carnal 'love' for the computer-generated cover girl's new face of America.[23]

But what of love's role in the technology of assimilation and nation building? What is the labor of love, if not to lose sight of the labor of the immigrant in the blinding bright light of patriotic gratitude for the possibility that there will be, if 'we' do not slip unawares into multiracial society, an intelligible national future after all? In the previous special issue, the female immigrant fleeing an archaic patriarchal family represented the limits of what immigration could do to alter America. To repeat, the narrative image of the woman in flight from intimate authoritarian structures translates into a figure of and desire for America, not the abject lived-in United States where suffering takes place and survival is decided locally, but abstract America, which foundationally authorizes an elastic language of love and happiness that incorporates and makes claim on any aspiring citizen's intimate desire, as long as the citizen is, in a deep way, 'legal.' Likewise, in 1993, an image of a sexualized cyborg gendered female explicitly bears the burden of mature and natural national love, which involves representing and effacing the transition the privileged classes of the United States must make to a new logic of national identity and narrative.

But love amounts to even more than this when it comes to revitalizing the national narrative. Desiring to read the immigrant like the fetus and the child, whose histories, if the world is 'moral,' are supposed to unfold from a genetic/ethical kernel or rhizome, *Time* in 1993 installs the future citizen, not in a family that has come from somewhere else, but in a couple form begotten by a desire to reproduce in private; that is to say, in a postpolitical domain of privacy authorized by national culture and law. It further illustrates this future through a series of photographic images, which are organized into a seven-by-seven square according to visible ethnicities now procreating in the United States. The principles by which an American ethnic type is determined are very incoherent: 'Middle Eastern,' 'Italian,' 'African,' 'Vietnamese,' 'Anglo-Saxon,' 'Chinese,' 'Hispanic.' These images are organized on the page following the model of those squares children use to learn the multiplication tables. Within these 'reproduction squares' the images are morphed onto each other so that their future American 'progeny' might be viewed in what is almost always its newly lightened form.[24] The nationalist heterosexuality signified by this racial chain is suffused with nostalgia for the feeling of a stable and dominant collective identity. In the now of the American future *Time* sets forth, the loving heart is a closed-off border open only to what intimacy and intercourse produce, and even American strangers cannot enter the intimate national future, except by violence.[25]

Love of the new face embodies three feelings less hopeful than the ones I've been following so far: disappointment in and disavowal of the cultural and economic violence of the present tense; a counterinsurgent rage at what has been called 'the new cultural politics of difference'; and an ambition for the nation's future.[26] Let me briefly address each of these. First, *Time* reinvents the 'new' but not yet achieved or experienced American future in the context of a more conventional engagement with issues of immigrant practice, never hesitating to trot out the same old categories (illegals, immigrant high culture, transformed metropolitan life, and so on) and the same old defensive bromides (Tocqueville and the *Federalist* papers are the real core of national identity that no immigrant culture can disturb). The ambition of the ex-privileged is to be able to narrate from the present a national scene of activity, accumulation, and reproduction that never becomes unintelligible, unmanageable: the wish of the dream cover is that American racial categories will have to be reinvented as tending toward whiteness or lightness, and whiteness will be reinvented as an ethnic minority (as in the story 'III Cheers for the WASPS,' which asserts that 'Americanization has historically meant specification. It is the gift that keeps on giving'; moreover, it is the essence of America's 'national character,' which is in danger of 'slipping into chronic malfunction').[27]

*Time,* admitting the bad science of its imaging technologies, nonetheless makes a claim that crossbreeding, in the reproductive sense, will do the work of 'melding' or 'melting' that diverts energy from subcultural identification to what will be the newly embodied national scene. 'For all the talk of cultural separatism,' it argues, 'the races that make the U.S. are now crossbreeding at unprecedented rates' such that 'the huddled masses have already given way to the muddled masses.'[28] 'Marriage is the main assimilator,' says Karen Stephenson, an anthropologist at UCLA. 'If you really want to effect change, it's through marriage and child rearing.' Finally, 'Those who intermarry have perhaps the strongest sense of what it will take to return America to an unhyphenated whole.'[29] This ambition about what 'the ultimate cultural immersion of interethnic marriage' will do for the nation is an ambition about the natural narrative of the national future.[30] The promise of this collective narrative depends on a eugenic program, enacted in the collective performance of private, intimate acts, acts of sex and everyday child-rearing. The American future has nothing to do with vital national world-making activities, or public life: just technologies of reproduction that are, like all eugenic programs, destructive in their aim.

Of course you wouldn't hear the violence of this desire in the tone of the special issue, which demonstrates an overarching optimism about the culturally enriching effects of all kinds of reproduction: the intimate private kind, and its opposite, from within the mass-mediated public sphere. You will remember that the special issue begins with the morpher's fantasy of cybersex with the fair lady's face he creates; it ends where 'The Global Village Finally Arrives.' *Time*'s excitement about globality is very specific: if the new national world of America will be embodied in private, the new global world will be public and abstract.

It would be easy, seeing all this, to say that the world is moving toward the *Raza Cósmica* (Cosmic Race), predicted by the Mexican thinker José Vasconcelos in the 20s – a glorious blend of mongrels and mestizos. It may be more relevant to suppose that more and more of the world may come to resemble Hong Kong, a stateless special economic zone full of expats and exiles linked by the lingua franca of English and the global marketplace.[31]

In other words, the melding of races sexually is not a property of the new world order, which *Time* describes as 'a wide-open frontier of polyglot terms and post-national trends.' This global scene is economic and linguistic, it has no narrative of identity, it is the base of capitalist and cultural expansion that supports the contraction of the intranational narrative into a space covered over by a humanoid face.

It remains to be asked why this national image of immigration without actual immigrants is marketed now, in the 1990s, and in a way that elides the optimism and anxiety about immigrant assimilation of the previous decade. To partly answer this, one must look at the essay by William A. Henry III 'The Politics of Separation,' which summarizes much in his subsequent book *In Defense of Elitism.* This essay blames multiculturalism, political correctness, and identity politics for the national fantasy *Time* promotes in this issue: 'one must be pro-feminist, pro-gay rights, pro-minority studies, mistrustful of tradition, scornful of Dead White European Males, and deeply skeptical toward the very idea of a "masterpiece,"' says Henry.[33]

Henry equates the discord of identity politics and its pressures on the terms of cultural literacy and citizenship competence with something like an antiassimilationist stance that might be taken by immigrants. Indeed, he bemoans the ways the dominant narratives that marked competency at citizenship themselves have become 'alien,' thanks to the allegedly dominant fanatical multiculture that reduces the complexity of culture and power to authoritarian countercultural simplicities. As a result, 'Patriotism and national pride are at stake,' for 'in effect, the movements demand that mainstream white Americans aged 35 and over clean out their personal psychic attics of nearly everything they were taught – and still fervently believe – about what made their country great.'[34]

Henry's passionately committed essay is not merely cranky. It is also a symptomatic moment in the struggle that motivates the 'new face of America' to be born. This is a culture war over whose race will be the national one for the policy-driven near future, and according to what terms. For example, if whites must be racialized in the new national order, racial identity must be turned into a national family value. If race is to be turned into a national family value, then the non-familial populations, the ones, say, where fathers are more loosely identified with the health of the family form, or affective collectivities not organized around the family, must be removed from the national archive, which is here organized around a future race of cyborgs, or mixed-race but still white-enough children. It is in this sense that the defensive racialization of national culture in this issue is genocidal. It sacrifices the centrality of African American history to American culture by predicting its demise; it sacrifices attention to the concrete lives of exploited immigrant and native people of color by fantasizing the future as what will happen when white people intermarry, thus linking racial mixing to the continued, but masked, hegemony of whiteness; it tacitly justifies the continued ejection of gays and lesbians and women from full citizenship, and deploys national heterosexuality to suppress the complex racial and class relations of exploitation and violence that have taken on the status of mere clichés – that is, accepted truths or facts of life too entrenched to imagine surpassing – by the panicked readership of *Time*. After all, the entire project of this issue is to teach citizens at the core culture to remain optimistic about the U.S. future, and this requires the 'new face' the nation is already becoming not to have a memory.

This epidemic of quasi-amnesia was sponsored by the Chrysler Corporation, a company sure to benefit from the translation of the immigrant into an image of an immigrant's future racially mixed granddaughter from a nice family in a white American suburb. And it should not be surprising that the 'new face of America' generated even more new faces: on the cover of the *National Review,* which shows a young African American child running away from a graffiti mustache he has drawn on the 'new face' of *Time*'s cover, accompanied by a story that blasts *Time*'s refusal to engage directly in the class and race war it is romancing away;[35] on the cover of *Mirabella,* in which a picture of a morphed woman and a computer chip makes explicit the desire to love and aspire only to faces that have never existed, unlike one's pitiful own; and in at least two marketing magazines,[36] which were directly inspired by *Time*'s 'new face' to think of new ethnic markets in cosmetics, so that 'ethnic' women might learn how simultaneously to draw on and erase the lines on their faces that distinguish them as having lived historically in a way that threatens their chances of making it in the new future present of America. [...]

In *Time* we have learned that the experience of the national future will be beautiful, will be administered by families, will involve intimate collective patriotic feelings, and will take place in the domestic private, or in foreign publics, places like Hong Kong or, say, CNN, the contemporary American postnation. In reinventing the national icon, embodied but only as an abstraction, *Time* delinks its optimism about national culture from the negativity of contemporary public politics: in the abstract here and now of *Time*'s America, the rhetorics of victimhood and minority that identity politics and multiculturalism have deployed are given over to the previously unmarked or privileged sectors of the national population; in the abstract here and now of this America, people at the bottom are considered American only insofar as they identify with and desire the status of the unmarked.

In this light we can better see more motives for official America's embrace of heterosexuality for national culture. For one thing, *Time*'s fantasy logic of a tacitly white or white-ish national genetic system integrated by private acts of consensual sex that lead to reproduction provides a way of naturalizing its separation of especially African American history and culture from the national future, and thus implicitly supports disinvestment in many contexts of African American life in the present tense. In making the main established taxonomy of race in the United States an archaic formation with respect to the future it is projecting as already here or 'new,' the issue of *Time* makes core national subjectivity itself racial along the lines of scientific racism through images of what it calls 'psychic genes' that mime the genes that splice during reproduction to produce new likenesses.

Second, heterosocial marriage is a model of assimilation like e pluribus unum, where sexual and individual 'difference' is obscured through an ideology/ethics of consensual 'melding' that involves channeling one's world-making desires and energy into a family institution through which the future of one's personhood is supposed to unfold effortlessly. So too the new face of America, having been bred through virtual sex acts, projects an image of American individuals crossbreeding a new citizenship form that will ensure the political future of the core national culture. In sum, the nationalist ideology of marriage and the couple is now a central vehicle for the privatization of citizenship: first, via moralized issues around privacy, sex, and reproduction that serve as alibis for white racism and patriarchal power; but also in the discourse of a United States that is not an effect of states, institutions, ideologies, and memories, but an effect of the private citizen's acts. The expulsion of embodied public spheres from the national future/present involves a process I have been describing as an orchestrated politics of nostalgia and sentimentality marketed by the official national culture industry, a politics that perfumes its cruelty in its claim to loathe the culture war it is waging, blaming social divisions in the United States on the peoples against whom the war is being conducted. [...]

## Notes

Much thanks to Arjun Appadurai, Carol Breckenridge, Cary Nelson, and Candace Vogler for goading me on to do this competently; and to Roger Rouse for his archival help, vast knowledge, intensive debate, and heroic labor of reading.

1. Benjamin, Walker (1973) 'Theses on the Philosophy of History', *Illuminations*. Trans. H. Zohn. Ed. H. Arendt. London: Fontana Press, p. 257.

2. See Foucault, 'Governmentality,' in *The Foucault Effect: Studies in Governmentaility*. (1991) Eds G. Burchell, C. Gordon and P. Miller. Chicago: University of Chicago Press, especially 100–104. Foucault argues that modern states substitute a relatively decentered economic model of population control for the familial model of the sovereign, pre-Enlightenment state, and at the same time become obsessed with maintaining intimacy and continuity with its governed populations, an obsession that results in a fetishism of the kinds of knowledge and feeling that support the security of the state. Thus the intimate identity form of national fantasy accompanies the increasing segmentation and dispersal of state force, violence, and capital.

3. The literature on the 'culture wars' is extensive. Inspiration for the conservative war to make a core national culture continues to be derived from Allan Bloom's *The Closing of the American Mind* (1987), London: Penguin; its current figurehead is former Secretary of Education, Chairman of the National Endowment for the Humanities, and director of the Office of National Drug Control Policy William J. Bennett. See *The De-Valuing of America*, New York: Simon and Schuster Inc., (1992), and *Our Children and Our Country*, New York: Simon and Schuster, Inc., (1988), particularly the chapters 'The Family as Teacher,' 61–68, and 'Public Education and Moral Education,' 69–76; and the section 'In Defense of the West,' 191–218. Some samples of the anti-core-culture side of the struggle (mainly over the content of educational curricula and youth-culture entertainment) are Richard Bolton, *Culture Wars*, New York: The New Press, (1992); Gates, *Loose Canons*, Oxford, Oxford University Press, (1992); Graff, *Beyond the Culture Wars*, New York: W. W. Norton and Company, (1993) and Jacoby, *Dogmatic Wisdom*, New York: Doubleday, (1994).

4. Coontz, *The Way We Never Were*, New York: Basic Books, (1992). See especially the chapters 'A Man's Home Is His Castle: The Family and Outside Intervention,' 122–48, and 'Strong Families, the Foundation of a Virtuous Society: The Family and Civic Responsibility,' 93–121.

5. *Time* 8 July 1985: 24, 36.

6. Bennett, *The De-Valuing of America*; Brimelow, P. (1995) *Alien Nation: Common Sense About America's Immigration Disaster*. New York: Random House. Henny, W.A. (1994) *In Defense of Elitism*. New York: Anchor Books.

7. *Time* 8 July 1985: I.

8. Ibid., 26.

9. Ibid., 3, 57.

10. Ibid., 33 ff.

11. Ibid., 29.

12. Ibid., 81.

13. Ibid., 82–83.

14. Ibid., 82, 100–101.

15. Ibid., 82.

16. Ibid., 26.

17. Ibid.

18. Barthes, Roland (1981) *Camera Lucida.* Trans. R. Howard. New York: Hill and Wang.

19. *Time* 8 July 1985: 24.

20. Ibid., 25.

21. There continues to be a vociferous debate on the right as to whether the benefit the United States might receive from immigrant 'blood' is not less than the cost their practices and histories pose to the maintenance of normal national culture. See, for example, Peter Brimelow's *Alien Nation*; the issue of the *National Review* titled 'Demystifying Multiculturalism' (21 February 1994); and William F. Buckley and John O'Sullivan, 'Why Kemp and Bennett Are Wrong on Immigration,' *National Review* 21 November 1994: 36–45, 76, 78; and Mills, *Arguing Immigration.*

22. *Time* 142, no. 21 (fall 1993): 5.

23. *Time* 8 July 1985: 100; *Time* 142, no. 21 (fall 1993): 3. Morphing as a model for humanity in general was apparently on *Time*'s 'mind': the cover story of the previous issue (8 November 1993) asks dramatically, 'Cloning Humans. The first laboratory duplication of a human embryo raises the question: Where do we draw the line?' 'The New Face of America' answers this question by performing an erasure of the traces of social desire and aversion that such hierarchical line drawing embodies. Thanks to Carol Breckenridge for alerting me to this continuity.

24. *Time* 142, no. 21 (fall 1993): 66–67.

25. *Time*'s impulse to taxonomize and therefore to make firmer borders around racial types in the United States prior to their 'melding' was evident in many places in the early 1990s. Another parallel example of the graphic unconscious is in the *Newsweek* cover story responding carefully to Richard Herrnstein and Charles Murray's reinvigoration of scientific racism in *The Bell Curve,* titled 'What Color is Black?' and illustrated by a four-by-five square of differently shaded African American faces. As though randomly related, the three faces on the upper-right-hand corner are partly obscured by a yellow slash that reads, 'Bailing Out Mexico.' *Newsweek* 13 February 1995.

26. West, 'The New Cultural Politics of Difference.'

27. *Time* 142, no. 21 (fall 1993): 79.

28. Ibid., 64–65.

29. Ibid., 65.

30. Ibid., 9.

31. Ibid., 87. Henry, *In Defense of Elitism.* See also Henry's much less extreme prophecy of xenophobia to come, in the brief *Time* cover story 'America's Changing Colors,' 9 April 1990: 28–31.

32. Henry, *In Defense of Elitism,* 74.

33. Ibid., 75

34. Ibid.

35. *National Review* 21 February 1994.

36. See *Cosmetics and Toiletries* 109, no. 2: 75; Ethnic Marketing 18 January 1993: 11.

# Chapter 27

# José Esteban Muñoz

## Pedro Zamora's *Real World* of Counterpublicity: Performing an Ethics of the Self

Pedro Zamora died on November 11, 1994. He was twenty-two. The day after his death, a cover story appeared in the *Wall Street Journal*. The article explained that Pedro received thousands of fan letters a week. It quoted one from a South Carolina woman, who wrote: 'I never thought anyone could change my opinion of homosexuals and AIDS. Because of you I saw the human side of something that once seemed so unreal to me.' The letter speaks to Pedro's intervention in the public sphere. It bears witness to the difference this young Latino's life's work made. I will suggest that although these interventions in the majoritarian public sphere were important, one would fail to understand the efficacy of the activist's tactics and the overall success of his life's work if one only considered such letters. Pedro's work enabled the possibility of queer and Latino counterpublics, spheres that stand in opposition to the racism and homophobia of the dominant public sphere. Through this labor one begins to glimpse new horizons of experience.

In what follows, I will outline the activism and cultural interventions of televisual activist Pedro Zamora and describe the way in which he performed what I understand as a Foucauldian ethics of the self. This 'working on the self' allowed Zamora to take a *next* step: a leap into the social through the public performance of an ethics of the self. I will also call attention to the ways in which this Cuban-American cultural worker's performances accomplished tasks that enabled the enactment of queer and Latino identity practices in a phobic public sphere. These

From: José Esteban Muñoz, *Disidentifications: Queers of Color and the Performance of Politics*. Minneapolis, MN: University of Minnesota Press, 1999.

tasks include the denouncement of the dominant public sphere's publicity that fixes images and understandings of queerness and *latinidad;* the enactment of resistance to the reductive multicultural pluralism that is deployed against them; the production of an intervention within the majoritarian public sphere that confronts phobic ideology; and the production of counterpublicity that allows the *possibility* of subaltern counterpublics.

In *The Care of the Self*, the third volume of his *History of Sexuality*, Michel Foucault elaborated, through a tour of antiquity and its philosophical underpinnings, an ethics of the self – a working on the self for others.[1] *The Care of the Self* emphasizes an ethics around nourishing and sustaining a self within civil society. It is ultimately expedient to cite one of Foucault's more elucidating interviews at some length for the purpose of explicating 'the care of the self' and its roots in Hellenistic and Greco-Roman culture:

> What interests me in the Hellenistic culture, in the Greco-Roman culture, starting from the third century BC and continuing until the second or third century after Christ, is a precept for which the Greeks had a specific word, *epimeleia heautou*, which means taking care of oneself. It does not mean simply being interested in oneself, nor does it mean having a certain tendency to self-attachment or self-fascination. *Epimeleia heautou* is a very powerful word in Greek which means 'working on' or 'being concerned with' something. For example, Xenophon used *epimeleia heautou* to describe agricultural management. The responsibility of a monarch for his fellow citizens was also *epimeleia heautou.* That which a doctor does in the course of caring for the patient is *epimeleia heautou.* It is therefore a very powerful word; it describes a sort of work, an activity; it implies attention, knowledge, technique.[2]

I consider the work of televisual activist Zamora to be just such a sort of 'work' that disseminated and 'publicized' 'attentions, knowledges, and techniques' that are consequential to the project of minoritarian subjectivity. I will suggest that Zamora worked within *The Real World*, which one should never forget is a product of the corporate entity MTV, and yet still managed to find ways to do this work *despite* the corporate ethos that ordered that program. Foucault had, at a later stage in his thinking, decided that our understanding of power could be augmented by richer discourse on the subject. Work on the ethics of self ultimately allows us a new vantage point to consider the larger games of truth that organize the social and the relations of these games to states of domination. Within the structure of MTV, and its corporate structure, Zamora performed his care of the self as a truth game that 'was for others,' letting them see and imagine a resistance to entrenched systems of domination.

It is important to note that Foucault's 'care of the self' is based on the lives of citizens and not slaves within antiquity. George Yúdice has pointed out this limit in Foucault's project and has gone on to theorize how an 'ethics of marginality' might be extracted from Foucault's project:

> The problem with Foucault's analysis, as I see it, is that the examples are drawn from the aesthetic practices of Greek freeman and, more important, modernist art. In both cases only elites engage in these particular types of self-analysis and self-formation. This does not mean, however, that Foucault's framework prohibits a priori other types of self-information related to different social groups. On the contrary,

insofar as knowledge, politics (power), and ethics mutually condition each other, despite their relative autonomy, the particularities of the group that engages in ethical practices (its knowledges, its politics) must be taken into consideration. If Foucault could trace the genealogy for dominant groups, it should be equally possible to trace that of dominated and oppressed peoples.[3]

Yúdice outlines the very specific origins of Foucault's paradigm. He suggests that even though elitist and First Worldist limitations exist within Foucault's paradigm, this does not mean that 'Foucault's framework prohibits a priori other types of self-formation related to different social groups.' Yúdice uses Rigoberta Menchú's *testimonio, I, Rigoberta Menchú: An Indian Woman in Guatemala*, as an example when unfolding his theory of an ethics of marginality. He uses the case of Menchú to amend Foucault's notion of 'an aesthetics of existence' and transform it into an ethics in which practical politics plays a central role. Yúdice explains that 'We might say that a "practical poetics" is the ethical "self-forming activity" in which the "self" is practiced in solidarity with others struggling for survival. Menchú, in fact, has turned her identity into a "poetics of defense."'[4] The example of Menchú and her *testimonio* potentially elucidates our understanding of the politics that undergirds Zamora's uses of the self, his care of the self for others. *The Real World* employs what it calls 'video confessionals.' These confessionals have been small rooms within the cast's living space where individual members are encouraged to 'confess' to the camera outside the space of social negotiation. These spaces have been used by the cast as sites where they could perform their selves solo and in private. Real Worlders have used these solo performances to argue for themselves and their identities. These spaces of self-formation are, of course, highly mediated by MTV, even more mediated than Menchú's *testimonio*, which was transcribed and heavily edited by Elisabeth Burgos-Debray. Yet, this corporate mediation does not foreclose the counterpublic building possibilities within these video *testimonios*. Whereas his housemates and cast members from other seasons used the video confessionals to weigh in on domestic squabbles, Zamora used them as vehicles to perform the self for others. Zamora's work, these quotidian video performances, function like video *testimonios* that convert identity into a 'poetics of defense.'

Following Yúdice's lead, I am disidentifying with Foucault's paradigm insofar as I am redeploying it and, to a certain extent, restructuring it, in the service of minoritarian identity. This chapter is interested in imagining an ethic of the minoritarian self. Within a Foucauldian framework recalibrated to consider the minoritarian subject's care of the self, to work on oneself is to veer away from models of the self that correlate with socially prescribed identity narratives. The rejection of these notions of the self is not simply an individualistic rebellion: resisting dominant modes of subjection entails not only contesting dominant modalities of governmental and state power but also opening up a space for new social formations. The performance of Latina/o, queer, and other minoritarian ontologies – which is to say the theatricalization of such ethics of the self – conjures the possibility of social agency within a world bent on the negation of minoritarian subjectivities. My project here is to map and document a minoritarian ethics of the self and, more important, the ways in which representations of and (simultaneously) by that self signal new spaces within the social. I will also suggest that the televisual dissemination of such performances allows for the *possibility of counterpublics* – communities and relational chains of resistance that contest the dominant public sphere. Within radical movements, Zamora's work may not register as progressive enough or may be seen as redundant. The fact that he agreed to work within the tepid multicultural frame of the corporate entity MTV might immediately diminish his significance to already-established activist communities. It is my contention that Zamora's work was not for other activists, queer or Latino, but was instead for a world of *potentially* politicized queers and Latinos; for a mass public that is structured by the cultural forces of homophobia and racism; for those who have no access to more subculturally based cultural production and grassroots activism. Thus, Zamora's activism preaches to the not yet converted, and in doing so may not seem as radical as the work of other activists, but should be acknowledged as frontline struggle and agitation. [...]

The act of performing counterpublicity in and through electronic/televisual sites dominated by the dominant public sphere is risky. Many representations of counterpublicity are robbed of any force by what Miriam Hansen has called the 'marketplace of multicultural pluralism.'[5] The practices of queer and Latino counterpublicity – acts that publicize and theatricalize an ethics of the self – that I am mapping present strategies that resist, often through performances that insist on local specificities and historicity, the pull of reductive multicultural pluralism.

The best way we can understand the categories *queer* and Latina/o or *latinidad* is as counterpublics that are in opposition to other social factions. What is primarily at stake is space. The mode of counterpublicity I am discussing makes an intervention in public life that defies the white normativity *and* heteronormativity of the majoritarian public sphere. Thus, I am proposing that these terms be conceptualized as social movements that are contested by and contest the public sphere for the purposes of political efficacy – movements that not only 'remap' but also *produce* minoritarian space.

The theoretical schools I am blending here – social theory influenced by Habermas and Foucault's discourse analysis – are more often than not pitted *against* each other. Habermas's thinking appeals to and attempts to reconstruct rationality. Foucault's, in its very premise, is a critique of rationality. The mappings that public-sphere social theory provide are extremely generative ones. Yet, as I leave the work of social theorists such as Negt and Kluge, Hansen, and Fraser and return to the major source of these paradigms, Habermas, I find myself having misgivings with his project's philosophical tenets – namely, his use of and investment in communicative reason.[6] Habermasian communicative reason presupposes that within the framing of all communicative gestures there exists an appeal to an undeniable 'good' that would alleviate all disagreements within the social. Foucauldians and others find the category of a universally defined good to be an exceedingly easy target.

My post-Habermasian use of the public sphere is primarily indebted to Negt and Kluge's critique of Habermas, especially their move to critique the underlying concepts of universal reason that they identify in his project. Their critique utilizes Immanuel Kant's critical philosophy to problematize the category of an abstract principle of generality. Their work then opens up space to conceptualize multiple publics, complete with their own particularities.

Jon Simmons has explained that it is indeed difficult to locate Foucault on any map of politics inherited from nineteenth-century philosophy. But he goes on to add that

Foucault does belong to a 'we,' though this 'we' is not easily classifiable according to traditional categories. How does one define the gay movement, feminism, youth protests, the movements of ethnic and national minorities, and the diffuse discontents of clients of educational, health and welfare systems who are identified as single mothers, unemployed, or delinquent? His transgressive practices of self with writing, drugs, gay friendship and S/M operate in the space opened by these movements. Those whose designated desires, genders, ethnic identities, or welfare categorizations do not seem to fit in this space. It is in this space where some women refuse to be feminine and become feminists; in which black-skinned people refuse to be Negroes and become African-Americans; and in which men who desire other men might refuse to be homosexuals and become gay. Like Foucault, they practice the politics of those who refuse to be who they are and strive to become other.[7]

The space that Simmons describes is what I consider the transformative political space of disidentification. Here is where Negt and Kluge function for me as valuable supplements to Foucault's mappings of the social. This space, what Simmons calls Foucault's 'we,' can be given a new materiality and substance when transcoded as counterpublics. Fredric Jameson, in a fascinating essay on Negt and Kluge, sees this connection between the German writers and Foucault, despite the fact that he is ultimately opposed to Foucault and valorizes Negt and Kluge:

The originality of Negt and Kluge, therefore, lies in the way in which the hitherto critical and analytical force of what is widely known as 'discourse analysis' (as in Foucault's descriptions of the restrictions and exclusions at work in a range of so-called discursive formations) is now augmented, not to say completed, by the utopian effort to create space of a new type.[8]

The definition of counterpublics that I am invoking here is intended to describe different subaltern groupings that are defined as falling outside the majoritarian public sphere; it is influenced by a mode of discourse theory that critiques universalities and favors particularities, yet it insists on a Marxian materialist impulse that *regrids* transgressive subjects and their actions as identifiable social movements. Thus, my notion of a counterpublic resonates alongside Simmons's description of 'those whose designated desires, genders, ethnic identities, or welfare categorizations do not seem to fit.' The object of my study, Pedro Zamora, was, from the purview of the dominant public sphere, one of those who did not seem to fit. In this way, his work can be understood as a counterpublic response to dominant publicity.

The young Cuban-American activist disidentified with that dominant publicity, working with *and* on one of its 'channels,' MTV. Habermas, following the example of Frankfurt school predecessor Theodor Adorno, would probably see MTV as the providence of monopoly capitalism, locked into a pattern of sameness that was only calibrated to reproduce the consumer. A strict Habermasian reading could never see MTV as a stage where radical work could be executed. Negt and Kluge understand that in this postmodern moment, the electronic media is essential to the reproduction of state capitalism and counterpublicity. Zamora also understood this. Using his keen sense of counterpublicity, he spotted *The Real World's* potential as an exemplary stage. One need only consider the cover letter he sent MTV when he was applying for the show to understand how the young activist immediately saw the political potential of the medium. I will first cite a section of the letter where his pitch challenges the producers to consider the possibility of having a person living with AIDS on the show:

> So why should I be on *The Real World?* Because in the real world there are people living productive lives who just happen to be HIV+. I think it is important for people my age to see a young person who looks and feels healthy, can party and have fun but at the same time needs to take five pills daily to stay healthy.
>
> On one of your episodes this season [season two] you had an HIV+ guy come in and talk about AIDS/HIV with the group. He was there a few hours and he left. I wonder what kind of issues would have come up if that HIV + guy would be living with the group, sharing the bathroom, the refrigerator, the bedroom, eating together? Everyday for six months. Things that make you go hmmmm.[9]

Here Zamora describes the dramatic and televisual energy his inclusion in the show would generate. He does not pitch his project in all its political urgencies. He understands that one needs to disidentify with the application process to be given access to the stage that the cable program provided him. He plays up the fact that his inclusion would make for good TV as well as be an important political intervention. He next speaks of his willingness to sacrifice his own privacy for the sake of his activism:

> I know that being on *The Real World* would mean exposing the most intimate details of my life on national television. How comfortable am I with that? Well, I do that through my job every day.
>
> If I can answer the questions of an auditorium full of fifth graders with inquiring minds, I am sure I could do it on national television.[10]

Zamora is willing to sacrifice his right to privacy because he understands that subjects like himself never have full access to privacy. Although the dominant public sphere would like to cast him in the zone of private illness, it is clear that any fantasy of real privacy, as *Bowers v. Hardwick* signals, is always illusory. In this statement, the young activist conveys his understanding that his desires, gender identifications, health, and national and ethnic minority status keep him from having any recourse to the national fantasy of privacy to which other subjects in the public sphere cling. [...]

Since its inception in 1991, MTV's *The Real World* has included queers in its 'real-life' ensemble cinema verité-style melodrama. The show's premise is simple: seven videogenic young people, all strangers, are chosen to live in a house together. The twenty-something group is usually racially diverse. Its gender breakdown is usually four men and three women. It has had five different 'casts' and five different incarnations, in five different cities: New York, Los Angeles, San Francisco, London, and Miami. Each season has included a gay or lesbian character. The New York cast included Norman, a white man who sometimes identified as bisexual and sometimes as gay. While being rather charismatic, Norman was something of a minor character on the show; most of that season focused on the contrived sexual tension between innocent country girl Julie and Eric, a New Jerseyan Herb Ritts model who was nominally straight and went on to host the illustrious MTV dance-party show

*The Grind.* Much steam was lost in the show's second season, in which the queer came as a mid-season replacement. Beth was a white lesbian who worked in B horror-movie production. Beth received probably less screen time than any other character in the show's five seasons. Norman and Beth both dated, but their sexual lives were relegated to 'special episodes.' The way in which these two characters were contained and rendered narratively subordinate to the show's straight characters is a succinct example of the inane multicultural pluralism that Hansen has described. It also clearly displays some of the ways in which queers and the counterpublicity they might be able to disseminate are rendered harmless within the channels of the electronic media and the majoritarian public sphere. Zamora was the third season's house queer. He did not, however, fall into obscurity the way his queer predecessors had. Rather, he managed to offer valuable counterpublicity for various subaltern counterpublics that included U.S. Latinos, queers, and people living with AIDS.

For five months Zamora was one of the few out gay men appearing regularly on television.[11] He was also one of the few Latinos seen regularly on national television. Furthermore, he was one of the few out people living with AIDS on television. There should be no mistake as to MTV's motives in selecting Zamora. He was as handsome as a model and rarely looked 'ill' in any way. He was a Cuban-American, a group that comes as close as any Latino community in the United States to qualifying as a 'model minority.' Although articulate and skilled as a public speaker, he had a thick Cuban accent that must have sounded very 'tropical' to North American ears. [...] Zamora was selected because of these features and his agency in this selection process was none. He fitted a larger corporate schema as to what MTV wanted for the show and these reasons led to his being represented. Yet, Zamora was more than simply represented; he used MTV as an opportunity to continue his life's work of HIV/AIDS pedagogy, queer education, and human-rights activism. Unlike his queer predecessors, he exploited MTV in politically efficacious ways; he used MTV more than it used him.

The fourth season of the show was set in London. At this point the show broke from its pattern of having an out house queer. *The Real World* London show was less contentious than the San Francisco show. It only included one ethnic minority, a black British jazz singer, and not one out lesbian, gay, bisexual, or transgendered person. It would seem that the ethnic, racial, and sexual diversity that characterized the show's first three seasons was put on hold after the explosive San Francisco season [...] I will argue that the soft multicultural pluralism that characterized the series was exploited and undermined by Zamora and some of his peers. I am suggesting that the fourth season of *The Real World* can be read as a backlash of sorts; which is to say that it was an escape from North American politics and social tensions to a storybook England, a fantasy Europe that had none of its own ethnic or sexual strife. (The roommates actually lived in a flat that was made up to look like a castle.)

The fifth season, set in Miami, represents a back-to-basics approach in which the tried-and-true formula of nominal racial and sexual diversity was reestablished. The Miami cast included two women of color: Cynthia, an African-American waitress from Oakland, California, and Melissa, 'the local girl,' a Cuban-American woman from the Miami area. The house queer spot went once again to a white man, as it did in the show's classic first season. Dan, a college student from Rutgers University, was raised in the Midwest, where he grew up watching the show like many queer kids in the United States. In a feature article in *Out* magazine, Dan spoke about the way in which he, as a pre-out youth, marveled at seeing an out Norman in the show's first season. In the article he expresses his understanding that he was now, thanks to the show, going to be the most famous gay man in America. The young Real Worlder's statement testifies to the counterpublic-making properties of the program. Dan aspires to be a model and a writer for flashy fashion magazines. His interviews on the program and in the print media indicate that he was cognizant of a need to be a public 'role model' for queers, but his performances fell short of the radical interventions that Zamora produced.

Dan understood the need to perform a positive image; Zamora, on the other hand, was conscious of the need to take the show's title seriously and be radically *real*. A coffee-table fan book that MTV published in 1995 while the fourth season was airing prints 'sound bites' by many of the show's stars, producers, and crew; the book's revenues go, in part, to the foundation started in Zamora's name. In that book, story editor Gordon Cassidy comments:

> The one thing I feel best about in this show is what Pedro enabled us to present to the rest of the country, and not just about AIDS, but about who he was as a person, things that networks can't get away with. You think of the problems networks have portraying gay relationships, interracial relationships, and he was all of those.[12]

The fact that Zamora was indeed all of these things is especially important. The 'realness' of Pedro and the efficacy and power of his interventions have as much to do with the manner in which he insisted on being a complicated and intersectional subject: not only gay but a sexual person; a person of color actively living with another person of color in an interracial relationship; a person living with AIDS. Although Cassidy's comments could be read as an example of MTV's patting itself on the back, much of what he is saying is accurate. As of this moment, with few exceptions, broadcast network television is unable and unwilling to represent queers who are sexual yet not pathological, interracial relationships, and stories about AIDS that portray the fullness and vibrancy of such a life narrative.

To understand Pedro's intervention one needs to survey the status of homosexuality on television at the time of his death in November 1994. A *Los Angeles Times* feature article cites Richard Jennings, executive director of Hollywood Supports, a group promoting positive gay portrayals in film and television, on the resurgence of gay characters in the media: 'As gays have increasingly 'come out,' many viewers have become aware of gay brothers, sisters and friends. Together with gay viewers, they are increasingly asking for sympathetic gay portrayals.'[13] This lobbying is opposed by right-wing activists such as the Reverend Louis Sheldon, head of the Orange County–based Traditional Values Coalition. Sheldon is quoted in the same article as saying that 'Homosexuals should not be portrayed at all on TV.' Sheldon, a bigot who is notorious for 'picketing' outside of AIDS memorials and funerals, feels that sympathetic gay role models confuse viewers and contends that 'If young males need to identify with someone, they should identify with Clint Eastwood.'[14] […]

Although some advertisers seem to have become more accepting of queer representation – Ellen DeGeneres's very public coming out in the spring of 1997 and the appearance of a black gay supporting character in ABC's *Spin City* are evidence of this – very few queer characters on television have, as of this writing, performed their sexualities on the screen. [...]

Within this context, Zamora's performance of self, his publicized 'care of the self,' especially as represented in an episode that featured an exchanging of rings ceremony with boyfriend Sean, can be seen as radical interventions. In that episode, originally broadcast on November 3, 1994, the two men kiss no fewer than seven times in the half-hour program. Zamora's romance was, according to producer John Murray, significant within the history of the show as it was, 'probably the deepest we've ever gotten into a relationship in our three seasons.'[15] [...] When I suggest that such performances function as counterpublicity, I am imagining the effect that they might have on a queer child or adult whose access to queer cultures or energies might be limited or nonexistent. These highly mediated images, brought into the fold through the highly mediated channels of corporate broadcasting, still served as a site where children and others could glimpse a queer *and* ethnic life-world. What started out as tokenized representation became something larger, more spacious – a mirror that served as a prop for subjects to imagine and rehearse identity. This, in part, enables the production of counterpublics.

It would be a mistake to elide the representational significance of Zamora's work on the mainstream. Pedro, as Bill Clinton put it, gave AIDS a very 'human face.' Beyond that, he gave it a vibrant, attractive, politicized, and brown face. He showed an ignorant and phobic national body that within the bourgeois public's fantasy of privacy, the binarism of public health and private illness could no longer hold – that the epidemic was no longer an abstract and privatized concern. He willfully embodied and called attention to all those things that are devastating and ennobling about possessing a minority subjectivity within an epidemic. Although MTV gave Zamora a stage to do this work of education and embodiment, however, it should not be too valorized for this contribution because it often attempted to undercut it. [...]

The show begins with Cory, a college student from California who rendezvoused with Pedro on a train.[16] The young Anglo woman is very taken with Pedro, and Pedro, for his part, as he explains in a voice-over, was expecting to meet a woman who would be very much like Cory, very 'all-American.' Soon all of the roommates are assembled: Judd, a Jewish cartoonist from Long Island; Pam, an Asian-American medical student; Mohammed, an African-American Bay Area musician and writer; Puck, a white man who was a bicycle messenger; and Rachel, a Republican Mexican-American from Arizona who is applying to graduate school.[17] [...] That first episode concluded with Pedro sharing his scrapbook with his roommates. The scrapbook consisted of newspaper clippings from around the nation of his activist work. This outed him to the rest of the cast not only as queer but also as a person living with AIDS. Rachel was put off by this display and proceeded, during an interview in the confessional,[18] to voice her AIDSphobic and homophobic concerns about cohabiting with Pedro. Thus, that first episode began with the 'all-American girl' meeting the handsome young stranger on a train and concluded with a conservative Latina expressing a phobic position against the young AIDS educator. This episode framed Pedro as one of the show's 'star' presences, unlike the queers from previous seasons.

Episode two presents an early confrontation between Pedro and the show's other star presence, Puck. Pedro objects to Puck's post-punk hygiene in the kitchen and throughout the living space. The show had hoped to frame this confrontation as a sort of odd couple dilemma, but it ignored the fact that Puck's lack of hygiene was nothing short of a medical risk for a person living with a compromised immune system. While Rachel goes to an 'Empower America' fund-raiser and meets the New Right's beloved Jack Kemp, one of her personal heroes, Pedro goes on a first date with Sean, an HIV-positive pastry chef with a disarming smile. Sean and Pedro's relationship advances and the couple falls in love by episode six. Puck makes homophobic jokes about Pedro during this episode. According to interviews with the cast after the series was completed, these comments from Puck were a regular household occurrence that was, through editing strategies, downplayed by the producers.

In episode eight, Pedro goes for a medical examination. He discovers that his T-cell count has dropped significantly. This moment represents an important moment in TV history: a painful aspect of a PWA's quotidian reality is represented as never before. This sequence is followed by one in which Pedro gives a safe-sex and risk-prevention seminar at Stanford University. Puck, always vying for the house's attention, schedules a beachcombing expedition at the same time. Pam and Judd choose to watch and support Pedro while Cory and Rachel join Puck. The show crosscuts both sequences, emphasizing the divisions in the house. Tensions mount during episode nine. Pedro and Sean become engaged and Puck reacts with what is by now predictable homophobia. The house confronts Puck on his behavioral problems in episode eleven. Puck will not listen and Pedro delivers an ultimatum to the house: it is either him or Puck. The members vote, and Puck is unanimously ejected from the house. [...]

Episode thirteen focuses on Pedro's returning home to Miami and his best friend Alex. The homecoming is cut short when Pedro becomes sick. Zamora, in a post–*Real World* interview, explained that he had wanted to show it all, the good days and the bad days.[19] Representing the totality of living with AIDS was very important for his ethics of the self, his performance of being a self *for* others. That episode gives a family history and background. Pedro emigrated to the United States in the Mariel boat lift in 1980. He lost his mother to cancer at the age of fifteen, a tragedy that rocked his family. His family is represented as a very typical blue-collar Cuban-American family. Cuban-Americans, especially Miami Cubans, are associated with right-wing politics and values. It is thus important to see this family embrace their son and brother without hesitation. The image of Cuban-Americans loving, accepting, and being proud of a gay son complicates the map of *latinidad* that is most available within U.S. media. The better-known map that positions Cubans on the far right and Chicanos on the far left, while demographically founded, is nonetheless a reductive depiction of *latinidad*. [...]

The second-to-last episode, episode nineteen, points out the restraints that the show's producers put on Zamora's performances and the way in which the young Cuban-American responded to them. Pedro's romance became the major romance of the show; Sean never fell out of the picture the way Norman's and Beth's partners and flirtations did. Sean became part of Pedro's quotidian reality. Both made their presence continuously known in the San Francisco flat. A few weeks into their relationship, Sean proposed marriage to Pedro and Pedro accepted. In response, the show's other 'star' presence, Puck, decided to one-up the queer couple by proposing marriage to his new girlfriend Toni. Puck stands as proof that not all counter-publics challenge the way in which the social is organized by the dominant culture.

Puck's counterpublic is a juvenile version of rugged individualism; it represents a sort of soft anarchism that relativizes all political struggles as equivalents to his own exhaustive self-absorption. The competing modes of counterpublicity between Pedro and Puck eventually contributed to the breakdown in the domestic space that concluded with Puck's being asked to leave.

Episode nineteen tracks Pedro's and Puck's respective romances. Pedro's queerness is played against Puck's heterosexuality. The episode crosscuts between the two pairings. One questions the producer's rationale for juxtaposing Puck and Toni's romantic relationship with Pedro and Sean's commitment ceremony. Because Puck was ejected from the house, producers continued to film his encounters with his former housemates Cory, Rachel, and Judd. But except for this penultimate episode, there had been no presentation of Puck independent of his housemates.

Early in the episode, Sean and Pedro are shown in bed together as they lie on top of each other and plan their commitment ceremony. To MTV's credit, there has never been any scene of queer sociality like it on television. The scene of two gay men of color, both HIV positive, in bed together as they plan what is the equivalent of a marriage is like none that was then or now imaginable on television. The transmission of this image throughout the nation and the world is a valuable instance of counterpublicity. Edited within this scene are individual video bites by both participants. Sean explains that

> [b]eing with Pedro, someone who is so willing to trust and love and sort of be honest with, is refreshing. I think that knowing that Pedro does have an AIDS diagnosis and has been getting sick makes me recognize the need to be here right now. I know that one of us may get sick at sometime but [it is this] underlying understanding or this underlying feeling that makes it a lot easier.

Sean's statement and his performance in front of the video camera explain their reason for having a formal bonding ceremony as being a response to a radically refigured temporality in the face of AIDS. This, too, is an important instance of nationally broadcast counterpublic theater that provides an important opportunity for the mass public to glimpse different life-worlds than the one endorsed by the dominant ideology.

Yet, the power of this image and Sean's statement is dulled when the program cuts to its next scene. The gay coupling scene is followed by Puck and Toni's coupling ritual. Puck, in a voice-over, announces that he and Toni are made for each other, that they are, in fact, 'a matched pair.' They go window-shopping for a wedding ring and Toni eyes a ring that she likes; Puck scolds her and tells her that the window item is a cocktail ring, not a traditional wedding ring. He then offers to buy her a tie clip instead. [...] Sean's voice-over is narratively matched with the playful Toni who explains that '[w]hen I first met Puck he was stinking and looking for a mate. I think we're in love. I know we're in love.' Whereas Sean and Pedro are preparing for an actual ceremony, Toni and Puck are shown hanging out. Toni and Puck are not planning any sort of ceremony. The producers' strategy of matching the story lines and making them seem equivalent is resolved by crosscutting the commitment ceremony with one of Puck's soapbox derby races. Toni is shown cheering Puck on as he races his green boxcar.

Since the inception of *The Real World,* its producers have always hoped for a romance to erupt on the set between cast members. That has yet to happen.[20] In lieu of such a relationship, the producers hope for an interesting relationship between a cast member and outsider. Sean and Pedro's romance emerged early on as the show's most significant relationship. I am arguing that the series producers were unable to let a queer coupling, especially one as radical as Sean and Pedro's, to stand as the show's actual romance. Pedro's and Sean's individual perform-ances and the performance of their relationship were narratively undermined by a strategy of weak multicultural crosscutting that was calibrated to dampen the radical charge that Pedro and Sean gave *The Real World*.

Despite these efforts by the show's producers to diminish the importance of Pedro and Sean's relationship, the ceremony itself stands as an amazingly pow-erful example of publicly performing an ethics of the self while simultaneously theatricalizing a queer counterpublic sphere.

The ceremony begins with a shot of a densely populated flat. Sean and Pedro are toasted by Eric, a friend of the couple who has not appeared on any previous episodes, and who delivers a touching toast:

> It gives me a lot of pleasure and I see it as a real pleasure to speak on behalf of Sean and Pedro and to them. In your love you remind us that life is about now and love is about being there for one another. It is with real bravery that you open your hearts *to each other* and I think it's with real hope that you promise your lives to each other. *We stand with you* defiantly and bravely and with real hope. To the adorable couple. (My emphasis)

This toast is followed by equally elegant statements by both Pedro and Sean. Eric's statement is significant because it marks the way in which Pedro and Sean's being for themselves ('to each other') is, simultaneously, a being for others ('We stand with you'). This ceremony is like none that has ever been viewed on com-mercial television. It is a moment of counterpublic theater. The commitment ceremony not only inspires the gathering of spectators at the ceremony to stand together bravely, defiantly, and with hope, but also, beyond the walls of the Lombard Street flat and beyond the relatively progressive parameters of San Francisco, it inspires a world of televisual spectators.

*The Real World* is overrun by queers. Queer bonds are made manifest in ways that have never been available on cable or broadcast television. Pedro's insistence on mastering the show's format through his monologues, domestic interventions, and continuous pedagogy are relaxed in the sequence just described. Here the public sphere is reimagined by bringing a subaltern counterpublic into represen-tation. The real world is overrun by queers – queers who speak about those things that are terrifying and ennobling about a queer and racialized life-world. The commitment ceremony sequence in many ways sets up the show's closure. Puck's antics, crosscut and stacked next to the commitment ceremony, are narratively positioned to lessen the queer spin put on *The Real World* by Pedro. Such a strat-egy is concurrent with the show's pluralist ethos. Queer commitments, energies, and politics are never quite left to stand alone.

The way Puck's relationship is used to relativize and diminish the emotional and political impact of Pedro and Sean's relationship is reminiscent of Pedro's selection to be included in the cast *with and in contrast to* Rachel, the young Republican Latina. Again, the ideologically bold move of representing an activist such as Pedro as a representative of *latinidad* is counterbalanced by a reactionary Latina. The fact that Rachel and Pedro later bond as Latinos, despite their ideological differ-ences, is narratively satisfying, producing a sense of hope for the spectator invested in pan-Latino politics.

The performance of a commitment ceremony itself might be read as an aping of heterosexual relationships. Such a reading would miss some important points. In a voice-over before the ceremony, Pedro discusses the need to 'risk' being with Sean. He points to the ways in which this relationship, within the confines of his tragically abbreviated temporality, forms a new space of self, identity, and relationality. It is, in Foucault's terms, a new form. The couple form, crystallized as the bourgeois heterosexual dyad, is shattered and reconfigured. Indeed, this is a disidentification with the couple form. When one is queer and knows that his or her loved one is dying, the act of 'giving oneself' to another represents an ethics of the self that does not cohere with the prescribed and normative coupling practices that make heterosexuals and some lesbians and gay men want to marry. Pedro and Sean's ceremonial bonding is *not* about aping bourgeois heterosexuality; rather, it is the enacting of a new mode of sociality. Foucault, in an often-cited interview on friendship, suggested that we understand homosexuality not so much as a desire, but rather as something that is *desirable.* He explains that we must 'work at becoming homosexual and not be obstinate in recognizing that we are.'[21] Homosexuality is desirable because a homosexual way of life allows us to reimagine sociality. The homosexual needs to 'invent from A to Z a relationship that is formless' and eventually to arrive at a 'multiplicity of relations.'[22]

Becoming homosexual, for Foucault, would then be a political project, a social movement of sorts, that would ultimately help us challenge repressive gender hierarchies and the structural underpinnings of institutions. Thus, mark Sean and Pedro's union as something new, a new form that is at the same time formless from the vantage point of established state hierarchies.[23] The new form that Sean and Pedro's performances of self bring into view is one that suggests worlds of possibility for the minoritarian subject who experiences multiple forms of domination within larger systems of governmentality.

When considering Zamora's lifework one is struck by his accomplishments, interventions within the dominant public sphere that had real effects on individuals [...] and other interventions as an activist. Zamora tested positive for HIV while still in high school, a few years after he arrived in the United States with his parents and two siblings in 1980 with some one hundred thousand other Cuban refugees who sailed to Florida in the Mariel boat lift. His activism began not long after he tested positive for the virus. Zamora testified before the Presidential Commission on AIDS and twice before congressional committees, took part in a public service ad campaign for the Centers for Disease Control and Prevention, and was appointed to a Florida government panel on AIDS. He also gave many interviews in the print and electronic media. I first encountered Zamora before his tenure on MTV. I saw him and his father on a local Spanish-language television news program in south Florida while I was visiting my parents during college. As I sat in the living room with my parents, I marveled at the televisual spectacle of this young man and his father, both speaking a distinctly Cuban Spanish, on television, talking openly about AIDS, safe sex, and homosexuality. I was struck because this was something new; it was a new formation, a being for others. I imagined countless other living rooms within the range of this broadcast and I thought about the queer children who might be watching this program at home with their parents. This is the point where I locate something other than the concrete interventions in the public sphere. Here is where I see the televisual spectacle leading to the possibility of new counterpublics, new spheres of possibility, and the potential for the reinvention of the world from A to Z.

# Notes

1. Michel Foucault, *The History of Sexuality,* vol. 3, *The Care of the Self,* trans. Robert Hurley (New York: Vintage Books, 1986). Also see Michel Foucault, 'The Ethic of the Care of the Self as a Practice of Freedom,' in *The Final Foucault,* ed. James Bernauer and David Rasmussen, trans. J. D. Gauthier (Cambridge: MIT Press, 1987).

2. Michel Foucault, 'On the Genealogy of Ethics: An Overview of Work in Progress,' in *Ethics: Subjectivity and Truth,* ed. Paul Rabinow, trans. Robert Hurley (New York: New Press, 1997), p. 269.

3. George Yúdice, 'Marginality and the Ethics of Survival,' in Andrew Ross, ed., *Universal Abandon? The Politics of Postmodernism* (Minneapolis: University of Minnesota Press, 1988), p. 220.

4. Ibid., p. 229.

5. Miriam Hansen, 'Foreword,' in Oskar Negt and Alexander Kluge, *Public Sphere and Experience: Toward an Analysis of the Bourgeois and Proletarian Public Sphere* (Minneapolis: University of Minnesota Press, 1999), p. xxxvii.

6. For an excellent reading of the political and philosophical disjunctures between Foucault and Habermas, see Jon Simmons, *Foucault and the Political* (New York: Routledge, 1995).

7. Ibid., p. 103.

8. Fredric Jameson. 'On Negt and Kluge,' in *The Phantom Public Sphere*, ed. Bruce Robbins (Minneapolis: University of Minnesota Press, 1993), p. 49.

9. Hillary Johnson and Nancy Rommelmann, *The Real* Real World (New York: MTV Books/Pocket Books/Melcher Media, 1995), p. 158.

10. Ibid.

11. Zamora has continued to be, even after his death, a beacon of queer possibility thanks to MTV's policy of continuously airing *The Real World* returns, from all five seasons.

12. Johnson and Rommelmann, *The Real* Real World, p. 90.

13. Joseph Hanania, 'Resurgence of Gay Roles on Television,' *Los Angeles Times,* November 3, 1994, p. 12.

14. Ibid.

15. Ibid.

16. The show used only first names. Thus, when I discuss the narratives of actual episodes, I will employ 'Pedro,' and when I refer mostly to the man and cultural worker outside of the show's narrative, I will use 'Zamora.'

17. I use the term *Mexican-American* to describe Rachel because I imagine that her political ideology would not be aligned with the politics of the Chicana/o movement.

18. The confessional is a room where house occupants perform a personal monologue for a stationary camera. The confessional footage is later intercut with the show's narrative.

19. Hal Rubenstein, 'Pedro Leaves Us Breathless,' *POZ* 1:3 (August–September 1994): 38–41, 79–81.

20. Judd and Pam did eventually begin dating, but only after the show stopped filming. Failed on-the-set couplings include Eric and Julie during the first season, Puck and Rachel in the third, and Kat and Neil in the fourth.

21. Michel Foucault, *Foucault Live,* ed. Sylvère Lotringer, trans. John Johnston (New York: Semiotext[e], 1989), p. 204.

22. Ibid.

23. The Pedro Zamora Memorial Fund was established after his death. The fund was set up to educate women, young people, minorities, and the poor about HIV/AIDS, and to fund AIDS service organizations. The fund, part of AIDS Action, can be reached at 202-986-1300 ext. 3013.

# Chapter 28

# Richard Fung

## Looking for my Penis: The Eroticized Asian in Gay Video Porn

Several scientists have begun to examine the relation between personality and human reproductive behaviour from a gene-based evolutionary perspective ... In this vein we reported a study of racial difference in sexual restraint such that Orientals > whites > blacks. Restraint was indexed in numerous ways, having in common a lowered allocation of bodily energy to sexual functioning. We found the same racial pattern occurred on gamete production (dizygotic birthing frequency per 100: Mongoloids, 4; Caucasoids, 8; Negroids, 16), intercourse frequencies (pre-marital, marital, extramarital), developmental precocity (age at first intercourse, age at first pregnancy, number of pregnancies), primary sexual characteristics (size of penis, vagina, testis, ovaries), secondary sexual characteristics (salient voice, muscularity, buttocks, breasts), and biologic control of behaviour (periodicity of sexual response, predictability of life history from onset of puberty), as well as in androgen levels and sexual attitudes. (Rushton and Bogaert 259)

This passage from *the Journal of Research in Personality* was written by University of Western Ontario psychologist Philippe Rushton, who enjoys considerable controversy in Canadian academic circles and in the popular media. His thesis, articulated throughout his work, appropriates biological studies of the continuum of reproductive strategies of oysters through to chimpanzees and posits that degree of 'sexuality' – interpreted as penis and vagina size, frequency of intercourse, buttock and lip size – correlates positively with criminality and sociopathic behavior and inversely intelligence, health, and longevity. Rushton sees race as *the* determining factor and places East Asians (Rushton uses the word *Orientals*) on one end of the spectrum and blacks on the other. Since whites fall squarely in the

From: *How Do I Look? Queer Film and Video.* Ed. Bad-Object Choices. Seattle, WA: Bay Press, 1991.

middle, the position of perfect balance, there is no need for analysis, and they remain free of scrutiny.

Notwithstanding its profound scientific shortcomings, Rushton's work serves as an excellent articulation of a dominant discourse on race and sexuality in Western society – a system of ideas and reciprocal practices that originated in Europe simultaneously with (some argue as a conscious justification for)[1] colonial expansion and slavery. In the nineteenth century these ideas took on a scientific gloss with social Darwinism and eugenics. Now they reappear, somewhat altered, in psychology journals from the likes of Rushton. It is important to add that these ideas have also permeated the global popular consciousness. Anyone who has been exposed to Western television or advertising images, which is much of the world, will have absorbed this particular constellation of stereotyping and racial hierarchy. [...]

The contemporary construction of race and sex as exemplified by Rushton has endowed black people, both men and women, with a threatening hypersexuality. Asians, on the other hand, are collectively seen as undersexed.[2] But here I want to make some crucial distinctions. First, in North America, stereotyping has focused almost exclusively on what recent colonial language designates as 'Orientals' – that is East and Southeast Asian peoples – as opposed to the 'Orientalism' discussed by Edward Said, which concerns the Middle East. This current, popular usage is based more on a perception of similar physical features – black hair, 'slanted' eyes, high cheek bones, and so on – than through a reference to common cultural traits. South Asians, people whose backgrounds are in the Indian subcontinent and Sri Lanka, hardly figure at all in North American popular representations, and those few images are ostensibly devoid of sexual connotation.[3]

Second, within the totalizing stereotype of the 'Oriental,' there are competing and sometimes contradictory sexual associations based on nationality. So, for example, a person could be seen as Japanese and somewhat kinky, or Filipino and 'available.' The very same person could also be seen as 'Oriental' and therefore sexless. In addition, the racial hierarchy revamped by Rushton is itself in tension with an earlier and only partially eclipsed depiction of *all* Asians as having an undisciplined and dangerous libido. I am referring to the writings of the early European explorers and missionaries, but also to antimiscegenation laws and such specific legislation as the 1912 Saskatchewan law that barred white women from employment in Chinese-owned businesses.

Finally, East Asian women figure differently from men both in reality and in representation. In 'Lotus Blossoms Don't Bleed,' Renee Tajima points out that in Hollywood films.

> there are two basic types: the Lotus Blossom Baby (a.k.a. China Doll, Geisha Girl, shy Polynesian beauty, et al.) and the Dragon Lady (Fu Manchu's various female relations, prostitutes, devious madames).... Asian women in film are, for the most part, passive figures who exist to serve men – as love interests for white men (re: Lotus Blossoms) or as partners in crime for men of their own kind (re: Dragon Ladies) (28)

Further:

> Dutiful creatures that they are, Asian women are often assigned the task of expendability in a situation of illicit love ... . Noticeably lacking is the portrayal of love relationships between Asian women and Asian men, particularly as lead characters. (29)

Because of their supposed passivity and sexual compliance, Asian women have been fetishized in dominant representation, and there is a large and growing body of literature by Asian women on the oppressiveness of these images. Asian men, however (at least since Sessue Hayakawa, who made a Hollywood career in the 1920s of representing the Asian man as sexual threat)[4] have been consigned to one of two categories: the egghead/wimp, or – in what may be analogous to the lotus blossom–dragon lady dichotomy – the kung fu master/ninja/samurai. He is sometimes dangerous, sometimes friendly, but almost always characterized by a desexualized Zen asceticsm. So whereas, as Fanon tells us, 'the Negro is eclipsed. He is turned into a penis. He *is* a penis,'[5] the Asian man is defined by a striking absence down there. And if Asian men have no sexuality, how can we have homosexuality?

Even as recently as the early 1980s, I remember having to prove my queer credentials before being admitted with other Asian men into a Toronto gay club. I do not believe it was a question of a color barrier. Rather, my friends and I felt that the doorman was genuinely unsure about our sexual orientation. We also felt that had we been white and dressed similarly, our entrance would have been automatic.[6]

Although a motto for the lesbian and gay movements has been 'we are everywhere,' Asians are largely absent from the images produced by both the political and the commercial sectors of the mainstream gay and lesbian communities. From the earliest articulation of the Asian gay and lesbian movements, a principal concern has therefore been visibility. In political organizing, the demand for a voice, or rather the demand to be heard, has largely been responded to by the problematic practice of 'minority' representation on panels and boards.[7] But since racism is a question of power and not of numbers, this strategy has often led to a dead-end tokenistic integration, failing to address the real imbalances.

Creating a space for Asian gay and lesbian representation has meant, among other things, deepening an understanding of what is at stake for Asians in coming out publicly.[8] As is the case for many other people of color and especially immigrants, our families and our ethnic communities are a rare source of affirmation in a racist society. In coming out, we risk (or feel that we risk) losing this support, though the ever-growing organizations of lesbian and gay Asians have worked against this process of cultural exile. In my own experience, the existence of a gay Asian community broke down the cultural schizophrenia in which I related, on one hand, to a heterosexual family that affirmed my ethnic culture and, on the other hand, to a gay community that was predominantly white. Knowing that there was support also helped me come out to my family and further bridge the gap.

If we look at commercial gay sexual representation, it appears that the antiracist movements have had little impact: the images of men and male beauty are still of *white* men and *white* male beauty. These are the standards against which we compare both ourselves and often our brothers – Asian, black, native, and Latino.[9] Although other people's rejection (or fetishization) of us according to the established racial hierarchies may be experienced as oppressive, we are not necessarily moved to scrutinize our own desire and its relationship to the hegemonic image of the white man.[10]

In my lifelong vocation of looking for my penis, trying to fill in the visual void, I have come across only a handful of primary and secondary references to Asian male sexuality in North American representation. Even in my own video work, the stress has been on deconstructing sexual representation and only marginally on creating erotica. So I was very excited at the discovery of a Vietnamese American working in gay porn.

Having acted in six videotapes, Sum Yung Mahn is perhaps the only Asian to qualify as a gay porn 'star.' Variously known as Brad Troung or Sam or Sum Yung Mahn, he has worked for a number of different production studios. All of the tapes in which he appears are distributed through International Wavelength, a San Francisco-based mail-order company whose catalog entries feature Asians in American, Thai, and Japanese productions. According to the owner of International Wavelength, about 90 percent of the Asian tapes are bought by white men, and the remaining 10 percent are purchased by Asians. But the number of Asian buyers is growing.

In examining Sum Yung Mahn's work, it is important to recognize the different strategies used for fitting an Asian actor into the traditionally white world of gay porn and how the terms of entry are determined by the perceived demands of an intended audience. Three tapes, each geared toward a specific erotic interest, illustrate these strategies.

*Below the Belt*, like most porn tapes, has an episodic structure. All the sequences involve the students and *sensei* of an all-male karate *dojo*. The authenticity of the setting is proclaimed with the opening shots of a gym full of *gi*-clad, serious-faced young men going through their weapons exercises. Each of the main actors is introduced in turn; with the exception of the teacher, who has dark hair, all fit into the current porn conventions of Aryan, blond, shaved, good looks.[11] Moreover, since Sum Yung Mahn is not even listed in the opening credits, we can surmise that this tape is not targeted to an audience with any particular erotic interest in Asian men. Most gay video porn uses white actors exclusively; those tapes having the least bit of racial integration are pitched to the specialty market through outlets such as International Wavelength.[12] This visual apartheid stems, I assume, from an erroneous perception that the sexual appetites of gay men are exclusive and unchangeable.

A karate *dojo* offers a rich opportunity to introduce Asian actors. One might imagine it as the gay Orientalist's dream project. But given the intended audience for this video, the erotic appeal of the *dojo*, except for the costumes and a few misplaced props (Taiwanese and Korean flags for a Japanese art form?), is completely appropriated into a white world.

The tape's action occurs in a gym, in the students' apartments, and in a garden. The one scene with Sum Yung Mahn is a dream sequence. Two students, Robbie and Stevie, are sitting in a locker room. Robbie confesses that he has been having strange dreams about Greg, their teacher. Cut to the dream sequence, which is coded by clouds of green smoke. Robbie is wearing a red headband with black markings suggesting script (if indeed they belong to an Asian language, they are not the Japanese or Chinese characters that one would expect). He is trapped in an elaborate snare. Enter a character in a black *ninja* mask, wielding a *nanchaku*. Robbie narrates: 'I knew this evil samurai would kill me.' The masked figure is menacingly running the *nanchaku* chain under Robbie's genitals when Greg, the teacher, appears and disposes of him. Robbie explains to Stevie in the locker room: 'I knew that I owed him my life, and I knew I had to please him [long pause] in any way that he wanted.' During that pause we cut back to the dream. Amid more puffs of smoke, Greg, carrying a man in his arms, approaches a low platform. Although Greg's back is toward the camera, we can see that the man is wearing the red headband that identifies him as Robbie. As Greg lays him down, we see that Robbie has 'turned Japanese'! It's Sum Yung Mahn.

Greg fucks Sum Yung Mahn, who is always face down. The scene constructs anal intercourse for the Asian Robbie as an act of submission, not of pleasure: unlike other scenes of anal intercourse in the tape, for example, there is no dubbed dialogue on the order of 'Oh yeah ... fuck me harder!' but merely ambiguous groans. Without coming, Greg leaves. A group of (white) men wearing Japanese outfits encircle the platform, and Asian Robbie, or 'the Oriental boy,' as he is listed in the final credits, turns to lie on his back. He sucks a cock, licks someone's balls. The other men come all over his body; he comes. The final shot of the sequence zooms in to a close-up of Sum Yung Mahn's headband, which dissolves to a similar close-up of Robbie wearing the same headband, emphasizing that the two actors represent one character.

We now cut back to the locker room. Robbie's story has made Stevie horny. He reaches into Robbie's pants, pulls out his penis, and sex follows. In his Asian manifestation, Robbie is fucked and sucks others off (Greek passive/French active/bottom). His passivity is pronounced, and he is never shown other than prone. As a white man, his role is completely reversed: he is at first sucked off by Stevie, and then he fucks him (Greek active/French passive/top). Neither of Robbie's manifestations veers from his prescribed role.

To a greater extent than most other gay porn tapes, *Below the Belt* is directly about power. The hierarchical *dojo* setting is milked for its evocation of dominance and submission. With the exception of one very romantic sequence midway through the tape, most of the actors stick to their defined roles of top or bottom. Sex, especially anal sex, as punishment is a recurrent image. In this genre of gay pornography, the role-playing in the dream sequence is perfectly apt. What is significant, however, is how race figures into the equation. In a tape that appropriates emblems of Asian power (karate), the only place for a real Asian actor is as a caricature of passivity. Sum Yung Mahn does not portray as Asian, but rather the literalization of a metaphor, so that by being passive, Robbie actually becomes 'Oriental.' At a more practical level, the device of the dream also allows the producers to introduce an element of the mysterious, the exotic, without disrupting the racial status quo of the rest of the tape. Even in the dream sequence, Sum Yung Mahn is at the center of the frame as spectacle, having minimal physical involvement with the men around him. Although the sequence ends with his climax, he exists for the pleasure of others.

Richard Dyer, writing about gay porn, states that

> although the pleasure of anal sex (that is, of being anally fucked) is represented, the narrative is never organized around the desire to be fucked, but around the desire to ejaculate (whether or not following from anal intercourse). Thus, although at a level of public representation gay men may be thought of as deviant and disruptive of masculine norms because we assert the pleasure of being fucked and the eroticism of the anus, in our pornography this takes a back seat. (28)

Although Tom Waugh's amendment to this argument – that anal pleasure is represented in individual sequences[13] – also holds true for *Below the Belt*, as a whole the power of the penis and the pleasure of ejaculation are clearly the narrative's organizing principles. As with the vast majority of North American tapes featuring Asians, the problem is not the representation of anal pleasure per se, but rather that the narratives privilege the penis while always assigning the Asian the role of bottom; Asian and anus are conflated. In the case of Sum Yung Mahn, being fucked may well be his personal sexual preference. But the fact remains that there are very few occasions in North American video porn in which an Asian fucks a white man, so few, in fact, that International Wavelength promotes the tape *Studio X* (1986) with the blurb 'Sum Yung Mahn makes history as the first Asian who fucks a non-Asian.'[14]

Although I agree with Waugh that in gay as opposed to straight porn 'the spectator's positions in relation to the representations are open and in flux' (33), this observation applies only when all the participants are white. Race introduces another dimension that may serve to close down some of this mobility. This is not to suggest that the experience of gay men of color with this kind of sexual representation is the same as that of heterosexual women with regard to the gendered gaze of straight porn. For one thing, Asian gay men are men. We can therefore physically experience the pleasures depicted on the screen, since we too have erections and ejaculations and can experience anal penetration. A shifting identification may occur despite the racially defined roles, and most gay Asian men in North America are used to obtaining pleasure from all-white pornography. This, of course, goes hand in hand with many problems of self-image and sexual identity. Still, I have been struck by the unanimity with which gay Asian men I have met, from all over this continent as well as from Asia, immediately identify and resist these representations. Whenever I mention the topic of Asian actors in American porn, the first question I am asked is whether the Asian is simply shown getting fucked.

*Asian Knights*, the second tape I want to consider, has an Asian producer-director and a predominantly Asian cast. In its first scenario, two Asian men, Brad and Rick, are seeing a white psychiatrist because they are unable to have sex with each other.

Rick:       We never have sex with other Asians. We usually have sex with Caucasian guys.
Counselor:  Have you had the opportunity to have sex together?
Rick:       Yes, a coupla times, but we never get going.

Homophobia, like other forms of oppression, is seldom dealt with in gay video porn. With the exception of safe-sex tapes that attempt a rare blend of the pedagogical with the pornographic, social or political issues are not generally associated with the erotic. It is therefore unusual to see one of the favored discussion topics for gay Asian consciousness-raising groups employed as a sex fantasy in *Asian Knights*. The desexualized image of Asian men that I have described has seriously affected our relationships with one another, and often gay Asian men find it difficult to see each other beyond the terms of platonic friendship or competition, to consider other Asian men as lovers.

True to the conventions of porn, minimal counseling from the psychiatrist convinces Rick and Brad to shed their clothes. Immediately sprouting erections, they proceed to have sex. But what appears to be an assertion of gay Asian desire is quickly derailed. As Brad and Rick make love on the couch, the camera cross-cuts to the psychiatrist looking on from an armchair. The rhetoric of the editing suggests that we are observing the two Asian men from his point of view. Soon the white man takes off his clothes and joins in. He immediately takes up a position at the center of the action – and at the center of the frame. What appeared to be a 'conversion fantasy' for gay Asian desire was merely a ruse. Brad and Rick's temporary mutual absorption really occurs to establish the superior sexual draw of the white psychiatrist, a stand-in for the white male viewer, who is the real sexual subject of the tape. And the question of Asian-Asian desire, though presented as the main narrative force of the sequence, is deflected, or rather reframed from a white perspective. [...]

*Asian Knights* is organized to sell representations of Asians to white men. Unlike Sum Yung Mahn in *Below the Belt*, the actors are therefore more expressive and sexually assertive, as often the seducers as the seduced. But though the roles shift during the predominantly oral sex, the Asians remain passive in anal intercourse, except that they are now shown to want it! How much this assertion of agency represents a step forward remains a question.

Even in the one sequence of *Asian Knights* in which the Asian actor fucks the white man, the scenario privileges the pleasure of the white man over that of the Asian. The sequence begins with the Asian reading a magazine. When the white man (played by porn star Eric Stryker) returns home from a hard day at the office, the waiting Asian asks how his day went, undresses him (even taking off his socks), and proceeds to massage his back.[15] The Asian man acts the role of the mythologized geisha or 'the good wife' as fantasized in the mail-order bride business. And, in fact, the 'house boy' is one of the most persistent white fantasies about Asian men. The fantasy is also a reality in many Asian countries where economic imperialism gives foreigners, whatever their race, the pick of handsome men in financial need. The accompanying cultural imperialism grants status to those Asians with white lovers. White men who for various reasons, especially age, are deemed unattractive in their own countries, suddenly find themselves elevated and desired.

From the opening shot of painted lotus blossoms on a screen to the shot of a Japanese garden that separates the episodes, from the Chinese pop music to the chinoiserie in the apartment, there is a conscious attempt in *Asian Knights* to evoke a particular atmosphere.[16] Self-conscious 'Oriental' signifiers are part and parcel of a colonial fantasy – and reality – that empowers one kind of gay man over another. Though I have known Asian men in dependent relations with older, wealthier white men, as an erotic fantasy the house boy scenario tends to work one way. I know of no scenarios of Asian men and white house boys. It is not the representation of the fantasy that offends, or even the fantasy itself, rather the uniformity with which these narratives reappear and the uncomfortable relationship they have to real social conditions.

*International Skin*, as its name suggests, features a Latino, a black man, Sum Yung Mahn, and a number of white actors. Unlike the other tapes I have discussed, there are no 'Oriental' devices. And although Sum Yung Mahn and all the men of color are inevitably fucked (without reciprocating), there is mutual sexual engagement between the white and nonwhite characters.

In this tape Sum Yung Mahn is Brad, a film student making a movie for his class. Brad is the narrator, and the film begins with a self-reflexive 'head and shoulders' shot of Sun Yung Mahn explaining the scenario. The film we are watching supposedly represents Brad's point of view. But here again the tape is not targeted to black, Asian, or Latino men; though Brad introduces all of these men as his friends, no two men of color ever meet on screen. Men of color are not invited to participate in the internationalism that is being sold, except through identification with white characters. This tape illustrates how an agenda of integration becomes problematic if it frames the issue solely in terms of black-white, Asian-white mixing, it perpetuates a system of white-centeredness.

The gay Asian viewer is not constructed as sexual subject in any of this work – not on the screen, not as a viewer. I may find Sum Yung Mahn attractive, I may desire his body, but I am always aware that he is not meant for me. I may lust after Eric Stryker and imagine myself as the Asian who is having sex with him, but the role the Asian plays in the scene with him is demeaning. It is not that there is anything wrong with the image of servitude per se, but rather that it is one of the few fantasy scenarios in which we figure, and we are always in the role of servant.

Are there then no pleasures for an Asian viewer? The answer to this question is extremely complex. There is first of all no essential Asian viewer. The race of the person viewing says nothing about how race figures in his or her own desires. Uniracial white representations in porn may not in themselves present a problem in addressing many gay Asian men's desires. But the issue is not simply that porn may deny pleasures to some gay Asian men. We also need to examine what role the pleasure of porn plays in securing a consensus about race and desirability that ultimately works to our disadvantage.

Though the sequences I have focused on in the preceding examples are those in which the discourses about Asian sexuality are most clearly articulated, they do not define the totality of depiction in these tapes. Much of the time the actors merely reproduce or attempt to reproduce the conventions of pornography. The fact that, with the exception of Sum Yung Mahn, they rarely succeed – because of their body type, because Midwestern-cowboy-porn dialect with Vietnamese intonation is just a bit incongruous, because they groan or gyrate just a bit too much – more than anything brings home the relative rigidity of the genre's codes. There is little seamlessness here. There are times, however, when the actors appear neither as simulated whites nor as symbolic others. There are several moments in *International Skin*, for example, in which the focus shifts from the genitals to hands caressing a body; these moments feel to me more 'genuine.' I do not mean this in the sense of an essential Asian sexuality, but rather a moment is captured in which the actor stops pretending. He does not stop acting, but he stops pretending to be a white porn star. I find myself focusing on moments like these, in which the racist ideology of the text seems to be temporarily suspended or rather eclipsed by the erotic power of the moment.

In 'Pornography and the Doubleness of Sex for Women,' Joanna Russ writes:

Sex is ecstatic, autonomous and lovely for women. Sex is violent, dangerous and unpleasant for women. I don't mean a dichotomy (i.e., two kinds of women or even two kinds of sex) but rather a continuum in which no one's experience is wholly positive or negative. (39)

Gay Asian men are men and therefore not normally victims of the rape, incest, or other sexual harassment to which Russ is referring. However, there is a kind of doubleness, of ambivalence, in the way that Asian men experience contemporary North American gay communities. The 'ghetto,' the mainstream gay movement, can be a place of freedom and sexual identity. But it is also a site of racial, cultural, *and* sexual alienation sometimes more pronounced than that in straight society. For me sex is a source of pleasure but also a site of humiliation and pain. Released from the social constraints against expressing overt racism in public, the intimacy of sex can provide my (non-Asian) partner an opening for letting me know my place – sometimes literally, as when after we come, he turns over and asks where I come from.[17] Most gay Asian men I know have similar experiences.

This is just one reality that differentiates the experiences and therefore the political priorities of gay Asians and, I think, other gay men of color from those of white men. For one thing we cannot afford to take a libertarian approach. Porn can be an active agent in representing *and* reproducing a sex-race status quo. We cannot attain a healthy alliance without coming to terms with these differences.

The barriers that impede pornography from providing representations of Asian men that are erotic and politically palatable (as opposed to correct) are similar to those that inhibit the Asian documentary, the Asian feature, the Asian experiment film and videotape. We are seen as too peripheral, not commercially viable – not the general audience. *Looking for Langston* (1988), which is the first film I have seen that affirms rather than appropriates the sexuality of black gay men, was produced under exceptional economic circumstances that freed it from the constraints of the marketplace.[18] Should we call for an independent gay Asian pornography? Perhaps I do in a utopian sort of way, though I feel that the problems in North America's porn conventions are manifold and go beyond the question of race. There is such a limited vision of what constitutes the erotic.

In Canada, the major debate about race and representation has shifted from an emphasis on the image to a discussion of appropriation and control of production and distribution – who gets to produce the work. But as we have seen in the case *of Asian Knights*, the race of the producer is no automatic guarantee of 'consciousness' about these issues or of a different product. Much depends on who is constructed as the audience for the work. In any case, it is not surprising that under capitalism, finding my penis may ultimately be a matter of dollars and cents. [...]

## Notes

*Acknowledgments*: I would like to thank Tim McCaskell and Helen Lee for their ongoing criticism and comments, as well as Jeff Nunokawa and Douglas Crimp for their invaluable suggestions in converting the original spoken presentation into a written text. Finally, I would like to extend my gratitude to Bad Object-Choices for inviting me to participate in *How Do I Look?*

1. See Williams.

2. The mainstream 'leadership' within Asian communities often colludes with the myth of the model minority and the reassuring desexualization of Asian people.

3. In Britain, however, more race-sex stereotypes of South Asians exist. Led by artists such as Pratibha Parmar, Sunil Gupta, and Hanif Kureishi, there is also a growing and already significant body of work by South Asians themselves that takes up questions of sexuality.

4. See Gong 37–41.

5. Fanon 120. For a reconsideration of this statement in the light of contemporary black gay issues, see Mercer 141.

6. I do not think that this could happen in today's Toronto, which now has the second-largest Chinese community on the continent. Perhaps it would not have happened in San Francisco. But I still believe that there is an onus on gay Asians and other gay people of color to prove our homosexuality.

7. The term 'minority' is misleading. Racism is not a matter of numbers but of power. This is especially clear in situations where people of color constitute actual majorities, as in most former European colonies. At the same time, I feel that none of the current terms is really satisfactory and that too much time spent on the politics of 'naming' can in the end be diversionary.

8. To organize effectively with lesbian and gay Asians, we must reject self-righteous condemnation of 'closetedness' and see coming out more as a process or a goal, rather than as a prerequisite for participation in the movement.

9. Racism is available to be used by anyone. The conclusion that – because racism = power + prejudice – only white people can be racist is Eurocentric and simply wrong. Individuals have varying degrees and different sources of power, depending on the given moment in a shifting context. This does not contradict the fact that, in contemporary North American society, racism is generally organized around white supremacy.

10. From simple observation, I feel safe in saying that most gay Asian men in North America hold white men as their idealized sexual partners. However, I am not trying to construct an argument for determinism, and there are a number of outstanding problems that are not easily answered by current analyses of power. What of the experience of Asians who are attracted to men of color, including other Asians? What about white men who prefer Asians sexually? How and to what extent is desire articulated in terms of race as opposed to body type or other attributes? To what extent is sexual attraction exclusive or changeable, and can it be consciously programed? These questions are all politically loaded, as they parallel and impact the debates between essentialists and social constructionists on the nature of homosexuality itself. They are also emotionally charged, in that sexual choice involving race has been a basis for moral judgment.

11. See Dyer. In his chapter on Marilyn Monroe, Dyer writes extensively on the relationship between blondness, whiteness, and desirability.

12. Print porn is somewhat more racially integrated, as are the new safe sex tapes – by the Gay Men's Health Crisis, for example – produced in a political and pedagogical rather than a commercial context.

13. Waugh 31.

14. *International Wavelength News.*

15. It seems to me that the undressing here is organized around the pleasure of the white man in being served. This is in contrast to the undressing scenes in, say, James Bond films, in which the narrative is organized around undressing as an act of revealing the woman's body, an indicator of sexual conquest.

16. Interestingly, the gay video porn from Japan and Thailand that I have seen has none of this Oriental coding. Asianness is not taken up as a sign but is taken for granted as a setting for the narrative.

17. Though this is a common enough question in our postcolonial, urban environments, when asked of Asians, it often reveals two agendas: first, the assumption that all Asians are newly arrived immigrants and, second, a fascination with difference and sameness. Although we (Asians) all supposedly look alike, there are specific characteristics and stereotypes associated with each particular ethnic group. The inability to tell us apart underlies the inscrutability attributed to Asians. This 'inscrutability' took on sadly ridiculous proportions when during World War II the Chinese were issued badges so that white Canadians could distinguish them from 'the enemy.'

18. For more on the origins of the black film and video workshops in Britain, see Pines 26.

## Works Cited

*Asian Knights.* Ed Sung, director. William Richhe Productions, 1985.

*Below the Belt.* Philip St. John, director. California Dream Machine Productions, 1985.

Dyer, Richard. 'Coming to *Terms.*' *Jump Cut* 30 (Mar. 1985): 27–29.

———. *Heavenly Bodies: Film Stars and Society.* New York: St. Martin's, 1986.

Fanon, Frantz. *Black Skin, White Masks.* London: Paladin, 1970.

Gong, Stephen. 'Zen Warrior of the Celluloid (Silent) Years: The Art of Sessue Hayakawa.' *Bridge* 8 (Winter 1982–83): 37–41.

*International Skin.* William Richhe, director. N'wayvo Richhe Productions, 1985.

*International Wavelength News* 2 (Jan. 1991).

*Looking for Langston.* Isaac Julien, director. U.K.: Sankofa Film and Video, 1988.

Mercer, Kobena. 'Imaging the Black Man's Sex.' *Photography/Politics: Two.* ed. Pat Holland, Jo Spence, and Simon Watney. London: Comedia/Methuen, 1987. Reprinted in *Male Order: Unwrapping Masculinity.* Ed. Rowena Chapman and Jonathan Rutherford. London: Lawrence and Wishart, 1988, 97–164.

Pines, Jim. 'The Cultural Context of Black British Cinema.' *Blackframes: Critical Perspectives on Black Independent Cinema.* Ed. Mybe B. Cham and Claire Andrade-Watkins. Cambridge: MIT P, 1988. 26–30.

Rushton, J. Philippe, and Anthony F. Bogaert, 'Race versus Social Class Difference in Sexual Behaviour: A Follow-Up Test of the r/K Dimension.' *Journal of Research in Personality* 22 (1988): 259–72.

Russ, Joanna. 'Pornography and the Doubleness of Sex for Women.' *Jump Cut* 32 (Apr. 1986): 38–41.

Said, Edward. *Orientalism.* London: Routledge and Kegan Paul, 1978.

*Studio X.* International Wavelength, 1986.

Tajima, Renee. 'Lotus Blossoms Don't Bleed: Images of Asian Women.' *Anthologies of Asian American Film and Video.* New York: Third World Newsreel, 1984. 28–33.

Waugh, Tom. 'Men's Pornography, Gay vs. Straight.' *Jump Cut* 30 (Mar. 1985): 30–35.

Williams, Eric. *Capitalism and Slavery.* New York: Capricorn, 1966.

# PART SIX

# STYLING:

# SUBCULTURE AND POPULAR PERFORMANCE

Subculture may no longer be that secret space where only the initiated gain a rite of passage. On the subject of subculture, Dick Hebdige once claimed that: 'as soon as the original innovations which signify "subculture" are translated into commodities and made generally available, they become "frozen". Once removed from their private contexts by the small entrepreneurs and big fashion interests who produce them on a mass scale, they become codified, made comprehensible, rendered at once public property and profitable merchandise.' In the last twenty years those 'small entrepreneurs' have expanded; the cultural industries market their products and packaged lifestyles according to knowledge accumulated from within (corporate graduates of subcultural style) and from outside (the corporate strategies of employing 'cool hunters' to seek out the latest youth culture styles). The period of 'translation' – from innovation to commodification – has rapidly sped up; and this may challenge the tactics of semiotic negation and claims to political agendas so pertinent to the study of subculture. The question to pose, then, is: What type of activity is styling? And relatedly, how does it relate to other activities of popular culture as identified by this *Reader*? In addition, this section ventures to ask what happens when new subjectivities occupy the spaces of subculture often attributed to white males? Can the processes that made British punk at the time of Hebdige's writing 'comprehensible ... on a mass scale' be said to work as well on queer subjectivities like riot grrrls, punk dykes, and drag kings? One thing is certain. The chapters in this section make clear that style is anything but inconsequential. The expression and understanding of style as a cultural and social force marks a complex relationship between time and place that is significant because of the immanent relationality of culture that it exemplifies. A key to the relational yet situated character of subcultural identification is the work and theorization of performance behind profound reconceptualizations of the work of identity within the cultural sphere. Contests over style – the ability to assert it, and through it to assert specific cultural and identificatory ties – functions as a both a performative and material intervention into a form of power/knowledge. Through style, knowledge and the manipulation of codes and meanings occur, and in its recognition resides the potential for the tangled dynamic of identity and community, as well as hegemony and counter-hegemony.

The influence of Dick Hebdige's *Subculture: The Meaning of Style* (1979) is unmatched in its subject. Drawing insights from writers like Claude Lévi-Strauss, Roland Barthes, Henri Lefebvre, Umberto Eco, Antonio Gramsci, Julia Kristeva, and scholars of the Birmingham Centre for Contemporary Cultural Studies, Hebdige offers a semiotic analysis of the subcultural styles and homological behaviors of punks, mods, teddy boys, and skinheads, to name a few. In his case studies of British youth subcultures, excerpted under the title **'Subculture'** from *Subculture: The Meaning of Style*, Hebdige seeks to articulate the political function of subculture; how signifying practices of *bricolage* ('the mods could be said to be functioning as *bricoleurs* when they appropriated another range of commodities by placing them in a symbolic ensemble which served to erase or subvert their original straight meanings') challenges hegemony through refusal, resistance, and reappropriation. The essays that follow Hebdige's in this section acknowledge his influence while extending as well as challenging his assertions by bringing them to bear on other subcultures, different relationships to popular culture, and additional subject positions – a revision that Hebdige himself participates in through subsequent works like *Hiding in the Light: On Image and Things* (London: Routledge, 1988) and *Cut 'n' Mix: Culture, Identity, and Caribbean Music* (New York: Methuen, 1987).

Angela McRobbie's more recent work – *Postmodernism and Popular Culture* (London: Routledge, 1994), *British Fashion Design: Rag Trade or Image Industry* (London: Routledge, 1998), *In the Culture Society: Art, Fashion, and Popular Music* (London: Routledge, 1999) – continues to work through the interstices of fashion, popular music, dance, feminism, and gender that she began in her work with the Birmingham Centre in the 1970s. Whereas 'Girls and Subcultures: An Exploration' (co-authored with Jenny Garber) was dedicated to recording girls' experiences in subculture in Stuart Hall and Tony Jefferson's early edited collection on British post-war subculture, *Resistance Through Rituals: Youth Subcultures in Post-war Britain* (London: Hutchinson, 1976), McRobbie's **'Second-Hand Dresses and the Role of the Ragmarket'** (1988), presented here, examines the post-punk subcultural entrepreneur. McRobbie, who in this essay maintains a dialogue with Hebdige's work on punk style, focuses on subcultural style as it relates to the mainstream fashion industry, as well as countercultural 'alternative shops' and market stalls selling 'vintage' and 'retrostyle': 'Girls and young women have played a major role, not just in providing youth subcultures with their items of style and dress, but also in rediscovering these items and imaginatively re-creating them.' McRobbie's major intervention has been to write girls into the (masculinist) contours of subculture and subcultural theory, which involved a renegotiation of concepts like 'participation'.

Where Hebdige's text studies how subculture practices are 'incorporated' into mainstream culture ('youth cultural styles may begin by issuing symbolic challenges, but they must inevitably end by establishing new sets of conventions...') and McRobbie asks her readers to consider subcultural style's place within the larger consumer culture, Sarah Thornton's **'The Media Development of Subcultures'** demonstrates how club/rave culture is dependent upon the media and culture industries. In her book,

*Club Cultures: Music, Media and Subcultural Capital* (1996), Thornton discusses the commonly accepted view that subcultures position themselves in opposition to mainstream media; often the imaginary space of the 'underground' is preferred and fiercely defended through accusations against would-be 'sell outs'. In the excerpted chapter provided here, Thornton argues that opposition between subculture and the media is not as prevalent as believed, and proceeds to examine the different media that she claims are 'integral to youth's social and ideological formations.' Thornton's investment in the study of subculture has also produced the valuable, *The Subcultures Reader* (London: Routledge, 1997), edited with Ken Gelder.

Sharing in the circles of subcultural debate prevalent in Hebdige's text is Tricia Rose's **'A Style Nobody Can Deal With: Politics, Style and the Postindustrial City in Hop Hop'**, taken from her collaboration with Andrew Ross in their excellent *Microphone Fiends: Youth Music and Youth Culture* (New York and London: Routledge, 1994) and found in her *Black Noise: Rap Music and Black Culture in Contemporary America* (1994). In contrast to Hebdige who addresses British subculture (mostly white, male, working-class and Afro-Caribbean), Rose concentrates on similar periods (the 1970s) within a US context. While the importance of style, dress, and the processes of incorporation are discussed in regards to hip hop culture, Rose places a stronger emphasis on the importance of 'place' than Hebdige. The post-industrial landscape of New York City and the depletion of social services in the 1970s, coupled with structural inequalities experienced by African-American and Hispanic communities within urban environs created certain conditions to which hip hop style responded: 'In the postindustrial urban context of dwindling low-income housing, a trickle of meaningless jobs for young people, mounting police brutality and increasingly demonic depictions of young inner-city residents, hip hop style *is* black urban renewal.' In brief, Rose establishes a relationship between culture and traditionally economic/material bases of urban renewal.

One of the most compelling contemporary interventions in considerations of subculture has been effected by queer theory. The emphasis on social class, that at one time functioned as 'the' defining attribute of subculture, has made way for equally important considerations of gender, race and ethnicity, as well as sexuality. Queer theory extends the means by which the relation of subcultures to counter-hegemonic processes may be understood and problematized. For example, the study of punk often premises itself on male practices, despite claims of play with conventional ideas of gender and representation. Cynthia Fuchs takes up just such a discrepancy in **'If I Had A Dick: Queers, Punks, and Alternative Acts'** (1998). Examining bands such as Bikini Kill, Tribe 8, and Pansy Division, Fuchs explores the space of queer performance to examine 'the productive interplay of performance and authenticity, the ways that sexualized acts and exchanges can 'speak,' display a range of identities that are otherwise rendered invisible precisely because they're attached to such acts and exchanges.' Ultimately, she suggests that claims to punk's performance aesthetics and anti-convention ethos by riot grrrl and queercore bands contributes to their revitalization, and, in some cases, to a valuable critique of the exclusivity that has marked aspects of subcultural practices.

The subject of performance in queer theory and its prevalence in popular culture is exemplified in Judith Halberstam's *Female Masculinity* (1998). (Other books include: *Skin Shows: Gothic Horror and the Technology of Monsters* (1995), *The Drag King Book* (with Del Lagrace Volcano, London: Serpent's Tail, 1999) and *In a Queer Time and Place: Transgender Bodies, Subcultural Lives*, New York: New York University Press,

2005). The chapter highlighted here, '**Drag Kings: Masculinity and Performance**' (2000), contributes to the conversation that this section advances. The figure of the 'Drag King' and the practice of 'kinging' (as an alternative to the specific historical qualities of camp) are held to challenge the implied 'naturalness' of masculinity ('the idea that masculinity "just is", whereas femininity reeks of the artificial …'). Popular culture is shown to pressure a radical rethinking of even the most normalized and normalizing of social codes – and the power mechanisms that operate through them. Drag king performance's ability to destabilize and denaturalize masculinity 'exposes the structure of dominant masculinity by making it theatrical and by rehearsing the repertoire of roles and types on which such masculinity depends.' This claim is evidenced in Halberstam's detailed investigation of drag king taxonomies: 'butch realness', 'femme pretender', 'male mimicry', 'fag drag', and 'denaturalized masculinity'.

# Play List

Ahearn, Charlie (dir.) (1982) *Wild Style*. DVD. Wea Corp.

Arnold, Jennifer (dir.) (2001) *American Mullet*. DVD. Palm Pictures.

Arnold, Rebecca (2001) *Fashion, Desire and Anxiety: Image and Morality in the Twentieth Century*. New Brunswick, NJ: Rutgers University Press.

Baur, Gabrielle (dir.) (2003) *Venus Boyz*. DVD. First Run Features.

Bennett, Andy and Kahn-Harris, Keith (2004) *After Subculture: Critical Studies in Contemporary Youth Culture*. London: Palgrave Macmillan.

Benstock, Shari and Suzanne Ferriss (eds) (1994) *On Fashion*. New Brunswick, NJ: Rutgers University Press.

Bikini Kill. *The Singles*. CD. Kill Rock Stars.

Bikini Kill. *Reject All American*. CD. Kill Rock Stars.

Blush, Steve (2001) *American Hardcore: A Tribal History*. Los Angeles: Feral House.

Bruzzi, Stella and Church Gibson, Pamela (2000) *Fashion Cultures: Theories, Explorations and Analysis*. London: Routledge.

Cashmore, Ellis (1983) *Rasta Man: The Rastafarian Movement in London*. London: Unwin Paperbacks.

Creekmur, Corey K. and Doty, Alexander (1995) *Out in Culture: Gay, Lesbian, and Queer Essays on Popular Culture*. Durham, NC: Duke University Press.

Delgado, Celeste Fraser and Muñoz, José Esteban (1997) *Every-Night Life: Culture and Dance in Latin/o America*. Durham, NC: Duke University Press.

DeMello, Margo (2000) *Bodies of Inscription: A Cultural History of the Modern Tattoo*. Durham, NC: Duke University Press.

Ewen, Stuart (1988) *All Consuming Images: The Politics of Style in Contemporary Culture*. New York: Basic Books.

Ferrell, Jeff (1996) *Crimes of Style: Urban Graffiti and the Politics of Criminality*. Boston, MA: Northeastern University Press.

Frank, Thomas (1997) *The Conquest of Cool: Business Culture, Counterculture, and the Rise of Hip Consumerism*. Chicago: University of Chicago Press.

Frith, Simon and Horne, Howard (1987) *Art into Pop*. London: Methuen.

Ganser, Lisa (dir.) (1999) *Homocore Minneapolis* (a queer punk documentary). Videocassette.

George, Nelson (1998) *Hip Hop America*. London: Penguin.

Healey, Murray (1996) *Gay Skins: Masculinity and Queer Appropriation*. London: Cassell.

Hebdige, Dick (1988) *Hiding in the Light: On Image and Things*. London: Methuen.

Henzell, Perry (dir.) (1972) *The Harder They Come*. DVD. Criterion Collection.

Hewitt, Paolo (2004) *The Soul Stylists: Six Decades of Modernism – From Mod to Casual*. London: Mainstream Publishing Co.

Hodkinson, Paul (2002) *Goth: Identity, Style and Subculture*. Oxford: Berg.

Hyder, Rehan (2004) *Brimful of Asia: Negotiating Ethnicity on the UK Music Scene*. Aldershot: Ashgate.

Julie Ruin (1998) *Julie Ruin*. CD. Kill Rock Stars.

Juno, Andra (1996) *Angry Women in Rock*. San Francisco:Juno Books.

Kaye, Tony (dir.) (1998) *American History X*. DVD. New Line Home Entertainment.

Lahickey, Beth (1998) *All Ages: Reflections on Straight Edge*. Hartford: Revelation.

Lathan, Stan (dir.) (1984) *Beat Street*. DVD. MGM.

Leblanc, Lauraine (1999) *Pretty in Punk: Girls' Gender Resistance in a Boy's Subculture*. New Brunswick, NJ: Rutgers University Press.

Lee, Spike (dir.) (1999) *Summer of Sam*. DVD. 40 Acres & A Mule Filmworks and Touchstone Pictures.

LeTigre (2004) *LeTigre*. CD. Mr. Lady.

LeTigre (2004) *This Island*. CD. Universal.

Macdonald, Nancy (2001) *The Graffiti Subculture: Youth, Masculinity and Identity in London and New York*. London: Palgrave Macmillian.

Marshall, George (1994) *Spirit of '69: A Skin Head Bible*. Dunoon, Scotland: S.T. Publishing.

Merendino, James (dir.) (1999) *SLC Punk*. DVD. Columbia/Tristar Studios.

Muggleton, David (2000) *Inside Subculture: The Postmodern Meaning of Style*. Oxford: Berg.

Neal, Mark Anthony (2002) *Soul Babies: Black Popular Culture and The Post-Soul Aesthetic*. London: Routledge.

O' Hara, Craig (1999) *The Philosophy of Punk*. Edinburgh: AK Press.

Peaches (2003) *Fatherfucker*. CD. Beggars XI Recording.

Perkins, William Eric (ed.) (1995) *Droppin' Science: Critical Essays on Rap Music and Hip Hop Culture*. Philadelphia, PA: Temple UP.

Polhemus, Tom (1996) *The Customized Body*. London: Serpent's Tail.

Pray, Doug (dir.) (2001) *Scratch*. DVD. Palm Pictures.

Robertson, Pamela (1996) *Guilty Pleasures: Feminist Camp from Mae West to Madonna*. Durham, NC: Duke University Press.

Roddam, Frank (dir.) (1979) *Quadrophenia*. DVD. Rhino Video.

Schnitzer, George (dir.) (2002) *What to do in the Case of Fire*. DVD. Columbia Tristar.

Shabazz, Jamal (2001) *Back in the Days*. New York: Power House Books.

Silver, Tony (dir.) (2003 [1983]) *Style Wars*. DVD. Plexifilm.

Sinker, Daniel (2001) *We Owe You Nothing, Punk Planet: The Collected Interviews*. New York: Akashic Books.

Small, Adam and Stuart, Peter (dirs) (1984) *Another State of Mind*. DVD. BMG Dist.

Spheeris, Penelope (dir.) (1983) *Suburbia*. DVD. New Concorde Home Video.

Suicide, Missy (2004) *Suicide Girls*. Los Angeles: Feral House. (www.suicide.girls.com).

Tribe 8 (1995) *Fist City*. CD. Alternative Tentacle.

Tribe 8 (1998) *Role Models for America*. CD. Alternative Tentacle.

*Rise Above: Tribe 8 Documentary* (2003) Tracy Flannign (dir.). Accenture Film. (www.riseabovethetribe8documentary.com)

Temple, Julien (dir.) (1980) *The Great Rock and Roll Swindle*. Videocassette. Wea/Warner Brothers.

Temple, Julien (dir.) (1986) *Absolute Beginners*. DVD. MGM.

Temple, Julien (dir.) (2000) *The Filth and the Fury – A Sex Pistols Film*. DVD. New Line Home Entertainment.

Toop, David (1999) *Rap Attack 3*. London: Serpent's Tail.

Whiteley, Sheila (ed.) (1997) *Sexing the Groove: Popular Music and Gender*. London: Routledge.

# Chapter 29

# Dick Hebdige

# Subculture

## Subculture: The Unnatural Break

[...] Subcultures represent 'noise' (as opposed to sound): interference in the orderly sequence which leads from real events and phenomena to their representation in the media. We should therefore not underestimate the signifying power of the spectacular subculture not only as a metaphor for potential anarchy 'out there' but as an actual mechanism of semantic disorder: a kind of temporary blockage in the system of representation. [...]

[...] Violations of the authorized codes through which the social world is organized and experienced have considerable power to provoke and disturb. They are generally condemned, in Mary Douglas' words (1967), as 'contrary to holiness' and Levi-Strauss has noted how, in certain primitive myths, the mispronunciation of words and the misuse of language are classified along with incest as horrendous aberrations capable of 'unleashing storm and tempest' (Levi-Strauss, 1969). Similarly, spectacular subcultures express forbidden contents (consciousness of class, consciousness of difference) in forbidden forms (transgressions of sartorial and behavioural codes, law breaking, etc.). They are profane articulations, and they are often and significantly defined as 'unnatural'. The terms used in the tabloid press to describe those youngsters who, in their conduct or clothing, proclaim subcultural membership ('freaks', 'animals ... who find courage, like rats, in hunting in packs'[1]) would seem to suggest that the most primitive anxieties concerning the sacred distinction between nature and culture can be summoned up by the emergence of such a group. No doubt, the breaking of rules is confused with the 'absence of rules' which, according to Levi-Strauss (1969), 'seems to provide

From: Dick Hebdige, *Subculture: The Meaning of Style*. London: Routledge, 1979.

the surest criteria for distinguishing a natural from a cultural process'. Certainly, the official reaction to the punk subculture, particularly to the Sex Pistols' use of 'foul language' on television[2] and record[3], and to the vomiting and spitting incidents at Heathrow Airport[4] would seem to indicate that these basic taboos are no less deeply sedimented in contemporary British society.

## Two Forms of Incorporation

[...] The emergence of a spectacular subculture is invariably accompanied by a wave of hysteria in the press. This hysteria is typically ambivalent: it fluctuates between dread and fascination, outrage and amusement. Shock and horror head-lines dominate the front page (e.g. 'Rotten Razored', *Daily Mirror*, 28 June 1977) while, inside, the editorials positively bristle with 'serious' commentary[5] and the centrespreads or supplements contain delirious accounts of the latest fads and rituals (see, for example, *Observer* colour supplements 30 January, 10 July 1977, 12 February 1978). Style in particular provokes a double response: it is alternately celebrated (in the fashion page) and ridiculed or reviled (in those articles which define subcultures as social problems). [...]

As the subculture begins to strike its own eminently marketable pose, as its vocabulary (both visual and verbal) becomes more and more familiar, so the refer-ential context to which it can be most conveniently assigned is made increasingly apparent. Eventually, the mods, the punks, the glitter rockers can be incorporated, brought back into line, located on the preferred 'map of problematic social reality' (Geertz, 1964) at the point where boys in lipstick are 'just kids dressing up', where girls in rubber dresses are 'daughters just like yours' (see pp. 98–9; 158–9, n. 8). The media, as Stuart Hall (1977) has argued, not only record resistance, they 'situate it within the dominant framework of meanings' and those young people who choose to inhabit a spectacular youth culture are simultaneously *returned,* as they are represented on T.V. and in the newspapers, to the place where common sense would have them fit (as 'animals' certainly, but also 'in the family', 'out of work', 'up to date', etc.). It is through this continual process of recuperation that the frac-tured order is repaired and the subculture incorporated as a diverting spectacle within the dominant mythology from which it in part emanates: as 'folk devil', as Other, as Enemy. The process of recuperation takes two characteristic forms:

(1)   the conversion of subcultural signs (dress, music, etc.) into mass-produced objects (i.e. the commodity form);
(2)   the 'labelling' and re-definition of deviant behaviour by dominant groups – the police, the media, the judiciary (i.e. the ideological form).

## The commodity form

The first has been comprehensively handled by both journalists and academics. The relationship between the spectacular subculture and the various industries which service and exploit it is notoriously ambiguous. After all, such a subculture is concerned first and foremost with consumption. It operates exclusively in the leisure sphere [...]. It communicates through commodities even if the meanings attached to those commodities are purposefully distorted or overthrown. It is therefore difficult in this case to maintain any absolute distinction between commercial exploitation on the one hand and creativity/originality on the other, even though these categories are emphatically opposed in the value systems of most subcultures. Indeed, the creation and diffusion of new styles is inextricably bound up with the process of production, publicity and packaging which must inevitably lead to the defusion of the subculture's subversive power – both mod and punk innovations fed back directly into high fashion and mainstream fashion. Each new subculture establishes new trends, generates new looks and sounds which feed back into the appropriate industries. [...]

[...] As soon as the original innovations which signify 'subculture' are translated into commodities and made generally available, they become 'frozen'. Once removed from their private contexts by the small entrepreneurs and big fashion interests who produce them on a mass scale, they become codified, made comprehensible, rendered at once public property and profitable merchandise. In this way, the two forms of incorporation (the semantic/ideological and the 'real'/commercial) can be said to converge on commodity form. Youth cultural styles may begin by issue symbolic challenges, but they must inevitably end by establishing new sets of conventions; by creating new commodities, new industries or rejuvenating old ones (think of the boost punk must have given haberdashery!). This occurs irrespective of the subculture's political orientation: the macrobiotic restaurants, craft shops and 'antique markets' of the hippie era were easily converted into punk boutiques and record shops. It also happens irrespective of the startling content of the style: punk clothing and insignia could be bought mail-order by the summer of 1977, and in September of that year *Cosmopolitan* ran a review of Zandra Rhodes' latest collection of couture follies which consisted entirely of variations on the punk theme. Models smouldered beneath mountains of safety pins and plastic (the pins were jewelled, the 'plastic' wet-look satin) and the accompanying article ended with an aphorism – 'To shock is chic' – we presaged the subculture's imminent demise.

## The ideological form

The second form of incorporation – the ideological – has been most adequately treated by those sociologists operate a transactional model of deviant behaviour. For example, Stan Cohen has described in detail how one particular moral panic (surrounding the mod–rocker conflict of the mid-60s) was launched and sustained.[6] Although this type of analysis can often provide an extremely sophisticated explanation of why spectacular subcultures consistently provoke such hysterical outbursts, it tends to overlook the subtler mechanisms through which potentially threatening phenomena are handled and contained. As the use of the term 'folk devil' suggests, rather too much weight tends to be given to the sensational excesses of the tabloid press at the expense of the ambiguous reactions which are, after all, more typical. As we have seen, the way in which subcultures are represented in the media makes them both more *and less ex*otic than they actually are. They are seen to contain both dangerous aliens and boisterous kids, wild animals and wayward pets. Roland Barthes furnishes a key to this paradox in his description of 'identification' – the one of the seven rhetorical figures which, according to Barthes, distinguish the meta-language of bourgeois mythology. He characterizes the petit-bourgeois as a person '... unable to imagine the Other ... the Other is a scandal which threatens his existence' (Barthes, 1972).

Two basic strategies have been evolved for dealing with this threat. First, the Other can be trivialized, naturalized, domesticated. Here, the difference is simply denied ('Otherness is reduced to sameness'). Alternatively, the Other can be transformed into meaningless exotica, a 'pure object, a spectacle, a clown' (Barthes, 1972). In this case, the difference is consigned to a place beyond analysis. Spectacular subcultures are continually being defined in precisely these terms. Soccer hooligans, for example, are typically placed beyond 'the bounds of common decency' and are classified as 'animals'. ('These people aren't human beings', football club manager quoted on the *News at Ten,* Sunday, 12 March 1977.) (See Stuart Hall's treatment of the press coverage of football hooligans in *Football Hooliganism* edited by Roger Ingham, 1978). On the other hand, the punks tended to be resituated by the press in the family, perhaps because members of the subculture deliberately obscured their origins, refused the family and willingly played the part of folk devil, presenting themselves as pure objects, as villainous clowns. Certainly, like every other youth culture, punk was perceived as a threat to the family. Occasionally this threat was represented in literal terms. For example, the *Daily Mirror* (1 August 1977) carried a photograph of a child lying in the road after a punk–ted confrontation under the headline 'VICTIM OF THE PUNK ROCK PUNCH-UP: THE BOY WHO FELL FOUL OF THE MOB'. In this case, punk's threat to the family was made 'real' (that could be my child!) through the ideological framing of photographic evidence which is popularly regarded as unproblematic.

None the less, on other occasions, the opposite line was taken. For whatever reason, the inevitable glut of articles gleefully denouncing the latest punk outrage was counter-balanced by an equal number of items devoted to the small details of punk family life. For instance, the 15 October 1977 issue of *Woman's Own* carried an article entitled 'Punks and Mothers' which stressed the classless, fancy dress aspects of punk.[7] Photographs depicting punks with smiling mothers, reclining next to the family pool, playing with the family dog, were placed above a text which dwelt on the ordinariness of individual punks: 'It's not as rocky horror as it appears'... 'punk can be a family affair' ... 'punks as it happens are non-political', and, most insidiously, albeit accurately, 'Johnny Rotten is as big a household name as Hughie Green'. Throughout the summer of 1977, the *People* and the *News of the World* ran items on punk babies, punk brothers, and punk– ted weddings. All these articles served to minimize the Otherness so stridently proclaimed in punk style, and defined the subculture in precisely those terms which it sought most vehemently to resist and deny. [...]

## Style as Intentional Communication

The cycle leading from opposition to defusion, from resistance to incorporation encloses each successive subculture. We have seen how the media and the market fit into this cycle. We must now turn to the subculture itself to consider exactly how and what subcultural style communicates. Two questions must be asked which together present us with something of a paradox: how does a subculture make sense to its members? How is it made to signify disorder? To answer these questions we must define the meaning of style more precisely. [...]

Umberto Eco writes 'not only the expressly intended communicative object ... but every object may be viewed ... as a sign' (Eco, 1973). For instance, the conventional outfits worn by the average man and woman in the street are chosen within the constraints of finance, 'taste', preference, etc. and these choices are undoubtedly significant. Each ensemble has its place in an internal system of differences – the conventional modes of sartorial discourse – which fit a corresponding set of socially prescribed roles and options.[8] These choices contain a whole range of messages which are transmitted through the finely graded distinctions of a number of interlocking sets – class and status self-image and attractiveness, etc. Ultimately, if nothing else, they are expressive of 'normality' as opposed to 'deviance' (i.e. they are distinguished by their relative invisibility, their appropriateness, their 'naturalness'). However, the intentional communication is of a different order. It stands apart – a visible construction, a loaded choice. It directs attention to itself; it gives itself to be read.

This is what distinguishes the visual ensembles of spectacular subcultures from those favoured in the surrounding culture(s). They are *obviously* fabricated (even the mods, precariously placed between the worlds of the straight and the deviant, finally declared themselves different when they gathered in groups outside dance halls and on sea fronts). They *display* their own codes (e.g. the punk's ripped T-shirt) or at least demonstrate that codes are there to be used and abused (e.g. they have been thought about rather than thrown together). In this they go against the grain of a mainstream culture whose principal defining characteristic, according to Barthes, is a tendency to masquerade as nature, to substitute 'normalized' for historical forms, to translate the reality of the world into an image of the world which in turn presents itself as if composed according to 'the evident laws of the natural order' (Barthes, 1972).

[...] By repositioning and recontextualizing commodities, by subverting their conventional uses and inventing new ones, the subcultural stylist gives the lie to what Althusser has called the 'false obviousness of everyday practice' (Althusser and Balibar, 1968), and opens up the world of objects to new and covertly oppositional readings. The communication of a significant *difference*, then (and the parallel communication of a group *identity*), is the 'point' behind the style of all spectacular subcultures. It is the superordinate term under which all the other significations are marshalled, the message through which all the other messages speak. [...]

## Style as Bricolage

The subcultures with which we have been dealing share a common feature apart from the fact that they are all predominantly working class. They are, as we have seen, cultures of conspicuous consumption – even when, as with the skinheads and the punks, certain types of consumption are conspicuously refused – and it is through the distinctive rituals of consumption, through style, that the subculture at once reveals its 'secret' identity and communicates its forbidden meanings. It is basically the way in which commodities are *used* in subculture which mark the subculture off from more orthodox cultural formations.

Discoveries made in the field of anthropology are helpful here. In particular, the concept of *bricolage* can be used to explain how subcultural styles are constructed. In *The Savage Mind* Levi-Strauss shows how the magical modes utilized by primitive peoples (superstition, sorcery, myth) can be seen as implicitly coherent, though explicitly bewildering, systems of connection between things which perfectly equip their users to 'think' their own world. These magical systems of connection have a common feature: they are capable of infinite extension because basic elements can be used in a variety of improvised combinations to generate new meanings within them. *Bricolage* has thus been described as a 'science of the concrete' in a recent definition which clarifies the original anthropological meaning of the term:

> [Bricolage] refers to the means by which the non-literate, non-technical mind of so-called 'primitive' man responds to the world around him. The process involves a 'science of the concrete' (as opposed to our 'civilised' science of the 'abstract') which far from lacking logic, in fact carefully and precisely orders, classifies and arranges into structures the *minutiae* of the physical world in all their profusion by means of a 'logic' which is not our own. The structures, 'improvised' or made up (these are rough translations of the process of *bricoler)* as *ad hoc* responses to an environment, then serve to establish homologies and analogies between the ordering of nature and that of society, and so satisfactorily 'explain' the world and make it able to be lived in. (Hawkes, 1977)

The implications of the structured improvisations of *bricolage* for a theory of spectacular subculture as a system of communication have already been explored. For instance, John Clarke has stressed the way in which prominent forms of discourse (particularly fashion) are radically adapted, subverted and extended by the subcultural *bricoleur*:

> Together, object and meaning constitute a sign, and, within any one culture, such signs are assembled, repeatedly, into characteristic forms of discourse. However, when the bricoleur re-locates the significant object in a different position within that discourse, using the same overall repertoire of signs, or when that object is placed within a different total ensemble, a new discourse is constituted, a different message conveyed. (Clarke, 1976)

In this way the teddy boy's theft and transformation of the Edwardian style revived in the early 1950s by Savile Row for wealthy young men about town can be construed as an act of *bricolage*. Similarly, the mods could be said to be functioning as *bricoleurs* when they appropriated another range of commodities by placing them in a symbolic ensemble which served to erase or subvert their original straight meanings. Thus pills medically prescribed for the treatment of neuroses were used as ends-in-themselves, and the motor scooter, originally an ultra-respectable means of transport, was turned into a menacing symbol of group solidarity. In the same improvisatory manner, metal combs, honed to a razor-like sharpness, turned narcissism into an offensive weapon. Union jacks were emblazoned on the backs of grubby parka anoraks or cut up and converted into smartly tailored jackets. More subtly, the conventional insignia of the business world – the suit, collar and tie, short hair, etc. – were stripped of their original connotations – efficiency, ambition, compliance with authority – and transformed into 'empty' fetishes, objects to be desired, fondled and valued in their own right.

At the risk of sounding melodramatic, we could use Umberto Eco's phrase 'semiotic guerilla warfare' (Eco, 1972) to describe these subversive practices. The war may be conducted at a level beneath the consciousness of the individual members of a spectacular subculture (though the subculture is still, at another level, an intentional communication (see pp. 100–2)) but with the emergence of such a group, 'war – and it is Surrealism's war – is declared on a world of surfaces' (Annette Michelson, quoted Lippard, 1970).

The radical aesthetic practices of Dada and Surrealism – dream work, collage, 'ready mades', etc. – are certainly relevant here. They are the classic modes of 'anarchic' discourse.[9] Breton's manifestos (1924 and 1929) established the basic premise of surrealism: that a new 'surreality' would emerge through the subversion of common sense, the collapse of prevalent logical categories and oppositions (e.g. dream/reality, work/play) and the celebration of the abnormal and the forbidden. This was to be achieved principally through a 'juxtaposition of two more or less distant realities' (Reverdy, 1918) exemplified for Breton in Lautréamont's bizarre phrase: 'Beautiful like the chance meeting of an umbrella and a sewing machine on a dissecting table' (Lautréamont, 1970). [...]

The subcultural *bricoleur,* like the 'author' of a surrealist collage, typically 'juxtaposes two apparently incompatible realities (i.e. "flag": "jacket"; "hole": "teeshirt"; "comb: weapon") on an apparently unsuitable scale ... and ... it is there that the explosive junction occurs' (Ernst, 1948), Punk exemplifies most clearly the subcultural uses of these anarchic modes. It too attempted through 'perturbation and deformation' to disrupt and reorganize meaning. It, too, sought the 'explosive junction'. But what, if anything, were these subversive practices being used to signify? How do we 'read' them? By singling out punk for special attention, we can look more closely at some of the problems raised in a reading of style.

## Style in Revolt: Revolting Style

[...] Although it was often directly offensive (T-shirts covered in swear words) and threatening (terrorist/guerilla outfits) punk style was defined principally through the violence of its 'cut ups'. Like Duchamp's 'ready mades' – manufactured objects which qualified as art because he chose to call them such, the most unremarkable and inappropriate items – a pin, a plastic clothes peg, a television component, a razor blade, a tampon – could be brought within the province of punk (un)fashion. Anything within or without reason could be turned into part of what Vivien Westwood called 'confrontation dressing' so long as the rupture between 'natural' and constructed context was clearly visible (i.e. the rule would seem to be: if the cap doesn't fit, wear it).

Objects borrowed from the most sordid of contexts found a place in the punks' ensembles: lavatory chains were draped in graceful arcs across chests encased in plastic bin-liners. Safety pins were taken out of their domestic 'utility' context and worn as gruesome ornaments through the cheek, ear or lip. 'Cheap' trashy fabrics (PVC, plastic, lurex, etc.) in vulgar designs (e.g. mock leopard skin) and 'nasty' colours, long discarded by the quality end of the fashion industry as obsolete kitsch, were salvaged by the punks and turned into garments (fly boy drainpipes, 'common' miniskirts) which offered self-conscious commentaries on the notions of modernity and taste. Conventional ideas of prettiness were jettisoned along with the traditional feminine lore of cosmetics. Contrary to the advice of every woman's magazine, make-up for both boys and girls was worn to be seen. Faces became abstract portraits: sharply observed and meticulously executed studies in alienation. Hair was obviously dyed (hay yellow, jet black, or bright orange with tufts of green or bleached in question marks), and T-shirts and trousers told the story of their own construction with multiple zips and outside seams clearly displayed. Similarly, fragments of school uniform (white bri-nylon shirts, school ties) were symbolically defiled (the shirts covered in graffiti, or fake blood; the ties left undone) and juxtaposed against leather drains or shocking pink mohair tops. The perverse and the abnormal were valued intrinsically. In particular, the illicit iconography of sexual fetishism was used to predictable effect. Rapist masks and rubber wear, leather bodices and fishnet stockings, implausibly pointed stiletto heeled shoes, the whole paraphernalia of bondage – the belts, straps and chains – were exhumed from the boudoir, closet and the pornographic film and placed on the street where they retained their forbidden connotations. Some young punks even donned the dirty raincoat – that most prosaic symbol of sexual 'kinkiness' – and hence expressed their deviance in suitably proletarian terms.

Of course, punk did more than upset the wardrobe. It undermined every relevant discourse. Thus dancing, usually an involving and expressive medium in British rock and mainstream pop cultures, was turned into a dumbshow of blank robotics. Punk dances bore absolutely no relation to the desultory frugs and clinches which Geoff Mungham describes as intrinsic to the respectable working-class ritual of Saturday night at the Top Rank or Mecca.[10] Indeed, overt displays of heterosexual interest were generally regarded with contempt and suspicion (who let the BOF/wimp[11] in?) and conventional courtship patterns found no place on the floor in dances like the pogo, the pose and the robot. Though the pose did allow for a minimum sociability (i.e. it could involve two people) the 'couple' were generally of the same sex and physical contact was ruled out of court as the relationship depicted in the dance was a 'professional' one. One participant would strike a suitable cliché fashion pose while the other would fall into a classic 'Bailey' crouch to snap an imaginary picture. The pogo forbade even this much interaction, though admittedly there was always a good deal of masculine jostling in front of the stage. In fact the pogo was a caricature – a *reductio ad absurdum* of all the solo dance styles associated with rock music. [...]

The robot, a refinement witnessed only at the most exclusive punk gatherings, was both more 'expressive' and 'less spontaneous' within the very narrow range such terms acquired in punk usage. It consisted of barely perceptible twitches of the head and hands or more extravagant lurches [...] which were abruptly halted at random points. The resulting pose was held for several moments, even minutes, and the whole sequence was as suddenly, as unaccountably, resumed and re-enacted.[...]

The music was similarly distinguished from mainstream rock and pop. It was uniformly basic and direct in its appeal, whether through intention or lack of expertise. If the latter, then the punks certainly made a virtue of necessity [...]. Typically, a barrage of guitars with the volume and treble turned to maximum accompanied by the occasional saxophone would pursue relentless (un)melodic lines against a turbulent background of cacophonous drumming and screamed vocals. Johnny Rotten succinctly defined punk's position on harmonics: 'We're into chaos not music'.

The names of the groups (the Unwanted, the Rejects, the Sex Pistols, the Clash, the Worst, etc.) and the titles of the songs: 'Belsen was a Gas', 'If You Don't Want to Fuck Me, fuck off', 'I Wanna be Sick on You', reflected the tendency towards wilful desecration and the voluntary assumption of outcast status which characterized the whole punk movement. [...]

It was in the performance arena that punk groups posed the clearest threat to law and order. Certainly, they succeeded in subverting the conventions of concert and night-club entertainment. Most significantly, they attempted both physically and in terms of lyrics and life-style to move closer to their audiences. This in itself is by no means unique: the boundary between artist and audience has often stood as a metaphor in revolutionary aesthetics [...] for that larger and more intransigent barrier which separates art and the dream from reality and life under capitalism.[12] The stages of those venues secure enough to host 'new wave' acts were regularly invaded by hordes of punks, and if the management refused to tolerate such blatant disregard for ballroom etiquette, then the groups and their followers could be drawn closer together in a communion of spittle and mutual abuse. At the Rainbow Theatre in May 1977 as the Clash played 'White Riot', chairs were ripped out and thrown at the stage. Meanwhile, every performance, however apocalyptic, offered palpable evidence that things could change, indeed were changing: that performance itself was a possibility no authentic punk should discount. Examples abounded in the music press of 'ordinary fans' (Siouxsie of Siouxsie and the Banshees, Sid Vicious of the Sex Pistols, Mark P of *Sniffin Glue*, Jordan of the Ants) who had made the symbolic crossing from the dance floor to the stage. [...]

If these 'success stories' were, as we have seen, subject to a certain amount of 'skewed' interpretation in the press, then there were innovations in other areas which made opposition to dominant definitions possible. Most notably, there was an attempt, the first by a predominantly working-class youth culture, to provide an alternative critical space within the subculture itself to counteract the hostile or at least ideologically inflected coverage which punk was receiving in the media. The existence of an alternative punk press demonstrated that it was not only clothes or music that could be immediately and cheaply produced from the limited resources at hand. The fanzines *(Sniffin Glue, Ripped and Torn,* etc.) were journals edited by an individual or a group, consisting of reviews, editorials and interviews with prominent punks, produced on a small scale as cheaply as possible, stapled together and distributed through a small number of sympathetic retail outlets. [...]

Even the graphics and typography used on record covers and fanzines were homologous with punk's subterranean and anarchic style. The two typographic models were graffiti which was translated into a flowing 'spray can' script, and the ransom note in which individual letters cut up from a variety of sources (newspapers, etc.) in different type faces were pasted together to form an anonymous message. The Sex Pistols' 'God Save the Queen' sleeve (later turned into T-shirts, posters, etc.) for instance incorporated both styles: the roughly assembled legend was pasted across the Queen's eyes and mouth which were further disfigured by those black bars used in pulp detective magazines to conceal identity (i.e. they connote crime or scandal). Finally, the process of ironic self-abasement which characterized the subculture was extended to the name 'punk' itself which, with its derisory connotations of 'mean and petty villainy', 'rotten', 'worthless', etc. was generally preferred by hardcore members of the subculture to the more neutral 'new wave'.[13]

## Style as Homology

The punk subculture, then, signified chaos at every level, but this was only possible because the style itself was so thoroughly ordered. The chaos cohered as a meaningful whole. We can now attempt to solve this paradox by referring to another concept originally employed by Levi-Strauss: homology.

Paul Willis (1978) first applied the term 'homology' to subculture in his study of hippies and motor-bike boys using it to describe the symbolic fit between the values and lifestyles of a group, its subjective experience and the musical forms it uses to express or reinforce its focal concerns. In *Profane Culture,* Willis shows how, contrary to the popular myth which presents subculture as lawless forms, the internal structure of any particular subculture is characterized by an extreme orderliness: each part is organically related to other parts and it is through the fit between them that the subcultural member makes sense of the world. For instance, it was the homology between an alternative value system ('Tune in, turn on, drop out'), hallucogenic drugs and acid rock which made the hippy culture cohere as a 'whole way of life' for individual hippies. In *Resistance Through Rituals,* Hall *et al.* crossed the concepts of homology and *bricolage* to provide a systematic explanation of why a particular subcultural style should appeal to a particular group of people. The authors asked the question: 'What specifically does a subcultural style signify to the members of the subculture themselves?'

The answer was that the appropriated objects reassembled in the distinctive subcultural ensembles were 'made to reflect, express and resonate … aspects of group life' (Hall *et al.,* 1976). The objects chosen were, either intrinsically or in their adapted forms, homologous with the focal concerns, activities, group structure and collective self-image of the subculture. They were 'objects in which (the subcultural members) could see their central values held and reflected' (Hall *et al.,* 1976). [...]

The punks would certainly seem to bear out this thesis. The subculture was nothing if not consistent. There was a homological relation between the trashy cut-up clothes and spiky hair, the pogo and amphetamines, the spitting, the vomiting, the format of the fanzines, the insurrectionary poses and the 'soulless', frantically driven music. The punks wore clothes which were the sartorial equivalent of swear words, and they swore as they dressed – with calculated effect, lacing obscenities into record notes and publicity releases, interviews and love songs. Clothed in chaos, they produced Noise in the calmly orchestrated Crisis of everyday life in the late 1970s – a noise which made (no) sense in exactly the same way and to exactly the same extent as a piece *of avant-garde* music. If we were to write an epitaph for the punk subculture, we could do no better than repeat Poly Styrene's famous dictum: 'Oh Bondage, Up Yours!', or somewhat more concisely: the forbidden is permitted, but by the same token, nothing, not even these forbidden signifiers (bondage, safety pins, chains, hair-dye, etc.) is sacred and fixed.

This absence of permanently sacred signifiers (icons) creates problems for the semiotician. How can we discern any positive values reflected in objects which were chosen only to be discarded? For instance, we can say that the early punk ensembles gestured towards the signified's 'modernity' and 'working-classness'. The safety pins and bin liners signified a relative material poverty which was either directly experienced and exaggerated or sympathetically assumed, and which in turn was made to stand for the spiritual paucity of everyday life. [...]

To reconstruct the true text of the punk subculture, to trace the source of its subversive practices, we must first isolate the 'generative set' responsible for the subculture's exotic displays. Certain semiotic facts are undeniable. The punk subculture, like every other youth culture, was constituted in a series of spectacular transformations of a whole range of commodities, values, common-sense attitudes, etc. It was through these adapted forms that certain sections of predominantly working-class youth were able to restate their opposition to dominant values and institutions. However, when we attempt to close in on specific items, we immediately encounter problems. What, for instance, was the swastika being used to signify?

We can see how the symbol was made available to the punks (via Bowie and Lou Reed's 'Berlin' phase). More over, it clearly reflected the punks' interest in a decadent and evil Germany – a Germany which had 'no future'. It evoked a period redolent with a powerful mythology. Conventionally, as far as the British were concerned, the swastika signified 'enemy'. None the less, in punk usage, the symbol lost its 'natural' meaning – fascism. The punks were not generally sympathetic to the parties of the extreme right. [...] We must resort, then, to the most obvious of explanations – that the swastika was worn because it was guaranteed to shock. [...] The signifier (swastika) had been wilfully detached from the concept (Nazism) it conventionally signified, and although it had been re-positioned (as 'Berlin') within an alternative subcultural context, its primary value and appeal derived precisely from its lack of meaning: from its potential for deceit. It was exploited as an empty effect. We are forced to the conclusion that the central value 'held and reflected' in the swastika was the communicated absence of any such identifiable values. Ultimately, the symbol was as 'dumb' as the rage it provoked. The key to punk style remains elusive. Instead of arriving at the point where we can begin to make sense of the style, we have reached the very place where meaning itself evaporates.

## Style as Signifying Practice

It would seem that those approaches to subculture based upon a traditional semiotics (a semiotics which begins with some notion of the 'message' – of a combination of elements referring unanimously to a fixed number of signifieds) fail to provide us with a 'way in' to the difficult and contradictory text of punk style. Any attempt at extracting a final set of meanings from the seemingly endless, often apparently random, play of signifiers in evidence here seems doomed to failure.

And yet, over the years, a branch of semiotics has emerged which deals precisely with this problem. Here the simple notion of reading as the revelation of a fixed number of concealed meanings is discarded in favour of the idea of *polysemy* whereby each text is seen to generate a potentially infinite range of meanings. Attention is consequently directed towards that point – or more precisely, that level – in any given text where the principle of meaning itself seems most in doubt. Such an approach lays less stress on the primacy of structure and system in language ('langue'), and more upon the *position* of the speaking subject in discourse ('parole'). It is concerned with the *process* of meaning-construction rather than with the final product. [...]

Julia Kristeva's work on signification seems particularly useful. In *La Revolution du Langage Poetique* she explores the subversive possibilities within language through a study of French symbolist poetry, and points to 'poetic language' as the 'place where the social code is destroyed and renewed' (Kristeva, 1975). She counts as 'radical' those signifying practices which negate and disturb syntax [...] and which therefore serve to erode the concept of 'actantial position' upon which the whole 'Symbolic Order,'*[14] is seen to rest.

Two of Kristeva's interests seem to coincide with our own: the creation of subordinate groups through *positioning in language* (Kristeva is specifically interested in women), and the disruption of the process through which such positioning is habitually achieved. In addition, the general idea of signifying practice (which she defines as 'the setting in place and cutting through or traversing of a system of signs'[15]) can help us to rethink in a more subtle and complex way the relations not only between marginal and mainstream cultural formations but between the various subcultural styles themselves. For instance, we have seen how all subcultural style is based on a practice which has much in common with the 'radical' collage aesthetic of surrealism and we shall be seeing how different styles represent different signifying practices. Beyond this I shall be arguing that the signifying practices embodied in punk were 'radical' in Kristeva's sense: that they gestured towards a 'nowhere' and actively *sought* to remain silent, illegible.

We can now look more closely at the relationship between experience, expression and signification in subculture; at the whole question of style and our reading of style. To return to our example, we have seen how the punk style fitted together homologically precisely through its lack of fit (hole: tee-shirt:: spitting: applause:: bin-liner: garment:: anarchy: order) – by its refusal to cohere around a readily identifiable set of central values. It cohered, instead, *elliptically* through a chain of conspicuous absences. It was characterized by its unlocatedness – its blankness – and in this it can be contrasted with the skinhead style.

Whereas the skinheads theorized and fetishized their class position, in order to effect a 'magical' return to an imagined past, the punks dislocated themselves from the parent culture and were positioned instead on the outside: beyond the comprehension of the average (wo)man in the street in a science fiction future. They played up their Otherness, 'happening' on the world as aliens, inscrutables. Though punk rituals, accents and objects were deliberately used to signify working-classness, the exact origins of individual punks were disguised or symbolically disfigured by the make-up, masks and aliases which seem to have been used, like Breton's art, as ploys 'to escape the principle of identity'.[16]

This workingclassness therefore tended to retain, *even in practice, even in its concretized forms,* the dimensions of an idea. It was abstract, disembodied, decontextualized. Bereft of the necessary details – a name, a home, a history – it refused to make sense, to be grounded, 'read back' to its origins. It stood in violent contradiction to that other great punk signifier – sexual 'kinkiness'. The two forms of

---

* The 'symbolic order' to which I have referred throughout should not be confused with Kristeva's 'Symbolic Order' which is used in a sense derived specifically from Lacanian psychoanalysis. I use the term merely to designate the apparent unity of the dominant ideological discourses in play at any one time.

deviance – social and sexual – were juxtaposed to give an impression of multiple warping which was guaranteed to disconcert the most liberal of observers, to challenge the glib assertions of sociologists no matter how radical. In this way, although the punks referred continually to the realities of school, work, family and class, these references only made sense at one remove: they were passed through the fractured circuitry of punk style and re-presented as 'noise', disturbance, entropy.

In other words, although the punks self-consciously mirrored what Paul Piccone (1969) calls the 'pre-categorical realities' of bourgeois society – inequality, powerlessness, alienation – this was only possible because punk style had made a decisive break not only with the parent culture but with its own *location in experience.* This break was both inscribed and re-enacted in the signifying practices embodied in punk style. The punk ensembles, for instance, did not so much magically resolve experienced contradictions as *represent* the experience of contradiction itself in the form of visual puns (bondage, the ripped tee-shirt, etc.). Thus while it is true that the symbolic objects in punk style (the safety pins, the pogo, the ECT hairstyles) were 'made to form a *"unity"* with, the group's relations, situations, experience' (Hall *et al.,* 1976), this unity was at once 'ruptural' and 'expressive', or more precisely it expressed itself through rupture.

This is not to say, of course, that all punks were equally aware of the disjunction between experience and signification upon which the whole style was ultimately based. The style no doubt made sense for the first wave of self-conscious innovators at a level which remained inaccessible to those who became punks after the subculture had surfaced and been publicized. Punk is not unique in this: the distinction between originals and hangers-on is always a significant one in subculture. Indeed, it is frequently verbalized (plastic punks or safety-pin people, burrhead rastas or rasta bandwagon, weekend hippies, etc. versus the 'authentic' people). For instance, the mods had an intricate system of classification whereby the 'faces' and 'stylists' who made up the original coterie were defined against the unimaginative majority – the pedestrian 'kids' and 'scooter boys' who were accused of trivializing and coarsening the precious mod style. What is more, different youths bring different degrees of commitment to a subculture. It can represent a major dimension in people's lives – an axis erected in the face of the family around which a secret and immaculate identity can be made to cohere – or it can be a slight distraction, a bit of light relief from the monotonous but none the less paramount realities of school, home and work. It can be used as a means of escape, of total detachment from the surrounding terrain, or as a way of fitting back in to it and settling down after a week-end or evening spent letting off steam. In most cases it is used, as Phil Cohen suggests, magically to achieve both ends. However, despite these individual differences, the members of a subculture must share a common language. And if a style is really to catch on, if it is to become genuinely popular, it must say the right things in the right way at the right time. It must anticipate or encapsulate a mood, a moment. It must embody a sensibility, and the sensibility which punk style embodied was essentially dislocated, ironic and self-aware.

Just as individual members of the same subculture can be more or less conscious of what they are saying in style and in what ways they are saying it, so different subcultural styles exhibit different degrees of rupture. The conspicuously scruffy, 'unwholesome' punks obtruded from the familiar landscape of normalized forms in a more startling fashion than the mods, tellingly described in a newspaper of the time as '... pin-neat, lively and clean', although the two groups had none the less engaged in the same signifying practice (i.e. self-consciously subversive *bricolage*). [...]

## Notes

1. This was part of a speech made by Dr George Simpson, a Margate magistrate, after the mod–rocker clashes of Whitsun 1964. For sociologists of deviance, this speech has become *the* classic example of rhetorical overkill and deserves quoting in full: 'These long-haired, mentally unstable, petty little hoodlums, these sawdust Caesars who can only find courage like rats, in hunting in packs' (quoted in Cohen, 1972).

2. On 1 December 1976 the Sex Pistols appeared on the Thames twilight programme *Today*. During the course of the interview with Bill Grundy they used the words 'sod', 'bastard' and 'fuck'. The papers carried stories of jammed switchboards, shocked parents, etc. and there were some unusual refinements. The *Daily Mirror* (2 December) contained a story about a lorry driver who had been so incensed by the Sex Pistols' performance that he had kicked in the screen of his colour television: 'I can swear as well as anyone, but I don't want this sort of muck coming into my home at teatime.'

3. The police brought an unsuccessful action for obscenity against the Sex Pistols after their first L.P. 'Never Mind the Bollocks' was released in 1977.

4. On 4 January, 1977 the Sex Pistols caused an incident at Heathrow Airport by spitting and vomiting in front of airline staff. The *Evening News* quoted a check-in desk girl as saying: 'The group are the most revolting people I have ever seen in my life. They were disgusting, sick and obscene.' Two days after this incident was reported in the newspapers, E.M.I. terminated the group's contract.

5. The 1 August 1977 edition of the *Daily Mirror* contained just such an example of dubious editorial concern. Giving 'serious' consideration to the problem of ted–punk violence along the King's Road, the writer makes the obvious comparison with the seaside disturbances of the previous decade: '[The clashes] must not be allowed to grow into the pitched battles like the mods and rockers confrontations at several seaside towns a few years back.' Moral panics can be recycled; even the same events can be recalled in the same prophetic tones to mobilise the same sense of outrage.

6. The definitive study of a moral panic is Cohen's *Folk Devils and Moral Panics*. The mods and rockers were just two of the 'folk devils' – 'the gallery of types that society erects to show its members which roles should be avoided' – which periodically become the centre of a 'moral panic'.

> Societies appear to be subject, every now and then, to periods of moral panic. A condition, episode, person or group of persons emerges to become defined as a threat to societal values and interests; its nature is presented in a stylised and stereotypical fashion by the mass media; the moral barricades are manned by editors, bishops, politicians and other right-thinking people; socially accredited experts pronounce their diagnoses and solutions; ways of coping are evolved or (more often) resorted to; the condition then disappears, submerges or deteriorates and becomes more visible. (Cohen, 1972)

Official reactions to the punk subculture betrayed all the classic symptoms of a moral panic. Concerts were cancelled; clergymen, politicians and pundits unanimously denounced the degeneracy of youth. Among the choicer reactions, Marcus Lipton, the late M.P. for Lambeth North, declared: 'If pop music is going to be used to destroy our established institutions, then it ought to be destroyed first.' Bernard Brook-Partridge, M.P. for

Havering-Romford, stormed, 'I think the Sex Pistols are absolutely bloody revolting. I think their whole attitude is calculated to incite people to misbehaviour.... It is a deliberate incitement to anti-social behaviour and conduct' (quoted in *New Musical Express*, 15 July 1977).

7. See also 'Punks have Mothers Too: They tell us a few home truths' in *Woman* (15 April 1978) and 'Punks and Mothers' in *Woman's Own* (15 October 1977). These articles draw editorial comment (a sign of recognition on the part of the staff of the need to reassure the challenged expectations of the reader?). The following anecdote appeared beneath a photograph showing two dancing teddy boys:

> The other day I overheard two elderly ladies, cringing as a gang of alarming looking punks passed them, say in tones of horror: 'Just imagine what their children will be like'. I'm sure a lot of people must have said exactly the same about the Teddy Boys, like the ones pictured ... and Mods and Rockers. That made me wonder what had happened to them when the phase passed. I reckon they put away their drape suits or scooters and settled down to respectable, quiet lives, bringing up the kids and desperately hoping they won't won't get involved in any of these terrible Punk goings-on.

8. Although structuralists would agree with John Mepham (1974) that 'social life is structured like a language', there is also a more mainstream tradition of research into social encounters, role-play, etc. which proves overwhelmingly that social interaction (at least in middle-class white America!) is quite firmly governed by a rigid set of rules, codes and conventions (see in particular Goffman, 1971 and 1972).

9. The terms 'anarchic' and 'discourse' might seem contradictory: discourse suggests structure. None the less, surrealist aesthetics are now so familiar (though advertising, etc.) as to form the kind of unity (of themes, codes, effects) implied by the term 'discourse'.

10. In his P.O. account of the Saturday night dance in an industrial town, Mungham (1976) shows how the constricted quality of working-class life is carried over into the ballroom in the form of courtship rituals, masculine paranoia and an atmosphere of sullenly repressed sexuality. He paints a gloomy picture of joyless evenings spent in the desperate pursuit of 'booze and birds' (or 'blokes and a romantic bus-ride home') in a controlled setting where 'spontaneity is regarded by managers and their staff – principally the bouncers – as the potential hand-maiden of rebellion'.

11. BOF = Boring old Fart
   Wimp = 'wet'.

12. Of course, rock music had always threatened to dissolve these categories, and rock performances were popularly associated with all forms of riot and disorder – from the slashing of cinema seats by teddy boys through Beatlemania to the hippy happenings and festivals where freedom was expressed less aggressively in nudity, drug taking and general 'spontaneity'. However punk represented a new departure.

13. The word 'punk', like the black American 'funk' and 'superbad' would seem to form part of that 'special language of fantasy and alienation' which Charles Winick describes (1959), 'in which values are reversed and in which "terrible" is a description of excellence'.

See also Wolfe (1969) where he describes the 'cruising' scene in Los Angeles in the mid-60s – a subculture of custom-built cars, sweatshirts and 'high-piled, perfect coiffure' where 'rank' was a term of approval:

> Rank! Rank is just the natural outgrowth of Rotten ... Roth and Schorsch grew up in the Rotten Era of Los Angeles teenagers. The idea was to have a completely rotten attitude towards the adult world, meaning, in the long run, the whole established status structure, the whole system of people organising their lives around a job, fitting into the social structure embracing the whole community. The idea in Rotten was to drop out of conventional status competition into the smaller netherworld of Rotten Teenagers and start one's own league.

14. I can only refer the reader to A. White's critique (1977) for an explication of Kristeva's use of terms like the 'symbolic' and of the dialectic between unity and process, the 'symbolic' and the 'semiotic' which forms the thematic core of her work:

> The symbolic is ... that major part of language which names and relates things, it is that unity of semantic and syntactic competence which allows communication and rationality to appear. Kristeva has thus divided language into two vast realms, the *semiotic* – sound, rhythm and movement anterior to sense and linked closely to the impulses (Triebe) – and the *symbolic* – the semantico-syntactic function of language necessary to all rational communication about the world. The latter, the *symbolic,* usually 'takes charge of' the semiotic and binds it into syntax and phonemes, but it can only do so on the basis of the sounds and movements presented to it by the semiotic. The dialectic of the two parts of language form the *mise en scene* of Kristeva's description of poetics, subjectivity and revolution.

(See also G. Nowell-Smith's introduction to 'Signifying Practice and Mode of Production' in the *Edinburgh '76 Magazine*, no. 1.)

15. The setting in place, or constituting of a system of signs requires the identity of a speaking subject in a social institution which the subject recognises as the support of its identity. The traversing of the system takes place when the speaking subject is put in process and cuts across, at an angle as it were, the social institutions in which it had previously recognised itself. It thus coincides with the moment of social rupture, renovation and revolution. (Kristeva, 1976)

Again, Kristeva is specifically concerned with positing a notion of the *subject in process* against the traditional conception of the single, unified subject, and she uses the terms 'significance', 'symbolic', 'semiotic' and 'imaginary' in the context of Jacques Lacan's theory of psychoanalysis. Her definition of 'signifying practice' none the less still holds when transplanted to the quite different context of the analysis of style in subculture.

16. 'Who knows if we are not somehow preparing ourselves to escape the principle of identity?' (A. Breton, Preface to the 1920 Exhibition of Max Ernst).

# References

Althusser, L. and Balibar, E. (1968) *Reading Capital.* New Left Books.

Barthes, Roland (1972) *Mythologies.* New York: Paladin.

Breton, A. (1924) 'The First Surrealist Manifesto', in R. Seaver and H. Lane (eds), *Manifestos of Surrealism.* Ann Arbor, MI: University of Michigan Press.

Breton, A. (1929) 'The Second Surrealist Manifesto', in R. Seaver and H. Lane (eds), *Manifestos of Surrealism.* Ann Arbor, MI: University of Michigan Press.

Clarke, J. and Jefferson, T. (1976) 'Working Class Youth Cultures' in G. Mungham and C. Pearson (eds), *Working Class Youth Culture.* London: Routledge and Kegan Paul.

Douglas, Mary (1967) *Purity and Danger: An Analysis of the Concepts of Pollution and Taboo.* Harmondsworth: Penguin Books.

Eco, U. (1972) 'Towards a Semiotic Enquiry into the Television Message', *Working Papers in Cultural Studies 3.* Birmingham: University of Birmingham.

Eco, U. (1973) 'Social Life as a Sign System', in D. Robey (ed.), *Structuralism: The Wolfson College Lectures 1972.* London: Cape.

Ernst, Max (1948) *Beyond Painting and Other Writing by the Artist and His Friends* (ed.), B. Karpel. New York: Sculz.

Geertz, Clifford (1964) 'Ideology as a Cultural System', in D.E. Apter (ed.), *Ideology and Discontent.* New York: The Free Press.

Goffman, E. (1971) *The Presentation of Self in Everyday Life.* London: Penguin.

Goffman, E. (1972) *Relations in Public.* London: Penguin.

Hall, Stuart (1977) 'Culture, the Media and the "Ideological Effect"', in J. Curran et al. (eds), *Mass Communication and Society.* London: Edward Arnold.

Hall, Stuart and Jefferson, Tony (eds.) (1993) *Resistance Through Rituals: Youth Subcultures in Post-War Britain.* London: Routledge. (First published in 1976 as *Working Papers in Cultural Studies* 7/8).

Hawkes, Terence (1977) *Structuralism and Semiotics.* London: Methuen.

Ingham, R. (ed.) (1977) *Football Hooliganism.* Interaction Imprint.

Kristeva, Julia (1975) 'The Speaking Subject and Poetical Language', paper presented at University of Cambridge.

Kristeva, Julia (1976) 'Signifying Practice and Mode of Production', *Edinburgh' 76 Magazine,* no. 1.

Lautréamont, Comte de (1970) *Chants du Maldoror.* Alison & Busby.

Levi-Strauss, C. (1966) *The Savage Mind.* Weidenfeld & Nicolson.

Levi-Strauss, C. (1969) *The Elementary Structures of Kinship.* London: Eyre & Spottiswood.

Lippard, L. (ed.) (1970) *Surrealists on Art.* Hemel Hampstead: Prentice Hall.

Mepham, J. (1974) 'The Theory of Ideology in "Capital"', *Working Papers in Cultural Studies,* no. 6. University of Birmingham.

Mungham, G. (1976) 'Youth in Pursuit of Itself' in G. Mungham and G. Pearson (eds), *Working Class Youth Culture.* London: Routledge and Kegan Paul.

Piccone, Paul (1969) 'From Youth Culture to Political Praxis', *Radical America.* 15 November.

Reverdy, P. (1918) *Nord-Sud.*

White, A. (1977) 'L'eclatement du sujet: The Theoretical Work of Julia Kristeva', paper available from University of Birmingham.

Willis, Paul (1978) *Profane Culture.* London: Routledge and Kegan Paul.

Winick, C. (1959) 'The Uses of Drugs by Jazz Musicians', *Social Problems,* vol. 7, no. 3 Winter.

Wolfe, T. (1969) *The Pump House Gang.* Bantham.

# Chapter 30

# Angela McRobbie

## Second-Hand Dresses and the Role of the Ragmarket

## Introduction

Several attempts have been made recently to understand 'retro-style'. These have all taken as their starting point that accelerating tendency in the 1980s to ransack history for key items of dress, in a seemingly eclectic and haphazard manner. Some have seen this as part of the current vogue for nostalgia while others have interpreted it as a way of bringing history into an otherwise ahistorical present. This article will suggest that second-hand style or 'vintage dress' must be seen within the broader context of post-war subcultural history. It will pay particular attention to the existence of an entrepreneurial infrastructure within these youth cultures and to the opportunities which second-hand style has offered young people, at a time of recession, for participating in the fashion 'scene'.

Most of the youth subcultures of the post-war period have relied on second-hand clothes found in jumble sales and ragmarkets as the raw material for the creation of style. Although a great deal has been written about the meaning of these styles little has been said about where they have come from. [...]

One reason for this is that shopping has been considered a feminine activity. Youth sociologists have looked mainly at the activities of adolescent boys and young men and their attention has been directed to those areas of experience which have a strongly masculine image. Leisure spheres which involve the wearing and displaying of clothes have been thoroughly documented, yet the hours

From: *Zoot Suits and Second-Hand Dresses: An Anthology of Fashion and Music.* Ed. Angela McRobbie. Boston, MA: Unwin Hyman, 1988.

spent seeking them out on Saturday afternoons continue to be overlooked. Given the emphasis on street culture or on public peer-group activities, this is perhaps not surprising, but it is worth remembering that although shopping is usually regarded as a private activity, it is also simultaneously a public one and in the case of the markets and second-hand stalls it takes place in the street. This is particularly important for girls and young women because in other contexts their street activities are still curtailed in contrast to those of their male peers. [...] Indeed, shopping has tended to be subsumed under the category of domestic labour with the attendant connotations of drudgery and exhaustion. Otherwise it has been absorbed into consumerism where women and girls are seen as having a particular role to play. [...]

Looking back at the literature of the late 1970s on punk, it seems strange that so little attention was paid to the selling of punk, and the extent to which shops like the *Sex* shop run by Malcolm McLaren and Vivienne Westwood functioned also as meeting places where the customers and those behind the counter got to know each other and met up later in the pubs and clubs. In fact, ragmarkets and second-hand shops have played the same role up and down the country, indicating that there is more to buying and selling subcultural style than the simple exchange of cash for goods. Sociologists of the time perhaps ignored this social dimension because to them the very idea that style could be purchased over the counter went against the grain of those analyses which saw the adoption of punk style as an act of creative defiance far removed from the mundane act of buying. The role of McLaren and Westwood was also downgraded for the similar reason that punk was seen as a kind of collective creative impulse. To focus on a designer and an art-school entrepreneur would have been to undermine the 'purity' or 'authenticity' of the subculture. The same point can be made in relation to the absence of emphasis on buying subcultural products. What is found instead is an interest in those moments where the bought goods and items are transformed to subvert their original or intended meanings. In these accounts the act of buying disappears into that process of transformation. Ranked below these magnificent gestures, the more modest practices of buying and selling have remained women's work and have been of little interest to those concerned with youth cultural resistance.[1] [...]

## The Role of the Ragmarket

Second-hand style owes its existence to those features of consumerism which are characteristic of contemporary society. It depends, for example, on the creation of a surplus of goods whose use value is not expended when their first owners no longer want them. They are then revived, even in their senility, and enter into another cycle of consumption. House clearances also contribute to the mountain of bric-à-brac, jewellery, clothing and furniture which are the staple of junk and second-hand shops and stalls. But not all junk is used a second time around. Patterns of taste and discrimination shape the desires of second-hand shoppers as much as they do those who prefer the high street or the fashion showroom. And those who work behind the stalls and counters are skilled in choosing their stock with a fine eye for what will sell. Thus although there seems to be an evasion of the mainstream, with its mass-produced goods and marked-up prices, the 'subversive consumerism' of the ragmarket is in practice highly selective in what is offered and what, in turn, is purchased. There is in this milieu an even more refined economy of taste at work. For every single piece rescued and restored, a thousand are consigned to oblivion. Indeed, it might also be claimed that in the midst of this there is a thinly-veiled cultural élitism in operation. The sources which are raided for 'new' second-hand ideas are frequently old films, old art photographs, 'great' novels, documentary footage and textual material. The apparent democracy of the market, from which nobody is excluded on the grounds of cost, is tempered by the very precise tastes and desires of the second-hand searchers. Second-hand style continually emphasizes its distance from second-hand clothing.

The London markets and those in other towns and cities up and down the country cater now for a much wider cross-section of the population. It is no longer a question of the *jeunesse dorée* rubbing shoulders with the poor and the down-and-outs.[2] Unemployment has played a role in diversifying this clientele, so also have a number of other less immediately visible shifts and changes. Young single mothers, for example, who fall between the teen dreams of punk fashion and the reality of pushing a buggy through town on a wet afternoon, fit exactly with this new constituency.[3] Markets have indeed become more socially diverse sites in the urban landscape. The Brick Lane area in London, for example, home to part of the Bangladeshi population settled in this country, attracts on a Sunday morning, young and old, black and white, middle-class and working-class shoppers as well as tourists and the merely curious browsers. It's not surprising that tourists include a market such as Brick Lane in their itinerary. In popular currency, street markets are taken to be reflective of the old and unspoilt, they are 'steeped in history' and are thus particularly expressive of the town or region.

The popularity of these urban markets also resides in their celebration of what seem to be pre-modern modes of exchange. They offer an oasis of cheapness, where every market day is a 'sale'. They point back in time to an economy unaffected by cheque cards, credit cards and even set prices. Despite the lingering connotations of wartime austerity, the market today promotes itself in the language of natural freshness (for food and dairy produce) or else in the language of curiosity, discovery and heritage (for clothes, trinkets and household goods). There is, of course, a great deal of variety in the types of market found in different parts of the country. In London there is a distinction between those markets modelled on the genuine fleamarkets, which tend to attract the kind of young crowd who flock each weekend to Camden Lock, and those which are more integrated into a neighbourhood providing it with fruit, vegetables and household items. [...]

The street market functioned as much as a daytime social meeting place as it did a place for transactions of money and goods. It lacked the impersonality of the department stores and thrived instead on the values of familiarity, community and personal exchange. This remains the case today. Wherever immigrant groups have arrived and set about trying to earn a living in a largely hostile environment a local service economy in the form of a market has grown up. These offer some opportunities for those excluded from employment, and they also offer some escape from the monotony of the factory floor. A drift, in the 1970s and 1980s, into the micro-economy of the street market is one sign of the dwindling opportunities in the world of real work. There are now more of these stalls carrying a wider range of goods than before in most of the market places in the urban centres. There has also been a diversification into the world of new technology, with stalls offering cut-price digital alarms, watches, personal hi-fis, videotapes, cassettes, 'ghetto-blasters' and cameras. The hidden economy of work is also supplemented here by the provision of goods obtained illegally and sold rapidly at rock-bottom prices.

This general expansion coincides, however, with changing patterns in urban consumerism and with attempts on the part of mainstream retailers to participate in an unexpected boom. In the inner cities the bustling markets frequently breathe life and colour into otherwise desolate blighted areas. This, in turn, produces an incentive for the chain stores to reinvest, and in places such as Dalston Junction in Hackney, and Chapel Market in Islington, the redevelopment of shopping has taken place along these lines, with Sainsbury's, Boots the Chemist and others, updating and expanding their services. The stores flank the markets, which in turn line the pavements, and the consumer is drawn into both kinds of shopping simultaneously. [...]

Otherwise, in those regions where the mainstream department stores are still safely located on the other side of town, the traditional street market continues to seduce its customers with its own unique atmosphere. Many of these nowadays carry only a small stock of second-hand clothes. Instead, there are rails of 'seconds' or cheap copies of high street fashions made from starched fabric which, after a couple of washes, are ready for the dustbin. Bales of sari material lie stretched out on counters next to those displaying make-up and shampoo for black women. Reggae and funk music blare across the heads of shoppers from the record stands, and hot food smells drift far up the road. In the Ridley Road market in Hackney the hot bagel shop remains as much a sign of the originally Jewish population as the eel pie stall reflects traditional working-class taste. Unfamiliar fruits create an image of colour and profusion on stalls sagging under their weight. By midday on Fridays and at weekends the atmosphere is almost festive. Markets like these retain something of the pre-industrial gathering. For the crowd of shoppers and strollers the tempo symbolises time rescued from that of labour, and the market seems to celebrate its own pleasures. Differences of age, sex, class and ethnic background take on a more positive quality of social diversity. [...]

## Subcultural Entrepreneurs

The entrepreneurial element, crucial to an understanding of street markets and second-hand shops, has been quite missing from most subcultural analysis. The vitality of street markets today owes much to the hippy counter-culture of the late 1960s. It was this which put fleamarkets firmly back on the map. Many of those which had remained dormant for years in London, Amsterdam or Berlin, were suddenly given a new lease of life. In the years following the end of World War Two the thriving black markets gradually gave way to the fleamarkets which soon signalled only the bleakness of goods discarded. For the generation whose memories had not been blunted altogether by the dizzy rise of post-war consumerism, markets for old clothes and jumble sales in the 1960s remained a terrifying reminder of the stigma of poverty, the shame of ill-fitting clothing, and the fear of disease through infestation, rather like buying a second-hand bed.

Hippy preferences for old fur coats, crêpe dresses and army great-coats, shocked the older generation for precisely this reason. But they were not acquired merely for their shock value. Those items favoured by the hippies reflected an interest in pure, natural and authentic fabrics and a repudiation of the man-made synthetic materials found in high street fashion. The pieces of clothing sought out by hippy girls tended to be antique lace petticoats, pure silk blouses, crêpe dresses, velvet skirts and pure wool 1940's-styled coats. In each case these conjured up a time when the old craft values still prevailed and when one person saw through his or her production from start to finish. In fact, the same items had also won the attention of the hippies' predecessors, in the 'beat culture' of the early 1950s. They too looked for ways of by-passing the world of ready-made clothing. In the rummage sales of New York, for example, 'beat' girls and women bought up the fur coats, satin dresses and silk blouses of the 1930s and 1940s middle classes. Worn in the mid-1950s, these issued a strong sexual challenge to the spick and span gingham-clad domesticity of the moment.

By the late 1960s, the hippy culture was a lot larger and much better off than the beats who had gone before them. It was also politically informed in the sense of being determined to create an alternative society. This subculture was therefore able to develop an extensive semi-entrepreneurial network which came to be known as the counter-culture. This was by no means a monolithic enterprise. It stretched in Britain from hippy businesses such as Richard Branson's Virgin Records and Harvey Goldsmith's Promotions to all the ventures which sprang up in most cities and towns, selling books, vegetarian food, incense, Indian smocks, sandals and so on. It even included the small art galleries, independent cinemas and the London listings magazine *Time Out*.

From the late 1960s onwards, and accompanying this explosion of 'alternative' shops and restaurants, were the small second-hand shops whose history is less familiar. These had names like 'Serendipity', 'Cobwebs' or 'Past Caring' and they brought together, under one roof, all those items which had to be discovered separately in the jumble sales or fleamarkets. These included flying jackets, safari jackets, velvet curtains (from which were made the first 'loon' pants) and 1920s flapper dresses. These second-hand goods provided students and others drawn to the subculture, with a cheaper and much more expansive wardrobe. (The two looks for girls which came to characterise this moment were the peasant 'ethnic' look and the 'crêpey' bohemian Bloomsbury look. The former later became inextricably linked with Laura Ashley and the latter with Biba, both mainstream fashion newcomers.) Gradually hippie couples moved into this second-hand market, just as they also moved into antiques. They rapidly picked up the skills of mending and restoring items and soon learnt where the best sources for their stock were to be found. This meant scouring the country for out-of-town markets, making trips to Amsterdam to pick up the long leather coats favoured by rich hippy types, and making thrice-weekly trips to the dry cleaners. The result was loyal customers, and if the young entrepreneurs were able to anticipate new demands from an even younger clientele, there were subsequent generations of punks, art students and others.

The presence of this entrepreneurial dynamic has rarely been acknowledged in most subcultural analysis. Those points at which subcultures offered the prospect of a career through the magical exchange of the commodity have warranted as little attention as the network of small-scale entrepreneurial activities which financed the counter-culture. This was an element, of course, vociferously disavowed within the hippy culture itself. Great efforts were made to disguise the role which money played in a whole number of exchanges, including those involving drugs. Selling goods and commodities came too close to 'selling out' for those at the heart of the subculture to feel comfortable about it. This was a stance reinforced by the sociologists who also saw consumerism within the counter-culture as a fall from grace, a lack of purity. They either ignored it, or else, employing the Marcusian notion of recuperation, attributed it to the intervention of external market forces.[4] It was the unwelcome presence of media and other commercial interests which, they claimed, laundered out the politics and reduced the alternative society to an endless rail of cheesecloth shirts.

There was some dissatisfaction, however, with this dualistic model of creative action followed by commercial reaction. Dick Hebdige[5] and others have drawn attention to the problems of positing a raw and undiluted (and usually working-class) energy, in opposition to the predatory youth industries. Such an argument discounted the local, promotional activities needed to produce a subculture in the first place. Clothes have to be purchased, bands have to find places to play, posters publicising these concerts have to be put up ... and so on. This all entails business and managerial skills even when these are displayed in a self-effacing manner. The fact that a spontaneous sexual division of labour seems to spring into being is only a reflection of those gender inequalities which are prevalent at a more general level in society. It is still much easier for girls to develop skills in those fields which are less contested by men than it is in those already occupied by them. Selling clothes, stage-managing at concerts, handing out publicity leaflets, or simply looking the part, are spheres in which a female presence somehow seems natural.[6]

  While hippy style had run out of steam by the mid-1970s the alternative society merely jolted itself and rose to the challenge of punk. Many of those involved in selling records, clothes and even books, cropped their hair, had their ears pierced and took to wearing tight black trousers and Doctor Martens boots. However, the conditions into which punk erupted and of which it was symptomatic for its younger participants were quite different from those which had cushioned the hippy explosion of the 1960s. Girls were certainly more visible and more vocal than they had been in the earlier subculture, although it is difficult to assess exactly how active they were in the do-it-yourself entrepreneurial practices which accompanied, and were part of, the punk phenomenon. Certainly the small independent record companies remained largely male, as did the journalists and even the musicians (though much was made of the angry femininity of Poly Styrene, The Slits, The Raincoats and others). What is less ambiguous is the connection with youth unemployment, and more concretely, within punk, with the disavowal of some of the employment which was on offer for those who were not destined for university, the professions or the conventional career structures of the middle classes.

  Punk was, first and foremost, cultural. Its self-expressions existed at the level of music, graphic design, visual images, style and the written word. It was therefore engaging with and making itself heard within the terrain of the arts and the mass media. Its point of entry into this field existed within the range of small-scale youth industries which were able to put the whole thing in motion. Fan magazines (fanzines) provided a training for new wave journalists, just as designing record sleeves for unknown punk bands offered an opportunity for keen young graphic designers. In the realm of style the same do-it-yourself ethic prevailed and the obvious place to start was the jumble sale or the local fleamarket. Although punk also marked a point at which boys and young men began to participate in fashion unashamedly, girls played a central role, not just in looking for the right clothes but also in providing their peers with a cheap and easily available supply of second-hand items. These included 1960s' cotton print 'shifts' like those worn by the girls in The Human League in the early 1980s (and in the summer of 1988 'high fashion' as defined by MaxMara and others), suedette sheepskin-styled jackets like that worn by Bob Dylan on his debut album sleeve, (marking a moment in the early 1960s when he too aspired to a kind of 'lonesome traveller' hobo look), and many other similarly significant pieces.

This provision of services in the form of dress and clothing for would-be punks, art students and others on the fringe, was mostly participated in by lower middle-class art and fashion graduates who rejected the job opportunities available to them designing for British Home Stores or Marks and Spencer. It was a myth then, and it is still a myth now, that fashion houses are waiting to snap up the talent which emerges from the end-of-term shows each year. Apart from going abroad, most fashion students are, and were in the mid-1970s, faced with either going it alone with the help of the Enterprise Allowance Schemes (EAS), or else with joining some major manufacturing company specialising in down-market mass-produced fashion. It is no surprise, then, that many, particularly those who wanted to retain some artistic autonomy, should choose the former. Setting up a stall and getting a licence to sell second-hand clothes, finding them and restoring them, and then using a stall as a base for displaying and selling newly-designed work, is by no means unusual. Many graduates have done this and some, like Darlajane Gilroy and Pam Hogg, have gone on to become well-known names through their appearance in the style glossies like *The Face, Blitz* and *iD,* where the emphasis is on creativity and on fashion-as-art. [...]

## Baby Dresses and Girls in Men's Suits

[...] Mainstream fashion has a lot to thank youth subcultures for. It can gesture back in time knowing that its readers have been well educated, through the media, in post-war pop culture history. Often it is enough just to signal Brian Jones's hairstyle, or Jimi Hendrix's hat and scarf, or Cathy McGowan's floppy fringe, as though they have already been immortalised as Andy Warhol prints. They remain recognisable as traces, signs or even as fragments of signs. This instant recall on history, fuelled by the superfluity of images thrown up by the media, has produced in style a non-stop fashion parade in which 'different decades are placed together with no historical continuity'.[7] Punk do-it-yourself fashion has transformed fashion into pop art, and collecting period fashion pieces into a serious hobby.

From the mid-1970s punk girls salvaged shockingly lurid lurex minis of the sort worn in Italian 'jet-set' films of the mid-1960s. They reinstated the skinny-rib jumper and plastic earrings (worn by Pauline of Penetration and Fay Fife of The Rezillos) as well as any number of 'shift' dresses into the fashion mainstream. They also reclaimed tarty fishnet stockings, black plastic mini skirts and, of course, ski pants.

When Debbie Harry first appeared in this country she was dressed in classic New York hooker style with white, knee-length, 'these boots are made for walkin' boots, micro skirt and tight black jumper. Television shows, even puppet TV shows, as well as 1960s movies such as *Blow Up* and, of course, all the old James Bond films, were continually raided by the 'new' stylists in search of ideas. Paul Weller, for example, joined this rush in the early 1980s and uncovered old pieces of 1960s 'Mod' clothing which were then installed as part of the 1980s 'soulboy' wardrobe ... Jon Savage has described this plundering of recent style history displayed each week at Camden Lock as follows: 'Fashion, cars, buildings from the last hundred years piled up in an extraordinary display ... a jungle where anything could be so worn, driven, even eaten as long as it was old.'[8] Savage reinforces Frederic Jameson's gloomy prognosis of the post-modern condition in this 'mass flight into nostalgia'.[9] Loss of faith in the future has produced a culture which can only look backwards and re-examine key moments of its own recent history with a sentimental gloss and a soft focus lens. Society is now incapable of producing serious images, or texts which give people meaning and direction. The gap opened up by this absence is filled instead with cultural bric-à-brac and with old images recycled and reintroduced into circulation as pastiche.

It is easy to see how this argument can be extended to include second-hand style, which in the early and mid-1980s did indeed appear to the observer like a bizarre pantomime parade where themes and strands from recognisable historical moments seemed to be combined at random. Against Savage and Jameson however, it might be argued that these styles are neither nostalgic in essence nor without depth. Nostalgia indicates a desire to recreate the past faithfully, and to wallow in such mythical representations. Nostalgia also suggests an attempt at period accuracy, as in a costume drama. While both of these are true, for example, of Laura Ashley fashions, they are certainly not apparent in contemporary second-hand style. This style is marked out rather by a knowingness, a wilful anarchy and an irrepressible optimism, as indicated by colour, exaggeration, humour and disavowal of the conventions of adult dress.

The best known examples of this are the two girl groups, Bananarama and Amazulu, and the pop presenter Paula Yates. The wardrobes of Yates and the others are still drawn in spirit, if not in practice, from the jumble sale or the second-hand market. Paula Yates's 'silly' dresses and gigantic hair bows are like outfits salvaged from a late 1950s children's birthday party. The huge baggy trousers worn by Bananarama, tied round the waist 'like a sack of potatoes', their black plimsolls and haystack hairstyles caught up with straggly cotton headscarves are equally evocative of an urchin childhood or a 'Grapes of Wrath' adolescence. It is as though the Bananarama girls tumbled out of bed and put on whatever came to hand without their mothers knowing. Amazulu's gypsy dresses worn with cascades of hair ribbons and Doctor Martens boots create a similar effect. Again and again they gesture back to a childhood rummage through a theatrical wardrobe and the sublime pleasure of 'dressing up'. There is a refusal of adult seriousness and an insistence on hedonism and hyperbole. The 1950s ball-gown glamour sought out by Paula Yates is undercut by the sheer excessiveness of it. Paula Yates's wardrobe exists within the realms of high camp. Her style of presentation and style of dress create an image of pure pastiche.

However this pastiche is celebratory rather than reflective of a sterile and depthless mainstream culture. It plays with the norms, conventions and expectations of femininity, post feminism. Each item is worn self-consciously with an emphasis on the un-natural and the artificial. Madonna remains the other best-known exemplar of this rags, ribbons and lace style. She wore her mid-1980s image like a mask and with what Kaja Silverman has described as a sense of 'ironic distance.[10]

The other most influential image in the fashion horizons of the 1980s which also drew on second-hand style flirted with the idea of androgyny. Punk androgyny was never unambiguously butch or aggressive, it was slim, slight and invariably 'arty'. The Robert Mapplethorpe cover of Patti Smith's first album made a strong impression on those who were less keen on studs, chains and bondage trousers. Smith appeared casual, unmade-up with a jacket slung over her shoulders and a tie loosened at her neck. The cuffs of her shirt were visibly frayed and she faced the camera direct with a cool, scrutinizing gaze. This cautious but somehow threatening androgyny had a much greater resonance than, for example, Diane Keaton's very feminine take-up of the male wardrobe in the Woody Allen film *Annie Hall*. She too ransacked the traditional gents' wardrobe but her image was New York 'kooky' and eccentric (ex-hippy), and not even vaguely menacing. Smith was unmistakably from the New York underground. She was pale-faced, dark, undernourished, intense and 'committed'.

Patti Smith sent bohemian girls off in search of these wide, baggy and unflattering clothes, while *Annie Hall* alerted others to the feminine potential of the male wardrobe. She made the do-it-yourself look attractive to those less familiar with the ragmarket, and balanced her shirts and ties with a soft, floppy, feminine hat. Suddenly all those male items which had lain untouched for years in second-hand shops, charity shops and street markets came to life. Nothing was left untouched including cotton pyjama tops, shirts, jackets, evening suits and tuxedos, overcoats, raincoats, trousers and even the occasional pair of shiny black patent evening shoes, small enough to fit female feet. Men's jackets replaced early 1970s figure-hugging jackets with an inverted pyramidic line. The exaggerated shoulders narrowed slowly down to below the hips creating a strong but none the less slimming effect. This was immediately taken up by fashion writers as 'liberating'. It covered all 'irregularities' in size, imposing instead a homogenously baggy look. It was a style open to all, not just the size 10s and 12s. As a result these jackets began to appear 'new', in chain stores and exclusive boutiques up and down the country. They were soon being worn by high-flying businesswomen as well as by secretaries, professionals and others. These 'new' jackets imitated what had been a necessary alteration on those bought second-hand. Instead of shortening male-length sleeves, these had simply been turned up revealing the high quality, soft, striped silk lining. Again, the effect of this was to lighten an otherwise dark and fairly heavy image. The same feature appeared in the second-hand winter coats found in 'Flip' and in markets like that at Camden Lock. The huge surplus of tweed overcoats kept prices low and the range of choice extensive. These too were adapted for female use by turning up the sleeves, as were their summer equivalents, the lightweight cotton raincoats of which there was, and still is, a vast discarded 'mountain'. This effect was soon copied in new overcoats for both men and women. It can be seen in outlets as exclusive as Joseph's and Paul Smith's and also in Warehouse and Miss Selfridge. However, the cost of such garments in fabric comparable to that found in their second-hand equivalents makes them prohibitively expensive. This in itself forces a much wider range of shoppers, including the so-called young professionals, back towards Flip and Camden Lock.

These items of male clothing never conferred on girls and women a true androgyny. There was instead a more subtle aesthetic at work. The huge, sweeping greatcoats imposed a masculine frame on what was still an unmistakably feminine form. All sorts of softening devices were added to achieve this effect – diamanté brooches, lop-sided berets, provocatively red lipstick, and so on. A similar process took place round the appropriation of the male shirt. It too seemed baggy and egalitarian and thus in keeping with 1970s feminist critiques of fashion. But these shirts were tightly tucked into a thick waistband which just as surely emphasised the traditional hour-glass figure. Men's shirts ushered in the new shape for female clothing. Their sleeve line fell far below the shoulder on women, often connecting with the body of the garment half-way down the arm. This produced a 'batwing' effect which in turn was taken up by manufacturers and marketed as such. The inverted pyramid shape here took the form of an elongated arm and shoulder line narrowing down at each side to a small and feminine waist.

Alongside these, other 'stolen' items began to appear in the high street. Tuxedos (favoured by Princess Diana), bow ties, silk evening shirts, and for everyday wear, flat, black patent, lace-up shoes. For two consecutive winters these were as ubiquitous as leggings were in the summer. And in both cases the point of origin was the man's wardrobe. Indeed, leggings offer a good example. These first appeared alongside the gent's vests, in a cream-coloured knitted cotton fabric, as winter underpants, again in places like Camden Market. They had an elasticated waistband and button opening at the front. Punk girls began to buy them as summer alternatives to their winter ski pants. Dyed black, they created a similar effect. Then, the stall-holders dyed them and sold them in a dark, murky, grey-black shade. But they still suffered from the design faults which arise from adapting male lower garments for women. They were cut too low at the waist and frequently slid down. The fly front cluttered the smooth line across the stomach and they were often too short at the crotch. It was not long, therefore, before the same stall-holders were making up their own models in the professionally-dyed brushed cotton fabric popularised through consumer demand for track suits and sweatshirts. By the summers of 1985 and 1986 these were being worn by what seemed to be the entire female population aged under thirty. They were combined with wide, baggy male-shaped shirts, headscarves knotted on top 1940s munitionsworker style, children's black plimsolls (or else smart walking shoes) and lightweight cotton jackets.

The popularity of the male wardrobe therefore reflects a similar confusion of meanings as those thrown up by second-hand 'baby' dressing. In this apparently androgynous context these meanings highlight an appreciation of high-quality fabrics of the sort rarely found in mass-produced goods, a desire also to reinstate them to their former glory, and even a desire to wear something 'socially useful'. By recycling discarded pieces of clothing new wearers are not only beating the system by finding and defining high fashion cheaply, they are also making good use of the social surplus. An ecological ideal thus resides alongside the desire for artifice, decoration and ambiguous, double-edged femininity. [...]

All of the styles described above have been seen as part of the contemporary interest in 'retro'. They have therefore been linked with other visual images which draw on and 'quote' from past sources or earlier genres. These are now most prominent in the world of advertising and in pop videos where some nebulous but nonetheless popular memory is evoked in the swirl of a petticoat or the sweep of a duster coat.

It is unwise however to place second-hand style unproblematically within that cultural terrain marked out by Fredric Jameson as the sphere of post modernity. This would be to conflate retro-dressing as merely yet another cultural re-run, no different from the nostalgic re-makes of 1940s 'B' movies, or the endless re-releases and revivals of old hit records.

These trends, including that of second-hand dress, require much more specific analysis. While pastiche and some kind of fleeting nostalgia might indeed play a role in second-hand style, these have to be seen more precisely within the evolution of post-war youth cultures. Second-hand style in this context reveals a more complex structure offering, among other things a kind of internal, unofficial job market within these 'enterprise subcultures'. Girls and young women have played a major role, not just in providing youth subcultures with their items of style and dress, but also in rediscovering these items and imaginately re-creating them. Despite being at the vanguard of style in this respect, these young women have been passed over and eclipsed in the fashion pages by the young 'geniuses' of fashion in the 1980s like John Galliano or John Flett. In fact fashion designers play a much less central role in setting fashion trends than is commonly imagined. There is even a case to be made for the 'death of the designer', since the main impetus for changes in fashion and in contemporary consumer culture, as this article has argued, comes from below, from those who keep an eye open for redeemable pieces which are then reinscribed into the fashion system.

## Notes and References

1. S. Hall *et al.*, *Resistance Through Rituals*, London, Hutchinson, 1977 and D. Hebdige, *Subculture: The Meaning of Style*, London, Methuen, 1979.

2. Paddy's Market in Glasgow, in the early 1970s, offered one of the best examples of absolute social polarity in second-hand shopping.

3. The Birmingham Ragmarket in the late 1970s provided many similar examples of social diversity in second-hand shopping.

4. J. Clarke, 'Style' in S. Hall (ed.) *et al.*, *Resistance Through Rituals*, London, Hutchinson, 1977.

5. D. Hebdige (1979) and A. McRobbie, 'Settling the Accounts with Subcultures: A Feminist Critique' in *Screen Education* no. 34, reprinted in T. Bennett (ed.) *Culture, Ideology and Social Process*, London, Academia Press, 1981.

6. A. McRobbie and J. Garber, 'Girls and Subcultures: An Exploration' in S. Hall *et al.*, *Resistance Through Rituals*, London, Hutchinson, 1977.

7. J. Savage, 'Living In The Past', *Time Out*, February 1983.

8. J. Savage (1983).

9. F. Jameson, 'Postmodernism, the Cultural Logic of Capital' in H. Foster (ed.) *Postmodern Culture*, London, Pluto Press, 1985.

10. K. Silverman, 'Fragments of a Fashionable Discourse', in T. Modeleski *Studies in Entertainment: Critical Approaches to Mass Culture*, Bloomington and Indianapolis, Indiana University Press, 1986.

# Chapter 31

# Sarah Thornton

# The Media Development of 'Subcultures' (or the Sensational Story of 'Acid House')

## The Underground Versus the Overexposed

The idea that authentic culture is somehow outside media and commerce is a resilient one. In its full-blown romantic form, the belief suggests that grassroots cultures resist and struggle with a colonizing mass-mediated corporate world. At other times, the perspective lurks between the lines, inconspicuously informing parameters of research, definitions of culture and judgements of value. [...]

[...] 'Acid house', a dance club culture which mutated into 'rave' after sensational media coverage about drug use, is particularly revealing of the cultural logics involved. In considering this case, I argue that there is, in fact, no opposition between subcultures and the media, except for a dogged ideological one. I do not uncover pure origins or organic homologies of sound, style and ritual, nor vilify a vague monolith called 'the media'. Instead, I examine how various media are integral to youth's social and ideological formations. Local micro-media like flyers and listings are means by which club organizers bring the crowd together. Niche media like the music press construct subcultures as much as they document them. National mass media, such as the tabloids, develop youth movements as much as they distort them. Contrary to youth subcultural ideologies, 'subcultures' do not germinate from a seed and grow by force of their

From: Sarah Thornton, *Club Cultures: Music, Media and Subcultural Capital.* Hanover, NH: Wesleyan University Press, 1996.

own energy into mysterious 'movements' only to be belatedly digested by the media. Rather, media and other culture industries are there and effective right from the start. [...]

The term 'underground' is the expression by which clubbers refer to things subcultural. More than fashionable or trendy, 'underground' sounds and styles are 'authentic' and pitted against the mass-produced and mass-consumed. Undergrounds denote exclusive worlds whose main point may not be elitism but whose parameters often relate to particular crowds. They delight in parental incomprehension, negative newspaper coverage and that best blessing in disguise, the BBC ban. More than anything else, then, undergrounds define themselves against the mass media. Their main antagonist is not the law which might suppress but the media who continually threaten to release their knowledges to others.

Like 'subcultures', undergrounds are nebulous constructions. They can refer to a place, a style, an ethos, and their crowds usually shun definitive social categorization. Mostly they are said to be 'mixed' but, although the subcultural discourses I describe do cross lines of class, race and sexuality, their holders are less likely to physically cross the relevant thresholds. [...]

The logic of the underground is aptly symbolized by its attitude to two product types. Its distinctive format is the 'white label' – a twelve-inch single produced in a limited edition without the colourful graphics that accompany most retailed music, distributed to leading disc jockeys for club play and to specialist dance record shops for commercial sale. The rarity of white labels guarantees their underground status, while accumulating them can contribute to their owner's distinction. [...] At the other end of the spectrum, the format with the least credibility is the television-advertised compilation album of already charted dance hits. [...] While these hit compilations may contain music that was on a white label only six months earlier, the sounds are corrupted by being accumulated and packaged.

The underground espouses a fashion system that is highly relative; it is all about position, context and timing. Its subcultural capitals have built-in obsolescence so that it can maintain its status not only as the prerogative of the young, but the 'hip'. This is why the media are crucial; they are the main disseminators of these fleeting capitals. They are not simply another symbolic good or indicator of distinction, but a series of institutional networks essential to the creation, classification and distribution of cultural knowledge. [...]

To understand the relations between youth subcultures and the media, one needs to pose and differentiate two questions. On the one hand, how do youth's subcultural ideologies position the media? On the other, how are the media instrumental in the congregation of youth and the formation of subcultures? The two questions are entwined but distinct. Youth's 'underground' ideologies imply a lot but understand little about cultural production. Their views of the media have other agendas to fill. Like other anti-mass culture discourses, they are not always what they purport to be, i.e. politically correct, moral or vanguard. [...] Subcultural ideologies are a means by which youth imagine their own and other social groups, affirm their distinction and confirm that they are not just 'attention spans' to be bought and sold by advertisers.

Similarly, the second question about how the media do not just represent but mediate within youth culture can only be fully understood in relation to club cultural ideologies. For the positioning of various media outlets – prime-time television chart shows versus late-night narrowcasts, BBC versus pirate radio, the music press versus the tabloids, flyers versus fanzines – as well as discourses about 'hipness', 'selling out', 'moral panic' and 'banning' are essential to the ways young people receive these media and, consequently, to the ways in which media shape subcultures.

## Mass Media: 'Selling Out' and 'Moral Panic'

Scholars all too often make generalizations about the media based on an analysis of television alone. In the mid-nineties, however, mass media are in decline and the dominance of television – or at least *broad*casting – is in question. We are in an age of proliferating media, of global narrowcasting and computer networks where anyone on-line is 'nearby'. To make sense of the complexity of contemporary communications, it is necessary to divide the media into at least three layers. From the point of view of clubbers and ravers, in particular, micro, niche and mass media have markedly different cultural connotations. Moreover, their diverse audience sizes and compositions and their distinct processes of circulation have different consequences for club cultures. With mass media, for instance, affirmative coverage of the culture is the kiss of death, while disapproving coverage can breathe longevity into what would have been the most ephemeral of fads. In this section, I examine these dynamics of 'selling out' and 'moral panic' in relation to three national media: prime-time television, national public service radio and mass circulation tabloid newspapers. [...]

Having been on the air for over twenty-five years, *Top of the Pops* has close to universal brand recognition; it is seen as the unrivalled nemesis of the underground and the main gateway to mass culture. This half-hour programme combines 'live vocal' performances attended by a free-standing studio audience with video clips – both of which are introduced according to their current position in that week's top forty. The show is considered so domestic, familial and accessible that the ultimate put-down is to say a club event was 'more *Top of the Pops* on E than a warehouse rave' (*i-D* June 1990). [...]

This disdain for *Top of the Pops* is tied up with a measure of contempt for the singles sales chart. Clubbers have a general antipathy to what they call 'chartpop' [...] which does not include everything in the top forty but rather the 'teenybop' material identified with girls between eight and fourteen [...]. However, when it comes to dance music, clubbers and ravers seem concerned less with actual sales figures than with concomitant media exposure – the ancillary effects of chart placement on television programming, radio playlists and magazine editorial policies. This is perhaps best demonstrated by the fact that clubbers and ravers tend to have deep admiration for tracks that got into the top ten without any radio or video play – simply on the strength of being heard in clubs, covered in the specialist press and bought on twelve-inch by clubbers alone.

*Top of the Pops*, rather than the singles chart *per se*, is seen as a key point of so-called 'selling out'. [...]

Dick Hebdige theorizes 'selling out' as a process of 'incorporation' into the hegemony. He describes this recuperative 'commercialization' as an aesthetic metamorphosis, an ideological rather than a material process whereby previously subversive subcultural signs (such as music and clothing) are 'converted' or 'translated' into mass-produced commodities (Hebdige 1979: 97). But as the popular rhetoric of 'selling out' assumes that records with low sales aren't 'commercial' (even though they are obviously products of commerce) and validates the proliferating distinctions of consumer capitalism, this fusion of populist and Marxist discourses is wistful.

Within club undergrounds, it seems to me that 'to sell' means 'to betray' and 'selling out' refers to the process by which artists or songs sell beyond their initial market which, in turn, loses its sense of possession, exclusive ownership and familiar belonging. In other words, 'selling out' means *selling* to *out*siders, which in the case of *Top of the Pops* means those younger and older than the club-going sixteen-to-twenty-four-year olds who do not form the bulk of the programme's audience, partly because they watch less television than any other age-group. [...]

Despite several academic arguments about the opposition of youth subcultures and television culture [...], British youth subcultures aren't 'anti-television' as much as they are against a few key segments of TV that expose youth subcultural materials to everybody else. The general accessibility of broadcasting, in the strict sense of the word, is at odds with the esotericism and exclusivity of club and rave cultures; it too widely distributes the raw material of youth's subcultural capitals. Other music-oriented television programmes which tie into club culture like MTV Europe or ITV's *Chart Show* have not accrued the connotations of *Top of the Pops*. First, these programmes are sufficiently narrow-cast to escape negative symbolization as the overground. Second, they have high video content – a form which is somehow seen to maintain the autonomy of music culture and has credibility amongst clubbers.

[...] Frith argues that 'the rise of pop video has been dependent on and accelerated the decline of the ideology of youth-as-opposition' (Frith 1988: 213). But many dance acts seem to think that videos help them resist 'selling out'. A couple of factors might contribute to this attitude. First, videos allow the band to present themselves (with the help of the marketing and promotions departments of their record company) in a controlled manner closer to their own terms. Videos enable them to avoid being tainted by the 'naff' context of *Top of the Pops*. The artists protect their authentic aura by refusing to make a physical appearance. Second, the practice of lip-synching and acting out songs which have no 'live' existence undermines the creative credibility of these artists. With few lyrics and few performers *per se*, much contemporary dance music (particularly house and techno) is still in the process of developing an effective style of 'live' presentation. [...]

Videos are considered by many to be an appropriate visual accompaniment to a music which is quintessentially recorded. This is particularly the case with dance videos that use animated or computer-generated graphics and abstract visuals which forego depicting the artist. It is now often forgotten that the music video had its debut in discos in the seventies and is still a feature of many clubs. [...]

Dance acts must nevertheless occasionally negotiate 'live' *Top of the Pops* appearances. For, as one television promotions manager put it, 'underground or not, major labels encourage their dance acts to appear because *Top of the Pops* shows hardly any videos, unless you're U2 or a breaker and then you only get twenty seconds' (Loraine McDonald, EMI: Interview, 2 September 1992). Two basic strategies for maintaining an underground sensibility and immunizing oneself against the domesticity of *Top of the Pops* are disguise and parody; dance acts frequently hide their faces with sunglasses, hoods and hats and/or go 'over the top' in their performance. Nothing is less 'cool' than taking *Top of the Pops* seriously. [...]

As a medium of image, print and sound which fills more leisure hours than any other form of communication, television is in a unique position to violate the esotericism and semi-privacies of club culture. Nevertheless, clubber and raver discourses about television programmes are intricate and full of discrepancies. They relate to the audience at home because undiscriminating exposure to outsiders is a betrayal. They concern the people depicted who can become objects of ridicule rather than points of identification, seeming incarnations of an ideological *other*. Underground discourses also involve issues of format and aesthetics in so far as music video and its stylistic practices are valued as means by which music culture can be televised but somehow preserve its rhetorical autonomy and authenticity.

Though these are the prevailing ideologies of club culture, they are not all determining nor without loopholes. For example, a *Top of the Pops* appearance is often seen by the dance act's original fans as an affirmation of their taste as well as something to be viewed with suspicions of 'selling out'. Ironically, nothing proves the originality and inventiveness of subcultural music and style more than its eventual 'mainstreaming'. Similarly, subcultures that never go beyond their initial base market are ultimately considered failures. Moreover, programmes like *Top of the Pops* are important for the recruitment of fifteen- and sixteen-year-olds to youth subcultures as its eclectic playlists frequently offer glimpses of otherworldly cult music cultures.

The betrayals of broadcasting and the aesthetics of atmosphere are but two cultural logics of club undergrounds. Negative coverage in the form of either wellpublicized omissions from programmes like *Top of the Pops* (sometimes characterized as censorship) or television news features on club and rave culture as a serious social problem (often framed as 'moral panic') are also important to the relationship between media and youth subcultures. Even though they are relevant to television, I will discuss these issues in relation to radio and tabloids where they constitute a more commanding dynamic.

Youth resent approving mass mediation of their culture but relish the attention conferred by media condemnation. How else might one turn difference into defiance, lifestyle into social upheaval, leisure into revolt? 'Moral panics' can be seen as a culmination and fulfilment of youth cultural agendas in so far as negative newspaper and broadcast news coverage baptize transgression. Whether the underground espouses an overt politics or not, it is set on being culturally radical. In Britain, the best guarantee of radicalism is rejection by one or both of the disparate institutions seen to represent the cultural *status quo*: the tempered, state-sponsored BBC (particularly pop music Radio One) and the sensational, sales-dependent tabloids (particularly the Tory-supporting *Sun*).

Although their audience share has declined markedly due to increased competition from newly licensed local stations, during the period in which I did the bulk of my research, Radio One was listened to by over thirty per cent of the British population every week – and notably more women than men. Unlike *Top of the Pops* (and contrary to common perception), the radio station did not limit its output to the top forty, but played an average of 1100 different titles a week, including dance catalogue, particularly from the more melodic end of the genre. Although it had specialist dance shows [...] the dance-oriented press tended to alternate between complaining that the station gave short shrift to dance music, and admiring genres like acid house and techno for not being radio musics. Either way, Radio One represented the accessible and safe mainstream.

Being 'banned' from Radio One was therefore a desirable prospect. It acted as expert testimony to the music's violation of national sensibilities and as circumstantial evidence of its transgression. Being banned was consequently the most reliable way to gain what is in theory a contradiction in terms, but in practice a relatively common occurrence – namely an underground smash hit. The Beatles' 'A Day in the Life' (1967), Donna Summer's 'Love to Love You Baby' (1976), 'The Sex Pistols' 'God Save The Queen' (1977), Frankie Goes to Hollywood's 'Relax' (1984), George Michael's 'I Want Your Sex' (1987) and The Shamen's 'Ebeneezer Goode' (1992) were all banned because of their references to sex, drugs or politics. All of them either became hit singles or were hit singles which went on to spearhead hit albums. In the case of tracks featuring the word 'acid', several climbed from the bottom forty to the top forty as a result of rumours alone.

For example, in October 1988, the first explicitly acid track to enter the top twenty, D-Mob's 'We call it Acieeed', caused some commotion. Radio One denied allegations, which emerged from the D-Mob's record company, of having banned the record, explaining that the single was not on the playlist because 'it wasn't right for the mood of some programmes such as the breakfast show'. However, as the Radio One playlist functioned only at peak times, the single had received fourteen plays from individual producers outside the playlist system, more times, in fact, than the Whitney Houston track that was number one that week. In other words, Radio One insisted that they had imposed no ban on acid house in the strict sense of the word, that is, they were *not censoring* acid house. However, the record company kept suggesting that the music was 'banned' in the conveniently loose sense of the word, namely that acid house was *not playlisted*. The subcultural consumer press favoured the more sensational record company line – it made better copy and kept things friendly with a main advertiser – and few clubbers took note of the story's sources or distinguished between the two kinds of 'banning'.

The BBC is conscious of the curiosity generated by anything alleged to be censored. As the executive producer of the station at the time explained, 'Radio One, as part of the BBC, is seen as the establishment … and anything considered antiestablishment has a head start as far as teenagers are concerned' (Stuart Grundy, Interview: 26 August 1992). As a result, the BBC tries to keep their gatekeeping low profile and if that fails it attempts to play down the offending issues. With reference to the 'acieeed' lyrics of the D-Mob single, a BBC spokesman stated that the radio service understood the song to be anti-drugs: 'it expresses the ideal sentiments for our forthcoming Drug Alert campaign' (*NME* 29 October 1988). Meanwhile the then Radio One DJ Simon Bates gave interviews asserting that 'Acid is all about bass-line in the music and nothing to do with drugs' (*Daily Mirror* quoted by *NME* 12 November 1988).

Back in January 1988, however, London Records (a subsidiary of Polygram) has successfully launched acid house as a genre on the coat-tails of its drug-oriented potential for scandal. The sleeve-notes to *The House Sound of Chicago Volume III: Acid Tracks* described the new music as 'drug induced', 'psychedelic', 'sky high' and 'ecstatic' and even concluded with a prediction of 'moral panic': 'The sound of acid tracking will undoubtedly become one of the most controversial sounds of 1988, provoking a split between those who adhere to its underground creed and those who decry the glamorization of drug culture.' In retrospect, this seems remarkably prescient, but the statement is best understood as hopeful. 'Moral panics' are one of the few marketing strategies open to relatively anonymous instrumental dance music.

While the BBC conducts its 'bans', the logic of 'moral panic' operates most conspicuously within the purview of the tabloids. Britons have a choice of eleven national daily newspapers which range between 'quality' broadsheets and 'popular' tabloids. Unlike papers like *The National Enquirer* or *USA Today*, the British tabloids are read by over half the British population every day. They cover political issues in dramatic, personal and often sexual terms (hence the biggest selling Sunday paper, *News of the World*, is nicknamed *News of the Screws*). They take a regular interest in youth culture which they tend to treat as either a moral outrage or a sensational entertainment, often both. In fact, in line with their interest in gaining and maintaining young readers, the *Sun's* favourite 'moral panics' would seem to be of the 'sex, drugs and rock'n'roll' variety – stories about other people having far *too much* fun – which allow their readers to vicariously enjoy the transgression one moment, and then to be shocked and offended the next. [...] Despite questions of credibility, the tabloids have a swift domino effect: their 'shock! horror!' headlines frequently make the news themselves, are relayed by television, radio and the quality newspapers and generate much word-of-mouth, so that one often knows what's going on in the tabloids without having read them.

Mods, rockers, hippies, punks and New Romantics have all had their tabloid front pages, so there is always the anticipation – the mixed dread and hope – that a youthful scene will be the subject of media outrage. Disapproving tabloid stories legitimize and authenticate youth cultures. In fact, without tabloid intervention, it is hard to imagine a British youth *movement*. For, in turning youth into news, the tabloids both frame subcultures as major events and also disseminate them. A tabloid front page, however distorted, is frequently a self-fulfilling prophecy; it can turn the most ephemeral fad into a lasting development.

Following London Records' sleeve-notes, the subcultural press repeatedly predicted that a 'moral panic' about acid house was 'inevitable'. In February 1988, a good six months before a daily paper ran a story and a few weeks after the compilation's release, the three main music weeklies ran stories about a new genre called 'acid house' that was liable to cause 'moral panic.' [...]

Some months later, innuendo about drug use in British clubs started to appear in the style and music press, but it was left to two music weeklies experiencing flagging sales ... to expose domestic drug-taking. In July 1988, *New Musical Express* (*NME*) ran several stories under the Timothy Leary slogan 'Tune in, Turn on, Drop Out' which exposed and investigated Ecstasy use in British clubs. Although they admitted that it was 'hardly a matter for public broadcast', they explained the appeal of the drug (it gave one the energy to dance all night and reduced inhibitions). They also offered proof of its prevalence [...] and they listed the possible negative effects like nausea and recurring nightmares, emphasizing however that the worst effect was 'making a complete and utter embarrassment of yourself by babbling E-talk and intimate confessions to whoever happens to be in earshot' (*NME* 16 July 1988). *Melody Maker* followed with stories like 'Ecstasy: a Consumer's Guide' which rated batches of MDMA. The legendary 'yellow capsules', they said, induced 'feelings of having being ripped off and a buzz akin to trapping your toe in the door', while the 'New York tablets' were the 'most ... reliable

Ecstasy ... the lasting sensation being one of unbruisability and general bliss' (*Melody Maker* 20 August 1988). [...]

When the 'inevitable' 'moral panic' ensued, the subcultural press were ready. They tracked the tabloids' every move, reproduced whole front pages, re-printed and analysed their copy and decried the misrepresentation of acid house by what they variously called 'moral panic', 'media hysteria', a 'gutter press hate campaign' and a 'moral crusade'. However much they condemned the tabloids, clubbers and club writers were fascinated by their representation and gloried in the sensational excess. [...]

Even well after the waves of tabloid coverage, dance magazines and fanzines compiled top ten charts of 'ridiculous platitudes' used by the popular press – 'Killer Cult', 'In the grip of E', 'Rave to the Grave' (Herb *Garden* June 1992). Others ran spoof scandals about millions of kids 'hooked on a mind bending drug called A' (for alcohol) or stories about the designer drug 'T' which was 'openly on sale in supermarkets and supplied in a small perforated bag' (*Herb Garden* June 1992; *Touch* February 1992). [...]

In 1991, however, when the negative stories had lost their news value, the tabloids started publishing positive articles with headlines like 'Bop to Burn: Raving is the Perfect Way to Lose Weight', 'High on Life' and 'Raves are all the Rage'. Needless to say, clubbers and their niche press were outraged. How could the tabloids about-face and ignore the abundant use of drugs? How did they think ravers stay up till 6 a.m., if it weren't for the numerous amphetamines inside them? [...]

Although negative reporting is disparaged, it is subject to anticipation, even aspiration. Positive tabloid coverage, on the other hand, is the subcultural kiss of death. In 1988, the *Sun* briefly celebrated acid house, advising their readers to wear T-shirts emblazoned with Smiley faces, the music's coat of arms, in order to 'dazzle your mates with the latest trendy club wear', before they began running hostile exposés. Had the tabloid continued with this happy endorsement of acid house, it is likely the scene would have been aborted and a movement would not have ensued. Similarly, rave culture would probably have lost its force with this second wave of positive reports had it not been followed by further disapproving coverage (about ravers converging on free festivals with 'travellers', namely, nomadic 'hippies' and 'crusties' who travel the countryside in convoys of 'vehicles').

Cultural studies and sociologies of 'moral panic' tend to position youth cultures as innocent victims of negative stigmatization. But mass media 'misunderstanding' is often an objective of certain subcultural industries, rather than an accident of youth's cultural pursuits. 'Moral panic' can therefore be seen as a form of hype orchestrated by culture industries that target the youth market. The music press seemed to understand the acid house phenomenon in this way, arguing that forbidden fruit is most desirable and that prohibition never works. The hysterical reports of the popular press, they argued, amounted to a 'priceless PR campaign' (*Q* January 1989). Perhaps the first publicist to court moral outrage intentionally was Andrew Loog Oldman who, back the mid-1960s, promoted the Rolling Stones as dirty, irascible, rebellious and threatening (cf. Norman 1993). Rather than some fundamental innovation, Malcolm McLaren's management of the image of the Sex Pistols in the 1970s followed an already well-trodden promotional path. In the 1980s and 1990s, acts as disparate as Madonna, Ice-T and Oasis have played with these marketing strategies, for 'moral panic' fosters widespread exposure at the same time as mitigating accusations of 'selling out'.

(Hence, the usefulness of 'Parental Advisory' stickers in marketing certain kinds of acts in the US.)

'Moral panic' is a metaphor which depicts a complex society as a single person who experiences sudden groundless fear about its virtue. Although the term serves the purposes of the record industry and the music press well by inflating the threat posed by subcultures, as an academic concept, its anthropomorphism and totalization mystify more than they reveal. It fails to acknowledge competing media, let alone their reception by diverse audiences. And, its concept of morals overlooks the youthful ethics of abandon.

Popular music is in perpetual search of significance. Associations with sex, death and drugs imbue it with a 'real life' gravity that moves it beyond light-weight entertainment into the realm of, at the very least, serious hedonism. Acid house came to be hailed as a movement bigger than punk and akin to the hippie revolution precisely because its drug connections made it newsworthy beyond the confines of youth culture. While subcultural studies have tended to argue that youth subcultures are subversive until the very moment they are represented by the mass media (Hebdige 1979 and 1987), here it is argued that these kinds of taste cultures (not to be confused with activist organizations) become politically relevant only when they are framed as such. In other words, derogatory media coverage is not the verdict but the essence of their resistance. [...]

## Micro-Media: Flyers, Listings, Fanzines, Pirates

Flyers, fanzines, flyposters, listings, telephone information lines, pirate radio, e-mailing lists and internet archive sites may not at first seem to have much in common. An array of media, from the most rudimentary of print forms to the latest in digital interactive technologies, are the low circulating, narrowly targeted micro-media which have the most credibility amongst clubbers and are most instrumental to their congregating on a nightly basis. Club crowds are not organic formations which respond mysteriously to some collective unconscious, but people grouped together by intricate networks of communications. Clubbers elect to come together by making decisions based on the information they have at hand *at the same time as* they are actively assembled by club organizers.

The media venerated for epitomizing the authenticity of dance subcultures are first and foremost word-of-mouth, word-on-the-street and fanzines. Although these media are romanticized as pure and autonomous, they are generally tainted by and contingent upon other media and other business. While they are assumed to be in the vanguard, they are just as likely to be belated and behind. Though these media are said to be closest to subcultures, various social and economic factors limit and complicate their intimate relations.

Word-of-mouth is considered the consummate medium of the underground. But conversations between friends about clubs often involve flyers seen, radio heard and features read. Rather than an unadulterated grassroots medium, word-of-mouth is often extended by or is an extension of other communications' media. For this reason, club organizers, like other marketers and advertisers, actively seek to generate word-of-mouth with their promotions. Likewise, romantic notions of the 'street' forget that it is a space of advertising and communication, subject to market research and given ratings called 'OTS' or 'opportunities to see'. The 'OTS' rating considers the details of people who pass particular poster and bill-board sites in cars or on foot, adjusting figures to take into account distractions such as rival sites or poor visibility. Although they do not survey illegal communications like flyposting or spray painting, we can infer a similar demographic bias of young, male and up-market viewers. [...]

More than any other medium, perhaps, fanzines have been celebrated as grass-roots – as the active voice of the consumer and as the quintessence of subcultural communications. While the former is undoubtedly true, the latter is open to question. Rave fanzines give vent to unruly voices, local slang, scatological juvenilia, moaning, ranting and swearing. First person narratives are common, particularly ones about drug experiences which recount stories of brilliant or nightmarish times on Ecstasy, tales of having one's 'gear' stolen by bouncers who then sell it back to you in the club, anecdotes about experiencing 'aggro' from 'charlie casuals' and 'lager louts' (namely, aggravation from abusers of cocaine and beer). [...]

Fanzines are the only place to find writing about clubbing from an explicitly female (though not always feminist) point of view. Several were edited by women (for example, *Duck Call* and *Gear*), while even the laddish *Boy's Own* has the occasional 'Girl's Own Nightmare' feature which discusses such problems as 'death by sisterhood on eight tabs', surviving the loo queue and the handbag problem. Similarly, *Herb Garden* ran a spoof of a woman's magazine quiz which determined whether you were a 'Sad Susan' who doesn't know a thing about dance culture, a 'Techno Tracy' who raves all the time but indiscriminately, or a 'Vicky Volante' (the name of the author of the mock quiz) who has the right attitude and knows how to have fun with style. [...]

While the rave fanzines are certainly outlets for clubber debate, they are not, as is often assumed, necessarily emergent. Most of the rave fanzines appeared in the aftermath of the tabloid 'moral panic' and did little to contribute to the early evolution of acid house. *NME* tried to explain the absence of fanzines by the fact that the music did not revolve around artists: 'That there isn't already a massive acid house fanzine scene is partly down to the anonymity of the idiom. It's rarely performed live, which is why the DJs who play the sounds in clubs have a higher profile than the musicians who make them' (*NME* July 16 1988). But the early fanzines could have focused on DJs as did the later ones which were full of hagiographic articles with titles like 'Seventeen things you never knew about Danny Rampling' (*Herb Garden* April 1992).

All but one fanzine appeared long after British acid house had been converted into a 'scene' by the subcultural consumer press because before the niche media baptism, the culture consisted of little more than a dozen tracks, a few clubs and DJs. Moreover, even when the numbers of people involved swelled through the summer of 1988, it was not long before the tabloids were on the case. Professional media are generally faster off the mark, working to monthly, weekly and daily deadlines rather than the slow productions and erratic schedules of amateur media. Even after their proliferation, then, the fanzines tended to write about events that happened months prior to their publication and were well behind the consumer press. [...]

Word-of-mouth and fanzines are likely to be residual as much as emergent means of communication. The idea that subcultural scenes are seeded with micro-media, cultivated by niche media and harvested by mass media describes the exception as much as the rule. There is no *natural* order to cultural development.

In competitive economies where sundry media work simultaneously, where global industries are local businesses and 'all that is solid melts into air' (cf. Berman 1983), organic metaphors about 'grassroots' and 'growth' eclipse as much as they explain. They are too unitary to make sense of the complex teleologies of contemporary popular culture. Culture emerges from above and below, from within and without media, from under- and overground.

Flyers are considered by many club organizers as the most effective means of building a crowd in so far as they are a relatively inexpensive way to target fine audience segments. Their distribution is conducted in three ways: they are mailed directly to clubbers (often members) in the form of invitations, handed to people in the street 'who look like they belong' or distributed to pubs, clothing and record shops in order that they might be picked up by the 'right crowd'. While the first method uses the means of the private party, the last two trace young people's routes through the city, exhibiting an understanding of what Michel de Certeau would call their 'practices of space' (de Certeau 1984). Club promoters talk about how the dissemination of flyers is a deceptively tricky business: one must be wary of printing too many and finding them littering the streets; of depositing them in unsuitable places and procuring a queue full of 'wallies'. The dispersal of flyers influences the assembly of dance crowds; the flow of one affects the circulation of the other. [...]

Mailing lists are compiled in a variety of ways. Sometimes, advertisements in fanzines and the subcultural consumer press invite people to send ten pounds to become a member, or one can pay for membership at the door. At other times, the addresses of regulars are requested by the club organizer or, in the case of a club called Rage (held at Heaven in London), people were chosen from amongst the crowd to have their picture taken, then were issued with a photo I.D. and placed on the mailing list.

Key recipients of flyers are local listings magazines which relay their information ... to preview or review clubs for their readers. Listings magazines contain at least three gradations of exposure: the relative obscurity of the listings themselves, the discreet disclosure of a column-mention or the open exhibition of a feature in the front pages. The listings are written in a kind of clubber jargon that is often incomprehensible to those who are not already familiar with clubbing. [...] When a club is singled out for recommendation or comment in the columns which precede the listings, overviews are offered and terms are occasionally defined. When the magazine runs a feature – usually on a new scene or 'vibe' – labels are translated and codes revealed; the culture is exposed and explained to non-clubbing outsiders.

Published listings need to be negotiated as carefully as flyer distribution. They can stimulate or stifle interest, under- or overexpose. While a crowd needs to be assembled, too much or the wrong kind of coverage can close down a club in a matter of weeks. Just enough and the right kind of publicity, on the other hand, can reserve a place in the annals of club cultural folklore. [...]

Listings magazines are available from any newsagent, so they manage the flow of information with degrees of cryptic shorthand, innuendo and careful omission. Their gatekeeping can often establish the boundaries of the esoteric, protect the feel of the underground and mitigate overexposure. Flyers, by contrast, follow the movement of people through the social spaces of the city, then attempt to guide them to future locations. Both are integral to the formation of club crowds.

Another micro-medium that requires discussion is pirate radio. Here, I will focus on one case which is particularly revealing of the logics of subcultural capital – the transition of KISS-FM from pirate to legal radio station, from micro- to niche medium. Until 1990, dance music radio was illegal in Britain; the only stations to offer a hundred per cent dance programming were the 'pirates'. From sharing the same DJ staff through to club tie-ins, reciprocal promotions and over-lapping audiences, pirate stations and dance clubs had been entangled in a web of financial and ideological affiliations that went back to the sixties. [...]

Pirate radio stations have long been positioned as the antithesis of the official, government-funded Radio One. Despite being for-profit narrowcasters, they are cloaked in the romance of the underground. Like fanzines, they are supposed to be the active voice of subcultures and like graffiti or sampling, their acts of unau-thorized appropriation are deemed 'hip'. To a large degree, the stations did indeed cater to those culturally disenfranchised by age and race. The black music press, in particular, championed the pirates; they published listings of their frequencies (even after it had been criminalized), recounted tricks for dodging the police and berated the DTI (Department of Trade and Industry, responsible for licensing the airwaves) as the 'Department of Total Idiots' (*Touch* October 1991; *Touch* March 1991). Moreover, pirate radio was celebrated as 'the bush telegraph of acid house – [it] keeps the revolutionaries informed' (*Soul Underground* December 1989–January 1990).

The Broadcasting Act of 1990, however, changed a long-standing state of affairs and propelled the pirates in one of two directions. By making it a criminal offence to advertise on pirate radio, many stations were driven from partial to total depend-ence on revenue generated by advertising clubs and raves. [...] The ties between clubs and pirates tightened to the extent that many stations became little more than communication units of the larger club organizations. The stations even took on the names of club nights and raves; for example, in September 1990, 'Future', 'Fantasy', 'Friends', 'Obsession', 'Lightning', 'Rave' and 'Sunrise' were all on the air.

The course for a few other pirates, however, was legalization. In London, Manchester and Bristol, for example, pirates with sizeable audiences and suffi-cient legal and financial backing won licences from the Independent Broadcasting Authority (IBA). Changes in government policy have generally been forced by the popularity of illegal radio. Radio One was established in 1967 as a reaction to the off-shore pirates, Radio Caroline and Radio London. While the 1990 Broadcasting Act intended de-regulation, the IBA was reluctant to license a dance music station, refusing KISS FM's first bid in favour of a jazz station to which few people tuned in. [...]

London's KISS-FM was the largest and most celebrated instance of a pirate station going legal, and consideration of their transition illuminates the subcul-tural logic which distinguishes between the thrill of the illicit and the banality of the condoned. Founded in 1985, the pirate KISS was ranked in 1987 as London's second most popular radio station, after Capital FM and ahead of Radio One, by a poll in the *Evening Standard*. With the million pound launch of KISS's legal version in 1990, Rogers and Cowan, its public relations firm, and BBDO, its advertising agency, tried to build on this audience by maintaining what they understood to be the station's appeal – its underground credibility and 'street' feel. They issued six marketing statements including 'KISS-FM reflects the sound of the street' and three slogans which declared that KISS was 'Radical Radio', 'The Station on Everyone's Lips' and 'The Voice of the Underground'. While the trade weeklies had no problem in accepting that 'KISS has deliberately kept its pirate station feel', most of the youth-oriented press were sure a combination of IBA restriction and business pressure would compromise KISS (Music Week 17 November 1990). Even amid the positive reviews, they repeatedly expressed doubt that the station could 'walk the fine line between credit and credibility' (*City Limits* 30 Aug.–6 Sept. 1990). KISS had always been 'commercial' but with licence fees, taxes and corporate backers, it would need to make more. Contrary to assumptions about the conservative role of bureaucratic bodies like the IBA, however, KISS-FM's 'Promise of Performance' contract went some way toward insisting that KISS maintain its underground feel. Their licence stipulated that at least fifty per cent of their playlist be new material, that is, pre-chart, on general release but not in the top forty, pre-release or unreleased in Britain at the time of broadcast (IBA document 1990).

Nevertheless, Lindsay Wesker, KISS's head of music and main spokesman, spent much of the station's first year of legal operation juggling the ideological contradictions between subcultures and commerce. Wesker repeatedly told the press that KISS both maintained its subcultural feel and offered a substantial target audience attractive to advertisers, that they were both uncompromising in their search for authentic dance sounds and unswerving in their accumulation of socially active listeners between fifteen to twenty-four years. Previously, legal radio stations hadn't bothered with 'hip' subcultural trappings because they enjoyed monopoly or duopoly markets. With KISS (and other incremental dance stations around the country), British radio had to confront the discursive inconsistencies for the first time. [...]

Five years after its launch, KISS-FM continues to promote dance events and club nights. They have club and rave listings several times throughout the day and advertisements at night and at the weekend when rates are cheaper. KISS represents a sizeable section of the London dance scene. It gives key club DJs their own evening shows in which to play a conspicuously high number of 'exclusives' and promote their own club nights. It also has a substantial portion of clubbers and ravers among its listeners. To talk about certain London dance subcultures without reference to KISS would be to omit a main point of reference, source of information, assimilator of sounds and disseminator of underground ideology. [...]

Finally, mention should be made of a new micro-medium which has come to the fore since I completed my research but has implications for the future development of music cultures: the internet. Electronic mail is an obvious improvement on traditional 'snail mailing' lists in so far as it is faster, cheaper and potentially interactive. The mailing list of 'UK-Dance' set up by Stephen Hebditch in 1993 is used by a small number of organizers to publicize clubs, by a larger number of clubbers to discuss forthcoming events and to review releases for one another, and even by a few ex-clubbers to discuss aspects of rave culture other than going out. The discussions here have the same personal flavour as the fanzines, with many being about drugs or the practicalities of dance events (like the lack of available water or the repulsive state of the portable toilets). Although this mailing list spawned an archive site, 'UK-Dance on the World Wide Web', the most elaborate site – and probably the first on the net – was Brian Behlendorf's techno/rave archive. First set up at Stanford University, then on Behlendorf's own San Francisco-based server called 'hyperreal', this world wide web site includes pictures of rave flyers, discographies and sound samples, as well as the opinions of its various experts and users. [...]

All the micro-media discussed here have different influences and impacts: the most venerated are not necessarily the most actively engaged in convening crowds or shaping subcultures. Whatever their exact effects, they are more than just representations of subcultures. Micro-media are essential mediators amongst the participants in subcultures. They rely on their readers/listeners/consumers to be 'in the know' or in the 'right place at the right time' and are actively involved in the social organization of youth.

## Niche Media: The Editorial Search for Subcultures

Britain saw a remarkable seventy-three per cent increase in consumer magazine titles in the 1980s – the result of more detailed market research, tighter target marketing and new technologies such as desk top publishing (*Marketing* 13 August 1992). By the end of the decade, about thirty magazines addressed youth, featured music and style editorial and drew advertising from the record, fashion, beverage and tobacco industries. While flyers and listings tend to deal in the corporeal world of *crowds*, and tabloids handle the sweeping and scandalous impact of *movements*, consumer magazines operate in *subcultures*. They categorize social groups, arrange sounds, itemize attire and label everything. They baptize scenes and generate the self-consciousness required to maintain cultural distinctions. They give definition to vague cultural formations, pull together and reify the disparate materials which become subcultural homologies. The music and style press are crucial to our conceptions of British youth; they do not just cover subcultures, they help construct them.

[...] It is worth asking why consumer magazines are involved in subcultures at all. One reason is that the *aficionados* who become the writers, editors and photographers of the subcultural consumer press have at one time or another been participants in subcultures and still espouse versions and variations of underground ideology. There is a fraternity of interest between the staff *and* readers of these magazines, not only because they are of the same sex, but because they share subcultural capital investments.

Another reason for the editorial interest in subcultures relates to the magazines' need to target and maintain readerships. The fortunes of the youth press have tended to fluctuate with the popularity of the scenes with which they're affiliated, so the monitoring of subcultures has become a financial necessity. For instance, *New Musical Express* peaked in circulation in 1980 when punk and post-punk rock held sway, then experienced steady decline until 1989 when its association with, and promotion of, the Manchester scene gave it a new lease on life (by pulling its circulation back above 100,000).

Similarly, *The Face* was an integral part of the New Romantics/New Wave London club scene in the early eighties. Its contributors roamed around 'clubland', celebrated posing and elaborated a subcultural ideology. By early 1988, the magazine had lost touch with club culture: it no longer contained its stock-in-trade club column and chose covers depicting established film stars (like Steve Martin and Woody Allen) rather than the budding dance acts of its past. Even when acid house started getting media attention elsewhere, *The Face* opted for rare groove and hiphop as if acid house were a fad too fleeting for its attention.

It ran the odd blurb or house-oriented cover story [...] but the magazine specialized in the 'House Post-Acid' and 'Club-land after Acid' story (*The Face* December 1988; *The Face* December 1990). [...]

The established magazine closest to clubland in 1988 was *i*-D. Though often grouped with *The Face* as a 'style monthly', the two periodicals are significantly different. Whereas *The Face* had come to specialize in personality profiles and celebrity interviews, *i*-D concentrated on scouting out talent and detecting early signs of subculture. The divergence is aptly represented by their front covers: *The Face* displayed familiar faces; *i*-D opted for enigmatic, winking unknowns. Since its inception, the mission of *i*-D has been to find and formulate subcultures. Back issues are a catalogue of club cultures – constructed, encapsulated and packaged. 'Club News' and 'DJ of the Month' columns as well as regular features excavate the youth cultural landscape and establish scenes. *i*-D is self-conscious about the history of youth culture, counter-culture and alternative style but, compared to the nostalgic fanzines, it is uninterested in origins. The monthly has to be careful to search for what's happening and what's next; it needs to ride the crest of cultural trends. [...]

Not all youth-orientated magazines are in the business of discovering and developing subcultures. *Smash Hits* is a top-selling fortnightly glossy that loves *Top of the Pops*, publishes poster pinups of the younger Radio One DJs and reiterates tabloid gossip with exclamations like 'Really?!!!'. With a target readership of females aged twelve to twenty-two, *Smash Hits* covers dance music but rarely discusses club culture or celebrates undergrounds. While not subcultural in any current sense of the word, these magazines certainly cater to niche taste cultures which are subject to fad and fashion.

Although the phrase 'subcultural consumer magazines' may at first seem to be a contradiction in terms, it accurately describes the editorial business of sustaining readerships by navigating the underground tributaries (which flow into the 'mainstream') as well as the common interpretative community to which staff and subcultural members belong. Another reason for the symbiotic relations between subcultures and the music and style press is that subcultures are a means by which consumer magazines create good copy, tell a story and make meaning out of music and clothes. The press envelop music in discourses (often instigated by relevant PR feeds from record companies) which don't reveal exact conditions of production but rather give acts a picturesque context, locate them agreeably underground, authenticate them with a scene. In other words, consumer magazines accrue credibility by affiliating themselves with subcultures, but also contribute to the authentication of cultural forms in the process of covering and constructing subcultures.

Authentication by a subculture is particularly important for musics which don't revolve around performing authors and their *oeuvres*. Acid house music was perceived as authentic partly because it was said to come out of Chicago's underground dance clubs. But exactly how did the genre come into being and how did its legend get into general circulation within British dance clubs? The answers to both questions lie with the commercial activities of London Records which coined the genre in the process of their importing, compiling and marketing several DJ International tracks on the third volume of their *House Sound of Chicago* series. Before the compilation's release in January 1988, all that existed was a technological sounding bleep produced by a Roland TB303 found on the 1987 house music hit 'Acid Tracks' by Phuture.

Hundreds of dance genres are coined every year. While most fail, acid house prospered; it got into circulation, gained currency and started drawing lines on people's aural, aesthetic and social maps. The album's sleeve-notes effectively set the agenda for the music press; they concentrated on three qualities that might be regarded as decisive for the authentication and promotion of a new dance genre. First, as discussed earlier in relation to 'moral panics', they emphasized acid house's drug-orientation and potential to be 'one of the most controversial sounds of 1988'. Second, they gave meaning to identifiable sounds and placed them in a genealogy. This new genre, they argued, took house music 'into an ecstatic, almost transcendental state, where slower rhythms, abstract sounds and expanded lyrics merge together into a kind of phuture funk'. The spelling of '*ph*uture' and the use of the subtitle 'Acid Tracks' deftly put a gestural genealogy in place, retrospectively claiming the 1987 hit as the origin of the genre. Third, acid house was positioned as the soundtrack of an American subculture with firm roots in Chicago: it had an 'underground creed' and 'came out of that city's underground dance studios'.

To be credible, new genres must be more than nominal; they must come across as genuine, seemingly natural, generations of sound. Only one, arguably two, of the compilation's eight tracks and fewer than a dozen singles in general circulation were acid house as the album's own sleeve-notes defined and described it. Moreover, the DJ-artists featured on the album contradicted each other about what was and wasn't 'acid house'. Given this, the success of the genre was no mean feat. Routinely suspicious of new genres, the music press believed in acid house because the existence of a Chicago scene had already been well established by London Records' two previous volumes of *The House Sound of Chicago*. [...]

London Records formulated a genre which played into underground ideology and framed the sound as authentic, psychedelic and transgressive. Features on a new genre called 'acid house' in *New Musical Express*, *Melody Maker*, *Record Mirror* and *Soul Underground* repeated the sleeve's three themes: it was a new generation of music with authentic subcultural roots and a potential for 'moral panic'. Later, when telling the story of acid house-cum-rave, however, these same periodicals excluded record company involvement from the early history, positioning them as 'bandwagon jumpers' producing last-minute acid remixes and pop singles with applied acid hook-lines. Contrary to the ideologies of both the underground and many subcultural studies, culture industries do not just co-opt and incorporate; they generate ideas and incite culture.

Both the publishing and record industries have sectors which specialize in the manufacture and promotion of 'anti-commercial' culture. This is not to say that acid house-cum-rave culture was not vibrant, nor that its youth were cultural dupes. On the contrary, business involvement does not make young people any less active or creative in their leisure. The argument here is that subcultural gestures are less grand and more contingent than subculturalists have argued. When appropriation is an industrial objective, it is whimsical to regard young people's use of cultural goods as 'profane' or 'subversive' (cf. Willis 1978; Hebdige 1979). Subcultural-studies often overstate the homogeneity and conformity of cultural industry output ... and as a consequence, exaggerate the presence of subcultural resistance (Willis 1978: 170). [...]

Although many listings and consumer magazines contributed to the construction of the subculture, *i*-D was the most productive. Throughout the early months of 1988, *i*-D ran stories on aspects of what would come to be clustered under the rubric of acid house. On the cover of its first issue of the year, *i*-D sported a winking Smiley face (the insignia which would be banned from high street shops that autumn because of its associations with drug-taking). Inside, a feature described the new penchant for Smiley T-shirts, purple turtle-necks, mutton chop side-burns, floppy fedoras and platform boots. These were the beginnings of the acid house wardrobe, but the garb was associated with rare groove (that is, original and remixed 1970s American funk music) and the crowd was emphatically urban and mixed-race (cf. *i*-D December 1987/January 1988).

In the ensuing months, *i*-D ran many articles about neo-hippie social types and subcultures. In a parodic manner that admits their creative writing and avoids any 'uncool' earnestness, the magazine portrayed the 'Yappy' or 'Young Artistic Previously Professional Yippy' who was said to fuse the materialism of yuppies with the rebellion of yippies and 'the Baldrics' (named after television character Blackadder's acne-faced sidekick) who were described as the 'psychedelic miscreants … of Manchester's latest surreal youth cult' and said to wear long hair and flares and 'roam the Haçienda in packs' (*i*-D February 1988; *i*-D April 1988). Twenty years after 1968, hippie attitudes and attire were in revival among many disparate groups of youth, to diverse soundtracks, with different ideologies – and *i*-D was busy picking scenes out of the cultural morass and labelling them as subcultures. […]

The subcultural consumer press compile what subculturalists turn around and interpret as revealing homologies. But, while not random, the distinct combination of rituals that came to be acid house was certainly not an unmediated reflection of the social structure. Magazines like *i*-D produced acid house subculture as much as the participating dancers and drug-takers. Like genres, subcultures are constructed in the process of being 'discovered'. Journalists and photographers do not invent subcultures, but shape them, mark their core and reify their borders. Media and other culture industries are integral to the processes by which we create groups through their representation. Just as national media like the BBC have been crucial to the construction of modern national culture (cf. Scannell 1989), so niche media like the music and style press have been instrumental in the development of youth subcultures.

## Conclusion

Although acid house and rave are unique phenomena, a few general lessons about music subcultures and the media can be gathered from their case study. First, communications media are inextricably involved in the meaning and organization of youth subcultures. Youth subcultures are not organic, unmediated social formations, nor are they autonomous, grassroots cultures which only meet the media upon recuperative 'selling out' or 'moral panic'. On the contrary, the media do not just represent but participate in the assembly, demarcation and development of music cultures.

Second, the reason for an absolute and essentialist ideological opposition between subcultures and media is, in one sense, simple. The stories that subcultural youth tell about media and commerce are not meant to give accurate accounts of media production processes, but to negotiate issues of subcultural capital and social structure.

Third, the stratifications of popular culture or, at least, these hierarchies of 'hipness' would seem to operate in symbiotic relation to the media. This is not only to say that assorted media act as symbolic goods – bestowing distinction upon their owners/readers/listeners – but also to contend that the media are a network or institution akin to the education system in their creation, classification and distribution of cultural knowledge. In other words, subcultural capital maintains its currency (or cultural worth) as long as it flows through channels of communication which are subject to varying degrees of restriction. The inaccessibility can be physical as in the case of carefully circulated flyers or intellectual in the case of indecipherable subcultural codes. Either way, media are involved in the determinations of cultural knowledge. The prestige of being 'in the know' is one way to make sense of young people's use of and attitudes towards different strata of contemporary communication.

Fourth, this is *not* to deprive clubbers and ravers of their agency or to argue a case for media manipulation. Neither would do justice to the labyrinthine interplay of media representations and authentic cultures, commerce and consumer. Clubbers and ravers are active and creative participants in the formation of club cultures, but myriad media are also involved. They are integral to clubber and raver perceptions of where they belong and to practices of where they actually go.

London may be an 'overexposed city', but it is not one without its darkened doorways, obscure recesses and unmapped circuits (cf. Virilio 1986). Club 'undergrounds' are distinguished by being in the shadow of mass-media spotlights. Unless the culture is cast in the 'negative light' of 'moral panic', such television or tabloid illumination leads to demystification, explication and access (processes often clustered under the negative banner of 'commercialization'). The circumspect highlighting of a culture by niche media and micro-media, however, doesn't threaten as much as shape and sustain the interest and activities of appropriate audiences. One basis for predicting the formation, longevity and even the revival of any British subculture is, therefore, the nature of its association with distinct layers of media. [...]

## References

Frith, Simon (1988) *Music for Pleasure*. London: Polity.

Hebdige, Dick (1979) *Subculture: The Meaning of Style*. London: Methuen.

Hebdige, Dick (1987) *Cut 'n' Mix: Culture, Identity and Caribbean Music*. London: Comedia.

Norman, Philips (1993) *The Stones*. London: Penguin Books.

Scannell, Paddy (1989) 'Public service broadcasting and modern public life.' *Media, Culture and Society*. X1/2, April.

Virilio, Paul (1986) 'The Overexposed city'. *Zone 1/2*. (eds.) M. Feher and S. Kwinter. New York: Urzone.

Willis, Paul (1978) *Profane Culture*. London: Routledge and Kegan Paul.

# Chapter 32

# Tricia Rose

## A Style Nobody can Deal With: Politics, Style and the Postindustrial City in Hip Hop

Life on the margins of postindustrial urban America is inscribed in hip hop style, sound, lyrics and thematics.[1] Emerging from the intersection of lack and desire in the postindustrial city, hip hop manages the painful contradictions of social alienation and prophetic imagination. Hip hop is an Afro-diasporic cultural form which attempts to negotiate the experiences of marginalization, brutally truncated opportunity and oppression within the cultural imperatives of African-American and Caribbean history, identity and community. It is the tension between the cultural fractures produced by postindustrial oppression and the binding ties of Black cultural expressivity that sets the critical frame for the development of hip hop.[2]

Worked out on the rusting urban core as a playground, hip hop transforms stray technological parts intended for cultural and industrial trash heaps into sources of pleasure and power. These transformations have become a basis for digital imagination all over the world. Its earliest practitioners came of age at the tail end of the Great Society, in the twilight of America's short-lived federal commitment to black civil rights, and during the predawn of the Reagan-Bush era.[3] In hip hop, these abandoned parts, people and social institutions were welded and then spliced together, not only as sources of survival, but as sources of pleasure.

From: *Microphone Fiends: Youth Music and Youth Culture*. Ed. Andrew Ross and Tricia Rose. New York and London: Routledge, 1994.

Hip hop replicates and reimagines the experiences of urban life and symbolically appropriates urban space through sampling, attitude, dance, style and sound effects. Talk of subways, crews and posses, urban noise, economic stagnation, static and crossed signals leap out of hip hop lyrics, sounds and themes. Graffiti artists spray-painted murals and (name) 'tags' on trains, trucks and playgrounds, claiming territories and inscribing their otherwise contained identities on public property.[4] Early breakdancers' elaborate, technologically inspired, street-corner dances, involving head spins on concrete sidewalks, made the streets theater-friendly, and turned them into makeshift youth centers. The dancers' electric, robotic mimicry and identity-transforming characterizations foreshadowed the fluid and shocking effect of morphing, a visual effect made famous in *Terminator 2*. DJs who initiated spontaneous street parties by attaching customized, makeshift turntables and speakers to streetlight electrical sources revised the use of central thoroughfares, made 'open-air' community centers in neighborhoods where there were none. Rappers seized and used microphones as if amplification was a life-giving source. Hip hop gives voice to the tensions and contradictions in the public urban landscape during a period of substantial transformation in New York, and attempts to seize the shifting urban terrain, to make it work on behalf of the dispossessed.

Hip hop's attempts to negotiate new economic and technological conditions, as well as new patterns of race, class and gender oppression in urban America, by appropriating subway facades, public streets, language, style and sampling technology are only part of the story. Hip hop music and culture also relies on a variety of Afro-Caribbean and Afro-American musical, oral, visual and dance forms and practices in the face of a larger society that rarely recognizes the Afro-diasporic significance of such practices. It is, in fact, the dynamic and often contentious relationship between the two – larger social and political forces and black cultural priorities – that centrally shape and define hip hop.

The tensions and contradictions shaping hip hop culture can confound efforts at interpretation by even the most skilled critics and observers. Some analysts see hip hop as a quintessentially postmodern practice, while others view it as a present-day successor to premodern oral traditions. Some celebrate its critique of consumer capitalism, while others condemn it for its complicity with commercialism. To one enthusiastic group of critics, hip hop combines elements of speech and song, of dance and display, to call into being through performance new identities and subject positions. Yet to another equally vociferous group, hip hop merely displays in phantasmagorical form the cultural logic of late capitalism. I intend to demonstrate the importance of locating hip hop culture within the context of deindustrialization and to show how hip hop's primary properties of flow, layering and rupture simultaneously reflect and contest the social roles open to urban inner city youth at the end of the twentieth century.

In an attempt to rescue rap from its identity as postindustrial commercial product, and situate it in the history of respected black cultural practices, many historical accounts of rap consider it a direct extension of African-American oral, poetic and protest traditions to which it is clearly and substantially indebted. This accounting, which builds important bridges between rap's use of boasting, signifying, preaching and earlier, related, black, oral traditions, produces multiple problematic effects. First, it reconstructs rap music as a singular oral poetic form which appears to have developed autonomously (outside hip hop culture) in the 1970s. Quite to the contrary, rap is one cultural element within the larger social movement of hip hop. Second, it substantially marginalizes the significance of rap as *music*. Rap's musical elements and its use of music technology are crucial aspects of the use and development of the form, and are absolutely critical to the evolution of hip hop generally. Finally, and most directly important for this discussion, it renders invisible the crucial role of the postindustrial city on the shape and direction of rap and hip hop and makes it difficult to trace the way hip hop revises and extends Afro-diasporic practices using postindustrial urban materials. Hip hop's styles and themes share striking similarities with many past and contiguous Afro-diasporic musical and cultural expressions; these themes and styles, for the most part, are revised and reinterpreted using contemporary cultural and technological elements. Hip hop's central forms – graffiti, break-dancing and rap music – developed, in relation to one another; within Afro-diasporic cultural priorities, and in relation to larger postindustrial social forces and institutions.

What are some of the defining aesthetic and stylistic characteristics of hip hop? What is it about the postindustrial city generally, and the social and political terrain in the 1970s in New York City specifically, that contributes to the emergence and early reception of hip hop? Even as today's rappers revise and redirect rap music, most understand themselves as working out of a tradition of style, attitude and form which has critical and primary roots in New York City in the 1970s. Substantial postindustrial shifts in economic conditions, access to housing, demographics and communication networks were crucial to the formation of the conditions which nurtured the cultural hybrids and sociopolitical tenor of hip hop's lyrics and music.

## The Urban Context

Postindustrial conditions in urban centers across America reflect a complex set of global forces which continue to shape the contemporary urban metropolis. The growth of multinational telecommunications networks, global economic competition, a major technological revolution, the formation of new international divisions of labor, the increasing power of finance relative to production, and new migration patterns from Third World industrializing nations have all contributed to the economic and social restructuring of urban America. These global forces have had direct and sustained impact on urban job opportunity structures, have exacerbated long-standing racial- and gender-based forms of discrimination and have contributed to increasing multinational corporate control of market conditions and national economic health.[5] Large-scale restructuring of the workplace and job market has had its effect upon most facets of everyday life. It has placed additional pressures on local, community-based networks of communication, and has whittled down already limited prospects for social mobility.

In the 1970s, cities across the country were gradually losing federal funding for social services, information service corporations were beginning to replace industrial factories, and corporate developers were buying up real estate to be converted into luxury housing, leaving working-class residents with limited affordable housing, a shrinking job market and diminishing social services. The poorest neighborhoods and the least powerful groups were the least protected and had the smallest safety nets. By the 1980s, the privileged elites displayed unabashed greed as their strategies to reclaim and rebuild downtown business and tourist zones with municipal and federal subsidies exacerbated the already widening gap between classes and races.

Given New York's status as hub city for international capital and information services, it is not surprising that these larger structural changes and their effects were quickly and intensely felt in New York.[6] As John Mollenkopf notes, 'during the 1970s, the U.S. system of cities crossed a watershed. New York led other old, industrial metropolitan areas into population and employment decline.'[7] The federal funds that might have offset this process had been diminishing throughout the 1970s. In 1975, President Ford's unequivocal veto to requests for a federal bail out to prevent New York from filing for bankruptcy made New York a national symbol for the fate of older cities under his administration. [...] Virtually bankrupt and in a critical state of disrepair, New York City and State administrators finally negotiated a federal loan, albeit one which accompanied an elaborate package of service cuts and carried harsh repayment terms. These dramatic social service cuts were felt most severely in New York's poorest areas and were part of a larger trend in unequal wealth distribution and were accompanied by a housing crisis which continued well into the 1980s. Between 1978 and 1986, the people in the bottom twenty percent of the income scale experienced an absolute decline in income while the top twenty percent experienced most of the economic growth. Blacks and Hispanics disproportionately occupied this bottom fifth. During this same period, thirty percent of New York's Hispanic households (for Puerto Ricans it is forty percent) and twenty five percent of black households lived at or below the poverty line. Since this period, low-income housing has continued to disappear, and blacks and Hispanics are still much more likely to live in overcrowded, dilapidated and seriously undermaintained spaces.[8] It is not surprising that these serious trends have contributed to New York's large and chronically homeless population.

In addition to housing problems, New York and many large urban centers faced other major economic and demographic forces which have sustained and exacerbated significant structural inequalities. While urban America has always been socially and economically divided, these divisions have taken on a new dimension. At the same time that racial succession and immigration patterns were reshaping the city's population and labor force, shifts in the occupational structure, away from a high-wage, high-employment economy grounded in manufacturing, trucking, warehousing and wholesale trade, and toward a low-wage, low-employment economy geared toward producer services, generated new forms of inequality. As Daniel Walkowitz suggests, New York has become

> sharply divided between an affluent, technocratic, professional, white-collar group managing the financial and commercial life of an international city and an unemployed and underemployed service sector which is substantially black and Hispanic.

Earlier divisions in the city were predominantly ethnic and economic. 'New York,' according to Mollenkopf, 'has been transformed from a relatively well-off, white, blue-collar city into a more economically divided, multi-racial, white-collar city.' This 'disorganized periphery' of civil service and manufacturing workers contributes to the consolidation of power among white-collar, professional, corporate managers, creating the massive inequalities in New York.[9]

The commercial imperatives of corporate America have also undermined the process of transmitting and sharing local knowledge in the urban metropolis. Ben Bagdikian's study, *The Media Monopoly,* reveals that monopolistic tendencies in commercial enterprises seriously constrain access to a diverse flow of information. For example, urban renewal relocation efforts not only dispersed central-city populations to the suburbs, they also replaced the commerce of the street with the needs of the metropolitan market. Advertisers geared newspaper articles and television broadcasts toward the purchasing power of suburban buyers – creating a dual 'crisis of representation' in terms of whose lives and images were represented physically in the paper, and whose interests were represented in the corridors of power.[10] These media outlet and advertising shifts have been accompanied by a massive telecommunications revolution in the information processing industry. Once the domain of the government, information processing and communication technology now lie at the heart of corporate America. As a result of government deregulation in communications via the break up of AT&T in 1982, communication industries have consolidated and internationalized. Today, telecommunications industries are global data transmittal corporations with significant control over radio, television, cable, telephone, computer and other electronic transmittal systems. Telecommunication expansion coupled with corporate consolidation has dismantled local community networks, and has irrevocably changed the means and character of communication.[11] Since the mid-1980s, these expansions and consolidations have been accompanied by a tidal wave of widely available communications products which have revolutionized business and personal communications. Facsimile machines, satellite-networked beepers, cordless phones, electronic mail networks, cable television expansions, VCRs, compact discs, video cameras and games and personal computers have dramatically transformed the speed and character of speech and of written and visual communication.

Postindustrial conditions had a profound effect on black and Hispanic communities. Shrinking federal funds and affordable housing, shifts in the occupational structure away from blue-collar manufacturing and toward corporate and information services, along with frayed local communication patterns, meant that new immigrant populations and the city's poorest residents paid the highest price for deindustrialization and economic restructuring. These communities are more susceptible to slumlords, redevelopers, toxic waste dumps, drug rehabilitation centers, violent criminals, mortgage redlining and inadequate city services and transportation. It also meant that the city's ethnic- and working-class-based forms of community aid and support were growing increasingly less effective against these new conditions.

In the case of the South Bronx, which has been frequently dubbed the 'home of hip hop culture,' these larger postindustrial conditions were exacerbated by disruptions considered an 'unexpected side effect' of a larger, politically motivated, 'urban renewal' project. In the early 1970s, this renewal [sic] project involved massive relocations of economically fragile people of color from different areas in New York City into parts of the South Bronx. Subsequent ethnic and racial transition in the South Bronx was not a gradual process that might have allowed already taxed social and cultural institutions to respond self-protectively; instead it was a brutal process of community destruction and relocation executed by municipal officials, under the direction of legendary city planner Robert Moses.

Between the late 1930s and the late 1960s Moses executed a number of public works projects, highways, parks and housing projects which significantly reshaped the profile of New York City. In 1959, city, state and federal authorities began the implementation of his planned Cross-Bronx Expressway, which would cut directly through the center of the most heavily populated working-class areas in the Bronx. While he could have modified his route slightly to bypass densely populated working-class ethnic residential communities, he elected a path that required the demolition of hundreds of residential and commercial buildings. In addition, throughout the 1960s and early 1970s, some sixty thousand Bronxites homes were razed. Designating these old blue-collar housing units as 'slums,' Moses's Title I slum clearance program forced the relocation of 170,000 people.[12] These 'slums' were in fact densely populated stable neighborhoods, comprised mostly of working- and lower-middle-class Jews, but they also contained solid Italian, German, Irish and black neighborhoods. Although the neighborhoods under attack had a substantial Jewish population, black and Puerto Rican residents were disproportionately affected. Thirty-seven percent of the relocated residents were non-white. This, coupled with the subsequent 'white flight,' devastated kin networks and neighborhood services. Between the late 1960s and mid-1970s the vacancy rates in the southern section of the Bronx skyrocketed. Some nervous landlords sold their property as quickly as possible, often to professional slumlords, others torched their buildings to collect insurance payments. Both strategies accelerated the flight of white tenants into northern sections of the Bronx and into Westchester. Equally anxious shopkeepers sold their shops and established businesses elsewhere. The city administration, touting Moses's expressway as a sign of progress and modernization, was unwilling to admit the devastation that had occurred. Like many of his public works projects, Moses's Cross-B ronx Expressway supported the interests of the upper classes against the interests of the poor, and intensified the development of the vast economic and social inequalities which characterize contemporary New York. The newly 'relocated' black and Hispanic residents in the South Bronx were left with few city resources, fragmented leadership and limited political power.

The disastrous effects of these city policies went relatively unnoticed in the media until 1977, when two critical events fixed New York and the South Bronx as national symbols of ruin and isolation. During the summer of 1977 an extensive power outage blacked out New York, and hundreds of stores were looted and vandalized. The poorest neighborhoods (the South Bronx, Bedford Stuyvesant, the Brownsville and Crown Heights areas in Brooklyn, the Jamaica area in Queens and Harlem) where most of the looting took place were depicted by the city's media organs as lawless zones where crime is sanctioned, and chaos bubbles just below the surface. The 1965 blackout, according to the New York Times, was 'peaceful by contrast,' suggesting that the blackout which took place during America's most racially tumultuous decade was no match for the despair and frustration articulated in the blackout of the summer of 1977.[13] The 1977 blackout and the looting which accompanied it seemed to raise the federal stakes in maintaining urban social order. Three months later, President Carter made his 'sobering' historic motorcade visit through the South Bronx, to 'survey the devastation of the last five years,' and announced an unspecified 'commitment to cities.' (Not to its inhabitants?) In the national imagination, the South Bronx became the primary 'symbol of America's woes.'[14]

Following this lead, images of abandoned buildings in the South Bronx became central popular cultural icons. Negative local color in popular film exploited the devastation facing the residents of the South Bronx and used their communities as a backdrop for social ruin and barbarism. As Michael Venture astutely notes, these popular depictions (and, I would add, the news coverage as well) rendered silent the people who struggled with and maintained life under difficult conditions:

> In roughly six hours of footage – *Fort Apache, Wolfen* and *Koyaanisqatsi* – we haven't been introduced to one soul who actually lives in the South Bronx. We haven't heard one voice speaking its own language. We've merely watched a symbol of ruin: the South Bronx [as] last act before the end of the world.[15]

Depictions of black and Hispanic neighborhoods were drained of life, energy and vitality. The message was loud and clear: to be stuck here was to be lost. And yet, while these visions of loss and futility became defining characteristics, the youngest generation of South Bronx exiles were building creative and aggressive outlets for expression and identification. The new ethnic groups who made the South Bronx their home in the 1970s began building their own cultural networks, which would prove to be resilient and responsive in the age of high technology. North American blacks, Jamaicans, Puerto Ricans and other Caribbean people with roots in other postcolonial contexts reshaped their cultural identities and expressions in a hostile, technologically sophisticated, multiethnic, urban terrain. While city leaders and the popular press had literally and figuratively condemned the South Bronx neighborhoods and their inhabitants, their youngest black and Hispanic residents answered back.

## Hip Hop

Hip Hop culture emerged as a source of alternative identity formation and social status for youth in a community whose older local support institutions had been all but demolished along with large sectors of its built environment. Alternative local identities were forged in fashions and language, street names and most importantly, in establishing neighborhood crews or posses. Many hip hop fans, artists, musicians and dancers continue to belong to an elaborate system of crews or posses. The crew, a local source of identity, group affiliation and support system, appears in virtually all rap lyrics and cassette dedications, music video performances and media interviews with artists. Identity in hip hop is deeply rooted in the specific, the local experience and one's attachment to and status in a local group or alternative family. These crews are new kinds of families forged with intercultural bonds which, like the social formation of gangs, provide insulation and support in a complex and unyielding environment and may, in fact, contribute to the community-building networks which serve as the basis for new social movements.

The postindustrial city, which provided the context for creative development among hip hop's earliest innovators, shaped their cultural terrain, access to space, materials and education. While graffiti writers' work was significantly aided by advances in spray-paint technology, they used the urban transit system as their canvas. Rappers and DJs disseminated their work by copying it on tape-dubbing equipment and playing it on powerful, portable 'ghetto blasters.' At a time when budget cuts in school music programs drastically reduced access to traditional forms of instrumentation and composition, inner-city youth increasingly relied on recorded sound. Breakdancers used their bodies to mimic 'transformers' and other futuristic robots in symbolic street battles. Early Puerto Rican, Afro-Caribbean and black American hip hop artists transformed obsolete vocational skills from marginal occupations into the raw materials for creativity and resistance. Many of them were 'trained' for jobs in fields that were shrinking or that no longer existed. Graffiti writer Futura graduated from a trade school specializing in the printing industry. But since most of the jobs for which he was being trained had already been computerized, he found himself working at McDonald's after graduation. Similarly, African-American DJ Red Alert (who also has family from the Caribbean) reviewed blueprints for a drafting company until computer automation rendered that job obsolete. Jamaican DJ Kool Herc attended Alfred E. Smith auto mechanic trade school while African-American Grand Master Flash learned how to repair electronic equipment at Samuel Gompers vocational high school. (One could say Flash 'fixed them alright'). Salt-N-Pepa (both with family roots in the West Indies) worked as phone telemarketing representatives at Sears while considering nursing school. Puerto Rican breakdancer Crazy Legs began breakdancing largely because his single mother could not afford Little League baseball fees.[16] All of these artists found themselves positioned with few resources in marginal economic circumstances, but each of them found ways to become famous as entertainers by appropriating the most advanced technologies and emerging cultural forms. Hip hop artists used the tools of obsolete industrial technology to traverse contemporary crossroads of lack and desire in urban Afro-diasporic communities.

Stylistic continuities were sustained by internal cross-fertilization between rapping, breakdancing and graffiti writing. Some writers, like black American Phase 2, Haitian Jean-Michel Basquiat, Futura and black American Fab Five Freddy produced rap records. Other writers drew murals that celebrated favorite rap songs (for example, Future's mural, 'The Breaks,' was a whole car mural that paid homage to Kurtis Blow's rap of the same name). Breakdancers, DJs and rappers wore graffiti-painted jackets and T-shirts. DJ Kool Herc was a graffiti writer and dancer first, before he began playing records. Hip hop events featured breakdancers, rappers and DJs as triple-bill entertainment. Graffiti writers drew murals for DJ's stage platforms, and designed posters and flyers to advertise hip hop events. Breakdancer Crazy Legs, founding member of the Rock Steady Crew, describes the communal atmosphere between writers, rappers and breakers in the formative years of hip hop:

> Summing it up, basically going to a jam back then was (about) watching people drink, (break) dance, compare graffiti art in their black books. These jams were thrown by the (hip hop) DJ ... it was about piecing while a jam was going on.[17]

Of course, sharing ideas and styles is not always a peaceful process. Hip hop is very competitive and confrontational; these traits are both resistance to and preparation for a hostile world which denies and denigrates young people of color. Breakdancers often fought other breakdance crews out of jealousy; writers sometimes destroyed murals, and rapper and DJ battles could break out in fights. Hip hop remains a never-ending battle for status, prestige and group adoration which is always in formation, always contested and never fully achieved. Competitions among and cross-fertilization between breaking, graffiti writing and rap music was fueled by shared local experiences and social position, and similarities in approaches to sound, motion, communication and style among hip hop's Afro-diasporic communities.

As in many African and Afro-diasporic cultural forms, hip hop's prolific self-naming is a form of reinvention and self-definition.[18] Rappers, DJs, graffiti artists and breakdancers all take on hip hop names and identities which speak to their role, personal characteristics, expertise or 'claim to fame.' DJ names often fuse technology with mastery and style: DJ Cut Creator, Jazzy Jeff, Spindarella, Terminator X Assault Technician, Wiz and Grand Master Flash. Many rappers have nicknames which suggest street smarts, coolness, power and supremacy: L.L. Cool J (Ladies Love Cool James), Kool Moe Dee, Queen Latifah, Dougie Fresh (and the Get Fresh Crew), D-Nice, Hurricane Gloria, Guru, MC Lyte, EPMD (Erick and Parrish Making Dollars), Ice-T, Ice Cube, Kid-N-Play, Boss, Eazy-E, King Sun, and Sir Mix-A-Lot. Other names serve as self-mocking tags, or critique society, such as Too Short, The Fat Boys, S1Ws (Security of the First World), The Lench Mob, N.W.A. (Niggas With Attitude) and Special Ed. The hip hop identities for breakdancers like Crazy Legs, Wiggles, Frosty Freeze, Boogaloo Shrimp, and Headspin highlight their status as experts known for special moves. Taking on new names and identities offered 'prestige from below' in the face of limited legitimate access to forms of status attainment.

In addition to the centrality of alternative naming, identity and group affiliation, rappers, DJs, graffiti writers and breakdancers claim turf and gain local status by developing new styles. As Hebdige's study on punk illustrates, style can be used as a gesture of refusal, or as a form of oblique challenge to structures of domination.[19] Hip hop artists use style as a form of identity formation which plays on class distinctions and hierarchies by using commodities to claim the cultural terrain. Clothing and consumption rituals testify to the power of consumption as a means of cultural expression. Hip hop fashion is an especially rich example of this sort of appropriation/critique via style. Exceptionally large, 'chunk,' gold and diamond jewelry (usually 'fake') mocks yet affirms the gold fetish in Western trade; fake Gucci and other designer emblems cut up and patch-stitched to jackets, pants, hats, wallets and sneakers in custom shops, work as a form of sartorial warfare (especially when fake Gucci-covered B-boys and B-girls brush past Fifth Avenue ladies adorned by the 'real thing.') Hip hop's late 1980s fashion rage – the large plastic (alarm?) clock worn around the neck over leisure/sweat suits – suggested a number of contradictory tensions between work, time and leisure.[20] Early 1990s trends – super-over-sized pants and urban warrior outer apparel, as in 'hoodies,' 'snooties,' 'tims' and 'triple fat' goosedown coats – make clear the severity of the urban storms to be weathered and the saturation of disposable goods in the crafting of cultural expressions.[21] As an alternative means of status formation, hip hop style forges local identities for teenagers who understand their limited access to traditional avenues of social status attainment. Fab Five Freddy, an early rapper and graffiti writer, explains the link between style and identity in hip hop and its significance for gaining local status:

You make a new style. That's what life on the street is all about. What's at stake is honor and position on the street. That's what makes it so important, that's what makes it feel so good – that pressure on you to be the best. Or to try to be the best. To develop a new style nobody can deal with.[22]

Styles 'nobody can deal with' in graffiti, breaking and rap music not only boost status and elevate black and Hispanic youth identities, they also articulate several shared approaches to sound and motion which are found in the Afro-diaspora. As black filmmaker and cultural critic Arthur Jafa has pointed out, stylistic continuities between breaking, graffiti style, rapping and musical construction seem to center around three concepts: *flow, layering* and *ruptures in line.*[23] In hip hop, visual, physical, musical and lyrical lines are set in motion, broken abruptly with sharp angular breaks, and yet sustain motion and energy through fluidity and flow. In graffiti, long winding, sweeping and curving letters are broken and camouflaged by sudden breaks in line. Sharp, angular, broken letters are written in extreme italics, suggesting forward or backward motion. Letters are double- and triple-shadowed in such a way as to illustrate energy forces radiating from the center – suggesting circular motion – and yet the scripted words move horizontally.

Breakdancing moves highlight flow, layering and ruptures in line. Popping and locking are moves in which the joints are snapped abruptly into angular positions. And yet, these snapping movements take place in one joint after the previous one – creating a semiliquid effect which moves the energy toward the fingertip or toe. In fact, two dancers may pass the popping energy force back and forth between each other via finger-to-finger contact, setting off a new wave. In this pattern, the line is both a series of angular breaks, and yet sustains energy and motion through flow. Breakers double each others' moves, like line-shadowing or layering in graffiti, intertwine their bodies into elaborate shapes, transforming the body into a new entity (like camouflage in graffiti's wild style) and then, one body part at a time, revert to a relaxed state. Abrupt, fractured, yet graceful footwork leaves the eye one step behind the motion, creating a time-lapse effect which not only mimics graffiti's use of line-shadowing, but also creates spatial links between the moves which give the foot series flow and fluidity.[24]

The music and vocal rapping in rap music also privileges flow, layering and ruptures in line. Rappers speak of flow explicitly in lyrics, referring to an ability to move easily and powerfully through complex lyrics, as well as to the flow in the music.[25] The flow and motion of the initial bass or drum line in rap music is abruptly ruptured by scratching (a process which highlights as it breaks the flow of the base rhythm), or the rhythmic flow is interrupted by other musical passages. Rappers stutter and alternatively race through passages, always moving within the beat or in response to it, often using the music as a partner in rhyme. These verbal moves highlight lyrical flow and points of rupture. Rappers layer meaning by using the same word to signify a variety of actions and objects; they call out to the DJ to 'lay down a beat,' which it is expected will be interrupted, ruptured. DJs layer sounds literally one on top of the other, creating a dialogue between sampled sounds and words.

What is the significance of flow, layering and rupture as demonstrated on the body and in hip hop's lyrical, musical and visual works? Interpreting these concepts theoretically, it can be argued that they create and sustain rhythmic motion, continuity and circularity via flow; accumulate, reinforce and embellish this continuity through layering; and manage threats to these narratives by building in ruptures which highlight the continuity as it momentarily challenges it. These effects at the level of style and aesthetics suggest affirmative ways in which profound social dislocation and rupture can be managed and perhaps contested in the cultural arena. Let us imagine these hip hop principles as a blueprint for social resistance and affirmation: create sustaining narratives, accumulate them, layer, embellish and transform them. But also be prepared for rupture, find pleasure in it, in fact, *plan* on social rupture. When these ruptures occur, use them in creative ways which will prepare you for a future in which survival will demand a sudden shift in ground tactics.

While accumulation, flow, circularity and planned ruptures exist across a wide range of Afro-diasporic cultural forms, they do not take place outside capitalist commercial constraints. Hip hop's explicit focus on consumption has frequently been mischaracterized as a movement *into* the commodity market (hip hop is no longer 'authentically' black if it is for sale). Instead, hip hop's moment(s) of 'incorporation' are a shift in the already existing relationship hip hop has always had to the commodity system. For example, the hip hop DJ frequently produces, amplifies and revises already recorded sounds, rappers prefer high-end microphones, and both invest serious dollars for the speakers that can produce the phattest beats. Graffiti murals, breakdancing moves and rap lyrics often appropriate and sometimes critique verbal and visual elements and physical movements from popular commercial culture, especially television, comic books and karate movies. If anything, black style through hip hop has contributed to the continued blackening of mainstream popular culture. The contexts for creation in hip hop were never fully outside or in opposition to commodities; they involved struggles over public space and access to commodified materials, equipment and products. It is a common misperception among hip hop artists and cultural critics that during the early days, hip hop was motivated by pleasure rather than profit, as if the two were incompatible. And it would be naive to think that breakdancers, rappers, DJs and writers were never interested in monetary compensation for their work. The problem was not that they were uniformly uninterested in profit, rather, many of the earliest practitioners were unaware that they could profit from their pleasure. Once this link was made, hip hop artists began marketing themselves wholeheartedly. Just as graffiti writers hitched a ride on the subways and used its power to distribute their tags, rappers 'hijacked' the market for their own purposes, riding the currents that are already out there, not just for wealth but for empowerment. During the late 1970s and early 1980s, the market for hip hop was still based inside New York's black and Hispanic communities. So while there is an element of truth to this common perception, what is more important about the shift in hip hop's orientation is not its movement from pre-commodity to commodity, but the shift in control over the scope and direction of the profit-making process, out of the hands of local black and Hispanic entrepreneurs and into the hands of larger, white-owned, multinational businesses. And, most importantly, while black cultural imperatives are obviously deeply affected by commodification, these imperatives are not in direct opposition to the market, nor are they 'irrelevant' to the shape of market-produced goods and practices.

Hebdige's work on the British punk movement identifies this shift as the moment of incorporation or recuperation by dominant culture, and perceives it to be a critical element in the dynamics of the struggle over the meaning(s) of popular expression. 'The process of recuperation,' Hebdige argues, 'takes two characteristic forms ... one of conversion of subcultural signs (dress, music and so on) into mass-produced objects and the 'labelling' and redefinition of deviant behavior by dominant groups – the police, media and judiciary.' Hebdige astutely points out, however, that communication in a subordinate cultural form, even prior to the point of recuperation, usually takes place via commodities, 'even if the meanings attached to those commodities are purposefully distorted or overthrown.' And so, he concludes, 'it is very difficult to sustain any absolute distinction between commercial exploitation on the one hand and creativity/originality on the other.'[26]

Hebdige's observations regarding the process of incorporation and the tension between commercial exploitation and creativity as articulated in British punk are quite relevant to hip hop. And hip hop has always been articulated via commodities and engaged in the revision of meanings attached to them. Conversely, hip hop signs and meanings are converted and behaviors relabeled by dominant institutions. Graffiti, rap and breakdancing are fundamentally transformed as they move into new relations with dominant cultural institutions.[27] In 1994, rap music is one of the most heavily traded popular commodities in the market, and yet it still defies total corporate control over the music, its local use and incorporation at the level of stable or exposed meanings.

These transformations and hybrids reflect the initial spirit of rap and hip hop as an experimental and collective space where contemporary issues and ancestral forces are worked through simultaneously. Hybrids in rap's subject matter, not unlike its use of musical collage and the influx of new, regional and ethnic styles, have not yet displaced the three points of stylistic continuity to which I referred earlier: approaches to flow, ruptures in line and layering can still be found in the vast majority of rap's lyrical and music construction. The same is true of the critiques of the postindustrial urban America context and the cultural and social conditions which it has produced. Today, the South Bronx and South Central Los Angeles are poorer and more economically marginalized than they were ten years ago.

Hip hop emerges from complex cultural exchanges and larger social and political conditions of disillusionment and alienation. Graffiti and rap were especially aggressive public displays of counterpresence and voice. Each asserted the right to write[28] – to inscribe one's identity on an environment which seemed Teflon-resistant to its young people of color; an environment which made legitimate avenues for material and social participation inaccessible. In this context, hip hop produced a number of double effects. First, themes in rap and graffiti articulated free play and unchecked public displays, and yet the settings for these expressions always suggested existing confinement.[29] Second, like the consciousness-raising sessions in the early stages of the women's rights movement and Black Power movement of the 1960s and 1970s, hip hop produced internal and external dialogues which affirmed the experiences and identities of the participants, and at the same time offered critiques of larger society which were directed to both the hip hop community and society in general.

Out of a broader discursive climate in which the perspectives and experiences of younger Hispanic, Afro-Caribbeans and African-Americans had been provided little social space, hip hop developed as part of a cross-cultural communication network. Trains carried graffiti tags through the five boroughs; flyers posted in black and Hispanic neighborhoods brought teenagers from all over New York to parks and clubs in the Bronx and eventually to events throughout the Metropolitan area. And characteristic of communication in the age of high-tech telecommunications, stories with cultural and narrative resonance continued to spread at a rapid pace. It was not long before similarly marginalized black and Hispanic communities in other cities picked up on the tenor and energy in New York hip hop. Boom boxes in Roxbury and Compton blasted copies of hip hop mix tapes made on high-speed, portable, dubbing equipment by cousins from Flatbush Avenue in Brooklyn. The explosion of local and national cable programming of music videos spread hip hop dance steps, clothing and slang across the country faster than brushfire. Within a decade, Los Angeles County (especially Compton), Oakland, Detroit, Chicago, Houston, Atlanta, Miami, Newark and Trenton, Roxbury and Philadelphia have developed local hip hop scenes which link (among other things) various regional postindustrial urban experiences of alienation, unemployment, police harassment and social and economic isolation to their local and specific experience via hip hop's language, style and attitude.[30] Regional and, increasingly, national differences and syndications in hip hop have been solidifying and will continue to do so. In some cases these differences are established by references to local streets and events, neighborhoods and leisure activities, preferences for dance steps, clothing, musical samples and vocal accents. At the same time, cross-regional syndicates of rappers, writers and dancers fortify hip hop's communal vocabulary. In every region, hip hop articulates a sense of entitlement, and takes pleasure in aggressive insubordination. Like Chicago and Mississippi blues, these emerging, regional, hip hop identities affirm the specificity and local character of cultural forms as well as the larger stylistic forces that define hip hop and Afro-diasporic cultures.

Developing a style nobody can deal with – a style that cannot be easily understood or erased, a style that has the reflexivity to create counterdominant narratives against a mobile and shifting enemy – may be one of the most effective ways to fortify communities of resistance and simultaneously reserve the right to communal pleasure. With few economic assets and abundant cultural and aesthetic resources, Afro-diasporic youth have designated the street as the arena for competition and style as the prestige-awarding event. In the postindustrial urban context of dwindling low-income housing, a trickle of meaningless jobs for young people, mounting police brutality and increasingly demonic depictions of young inner-city residents, hip hop style *is* black urban renewal.

## Notes

This essay is excerpted from *Black Noise: Rap Music and Black Culture in Contemporary America* (Wesleyan Press, 1994).

1. I have adopted Mollenkopf's and Castell's use of the term postindustrial as a means of characterizing the economic restructuring that has taken place in urban America over the past twenty-five years. By defining the contemporary period in urban economies as postindustrial, Mollenkopf and Castells are not suggesting that manufacturing output has disappeared, nor are they adopting Daniel Bell's formulation that 'knowledge has somehow replaced capital as the organizing principle of the economy.' Rather Mollenkopf and Castells claim that their use of postindustrial 'captures a crucial aspect of how large cities are being transformed: employment has shifted massively away from manufacturing toward corporate, public and nonprofit services; occupations have similarly shifted from manual worker to managers, professionals, secretaries and service workers.' John Mollenkopf and

Manuel Castells, eds., *Dual City: Restructuring New York* (New York: Russel Sage Foundation, 1991), p. 6. Similarly, these new postindustrial realities, entailing the rapid movement of capital, images and populations across the globe, have also been referred to as 'post-Fordism' and 'flexible accumulation.' See David Harvey, *Social Justice and the City* (Oxford: Basil Blackwell, 1988). For an elaboration of Bell's initial use of the term, see Daniel Bell, *The Coming of Post-Industrial Society* (New York: Basic Books, 1973).

2. My arguments regarding Afro-diasporic cultural formations in hip hop are relevant to African-American culture as well as Afro-diasporic cultures in the English- and Spanish-speaking Caribbean, each of which has prominent and significant, African-derived, cultural elements. While rap music, particularly early rap, is dominated by English-speaking blacks, graffiti and breakdancing were heavily shaped and practiced by Puerto Ricans, Dominicans and other Spanish-speaking Caribbean communities which have substantial Afro-diasporic elements. (The emergence of Chicano rappers took place in the late 1980s in Los Angeles.) Consequently, my references to Spanish-speaking Caribbean communities should in no way be considered inconsistent with my larger Afro-diasporic claims. Substantial work has illuminated the continued significance of African cultural elements on cultural production in both Spanish- and English-speaking nations in the Caribbean. For examples, see Herbert S. Klein, *African Slavery in Latin America and the Caribbean* (New York: Oxford Press, 1986); Ivan G. Van Sertima, *They Came Before Columbus* (New York: Random House, 1976) and Robert Farris Thompson, *Flash of the Spirit* (New York: Random House, 1983).

3. See Allen J. Matusow, *The Unravelling of America: A History of Liberalism in the 1960s* (New York: Harper and Row, 1984).

4. In hip hop, the train serves both as means of inter-neighborhood communication and a source of creative inspiration. Big Daddy Kane says that he writes his best lyrics on the subway or train on the way to producer Marly Marl's house. See Barry Michael Cooper, 'Raw Like Sushi,' *Spin* (March, 1988), p. 28. Similarly, Chuck D claims that he loves to drive; that he would have been a driver if his rapping career had not worked out. See Robert Christgau and Greg Tate, 'Chuck D All Over the Map,' *Village Voice, Rock n Roll Quarterly*, vol. 4, no. 3 (Fall, 1991).

5. See John H. Mollenkopf, *The Contested City* (Princeton, NJ: Princeton U. Press, 1983), especially pp. 12–46 for a discussion of larger twentieth century transformations in U.S. cities throughout the 1970s and into the early 1980s. See, also, John Mollenkopf and Manuel Castells, eds., *Dual City: Restructuring New York* (New York: Russell Sage Foundation, 1991); Michael Peter Smith and Joe R. Feagin, eds., *The Capitalist City: Global Restructuring and Community Politics* (London: Basil Blackwell, 1987); Michael Peter Smith, ed., *Cities in Transformation: Class, Capital and the State* (Beverly Hills: Sage Publications, 1984); and Saskia Sassen, *The Mobility of Labor and Capital: A Study in International Investment and Labor Flow* (Cambridge: Cambridge University Press, 1988).

6. I am not suggesting that New York is typical of all urban areas, nor that regional differences are insignificant. However, the broad transformations under discussion here have been felt in all major U.S. cities, particularly New York and Los Angeles – hip hop's second major hub city – and critically frame the transitions that, in part, contributed to hip hop's emergence. In the mid-1980s very similar postindustrial changes in job opportunities and social services in the Watts and Compton areas of Los Angeles became the impetus for Los Angeles' gangsta rappers. As Robin Kelley notes: 'The generation who came of age in the 1980s, under the Reagan and Bush era, were products of devastating structural changes in the urban economy that date back at least to the late 1960s. While the city as a whole experienced unprecedented growth, the communities of Watts and Compton faced increased economic displacement, factory closures, and an unprecedented deepening of poverty.... Developers and city and county government helped the process along by infusing massive capital into suburbanization while simultaneously cutting back expenditures for parks, recreation, and affordable housing in inner city communities.' Robin D.G. Kelley, 'Kickin'

Reality, Kickin' Ballistics' forthcoming in Eric Perkins, ed., *Droppin' Science: Critical Essays on Rap Music and Hip Hop Culture* (Philadelphia: Temple, 1994). See, also, Mike Davis, *City of Quartz: Excavating the Future of Los Angeles* (London: Verso, 1989).

7. Mollenkopf, *Contested City*, p. 213.

8. Philip Weitzman, '"Worlds Apart": Housing Race/Ethnicity and Income in New York City.' *Community Service Society of New York* (CSS), 1989. See, also, Terry J. Rosenberg, 'Poverty in New York City: 1980–1985' (CSS), 1987; Robert Neuwirth 'Housing After Koch' *Village Voice* 7 (November 7, 1989) pp. 22–24.

9. Daniel Walkowitz 'New York: A Tale of Two Cities' in Richard M Bernard ed., *Snowbelt Cities: Metropolitan Politics in the Northeast and Midwest Since World War II* (Bloomington: Indiana Press, 1990); Mollenkopf and Castells, eds., *Dual City* p. 9. See, also, parts 2 and 3 *Dual City*, which deal specifically and in greater detail with the forces of transformation, gender and the new occupational strata.

10. Ben Bagdigian, *The Media Monopoly* (Boston: Beacon Press, 1987). Despite trends towards the centralization of news and media sources, and the fact that larger corporate media outfits have proven unable to serve diverse ethnic and racial groups, a recent study on New York's media structure in the 1980s suggests that a wide range of alternative media sources serve New York's ethnic communities. However, the study also shows that black New Yorkers have been less successful in sustaining alternative media channels. See Mitchell Moss and Sarah Ludwig, 'The Structure of the Media,' in *Dual City*, pp. 245–265.

11. See Tom Forester. *High-Tech Society* (Cambridge, MIT Press, 1988) and Herbert Schiller, *Culture, Inc.: The Corporate Takeover of Public Expression* (New York: Oxford Press, 1989).

12. Similar strategies for urban renewal via 'slum clearance' demolition took place in a number of major metropolises in the late 1960s and 1970s. See Mollenkopf, *Contested City*, especially ch. 4, which describes similar processes in Boston and San Francisco.

13. Robert D. McFadden, 'Power Failure Blacks Out New York; Thousands Trapped in Subways; Looters and Vandals Hit Some Areas,' *New York Times* (July 14, 1977) p. A1, col. 5; Lawrence Van Gelder, 'State Troopers Sent Into City as Crime Rises,' *New York Times* (July 14, 1977) p. A1, col. 1; Charlayne Hunter-Gault, 'When Poverty is Part of Life, Looting is Not Condemned,' *New York Times* (July 15, 1977) p. A4, col. 3; Selwyn Raab, 'Ravage Continues Far Into Day; Gunfire and Bottles Beset Police,' *New York Times* (July 15, 1977) p. A1, col. 1; Editorial, 'Social Overload,' *New York Times* (July 22, 1977) p. A22.

14. Lee Dembart, 'Carter Takes 'Sobering' Trip to South Bronx,' *New York Times* (October 6, 1977) p. A1, col. 2, B18, col. 1; Richard Severo, 'Bronx a Symbol of America's Woes.' *New York Times* (October 6, 1977) p. B18, col. 1; Joseph P. Fried, 'The South Bronx USA: What Carter Saw in New York City is a Symbol of Complex Social Forces on a Nationwide Scale,' *New York Times* (October 7, 1977) p. A22, col. 1.

15. Michael Ventura, *Shadow Dancing in the USA* (Los Angeles: J.P. Tarcher Press, 1986) p. 186. Other popular films from the late 1970s and early 1980s which followed suit included *1990: The Bronx Warriors and Escape From New York*. This construction of the dangerous ghetto is central to Tom Wolfe's 1989 best-seller and the subsequent film *Bonfire of the Vanities*. In it, the South Bronx is constructed as an abandoned, lawless territory from the perspective of substantially more privileged, White outsiders.

16. Rose interviews with all artists named except Futura, whose printing trade school experience was cited in Steve Hager, *Hip Hop: The Illustrated History of Breakdancing, Rap Music, and Graffiti* (New York: St. Martin's Press, 1984), p. 24. These artist interviews were conducted for my book on rap music, entitled *Black Noise: Rap Music and Black Culture in Contemporary America* (Wesleyan Press, 1994).

17. Rose interview with Crazy Legs, November 1991. 'Piecing' means drawing a mural or masterpiece.

18. See Henry Louis Gates, Jr., *The Signifying Monkey: A Theory of Afro-American Literary Criticism*. Gates's suggestion that naming be 'drawn upon as a metaphor for black

intertextuality' is especially useful in hip hop, where naming and intertextuality are critical strategies for creative production. See pp. 55, 87.

19. Dick Hebdige, *Subculture: The Meaning of Style* (London: Methuen, 1979). See, especially, pp. 17–19, 84–89.

20. For an interesting discussion of time, the clock and nationalism in hip hop, see Jeffrey L. Decker's article in this collection.

21. Hoodies are hooded jackets or shirts, snooties are skull caps and tims are short for Timberland brand boots.

22. Nelson George, et al., eds., *Fresh: Hip Hop Don't Stop* (New York: Random House, 1985) p. 111.

23. While I had isolated some general points of aesthetic continuity between hip hop's forms, I did not identify these three crucial organizing terms. I am grateful to Arthur Jafa, black filmmaker and cultural critic, who shared and discussed the logic of these defining characteristics with me in conversation. He is not, of course, responsible for any inadequacies in my use of them here.

24. For a brilliant example of these moves among recent hip hop dances, see 'Reckin'' Shop In Brooklyn' directed by Diane Martel (Epoch Films, 1992). Thanks to Arthur Jafa for bringing this documentary film to my attention.

25. Some examples of explicit attention to flow are exhibited in Queen Latifah's *Ladies First:* 'Some think that we can't flow, stereotypes they got to go'; in Big Daddy Kane's *Raw:* 'Intro I start to go, my rhymes will flow so'; in Digital Underground's *Sons of the P:* 'Release your mind and let your instincts flow, release your mind and let the funk flow.' Later, they refer to themselves as the 'sons of the flow.'

26. Hebdige, *Subculture* pp. 94–95.

27. Published n 1979, *Subculture: The Meaning of Style* concludes at the point of dominant British culture's initial attempts at incorporating punk.

28. See Duncan Smith, 'The Truth of Graffiti', *Art & Text* 17, pp. 84–90.

29. For example, Kurtis Blow's 'The Breaks' (1980) was both about the seeming inevitability and hardships of unemployment and mounting financial debt, and the sheer pleasure of 'breaking it up and down,' of dancing and breaking free of social and psychological constrictions. Regardless of subject matter, elaborate graffiti tags on train facades always suggested that the power and presence of the image was possible only if the writer had escaped capture.

30. See Bob Mack, 'Hip-Hop Map of America', *Spin* (June 1990).

# Chapter 33

# Cynthia Fuchs

# If I had a Dick: Queers, Punks, and Alternative Acts

Once sex and gender are placed on equally fictive footing, the possibilities for multiple identities (and alliances) are enormous.

—Cathy Schwichtenberg,
'Madonna's Postmodern Feminism'

I watch it like a movie
the details so consume me
what's real will surface when it's gone
(and then it's gone).

—Bikini Kill, 'For Only'

Would you like me if I talked with a lisp?
if I had a dick, put it away,
always had something to say.

—Tribe 8, 'What?'

During the winter of 1995, I attended a show at Washington D.C.'s old 9:30 Club. The three bands appearing that night – Sexpod, Tribe 8, and Pansy Division[1] – might all be called punk, though their musical styles were quite different, ranging from three-chord rock to DIY to perky pop-punk. They might also all be called queer. Their attitudes ranged from pissed off to charming to seductive to comic, and their topics from 'dykes on bikes' to 'cocksucker clubs.' In other words, for

From: *Mapping the Beat: Popular Music and Contemporary Theory*. Ed. Thomas Swiss, John Sloop and Andrew Herman. Oxford: Blackwell Publishers, 1998.

all their differences, they shared an identifiable set of concerns with each other and with their audience [...]. While these concerns – with sex and sexuality, gender transgressions, unruly bodies, social offenses, and systemic oppressions, among other things – directly inform punk, postpunk, and queer sensibilities, they also illustrate the definitional messiness of punk, queer, queercore, and riot grrrl cultures, their predilections for mutation and motion, and their diverse modes of resistance to what might be understood as a dominant culture.[2]

I also want to suggest that for the brief time and space of the show at the 9:30 Club, band and audience members were aligned through a series of mutually appreciative acts, forging a loose community that was particular and performative, coalitional and conditional. I'm not saying that the experience constituted some kind of queerpunk mini-nation, that there was ever a moment when the crowd swayed as one body with their hands in the air, or that the room was continually awash in a tide of uniformly good will. But even while everyone looked, moved, and responded in individual ways, there were discernible moments of consensus. Spectators were clamorously enthusiastic, occasionally raucous: the mostly teens and twentysomethings danced, moshed (soft style, the kind dictated by a small space with wide hard columns), applauded, and sweated together. Like many punk shows, this one was premised on an ongoing exchange of energies and vexations: band and audience members tossed phrases – 'Fuck you,' 'Suck me' – and plastic beer cups back and forth in a ritual that, for all its potent language and contentious gesticulating, was about community and shared identity. For this night, anyway, everyone here was 'queer.'

Of course, any claim for such 'queerness' – and the quotation marks indicate both contingency and irony – is complicated by a variety of factors, not the least being the fact that some participants were heterosexual. But if this evening's queerness wasn't 'literal' or even sustained once participants walked out the door, if it was 'performative' in the most mundane sense, it was effective. It moved those of us who were there. This effect was as visceral as it was vocal, a volatile mix of sound [...] and movement, plus some wilder, in-between moments, approximating what Michel de Certeau calls 'enunciative gaps.' These '"obscene" citations of bodies,' he writes, 'these sounds waiting for a language, seem to certify, by a "disorder" secretly referred to an unknown order, that there is something else, something other' (de Certeau, 1984: 163–4). Granted, this experience of 'something else' may have been the function of a particularly hot moment. But what I want to stress here is the productive interplay of performance and authenticity, the ways that sexualized acts and exchanges can 'speak,' display a range of identities that are otherwise rendered invisible precisely because they're attached to such acts and exchanges. [...]

The usefulness of punk aesthetics and politics for queer performers is in part premised on the genre's well-known rough-and-ready rebelliousness (not to mention its openness to a range of conventional and unconventional musical skills), a commitment to social protest that was simultaneously produced and consumed by a lack of polish and cash. It's frequently been asserted that since Nirvana's crossover success made punk bands common-place – with platinum albums and labeled slots in Tower Records – whatever subversiveness was once assumed for it is now less obvious. As punk (and more generally, alternative music) has invaded, forever altered, and even become the Mainstream, the question of 'authenticity' is both more and less important with regard to understanding fandom or possibilities for activism and social change.

In his famous study of subculture, Dick Hebdige observes that punk, from its inception, engaged with the perceived dominant culture, consuming and reinventing that culture, reconfiguring its restrictions as a means to exhibit frustration, innovation, and resistance. He writes that punk in its early forms narrated and communicated a sense of crisis by marking an edge of appropriable, understandable language, 'challenging at a symbolic level the "inevitability," the "naturalness" of class and gender stereotypes' (Hebdige, 1979: 89). While attempts to define punk typically set it against a fixed opposite (say, punk versus metal, or punk versus classic rock), its flexibility and resilience are typically matched by those of so-called dominant culture. Punk traditionally presumed a white, working-to middle-class, left-leaning, heterosexual male performer-and-fan base (not unlike most regular rock), but more recently (also like regular rock), it has shifted to include and appeal to a diversely raced, gendered, sexed, and classed set of artists and audiences (including girl and girl-fronted bands, mixed-race bands, and punk-hybrid bands, like punk-ska, punk-folk, punk-blues, punk-hiphop, etc.). [...]

The shift has produced neo-lite-punks (like Green Day, Offspring, Rancid, or Veruca Salt), whose derision by hardcore fans is understandable and politically important (as informed critiques of industry practices), but also potentially reductive and counterproductive, because it misses the ways that punk's incursions into commercial viability can complicate conventional oppositions. Hebdige proposes that punk's emphasis on 'style' signals not straight-up capitulation, but simultaneous assimilation and resistance. 'It is therefore difficult,' he writes, 'to maintain any absolute distinction between commercial exploitation on the one hand and creativity/originality on the other, even these categories are emphatically opposed in the value systems of most subcultures' (Hebdige, 1979: 95). A similar rejection of 'absolute distinction' also characterizes many queer and grrrl artists, audiences, and theorists, a diverse 'community' whose markers of identity can be (deliberately) ambiguous as well as unmistakable, embracing a continuum of activism and incorporation, visibility and invisibility, private and public spheres, working against and through strictly oppositional structures.[3]

## 'Don't Need your Dick to Fuck!'

As the above lyric from Bikini Kill's 'Don't Need You' implies, the rejection of dominant cultural forms is a central theme for queercore and riot grrrl acts. If such protest is familiar from earlier incarnations of punk and rock more generally, its particular permutations in queercore and riot grrrl are less strictly oppositional, more disruptive. This practice allows for a range of alliances, in performances and audiences. Consider, for example, the striking display of collectivity when Tribe 8 singer Lynn Breedlove takes off her T-shirt: viewers typically respond in ways that suggest that they identify her as same and other, that they can imagine wanting and being her. Girls us front, near the stage, also take off their shirts – and often their bras, if they're wearing them – performing their solidarity with the dykes on stage, sometimes moshing hard enough to push boys out of the pit.[4] And when Breedlove pushes her hand down into her jeans, simulating masturbation, the crowd also reacts enthusiastically, though usually not by mirroring her act.

The performance raises all kinds of questions about identity and authenticity. How, for instance, is Breedlove's authenticity entangled with that of her audience? Does she become a real dyke in and as her act, in taking of her shirt or in masturbating? Do her viewers also become authentic dykes if their responses conform to some idea of authentic dykeness? And how do these acts read differently for the women, straight or gay men who are watching her? The moment plays like drag at the same time that it's a punk-rock salvo, turning straight-porn conventions (the woman on display for a presumed male viewer) upside down, inviting girls to participate in sex fantasies, insisting on the fluidity of viewing and performing positions, and creating a continuum of gender and sexual identities.

At the 9:30 Club, for 'Romeo and Julio' – a song about two gay boys 'down by the schoolyard' – Breedlove pulled a dildo from out of her fly, put on a condom, and invited Pansy Division's bassist, Chris Freeman, to come on stage and suck her off, which he proceeded to do with comically exaggerated zeal while men and women in the audience rooted them on. Then, during 'Frat Pig,' a song about gang rape ('In the name of male-bonding/in the name of fraternity') and revenge, Breedlove yelled, 'Let's play a game called cas-trate!' and sawed off that faux dick with a hunting knife. Spectators cheered again as she held the pathetic item up on the tip of the knife, then grabbed for it when she tossed it into the pit. Tribe 8's set ended with a series of stereotypically masculine rock-star moves, with guitar players Lynn Flipper and Leslie Mah's and bassist Lynn Payne's legs thrust forward to the edge of the stage, available for fans' caresses.

Tribe 8's genderbending set turned out to be a provocative introduction for Pansy Division's. While the Pansies' on-stage style is more conspicuously and consistently playful than Tribe 8's, the boys' lyrics can be equally 'lewd' [...]. At the 9:30 Club, they sang 'Surrender Your Clothing' ('Zippers down, the prize revealed') and 'Anthem' ('We wanna sock it to your hole'), sentiments clearly addressed to men, but also readable as paeans to queerness (or gloriously 'deviant' sexual behaviors). Still, it's clear enough that the bands have very different takes on dicks and dick practices. How do audience members process this range of politics and performance, so they can applaud them within the space of a single evening?

Breedlove's donning of the dildo, for instance, can play differently for different crowds. I've seen the band perform for a mostly straight audience in Madison, Wisconsin, as well as for mostly lesbian audiences at other sites in D.C., and in each instance, she has pulled out the dildo and solicited an audience member to come on stage to 'suck my dick!' While the possible meanings of this scene shift, depending on the gender and sexuality of the volunteer (and these may not always be immediately or ever clear), the easy read is that it constitutes a kind of continuum, of act and reaction, of attractive illusion and material reality. [...]

Breedlove's literal apprehension of the (fake) penis brings various cultural assumptions to bear on the always complicated relationship between queer sexual acts and queer identity, or between performativity and authenticity. As Colleen Lamos argues, 'the significance of the dildo is the manner in which it questions the nature of sexual difference' (Lamos, 1995: 110). Certainly this question is pervasive at a Tribe 8 show, as Breedlove all but embodies it. Her ironic self-display can, after all, be threatening to some boys, as when she warns them that their 'cute girlfriends' might go home with her. Shirtless to expose her long torso, wearing sunglasses, blue or pink hair, baggy jeans, and her baseball cap backwards when she sings 'Oversize Ego' ('I'm a real big deal!'), from the back she might pass for a guy. And then she turns around, displaying the A for Anarchy written on her belly, her breasts and nipple-ring, and her dildo. Perhaps needless to say, the dilemma of authenticity is repeatedly foregrounded by this body that won't conform to conventions.[5] You can't help but look at the rubber dick that's swinging from her crotch. As Lamos writes, 'The dildo denaturalizes and renders perverse its subject so that the dildo's representation must continue to provoke uneasiness, especially the uneasiness of the loss of a secure gender identity' (Lamos, 1995: 118). Uneasiness, yes. At the end of some performances of 'Frat Pig,' I've seen Breedlove haul out a chainsaw, revving loudly, to chop the thing off.

Tribe 8's performances insist that authenticity is a perpetual act, not 'artificial' as opposed to 'true' or 'real,' but an act that carries with it consequences, meanings, and possibilities for transformation. For queers who are tired of trying to gain access to entrenched cultural hierarchies defined by (and defining) 'original' and 'copy,' asserting an authentic (sometimes, though not always, formulated as 'genetic') identity has been, in the recent past, politically significant and effective. At the same time however, drawing attention to the performances of everyday life has proven to be a useful tool for progressive social critique. As one measure of resistance to a commercializing and co-opting system, authenticity both establishes and diffuses the limits of popular representation. By the same token, punk's overt investment in affective cynicism, irony, and self-consciousness complicates any singular notion of authenticity, and insists on multiple identifications and fluid identities.

At least part of queercore's 'subversiveness' is manifest in its self-ascribed authentic outrage, its rejection of orthodox conduits to success, financial and popular. 'Contemporary gay punk,' writes Matias Viegener (1994), insists not only on a generalized, transcultural 'gender dysphoria,' but as well rejects '"nice," post-Stonewall gay culture, as it is manifested in disco, gay marriages, *The Advocate,* polo shirts, David Leavitt's fiction, and Calvin Klein advertisements' (117). Queer punk communities, he continues, 'tend to be specific and local, centered in San Francisco, Toronto, and Los Angeles, among other cities, placed willfully beyond the "mainstream"' (117). Such specificity grants queercore a sense of simultaneous risk and threat, vulnerability and aggression, as well as a 'decentralization' that, Viegener argues, prevents any linear climbs to stardom or 'typical' fan behaviors (118).

But insisting on the 'beyond the mainstream' purity of this resistance can obscure what seems to me its potential to transform how 'we' think about politics and products in contingent their relationship. That is, while Viegener's version of radical transience designates a specific authenticity in underground scenes, it also problematizes visibility outside immediate venues, and visibility is, after all, what being out is all about. And so, queer punks must negotiate among ironies, authenticities, and appearances that count.

## 'Against All Odds We Appear'

In 1994, Pansy Division became particularly visible when they went on tour as the opening band for Green Day (the quotation above is from the Pansies). In doing so, they confronted a question that hasn't yet come up for most queercore bands: how is it possible to be visibly and actively political (as *being* queer would seem to demand) in a meta-media-universe? Is it possible to sell out when you're out, as a queer person and performer? What determines being out or selling out? Within the music business, answers to these questions are necessarily connected to the measures and readability of authenticity. Fans, record labels, promoters, and performers all have vested interests in claiming and defining authenticity. In a postmodern environment, Lawrence Grossberg has argued, there can be no such thing as authentic authenticity (if such a thing was ever possible, which is, at the least, debatable), only 'authentic inauthenticity,' a series of poses, mediations, and performances, alternately narrated by artists and judged by audiences who are, in turn, affiliated (or not) through taste, style, and affect (Grossberg, 1992).

Identification through such affiliation, as differentiated from, say, some notion of a shared inherent identity, makes people nervous. It doesn't seem committed, it could be faked, it might turn over tomorrow. But it also suggests another way to understand processes of identity and identification, one less invested in what appears to be real and more flexible with regard to lived experiences. Noting that it 'became clear, particularly after punk, that this romanticism of authenticity was a false and idealized view,' Angela McRobbie (1994) proposes that 'subcultural life' combines commercial, aesthetic, and identificatory experiences, and these experiences, even if they aren't overtly 'resistant,' provide 'young people in youth cultures with a way of achieving social subjectivity and therefore identity' (161).

Pansy Division is a case in point. They mix basic pop tunes and explicitly gay-sex lyrics, a combination that, depending on the venue, can be pretty regular or pretty outrageous. You could hardly call them intellectually complex or musically innovative, yet their expanding audience (in numbers and in demographic range) suggests that their charming and yet in-your-face performances of queerness are effectively creating affiliations, or what Robin Balliger aptly calls 'sounds of resistance.' Local and strategic, these 'sounds,' Balliger argues, constitute art that is not difficult or overtly 'political,' but rather appeal 'to the senses, to physical pleasure.' Balliger suggest that while it is typically dismissed by critics and theorists, this kind of pleasure is a means to conceive and build resistance (Balliger, 1995: 21).

Pansy Division seems especially able to faciliate such affiliations as resistance. At one point during their set at the 9:30 Club, for example, Pansy singer Jon Ginoli introduced the band's new drummer, Dustin Donaldson, as 'heterosexual, but wearing a dress in solidarity' (a decidedly femme number he had borrowed from Leslie Mah). Donaldson stood up and bowed deeply, as viewers roundly applauded the courage of this outed 'outsider.' In this context, I think it's instructive to recall that a few months before this, I had been to another show at the same club, this one featuring Ice T's thrash-metal band, Body Count.[6] At this show I was surrounded by a spirited assembly of almost all white youths, who were more than happy to join in Ice T's call to 'Fuck the police!' At one level this gleeful aggression seemed almost absurd: it's likely that most of these middle-class white fans had no experience with the cops resembling that described by Ice T in 'Cop Killer'. But they were more than willing to make an imaginative leap – whether to be cool or appropriative. [...]

I witnessed a similar unlikely crossover effect when I attended a Green Day show at the Patriot Center, a sports and concert arena in suburban Northern Virginia.[7] The audience was primed for Green Day, then enjoying the enormous success of their album, *Dookie,* and a quite hilarious punk performance at Woodstock II (during which frontperson Billie Joe Armstrong had exchanged insults and gobs of mud with his audience), many wearing Green Day T-shirts, some just purchased at the arena – looked to be almost entirely white boys (teenagers and preteens), several of whom sat with parents [...]. I doubt that most of them know that Green Day front-person Billie Joe Armstrong had recently come out as 'not fully straight' in a *Village Voice* piece about Pansy Division's 'full steam ahead' gay punk activism (Herman, 1995: 57). (And besides, the glossy national magazines, like *Rolling Stone* and *Spin*, were leading with stories about his happy marriage and new baby.) And the major-ity certainly didn't recognize the warm-up band. But by the time Green Day came on, everyone in that space knew something about Pansy Division.

In fact, from the distance dictated by arena seating, the Pansies even looked like Green Day, three guys with shortish hair, dressed in jeans and T-shirts, and com-bining comic poise, nonthreatening aggression, and humorous self-deprecation on stage. Both bands depend on power chords, driving drums, and, between songs, well-rehearsed tirades by their respective front-men. During both bands' sets, eager listeners reciprocated, throwing pieces of clothing onto the stage, along with cups half full of soda and (mostly empty) food containers. But for all their formal resemblances, the two bands part ways when it comes to subject matter. Though they both focus on young male experiences, where Armstrong sings about masturbation in 'Long View' and angst-ridden insanity in 'Basket Case' (both songs for which the spectators seemed to know all the words), Ginoli was describing gay club scenes ('Rock & Roll Queer Bar') and the ups and downs of gay roman-tic coupledom ('Hippy Dude'), with very little ambiguity regarding sexual acts ('We're butt-fuckers! Fuck you!').

It was, unsurprisingly, a very dissimilar show from the one I saw at the smaller club in D.C., where the audience was enchanted by the drummer's dress. The set list was similar – they sang 'Fem in a Black Leather Jacket,' 'Bunnies' ('I got the carrot, you got the stick') and 'Fuck Buddy' at both sites – but in Virginia, the crowd might have been from another planet, and Ginoli worked it differently (which is not to say he was less vigorous; rather, he was more cajoling, and even more energetic). I mean, he worked it like a hostile gathering, folks who probably wouldn't be converted to full-on support, but who might be convinced to be tolerant. Within a few minutes of stepping on stage, Ginoli asked them to identify themselves: 'How many of you out there are homophobic?' Several dozen hands went up, and you could hear the groans and jeers as well. In front of me, four boys in baseball caps, knee-length shorts, and Chucks, yelled back to Ginoli, 'Fuck you, homo!'

It seemed clear that such a response was routine for this tour. Most of the kids were there to mosh, however, so lyrics and pronouncements of identity ('homos' or 'homophobes') were mostly beside the point. Shut up and dance. The Pansies launched into 'Vanilla,' their chords relentlessly bouncy ('People should do in bed whatever pops into their heads!') and then, 'Anthem': 'We can't relate to Judy Garland/It's a new generation of music calling.' You could say that. 'Basically,' Freeman has said, 'what we're doing is de-masculating men by telling them to bend over and take it. Come on, *enjoy* it, it's fun!' (Herman, 1995: 57). I've heard of a show where Freeman wore a nightgown and at the end of the night pulled it up to reveal that he was naked: the band is fun, no doubt about it. They sing about 'getting tied up, and my boyfriend, Sean Connery' in 'James Bondage,' nonlethal

STDs in 'Crabby Day,' and always, always, elusive 'cute guys.' And for all the potential and real tensions in the Patriot Center, that show actually seemed more compelling than the queer-identified one. [...]

It wasn't as if there was a politically committed collective formed this night, or that the young (or older) phobes were reformed or enlightened. But the overwhelming effect of the spectacle on stage, the similarity of motion and emotion represented by the pit, was that change was possible, if not inevitable. Lynn Breedlove puts it this way in an interview: 'There are different stages in revolution. The first stage is identity. That means you all have to get together very narrowly and limit yourself to just hanging out with people who are exactly like you. Once you're secure in who you are, and who your friends are, then you can start reaching out and building alliances. Once you have *alliances* you have power. Because there's numbers' (Juno, 1996: 66–7).

## 'I Can Sell my Body if I Wanna'

As Kathleen Hanna sings in 'Jigsaw Youth,' making and having options is key to this idea of 'revolution.' The differences among Tribe 8, Pansy Division, and Bikini Kill demonstrate the need for more than one 'alternative.' The rawness of Bikini Kill shows is a long way from the orchestrations of the Pansies or Tribe 8. Each time I've seen them, Bikini Kill has made do with lousy sound systems (one show, a benefit for a local organization to help young prostitutes, was in a room with gymnasium-style acoustics). Each time they've played with three to four other grrrl bands. While Bikini Kill is by now very well-known as one of the initial acts in the movement afterwards called 'riot grrrl,' they have also resolutely refused to record for a major label, to claim a singularly 'representative' position. Their album, *Reject All American* (1996) has been praised by music critics (for *Rolling Stone*, *AP*, and other publications), but the crucial energy of the band remains focused through and at their live shows.

The first time I saw them, they appeared as the last band, after Slant 6 and Team Dresh. The second time I saw them, they also served as anchor, for a four-band lineup including Team Dresch. While Team Dresch's lyrics focused on women's relations, their act was consistently rough and overtly politicized. Their first album, *Personal Best*, features cover art recalling the poster for Robert Townsend's movie: two girl runners posed on a track, looking at each other, ready to 'break all the rules,' as the accompanying text has it. But there are other rules at stake in punk, imperatives to disorder, or at least a convincing show of same. The Team Dresch–Slant 6–Bikini Kill show, at a small D.C. club called the Black Cat, opened with a demonstration of self-defense for women.[8] Without microphones or props, members of all the bands acted out various parts, including would-be victims and aggressors, male and female (including a scenario where a lesbian imposes on a straight woman). As Team Dresch then started their set, the mostly white and female audience was more than ready to appreciate their every pro-girl gesture and inflection.

As the night went on, the audience became more gender-mixed, men arriving late, in time to hear Bikini Kill, the biggest name up that night. By the time frontperson Kathleen Hanna took the stage, the crowd was restless and excited. She instructed the men in the audience to step to the back so women could see the stage (only a few men complied). 'Girl power now!' she screamed, leading into 'Rebel Girl' ('You are the queen of my world'). When Hanna erupted into 'White Boy' – 'I'm so sorry if I've alienated some of you! Your whole fucking culture alienates me!' – it was clear that no one in the audience was going to be identifying as a 'white boy.' 'It's hard to talk with your dick in my mouth,' sang Hanna, and all heads in the audience nodded, as if swept up by a single rhythm, moved by a single cause and lively chorus: 'White boy, don't laugh, don't cry. Just die!' Some of the guy moved off to the sides of the room, as if to fade into the crowd or walls. But most of them hung with their girl companions, their flannel shirts and baggy pants providing precious little camouflage. And yet this apparent capacity to make white-boy-ness invisible, or at least negotiable, becomes more complicated when you consider that I also saw several girls at the front, in the very small pit, being shoved by boys. Hanna stopped the show, and refused to continue until the rest of the audience stopped these guys from misbehaving.[9]

There seem to be at least two ways to read this scene, and both have to do – perhaps ironically – with knowing your options, with understanding what constitutes a 'crisis' (as Hebdige uses the term), and with negotiating between authentic and performative transgressions: the white boys in the audience are in deep denial, or they are quite self-aware and able to make a serious leap, of faith, of imagination, of empathy. (Actually, there are a number of other ways to read the scene that fall in between these poles, and each of the young men in the audience must have his own perspective on his experience of the evening.) What I'd like to suggest, though, derives from Eve Kosofsky Sedgwick's (1995) proposition that 'masculinity and femininity are threshold effects.' She defines these effects as 'places where quantitative increments along one dimension can suddenly appear as qualitative differences somewhere else on the map entirely' (16). I find this spatial metaphor useful, in the sense that it might address the various spaces (though the differences among them are worth noting, as they indicate and shape audience responses, the bigger venues allowing more room for less unified-looking reactions), because of the surprise she describes – 'suddenly,' as if gendered and sexual identities might 'show up,' uninvited and unanticipated, complicating and challenging expectations.

This effect seemed, perhaps, most obvious during Pansy Division's appearance at the arena, but there was a way in which the Bikini Kill show pressed its audience to make choices about their identifications, which were immediate and temporary, but choices with consequences nevertheless. This wasn't an atmospheric shift that changed the world forever. Granted, some made lousy choices: they pushed girls even as Hanna was singing (or rather, yelling, which is closer to describing her performance style), 'It's about wanting you dead' (in 'Outta Me'). But everyone (or nearly everyone) in the room acted as if they were aware of the stakes inherent in his or her behavior. Hanna is nothing if not an aggressive and 'confessional' performer, incorporating her own experiences into her work, and also laying responsibility onto her audience, making them into a 'community' that can act to stop violence or abuse.[10]

While an ostensible singleness of purpose is surely integral to punk's aesthetics and politics, confusion has also long been an important factor, mounting a particular challenge to linearity, binarism, and coherence. The increasing availability and accessibility of a popular, 'commodity' queerness (lesbian chic in *New York* magazine [Kasindorf, 1993], for instance, a 'gay' episode of MTV's *Dating Game* ripoff series, *Singled Out* [1995], Ellen's coming out [1997], or a wholly sympathetic, even heroic, gay boy in Amy Heckerling's *Clueless* [1995]) seem less a loss of authentic marginality than an invasion and expansion of the mainstream. Punk emulates a kind of acting out and giving in, simulating resistance to exacerbate linguistic and generic instabilities, acting out and acting up to kick listeners into gear. Transforming the mainstream – injecting it with good music, no less – queer punk translates experience into performance and vice versa, collapsing expression onto identity, fiction onto productive politics. As Kathleen Hanna sings, 'There's more than one way of going somewhere.'

## Notes

1. Sexpod's members are Karyn Kuhl on guitar and lead vocals, Alice Genese on bass and vocals, Billy Loose on drums; Tribe 8 is Lynn Breedlove on vocals (and chainsaw), Lynn Flipper on guitar, Leslie Mah on guitar, Lynn Payne/Tantrum on bass, and Slade Bellum on drums; and Pansy Division is currently composed of Jon Cinoli on guitar and vocals, Chris Freeman on bass and vocals, and Dustin Donaldson on drums. Donaldson, who replaced Patrick Hawley and has been with the band for a little over a year, is the only straight member of the group.

2. For the sake of drawing some broad generic lines, I'm using the labels punk, queer-core, and riot grrrl, even though they are notoriously inaccurate and many bands reject them on principle (that such labeling is designed to enable more effective marketing rather than describe music or performance styles). And yet, as Tom Frank points out, the 'expression of dissent' that characterizes such 'alternative' cultures retains a persuasive power for its local, immediate constituencies. He writes, 'through its noise comes the scream of torment that is this country's only mark of health: the sweet shriek of outrage that is the only sign that sanity survives amid the stripmalls and hazy clouds of Hollywood desire' (Frank, 1995: 118). Pretty to think so, and sometimes effective.

3. John Champagne, in his formulation of an 'ethics of marginality,' describes a difference between 'liberal criticism' and an 'ethical criticism.' The first 'extends to the Other a greater subjectivity' (working within an established, hierarchical social and political system), the second 'deploys the Other towards a resistance to subjectivity' as subjectivity constitutes a restrictive dichotomy of subject and object, in order to challenge this established system (Champagne, 1995: xxxiii).

4. A friend of mine overheard one young man at the Madison, Wisconsin show complaining to his male friend that 'some chick' had pushed him so hard and aggressively he was reluctant to return to the pit unless his friend accompanied him, as a kind of reinforcement: they decided to hang back in the crowd.

5. And the band, which identifies itself as 'pro-SM,' has been challenged by other feminists. The most famous instance of this occurred at the 1994 Michigan Womyn's Music Festival, when their performance was interrupted by women carrying banners that read, 'Tribe 8 promotes violence against women and children' and 'If you're a sexual abuse survivor you may not want to attend this concert' (Thomas, 1995: 22). And Evelyn McDonnell (1995) reports that one speaker at an antiviolence workshop at the festival called the band 'pornographers.'

6. While the 9:30 Club is a self-designated site for 'alternative' music (that famously bland and amorphous category) and tends to attract a caucasian, middle-class, straight

clientele, such demographic generalizations make presumptions (sometimes warranted, sometimes not) about performative possibilities.

7. I've written elsewhere about this show, with more specific focus on Green Day (Fuchs, 1996).

8. This educational 'self-defense' performance is part of an ongoing collaborative project, with other women's bands, which has produced two recent CDs, *Free To Fight* (Portland, OR: Candy Ass, 1995), and *Home Alive: The Art of Self-Defense* (New York: Sony Music, 1996). The latter comes with a 'People Advisory Sticker,' which reads: 'Contents of this record represent the views of people who have been affected by violence. This is a topic that inspires various responses. Some people may be offended by the language and views on this record. Home Alive believes that awareness, communication and responsibility, rather than silence, censorship or denial of these complex issues, will lead to change. We all have a lot to learn. Warning: This world contains people and events that can be harmful to your health.'

9. I've seen Tribe 8 and other women's bands deal with this behavior as well: L7 stopped singing and playing at one performance, to demand that a singled-out young man stop sticking his elbow in a woman's face. He complied, they played on.

10. See also Hanna's project with a group called the Fakes, *Real Fiction* (Portland, OR: Chainsaw Records, 1995), which the liner notes describe as a 'rock opera' (not unlike the Who's *Tommy*), about a girl's abuse by her father. She also discusses this notion of audience as 'community' in an interview with Andrea Juno (Juno, 1996: 90).

## References

Balliger, R. 1995. 'Sounds of Resistance.' In *Sounding Off! Music as Subversion/Resistance/Revolution*, edited by R. Sakolsky and F. Wei-Han Ho. New York: Autonomedia.

Butler, J. 1989. 'Imitation and Gender Insubordination.' In *Inside/Out: Lesbian Theories, Gay Theories*, edited by D. Fuss. New York: Routledge.

————. 1993. *Bodies that Matter: On the Discursive Limits of 'Sex.'* New York: Routledge.

Champagne, J. 1995. *The Ethics of Marginality: A New Approach to Gay Studies*. Minneapolis: University of Minnesota Press.

de Certeau, M. 1984. *The Practice of Everyday Life*. Berkeley, CA: University of California Press.

Frank, T. 1995. 'Alternative to What?' In *Sounding Off Music as Subversion/Resistance/Revolution*, edited by R. Sakolsky and F. Wei-Han Ho. Brooklyn, NY: Autonomedia.

Fuchs, C. 1996. '"Beat me outta me": Alternative Masculinities.' In *Boys: Masculinities in Contemporary Culture*, edited by P. Smith, 171–97. New York: Westview Press.

Fuss, D. 1989. *Essentially Speaking: Feminism, Nature, and Difference*. New York: Routledge.

Grossberg, L. 1992. *We Gotta Get Out of This Place: Popular Conservatism and Postmodern Culture*. New York: Routledge.

————. 1993. 'The Framing of Rock: Rock and the New Conservatism.' In *Rock and Popular Music: Politics, Policies, Institutions*, edited by T. Bennett, S. Frith, L. Grossberg, J. Shepherd, and G. Turner. London: Routledge.

Hebdige, D. 1979. *Subculture: The Meaning of Style*. London: Routledge.

Herman, J.P. 1995. 'Orgasm Addicts.' *Village Voice*, January 10, 57–8.

Juno, A. 1996. *Angry Women in Rock, Volume 1*. New York: Juno Books.

Kasindorf, J.R. 1993. 'Lesbian *Chic*.' *New York*, May 10, 30–7.

Lamos, C. 1995. Taking on the Phallus.' In *Lesbian Erotics*, edited by Karla Jay, 101–24. New York: New York University Press.

McDonnell, E. 1995. 'Riot Grrrls Invade the 'Lesbian Woodstock.' *Addicted to Noise* [on-line magazine at http://www.addict.com/].

McRobbie, A. 1994. *Postmodernism and Popular Culture.* London: Routledge.

Schwichtenberg, C. 1993. 'Madonna's Postmodern Feminism: Bringing the Margins to the Center.' In *The Madonna Connection: Representational Politics, Subcultural Identities, and Cultural Theory,* edited by C. Schwichtenberg: 129–45. Boulder, CO: Westview Press.

Sedgwick, E.K. 1995. 'Gosh. Boy George, You Must Be Awfully Secure in Your Masculinity!' In *Constructing Masculinity,* edited by M. Berger, B. Wallis and S. Watson, 11–20. New York: Routledge.

Thomas, T. 1995. 'Music for the Tribe: Interview with Tribe 8.' *Girlfriends,* July–August, 20–22, 46.

Viegener, M. 1994. '"The Only Haircut That Makes Sense Anymore": Queer Subculture and Gay Resistance.' In *Queer Looks: Perspectives on Lesbian and Gay Film and Video,* edited by M. Gever, J. Greyson and P. Parmar. New York: Routledge.

## CD/s listed in this article

1. Bikini Kill. 1993. *Bikini Kill: The CD Version of the First Two Records* [compact disc]. Olympia, WA: Kill Rock Stars.

2. ———.1994. *Pussywhipped* [compact disc]. Olympia, WA: Kill Rock Stars.

3. ———. 1996. *Reject All American* [compact disc]. Olympia, WA: Kill Rock Stars.

4. Pansy Division. 1993a. *Deflowered* [compact disc]. Berkeley, CA: Lookout Records.

5. ———. 1993b. *Undressed* [compact disc]. Berkeley, CA: Lookout Records.

6. ———. 1995. *Pile Up* [compact disc]. Berkeley, CA: Lookout Records.

7. ———. 1996. *Wish I'd Taken Pictures* [compact disc]. Berkeley, CA: Lookout Records.

8. The Fakes. 1995a. *Real Fiction* [compact disc]. Portland, OR: Chainsaw.

9. ———. 1995b. *Home Alive* [compact disc]. Portland, OR: Chainsaw.

10. ———. 1995c. *Free to Fight* [compact disc]. Portland, OR: Chainsaw.

11. Tribe 8. 1995a. *By The Time We Get To Colorado* [compact disc]. San Francisco: Outpunk.

12. ———. 1995b. *Fist City* [compact disc]. San Francisco: Alternative Tentacles.

13. ———. 1996. *Snarkism* [compact disc]. San Francisco: Alternative Tentacles.

# Chapter 34

# Judith Halberstam

## Drag Kings: Masculinity and Performance

## What is a Drag King?

In clubs and cabarets, theaters and private parties, in movies and on TV, the drag queen has long occupied an important place in the American drama of gender instability. Drag queens have been the subject of mainstream and independent movies,[1] and straight audiences are, and historically have been, willing to pay good money to be entertained by men in drag. And not only in performance arenas have drag queens been an important part of social negotiations over the meaning of gender. In academia, ever since Esther Newton's 1972 classic anthropological study of female impersonators in America, scholars have been vigorously debating the relation of camp to drag, of drag to embodiment, and of camp humor to gay culture.[2] But in all the articles and studies and media exposés on drag queen culture, very little time and energy has been expended on the drag queen's counterpart, the drag king. [...] The history of public recognition of female masculinity is most frequently characterized by stunning absences. And the absence of almost all curiosity about the possibilities and potentiality of drag king performance provides conclusive evidence of precisely such widespread indifference.

A drag king is a female (usually) who dresses up in recognizably male costume and performs theatrically in that costume. Historically and categorically, we can make distinctions between the drag king and the male impersonator. Male

From: Judith Halberstam, *Female Masculinity*. Durham, NC: Duke University Press, 2000.

impersonation has been a theatrical genre for at least two hundred years, but the drag king is a recent phenomenon. Whereas the male impersonator attempts to produce a plausible performance of maleness as the whole of her act, the drag king performs masculinity (often parodically) and makes the exposure of the the-atricality of masculinity into the mainstay of her act. Both the male impersonator and the drag king are different from the drag butch, a masculine woman who wears male attire as part of her quotidian gender expression. Furthermore, whereas the male impersonator and the drag king are not necessarily lesbian roles, the drag butch most definitely is.

In the 1990s, drag king culture has become something of a subcultural phe-nomenon. Queer clubs in most major American cities feature drag king acts: for example, there is a regular weekly drag king club in New York called Club Casanova whose motto is 'the club where everyone is treated like a king!' There is a monthly club in London called Club Geezer and a quarterly club in San Francisco called Club Confidential. [...] But although drag kings seem to have become a major part of urban queer scenes, there are no indications that drag king culture is necessarily about to hit the mainstream any time soon. [...]

I know at least three people who like to claim that *they*, and they alone, coined the name 'drag king.' But the truth is that as long as we have known the phrase 'drag queen,' the drag king has been a concept waiting to happen.[3] Some scholars have traced the use of the word 'drag' in relation to men in women's costume back to the 1850s, when the term was used for both stage actors playing female roles and young men who just liked to wear skirts.[4] Male impersonation as a theatrical tradition extends back to the Restoration stage, but more often than not, the trouser role was used to emphasize femininity rather than to mimic maleness. In 'Glamour Drag and Male Impersonation,' Laurence Senelick comments on the function of the breeches role as 'a novelty' or as 'a salacious turn' until the 1860s in America, when the male impersonator and the glamour drag artists brought to the stage 'a plausible impression of sexes to which they did not belong.'[5] Much male impersonation on the nineteenth-century stage involved a 'boy' role in which a boyish woman represented an immature masculine subject; indeed, the plausible representation of mannishness by women was not encouraged. Because boys played women on the Shakespearean stage and women played boys on the nineteenth-century stage, some kind of role reversal symmetry seems to be in effect. But this role reversal actually masks the asymmetry of male and female impersonation. If boys can play girls and women, but women can play only boys, mature masculinity once again remains an authentic property of adult male bodies while all other gender roles are available for interpretation.

Male impersonation became an interesting phenomenon at the turn of the century in America with actors such as Annie Hindley developing huge female followings.[6] On and off the stage, cross-dressing women in the early twentieth century, from Annie Hindley to Radclyffe Hall, began to steady assault on the naturalness of male masculinity and began to display in public the signs and sym-bols of an eroticized and often (but not inevitably) politicized female masculinity. That some male impersonators carried over their cross-dressing practices into their everyday lives suggests that their relation to masculinity extended far beyond theatricality. Furthermore, the cross-dressing actress represents only the tip of the iceberg in terms of an emergent community of masculine-identified women.

The theatrical tradition of male impersonation continued and flourished for the first two decades of this century and then declined in popularity. After the passing of the 1933 Hollywood Motion Picture Production Code, which [...] banned all performances of so-called sexual perversion, male impersonation died out as a mainstream theatrical practice.[7] Some critics have traced the careers of one or two male impersonators such as Storme DeLaverie to show that pockets of male impersonation still existed within subcultural gay male drag culture between the 1930s and the 1960s. However, there is general agreement that no extensive drag king culture developed within lesbian bar culture to fill the void left by the disappearance of male impersonators from the mainstream theater. Indeed, Elizabeth Kennedy and Madeline Davis comment in their Buffalo oral histories that the masculinity constructed by butches in the 1940s and 1950s was accompanied by a 'puzzling lack of camp.'[8] Kennedy and Davis observe a notable lack of anything like drag king culture in the butch-femme bar world: 'Few butches performed as male impersonators, and no cultural aesthetic seems to have developed around male impersonation' (75). Kennedy and Davis use the absence of a camp or drag aesthetic to caution against the conflation of gay and lesbian histories. The queen and the butch, they argue, do not share parallel histories. Like many other cultural commentators, Kennedy and Davis tend to attribute the lack of lesbian drag to the asymmetries of masculine and feminine performativity in a male supremacist society. Accordingly, because the business of survival as a butch woman is often predicated on one's ability to pass as male in certain situations, camp has been a luxury that the passing butch cannot afford.

While it seems very likely that the lack of a lesbian drag tradition has much to do with the need for butches to pass, at least one other reason that male impersonation did not achieve any general currency within lesbian bar culture must also be attributed to mainstream definitions of male masculinity as nonperformative. Indeed, current representations of masculinity in white men unfailingly depend on a relatively stable notion of the realness and the naturalness of both the male body and its signifying effects. Advertisements for Dockers pants and Jockey underwear, for example, appeal constantly to the no-nonsense aspect of masculinity, to the idea that masculinity 'just is,' whereas femininity reeks of the artificial. Indeed, there are very few places in American culture where male masculinity reveals itself to be staged or performative; when it does, however, the masculine masquerade appears quite fragile. In TV sitcoms such as *Seinfeld,* for example, men apply comic pressure to the assumed naturalness of maleness, and a truly messy, fragile, and delegitimized masculinity emerges. In one particularly memorable *Seinfeld* episode highlighting abject male inadequacy, for example, George confesses to Jerry: 'I always feel like lesbians look at me and say, "That's the reason I am not into men!"' Such Woody Allenesque proclamations expose momentarily the instability of mainstream fictions of fortified male masculinities.

Outside of *Seinfeld,* unfortunately, white men derive enormous power from assuming and confirming the nonperformative nature of masculinity. For one thing, if masculinity adheres 'naturally' and inevitably to men, then masculinity cannot be impersonated. For another, if the nonperformance is part of what defines white male masculinity, then all performed masculinities stand out as suspect and open to interrogation. For example, gay male macho clones quite clearly exaggerate masculinity, and in them, masculinity tips into feminine performance. And the bad black gangsta rapper who bombastically proclaims his masculinity becomes a convenient symbol of male misogyny that at least temporarily exonerates less obviously misogynistic white male rock performances.[9] These clear differences between majority and minority masculinities make the drag king act different for different women. For the white drag king performing conventional heterosexual maleness, masculinity has first to be made visible and theatrical before it can be performed. Masculinities of color and gay masculinities, however, have already been rendered visible and theatrical in their various relations to dominant white masculinities, and the performance of these masculinities presents a somewhat easier theatrical task. Furthermore, although white masculinity seems to be readily available for parody by the drag kings, black masculinities or queer masculinities are often performed by drag kings in the spirit of homage or tribute rather than humor. [...]

Performances of masculinity seem to demand a different genre of humor and performance. It is difficult to make masculinity the target of camp precisely because masculinity tends to manifest as nonperformative. When drag king performances are campy, it is generally because the actor allows her femininity to inform and inflect the masculinity she performs. Performances of humorous masculinity demand another term, not only to distinguish them from the camp humor of femininity but also to avoid the conflation of drag and camp with butch-femme. I want to propose the term 'kinging' for drag humor associated with masculinity, not because this is a word used by drag kings themselves but because I think that a new term is the only way to avoid always collapsing lesbian history and social practice associated with drag into gay male histories and practices. Accordingly, femme may well be a location for camp, but butch is not. For drag butches and drag kings who perform masculinity from a butch or masculine subject position, camp is not necessarily the dominant aesthetic. Some drag king performances, of course, may well contain a camp element, but the kinging effect depends on several different strategies to render masculinity visible and theatrical.

The difference between men performing femininity and women performing masculinity is a crucial difference to mark out: the stakes in each are different, the performances look different, and there is a distinct difference between the relations between masculinity and performance and femininity and performance. To give one example of what I am saying about the difference between camp and kinging, I think it helps to examine an actual drag show. In a performance I saw at Club Casanova, the weekly drag king club in New York, in December 1996, the show combined both drag kings and drag queens onstage. The effect was startling. The four impersonators were performing as the B52'S, and the two men in the band were played by drag kings Pencil Kase and Evil Cave Boy. The two women, with bouffant hairdos and five-inch heels, were played by drag queens: Miss Kitten played Kate, and Corvette played Cindy. While the drag queens bounced and bobbed, stumbled and slipped around the small stage, they almost blocked out the more understated drag kings. Evil Cave Boy as the lead singer, Fred, jumped up and down, but his performance was marked by restraint and containment; Pencil Kase similarly played down his role as Keith and sulked in the back with his air bass guitar. The queens towered over the kings and barely restrained their impulses to take over the entire stage. The effect of placing drag femininity and drag masculinity side by side was positively vertiginous; on the one hand, the juxtaposition made clear the difference between a camp femininity and a very downplayed masculinity (an almost antitheatrical performance), and on the other hand, it made all gender unreadable. The kings were very convincing as men, and this made the drag queens more plausible despite the height differentials. A rather trendy bald person with shades and many visible piercings was standing next to me during the show, and after five minutes, this person called out: 'I don't get it! Who are the men and who are the women?' It is a frequent event at Club Casanova for drag queens to take the stage with the drag kings, and their performances literally spill over into the drag kings' careful and hilariously restrained acts, which are noticeably sincere, or, to use a Wildean term that tends to typify the very opposite of camp, 'earnest.' This is one part of what I call kinging: where all the emphasis is on a reluctant and withholding kind of performance.

While the spectacle of feminine and masculine drag onstage simultaneously allows for an interesting clash of gender-bending styles, the solo appearance of the drag king allows for an unusual confrontation between male and female masculinity and provides a rare opportunity for the wholesale parody of, particularly, white masculinity. The drag king performance, indeed, exposes the structure of dominant masculinity by making it theatrical and by rehearsing the repertoire of roles and types on which such masculinity depends. In the rest of this chapter, I outline the ways in which dominant forms of male masculinity manage to appear authentic and all other forms of masculinity are consequently labeled derivative. This relation is actually not reproduced within dominant femininities: as a film such as *Paris Is Burning* proved, much of what we understand to be original about female femininity already has been channeled through queer male bodies. The startling image of drag queen Willie Ninja teaching female models how to walk the catwalk in *Paris Is Burning* perhaps provides the best example of the lack of originality that we associate with female femininities. Another example of this would be recent films about young women such as *Clueless* (1995) and *Romy and Michelle's High School Reunion* (1997). In both films, the spectacle of exaggerated femininity creates a kind of heterosexual camp humor that depends totally on a prior construction of femininity by drag queens. This is particularly true in *Romy and Michelle's High School Reunion,* in which Lisa Kudrow and Mira Sorvino, as the two women preparing for their reunion, present a spectacle of loud and outrageous femininity that is only made more camp and more evocative of a drag queen aesthetic because they are both very tall and tower over their classmates. Finally, the British TV show *Absolutely Fabulous* completely appropriates camp and drag queen motifs to portray the humorous lives of two middle-aged women in the design business. In all of these representations, humorous femininity is relayed through a gay male aesthetic. By way of comparison, it would be almost impossible to imagine a mainstream depiction of masculinity that acknowledged that it had been routed through lesbian masculinity.

The notion of female femininity as derivative, furthermore, echoes the wholesale depiction of lesbianism as epitomizing the derivative or unauthentic. According to such logic, butch lesbians are supposedly imitating men; femme lesbians are wanna-be drag queens, or else they are accused of blending seamlessly into heterosexual femininity; the androgynous lesbian has 'borrowed' from both male and female; and the leather dyke or club girl parasitically draws from gay male leather culture. Drag king performances, however, provide some lesbian performers (although all drag kings are by no means lesbians) with the rare opportunity to expose the artificiality of all genders and all sexual orientations and therefore to answer the charge of inauthenticity that is usually made only about lesbian identity. [...]

## The 1995–1996 Hershe Bar Drag King Contests

On the night I attended my first drag king contest, I was asked on my way into the club whether I would like to compete. I thought long and hard about this question but said finally, 'No thanks, I don't have an act.' As it turned out, neither did any of the other drag kings, but this did not stop them from going onstage. I took my place in the audience and waited for the show. The club, Hershe Bar, was packed with a very diverse crowd, and the show was the center of the evening's entertainment. Finally the lights dimmed, and the evening's emcee, lesbian comic Julie Wheeler, took the stage in her own Tony Las Vegas drag and began the evening by performing an Elvis song. Soon afterward, ten drag kings filed out in various states of dress and flaunted many different brands of masculine display. Like champion bodybuilders, the drag kings flexed and posed to the now wildly cheering audience: the winner was to receive prize money of $200, and she earned the right to compete in the grand finale for a prize of $1,000. The show was a huge success in terms of producing a spectacle of alternative masculinities; however, it was ultimately a big letdown in terms of the performative. The drag kings, generally speaking, seemed to have no idea of how to perform as drag kings, and when called on to 'do something,' one after the other just muttered his name. When compared to the absolutely exaggerated performances featured within drag queen shows, these odd moments of drag king stage fright read as part of a puzzle around masculine performativity. While certainly part of the drag king stage fright had to do with the total lack of any prior role models for drag king performance, and while certainly this inertia has been replaced in recent months by lavish drag king acts, at least in these early contests, the stage fright was also a sign of the problem of masculine nonperformativity. The drag kings had not yet learned how to turn masculinity into theater. There were other contributing factors at work, though, including that many of the women onstage seemed to be flaunting their own masculinity rather than some theatrical imitation of maleness.

The drag king contest is a difficult scene to read because we need a taxonomy of female masculinities to distinguish carefully between the various types of identification and gender acts on display. I would like, therefore, to spend some time charting some of the masculine gender variations within the drag king contests. My models are quite particular to the contests and have not necessarily carried over into the regular performances. Drag king contests, it is worth noting, function less like traditional drag queen shows and have more in common with the various performances staged by the queens in *Paris Is Burning*. Like the Harlem balls documented in this film, these drag king contests had a cash prize and drew a largely black and Latino pool of contestants. Unlike the ball scene, the drag king events do not necessarily open out into an elaborate culture of gay houses and sex work.[10] [...]

## Butch realness

In the drag king contests, the winner would very often be a biological female who was convincing in her masculinity (sometimes convincing meant she could easily pass as male, but sometimes it meant her display of a recognizable form of female masculinity). [...] To describe the 'convincing' aspect of the butch realness look I offer the example of the contestant who won on the first night I attended Hershe Bar. The butch who won was a very muscular black woman wearing a basketball shirt and shorts. In her 'sports drag' and with her display of flexed muscles, the contestant could easily have passed as male, and this made her 'convincing.' This contestant won through her display of an authentic or unadorned and unperformed masculinity; she was probably a walk-on rather than someone who prepared elaborately for the contest. Interestingly enough, the category of butch realness is often occupied by nonwhite drag kings, attesting specifically to the way that masculinity becomes visible as masculinity once it leaves the sphere of normative white maleness. Furthermore, the relative invisibility of white female masculinity may also have to do with a history of the cultivation of an aesthetic of androgyny by white middle-class lesbians. The white drag kings in this particular contest were at something of a loss: they were not at all performative in the way some of the black and latino drag kings were (dancing and rapping) and tended to wear tuxedos as part of their drag king look. Every now and then, a white drag king would attempt a construction worker aesthetic or strike a James Dean pose. [...]

Because of its reliance on notions of authenticity and the real, the category of butch realness is situated on the sometimes vague boundary between transgender and butch definition. The realness of the butch masculinity can easily tip, in other words, into the desire for a more sustained realness in a recognizably male body. There is no clear way of knowing how many of the drag kings at this club had any transgender modes of identification, and because the whole show took place under the auspices of a lesbian club, one might assume that most identified at least in some way with the label of dyke or lesbian.

One way of describing the relationship between butch realness and male masculinity is in terms of what José Muñoz has called an active disidentification, or 'a mode of dealing with dominant ideology, one that neither opts to assimilate within such a structure nor strictly opposes it.'[11] Similarly, within butch realness, masculinity is neither assimilated into maleness nor opposed to it; rather it involves an active disidentification with dominant forms of masculinity, which are subsequently recycled into alternative masculinities.

## Femme pretender

Butch realness is clearly opposed to femme drag king performances. These may be termed 'femme pretender' performances, and they look more like drag queen shows, not simply because the disjuncture between biological sex and gender is the basis for the gender act but because irony and camp flavor the performance. [...] A femme pretender who has garnered much attention in New York is Buster Hymen. Hymen has a song-and-dance act and often disrobes halfway through and transforms herself into a lounge kitten. Clearly, the performance is all about transformation, and it capitalizes on the idea that, as Newton puts it, 'the appearance is an illusion.'[12] Whereas a few male drag performers create drag drama by pulling off their wigs or dropping their voices a register or two, the femme pretender often blows her cover by exposing her breasts or ripping off her suit in a parody of classic striptease.

One or two femme pretenders would appear in every drag king contest, and their performances often revolved around a consolidation of femininity rather than a disruption of dominant masculinity. The femme pretender actually dresses up butch or male only to show how thoroughly her femininity saturates her performance – she performs the failure of her own masculinity as a convincing spectacle. These performances tend to be far more performative than butch realness ones, but possibly less interesting for the following reasons: first, the femme drag king has not really altered the structure of drag as it emerged within gay male contexts as camp; second, the femme pretender offers a reassurance that female masculinity is just an act and will not carry over into everyday life. Many femme drag kings talk about the power they enjoy in accessing masculinity through a drag act, but they return ultimately to how confirmed they feel in their femininity. Ultimately, femme drag kings tend to use drag as a way to, as Buster Hymen puts it, 'walk both sides of the gender fence,'[13] and this tends to reassert a stable binary definition of gender. It is worth noting that the drag kings who have managed to garner the most publicity tend to be the femme pretenders.[14] Even some gay male writers who are conversant with the gender-bending tactics of drag tend to identify all drag kings as femme drag king. Michael Musto, in an article on drag kings for the *New York Post,* concluded his piece with a reassurance for his straight readers: he notes that very butch looking drag king Mo B. Dick 'happens to love lipstick as much as any girl.'[15]

## Male mimicry

In male mimicry, the drag king takes on a clearly identifiable form of male masculinity and attempts to reproduce it, sometimes with an ironic twist and sometimes without. In one of the few performances of white masculinity at the Hershe Bar shows, for example, a drag king contestant performed a mock priest act that had the nice effect of exposing the theatricality of religion. Male mimicry is often at work in the femme pretender performances but actually can be performed by butches or femmes. It is the concept of male mimicry that props up an enterprise such as Diane Torr's Drag King Workshop. Although the workshop takes us a little off the topic of the drag king contests, the concept of male mimicry as produced by the workshops did influence some of the white contestants in the Hershe Bar contests. Indeed, many news articles attribute the origins of New York drag king culture to Diane Torr (as does Torr herself), and some drag kings such as Buster Hymen credit Torr with inspiring them to begin performing.[16] Diane Torr is a New York–based performance artist who, as Danny Drag King, runs a workshop in which women can become men for a day.[17] Torr's workshop advertisement tells potential participants that they can 'explore another identity–you will learn the basic male behavioral patterns. How to walk, sit, talk and lie down like a man.'[18]

In the workshop, which has been written up in many different magazines and newspapers and filmed for the BBC, Torr instructs her students in the manly arts of taking up space, dominating conversations, nose picking, and penis wearing, and she gives them general rudeness skills. Torr's students become men for the day by binding and jockey stuffing, and then she shows them how to apply facial hair and create a credible male look. Finally, Torr takes her charges out into the mean streets of New York City and shows them how to pass. Torr herself articulates no particular masculine aspirations; she, like many of her workshop participants, avows over and over that she has no desire to *be* a man; she just wants to pass as a man within this limited space of experimentation.'[19] Torr says that her reasons for cross-dressing are quite clear; she wants to experience 'male authority and territory and entitlement.'[20] Many workshop women discuss the feeling of power and privilege to which the masquerade gives them access, and many are titillated by the whole thing but relieved at the end of the day to return to a familiar femininity.

One account of the drag king workshop describes it as a spin on the everyday practice of gender performance. Shannon Bell claims to be what we might call 'a gender queen,' someone who plays butch one day and femme the next.[21] She used the Drag King Workshop to explore one of her many genders, her queer fag self. Obviously, this sense of gender as costume and voluntary performance is not at all related to the butch realness mode of female masculinity. Bell plays gender like a game precisely because her gender normativity provides a stable base for playing with alterity. Bell represents the typical workshop participant in that she understands its function as an exercise in gender fluidity and a political exposé of male privilege. Bell asks Torr why people take the workshop, and Torr provides a political justification intended to make the workshop respectable within the terms of feminist consciousness: 'Part of what happens at the Drag King Workshop is that women learn certain things: we don't have to smile, we don't have to concede ground, we don't have to give away territory' (96). In this way, the workshop functions rather like a feminist consciousness-raising group but seems to have very little to do with the reconstruction of masculinity.

Diane Torr goes so far as to claim that she invented the term 'drag king' and she tells interviewer Amy Linn: 'It came to me in about 1989.... It was a day that I had done a photo shoot in male clothes, and I had an opening to go to at the Whitney. I decided to go dressed as a man.'[22] When Torr found herself easily passing and receiving much attention from women, she decided to make this defamiliarizing experience available to women in the form of a workshop for assertiveness training. The workshop, obviously, has little to do with drag kings or kinging. It is a simple lesson in how the other half lives, and it usefully opens a window on male privilege for women who suffer the effects of such privilege every day. As I suggested earlier, however, it is hard to lay claim to the term 'drag king,' and certainly we would not want to attribute the origins of modern drag king culture to a workshop that is primarily designed for heterosexual women and unproblematically associates masculinity with maleness. For masculine women who walk around being mistaken for men every day, the workshop has no allure. The Drag King Workshop emphasizes for me the divide between a fascination in male masculinity and its prerogatives and an interest in the production of alternate masculinities.

## Fag drag

Like other forms of minority masculinity, gay male masculinity stands apart from mainstream formulations of maleness and is very available for drag king imitation. Furthermore, some lesbians in recent years have positively fetishized gay male sex culture, and some women base their masculinity and their sex play on gay male models. This may mean copying a gay male aesthetic such as the 'Castro clone.' The Castro clone refers to a popular masculine aesthetic within urban gay ghettos that depends on leather and denim and a queer biker look. That the image is already identified as a clone suggests that imitation and impersonation are already part of its construction; this makes it easy for drag kings to take on fag drag. Some of the drag kings in the Hershe Bar contest cultivated a gay male look with leather or handlebar mustaches, and they often routed these looks through a Village People type of performance of hypermasculinity.

## Denaturalized masculinity

Last in my taxonomy of female masculinities, I want to identify a category that often disappears into the other categories I have outlined. Denaturalized masculinity plays on and within both butch realness and male mimicry but differs from butch realness in its sense of theatricality and hyperbole and remains distinct from male mimicry by accessing some alternate mode of the masculine. Dred, [winner of] the 1996 Hershe Bar contest, [pulled] off a tribute to blaxploitation macho with a butch twist. Dred is an interesting drag king because she plays the line between the many different versions of drag king theater. On the one hand, she appears in the bar contests heavily made up as Superfly; on the other hand, she also plays in staged drag king theatrical performances in a much more campy role in which she metamorphs from Superfly to Foxy Brown. Then again, she regularly performs with another drag king, Shon, as part of rap duo Run DMC. Dred represents the fluid boundaries between the many different drag king performances. I include her in my section on denaturalized masculinity because she combines appropriation, critique, and alternative masculinity in her presentation.

Denaturalized masculinity in many ways produces the most successful drag king performances. In Julie Wheeler's act as Tony Las Vegas, the emcee for the drag king contest, for example, she wore slicked-back hair and a lounge suit. Tony made sleazy asides throughout the contest, and in the show I was at, he moved in way too close on a drag king who was clearly a femme pretender, breathing in her ear and asking what she had on under her suit. He periodically called out to the audience, 'Show us yer tits,' and generally made a spectacle of slimy masculinity and misogyny. Whereas the Drag King Workshop mimics maleness without necessarily parodying it Tony makes male parody the center of his act by finding the exact mode in which male masculinity most often appears as performance: sexism and misogyny. The drag king demonstrates through her own masculinity and through the theatricalization of masculinity that there are no essential links between misogyny and masculinity: rather, masculinity seems bound to misogyny structurally in the context of patriarchy and male privilege. For masculine women who cannot access male privilege, the rewards of misogyny are few and far between, and so she is very likely to perform her masculinity without misogyny. But sexism makes for good theater, and the exposure of sexism by the drag king as the basis of masculine realness serves to unmask the ideological stakes of male nonperformativity. [...]

## Notes

1. To just name a few mainstream and independent films that have been about, or have prominently featured, drag queens: *Some Like It Hot* (1959, dir. Billy Wilder), *Tootsie* (1982, dir. Sydney Pollack), *Wigstock* (1993, dir. Tom Rubnitz), *Priscilla: Queen of the Desert* (1994, dir. Stephan Elliot), *The Crying Game* (1992, dir. Neil Jordan), *Mrs. Doubtfire* (1993, dir. Chris Columbus). Drag queen Ru Paul also currently has his own talk show. By comparison, there is not a single mainstream film that features a drag king or a male impersonator who produces anything like credible masculinity. *Victor/Victoria* (1982, dir. Blake Edwards), for example, is really still about drag queens, and Julie Andrews totally fails to pass.

2. See two anthologies for examples of such academic work on drag: David Bergman, ed., *Camp Grounds: Style and Homosexuality* (Amherst: University of Massachusetts Press, 1993); Moe Meyer, ed., *The Politics and Poetics of Camp* (New York: Routledge, 1994).

3. Esther Newton had the following to say about the history of the term 'drag king': 'As one segment of a drag queen context I witnessed in the late sixties in Chicago, there was a 'drag king' competition (and although I wrote earlier that this term was never used then, I seem to remember that in this one context, on stage, it was), and I do have slides of it. I agree that the concept was always available but, as Sarah Murray has noted, it never developed into a continuously generating tradition the way drag queen has.' Newton, in personal correspondence with the author (July 1997).

4. See Elizabeth Drorbaugh, 'Sliding Scales: Notes on Storme DeLaverie and the Jewel Box Revue, the Cross-Dressed Woman on the Contemporary Stage, and the Invert,' in *Crossing the Stage: Controversies on Cross-Dressing,* ed. Lesley Ferris (London: Routledge, 1993), 120–43.

5. Laurence Senelick, 'Boys and Girls Together: Subcultural Origins of Glamour Drag and Male Impersonation on the Nineteenth-Century Stage,' in *Crossing the Stage: Controversies on Cross-Dressing,* ed. Lesley Ferris (London: Routledge, 1993), 82.

6. Lisa Duggan reads female-to-male cross-dressing practices of this period as 'the seeds of a new identity' and as a practice far more complex than 'temporary or superficial disguise' (Duggan, 'The Trials of Alice Mitchell: Sensationalism, Sexology, and the Lesbian Subject in Turn-of-the-Century America,' *Signs* 18, no. 4 [summer 1993]: 809).

7. Drorbaugh, 'Sliding Scales,' 124.

8. Elizabeth Lapovsky Kennedy and Madeline Davis, *Boots of Leather and Slippers of Gold: The History of a Lesbian Community* (New York: Routledge, 1993), 62.

9. See my article on drag kings and rap for an elaboration on this point: 'Mackdaddy, Superfly, Rapper: Gender, Race, and Masculinity in the Drag King Scene,' *Social Text* (fall 1997), Special Issue on Race and Sexuality, edited by José Muñoz and Ann McClintock.

10. Although I do not have any specific information about the relationship between these drag king performers and their involvement or lack of involvement in sex work, I am trying to establish here the lack of an organized 'house' system as the productive matrix for these contests. The contests featured random women, mostly butch women who went up on stage mostly to try to win $200. That most of the contestants were butch should also suggest that sex work is not the obvious backdrop for the contests.

11. José Muñoz, 'Famous and Dandy like B. 'n' Andy: Race, Pop, and Basquiat,' in *Pop Out: Queer Warhol* (Durham, N.C.: Duke University Press, 1996), 147. Muñoz articulates the

complex relations between minority subjects and mainstream culture, and he finds that very often the forms of cultural resistances produced by such subjects are constructed out of contradictory relations between dominant and minority identifications. Disidentification, Muñoz writes, 'is a strategy that tries to transform a cultural logic from within' (148).

12. Newton, Ester (1972) *Mother Camp.* Chicago: University of Chicago Press, 101.

13. Kimberly Pittman, 'Walk like a Man: Inside the Booming Drag King Scene,' *Manhattan Pride,* June 1996, 4.

14. The femme drag kings, it must be said, garner both the good and the bad publicity. In a truly offensive article for *Penthouse,* Ralph Gardner Jr. went in search of a 'beautiful lesbian' by exploring the drag king scene and spent time hanging out with Buster Hymen and villain. This did not save them from becoming the objects of Gardner's lascivious attention in print. He also made racist remarks about Dred ('Drag Kings,' *Penthouse,* February 1997, 85, 86, 128).

15. Michael Musto, *New York Post,* Arts Section, 20 February 1997, 43–44.

16. Buster Hymen is described as a 'graduate of Torr's testosterone training' by Kimberly Pittman ('Drag Kingdom Come,' *Manhattan Pride,* June 1996, 3).

17. Torr has been running the workshop since about 1989, and she charges $100 a session. Torr is a performance artist and has performed as a go-go dancer and in cross-dressing performances for many years in New York City.

18. Copy from a flyer advertising the workshop in March 1997. On the flyer, Torr describes herself as 'a performance artist' and states that 'she lives and works in New York where as a cross-dresser, she is a member of the F2M (female-to-male) fraternity.' Because Torr is not an FTM transsexual and not an 'out' lesbian, it is not altogether clear what this self-positioning statement means.

19. See, for example, Julie Wheelwright, 'Out of My Way, I'm Man for a Day,' *Independent,* 11 November 1994, 27–28; Anna Burnside, 'Walk like a Man,' *Scotland on Sunday,* 24 May 1995, 5.

20. As quoted in Phyllis Burke, 'Diane Ton's Drag King Workshop,' in *Gender Shock: Exploding the Myths of Male and Female* (New York: Anchor Books, 1996), 147.

21. Shannon Bell, 'Finding the Male Within and Taking Him Cruising,' in *The Last Sex,* ed. Arthur Kroker and Marilouise Kroker (New York: St. Martin's Press, 1993), 91–97.

22. Linn, Amy (1995) 'Drag Kings', *San Fransisco Weekly,* 27 September–3 October, 10–11, 13–16, 18.

# PART SEVEN

# LOCATING:

# SPACE, PLACE, AND POWER

Spatial metaphors abound within the study of popular culture. Most notably the usage of 'site' as in Hall's Gramsci-influenced statement that popular culture is 'one of the sites where … [the] struggle for and against a culture of the powerful is engaged' or Lowe and Lloyd's related claim about culture as 'a terrain in which politics, culture, and the economic form an inseparable dynamic'. However, the subject of space can be limited neither to metaphor nor simile. In basic terms, popular culture is not practiced and experienced in an abstract sense. Our section on *Commodifying* speaks to both the tangible and intangible qualities of the commodity form. It foregrounds how popular culture, understood as product, helps us ascertain the socio-economic relations between cultural production and cultural industry as explored in our *Marketing* section. Within the study of popular culture (and especially subculture) space and place are highly visible research areas. They may comprise a central subject of study or be considered tangentially as a component within a larger research emphasis. The following survey illustrates how scholars have understood space and place, as well as the specific phenomenon to which they have applied this knowledge: urban pool halls (Ned Polsky, 1967), working-class amusements (Kathy Peiss, 1986), the tearoom (Laud Humphreys, 1970), post-war reconstruction and working-class community in London's East End (Phil Cohen, 1972), girls' bedroom culture (Angela McRobbie and Jenny Carter, 1976), the beach (John Fiske, 1989 and Meaghan Morris, 1992), Hip Hop and New York City (Tricia Rose, 1994 and Juan Flores, 1994), the dance club (Sarah Thornton, 1996), Gangsta Rap in South Central, Los Angeles (Robin D. G. Kelley, 1994), and the record shop (Will Straw, 1997).

In addition, the humanities and social sciences began to consider the importance of space, place, area studies, and geography for understandings of popular culture and cultural experience with the publication of various influential texts in the early 1990s. These included: Mike Davis's *City of Quartz* (London: Verso, 1990), Edward W. Soja's *Postmodern Geographies: The Reassertion of Space in Critical Social Theory* (London: Verso, 1989), Fredric Jameson's *Postmodernism or, The Cultural Logic of Late Capitalism* (Durham, NC: Duke University Press, 1991), and David Harvey's *The Condition of Postmodernity: An Enquiry into the Origin of Cultural Change* (Oxford: Blackwell, 1991). It is also worth pointing out that French intellectuals have also been influential in foregrounding the subject of space in relation to practices of power. Both Soja and Harvey have drawn from Henri Lefebvre's *The Production of Space* (Oxford: Blackwell, 1991 [1974]), Michel Foucault's various books, lectures, and interviews on discipline and power as well as his (1986) 'Of Other Spaces', *Diacritics* (Spring): 22–7, within which he develops his notion of 'heterotopia', and of course Michel de Certeau's *The Practice of Everyday Life* (Berkeley, CA: University of California Press, 1984) whereby he distinguishes place from space in order to elaborate on his concept of 'spatial practices'.

As we have stated in the general introduction to *Popular Culture: A Reader,* no common canon exists in the academy through which study of popular culture is exclusively channeled. The same may be said of space and place in that their critical function has continued to develop as popular culture and cultural politics become the lens through which both are made visible. Inversely, when space and place become a measure through which questions of identity are raised, it becomes possible to use them to cut across certain national, racial, gender, sexual, and ethnic boundaries. Here we have in mind seminal work that has broadened our understanding of the importance of space and place in relation to time, memory, history, diaspora, movement, experience, and performance that defy easy mapping. Such work, which exceeds easily recognized boundaries and parameters, has taken diverse forms. Among them are the interventions of: George Lipsitz's *Time Passages: Collective Memory and American Popular Culture* (Minneapolis, MN: University of Minnesota Press, 1990), Paul Gilroy's *The Black Atlantic: Modernity and Double Consciousness* (Cambridge, MA: Harvard University Press, 1993), and Joseph Roach's *Cities of the Dead: Circum-Atlantic Performances* (New York: Columbia Press, 1996), Norman M. Klein's *The History of Forgetting: Los Angeles and the Erasure of Memory* (London: Verso, 1977) and Samuel R. Delany's *Times Square Red Times Square Blue* (New York: New York University Press, 1999).

The last section of the *Reader* constructs itself from the critical work on space and place that came into prominence within the 1990s. Instead of limiting our investment in *locating* to a direct reflection of the seminal work that we have just mentioned, we have sought to complement and expand this trajectory. Here we are most interested in taking the broadest possible use of place and space through which visibility of identity is negotiated: the act of physical movement in the everyday practice of walking (de Certeau), questions of passing and identity tourism within the spaces of the Internet (Nakamura), the circulation of black ephemera and its communicative abilities (Gilroy), sonic dialogues and travel (Lipsitz), critiques of urbanism through tricks and gestures associated with skateboarding (Willard), and the liminal practices of 'Ozomatli' and the place of LA's Greater Eastside (Viesca).

Michel de Certeau's influence on the study of popular culture and cultural studies' indebtedness to his *The Practices of Everyday Life* (English trans, Berkeley, CA: University of California Press, 1984) has already been touched upon in the general introduction. However, de Certeau's intellectual contributions must not be seen solely through the lens of US cultural studies' investments in pleasure and active reading practices. Like his anonymous pedestrian – walking in countless thousands on the street – from '**Walking in the City**', de Certeau's *oeuvre* is elusive. The subject matter of his numerous books – *Culture in the Plural* (orig. 1974; English trans., Minneapolis, MN: University of Minnesota Press, 1998), *The Writing of History* (orig. 1975; English trans., New York: Columbia University Press, 1988), *The Mystic Fable. Vol. 1, The Sixteenth and Seventeenth Centuries* (orig. 1982; English trans., Chicago: University of Chicago Press, 1992), *Heterologies: Discourses on the Other* (Minneapolis, MN: University of Minnesota Press, 1986), *The Capture of Speech and Other Political Writings* (Minneapolis, MN: University of Minnesota Press, 1998), *The Practices of Everyday Life, Vol. 2, Living and Cooking* (written with Luce Giard and Pierre Mayol, Minneapolis, MN: University of Minnesota Press, 1998), *The Possession at Loudon* (Chicago: University of Chicago Press, 2000) – range from historiography to sociology, cultural history to philosophy, mysticism to everyday life, psychoanalytic theory to linguistics, urbanism to religion. Detailed examinations of the diverse works of writers such as Freud, Bourdieu, and Foucault occupy a great deal of his writing. Foucault, in particular his theorization of panoptic power, is instrumental for de Certeau's articulation of spatial practices that both operate within and outside disciplinary technology. De Certeau is invested in enunciating the ordinary tactics, practices, or the 'arts of making do' that demonstrate the 'multiform, resistance, tricky and stubborn procedures that elude discipline without being outside the field in which it is exercised, and which should lead us to a theory of everyday practices, of lived space, of the disquieting familiarity of the city'.

Two chapters in this section concentrate on the importance of critical considerations of space and spatialized politics for understanding popular culture in regards to identity and community, reconfigurations of public space through cultural practices, social experience and urbanism, and the categories of local and global. Both essays carry out their analysis on and within the multifarious place of Los Angeles. Michael Nevin Willard's '**Séance, Tricknowlogy, Skateboarding, and the Space of Youth**' originally appeared in *Generations of Youth: Youth Cultures and History in Twentieth Century America* (1998) (co-edited with Joe Austin). Willard's piece examines downtown Los Angeles – within the sharp contrasts between the Bunker Hill area and Broadway – in regards to the spatial limitations placed upon those who occupy the streets, as well as how the action of skateboarding ('tricks') challenges these limitations through reinvention while revealing the social constructedness of these imposed limitations. 'Whenever skaters perform their 'tricks' they make their own meanings, critiques of power, and interpretations of urban life.'

'**Straight Out of the Barrio: Ozomatli and the Importance of Place in the Formation of Chicano/a Popular Culture in Los Angeles**' (2000), by Victor Hugo Viesca, discusses the spatial context within which the politically engaged and 'interethnic sensibility' of the band Ozomatli formed. Viesca provides a telling overview of the socio-economic conditions that construct the Greater Eastside of Los Angeles and Los Angeles as a global city, as well as the cultural emphasis ('rather than nationality or color') played out in/around contemporary Chicano popular culture, memory, history, and intercultural social identities formed through the circumstances of place. As Viesca argues:

> The barrio is a vibrant mix of the traditional *and* popular. It is a product of local history as much as global change. It is a place where the life of the city streets mixes with the memories of the past, of Mexico or the Chicano *movimiento*, echoed in the sounds and imagery of the music. This is where the ties of Ozomatli to the city are especially pertinent. Rather than discarding the popular sounds of the barrio, from *banda* to *cumbia* to hip hop, Ozo has fused them into a musical language that reflects sonically the transformations of space, place, and identity that are taking place in the city.

It is precisely this type of complexity that considerations of space and place afford the study of popular culture.

Best known for his seminal books, *There Aint No Black in the Union Jack: The Cultural Politics of Race and Nation* (Chicago: University of Chicago Press, 1987) and *The Black Atlantic: Modernity and Double Consciousness* (Cambridge, MA: Harvard University Press, 1993) as well as his more recent, *Against Race: Imagining Political Culture Beyond the Color Line* (Cambridge, MA: Harvard University Press, 2001) and for his part as an editor for *Without Guarantees: In Honor of Stuart Hall* (London: Verso, 2000), Paul Gilroy is a major figure within the study of popular culture as well as within ethnic, critical race studies, and cultural studies. Included here is an often overlooked article on black music, history, memory, and experience from his *Small Acts: Thoughts on the Politics of Black Cultures* (1993). In **'Wearing Your Art on Your Sleeve: Notes Towards a Diaspora History of Black Ephemera'**, Gilroy studies the political relationships between diasporic people and commercial culture. His 'object' of analysis is the now marginal LP record sleeve and its communicative abilities to bestow visual as well as textual information on black social history, struggles, and black political discourse. With the replacement of the record sleeve by CD packaging, Gilroy draws his readers' attention to the significance of the sleeve's importance for racial representation within the music industry: 'The cultural significance of record covers as a form of folk art is therefore enhanced simply because they offer one of very few opportunities to see and enjoy images of black people outside the stereotyped guises in which the dominant culture normally sanctions their presence.' Gilroy extends his analysis to also consider the importance of record cover display within the social space of the black record shop.

'The dialogue of the African diaspora informs the politics and culture of countries across the globe. It draws upon ancient traditions and modern technologies, on situated knowledge and a nomadic sensibility.' George Lipsitz's **'Diasporic Noise: History, Hip Hop, and the Post-colonial Politics of Sound'** (1994), carefully examines the communicative abilities of popular culture; how hip hop and other black musical forms engage in cultural politics through the exchanges of sound, history, and knowledge in music production. Conversations travel throughout postcolonial culture and are instrumental in assisting in the creation and maintance of 'new social movements' via commercialized forms, forms that are also, Lipsitz argues, expressive of 'the potential for contemporary commercialized leisure to carry images, ideas, and icons of enormous political importance between cultures'. George Lipsitz's writings on race, history, identity, place and popular culture are invaluable to the area. Notable works include: *The Possessive Investment in Whiteness: How White People Profit from Identity Politics*

(Philadelphia, PA: Temple University Press, 1998), *Time Passages: Collective Memory and American Popular Culture* (1990), *The Sidewalks of St. Louis: Places, People, and Politics in an American City* (St. Louis: University of Missouri Press, 1991), and *Dangerous Crossroads: Popular Music, Postmodernism and the Poetics of Place* (New York and London: Verso, 1994), from which the excerpted piece is taken.

Lisa Nakamura's '**Head-Hunting on the Internet: Identity Tourism, Avatars, and Racial Passing in Textual and Graphic Chat Spaces**' (2002) easily eludes the themes used to organize the study of popular culture in this *Reader*. Although placed in the *Locating* section, on account of its direct engagement with online social spaces, 'Head-Hunting on the Internet' also speaks very well to concerns around identity and popular culture expressed in previous sections: *Practicing* (role-playing, online gaming, MOOs & MUDs), *Styling* (performance, avatars), and *Voicing* (chat, racial otherness). Like the subjects of her piece – tourism, racial passing, identity performance, subjectivity, cyberspace and the Internet – Nakamura's research speaks to various academic interests, thus further entangling the popular. For example, earlier versions of the work presented here (taken from her *Cybertypes: Race, Ethnicity, and Identity on the Internet* (New York and London: Routledge, 2002) appeared in *The Cybercultures Reader* (edited by David Bell and Barbara M. Kennedy (New York and London: Routledge, 2000)), while complementary research has been included in *The Visual Culture Reader* (2nd edition, edited by Nicholas Mirzoeff, New York and London: Routledge, 2002). Nakamura's *Race in Cyberspace* (co-edited with Beth E. Kolko and Gilbert B. Rodman (New York and London: Routledge, 2000)) marks a vital intervention into discussions and debates on identity and new media. While scholars have raised important questions concerning identity, space, and the Internet, 'online communities', cybernetics, and immersive environments – the 'second self' (Turkle), the body (Stone, Bukatman, Hayles), feminism and sexuality (Haraway, Balsamo, Plant), race and ethnicity have often been overlooked in this history. Research by Anna Everett, Guillermo Gómez-Peña, Paul D. Miller (aka DJ Spooky That Subliminal Kid), Alondra Nelson, Kalí Tal, Alexander G. Weheliye and others, promises to center questions of race and ethnicity within the vast expanse of new media theory and history. Critical of the Internet as a 'race-less space' where identities can be 'tried on', exchanged, rejected, recreated, or occupied at the speed of a mouse click, Nakamura insists that 'the choice to enact oneself as a samurai warrior in LambdaMOO constitutes identity tourism that allows a player to appropriate an Asian racial identity without any of the risks associated with being a racial minority in real life'.

# Play List

Afrika Bambaataa and the Soul Sonic Force. *Dont Stop … Planet Rock (92 remix)*. Tommy Boy (1992). CD.

Anzaldúa, Gloria (1987) *Borderlands: The New Mestiza = La Frontera*. San Francisco: Spinsters/Aunt Lute.

Balsamo, Anne (1996) *Technologies of the Gendered Body: Reading Cyborg Women*. Durham, NC: Duke University Press.

Borden, Iain (2001) *Skateboarding, Space and the City: Architecture and the Body*. Oxford: Berg.

Bukatman, Scott (1993) *Terminal Identity: The Virtual Subject in Post-Modern Science Fiction*. Durham, NC: Duke University Press.

Bull, Michael (2000) *Sounding Out the City: Personal Stereos and the Management of Everyday Life*. Oxford: Berg.

Cohen, Phil (1972) 'Subcultural Conflict and Working Class Community', *Working Papers in Cultural Studies* 2, University of Birmingham: Centre for Contemporary Cultural Studies.

Davis, Mike (1990) *City of Quartz: Excavating the Future of Los Angeles*. London: Verso.

Davis, Mike (2001) *Magical Urbanism: Latinos Reinventing the US City*. London: Verso.

Delany, Samuel R. (1999) *Times Square Red Times Square Blue*. New York: New York University Press.

Everett, Anna (2005) *Digital Diaporas: The Race for Cyberspace*. Albany, NY: SUNY Press.

Fiske, John (1989) *Reading the Popular*. London: Unwin Hyman.

Flores, Juan (2000) *From Bomba to Hip-Hop: Puerto Rican Culture and Latino Identity*. New York: Columbia University Press.

Foucault, Michel (1986) 'Of Other Spaces', *Diacritics* (Spring): 22–7.

Fyfe, Nicholas R. (1998) *Images of the Street: Planning, Identity and Control in Public Space*. London: Routledge.

Gómez-Peña, Guillermo (2000) 'The Virtual Barrio @ The Other Frontier (or the Chicano *interneta*)' in *Electronic Media and Technoculture*. John Thornton Caldwell (ed) New Brunswick, NJ: Rutgers University Press.

Haraway, Donna J. (1991) *Simians, Cyborgs, and Women: The Reinvention of Nature*. London: Routledge.

Hayles, N. Katherine (1999) *How We Became Posthuman: Virtual Bodies in Cybernetics, Literature, and Informatics*. Chicago: University of Chicago Press.

Humphreys, Laud (1970) *Tearoom Trade: Impersonal Sex in Public Places*. Chicago: Aldine.

Ingram, Gordon Brent (1997) *Queers in Space: Communities, Public Places, Sites of Resistance*. Seattle, WA: Bay Press, 1997.

Keith, Michael and Pile, Steve (eds) (1993) *Place and the Politics of Identity*. London: Routledge.

Kelley, Robin D. G. (1994) *Race Rebels: Culture, Politics, and the Black Working Class*. New York: The Free Press.

Lipsitz, George (1990) *Time Passages: Collective Memory and American Popular Culture*. Minneapolis, MN: University of Minnesota Press.

McRobbie, Angela and Garber, Jenny (1976) 'Girls and Subcultures' in Hall, Stuart and Jefferson, Tony (eds.) (1993) *Resistance Through Rituals: Youth Subcultures in Post-War Britain*. London: Routledge. (First published in 1976 as *Working Papers in Cultural Studies* 7/8).

Massey, Doreen (1994) *Space, Place, and Culture*. Minneapolis, MN: University of Minnesota Press.

Miller, Paul D. (2004) *Rhythm Science*. Cambridge, MA: MIT Press.

Morris, Meaghan (1992) 'On the Beach' in Lawrence Grossberg et al. *Cultural Studies*. London: Routledge.

Morris, Meaghan (1998) *Too Soon Too Late: History in Popular Culture*. Bloomington, IN: Indiana University Press.

Nelson, Alondra (ed.) (2002) 'Afrofuturism: Special Themed Issue.' *Social Text* 71 (Summer) 2002.

Nelson, Alondra et al. (ed.) (2001) *Technicolor: Race, Technology, and Everyday Life*. New York: New York University Press.

Ozomatli. (1998) *Ozomatli*. CD. Almo Sounds.

Ozomatli. (2001) *Embrace the Chaos*. CD. Almo Sounds.

Parliament. (1976) *Mothership Connection*. CD. Polygram.

Peiss, Kathy (1986) *Cheap Amusements: Working Women and Leisure in Turn-of-the-Century New York*. Philadelphia, PA: Temple University Press.

Plant, Sadie (1997) *Zeros and Ones: Digital Women and the New Technoculture*. London: Doubleday.

Polsky, Ned (1967) *Hustlers, Beats, and Others*. New York: Anchor Books.

Roach, Joseph (1996) *Cities of the Dead: Circum-Atlantic Performance*. New York: Columbia University Press.

Rose, Tricia (1994) *Black Noise: Rap Music and Black Culture in Contemporary America*. Hanover & London: Wesleyan University Press.

Ross, Kristin (1996) 'Streetwise: The French Invention of Everyday Life', *Parallax* 2 (February): 67–76.

Skelton, Tracey and Valentine, Gill (eds) (1997) *Cool Places: Geographies of Youth Culture*. London: Routledge.

Sorkin, Michael (ed.) (1992) *Variations on a Theme Park: The New American City and the End of Public Space*. New York: Hill and Wang.

Spigel, Lynn (2001) *Welcome to the Dreamhouse: Popular Media and Postwar Suburbs*. Durham, NC: Duke University Press.

Stone, Allucquère Rosanne (1995) *The War of Desire and Technology at the Close of the Mechanical Age*. Cambridge, MA: MIT University Press.

Straw, Will (1997) '"Organized Disorder": The Changing Space of the Record Shop' in Steve Redhead et al. (ed.) *The Clubcultures Reader: Readings in Popular Cultural Studies*. Oxford: Blackwell Publishing.

Tal, Kalí (1996) 'The Unbearable Whiteness of Being: African American Critical Theory and Cyberculture' Online at http://www.kalital.com/Text/Writing/Whitenes.html.

Thornton, Sarah (1996) *Club Cultures: Music, Media and Subcultural Capital*. Hanover & London: Wesleyan University Press.

Turkle, Sherry (1995) *Life on the Screen: Identity in the Age of the Internet*. New York: Simon and Schuster.

Wachs, Martin and Crawford, Margaret (eds) (1992) *The Car and the City: The Automobile, the Built-environment, and Daily Urban Life*. Ann Arbor, MI: University of Michigan Press.

# Chapter 35

# Michel de Certeau

## Walking in the City

Seeing Manhattan from the 110th floor of the World Trade Center. Beneath the haze stirred up by the winds, the urban island, a sea in the middle of the sea, lifts up the skyscrapers over Wall Street, sinks down at Greenwich, then rises again to the crests of Midtown, quietly passes over Central Park and finally undulates off into the distance beyond Harlem. A wave of verticals. Its agitation is momentarily arrested by vision. The gigantic mass is immobilized before the eyes. It is transformed into a texturology in which extremes coincide – extremes of ambition and degradation, brutal oppositions of races and styles, contrasts between yesterday's buildings, already transformed into trash cans, and today's urban irruptions that block out its space. Unlike Rome, New York has never learned the art of growing old by playing on all its pasts. Its present invents itself, from hour to hour, in the act of throwing away its previous accomplishments and challenging the future. A city composed of paroxysmal places in monumental reliefs. The spectator can read in it a universe that is constantly exploding. In it are inscribed the architectural figures of the *coincidatio oppositorum* formerly drawn in miniatures and mystical textures. On this stage of concrete, steel and glass, cut out between two oceans (the Atlantic and the American) by a frigid body of water, the tallest letters in the world compose a gigantic rhetoric of excess in both expenditure and production.[1]

### Voyeurs or Walkers

To what erotics of knowledge does the ecstasy of reading such a cosmos belong? Having taken a voluptuous pleasure in it, I wonder what is the source of this

From: Michel de Certeau, *The Practice of Everyday Life*. Berkeley, CA: University of California Press, 1984.

pleasure of 'seeing the whole,' of looking down on, totalizing the most immoderate of human texts.

To be lifted to the summit of the World Trade Center is to be lifted out of the city's grasp. One's body is no longer clasped by the streets that turn and return it according to an anonymous law; nor is it possessed, whether as player or played, by the rumble of so many differences and by the nervousness of New York traffic. When one goes up there, he leaves behind the mass that carries off and mixes up in itself any identity of authors or spectators. An Icarus flying above these waters, he can ignore the devices of Daedalus in mobile and endless labyrinths far below. His elevation transfigures him into a voyeur. It puts him at a distance. It transforms the bewitching world by which one was 'possessed' into a text that lies before one's eyes. It allows one to read it, to be a solar Eye, looking down like a god. The exaltation of a scopic and gnostic drive: the fiction of knowledge is related to this lust to be a viewpoint and nothing more.

Must one finally fall back into the dark space where crowds move back and forth, crowds that, though visible from on high, are themselves unable to see down below? An Icarian fall. On the 110th floor, a poster, sphinx-like, addresses an enigmatic message to the pedestrian who is for an instant transformed into a visionary: *It's hard to be down when you're up*.

The desire to see the city preceded the means of satisfying it. Medieval or Renaissance painters represented the city as seen in a perspective that no eye had yet enjoyed.[2] This fiction already made the medieval spectator into a celestial eye. It created gods. Have things changed since technical procedures have organized an 'all-seeing power'?[3] The totalizing eye imagined by the painters of earlier times lives on in our achievements. The same scopic drive haunts users of architectural productions by materializing today the utopia that yesterday was only painted. The 1370 foot high tower that serves as a prow for Manhattan continues to construct the fiction that creates readers, makes the complexity of the city readable, and immobilizes its opaque mobility in a transparent text.

Is the immense texturology spread out before one's eyes anything more than a representation, an optical artifact? It is the analogue of the facsimile produced, through a projection that is a way of keeping aloof, by the space planner urbanist, city planner or cartographer. The panorama-city is a 'theoretical' (that is, visual) simulacrum, in short a picture, whose condition of possibility is an oblivion and a misunderstanding of practices The voyeur-god created by this fiction, who, like Schreber's God, knows only cadavers,[4] must disentangle himself from the murky intertwining daily behaviors and make himself alien to them.

The ordinary practitioners of the city live 'down below,' below the thresholds at which visibility begins. They walk – an elementary form of this experience of the city; they are walkers, *Wandersmänner,* whose bodies follow the thicks and thins of an urban 'text' they write without being able to read it. These practitioners make use of spaces that cannot be seen; their knowledge of them is as blind as that of lovers in each other's arms. The paths that correspond in this intertwining, unrecognized poems in which each body is an element signed by many others, elude legibility. It is as though the practices organizing a bustling city were characterized by their blindness.[5] The networks of these moving, intersecting writings compose a manifold story that has neither author nor spectator, shaped out of fragments of trajectories and alterations of spaces: in relation to representations, it remains daily and indefinitely other.

Escaping the imaginary totalizations produced by the eye, the everyday has a certain strangeness that does not surface, or whose surface is only its upper limit, outlining itself against the visible. Within this ensemble, I shall try to locate the practices that are foreign to the 'geometrical' or 'geographical' space of visual, panoptic, or theoretical constructions. These practices of space refer to a specific form of *operations* ('ways of operating'), to 'another spatiality'[6] (an 'anthropological,' poetic and mythic experience of space), and to an *opaque and blind* mobility characteristic of the bustling city. A *migrational,* or metaphorical, city thus slips into the clear text of the planned and readable city.

## 1. From the Concept of the City to Urban Practices

The World Trade Center is only the most monumental figure of Western urban development. The atopia-utopia of optical knowledge has long had the ambition of surmounting and articulating the contradictions arising from urban agglomeration. It is a question of managing a growth of human agglomeration or accumulation. 'The city is a huge monastery,' said Erasmus. Perspective vision and prospective vision constitute the twofold projection of an opaque past and an uncertain future onto a surface that can be dealt with. They inaugurate (in the sixteenth century?) the transformation of the urban *fact* into the *concept* of a city. Long before the concept itself gives rise to a particular figure of history, it assumes that this fact can be dealt with as a unity determined by an urbanistic *ratio*. Linking the city to the concept never makes them identical, but it plays on their progressive symbiosis: to plan a city is both to *think the very plurality* of the real and to make that way of thinking the plural *effective*; it is to know how to articulate it and be able to do it.

### An operational concept?

The 'city' founded by utopian and urbanistic discourse[7] is defined by the possibility of a threefold operation:

1.  The production of its *own* space (*un espace propre*): rational organization must thus repress all the physical, mental and political pollutions that would compromise it;
2.  the substitution of a nowhen, or of a synchronic system, for the indeterminable and stubborn resistances offered by traditions; univocal scientific strategies, made possible by the flattening out of all the data in a plane projection, must replace the tactics of users who take advantage of 'opportunities' and who, through these trap-events, these lapses in visibility, reproduce the opacities of history everywhere;
3.  finally, the creation of a *universal* and anonymous *subject* which is the city itself: it gradually becomes possible to attribute to it, as to its political model, Hobbes' State, all the functions and predicates that were previously scattered

and assigned to many different real subjects – groups, associations, or individuals. 'The city,' like a proper name, thus provides a way of conceiving and constructing space on the basis of a finite number of stable, isolatable, and interconnected properties.

Administration is combined with a process of elimination in this place organized by 'speculative' and classificatory operations.[8] On the one hand, there is a differentiation and redistribution of the parts and functions of the city, as a result of inversions, displacements, accumulations, etc.; on the other there is a rejection of everything that is not capable of being dealt with in this way and so constitutes the 'waste products' of a functionalist administration (abnormality, deviance, illness, death, etc.). To be sure, progress allows an increasing number of these waste products to be reintroduced into administrative circuits and transforms even deficiencies (in health, security, etc.) into ways of making the networks of order denser. But in reality, it repeatedly produces effects contrary to those at which it aims: the profit system generates a loss which, in the multiple forms of wretchedness and poverty outside the system and of waste inside it, constantly turns production into 'expenditure.' Moreover, the rationalization of the city leads to its mythification in strategic discourses, which are calculations based on the hypothesis or the necessity of its destruction in order to arrive at a final decision.[9] Finally, the functionalist organization, by privileging progress (i.e., time), causes the condition of its own possibility – space itself – to be forgotten; space thus becomes the blind spot in a scientific and political technology. This is the way in which the Concept-city functions; a place of transformations and appropriations, the object of various kinds of interference but also a subject that is constantly enriched by new attributes, it is simultaneously the machinery and the hero of modernity.

Today, whatever the avatars of this concept may have been, we have to acknowledge that if in discourse the city serves as a totalizing and almost mythical landmark for socioeconomic and political strategies, urban life increasingly permits the re-emergence of the element that the urbanistic project excluded. The language of power is in itself 'urbanizing,' but the city is left prey to contradictory movements that counter-balance and combine themselves outside the reach of panoptic power. The city becomes the dominant theme in political legends, but it is no longer a field of programmed and regulated operations. Beneath the discourses that ideologize the city, the ruses and combinations of powers that have no readable identity proliferate; without points where one can take hold of them, without rational transparency, they are impossible to administer.

## The return of practices

The Concept-city is decaying. Does that mean that the illness afflicting both the rationality that founded it and its professionals afflicts the urban populations as well? Perhaps cities are deteriorating along with the procedures that organized them. But we must be careful here. The ministers of knowledge have always assumed that the whole universe was threatened by the very changes that affected their ideologies and their positions. They transmute the misfortune of their theories into theories of misfortune. When they transform their bewilderment into 'catastrophes,' when they seek to enclose the people in the 'panic' of their discourses, are they once more necessarily right?

Rather than remaining within the field of a discourse that upholds its privilege by inverting its content (speaking of catastrophe and no longer of progress), one can try another path: one can try another path: one can analyze the microbe-like, singular and plural practices which an urbanistic system was supposed to administer or suppress, but which have outlived its decay; one can follow the swarming activity of these procedures that, far from being regulated or eliminated by panoptic administration, have reinforced themselves in a proliferating illegitimacy, developed and insinuated themselves into the networks of surveillance, and combined in accord with unreadable but stable tactics to the point of constituting everyday regulations and surreptitious creativities that are merely concealed by the frantic mechanisms and discourses of the observational organization.

This pathway could be inscribed as a consequence, but also as the reciprocal, of Foucault's analysis of the structures of power. He moved it in the direction of mechanisms and technical procedures, 'minor instrumentalities' capable, merely by their organization of 'details,' of transforming a human multiplicity into a 'disciplinary' society and of managing, differentiating, classifying, and hierarchizing all deviances concerning apprenticeship, health, justice, the army, or work,[10] 'These often miniscule ruses of discipline,' these 'minor but flawless' mechanisms, draw their efficacy from a relationship between procedures and the space that they redistribute in order to make an 'operator' out of it. But what *spatial practices* correspond, in the area where discipline is manipulated, to these apparatuses that produce a disciplinary space? In the present conjuncture, which is marked by a contradiction between the collective mode of administration and an individual mode of reappropriation, this question is no less important, if one admits that spatial practices in fact secretly structure the determining conditions of social life. I would like to follow out a few of these multiform, resistance, tricky and stubborn procedures that elude discipline without being outside the field in which it is exercised, and which should lead us to a theory of everyday practices, of lived space, of the disquieting familiarity of the city.

## 2. The Chorus of Idle Footsteps

'The goddess can be recognized by her step'

Virgil, *Aeneid*, 1, 405

Their story begins on ground level, with footsteps. They are myriad, but do not compose a series. They cannot be counted because each unit has a qualitative character: a style of tactile apprehension and kinesthetic appropriation. Their swarming mass is an innumerable collection of singularities. Their intertwined paths give their shape to spaces. They weave places together. In that respect, pedestrian movements form one of these 'real systems whose existence in fact makes up the city.'[11] They are not localized; it is rather they that spatialize. They are no more inserted within a container than those Chinese characters speakers sketch out on their hands with their fingertips.

It is true that the operations of walking on can be traced on city maps in such a way as to transcribe their paths (here well-trodden, there very faint) and their trajectories (going this way and not that). But these thick or thin curves only refer, like words, to the absence of what has passed by. Surveys of routes miss what was: the act itself of passing by. The operation of walking, wandering, or 'window shopping,' that is, the activity of passers-by, is transformed into points that draw a totalizing and reversible line on the map. They allow us to grasp only a relic set in the nowhen of a surface of projection. Itself visible, it has the effect of making invisible the operation that made it possible. These fixations constitute procedures for forgetting. The trace left behind is substituted for the practice. It exhibits the (voracious) property that the geographical system has of being able to transform action into legibility, but in doing so it causes a way of being in the world to be forgotten.

## Pedestrian speech acts

A comparison with the speech act will allow us to go further[12] and not limit ourselves to the critique of graphic representations alone, looking from the shores of legibility toward an inaccessible beyond. The act of walking is to the urban system what the speech act is to language or to the statements uttered.[13] At the most elementary level, it has a triple 'enunciative' function: it is a process of *appropriation* of the topographical system on the part of the pedestrian (just as the speaker appropriates and takes on the language); it is a spatial acting-out of the place (just as the speech act is an acoustic acting-out of language); and it implies *relations* among differentiated positions, that is, among pragmatic 'contracts' in the form of movements (just as verbal enunciation is an 'allocution,' 'posits another opposite' the speaker and puts contracts between interlocutors into action).[14] It thus seems possible to give a preliminary definition of walking as a space of enunciation. [...]

Considered from this angle, the pedestrian speech act has three characteristics which distinguish it at the outset from the spatial system: the present, the discrete, the 'phatic.'

First, if it is true that a spatial order organizes an ensemble of possibilities (e.g., by a place in which one can move) and interdictions (e.g., by a wall that prevents one from going further), then the walker actualizes some of these possibilities. In that way, he makes them exist as well as emerge. But he also moves them about and he invents others, since the crossing, drifting away, or improvisation of walking privilege, transform or abandon spatial elements. Thus Charlie Chaplin multiplies the possibilities of his cane: he does other things with the same thing and he goes beyond the limits that the determinants of the object set on its utilization. In the same way, the walker transforms each spatial signifier into something else. And if on the one hand he actualizes only a few of the possibilities fixed by the constructed order (he goes only here and not there), on the other he increases the number of possibilities (for example, by creating shortcuts and detours) and prohibitions (for example, he forbids himself to take paths generally considered accessible or even obligatory). He thus makes a selection. [...]

In the framework of enunciation, the walker constitutes, in relation to his position, both a near and a far, a *here* and a *there*. To the fact that the adverbs *here* and *there* are the indicators of the locutionary seat in verbal communication[15] – a coincidence that reinforces the parallelism letween linguistic and pedestrian enunciation – we must add that this location (*here* – *there*) (necessarily implied by walking and indicative of present appropriation of space by an 'I') also has the function of introducing an other in relation to this 'I' and of thus establishing a conjunctive and disjunctive articulation of places. Walking, which alternately follows a path and has followers, creates a mobile organicity in the environment, a sequence of phatic *topoi*. And if it is true that the phatic function, which is an effort to ensure communication, is already characteristic of the language of talking birds, just as it constitutes the 'first verbal function acquired by children,' it is not surprising that it also gambols, goes on all fours, dances, and walks about, with a light or heavy step, like a series of 'hellos' in an echoing labyrinth, anterior or parallel to informative speech.

The modalities of pedestrian enunciation which a plane representation on a map brings out could be analyzed. They include the kinds of relationship this enunciation entertains with particular paths (or 'statements') by according them a truth value ('alethic' modalities of the necessary, the impossible, the possible, or the contingent), an epistemological value ('epistemic' modalities of the certain, the excluded, the plausible, or the questionable) or finally an ethical or legal value ('deontic' modalities of the obligatory, the forbidden, the permitted, or the optional).[16] Walking affirms, suspects, tries out, transgresses, respects, etc., the trajectories it 'speaks.' All the modalities sing a part in this chorus, changing from step to step, stepping in through proportions, sequences, and intensities which vary according to the time, the path taken and the walker. These enunciatory operations are of an unlimited diversity. They therefore cannot be reduced to their graphic trail.

## Walking rhetorics

The walking of passers-by offers a series of turns (*tours*) and detours that can be compared to 'turns of phrase' or 'stylistic figures.' There is a rhetoric of walking. The art of 'turning' phrases finds an equivalent in an art of composing a path (*tourner un parcours*). Like ordinary language,[17] this art implies and combines styles and uses. *Style* specifies 'a linguistic structure that manifests on the symbolic level ... an individual's fundamental way of being in the world';[18] it connotes a singular. Use defines the social phenomenon through which a system of communication manifests itself in actual fact; it refers to a norm. Style and use both have to do with a 'way of operating' (of speaking, walking, etc.), but style involves a peculiar processing of the symbolic, while use refers to elements of a code. They intersect to form a style of use, a way of being and a way of operating. [19]

In introducing the notion of a 'residing rhetoric' ('*rhétorique habitante*'), the fertile pathway opened up by A. Médam [20] and systematized by S. Ostrowetsky [21] and J.-F. Augoyard,[22] we assume that the 'tropes' catalogued by rhetoric furnish models and hypotheses for the analysis of ways of appropriating places. Two postulates seem to me to underlie the validity of this application: 1) it is assumed that practices of space also correspond to manipulations of the basic elements of a constructed order; 2) it is assumed that they are, like the tropes in rhetoric, deviations relative to a sort of 'literal meaning' defined by the urbanistic system. There would thus be a homology between verbal figures and the figures of walking (a stylized selection among the latter is already found in the figures of dancing) insofar as both consist in 'treatments' or operations bearing on isolatable units,[23] and in 'ambiguous dispositions' that divert and displace meaning in the direction of equivocalness[24] in the way a tremulous image confuses and multiplies the photographed object. In these two modes, the analogy can be accepted. I would add that the geometrical space of urbanists and architects seems to have the status of the 'proper meaning' constructed by grammarians and linguists in order to have a normal and normative level to which they can compare the drifting of 'figurative' language. In reality, this faceless 'proper' meaning (*ce 'propre' sans figure*) cannot be found in current use, whether verbal or pedestrian; it is merely the fiction produced by a use that is also particular, the metalinguistic use of science that distinguishes itself by that very distinction.[25]

The long poem of walking manipulates spatial organizations, no matter how panoptic they may be: it is neither foreign to them (it can take place only within them) nor in conformity with them (it does not receive its identity from them). It creates shadows and ambiguities within them. It inserts its multitudinous references and citations into them (social models, cultural mores, personal factors). Within them it is itself the effect of successive encounters and occasions that constantly alter it and make it the other's blazon: in other words, it is like a peddler, carrying something surprising, transverse or attractive compared with the usual choice. These diverse aspects provide the basis of a rhetoric. They can even be said to define it.

By analyzing this 'modern art of everyday expression' as it appears in accounts of spatial practices,[26] J.-F. Augoyard discerns in it two especially fundamental stylistic figures: synecdoche and asyndeton. The predominance of these two figures seems to me to indicate, in relation to two complementary poles, a formal structure of these practices. *Synecdoche* consists in 'using a word in a sense which is part of another meaning of the same word.'[27] In essence, it names a part instead of the whole which includes it. Thus 'sail' is taken for 'ship' in the expression 'a fleet of fifty sails'; in the same way, a brick shelter or a hill is taken for the park in the narration of a trajectory. *Asyndeton* is the suppression of linking words such as conjunctions and adverbs, either within a sentence or between sentences. In the same way, in walking it selects and fragments the space traversed; it skips over links and whole parts that it omits. From this point of view, every walk constantly leaps, or skips like a child, hopping on one foot. It practices the ellipsis of conjunctive *loci*.

In reality, these two pedestrian figures are related. Synecdoche expands a spatial element in order to make it play the role of a 'more' (a totality) and take its place (the bicycle or the piece of furniture in a store window stands for a whole street or neighborhood). Asyndeton, by elision, creates a 'less,' opens gaps in the spatial continuum, and retains only selected parts of it that amount almost to relics. Synecdoche replaces totalities by fragments (a *less* in the place of a *more*); asyndeton disconnects them by eliminating the conjunctive or the consecutive (nothing in place of something). Synecdoche makes more dense: it amplifies the detail and miniaturizes the whole. Asyndeton cuts out: it undoes continuity and undercuts its plausibility. A space treated in this way and shaped by practices is transformed into enlarged singularities and separate islands.[28] Through these swellings, shrinkings, and fragmentations, that is, through these rhetorical operations a spatial phrasing of an analogical (composed of juxtaposed citations) and elliptical (made of gaps, lapses, and allusions) type is created. For the technological system of a coherent and totalizing space that is 'linked' and simultaneous, the figures of pedestrian rhetoric substitute trajectories that have a mythical structure, at least if one understands by 'myth' a discourse relative to the place/nowhere (or origin) of concrete existence, a story jerry-built out of elements taken from common sayings, an allusive and fragmentary story whose gaps mesh with the social practices it symbolizes.

Figures are the acts of this stylistic metamorphosis of space. Or rather, as Rilke puts it, they are moving 'trees of gestures.' They move even the rigid and contrived territories of the medico-pedagogical institute in which retarded children find a place to play and dance their 'spatial stories.'[29] These 'trees of gestures' are in movement everywhere. Their forests walk through the streets. They transform the scene, but they cannot be fixed in a certain place by images. If in spite of that an illustration were required, we could mention the fleeting images, yellowish-green and metallic blue calligraphies that howl without raising their voices and emblazon themselves on the subterranean passages of the city, 'embroideries' composed of letters and numbers, perfect gestures of violence painted with a pistol, Shivas made of written characters, dancing graphics whose fleeting apparitions are accompanied by the rumble of subway trains: New York graffiti.

If it is true that *forests of gestures* are manifest in the streets, their movement cannot be captured in a picture, nor can the meaning of their movements be circumscribed in a text. Their rhetorical transplantation carries away and displaces the analytical, coherent proper meanings of urbanism; it constitutes a 'wandering of the semantic'[30] produced by masses that make some parts of the city disappear and exaggerate others, distorting it, fragmenting it, and diverting it from its immobile order.

## 3. Myths: What 'Makes Things Go'

The figures of these movements (synecdoches, ellipses, etc.) characterize both a 'symbolic order of the unconscious' and 'certain typical processes of subjectivity manifested in discourse.'[31] The similarity between 'discourse'[32] and dreams[33] has to do with their use of the same 'stylistic procedures'; it therefore includes pedestrian practices as well. The 'ancient catalog of tropes' that from Freud to Benveniste has furnished an appropriate inventory for the rhetoric of the first two registers of expression is equally valid for the third. If there is a parallelism, it is not only because enunciation is dominant in these three areas, but also because its discursive (verbalized, dreamed, or walked) development is organized as a relation between the *place* from which it proceeds (an origin) and the nowhere it produces (a way of 'going by').

From this point of view, after having compared pedestrian processes to linguistic formations, we can bring them back down in the direction of oneiric figuration, or at least discover on that other side what, in a spatial practice, is inseparable from the dreamed place. To walk is to lack a place. It is the indefinite process of being absent and in search of a proper. The moving about that the city multiplies and concentrates makes the city itself an immense social experience of lacking a place – an experience that is, to be sure, broken up into countless tiny deportations (displacements and walks), compensated for by the relationships and intersections of these exoduses that intertwine and create an urban fabric, and placed under the sign of what ought to be, ultimately, the, place but is only a name, the City. The identity furnished by this place is all the more symbolic (named) because, in spite of the inequality of its citizens' positions and profits, there is only a pullulation of passer-by, a network of residences temporarily appropriated by pedestrian traffic, a shuffling among pretenses of the proper, a universe of rented spaces haunted by a nowhere or by dreamed-of places.

## Names and symbols

An indication of the relationship that spatial practices entertain with that absence is furnished precisely by their manipulations of and with 'proper' names. The relationships between the direction of a walk (*le sens de la marche*) and the meaning of words (*le sens des mots*) situate two sorts of apparently contrary movements, one extrovert (to walk is to go outside), the other introvert (a mobility under the stability of the signifier). Walking is in fact determined by semantic tropisms; it is attracted and repelled by nominations whose meaning is not clear, whereas the city, for its part, is transformed for many people into a 'desert' in which the meaningless, indeed the terrifying, no longer takes the form of shadows but becomes, as in Genet's plays, an implacable light that produces this urban text without obscurities, which is created by a technocratic power everywhere and which puts the city-dweller under control (under the control of what? No one knows): 'The city keeps us under its gaze, which one cannot bear without feeling dizzy,' says a resident of Rouen.[34] In the spaces brutally lit by an alien reason, proper names carve out pockets of hidden and familiar meanings. They 'make sense'; in other words, they are the impetus of movements, like vocations and calls that turn or divert an itinerary by giving it a meaning (or a direction) (*sens*) that was previously unforeseen. These names create a nowhere in places; they change them into passages.

A friend who lives in the city of Sevres drifts, when he is in Paris, toward the rue des Saints-*Pères* and the rue de *Sévres,* even though he is going to see his mother in another part of town; these names articulate a sentence that his steps compose without his knowing it. Numbered streets and street numbers (112th St., or 9 rue Saint-Charles) orient the magnetic field of trajectories just as they can haunt dreams. Another friend unconsciously represses the streets which have names and, by this fact, transmit her – orders or identities in the same way as summonses and classifications; she goes instead along paths that have no name or signature. But her walking is thus still controlled negatively by proper names.

What is it then that they spell out? Disposed in constellations that hierarchize and semantically order the surface of the city, operating chronological arrangements and historical justifications, these words (*Borrégo, Botzaris, Bougainville ...*) slowly lose, like worn coins, the value engraved on them, but their ability to signify outlives its first definition. *Saints-Pères, Corentin Celton, Red Square ...* these names make themselves available to the diverse meanings given them by passers-by; they detach themselves from the places they were supposed to define and serve as imaginary meeting-points on itineraries which, as metaphors, they determine for reasons that are foreign to their original value but may be recognized or not by passers-by. A strange toponymy that is detached from actual places and flies high over the city like a foggy geography of 'meanings' held in suspension, directing the physical deambulations below: *Place de l'Étoile, Concorde, Poissonnière* ... These constellations of names provide traffic patterns; they are stars directing itineraries. 'The Place de la Concorde does not exist,' Malaparte said, 'it is an idea.'[35] It is much more than an 'idea.' A whole series of comparisons would be necessary to account for the magical powers proper names enjoy. They seem to be carried as emblems by the travellers they direct and simultaneously decorate.

Linking acts and footsteps, opening meanings and directions, these words operate in the name of an emptying-out and wearing-away of their primary role. They become liberated spaces that can be occupied. A rich indetermination gives them, by means of a semantic rarefaction, the function of articulating a second, poetic geography on top of the geography of the literal, forbidden or permitted meaning. They insinuate other routes into the functionalist and historical order of movement. Walking follows them; 'I fill this great empty space with a beautiful name.'[36] People are put in motion by the remaining relics of meaning, and sometimes by their waste products, the inverted remainders of great ambitions.[37] Things that amount to nothing, or almost nothing, sym-bolize and orient walkers' steps: names that have ceased precisely to be 'proper.'

In these symbolizing kernels three distinct (but connected) functions of the relations between spatial and signifying practices are indicated (and perhaps founded): the *believable,* the *memorable,* and *the primitive.* They designate what 'authorizes' (or makes possible or credible) spatial appropriations, what is repeated in them (or is recalled in them) from a silent and withdrawn memory, and what is structured in them and continues to be signed by an in-fantile (*in-fans*) origin. These three symbolic mechanisms organize the topoi of a discourse on/of the city (legend, memory, and dream) in a way that also eludes urbanistic systematicity. They can already be recognized in the functions of proper names: they make habitable or believable the place that they clothe with a word (by emptying themselves of their classifying power, they acquire that of 'permitting' something else); they recall or suggest phantoms (the dead who are supposed to have disappeared) that still move about, concealed in gestures and in bodies in motion; and, by naming, that is, by imposing an injunction proceeding from the other (a story) and by altering functionalist identity by detaching themselves from it, they create in the place itself that erosion or nowhere that the law of the other carves out within it.

## Notes

1. See Alain Médam's admirable 'New York City,' *Les Temps modernes,* August–September 1976, 15–33; and the same author's *New York Terminal* (Paris: Galilée, 1977).

2. See H. Lavedan, *Les Représentations des villes dans l'art du Moyen Age* (Paris: Van Oest, 1942); R. Wittkower, *Architectural Principles in the Age of Humanism* (New York: Norton, 1962); L. Marin, *Utopiques: Jeux d'espaces* (Paris: Minuit, 1973); etc.

3. M. Foucault, 'L'Oeil du pouvoir,' in J. Bentham, *Le Panoptique* (Paris: Belfond, 1977), 16.

4. D.P. Schreber, *Mémoires d'un névropathe* (Paris: Seuil, 1975), 41, 60, etc.

5. Descartes, in his *Regulae,* had already made the blind man the guarantor of the knowledge of things and places against the illusions and deceptions of vision.

6. M. Merleau-Ponty, *Phénoménologie de la perception* (Paris: Gallimard Tel, 1976), 332–333.

7. See F. Choay, 'Figures d'un discours inconnu,' *Critique,* April 1973, 293–317.

8. Urbanistic techniques, which classify things spatially, can be related to the tradition of the 'art of memory': see Frances A. Yates, *The Art of Memory* (London: Routledge and Kegan Paul, 1966). The ability to produce a spatial organization of knowledge (with 'places' assigned to each type of 'figure' or 'function') develops its procedures on the basis of this 'art.' It determines utopias and can be recognized even in Bentham's *Panopticon.* Such a form remains stable in spite of the diversity of its contents (past, future, present) and its projects (conserving or creating) relative to changes in the status of knowledge.

9. See André Glucksmann, 'Le Totalitarisme en effet,' *Traverses,* No. 9, 1977, 34–40.

10. M. Foucault, *Surveiller et punir* (Paris: Gallimard, 1975); *Discipline and Punish,* trans. A. Sheridan (New York: Pantheon, 1977).

11. Ch. Alexander, 'La Cité semi-treillis, mais non arbre,' *Architecture, Mouvement, Continuité,* 1967.

12. See R. Barthes's remarks in *Architecture d'aujourd'hui.* No. 153, December 1970 – January 1971, 11–13: 'We speak our city ... merely by inhabiting it, walking through it, looking at it.' Cf. C. Soucy, *L'Image du centre dans quatre romans contemporains* (Paris: CSU, 1971), 6–15.

13. See the numerous studies devoted to the subject since J. Searle's 'What is a Speech Act?' in *Philosophy in America,* ed. Max Black (London: Allen & Unwin; Ithaca, N.Y.: Cornell University Press, 1965), 221–239.

14. E. Benveniste, *Problèmes de linguistique générale* (Paris: Gallimard, 1974), 11, 79–88, etc.

15. R. Barthes, quoted in C. Soucy, *L'Image du centre,* 10.

16. '*Here* and *now* delimit the spatial and temporal instance coextensive and contemporary with the present instance of discourse containing I': E. Benveniste, *Problèmes de linguistique générale* (*Paris:* Gallimard, 1966), I, p. 253.

17. R. Jakobson, *Essais de linguistique générale* (Paris: Seuil Points, 1970), p. 217.

18. On modalities, see H. Parrel, *La Pragmatique des modalités* (Urbino: Centro di Semiotica, 1975); A.R. White, *Modal Thinking* (Ithaca, N.Y.: Cornell University Press, 1975).

19. See Paul Lemaire's analyses, *Les Signes sauvages. Une Philosophie du langage ordinaire* (Ottawa: Université d'Ottawa et Université Saint-Paul, 1981), in particular the introduction.

20. A.J. Greimas, 'Linguistique statistique et linguistique structurale,' *Le Français moderne,* October 1962, 245.

21. In a neighboring field, rhetoric and poetics in the gestural language of mute people, I am grateful to E.S. Klima of the University of California, San Diego and U. Bellugi, 'Poetry and Song in a Language without Sound,' an unpublished paper; see also Klima, 'The Linguistic Symbol with and without Sound,' in *The Role of Speech in Language,* ed. J. Kavanagh and J.E. Cuttings (Cambridge, Mass.: MIT, 1975).

22. *Conscience de la ville* (Paris: Anthropos, 1977).

23. See Ostrowetsky, 'Logiques du lieu,' in *Sémiotique de l'espace* (Paris: Denoël-Gonthier Médiations, 1979), 155–173.

24. *Pas à pas. Essai sur le cheminement quotidien en milieu urbain* (Paris: Seuil, 1979).

25. In his analysis of culinary practices, P. Bourdieu regards as decisive not the ingredients but the way in which they are prepared and used: 'Le Sens pratique,' *Actes de la recherche en sciences sociales,* February 1976, 77.

26. J. Sumpf, *Introduction à la stylistique du français* (Paris: Larousse, 1971), 87.

27. On the 'theory of the proper,' see J. Derrida, *Marges de la philosophie* (Paris: Minuit, 1972), 247–324; *Margins of Philosophy,* trans. A. Bass (Chicago: University of Chicago Press, 1982).

28. Augoyard, *Pas à pas.*

29. T. Todorov, 'Synecdoques,' *Communications,* No. 16 (1970), 30. See also P. Fontanier, *Les Figures du discours* (Paris: Flammarion, 1968), 87–97; J. Dubois et al., *Rhétorique générale* (Paris: Larousse, 1970), 102–112.

30. On this space that practices organize into 'islands,' see P. Bourdieu, *Esquisse d'une théorie de la pratique* (Genève: Droz, 1972), 215, etc.; 'Le Sens pratique,' 51–52.

31. See Anne Baldassari and Michel Joubert, *Pratiques relationnelles des enfants à l'espace et institution* (Paris: CRECELE-CORDES, 1976); and by the same authors, 'Ce qui se trame,' *Parallèles,* No. 1, June 1976.

32. Derrida, *Marges,* 287, on metaphor.

33. Benveniste, *Problèmes,* I, 86–87.

34. For Benveniste, 'discourse is language considered as assumed by the person who is speaking and in the condition of intersubjectivity' (ibid., 266).

35. See for example S. Freud, *The Interpretation of Dreams,* trans. J. Strachey (New York: Basic Books, 1955), Chapter VI, § 1–4, on condensation and displacement, 'processes of figuration' that are proper to 'dreamwork.'

36. Ph. Dard, F. Desbons et al., *La Ville, symbolique en souffrance* (Paris: CEP, 1975), 200.

37. See also, for example, the epigraph in Patrick Modiano, *Place de l'Étoile* (Paris: Gallimard, 1968).

38. Joachim du Bellay, *Regrets,* 189.

39. For example, *Sarcelles,* the name of a great urbanistic ambition (near Paris), has taken on a symbolic value for the inhabitants of the town by becoming in the eyes of France as a whole the example of a total failure. This extreme avatar provides its citizens with the 'prestige' of an exceptional identity.

40. *Superstare*: 'to be above,' as something in addition or superfluous.

41. See F. Lugassy, *Contribution à une psychosociologie de l'espace urbain. L'Habitat et la forêt* (Paris: Recherche urbaine, 1970).

42. Dard, Desbons et al., *La Ville, symbolique en souffrance.*

43. Ibid., 174, 206.

44. C. Lévi-Strauss, *Tristes tropiques* (Paris: Plon, 1955), 434–436; *Tristes tropiques,* trans. J. Russell (New York: Criterion, 1962).

45. One could say the same about the photos brought back from trips, substituted for and turned into legends about the starting place.

46. Terms whose relationships are not thought but postulated as necessary can be said to be symbolic. On this definition of symbolism as a cognitive mechanism characterized by a 'deficit' of thinking, see Dan Sperber, *Le Symbolisme en général* (Paris: Hermann, 1974); *Rethinking Symbolism,* trans. A.L. Morton (Cambridge: Cambridge University Press, 1975).

47. F. Ponge, *La Promenade dans nos serres* (Paris: Gallimard, 1967).

48. A woman living in the Croix-Rousse quarter in Lyon (interview by Pierre Mayol): see *L'Invention du quotidien,* II, *Habiter, cuisiner* (Paris: UGE 10/18, 1980).

49. See *Le Monde* for May 4, 1977.

50. See note 48.

51. See the two analyses provided by Freud in *The Interpretation of Dreams* and *Beyond the Pleasure Principle,* trans. J. Strachey (New York: Liveright, 1980); and also Sami-Ali, *L'Espace imaginaire* (Paris: Gallimard, 1974), 42–64.

52. J. Lacan, 'Le Stade du miroir,' *Écrits* (Paris: Seuil, 1966), 93–100; 'The Mirror Stage,' in *Écrits: A Selection,* trans. A. Sheridan (New York: Norton, 1977).

53. S. Freud, *Inhibitions, Symptoms and Anxiety* (New York: Norton, 1977).

54. V. Kandinsky, *Du spirituel dans l'art* (Paris: Denoël, 1969), 57.

# Chapter 36

# Michael Nevin Willard

# Séance, Tricknowlogy, Skateboarding, and the Space of Youth

In much of Los Angeles, the casual pedestrian was an oddity—or a walking threat to the civic order.

> —Edward Soja, Rebecca Morales, and Goetz Wolff,
> "Urban Restructuring,' *Economic Geography* 59, no.2 (1983)

[If I won the lottery] I'd like to help people who really need it. Like, I'd give to a homeless person before I'd give to a relative or something ... Some people think the homeless deserve to be where they are because they could just get up and get off the street if they wanted it bad enough. But I don't think that way.

> —Daewon Song, skateboarder, in
> *Transworld Skateboarding* 12, no. 9 (1994)

## Angles of history in the City of Angels

Wing Ko and I stand on the corner of Third and Broadway, once-downtown Los Angeles, loitering in the shadows of postmodernism. Behind our backs to the west the new downtown skyline of eclectic history, glass, and aluminum grows upon

From: *Generations of Youth: Youth Cultures and History in Twentieth-century America*. Ed. Joe Austin and Michael Nevin Willard. New York: New York University Press, 1998.

itself as it piles skyward. Hovering over us from atop Bunker Hill, and announcing Los Angeles as a global city, it melts into air.

Wing is a filmmaker and skateboarder. We are waiting for Rodney Mullen, a professional skateboarder, and Socrates Leal, a video maker and skateboarder, who have been on Broadway all day shooting footage for Rodney's segment of the next Plan B skateboard company video. 'Soc' works with Rodney on the skateboarding segments of the video. Wing films the segments for the 'feeling' and storyline of the video. Later Rodney tells me that the 'feeling' of a skate video is crucial these days when there aren't as many contests to differentiate skaters. The tricks that win contests often aren't as good as the tricks in the videos. What with so many good skateboarders all of whom can do the most difficult tricks, it becomes even more important that each skater in a video have an 'identity.'

Today Wing will shoot footage of Rodney carrying his skateboard and walking among the dense crowds who fill the sidewalks along Broadway: families, youth, elderly, mostly working-class, mostly Latino; fewer Asian and Black shoppers; present though much fewer still, lunch-hour, predominantly Anglo business people, though almost never shoppers; equally diverse, all-adult homeless people; and civil servants from the Ronald Reagan office building located a block away on Spring Street.[1]

Across Third Street, on the corner opposite from Wing and me, stands the renovated Bradbury building, anchor of the redevelopment project sometimes known as 'Bunker Hill East,' which appears to be fulfilling Mike Davis's predictions for this corner of Broadway. In his 1990 book *City of Quartz*, he identified Community Redevelopment Agency (CRA) strategies for recolonizing the northern end of Broadway, this 'two way street' that runs south culturally and transnationally all the way to Mexico and back.[2] Along with the Bradbury, the Grand Central Square Market[3] and Apartments and the Million Dollar Theater[4] anchor owner Ira Yellin's Grand Central Square redevelopment plan.[5] Over the last thirty years corporate tenants and urban renewers have abandoned Broadway in favor of insular citadels of higher finance built on the razed and renewed, formerly Filipino, Mexican American, and working-class neighborhoods of Bunker Hill. Now some of these 'off-world' corporate privateers are beginning to return, lured back down to the ground, as lunch-hour tourists[6] – to consume the more diverse, if not more public and democratic, street life of Mexican Americans and immigrant Latinos who have reclaimed Broadway as their own. [...]

On Sunday afternoons, the bustle and hustle remind me of what I think New York must be like, though I imagine that the recently immigrated Latino shoppers may find more similarities to shopping districts in their native countries. The stores on Broadway open right onto the sidewalk, many of them wedged and retrofitted into the abandoned lobbies of the many palatial two thousand-seat movie palaces of early twentieth-century Los Angeles that line Broadway. Now, with *banda* and *ranchera* recordings trumpeting out pop and disco '*ritmos Latinos*' from banks of three-foot-tall speakers positioned on the sidewalks in front of the music and audio equipment shops that dot the street at half-block intervals, shopping on Broadway is less formal than in the early twentieth century. Now Sunday shopping on Broadway is more like a celebration. Families doing their shopping after church are dressed up, but they mix unconcernedly with less formally dressed homeless people and other Sunday strollers, all of whom soak in the music and commotion.

On this day Wing and Rodney work to get a few more shots of Rodney among the crowds of shoppers that will establish his 'identity'[7]. Wing has told me, and I have also learned from reading magazine interviews and watching videos, that Rodney is sometimes known in the skateboarding subculture as a mad scientist, a 'brainiac' who finds more entertainment in doing calculus problems than in hanging out on the beach. All skaters exhibit a high degree of intellectual expertise when they skate. Rodney's is incredibly technical and uniquely inventive.[8]

For example, most skaters execute boardslides using the underside of their decks to slide along the edge of benches, down staircase handrails, or down the slides of concrete that are sometimes built alongside staircases. Rodney, on the other hand, rolls up to the sloped concrete on the side of a staircase and as he ollies onto it, in a pique of inspiration, he flips his board upside down to theorize a version of his trademark 'darkslide' down the concrete. Standing on what is normally the underside of the board to either side of the wheels that now face up, he slides topside down, descending the sloping incline of concrete on the 'dark' black grip tape, only to flip the board over at the last nanosecond of the slide, to land topside up and roll away.[9]

Back on Broadway Wing and Rodney discuss their objectives in these shots. They work to construct an image of Rodney appropriate to the persona of the introverted, solitary genius – whose inspiration borders on madness and spirituality – that he expresses in his skating and his trademark 'darkslide.' Rodney walks up the block and disappears into the crowd. He returns sometimes as much as five minutes later. Wing films him as he comes into view. Every time Rodney emerges from the crowd, he is walking a few steps behind one of the frequent homeless men whose spatial privation is so visually communicated through his clothing, mussed hair, and bodily posture. Nevertheless, the homeless prefer the relatively greater freedom of Broadway to what can be found on Bunker Hill or in other shopping districts in the city. At first I don't notice this, but after watching Wing and Rodney repeat this shot a few times and listening to them talk between shots, I realize that the delays between Rodney walking up the street and coming back into view are due to his waiting to find a homeless person to walk behind. When I ask Rodney why he chose to shoot on Broadway, he tells me that his video segments usually show him skating alone at the beach. This time he wanted to be seen skating in the city, among many people, but still alone.

While Rodney cultivates his image of the lone intellectual, in this instance by juxtaposing his sense of isolation with similarly isolated homeless men, his identification with the homeless is not unique. Scenes of homeless people talking to skaters and expressing enthusiasm for their tricks are common in skate videos. Shooting in urban settings brings skaters into close contact with the homeless. While many of these scenes occur as chance encounters during skate sessions or during the work of making videos, it is important to note that skaters use the chance documentation of these moments of everyday urban life to call attention to the similarities of spatial exclusion that both skaters and the homeless experience.

In the process of making a skate video, the camera also inevitably documents encounters between skaters and security/police forces or irate adults. Inclusion of such scenes in skate videos is also common. Such scenes of both the police and the homeless suggest that skaters create relationships of affinity with the homeless to intentionally dramatize their own kind (but not degree) of spatial poverty. I have witnessed both on video and on the street that, unlike most urban pedestrians, the homeless often stop to watch and express interest in skaters' activities.

In sharp contrast to Broadway, Bunker Hill is coated with redundant kevlar layers of high-tech security. As Mike Davis explains, 'The occasional appearance of a destitute street nomad ... in front of the Museum of Contemporary Art sets off a quiet panic; video cameras turn on their mounts and security guards adjust their belts.'[10] Increasingly in most urban areas, multiple levels of cooperation and coordination between private and public police forces, building security guards, video surveillance cameras, computer databases, and, in Los Angeles, barrel-shaped, bum-(in both senses of the word)-proof,[11] bus-stop benches define space as a prec(ar)ious material (and cultural) condition of urban life.[12] In L.A. this security apparatus effectively sweeps undesirables off Bunker Hill and further reduces the geographical scale of urban space available to people without homes.

By comparison the physically crumbling yet culturally recycled, vibrant, and retro-fitted Broadway seems humanitarian. But for the present – until gentrification remakes Broadway in the image of rehistoricized shopping districts and tourist bubbles such as Old Town Pasadena or the more tolerant, though still vigilant, Third Street Promenade in Santa Monica, where the homeless and 'idle' youth are permitted to occupy public benches and pedestrian space for hours on end – Broadway is well within the space of downtown Los Angeles that has been cordoned off to contain and limit the mobility of the homeless, Latino transnationals, and sometimes even skateboarders.

What I come to understand more fully later is that both skaters and downtown redevelopment agencies employ images of 'the urban' to generate cultural coherence among their respective constituents. Sharing similar images of 'the urban' within the structures of their respective communities and corporations enables skaters and downtown developers to construct space to match their value-producing activities – as profitable historical nostalgia and a simulated 'public' for developers; and as variable, in-constant space for skaters. The restructuring of urban space – which makes the global scale of transnational capitalism possible – also makes a new status of 'youth' possible. On the level of a global scale, skateboarders (youth) and business/development coalitions coincide and constitute each other; at the level of the production of scales of the body and the urban, skaters (youth), corporate redevelopers, and municipal officials often conflict. I will elaborate on this point below.

When I ask Rodney whether the cops have ever hassled him while he was on Broadway shooting his video, he says that they never said a word: 'And we [Rodney and Soc] were really in the way. Sometimes for thirty minutes in one spot.'[13] For skateboarders space is something temporary, but their use of the media 'constructs' larger spatial scales that help to overcome such a transient and transitory existence.

## Jumping Scale

It may be an unusual comparison to draw parallels among the homeless, immigrants of Latin American diasporas, and skateboarders. The vast dissimilarities of class privilege, opportunity, and access to media and social infrastructures among these groups are more important than the similarities. However, the very same processes of global economic restructuring that have dislocated entire communities from

Bunker Hill to 'renew' it[14] have also fundamentally restructured the social and spatial conditions of youth. 'In the wake of the Watts rebellion' in 1965, businesses abandoned Broadway for fear of the 'Black and Mexican poor.' Now in the wake of Proposition 187 and despite the presence of sales-tax-paying immigrant shoppers – whom Southern California businesses are happy to employ, but along with most California voters would deny citizenship to, let alone basic human services such as health care and education – real estate developers and gentrification have returned to Broadway to inoculate and pacify it.[15] The way that skateboarders interact with the forces of global restructuring is the subject of the rest of this essay.

It is significant that Rodney, Soc, and Wing were never hassled by cops and security guards while they were shooting on Broadway. So often, skaters must contend with security guards in practically every place they find to skate. During the past thirty years of urban renewal, Broadway has been spatially cut off from newer downtown Los Angeles. Despite the unexpected comparison, it becomes especially important to recognize the significance of a moment where socially dissimilar groups who share the experience of spatial exclusion occupy the same space.

The possibilities for these groups to assert their presence beyond tightly controlled and partitioned urban spaces such as Broadway, has much to do with their ability to jump scale, to expand the spatial range and scope of their self-activity – beyond the limits imposed by external organizations of power – to larger internally defined extensions of community and affective experience.[16]

Geographer Neil Smith explains scale as a social and geographical 'contest to establish boundaries between different places, locations and sites of experience.' Whenever a place is constructed – both architecturally and socially – scale is also produced. When real-estate developers build plazas to project an image of public space they also produce multiple scales. For example, they produce a scale of the body that organizes and limits mobility (walking vs. running), postures (sitting, leaning, standing), and appearance (the quality of one's clothing or the color of one's skin, which catches the attention of surveillance cameras).

Scale is open-ended and extends in an indefinite series of nested levels from the smallest scale of the body to the largest scale of the global. For Neil Smith, 'scale is the criterion of difference not so much between places as between different kinds of places.'[17] A single place is made up of multiple (if not infinite) scales. In Smith's formulation, both places and people have and produce scale. 'Scale both *contains* social activity, and at the same time provides an already partitioned geography within which social activity *takes place*. Scale demarcates the sites of social contest, the object as well as the resolution of contest.'[18]

Skaters, like their Latino and homeless counterparts on Broadway, experience scale as separation, as the attempt by those with greater power to produce scale that limits the extent of their social activity and everyday life. Smith's explanation of scale jumping in regard to the homeless is useful for understanding the implications of skaters' movement on the urban landscape: 'The importance of "jumping scales" lies precisely in [the] active social and political connectedness of apparently different scales, their deliberate confusion and abrogation.'[19] Skaters' similar experience of the imposition of scale is likewise overcome by their ability to connect apparently different scales.

Jumping scale is a process of circulating images of self and community that can be cast broadly to the rest of the social hierarchy. This is the basis for the production of larger scales that insure continued inclusion in, and ability to shape, urban spaces. For skateboarders the production of 'translocal' community within mass-mediated networks of subcultural skills/knowledge has become the most significant scale of identity formation.[20] One of the first steps that the spatially marginalized can take to counter the spatial limitations of their identity is to call attention to the fact that space is socially constructed according to specific imaginings of who may occupy it and who may not.

In the rest of the essay I will focus on the production of some of the many scales that skaters jump whenever they skate. In each case the geographical production of scale functions as common knowledge among skaters that is circulated among them to establish the existence of 'translocal' subcultural community, one of the larger scales that has become available to skaters through global economic restructuring, economies of information, and resultant changes in the status of youth.

First, as they construct a scale of the body (as well as 'local' community) that is radically different from the scale of the body produced by urban planners and built into 'public' spaces, skaters teach us about the social construction of space. Second, skaters teach us about the history of the spatial construction of youth. Third, I will consider how skaters reproduce the global scale of youth itself, according to values created through skating.

## Big Trees Small Acts

> Gaps, blocks, handrails, benches, ramps, street. I like to skate things that are not built for skateboarding.
>
> —John Reeves, interviewed by Kien Lieu in
> *Transworld Skateboarding* 12, no. 9 (1994)

We have all noticed, perhaps dismissed as 'boys' stuff,' but definitely marveled at, the clatterous, noisy moments of skateboarding that have become a predictable part of the everyday urban landscape. Skaters interact spectacularly with the built environment in a way that denaturalizes its fixity, wears its welcome 'out,' embellishes the functional, operationalizes the ornamental, disobeys architectural modifications of behavior, re-bounds decency in a single leap, liberates the strictures of structure, and breaks out of the channeled flows (commerce, transportation) of city life.[21]

Whenever skaters perform their 'tricks' they make their own meanings, critiques of power, and interpretations of urban life. When a skater ollies into a frontside tailslide down a thirteen-stair handrail, the genius of such tricknowlogy is that it makes the unexamined assumptions of otherwise inconsequential architectural elements become strange, and stand out in stark relief. Is a handrail *only* for safety, or is it also intended to keep people off the grass? Is a bus-stop bench barrel-shaped because it is meant to be aesthetically pleasing?

The basis of skaters' alchemical estrangement of urban space and critique of urban life is the ollie. As the skater nears the object (bench, fire hydrant, curb, handrail, staircase, planter box, trash can) the ollie begins by thrusting the back foot down and quickly slapping the tail of the skateboard on the pavement, while at the same time unweighting the front foot and raising the front wheels off the ground. At the full extension of the back foot's downward thrust, the skater quickly jumps off the same foot, bending the knees and quickly pulling them up, allowing the tail to rebound from the force of the tailslap. Rear wheels follow front wheels into the air so that board and skater are spectacularly airborne – sometimes four or five feet above flat ground, or even 'phatter' yet, ten to fifteen feet above a flight of stairs, off a wall or building. Reversing this sequence, first thrusting the nose of the board down to elevate the tail followed by the nose rebounding into the air, is known as a 'nollie' (nose ollie).

Increasingly difficult ollie variations include kick-flipping and/or spinning the board, once airborne, so that board and rider are momentarily separated in midair. Riffs on these ollie variations proliferate further when a skater rides switch-stance, reversing the original foot placement to execute ollies, nollies and kick flips with back foot forward. When a skater learns to skate, foot placement is determined with similar left- or right-handed preference exhibited when learning to write or play a guitar. Executing a complex switch-stance trick is comparable to playing a Jimi Hendrix solo in the first-learned, right-handed position, then flipping the guitar over and playing the solo left-handed with equal virtuosity. Skaters' revision of urban space calls into question the seeming fixity of distance and the directional stability of forward and backward, right and left, perhaps even of up and down.[22] By producing their own body scale, skaters create variable space.

When a skater ollies, without any banked transition, from horizontal sidewalk to the vertical wall of an office building, the social construction of space changes radically. In these moments skaters become urbanologists with perhaps as much 'expertise' and facility for the construction of space according to concepts of 'multiple use' as architects or urban planners. What may seem, to passersby, to be repetitive tricks performed by different skaters are, to the eyes of other skaters, variations on one another's techniques. Through the mutual enjoyment and recognition of variations between these tricks as they are inventively planned (as opposed to childishly played) on the urban landscape, skaters' ability to understand these variations allows them to create local and translocal subcultural communities.

One Sunday morning I witnessed moments of variable space creation. Passing the Arco Plaza in new downtown L.A., I heard telltale tailslaps and boardslides. In the recesses of this plaza – one of the first statements of L.A. 'public' space resulting from downtown urban removal/renewal – I witnessed objects such as benches and handrails become transformed. While skaters were using them, the architectural elements of the plaza could no longer be seen and assigned a place within a stable set of elements according to urban planners' or corporate tenants' definitions of 'public space.' A bench was no longer an invitation to inclusion through the act of sitting, nor was a sculpture intended as a shared viewing experience.

On this strategically chosen Sunday morning there were no security guards to chase the skaters away. In both their after-hours timing of this skate session and in other instances when security guards do eject them, skaters reveal the limits of 'the public' that postmodern architecture and shopping zones typical of new-downtown L.A. project. If it were really a diverse 'public' space there would be reason for people to make multiple use of the Arco Plaza during and after business hours. Every day. Moments when undesirables such as skaters or the homeless are ejected from such places also show that the 'public inclusion' projected so invitingly by postmodern plazas of high finance, in fact, is a 'public illusion' limited to narrow definitions of who may enter and how they may participate in this fiction of public space. Skaters reveal spatial artifice, but they also bring their own social meaning to their constructions of space.

During any instance of skateboarding, as on that Sunday morning, the technology of vision at the interface between skateboard, human body, and built environment is linked to the group of skaters who created space 'up close,' more tactilely according to perceptions of foot placement on the board and board placement on the object than according to optical perceptions and overall organizing vision employed by architects or planners who create space to communicate a visual definition – as well as a limitation – of 'the public.' [...]

In such instances the body scale produced by skaters is not identical to that of developers and planners, whose plans may limit bodies as fixed points within the static relations of architectural objects in a public plaza. Skaters' production of body scale overlaps developers' and becomes a kind of knowledge that in place-specific instances of skateboarding produces a 'local' community, which in turn also allows skaters to jump the local scale of place contained in the developers' narrow definitions of 'the public' to produce a translocal community.

Rather than simply ollieing over the dead space between objects, ollie variations fill gaps with social relations constituted through shared knowledge of variable space. Frozen on film in magazine or video, but circulated among translocal communities, the impossibly chaotic angles of board and body that 'take place and make space' during ollie variations provide a theorization of space simultaneous to and independent of theorizations advanced by philosophers and critical theorists of space in 1970s France and in 1980s–1990s America and Britain.[23]

While most of the photos in skateboard magazines primarily produce the scale of the body through detailed sequences of body movement captured with high-speed film advance motors, this is not the only scale that skateboard magazines produce.[24] Two such pictures are worth more than the brief description I give them here. The Solar clothing ad in the February 1997 issue of Thrasher features skater Jackson Taylor ollieing over a five foot high, closed (and locked?) wrought iron gate. The photo is labeled 'surveillance image h5;Tx1l1' and calls attention to both the limits of scale imposed on skaters as well as an increasing trend toward gated communities that lock in their own scale through active policing of their borders. In the Gullwing ad in the April 1997 issue of *Slap*, Malcolm Watson and photographer Chris Otiz construct Los Angeles urban space as collective memory by juxtaposing two generations of youth: the Black Panther mural on Jefferson Boulevard in the Jefferson Park neighborhood, and Malcolm Watson ollieing over a fire hydrant in the foreground.

What skaters explain if we know how to see it is that space is not absolute, not a 'field, container, [or] co-ordinate system of discrete and mutually exclusive locations.'[25] If French, American, and British theorists and urban planners such as Henri Lefebvre, Edward Soja, Doreen Massey, and Neil Smith use concepts of scale and variable space to argue for more inclusive constructions of public space, skate-urbanologists' argument for the same is no less valuable[26] – though communicated in a vocabulary of gesture and image that is less comprehensible to those outside their subcultural communities.

## A Handrail is not a Toy

So far, skaters have shown us how the 'uses' of space are socially constructed and accepted as self-evident. A handrail is not a toy; it is only for safety; but we aren't meant to know that it is also a mechanism of discipline and separation. Even here, once skaters have shown the artificiality of the built environment, we also catch glimpses of other processes at work, here the spatial construction of the social. By 'the social' I mean the commonsense understandings of, for example, 'the public' or of 'youth.'

As geographer Doreen Massey puts it, 'Society is necessarily constructed spatially, and that fact – the spatial organization of society – makes a difference in how it works ... All social (and indeed physical) phenomena/activities/relations have a spatial form and relative spatial location.'[27] 'Space' is created 'out of the vast intricacies, the incredible complexities, of the interlocking and the non-interlocking, and the networks of relations at every scale from local to global. What makes a particular view of these social relations specifically spatial is their simultaneity.'[28]

If a handrail is not a toy, then stairs are not a place where skateboarders should be, and because skaters use handrails for pleasure – as 'toys' in the eyes of local authorities – their actions are constru(ct)ed as expressions of youth, but youth defined as people who need supervision and warnings, people who cannot take care of themselves and who must be limited in their spatial mobility.

Skateboarders show that city planners, architects, and corporate members of redevelopment agencies may often construct urban spaces according to rather narrow principles of multiple use. What is important for the purposes of this essay is that historically, youth have been limited in their spatial mobility according to a logic that says that a handrail is not a toy. Historically youth have been located within spaces that are safe, where it is O.K. to 'play,' the assumption being that when they grow out of playing with toys they can leave such enclosed spaces of containment. Historically, 'youth' has been located within a logic of moral reform.

The corresponding assumption built into this spatial production of youth is that, if left unsupervised, youth will become immoral or delinquent, because every young person has within him the potential to become delinquent and within him or her the potential to become immoral. The history of spaces constructed according to the logic of moral reform is a history of spaces constructed to limit youth to the geographical scale of the home and to stay within parental control.[29] [...]

Moral reform, supervision and containment often inform city officials' attitudes toward skateboarders specifically and youth generally; and they are often derived from the past, from a historical period that constructed the space of youth according to a conception of youth based on the logic of moral reform. A significantly different concept of youth is now emerging from global economic restructuring.

## Whosoever Diggeth a Pit: Skateboarding and the Status of Youth

Skateboarding is one of the most spectacular forms of urban cultural expression to emerge in postindustrial America. Along with hip-hop culture, punk rock, graffiti, heavy metal, gangsta' rap, riot grrrl, and low riding, skateboarding provides an important record of, and insight into, the history of youth and urban space. This youth-produced history is quite often absent from the 'public' record produced by more powerful adults.

This absence is doubly reinforced when youth's expertise and their complex interpretations of the urban hierarchy are constructed by police, media, and city officials as 'juvenile.' Such trivialization fails to recognize that these popular-culture practices express a complex, insightful, and sophisticated understanding of history, power, and the structuring of urban space. Too often authorities are quick to locate the source of urban problems in what they perceive to be the questionable morals of the youth culture. Given the spatial outcomes (containment, enclosure, supervision) of the history of youth and moral reform, it is worth suggesting, given the topic of this essay, that dismissal of youth on the basis of moral disapproval may be more than a simple misunderstanding, it may be evidence of the desire to contain and enclose youth in spaces over which they have little control.

The images of urban density, of the homeless, and of Latino ethnicity that Rodney, Soc, and Wing created in order to give Rodney's five-minute video sequence an 'identity' may echo relationships of tourists visiting a foreign culture for a photo opportunity. However, we can also see that they were using communication and 'information technology to create unexpected (though not without differences of power and privilege) relationships of affinity. These can call attention to similarities of spatial positioning and exclusion. These relationships are gaining increasing importance within economies of global urban restructuring.

In her brilliant study of British Rave culture, Sara Thornton points out that the subcultures that youth create within information societies can exist only because of the availability of niche-, micro- and mass media.[30] Thornton's explanation is useful because it shows precisely the (im)material basis of the new youth status. The status of youth has changed from a life stage to be contained and protected – as a reserve army of labor – until they assume adult status, to one where coming of age matters much less because youth already engage in labor that, in addition to producing subcultural values, is already a highly sophisticated form of techno-scientific, information management, and value-producing labor within the global information economy. The circulation of situated knowledges such as skateboarders' critiques of urban space allows youth to reproduce the global scale of immaterial (because its products are images and information) labor, as a little-remarked result of the same processes that have deindustrialized central and south-central Los Angeles, replaced manufacturing jobs with automation, and replaced desk jobs with computers.[31]

When youth produce a global scale, through the immaterial labor of media and information circulation, they have explicit permission to form translocal communities on the basis of values produced *within* such networks of knowledge. Thornton further points out that most often the formation of a subcultural community is based on the ability of young people to exploit the moral panic that adults are still prone to when they encounter the alternative values of internally coherent youth subcultures. Skateboarders show us that their exploitation of moral panic – as is evident in a magazine titled *Thrasher* – or, to adult eyes, monstrous and terrifying graphics on the bottom of a skateboard, is not simply rebellion for the sake of rebellion.[32] At the same time that skaters use the impetus to moral reform, which is still espoused by some adults, against itself, their sometimes shocking statements also express profound, sophisticated, but highly coded understandings of the spatial relations that global capitalism has produced.[33]

Outsiders often cannot understand skaters' production of the scale of the body as an intimate expression of variable space. This works to the skaters' advantage because their ability to differentiate between a nollie and a fakie ollie is one way to gain control of the boundaries of 'local' and translocal scales of community.

On another day of filmmaking with Wing, this time in Huntington Beach, Phil of Clockwork Skateboards tells me something similar: every skateboard company has to have its own image, or icon, in order to get kids to buy their products; but because skateboarding is 'punk rock,' it is very difficult to keep an icon and one's image fresh. I take 'punk rock' to mean anti-commercial and anti-sellout, but more importantly D.I.Y. (do-it-yourself) and 'anti-mass culture.' Within micromarkets of the skateboarding subculture, processes of distinction and style are intense. Many skaters carefully choose ensembles of shoes, everyday clothing, and brands of skateboard decks, trucks, and wheels. Important in this process are brand logos and the ubiquitous decals that skaters use to code and recode their decks, cars, and skate spaces. A collage of stickers on the bottom of a board can become, in the hands of a skilled applicator, an important form of subcultural expression. Like the underground of the British Rave culture that Sara Thornton discusses, Phil's (and skaters') concern is 'popularization.' To paraphrase Phil, 'If too many kids have the same board [or brand of shoes, clothes] it will become stale and they won't want it anymore, because everyone has it.' Skateboards, or 'decks,' feature amazing graphic art – movable micromurals – on the underside of the deck. A majority of skaters are themselves self-trained and awesome graphic artists, and as of this writing a traveling exhibit of skateboard art has been organized in Southern California.

Because skateboarding is punk rock, it creates opportunities for skaters to form clothing, graphics, and equipment companies (usually all of the above), and, at least for the youth involved in these microbusinesses, to move beyond – while still perpetuating – the primarily cultural economy of subcultural distinction to a subcultural 'career,' a means of economic survival. However, because skateboarding is punk rock, companies are limited, and it becomes difficult to sustain the business as a means of cultural survival without growing too big and becoming stale.[34]

Skaters are often misunderstood in their production of the scale of translocal community. Because their subcultural activities are sanctioned by global economic restructuring and because the status of youth is much less stringently defined by the logic of containment and moral reform, skateboarders have been able to participate in urban restructuring to demand that municipalities build spaces for them. Planners and developers have listened to skaters' demands, but they have usually missed the fact that economies of information and global economic restructuring have changed the status of 'youth.' Some of these spaces are organized, if not according to the logic of moral reform and containment, then still according to the logic of organized sport. This organization also functions as a means of control by making skateboarding conform to more mainstream values of individual competition.

Recently, in the California state legislature, assembly bill 2357 was introduced to add skateboarding to the state's list of 'hazardous recreational activities.'[35] Declaring skateboarding a hazardous sport would absolve municipalities of liability for injury. In anticipation of the passage of this bill, cities around the state have begun to build skate parks. While legislation has given cities the confidence to build parks, all have done so as a means of alleviating the spatial crisis between skaters, business people, and property owners. The cities of Huntington Beach, Temecula, Glendale, and Ventura have all built skate parks in the last five years.

Because skateboarding exists at the global scale of immaterial labor, skaters have gained the means to jump previous scales of youth, to form translocal communities. As they have become both subcultures defined by the circulation of sophisticated understandings of urban space and corresponding productions of scale, skaters have also produced their own institutional stability. Herein small skater-run businesses also construct a market equal in expanse to the scale of the subcultural community, because skateboarders exist as a coherent community held together through the circulation of style, products, and most important, translocal community-producing knowledge. I would argue that this new status of youth is as much responsible for the recent construction of municipal skate parks as is the more often cited 'public nuisance' that skaters create.

While it is beyond the scope of this essay to detail the ways in which scale has been contested in city officials' explanations of their reasons for building skateparks, a brief comparison of the ways in which the actual parks themselves have been organized is instructive for what it reveals about the new status of youth.

The cities of Santa Cruz, Palo Alto, and Marin in northern California have had skate parks for a number of years when skateboarding was in relative decline. These cities chose simply to risk the threat of liability. Since it opened, the Derby Park skate track in Santa Cruz has had one serious injury and one liability suit, which the plaintiffs lost.

What is more significant for the purposes of this essay is that these skate parks have permitted skaters to construct the meanings of their activities according to the values that result from their use of the built environment. For example, graffiti is permitted on the concrete of the skate parks, and the parks are free. Parks built in the cities of Temecula and Glendale, on the other hand, have chosen instead to try to reform skateboarding and, to varying degrees, contain it within the legitimacy of sport. Both cities have taken a zero tolerance approach to graffiti, maintaining that it would be impossible to control the kinds of messages that skaters would write and that it would be impossible to keep graffiti only on skateboarding surfaces. By comparison, derby skate track designer Ken Wormhoudt maintains that the cities of Santa Cruz, Palo Alto, and Marin have had no problems with the spread of graffiti. Temecula runs its skate park on a per hour fee basis, and with the police department it co-sponsors a skateboard club at the high-school. The club cleans the park on weekend mornings in exchange for free skate time.[36]

What is most significant about these two different attitudes toward graffiti is that they suggests two different understandings of skateboarding. While all of the parks mentioned here are administered by recreation departments, Glendale and Temecula have organized their skate parks according to an older perception of youth where the elders must save young people from themselves while carrying out a program of moral reform.

I realize that I have not given voice to the views of planners and city officials regarding urban space. In the book-length version of this article I will. Perhaps some would agree that skaters have something to teach us about concepts of multiple use and the ways that the social can be spatially constructed to make the production of variable space more possible. Those who disagree with skaters' (and my own) explanations and critiques of space-as-power and argue that the spatial exclusion of skateboarders from urban space has more to do with issues of functionality, vandalism, and public safety and liability only prove my (and the skaters') point. First, they misunderstand youth, especially now when youth have an amplified and expanded ability to comment on the conditions of urban life. Second, they can only say this if they assume that space is static and universally perceived by all people in the same way. It should be possible to plan and build spaces for skateboarding that are not segregated according to older histories of youth or spaces of separation and enclosure, but rather that coexist with and are next to places of public gathering.

As global restructuring reconfigures the potentials of youth, and as youth, in the coded language of a translocal community, critique the present spatial order and demand spaces of their own, the possibility remains that spaces configured to contain youth may not work. On the other hand, one of the most spectacular instances of skaters' taking control of urban space occurred in Portland, Oregon, in 1989, when Mark Scott and Brett Taylor took space into their own hands: they excavated and cemented a skate bowl under a city-owned highway overpass. They continued to build more bowls until this space became known as the Burnside Project. The choice between skate parks built according to containment and enclosure or governed by the formation of a translocal community seems obvious. If you dig a pit, you can fall in it, or skate it.[37]

## Notes

This article has benefitted immeasurably from the wisdom, seance, and tricknowlogy of Mary Kay Van Sistine, Joe Austin, Michael Steiner, Alejandra Marchevsky, Jason Elias, Linda Maram, Jonathan Sterne, Carrie Rentschler; Rodney Mullen and Socrates of Plan B Skateboards; Julie Pelletier, Scott Reese, Ken Wormhoudt; and the all-terrain-vehicle, cross-training, hybrid, vert-street-cope-slope you-name-it-we'll-skate-it, super morphin' skaters of Clockwork Skateboards: Brian Patch, Christian, Jeff Patch, and Phil. Edward Soja commented on an earlier version of this essay delivered at the meetings of the American Studies Association in 1992. Special thanks go to Joe Austin, Joe Austin, Joe Austin; and Jeff Rangel for conversations about skateboarding and surfing. Martin Wong (and *Giant Robot* magazine) got me skating after years away and knew all the right people at exactly the right times; Jason Loviglio read drafts of this essay and offered indispensable criticism and rare insight; Wing Ko, skater with a camera and the Sergei Eisenstein of skate filmmakers, patiently answered my endless questions, listened to me propound my theories of skateboard discourse, and taught me much as I watched him at work. Socrates Leal and Daewon Song, who work tirelessly to redesign Los Angeles every day, came through on the shortest notice.

1. The Reagan building was completed after the publication of Mike Davis's *City of Quartz: Excavating the Future in Los Angeles* (London: Verso, 1990). As has happened so often with his book, Davis's analysis of Los Angeles has proven to be prophetic, the rebellion and civil unrest of 1992 being only the most obvious example. Based on my own observations I am convinced that Davis's prophecy about the Reagan building has become reality. In his book Davis explained that the Los Angeles Community Redevelopment Agency spent $20 million inducing the State to build the 'Ronald Reagan Office Building' a block away from the corner of Third and Broadway, while simultaneously bribing the Union Rescue Mission $6 million to move its homeless clientele out of the neighborhood. The 3,000 civil servants from the Reagan Building are intended as shock troops to gentrify the strategic corner of Third and Broadway where developer Ira Yellin has received further millions in subsidies from the CRA to transform the three historic structures he owns (the Bradbury Building, Million Dollar Theater and Grand Central Market) into 'Grand Central Square.' The 'Broadway-Spring Center' … provides 'security in circulation' between the Reagan Building and Square.' (Davis, *City of Quartz*, 261, n. 8)

2. Such processes of redevelopment are not totally predictable. When I called the Grand Central Square Apartments I found out that the CRA has required the owner of the building to rent half of the one- and two-bedroom apartments to 'income qualified' people at roughly half the market rate. For example, a one-bedroom apartment rents for $460 to renters with an income of less than $17,000 a year, and slightly above $500 for those with an income between $17,000 and $20,000. Two-bedroom apartments also go at approximately half the market rate, depending on level of income.

3. A large Spanish-language produce, meat, and seafood market, where local residents do their daily shopping and browse among the many stalls.

4. At present, a Spanish-language evangelical church.

5. Much of the urban history of Los Angeles that informs my physical and written wanderings on Broadway comes from Davis, *City of Quartz*, 230–31, 261, n. 8. See also Margaret Crawford, 'The Fifth Ecology: Fantasy, the Automobile, and Los Angeles,' in Martin Wachs and Margaret Crawford, eds., *The Car and the City: The Automobile, the Built-environment, and Daily Urban Life* (Ann Arbor: University of Michigan Press, 1992), 233.

6. Pedestrians are now carried up and down Bunker Hill by the recently refurbished Angels' Flight incline railroad. This incline railroad, a formerly much-used vehicle that facilitated movement between Bunker Hill and the old downtown shopping district, has been re-created for use mostly as a trendy tourist route. There are, however, high-rent, high-rise apartment buildings on Bunker Hill, and it is possible that their occupants may also be using the railroad to gain somewhat easier access to Grand Central Square.

7. Identity is usually created through the skater's choice of music that accompanies his video segment.

8. See, for example, Rodney Mullen, interviewed by Thomas Campbell, *Transworld Skateboarding* (December 1993); Plan B, advertisement, *Transworld Skateboarding* (September 1996). See also Plan B Videos, *Questionable* (1992), *Virtual Reality* (1993), *Second Hand Smoke* (1995).

9. *Virtual Reality*, Plan B Video (1993).

10. Davis, *City of Quartz*, 231.

11. Robert Morrow, '"Bum-Proof" Bus Bench Hill Street Downtown,' photograph in Davis, *City of Quartz*, 235.

12. I use nested and parenthetical words such as 'prec(ar)ious' primarily for economy, and not proliferation, of mean(der)ing.

13. In interviews with recreation officials from the cities of Glendale and Temecula, I learned that the police hate to 'bust' skaters. The police come out looking like villains when skaters are not really doing anything seriously wrong. In the cities of Temecula and Glendale, the police were the most vocal and ardent supporters of the skaters' repeated requests that the city provide them with a place to skate.

14. For a more developed angle on the history of urban renewal and the disastrous 'civic development' of 'big league' cities that characterized the widespread clearance and renewal projects of the 1950s and 1960s, including the clearance of Mexican American neighborhoods in Chavez Ravine in order to build Dodger Stadium, which is only minutes to the northwest of Bunker Hill, see George Lipsitz, 'Sports Stadia and Urban Development: A Tale of Three Cities,' *Journal of Sport and Social Issues* 8, no. 2 (Summer/Fall 1984). Sports stadia become one of the elements in a larger pattern of faux-public-foe tourist attractions anchoring contemporary downtown developments that Dennis Judd refers to as 'tourist bubbles.' See Dennis R. Judd, 'Enclosure, Community, and Public Life,' *Research in Community Sociology* 6 (1996), 230.

15. On developers' fears of 'the Black and Mexican poor' in the wake of the 1965 civil unrest, see Davis, *City of Quartz*, 230. Many scholars and politicians see proposition 187 as the first salvo in a concerted effort to create two tiers of citizenship. See Leo R. Chavez, 'Immigration Reform and Nativism: The Nationalist Response to the Transnationalist Challenge,' *The New Nativism* (New York: New York University Press, 1996). On the relationship between global-economic urban restructuring and anti-immigrant attitudes, see Alejandra Marchevsky, 'The Empire Strikes Back: Globalization, Nationalism, and California's Proposition 187,' *Critical Sense* 4, no. 1 (Spring 1996), 8–51.

16. I am not arguing that the ability to 'jump scale' constitutes the new status of youth. Young people have always jumped scale. See, for example, David Nasaw, *Children of the City: At Work and Play* (New York: Anchor/Doubleday, 1985). Instead, I am arguing that the horizon for jumping has expanded.

17. Neil Smith, 'Contours of a Spatialized Politics: Homeless Vehicles and the Production of Geographical Scale,' *Social Text*, vol. 10, no. 4 (1992), 64.

18. Ibid., 66.

19. On the spatial politics of scale, the homeless, and the 'strategic political geography' of scale jumping, see Neil Smith, 'Homeless/Global: Scaling Places,' in Jon Bird, Barry Curtis, George Robertson, and Lisa Tickner, eds., *Mapping the Futures: Local Cultures, Global Change* (New York: Routledge, 1993), and idem, 'Contours of a Spatialized Politics.' On Latin American immigrants and citizenship in Southern California, see Chavez, 'Immigration Reform and Nativism'; S. Pincetl, 'Challenges to Citizenship: Latino Immigrants and Political Organizing in the Los Angeles Area,' *Environment and Planning A* 26 (1994), 895–914. The source of the phrase 'translocal community' is Brenda Bright's essay 'Nightmares in the New Metropolis: The Cinematic Poetics of Low Riders,' in Joe Austin and Michael Nevin Willard, eds., *Generations of Youth: Youth Cultures and History in Twentieth-Century America* (New York: New York University Press, 1998), Chapter 25.

20. For Latino immigrants, expanding the geographical scale of daily life to the scale of the nation and the rights of citizenship has become one of the most significant scales. For the homeless, the scale of community has become one of the most significant scales of spatial and identity formation.

21. Iain Borden, a former Skatopia (a Southern California skate park built in the late 1970s) denizen and now urban planner, explains skateboarding similarly. 'Skateboarders threaten accepted definitions of space, [by] taking over space conceptually as well as physically and so striking at the very heart of what everyone else understands by the city.' Iain Borden, 'Beneath the Pavement, the Beach: Skateboarding, Architecture and the Urban Realm,' in Iain Borden et al., eds., *Strangely Familiar: Narratives of Architecture in the City* (London: Routledge, 1996), 85. For a much more developed discussion of the relationship between architecture, power, knowledge, and the possibilities for the kinds of 'freespaces' that skateboarders produce, see Lebbeus Woods, 'The Question of Space,' and Michael Menser, 'Becoming-Heterarch: On Technocultural Theory, Minor Science, and the Production of Space,' in Stanley Aronowitz et al., eds., *Technoscience and Cyberculture* (New York: Routledge, 1996).

22. This and the following paragraph are influenced by the analysis of space in Gilles Deleuze and Felix Guattari, *A Thousand Plateaus: Capitalism and Schizophrenia*

(Minneapolis: University of Minnesota Press, 1987), especially their discussion of nomad art, pp. 492–500.

23. For discussion of French spatial theorizations by Henri Lefebvre and Michel Foucault, see Smith 'Contours of Spatialized Politics,' and Soja, *Postmodern Geographies* (London: Verso); also Michel de Certeau, *The Practice of Everyday Life* (Minneapolis: University of Minnesota Press, 1988); Gilles Deleuze, 'Postscript on the Societies of Control,' *October* 59 (1992); and Deleuze and Guattari, *A Thousand Plateaus*. For more-recent work by Americans and Britons see Smith, 'Contours of a Spatialized Politics' and 'Homeless/Global' in Jon Bird et al. eds. *Mapping the Futures*. London: Routledge; and Neil Smith and Cindi Katz, 'Grounding Metaphor: Towards a Spatialized Politics,' in Michael Keith and Steve Pile, eds., *Place and the Politics of Identity* (New York: Routledge, 1993); Soja, *Postmodern Geographies;* and Doreen Massey, 'Politics and Space/Time,' in *Place and the Politics of Identity*.

24. See, for example, the covers of *Transworld Skateboarding*, for June 1996, April 1997, and June 1997, which are highly staged commentaries on the urban location of the photos in addition to showing the action in them. Such photos required an incredibly creative and sophisticated understanding of the multiple possibilities for using any space.

25. Smith and Katz, 'Grounding Metaphor,' 75.

26. While skaters align themselves with the homeless and advance critiques of 'public' space, at the same time they also reproduce spaces of masculinity. In her ethnography of skateboarding, Becky Beal asserts that, when considered in relation to the masculinity of organized sports, skaters exhibit a cooperative form of masculinity that is not included in the values of competition and performance of more 'legitimate' sports. Beal also considers moments of contradiction when skaters' masculinity can be seen as a situational construct that reinforces traditional, competitive masculinity. To supplement my argument I cite Beal's explanation here to point out that often skaters' challenges to power and security forces reproduce the kind of masculinity that informs constructions of space that do not account for the subjectivity of women. See Beal, 'The Subculture of Skateboarding: Beyond Social Resistance'; 'Disqualifying the Official: An Exploration of Social Resistance through the Sub-culture of Skateboarding,' *Sociology of Sport Journal* 12 (1995), 252–67, and 'Alternative Masculinity and Its Effects on Gender Relations in the Subculture of Skateboarding, *Journal of Sport Behavior* 19, no. 3 (August 1996). For a very useful consideration of the ways that masculinity gets produced in contestations between urban governments and male youth subcultures, see Joe Austin, 'Taking the Train: Youth Culture, Urban Crisis, and the "Graffiti Problem" in New York City, 1970–1900' (Ph.D. diss., University of Minnesota, 1996). See also Rosalyn Deutsche, 'Men in Space,' *Strategies: A Journal of Theory, Culture and Politics* 3 (1990); Mary Jo Deegan, 'The Female Pedestrian: The Dramaturgy of Structural and Experimental Barriers in the Street,' *Man-Environment Systems* 17 (1987), 79–86.

27. Massey, 'Politics and Space/Time,' 146.

28. Ibid., 155–56.

29. On the history of constructions of youth, see Susan Ruddick, *Young and Homeless in Hollywood: Mapping Social Identities* (New York: Routledge, 1996). Ruddick finds the origins of the status of youth as the subject of moral reform in the formation of the juvenile-care system at the beginning of the twentieth century.

30. Sarah Thornton, ' Moral Panic, the Media and British Rave Culture,' in Andrew Ross and Tricia Rose, eds., *Microphone Fiends: Youth Music and Youth Culture* (New York: Routledge, 1994); Sarah Thornton, *Club Cultures: Music, Media and Subcultural Capital* (Hanover, N.H.: Wesleyan/University of New England Press, 1996).

31. On immaterial labor, see Michael Hardt and Antonio Negri, *Labor of Dionysus: A Critique of the State-Form* (Minneapolis: University of Minnesota Press, 1994).

32. Now graphics have expanded beyond heavy-metal-influenced terror and horror imagery to include cartoon kid figures. This is an important recuperation of 'kid' status by

linking it to the serious work of subcultural formation. On terror imagery as a means to symbolically challenge the imbalance of power that youth experience see Robert Walser, *Running with the Devil: Power, Gender and Madness in Heavy Metal Music* (Hanover, N.H.: Wesleyan/University Press of New England, 1993).

33. On the mediation and construction of 'opposition' as a strategy for the formation of youth culture and subcultural capital, see Thornton, 'Moral Panic, the Media and British Rave Culture'; Thornton, *Club Cultures: Music, Media and Subcultural Capital*; Dick Hebdige, *Hiding in the Light: On Images and Things* (London: Comedia/Routledge, 1988), 17–36.

34. For more on the subcultural dynamics of being 'punk rock,' see Steve Duncombe's essay, 'Lets All be Alienated Together: Zines and the Making of the Underground Community', in Joe Austin and Michael Nevin Willard, eds., *Generations of Youth: Youth Cultures and History in Twentieth-Century America* (New York: New York University Press, 1998), chapter 26. On youth culture, selling out, and cultural economies of distinction, see Thornton, 'Moral Panic, the Media and British Rave Culture'; Thornton, *Club Cultures*. On the dangers of overexposure in the surfing and skateboarding industries, see Mary Ann Galante, 'Surfwear Firms Jump on the Skateboard Bandwagon,' *Los Angeles Times*, April 17, 1988.

35. Bill Billiter, 'Council Endorses Skateboarding Bill,' *Los Angeles Times*, Orange County Edition, July 23, 1996, Metro Section, 3.

36. Interview, Julie Pelletier, Temecula Recreation Department, March 1997.

37. Mark Scott, 'Burnside Project,' *Transworld Skateboarding* 10, no. 9 (September 1992), 52–55.

# Chapter 37

# Victor Hugo Viesca

## *Straight Out the Barrio*: Ozomatli and the Importance of Place in the Formation of Chicano/a Popular Culture in Los Angeles

Have you wondered how Run D.M.C., layered with Mexican folk singers, with a touch of Tito Puente sounds like? (DJ Alex Camu, 1998) .

En español, con distintos acentos y colores, ofrecíeron canciones a Cuba, protestaron contra el imperialismo, y apoyaron a los presos políticos que pueblan nuestras naciones. Corazoncito de emigrante, las ganas de vivír. Qué se puede esperar de este fin de siglo?: mestizaje radical: Ozomatli! (Rita Robles, 1999)

At the dawn of the twenty-first century, and a generation after the emergence of the Chicano *movimiento* of the 1960s, popular culture and especially popular music functions as a vital marker of the changing shape of Chicano/a identity in the 1990s. The music of Ozomatli reveals much about an important moment in the changing nature of Chicano culture while providing a window as well into the cultural and social dynamics of contemporary Los Angeles as a whole. The spatial context of Ozomatli's emergence and their links to past musical movements helps historicize these changes and clarifies their impact on Chicano/a identity in turn-of-the-century Los Angeles. Most importantly, perhaps, Ozomatli's history of formation, the multiplicity of its sounds, and the role played by its music in enabling political activism and political coalitions all illuminate the relations

From: *Cultural Values* 4.4 (October), 2000, pp. 445–473.

between identities and politics at the present moment. The band's success shows how some of the mechanisms of oppression like displacement, segregation, and commercial culture can be hijacked and used against the grain by grass roots activists, artists, and intellectuals.

One of the better known groups to emerge from the burgeoning underground music scene in Los Angeles, Ozomatli brings together a number of eclectic instruments ranging from congas to *claves,* from *bajo sextos* to bass guitars, from turntables to *tablas* – into an infectious blend of poly-rhythms and politically engaged bilingual lyrics. The words and sounds of the group evoke a controlled chaos, mixing sonic styles and lyrical flows into a tight soundtrack of everyday life in the urban landscape of this metropolis on the edge of the millennium.

Ozomatli also represents a form of political possibility that inheres in post-industrial culture, a possibility that is specific to the current historical moment of globalization. The very conditions of oppression and disenfranchisement that characterize the new economy have enabled (and required) a particular counter-response, a response that is necessarily different from older forms of struggle. Ozomatli is both the product of – and a means for countering – the impact of globalization on low-wage workers and aggrieved racialized populations. Not just a band with a new and eclectic repertoire, Ozomatli is an institution that emerged out of collective political mobilization, a repository of social memory about past struggles for social change, and a site for imagining and enacting new social relations. The members of Ozomatli first encountered each other as worker/activists organizing for trade union representation in collective bargaining negotiations with their employer. They did not win union recognition, but they did secure an important concession from city officials – use of an abandoned building for one year. They used that space as a non-profit cultural arts center, as a space to incubate a band rather than a radical party or a trade union. The musical group they formed serves as a floating site of resistance, a mechanism for calling an oppositional community into being through performance. Ozomatli links together diverse parts of a spatially dispersed community through the activities of live performance, listening to recordings and radio, and following the band to marches, demonstrations, and direct action protests.

As a cultural phenomenon, Ozomatli occupies a liminal space, not quite fitting within the categories of commercial culture and yet not quite conforming to reigning definitions of 'folk' culture. They dissolve the binary oppositions between folk and commercial culture, between social movement culture and popular culture, between assimilation and ethnic nationalism. The music they perform echoes the dislocations and displacements endemic to global cities in the transnational era, but it also announces the emergence of new forms of resistance that find counter-hegemonic possibilities within contradictions. In culture and in politics, Ozomatli proceeds through immanent critiques and creative reworkings of already existing social relations rather than through transcendant teleologies aimed at the establishment of utopian sites and subjects. Rather than a politics of 'either/or' that asks people to choose between culture and politics, between class and race, or between distinct national identities, Ozomatli embraces a politics of 'both/and' that encourages dynamic, fluid, and flexible stances and identity categories.

Ozomatli's first album *(Ozomatli,* Almosounds/Interscope, 1998) combines Afro-Cuban styles, Mexican folk forms, and the breakbeats of funk and hip hop music of the United States with traces of Jamaican dub-reggae and traditional Indian music.

They present a syncretic sound created by blending together the diverse influences found within the group. Jiro Yamaguchi, a resident of the largely Latino Echo Park neighborhood, brings his training in Indian classical music in Japan and New York City to the group, especially through his use of sitar and tabla on the band's first album (Shuster, 1998). DJ Cut Chemist from Scotland and the 'Black Socrates' of rap, Chali 2na, both of whom are also members of the Los Angeles hip hop crew Jurrassic 5, provide the hip hop elements with rapping, sampling and turntable musicianship. Guitarist Raul Pacheco, from East L. A., and trumpeter Asdru Sierra, from Highland Park, sing Spanish songs in the popular Latin styles of *cumbia* and Mexican *norteño*. Jose Espinosa, also from East L. A., plays saxophone and Ulises Bella, from the Southeast suburb of Bell, plays tenor sax. The percussion of William Marufo, Justin 'Niño' Poree and Yamaguchi expertly mixes tempos between salsa and funk, hip hop and *norteño* while Pico Union's Wil-Dog Abers' funky bass provides a steady bounce of Latin and jazz-funk rhythms.

Ozomatli's bilingualism, their deft blend of global sounds, and their politically engaged lyrics reveal distinctive characteristics of Chicano music in Los Angeles. Like earlier Chicano groups from East L. A., as well as their cohorts in the Chicano underground music scene today, including groups like Quetzal, Blues Experiment, Ollin, Yeska and Aztlán Underground, Ozomatli does not fit any existing categorizations of popular music currently set up by the mainstream music industry, which leads, in part, to their neglect by major record labels (Loza, 1993, p. 138). Yet Ozomatli's first release has met with both popular and critical success. Their eponymous album has sold over 100,000 copies based primarily on word of mouth and relentless touring, having received virtually no commercial radio support and little music video play (Valdes-Rodriguez, 1999, p. 78). […]

How has Ozo, as they are also known, managed to reach such heights so quickly with a sound that has no place in mainstream music? While the growing international appeal of Latin music has opened up space for Latino artists, Ozomatli's popularity has more to do with their ties to Los Angeles, where they have garnered over one quarter of their sales (Valdes-Rodriguez, 1998, p. 78). The city from which they come is also the city in which their music seems to register most. The band's success in making a connection with the people of Los Angeles derives, at least in part, from their grounding in Los Angeles' contemporary Chicano culture and in the new social relations, new knowledges, and new sensibilities of an emerging global city in the transnational era. This identity-in-formation has been taken up by young, mostly second or third generation Mexican Americans from the predominately working class spaces of Latino Los Angeles.

Latino Los Angeles, urban historian Mike Davis (1999) has recently argued, is a 'city within a city' (p. 20). People of Mexican descent made up 80 percent of the Latino population in Los Angeles at the time of the 1990 U. S. Census. The two national groups that follow, Salvadorans at six percent and Guatemalans at three percent, make up the largest concentrations of the rest of the Latino population. The vast majority of Latinos are concentrated on the east side of central Los Angeles County.' Political scientists Victor Valle and Rodolfo D. Torres (1993) have labeled the region 'The Greater Eastside' to describe the concentration of Latinos, predominately of Mexican descent, in the small and medium-sized cities and industrial suburbs that radiate east and south of the traditional Chicano core super barrio of East Los Angeles. […]

While the members of Ozomatli are from various neighborhoods around Los Angeles, many of the members come from, and the formation of the band itself took place in, the Greater Eastside. Ozo's first album portrays a particularly radical vision of the emerging social world from the vantage point of these spaces. Several songs from the first album shed light on some of the more pressing issues affecting the working-class communities of color in this post-industrial city, such as youth violence ('Cumbia de los Muertos' and 'O Le Le'), police brutality ('Chota'), and the growing disaffection with the inequities and biases of the political and economic system of 'Uncle Sam' ('Coming War'). On the Latin/funk inspired 'Coming War', Chali 2na raps: 'It makes me wonder sometimes are we in hell or inches away from confronting the powers that be'. Yet there is a constant positive energy in the music that portends a future of cultural exchange within the diversity of the global city. Ozo's oeuvre offers an inventory of hybrid and heterogeneous musics from the Americas that have themselves emerged from international and intercultural collisions and coalitions, including the Afro-Latin musics of Dominican *merengue*, Colombian *cumbia*, Cuban salsa and rumba, the reggae of Jamaica, Mexican *norteño*, and hip hop and funk from the United States. All of this, of course, is also the music of the contemporary Chicano barrio in Los Angeles.

## New World Barrio: Globalization and the Making of the Greater Eastside

*Como ves, como ves/la historia no es como crees.* (Ozomatli, 'Como Ves')

Ozomatli and the alternative Chicano culture from which they emerged have been shaped by the contradictory conditions of the global city that Los Angeles has become. The rise of a service-dominated, global economy and the parallel trans-national movements of people, culture and capital has dramatically changed the urban landscape as well as the meaning of Mexican ancestry in a city that has become one of the most diverse sites of the planet (Naficy, 1994, p. 6). Going beyond regional or even national centers, 'global' or 'world' cities are increasingly integrated into the international networks of the transnational economy. They are central nodal points, or hubs, in the processes of globalization, including the liberalization of world trade, the increasing transnational flow of capital, growing immigration and the formation of global culture. [...]

Viewing Ozomatli as a 'global' band, however, as a product of the 'border' culture, or even as an example of the transnationalism that purportedly permeates Chicano culture, can obscure the important role played by local places and spaces in shaping their sound and vision. Although it is important to acknowledge the transnational experiences of Latinos – the links across national borders created by remittances sent home from migrant workers' wages, by telecommunications, and by inexpensive travel – the particular dynamics and local histories of global cities should not be neglected. The development of Chicano popular culture has been shaped as much by the local histories of the particular spaces where Latinos have concentrated as it has been shaped by the dramatic transformations generated by globalization. [...]

Ozomatli, and the larger Chicano musical subculture to which Ozo belongs, has itself emerged from the changing nature of work and the new formations of Latino culture wrought by the urban and economic transformation of the post-industrial city. Moreover, this musical subculture has been shaped by both the Mexicanization of Los Angeles in the 1990s and the overwhelming and creative response by the Latino community to the racialized scapegoating of immigrants in early 1990s California, when the state was in the midst of a prolonged recession. It is critical that we consider these cultural manifestations of change as integral components of imagining and building the struggle against working-class poverty and iniquitous social change in Los Angeles. Through their music and political activism, Ozo and the Chicano underground remain invested in the working-class communities throughout Los Angeles. Indeed, the very convergence and creation of Ozo was precipitated by a protest against the precarious circumstances facing the working-class youth of post-industrial Los Angeles.

In the aftermath of an explosive rebellion that was due in large part to the ravages of economic restructuring, Wil-Dog worked for the Los Angeles Conservation Corps, a federally funded jobs program set up in response to the 1992 insurrection (Oliver et al., 1993). In March, 1995, Wil-Dog, along with several others attempted to organize a union among the (mostly Latino) youth who worked in the Emergency Resources Unit of the Corps located in downtown. The Emergency Resources Unit trained and employed local inner-city youth at minimum wages with no benefits and offered few long term job prospects. At the same time, upper-level management received high wages and lavish benefits. As the young workers began protesting this discrepancy, the Corps management fired Carmelo Alvarez, Wil-Dog's boss, and the Corps' only Latino site director. Agency managers also shut down the Emergency Resources Unit's downtown building. Wil-Dog joined with the other members of his Corps unit to stage a takeover of the building and to mount a two month sit-in. These actions were aimed at securing union representation, better wages, stable employment and the chance for advancement for those involved in the Corps. As Josh Kun (1998) notes, 'Wil-Dog was raised by active members of the Revolutionary Communist Party and he knew a labor sham when he saw one' (p. 38). Those attempting to organize the youth – 30 workers in all – were fired. Negotiations, prompted by bad publicity for the Corps, did not bring about a union but did manage to secure access to the locked out downtown building for a period of twelve months. The activists quickly renamed the building the Peace and Justice Center and transformed it into a nonprofit community arts center (Martinez, 1995; Valdes-Rodriguez, 1999; Kun, 1998; Shuster, 1998). The first benefit concert held at the new Peace and Justice Center was for the Revolutionary Communist Youth Brigade and it was Ozomatli's first public appearance.

This local struggle was the impetus for the formation of Ozomatli, which initially had been named Todos Somos Marcos after the Zapatista movement in Chiapas, Mexico and its spokesperson's eloquent critiques and strategic organizing against the North American Free Trade Agreement and other aspects of globalization. As Wil-Dog notes:

> After the strike, we were given access to this new community center dedicated to youth and art. We had to raise money for the building, so I called all these musicians I knew. Ozomatli got together during the first five gigs. It was a jam thing where everyone's musical past came out. We never set out to play this style. It's just what everybody knew. (Shuster, 1998)

Ozomatli was one of several bands that emerged from this experiment in urban cultural politics at the Peace and Justice Center. Several Chicano groups like Blues Experiment, Rice and Beans. Ollin, and Quetzal, as well as multi-racial groups like Black Eyed Peas and Rage Against the Machine performed at the Center on weekends, while the week was dedicated to workshops in studio mixing, theater production, poetry writing, and community organizing led by many of these same musicians. Blues Experiment, like Ozomatli, was actually born from this work at the Center (Doss, 1998b, pp. 4–5). Although the Center no longer exists, its impact is still being felt. The Peace and Justice Center contributed a great deal to the development of local bands, and its legacy is readily seen in the activism of Zack de la Rocha, from Rage Against the Machine, who has since organized The People's Resource Center. Located in the predominately Latino neighborhood of Highland Park, just northeast of downtown, this community-arts venue grew out of work done at the Peace and Justice Center (Grant, 1999). Meanwhile, several groups with ties to the Peace and Justice Center remain a proactive part of the local community, not only playing at local venues but also playing at festivals raising awareness against police abuse and raising money for Californian high school music programs (Kun, 1998, p. 40).

Chicano and other local artists of color are expressing politics through a cultural practice that attempts to serve – not distract from – the need to deal collectively with expanding poverty and the racist scapegoating of immigrants that disproportionately affect their communities. Chicanos are looking to the past, using the traditional styles, not to mention instruments, of their communities, and through the vehicles of commercial culture are making the interrelationship between 'politics' and 'culture' transparent. As Wil-Dog puts it, 'I think more protests need music. I mean, every revolution has a soundtrack, bro, and that's where we come in' (Grant, 1999).

## Post-Nationalist Chicanismo, or the Logic of Chicano Pop Culture

What is a DJ if he can't scratch – to a ranchera? (Ozomatli, 'La Misma Cancion')

Ozomatli do not directly refer to themselves as a 'Chicano Band'. As Ulises Bella, tenor saxophonist, put it, 'As much as I want to say we're a Chicano band, we can't because we're not. We can't say that and have a Japanese dude, a black dude and a Scottish dude in the band. Ozomatli is very L. A. in its racial mix … It's very universal' (Doss, 1998a, p. 4). For Raul Pacheco, Ozomatli's inclusive nature is a vital part of their overall trajectory beyond the barrio to reach the rest of Los Angeles with music and a message. According to Pacheco, 'We're an inclusive band. We want to include people in our experience. Some of the messages may be hard for people to swallow, but we're going to try and win them over. If they're able to enjoy our show, we may be able to open them to our ideas' (Doss, 1998a, p. 4).

Ozomatli's inter-ethnic sensibility as reflected in their music and their makeup has gained them a broad audience. Between 1997 and 1999 they played in several diverse musical spaces participating in two punk tours, one swing tour, a hip hop tour, and a ska tour. They have opened for groups as wide ranging as Dave

Matthews and Maná, The Roots, and Red Hot Chili Peppers. Their popularity among Latino youth, however, is especially strong. This Chicano connection has been actively cultivated by the group and their label. Almo Sounds has constructed a 'multi-pronged marketing strategy' that not only attempts to work existing hip hop and alternative radio stations, but also traditional Mexican and crossover, 'Chicano urban' radio (Doss, 1998a, p. 4). Ozo have appeared in a Los Angeles-based Spanish-language show called 'Cuanto Cuesta El Show', and while their videos are rarely played on MTV in the United States, they are seen on MTV Latin America (not to mention BET and the viewer controlled video show The Box). [...]

More directly, Ozomatli's investment in and their emergence from the barrios of the Eastside of Los Angeles and their identification with Chicano culture are important elements of the group. Although members of Ozo have described their band as 'inclusive' and 'universal', such notions are deeply informed by Ozomatli's Chicano affiliations. The name Ozomatli, for example, comes from the indigenous Mexican language of Nahuatl. It refers to the monkey-figure found on the Aztec sun calendar which, from adaptations, has come to refer to the God of Dance (Doss, 1998b, p. 82). Historically, the Aztecs have been identified with the Mexican people and, since the Chicano *movimiento* of the 1960s, with the Chicano population of the Southwest, the latter location having been interpreted by *movimiento* ideology as the mythological Aztec nation-Utopia of the Chicano people called Aztlán. Ozo's different (and definitive) sounds and related instrumentation choices are informed by Mexican/Chicano culture. The use of the *bajo sexto* throughout the album, or the use of the accordion and the *requinto doble* by David Hidalgo, from Los Lobos, in his featured appearance on 'Aquí No Será' and 'La Misma Cancíon', reveals their music's roots in Mexican working-class musics. Along with the accordion, the *bajo sexto* (a guitar that includes bass strings) is used in the popular Mexican musics of *norteño* and *conjunto* from Northern Mexico and South Texas, respectively. And the *requinto doble* (a smaller version of the Spanish guitar which is 'tuned up to a fourth') was the standard instrument of the trio format popular in Mexico and Latin America during the 1940s and 1950s (Loza 1993, p. 255). Furthermore, the vision of Ozo's political activism has an important connection to the broader Mexican community. They have played at fundraisers for the *Ejercito Zapatista de Liberación National* (EZLN) and the United Farm Workers (UFW), two organizations fighting for the rights of Mexican people on both sides of the United States-Mexico border (Kun, 1998, p. 38). The EZLN of Chiapas, Mexico, has been waging a revolt against the Mexican government for the rights of Mexico's indigenous population since 1994, and the UFW has been struggling for the unionization of Mexican agricultural laborers in the U.S. for over thirty years.

This focus on the meaning of Ozomatli for Chicano identity is not intended to erase the cultural backgrounds of the non-Chicanos in the group, nor the existence of their growing multiracial fanbase. But it is meant to clarify the history and circumstances of Ozomatli's formation within the context of the changing Chicano/Latino community that is fast becoming the majority of the city. More importantly for my purposes, however, is the context of their formation within a larger cultural movement that is engaged in the recovery and revision of Chicano identity. While members of Ozomatli might resist labeling their diverse band, they are certainly involved in the current transformations of what it means to be Chicano in Los Angeles at the dawn of the twenty-first century. The use of

Chicano cultural forms by contemporary artists may well reflect Chicano culture's function as a resource for oppositional culture in Los Angeles, where its language of *mestizaje,* or cultural mixing, can be especially useful for global city dwellers. Chicano culture becomes a means whereby other aggrieved groups or individuals in the city derive some alternative knowledge, as well as an oppositional language, in which to ground themselves. [...]

Although Chicano culture speaks to the shared social experiences, institutions and cultural practices of Mexican Americans, there are other expressions of identification and identity co-existing within it. Inter-ethnic unity through culture rather than nationality or color is an integral part of this contemporary Chicano identity (Lipsitz, 1999a, pp. 213–31; 1999b, pp. 193–212; 1992, pp. 267–80). Yvette C. Doss, one of the main chroniclers of the Eastside Chicano underground scene and co-publisher and editor of the Chicano/Latino music and culture magazine *frontera,* argues that this emerging Chicano identity is more wide ranging and less rigid than the Chicano nationalism of the past. According to Doss (1999), the Chicano musicians who make up the Chicano underground 'have chosen to call themselves Chicano, salvaging the term from its previous, hyperpolitical essentialist confines and letting it loose on the modern world to evolve and take on new, broader permutations' (p. 148). Sometimes it takes a group like Ozomatli to remind us that Chicano identity is not static, nor is Chicano music simply reconstructed Mexican music. As Raúl Pacheco, lead singer of Ozo, describes it, 'What represents us, as Ozomatli, is I find beauty in the African American culture as well as my own. In the Japanese culture and the white culture. When Chali 2na raps, man, that's us, too. Whatever he's saying that's me' (Cuda, 1997, p. 8). [...]

The barrio is a vibrant mix of the traditional *and* popular. It is a product of local history as much as global change. It is a place where the life of the city streets mixes with the memories of the past, of Mexico or the Chicano *movimiento,* echoed in the sounds and imagery of the music. This is where the ties of Ozomatli to the city are especially pertinent. Rather than discarding the popular sounds of the barrio, from *banda* to *cumbia* to hip hop, Ozo has fused them into a musical language that reflects sonically the transformations of space, place, and identity that are taking place in the city.

Not strictly alternative, hip hop, or even *roq en español,* Ozomatli are part of a growing circle of artists and musicians in Los Angeles (and California) who have self-consciously identified themselves as 'Chicano' and attempted to bring the militant political consciousness of Chicanismo up to date through humor, art, and especially music. It is an emerging culture based on the everyday experiences, struggles and pleasures of the broader Chicano and Latino communities of Southern California. Many of the most promising artists of this Chicano cultural movement attempt to adapt the pride, history and connection to *La Raza* that was articulated by the Chicano nationalism of the 1960s and 1970s, to the changing circumstance of 1990s Los Angeles. Neither assimilationist nor separatist, this site of contemporary Chicano cultural production affirms its cultural heritage and its history of place in Los Angeles while creatively engaging in the adaptation of the diversity of cultural forms that cross the city. Of particular importance is the music of the Afro-diaspora. The influence of African music is apparent in Ozomatli's Afro-Latin, funk, and hip hop repertoire. [...]

This identification and performance of Chicano culture continues to have commercial and cultural consequences. Doss (1998b) has noted that the Latin-based sound and the self-identification of these groups as Chicano has rendered them too 'ethnic' or 'Latin' in the eyes of mainstream companies. At the same time, the bilingual lyricism of Chicano groups presents a challenge to the Latin-divisions of major labels who are only equipped to market music in Spanish (p. 82). The formation of a loosely united Chicano musical underground from the Greater Eastside has been inspired by this resistance to existing musical boundaries. According to Doss (1999), the current Chicano underground music scene 'is the product of a generation of fans and artists whose cultural and musical sensibilities haven't been expressed by either the Latin America-oriented *rock en español* or traditional 'Anglo' rock scenes, nor by the popular Mexican sounds of *banda* or *mariachi* (p. 144).

The local public and political culture of 1990s California is also an important part of formation of Chicano popular culture and its investment in the on-going re-creation of Chicano identity. The coming of age of the Chicano generation from which the underground musical movement comes is taking place during a time of an organized political repression against people of color in the state driven by its shrinking, but still electorally dominant, white population. In the last six years alone (1994–2000) California voters have been presented with and passed a set of 'propositions' that can only have adverse consequences for the non-white population: Proposition 187 (which restricts the rights to education and health care for undocumented immigrants); the anti-affirmative action Proposition 209; the anti-bilingual education Proposition 227; and in March, 2000, California voters overwhelmingly passed Proposition 21, meant to stiffen penalties for juvenile offenders while allowing more juveniles to be tried as adults. Los Angeles County will be especially impacted since it is the source for nearly one-third of the state's juvenile offenders, most of whom are Black or Chicano (Beiser and Solhei, 2000).

Undergirded by 'the possessive investment in whiteness', California public policies as well as private prejudice have been organized against the burgeoning population of color since the 1960s (Oliver and Johnson, 1984; Nicolaides, 1999; Soja et al., 1987; Davis, 1995; Lipsitz, 1998). They manifest a form of white identify politics that works to maintain, and increase, white privilege. These political campaigns, intended for white voters from both the Republican and Democratic Parties, are an orchestrated scapegoating of people of color, who have been made responsible for California's economic woes, its crime, and even insecurities about higher education by white citizens. This scapegoating is exemplified in the voter initiatives mentioned above but also in the militarization of the United States-Mexico border and its construction of the undocumented Mexican immigrant as an 'illegal alien', while the 'illegal businesses' that hire and exploit this necessary but marginalized labor force are left unacknowledged and unprosecuted (Dunn, 1996).

It is important to note that these initiatives, and their consequent criminalization of Latinos, emerged in the wake of the multiracial uprising of late April 1992 in California's largest city. Latinos made up the largest group of arrestees during the 'civil unrest' which followed the not guilty verdict of the LAPD officers who were videotaped in the gang-beating of Black motorist Rodney King. The true participation of Latinos can never be known, since several of those arrested were not charged but deported by 1,000 Border Patrol and Immigration and Naturalization Service agents who descended on the Latino immigrant enclave of Pico Union during the latter days of the uprising (Davis, 1993, p. 145).

While anti-immigrant sentiment deflects attention away from the consequences of urban austerity and economic restructuring on the state economy, people of color, particularly immigrants, have been targeted by the Republican Party, with the financial support of wealthy state citizens, as drains on the state with unrivaled access to public resources (Lipsitz, 1998, pp. 47–56, 224–33). The electoral campaign by Governor Pete Wilson in 1994, for example, directed attention away from a massive recession (which had helped the governor's approval ratings fall below 20 percent) by broadcasting video footage of Mexican immigrants crossing the United States-Mexico border and delivering campaign speeches that stressed the burdens imposed on U.S. hospitals by undocumented Mexican immigrant women giving birth inside them. By supporting the anti-immigrant Proposition 187 and making it the focus of his re-election campaign, Wilson relied more on his whiteness than his political record. This helped secure his re-election in 1994 despite his low approval. White voters for the proposition conveniently forgot their reliance on Latino and Asian immigrant labor as farmers, low-wage labor, domestics, etc., and remained ignorant of the fact that undocumented immigrants pay more in taxes than they receive in services (McDonnell, 1997). Additionally, the overwhelming support of Proposition 187 by wealthy white voters can be seen as a measure to control labor and prevent free bargaining over wages, hours, and working conditions. In supporting Proposition 187, such voters were criminalizing low-wage immigrant laborers likely to become active in growing unionization efforts throughout the state.

The affiliation of Chicano popular culture with the Chicano/Latino community, as well as other communities of color, has been shaped by the right turn in Californian electoral politics. In and against such a political climate, much of the work on the part of Chicano popular culture producers has an important critical function, attempting not only to fill in the gaps of a media industry that inexplicably ignores the indigenous culture of the city to be found on the Eastside, but also to face up and talk back to the growing inequalities of the global city and the concurrent scapegoating of people of color.[1] [...]


## la Musica es el Mensaje: Audible L.A.

> Everyone else in the band says, 'we take you around the world'. But for me it's like we just take you around L.A. (Wil-Dog, in Kun, 1998, p: 39)

Ozomatli emerge from the contemporary music scene of Los Angeles. As Wil-Dog notes in an interview with the music magazine *The Synthesis*, Ozomatli's range of styles is peculiarly 'L.A.':

> *The Synthesis:* Is your music influenced by what you see on the [L.A.] streets every day?

*Wil-Dog.* I think that's one aspect of it. Just growing up there, you'll hear somebody next door playing *Ranchettas*, you know, and then all of a sudden, a car will drive by bumping some hip-hop. That's partially where it comes from, and then, well, we all really respect all the types of music we play. (Sidman, 1999)

Wil-Dog's pointing to *rancheras* and hip hop as important influences on the sound of Ozomatli speaks not only to the contemporary mix of cultures to be found in the global city, but to the continuing role of popular music as a vital source of expression among Chicanos in Los Angeles.

Ozomatli's relationship to the broader contemporary Chicano music scene is quickly evident in the production credits of their first album. Ozomatli's self-titled debut was produced by T-Ray who has also worked with the popular rap group, Cypress Hill, whose own ties to the Chicano culture of the Greater Eastside are integral to their music and success (Cross, 1994). Cypress Hill's gangster tales of life in the southeast Los Angeles barrio of South Gate uses the slang (*cálo*), imagery and sounds of Chicano gang culture, such as the loop of the *Cholo* soul anthem 'Duke of Earl' in their song 'How I Could Just Kill a Man', to participate in the popular cultural world of hip hop. Rooted in Afro-diasporic cultural practices and one of the few spaces in which Black and Puerto Rican people were able to express themselves and protest their continuing marginalization in post-industrial New York City, hip hop has become a vital space in fostering adaptation and innovation, the use of old and new, in the formation of new, urban music. Rap music has been utilized by several distinct social groups in affirming their own cultural roots (Rose, 1994, pp. 21–61; Lipsitz, 1994, pp. 24–45). Cypress Hill, and other more explicitly Chicano groups like Kid Frost, Delinquent Habits, Mexakinz, 2Mex, Aztlán Underground, Of Mexican Descent (OMD), and A Lighter Shade of Brown, adapt hip hop as a vehicle for a *Chicano* mode of expression that connects them not only with the wider world of hip hop and urban culture, but to the everyday lives of Chicanos in Los Angeles. Their samples of older Mexican or Chicano music, such as the *mariachi* in the Delinquent Habits recent single, 'Here Come the Horns' (1998), or Frost's best-selling single, 'La Raza' (1991), which samples El Chicano's rendition of 'Viva Tirado', are reconstructed and lay the foundation for their contemporary observations of the Chicano social world through rap. Ozomatli's raps are delivered by Chali 2na, an African American with an explicitly 'Black' consciousness. Chali 2na's flow over Mexican and Latin musical forms exemplifies the historical relationship between Chicanos and African Americans in music, politics, and in the everyday struggles that besiege these racialized, predominately working-class communities. It is a relationship that Ozomatli is actively cultivating in music and politics. Ozo has also played at protests, rallies and fundraisers that focus on issues central to both communities, such as police brutality and affirmative action. [...]

At the same time, while being one of the newest hip hop groups out of the growing rap music scene, Ozomatli is also one of the newest *conjuntos* out of the exploding *banda* scene in Mexican Los Angeles. The *norteño* and *banda* music (what Wil-Dog refers to as *rancheras)* popular in the Mexican states of Sinaloa, Nayarit, Michoacan and Jalisco, has become one of the most popular sounds of the Chicano/Mexican working classes in Los Angeles, and it can be heard in Mexican immigrant barrios throughout the country. Ozo pays tribute to this popular Mexican music in 'La

Misma Cancion' and 'Aqui No Sera'. *Banda* arose in the nineteenth century from the cultural exchange of Mexicans and Europeans in nineteenth century Mexico. European immigrants to northern Mexican states like Sinaloa introduced polkas, the waltz and the instruments that accompanied them, such as the accordion, to the region. Popular throughout Mexico in the 1940s, *banda* traditionally consisted of the rhythms of tubas and bass drums under dominant brass and woodwind instruments but was transformed into techno-*banda* in the 1990s, adapting elements of rock and roll and replacing traditional instruments with the electric bass, modern drums, *timbales,* and synthesizers (Lipsitz, 1999b, p. 200).

While originally from Mexico, *banda's* recent popularity has been fostered by Mexicans in Los Angeles, where the music has developed its own subculture. [...] Working-class Chicanos and Mexican immigrants flock to *banda* dances throughout Los Angeles, where eight hundred *quebradita* (little break) clubs, named after the distinct dance style of the music, with over thirty thousand members have been established to stage parties and dances in the backyards, dancehalls, and warehouses throughout the area (Martinez, 1998).

*Banda's* popularity is especially evident in the explosive ratings of local radio stations programming the music. In 1993, the Spanish-language KLAX 97.9 went from the twentieth to the number one-rated station in the city by placing the music in regular rotation. As the nation's largest radio market, Los Angeles made KLAX the top-rated station in the United States by playing Mexican *banda* music (Lipsitz, 1999b, pp. 197–8).

Although it is predominately the favored music of Los Angeles's most recent Mexican immigrants, post-1984, many of the music's newest fans and artists are young Chicanos who have turned to this Mexican folk music at a time when Mexicans became the favorite scapegoat of California politics. Like Ozomatli, and the *drywalleros* mentioned earlier, one way young Chicanos forge a sense of collective and affirmative identity is by looking to their traditions, as real or imagined as they may be.

One of the more prolific *banda* artists from Los Angeles, Saul Viera, a.k.a. El Gavilancillo (the Little Hawk), expressed this desire to turn to the roots of his identity in his decision to become a *banda* musician. Viera, a Chicano from the small city of Paramount in southeast L. A., recalled that 'When I was in junior high and my dad would play *banda* music, I'd be like, "Turn it down. My friends are going to hear". Now it's the other way around. I'm turning it up, and my parents are turning it down. When I was younger, I was ashamed of Mexican music. Now I know who I am. I'm not afraid of my race' (Quiñones, 1998). Viera produced 15 albums in his short career of four years, tragically cut short by his unsolved murder in 1998. Sam Quiñones (1998), one of the historians of this recent *banda* resurgence, described Viera as a 'wonderful urban-immigrant anomaly' that was becoming more frequent among working-class Mexican males in Los Angeles in the 1990s: 'a young man who listened to rap and made a living singing polkas about Mexican drug smugglers'.

Moreover, while *banda* may seem to have little in common with hip hop, it shares important histories with rap music in Los Angeles. *Banda's* cultivation has been developed in the same ethnic retail and distribution networks within the local economy of working-class Los Angeles. Like the early dissemination of rap music in the mid-1980s, the marketing of *banda* music was initially a grassroots strategy that took advantage of specific consumption spaces of the city's working-class lanscape. Quiñones argues that for the initial artists of *banda:*

> Cracking the established L.A. record distribution system was nearly impossible, so the racks (or *raquitas*) at car washes, bakeries, butcher shops and above all, swap meets became the primary outlets. For most Angelenos, the dozens of swap meets dotting the Southland are places to unload unwanted junk – or pick up someone else's. But for many Mexican immigrants, who don't understand banking or have no hope for a business loan, swap meets are a shot at capital formation. They get the product directly to the public, without having to rely on advertising, big distributors or credit lines.

The mix tapes of local DJs and aspiring producers like Dr. Dre and the initial recordings of local rap pioneers like N.W.A., King T, Ice T, and Mixmaster Spade, all from the working-class neighborhoods of South Central and southeast Los Angeles, first sold their music in swap meets as well (Cross, 1994).

Another significant similarity with hip hop is the development of *narco-corridos* within the *banda* style. Like the sub-genre of gangsta rap that Los Angeles, with groups like N.W.A. and Cypress Hill, made internationally famous, *narco-corridos* are Spanish tales of the Mexican drug world that carry themes of violence, the treachery of police on both sides of the border, and the fearless heroism of drug smugglers. This type of music was originally produced by Chalino Sanchez, an undocumented immigrant from Sinaloa who settled in Paramount and played in bars and nightclubs throughout the southeast. Quiñones (1998) describes Chalino as 'the most influential music figure to emerge in Los Angeles in decades'. After selling thousands of recordings of his music about the drug life in his home state of Sinaloa, an area notorious for drug cultivation and smuggling run by a local Mexican drug cartel, Chalino was murdered upon his return there in 1992 by unknown assailants. He was shot after his performance in front of a packed audience of 2,000 in the capital city of Culiacan, where Chalino's tales about drug running may have been considered too revealing. [...]

Yet *banda* music is only a part of the musical environment that is remaking Chicano culture. *Banda* is often played alongside hip hop, *merengue, cumbias* and house music at dances and private parties among the Mexican working class. Ozomatli's expression and production of Chicano cultural identity are rooted in these diverse traditions. The sound of the barrio crosses several generations and musical expressions, and is produced as much by cultural exchanges with other groups as it is by its roots in Mexican musical tradition. As Los Angeles fast becomes a Latino majority city, and the influence and sounds of Chicano culture in the city becomes more obvious, maybe the claim that Ozomatli is 'very L. A.' is quite appropriate after all. It is, in the end, the music which expresses most eloquently Ozomatli's connection to Chicano culture and the importance of place, in this case the musical environment of the contemporary barrio, in the formation of Chicano music at this moment.

The polyglot, dialogical and category-resistant quality of Ozomatli's musical (con)fusions register in precise and detailed fashion the injuries done to low-wage workers and racial others by globalization and transnationalism. But new social structures create new social subjects who in turn create new social imaginaries.

At the very moment when political and economic leaders scapegoat multilingual 'mongrel' communities and cultures, groups like Ozomatli challenge the cultural and political pretensions of white/Anglo culture and exploit the contradictions between the nation's political reliance on fictions of cultural homogeneity and the nation's economic dependence on securing low-wage labor, markets, and raw materials from Latin America, Asia, and Africa. Speaking from the interstices between commercial culture and the new social movements, Ozomatli's music and political work offer us invaluable bottom-up perspectives on the terrain of counter-politics and cultural creation at the beginning of the twenty-first century.

## Note

1 The racialization of California politics has much to do with the increasing racial diversity of the state since the 1960s but particularly since the explosion of Asian and Latin American immigration in the 1980s and 1990s. Asian and Pacific Islanders increased their population in the state by over 116 percent between 1980 and 1990 to almost three million, or almost 10 percent of the overall population. Latinos in California have increased by over 66 percent in the same period, to become a quarter of the state's population. The African American population has grown by 20 percent to over 2 million, although the proportion of their population has fallen to 7.4 percent in 1990 from 7.7 percent in 1980 (Saito, 1998, p. 2). Meanwhile, the Los Angeles region is rapidly becoming a majority Latino metropolis.

## References

Almosounds 2000: http://www.almosounds.com/ozomatli/
Anaya, Rodolfo A. and Lomeli, Francisco (eds) 1991: *Aztlán: Essays on the Chicano Homeland*. Albuquerque, NM: University of New Mexico Press.
Anonymous 1997: Schools Brief: One World? *The Economist* (October 18), 79–80.
Beiser, Vince and Solhei, Karla 2000: Juvenile Injustice: Proposition 21 Aims to Send Thousands of California Teenagers to Adult Prisons. *Los Angeles Weekly* (Feb. 11–17).
Camu, DJ Alex 1998: *models.com*, (May). http://www.models.com/groove/hot_picks/index.html.
Castillo, Jaime 1999: Ozomatli Interview, *salsazine.com*, (September 15). http://www.salsazine.com/.
*CMJ New Music Report*, 573. June 8, 1998.
Cross, Brian 1994: It's Not About a Salary ... Rap, Race + Rap, Race + Resistance In *Los Angeles*. New York and London: Verso.
Cuda, Heidi Sigmund 1997: The Wild Bunch. *Los Angeles Times (Calendar Section)* (July 10), p. 8.
Davis, Mike 1993: Uprising and Repression in L.A. In Robert Gooding-Williams (ed) *Reading Rodney King/Reading Urban Uprising*. New York: Routledge, pp. 142–54.
Davis, Mike 1995: Hell Factories in the Field. *The Nation*, pp. 229–34, 260–7 (February 20).
Davis, Mike 1999: Magical Urbanism: Latinos Reinvent the US Big City. *New Left Review*, 234 (March–April).
Delinquent Habits 1998: *Here Come the Horns*. PMP/Loud.
Doss, Yvette C. 1998a: Música for the Masses. *Los Angeles Times (Calendar Section)*, (June 8).

Doss, Yvette C. 1998b: Unbound by Tradition. *Los Angeles Times (Sunday Calendar),* (January 11).

Doss, Yvette C. 1999: Choosing Chicano in the 1990s: The Underground Music Scene of Los(t) Angeles. In Gustavo Leclerc, Raúl Villa, and Michael J. Dear (eds) *La Vida Latina en L.A.: Urban Latino Cultures.* Thousand Oaks, CA: Sage, pp. 143–56.

Dunn, Timothy 1996: *The Militarization of the U. S.-Mexico Border, 1978–1992.* Austin, TX: University of Texas Press.

*frontera 2000*: http://www.fronteramag.com.

Grant, Kieran 1999: Multiculturalism Thrives in L. A.'s Ozomatli. *Toronto Sun* (July 9).

Kid Frost 1990: *Hispanic Causing Panic.* Virgin.

Kun, Josh 1998. Around the World in L. A.: The Anomalies of Ozomatli. *ColorLines,* 1 (2), (Fall), pp. 38–40.

*latinolink.com* 1999: Review: Latin Rock's Maná Joins Legendary Santana. *Latino Link, Arts and Entertainment Section,* (August 26). http://www.latinolink.com/arts_entertainment/music/0826sant.htm.

Lipsitz, George 1992: Chicano Rock: Cruisin' Around the Historical Bloc. In Reebee Garofalo (ed) *Rockin' the Boat: Mass Music and Mass Movements.* Boston, MA: South End Press, pp. 267–80.

Lipsitz, George 1994: *Dangerous Crossroads.* London and New York: Verso.

Lipsitz, George 1998: *The Possessive Investment in Whiteness: How White People Profit from Identity Politics.* Philadelphia, PA: Temple University Press.

Lipsitz, George 1999a: World Cities and World Beat: Low-Wage Labor and Transnational Culture. *Pacific Historical Review,* pp. 213–31.

Lipsitz, George 1999b: 'Home is Where the Hatred Is': Work, Music, and the Transnational Economy. In Hamid Naficy (ed) *Home, Exile, Homeland: Film, Media, and the Politics of Place.* New York: Routledge, pp. 193–212.

Lonidier, Fred 1994: *Los Drywalleros: Huelgistas.* Labor Link TV.

*Los Angeles Weekly,* http://www.laweekly.com.

Los *Angeles Weekly* 1999: Music Feature: And the LAWMA Goes To … July 2–8). http://www.laweekly.com/ink/99/32/music-.shtml.

Loza, Steven 1993: *Barrio Rhythms: Mexican American Music in Los Angeles.* Urbana and Chicago, IL: University of Illinois Press.

Martinez, Rubén 1998: The Shock of the New. In Antonia Darder and Rodolfo D. Torres (eds) *The Latino Studies Reader: Culture, Economy, and Society.* Malden, MA: Blackwell, pp. 170–79.

Martinez, Marilyn 1995: Strike at Jobs Program: L.A. Conservation Corps Workers Stage Sit-in, Demand Benefits and Better Pay. *Los Angeles Times* (March 22), B1.

McDonnell, Patrick J. 1997: Immigrants a Net Economic Plus, Study Says. *Los Angeles Times* (May 18), A1.

Moore, Joan and Vigil, James Diego 1993: Barrios in Transition. In Joan Moore and Rachel Pinderhughes (eds) *In the Barrios: Latinos and the Underclass Debate.* New York: Sage, pp. 27–49.

Naficy, Hamid 1994: *The Making of Exile Culture.* Minneapolis, MN: University of Minnesota Press.

Nicolaides, Becky M. 1999: *Making the Suburban Crisis in Postwar Working-Class Los Angeles.* Paper presented for the conference Unimagined Futures: The Racial Economy of Postwar Metropolitan California. Stanford University (May).

Oliver, Melvin and Johnson, Jr., James H. 1984: Inter-Ethnic Conflict in an Urban Ghetto: The Case of Blacks and Latinos in Los Angeles. Research in Social Movements. *Conflict and Change,* pp. 57–94.

Oliver, Melvin L., Johnson, Jr., James H., and Farrell, Jr., Walter C. 1993: Anatomy of a Rebellion: A Political-Economic Analysis. In Robert Gooding-Williams (ed) *Reading Rodney King/Reading Urban Uprising.* New York and London: Routledge, pp. 117–41.

*Ozomatli* 1998: Almo Sounds/Interscope.

*ozomatli.com:* http://www.ozomatli.com.

Quiñones, Sam 1998: 'Sing Now, Die Later'. The Ballad of Chalino Sanchez. *Los Angeles Weekly* (July 31–August 6). http//www.laweekly.com/ink/98/36/quinones1.shtml.

Robles, Rita 1999: Ozomatli (Concert review, Madrid, Spain), *indyrock magazine* (November). http://www.ideal.es/indyrock/ozomatli.html.

Rose, Tricia 1994: *Black Noise: Rap Music and Black Culture in Contemporary America.* Hanover, NH: Wesleyan University Press.

Rouse, Roger 1991: Mexican Migration and the Social Space of Postmodernism. *Diaspora,* 1 (1), (Spring), pp. 8–23.

Saito Leland 1998: *Race and Politics: Asian Americans, Latinos, and Whites in a Los Angeles Suburb.* Urbana and Chicago, IL: University of Illinois Press.

Saldívar, José David 1997: *Border Matters: Remapping American Cultural Studies.* Berkeley, CA: University of California Press.

Shuster, Fred 1998: Taste the New Salsa. *Los Angeles Daily News* (July 22).

Sidman, Max 1999: Soundtrack to the People's Revolution. *The Synthesis,* http://www.thesynthesis.com/interviews/ozomatli.

Soja, Edward, Morales, Rebecca, and Wolff, Goetz 1987: Industrial Restructuring: An Analysis of Social and Spatial Change. In Richard Peet (ed) *International Capitalism and Industrial Restructuring.* Boston, MA: Allen and Unwin, pp. 145–74.

Utne Reader 1996 (December): http://www.utne.com.

Valdes-Rodriguez, Alisa 1999: Ozo Rising. *Los Angeles Times, Sunday Calendar* (July 25).

Valle, Victor and Torres, Rodolfo D. 1993: Latinos in a Post-Industrial Disorder. *Socialist Review,* 93 (4), pp. 1–28.

# Chapter 38

# Paul Gilroy

# Wearing Your Art on Your Sleeve: Notes Towards a Diaspora History of Black Ephemera

As perhaps the first of the technological artistic inventions, it [the phonograph record] already stems from an era that cynically acknowledges the dominance of things over people through the emancipation of technology from human requirements and human needs and through the presentation of achievements whose significance is not primarily humane; instead, the need is initially produced by advertisement, once the thing already exists and is spinning in its own orbit.

T. W. Adorno

While we were in Lagos we visited Fela Ransome Kuti's club the Afro Spot, to hear him and his band. He'd come to hear us, and we came to hear him. I think when he started as a musician he was playing a kind of music they call Highlife, but by this time he was developing Afro-beat out of African music and funk. He was kind of like the African James Brown. His band had strong rhythm ... Some of the ideas my band was getting from that band had come from me in the first place, but that was okay with me. It made the music that much stronger.

James Brown

Special cultural and political relationships have been created in the Atlantic 'triangle' of the African diaspora. They are the outcome of long processes in which the cultures of Africa, the Americas, Europe and the Caribbean have interacted and

From: Paul Gilroy, *Small Acts: Thoughts on the Politics of Black Cultures*. London: Serpent's Tail, 1993.

transformed each other. Their complex history cannot be presented in detail here[1] but it has involved struggles that dissolve the separation between politics and cultural expression. They have been concerned with the abolition of slavery and the acquisition of political rights for black Americans, the independence of colonial countries and the solidarity of diaspora blacks with movements for the destruction of racist settler regimes in Africa. These struggles are notable for the way they have been infused with the spiritual rhetoric and messianic visions of the black Church. They have involved the movement of key individuals, the international circulation of books, tracts and pamphlets and, perhaps above all, they have been signalled through the transnational power of black musics which have reached out beyond the boundaries of the nation-state. These struggles have also relied on the circulation of images and symbols.

Against this background, I want to explore one means through which cultural and aesthetic exchanges between different populations across the diaspora have been constructed – one population providing cultural and philosophical fuel for another and vice versa. It may, at first sight, appear to be trivial and inconsequential to focus on gramophone records as a medium through which these diasporic conversations have been conducted, particularly as they are commodities that are designed to be ephemeral, giving way to replacements once boredom has set in or fashions have changed. Black music has, however, only partially obeyed the ground rules of reification and planned obsolescence. Its users have sometimes managed to combine the strongest possible sense of fashion with a respectful, even reverent approach to the historical status of their musical culture which values its longevity and its capacity to connect them to their historical roots. The music has thus often been prized more for its sublimity and the racial probity of its witness to their lives than for its precarious status as a disposable and replaceable fragment of pop culture.

I will not, however, examine records solely for the music that they contain. They should be understood as complex cultural artefacts – objects – in their own right. The music recorded and encoded onto the surface of the discs may be the primary inducement to acquire a record, but the sleeve with its combination of text and images comprises an important, if secondary, element that so far seems to have escaped sustained consideration from cultural historians of black experience.

The rise of the long-playing, 33 rpm, vinyl gramophone record coincides neatly with turbulent years of black struggle in the United States and it provides a valuable means to examine both that history and its international impact. The corporate replacement of LP records by cassettes, CDs and other new digital formats is having profound and dismal consequences for the circulation and use of black music. CDs do their work in secret, shut away from the disruptive, creative power of black hands once that mysterious drawer is closed. But it is not only that the specific forms of vernacular creativity constituted around vinyl discs cannot be maintained in the newer formats. Reissues of back catalogue are selective and completely out of step with the needs of the black underground, let alone the demands of cultural history. This means that some of the most dynamic traffic in our cultural heritage comes to an abrupt halt as more and more records simply cannot be replaced. We are left with different kinds of commodity which are experienced and used differently. Images and text have been shrunk. Both the ratio between them and their relationship to the music have been transformed.

The text and images found on sleeves existed in relation to the music they enclosed but these different dimensions of communication had a significant measure of independence from each other. Together they constituted an intricate commodity that fused different components of black cultural and political sensibility in an unstable and unpredictable combination. In the 1960s and 1970s, black political discourse migrated to and colonized the record sleeve as a means towards its expansion and self-development. That era is now over.

I have argued elsewhere[2] that the social relations that surround the consumption of African diaspora musics and the forms that these musics assume, do not fit easily into the saleable segments that their status as cultural commodities requires. The history of black musical forms includes a constant struggle against both the constraints of the technology of musical reproduction and dominant expectations of how music, packaged and sold in this way, should be heard. The imagery on record sleeves was a minor, though still significant, part of this struggle. Those who provide the means that can translate the substance of black creativity into two ounces of plastic with a hole in the middle, wrap it in paper, cardboard and plastic, and then ship it around the world in order to maximize their profit, have been unable to command this convoluted distributive process in its entirety. The musicians who created the music did not always control its packaging, but they were sometimes able to use cover art to collude with their preferred audiences in telling ways which the multinational companies who circulated these products either did not care about or were unable to foresee. For example, the prevalence of images of ancient Egypt during the 1960s and 1970s proved to be an important means for communicating pan-African ideas in an inferential, populist manner. It is worth noting that, appropriated in this way, the 'traditional' imagery of ancient Egypt was not counterposed to views of 'modern' reality but rather presented in a way that emphasized its continuity with contemporary technological and scientific developments.

It is noteworthy that, although these images are still part of the visual culture that supports African-American music, they were used in a number of rather different ways during the 1980s. One recent version mediates the heritage of Nile Valley civilizations by inserting the borrowed and 'blackened' image of Indiana Jones, the superhuman hero from Steven Spielberg's adventure films, between the cartouche and the viewer.

African-American music has frequently been sent out into the world in open, 'provisional' formats which anticipate the supplementary work that active consumers must bring to the ritual settings in which it will be played, if it is to reveal its full power. This argument can be extended beyond the specifically musical dimensions of the record as a cultural commodity. Parallel and essentially similar processes of aesthetic and political grounding can be shown to be at work in the invitation to 'read' and make active use of images and text on record sleeves. In order to appreciate the significance of the imagery of race that record sleeves project, it is essential to remember that we are dealing with a dispossessed and economically exploited population which does not enjoy extensive opportunities to perceive itself or see its experiences imaginatively or artistically reflected in the visual culture of urban living. As far as Britain is concerned, blacks have been seldom seen in advertisements or on television. The pictorial symbols inherent in the political agitation of their communities, in independently published magazines or the minority markets in specialized items like cosmetics which have displayed the cultural assets and distinctiveness of the 'racial' group, are limited and meagre visual resources by comparison with the mainstream media. The cultural significance of record covers as a form of folk art is therefore enhanced simply because they offer one of very few opportunities to see and enjoy images of black people outside the stereotyped guises in which the dominant culture normally sanctions their presence. For example, this simple family snapshot of the Marleys would never have emerged while his record company was promoting him as a swaggering and sexually available Rastaman shrouded by a cloud of ganga smoke. This variety of hyper-masculine representation had been thought essential to the development of Marley's appeal to rock audiences. This picture only appeared as a curiosity in the nostalgic moment after his death in 1981.

Showing something of how the record sleeve fits into vernacular cultural and political history is relatively easy in black America. There, the depth and vitality of musical traditions means that the recent history of black life has been registered in the most minute detail through the imagery found on disc sleeves, the titles of the records and their changing appeals to different groups of black and white consumers. The formation and transcendence of the market for 'race records' is there to behold. The secularization of black music which led to soul, the civil rights struggles and, in particular, the Black Power movement, can all be apprehended by this means. The ebbs and flows in black political culture have been faithfully transcribed through the text, imagery and artwork of the record sleeve.

This story is made more complex by questions of musical genre[3] and of course, by the shifting relationship between independent black record production and the multinational companies that dominate the music industries. Marketing jazz is necessarily different from marketing soul, hip-hop, house or reggae. Each sub-category creates its own rules, styles and strategies of visual communication which require detailed consideration. However, some tentative generalizations can be made. On the most basic level, sleeves have been used to define artists and to assist in the process of locating them into the particular area of the market to which they have been assigned by the record company, but this has not been their sole function. Apart from their use as a means to tell an audience how to hear and comprehend the music they enclose, sleeves have been developed as an agitational or educational tool which can, for example, encourage people to register to vote, to grow their hair a certain way, to wear a particular garment or to employ a familiar item of clothing in an unfamiliar and 'sub-culturally' distinctive way. Album jackets may also convey useful information to a specially targeted audience which is not the same as the one in which the record company is interested. They may also help to solicit this audience into specific modes of cultural and political identification. Most importantly for my purposes here, record sleeves have been employed to address the black public and to induce that public to assess and possibly to share in the styles and symbols that constitute the idea of blackness itself. The music facilitates the circulation of styles and symbols, creating an aura of pleasure and desire around them which is an important political phenomenon. This process has not always been a simple extension of the sale of records.

These developments may have been most obvious during the 1960s when the presentation of the black body had a crucial symbolic significance in the ideology of Black Power and its cultural correlates. However, the recent controversy over the cosmetic surgical operations undertaken by performers like Michael Jackson and George Benson shows that these issues are still politically charged and articulated into a broader network of American racial politics.[4] Arguments over surgical 'Europeanization' also apply to the lesser but more widespread practice of photographical whitening which has been a notable feature of the marketing of rhythm-and-blues artists as pop singers to white audiences during the 1980s.

The sheer intensity of feeling generated by these issues needs to be explained. It derives not simply from the belief that these ploys place the racial identity of black artists in jeopardy. It stems from the special conception of responsibility allocated to the artist in black expressive culture whereby musicians are seen as a priestly caste charged (among other things) with the custodianship of the racial group's most intimate self-identity. The black body, publicly displayed by the performer, becomes a privileged 'racial' sign. It makes explicit the hidden links between blacks and helps to ground an oppositional aesthetic constituted around our phenotypical difference from 'white' ideals of beauty and a concept of the body in motion which is the residue of our African cultures. When Prince, whose faithful adherence to the performative and aesthetic strategies of black America is thought by some commentators to contrast sharply with his calculated androgyny,[5] declares himself to be the son of a white woman in the 'autobiographical' film *Purple Rain,* a further layer of difficulty begins to take shape. This cover was produced prior to his marketing to whites as a rock artist.

Hair has provided the primary means to express these aesthetic and stylistic concerns[6] but the public display of Afrocentric *styles* – of dress, language and social conduct – remains a major consideration for both men and women. Long before the mass marketing of recorded music, black musicians, sacred and profane, had a special role in signifying black style in general and coolness[7] in particular to the black publics constituted in the dynamic act of performance. Ralph Ellison put it like this in 1964:

> Bessie Smith might have been a 'blues queen' to the society at large, but within the tighter Negro community where the blues was part of a total way of life, and a major expression of an attitude toward life, she was a priestess, a celebrant who affirmed the values of the group and man's ability to deal with chaos.[8]

Images of Aretha Franklin, presented, fifteen years apart, on the covers of her two double albums of religious music, actualize this role in strikingly different ways that convey much of how black America changed between 1972 and 1987. The African costume on the earlier sleeve is only the most obvious clue to the different notions of femininity that are being invoked. In the first picture she waits outside the church, possibly for baptism. In the second she is inside, her garments of heavenly white convey the fact that she has now been saved. These changes can be explained, not simply by the fact that Aretha has aged, but by the way that the Jackson presidential candidacy, which took black politics to a new position within the official political culture, recomposed the relationship between sacred and secular elements of black cultural struggle. If the church building represents America, what are we to make of Aretha's entry? The later record included a lengthy oration by Jackson himself. With Aretha's help, he was able to address her audience directly rather than rely on her art to transpose his message, 'I know it's dark but the morning had to come', into another *musical* discourse.

These pictures of Aretha are also a means to emphasize that men and women may encounter these images of blackness in different ways and put them to different kinds of use. Blackness appears in gender-specific forms that allow for the construction of distinctive modes of masculinity and femininity which, though connected by a common 'racial' identity, may be actively antagonistic. Sometimes the mode of this antagonism is taken to represent an internal truth of the black condition. Particularly in rhythm and blues, ritual conflict between men and women is dramatized so that it becomes a heavily encoded symbol of racial difference and racial distinctiveness. Some covers realize this visually, signifying blackness through the special intensity at which, it is believed, both gender difference and the conflict between men and women can be experienced.

The black population of Britain has a unique place within these complicated discursive relationships. Although there have been substantial black populations in Britain for a considerable period of time, the bulk of contemporary settlement is a post-war phenomenon. This means that the black British are a comparatively new and fragmented population. Black Britain has been heavily reliant on the output of black populations elsewhere for the raw materials from which its own distinctive, cultural and political identities could be assembled. The proximity of Britain's black settlers to the experience of migration also means that the cultures of the Caribbean have provided important resources which enabled people to retain and re-create links with the cultures from which they came. This has not, however, been a one-way street.

The different varieties of visual imagery used to sell Jimi Hendrix's music on the different sides of the Atlantic can be cited as an example here. In Britain Hendrix, a black American, was sold in conjunction with images of exoticism and transgression. In Britain, for example, his portrait was banished to the interior of the 'Electric Ladyland' sleeve by David King's celebrated photograph of nineteen naked women. Eighteen of them are 'white'; a lone black woman sits vacantly in the right mid-ground, offering a striking image of Hendrix's own displacement and isolation.

The cover of his second album release, 'Axis Bold As Love' went so far as to offer a painting of him in the guise of a Hindu deity. On the other side of the ocean, he was projected as a flower child produced from the womb of swinging London rather than a veteran rhythm-and-blues player. Indeed, his pedigree in the traditions of black music-making was perceived as an active hindrance to his serious status as a successful rock artist.[9] Finding two competent white sidemen who could also backcomb their hair into an approximation of his grown-out process-cum-proto 'fro style, became a means to undermine any lingering residues of blackness. Hendrix is an important, if exceptional, case because in neither place was he primarily marketed to a black audience.

The diasporic relationship between American and Caribbean cultures is also an increasingly complicated one. It is made yet more so by the cross-fertilization of musical styles that has followed the relocation of Caribbean people in the US, particularly in New York.[10] It is essential to remember that reggae is itself a composite, hybrid form which derives in part from jazz, rhythm and blues and soul styles. The cultures of black America have also supplied a political language to the world-wide black public. First the rhetoric of rights and justice, then the discourse of Black Power crossed the seas and enabled black folks here, there and everywhere to make sense of the segregation, oppression and exploitation they experienced in their countries of residence. With this in mind, it is perhaps unsurprising that the style of reggae culture in its reggae and its raggamuffin phases has been imported into the mainstream of black America through the visual culture of hip-hop.

The meaning of these imported cultural forms was not fixed or finally established at their point of origin, and it bears repetition that they too were offered outwards to the wider black world in radically unfinished forms that anticipated, even expected, supplementary input and further developmental work. In the cultural and aesthetic histories of diaspora populations, this anticipation of supplementation applies as readily to the visual meanings through which blackness is articulated as it does to its textual, verbal and performative figurations. The secret codes of black style and fashion have operated as a silent anti-language that connected us to each other in spite of wide variations in culture and lived experience.

In the past, I described the role of music in constituting an alternative public sphere in which the self-understanding of particular black populations has been negotiated. The public institutions in which the music is actively and socially consumed are an essential part of this process but they do not exhaust it. My previous discussion of these issues centred on the affirmative potency of the dancehall and the medley of social and cultural practices – dance, word play, scratching, dubbing and mixing – that are assembled and rearticulated there. To conclude, I want to take this argument back one step by looking at the black record shop as a similar kind of cultural institution, distinguished from the dancehall by the way that the music is complemented there by a proliferation of *visual* signs of blackness.

Like the barbershop, the record shop was a special social place. In Britain, where 'front lines' exist without ghetto communities comparable with those of America or the Caribbean, the role of the record shop as a popular cultural archive and repository of folk knowledge is especially significant. It stores some of the key cultural resources of the racial group and provides an autonomous space in which the music, language and style that enable people to bring meaning and order to their social lives can be worked out and worked on. Unlike America, black Britain also lacked any significant opportunities for the radio play of black music until the pirate radio movement of the 1980s. Without radio, record shops and clubs had an additional significance in that they were the principal places where music, denied overground exposure, could be heard. They provided centres for its dissemination within the cultural underground and constituted the pathways through which communities of sentiment and interpretation could develop. I am suggesting, then, that the untidy 'patchwork' effect of record sleeves on the walls of these shops contributes substantially to the grounded, profane aesthetics of Britain's black cultural idiom. How the images are grouped together – whether, for example, styles like reggae, soul or hip-hop appear together or are separated – become significant issues. The pressure of space is itself a factor in this. The shops are often extraordinarily small[11] and the lack of any browsing or rack space for displaying the product means that the walls take on an enhanced function in revealing what is on sale and in providing an ever-changing and seemingly organic agglomeration of covers, posters and advertisements which complement the power of sound with a montage of vernacular visual codes.

The urban location of the record shop, like the urban connotations of the music itself, is also a powerful means to draw together the discrepant sensibilities of scattered black populations. A sense of the city as a place where racial particularity grows into unique patterns is something central to the tradition of music-making which culminated in rhythm and blues. It comes across strongly in three strikingly different images from each of the preceding decades. All of them use the same urban environment to make their statements but in dissimilar ways.

The first shows The Impressions, photographed amidst the rubble of Chicago's South Side. The acoustic guitar that Curtis Mayfield clutches is an emblem of the trio's historical rootedness. They are an absolutely 'natural' presence in this landscape. It is their territory and the viewer is asked whether the title of the record refers to the ghetto in which we see them or to America as a whole. The band could have just emerged from a cellar, prepared to make their beautiful music in what remains of the street. The presence of an instrument also emphasizes the decline of images of performance in contemporary packaging. The second picture, from the mid-1970s shows George Clinton and his spaceship. Is he arriving or departing? I have argued before that images like this express a utopian desire to escape from the order of racial oppression, as well as a cosmic pessimism that despairs over the possibility of actual flight. In Clinton's hands, the hi-tech imagery of interplanetary travel is tamed by its association with the ancient wisdom of African civilizations. Clinton's image has been superimposed on his ghetto environment – the organic link which tied Curtis to it has been broken. The picture works through the contrast between the spaceship and its downbeat context, and this tension is repeated in the gulf that appears to separate the music from the social location in which the listener is likely to encounter it. The third picture comes from Alyson Williams's 1989 album 'Raw'. This cover is clearly the product of a period where record companies gained a much greater degree of corporate control over the image-making process and where the importance of video, particularly for artists who might sell to white audiences, demands a close coordination of cover art with television imagery. Alyson is, significantly, a much a larger presence in the sleeve photograph than either of the other artists. Although her image has, like Clinton's, been superimposed, it is somehow much more closely tied to its artificial background. She may have walked up the alley on her way to a party or a modelling assignment. However, the street is once again being used to convey something fundamental about the nature of the music itself. The combination of decay and sophistication in the image conveys the blend of upmarket soul and homegirl hip-hop that characterizes her music. The radical implications of the picture become clearer if we set it alongside some images taken from competing black pop releases by female singers from the same period. Unlike Alyson, who is assertively at home in the street, Karyn White is happier and most fully herself in the private sphere. She was photographed, apparently in the throes of pre-coital rapture, by an unmade bed. Vanessa Williams is pictured without any background at all, her notoriety as a disgraced Miss America being all the prospective chaser of her record needed to put it in the right context.

The continuity of the street as a backdrop for these three covers is much more significant than their obvious differences. It offers a valuable glimpse of the structure of feeling that underlies the political culture to which these images contribute and of which they are part.

'Consumption' is a vague word that trips far too easily off the dismissive tongue. People *use* these images and the music that they enclose for a variety of reasons. For the black user of these images and products, multivariant processes of 'consumption' may express the need to belong, the desire to make the beauty of blackness intelligible and somehow to fix that beauty and the pleasures it creates so that they achieve, if not permanence, then at least a longevity that retrieves them from the world of pop ephemera and racial dispossession. However trivial the black music record sleeve may seem to the outsider, it points to a fund of aesthetic and philosophical folk knowledge which the record as a commodity has been made to contain *in addition* to its reified pleasures. The presence of this extra cultural resource does not, of course, negate or deny the act of capitalistic exchange through which the record is usually acquired. But the guidance, solace and pleasures which that commodity may impart cannot be understood as an incidental adjunct to the sometimes solitary act of purchasing it.

## Notes

1. Joseph Harris, *Global Dimensions of the African Diaspora,* Howard University Press, Washington D.C., 1982. Martin Kilson and Robert Rotberg (eds), *The African Diaspora: Interpretive Essays,* Harvard University Press, 1976.
2. *There Ain't No Black in the Union Jack, Hutchinson,* London, 1987.
3. Herman Gray, *Producing Jazz: The Experience of an Independent Record Company,* Temple University Press, Philadelphia, 1988.
4. Nelson George, *The Death of Rhythm and Blues,* Omnibus Press, London, 1988.
5. Ibid. Amiri Baraka, 'Class Struggle in Music', *The Black Nation,* vol. 5, no. 1, Summer/Fall 1986.
6. Kobena Mercer, 'Black Hair Style Polities', *New Formations,* no. 3, 1987.
7. Robert Farris Thompson, 'An Aesthetic of the Cool: West African Dance', *African Forum,* vol. 2, pt 2, Fall 1966.
8. *Shadow and Act,* Random House, New York, 1964, p. 157.
9. Charles Shaar Murray, *Crosstown Traffic,* Faber, London, 1989.
10. Steven Hager, 'Africa Bambaataa's Hip Hop', *Village Voice,* 21 September 1982.
11. Dub Vendor in Ladbroke Grove, Footprintz, Quaff and Light and Sound in Finsbury Park or Don Christie's original shop in the Ladypool Road, Birmingham, are some of the examples that I have in mind here.

# Chapter 39

# George Lipsitz

## Diasporic Noise: History, Hip Hop, and the Post-Colonial Politics of Sound

In 1989, a nineteen-year-old African-American woman from Irvington, New Jersey performing under the name Queen Latifah starred in a music video promoting her rap song 'Ladies First.' At a time when politicians, journalists, and even most male rappers presented few positive images of Black women, Queen Latifah drew upon the diasporic history of Black people around the world to fashion an affirmative representation of women of African descent. Assisted by Monie Love, an Afro-Caribbean rapper from London, as well as Ms. Melody and a chorus of other Black female rappers from the U.S.A., Latifah appeared in a video that interspersed still photos of Angela Davis, Sojourner Truth, and Madame C.J. Walker with newsreel films of women prominent in the struggle against apartheid in South Africa. Uniting Black people across generations and continents, the young rap artist from New Jersey situated claims about her prowess with rap rhythms and rhymes within a broader story of diasporic struggle.

In telling its story about the achievements, ability, and desirability of Black women, 'Ladies First' inverted and subverted existing representations with wide circulation in mass media and popular culture. During a decade when politicians and journalists in the U.S.A. regularly depicted Black women as unwed mothers and 'welfare queens,' Latifah's video presented them as 'queens of civilization' and 'mothers' who 'give birth' to political struggle. At a time when 'gangsta rap' glamorized the aggression and violence of street criminals, 'Ladies First' celebrated

From: George Lipsitz, *Dangerous Crossroads: Popular Music, Postmodernism and the Poetics of Place*. New York and London: Verso, 1994.

the militancy of collective struggles for social change. In an era when some Black nationalists belittled the gains made by Black women as detrimental to the community as a whole and urged them to accept subordinate places behind Black men, Latifah hailed the historic accomplishments of African-American women and emphasized the need for equal dedication and commitment from Black men and Black women in their common struggle against racism. Most important, in an American culture increasingly dismissive of African-American appeals for justice, dignity, and opportunity as 'minority' concerns, Latifah's deployment of images from the African diaspora demonstrated that the 'minority' populations of the U.S.A. are part of the global majority who have been victimized and oppressed by Euro-American racism and imperialism.

Queen Latifah's effort to map out discursive and political space through the trope of the African diaspora builds on historical practices within hip-hop culture as well as within the broader history of Afro-America. The first visible manifestations of what we have come to call hip hop culture (rap music, break dancing, graffiti, B Boy and wild style fashions) appeared in the early 1970s when a member of a New York street gang (The Black Spades) calling himself Afrika Bambaataa organized 'The Zulu Nation.' Confronted by the ways in which displacement by urban renewal, economic recession, and the fiscal crisis of the state combined to create desperate circumstances for inner-city youths, Bambaataa tried to channel the anger and enthusiasm of young people in the South Bronx away from gang fighting and into music, dance, and graffiti. He attracted African-American, Puerto Rican, Afro-Caribbean, and Euro-American youths into his 'nation.' He staged dances featuring his estimable talents as a 'mixer' and sound system operator capable of providing a non-stop flow of danceable beats from an enormous range of musical style. In 1982, he recorded 'Planet Rock' under the name Afrika Bambaataa and Soulsonic Force, and sold more than a million copies on twelve-inch vinyl of his song 'Planet Rock.'

Part of a generation of inner-city youths who found themselves unwanted as students by schools facing drastic budget cuts, unwanted as citizens or users of city services by municipalities imposing austerity regimens mandated by private financial institutions, and even unwanted as consumers by merchants increasingly reliant on surveillance and police power to keep urban 'have-nots' away from affluent buyers of luxury items, Bambaataa and his Zulu nation used their knowledge as consumers of popular music to become skilled producers of it. They used the conduits of popular culture to bring the expressive forms of their isolated and largely abandoned neighborhoods to an international audience. Hemmed in by urban renewal, crime, and police surveillance, and silenced by neglect from the culture industry, the school system, and city government, they found a way to declare themselves part of a wider world through music. 'You can go do anything with rap music,' Bambaataa has argued, 'you can go from the past to the future to what's happening now.'[1]

Bambaataa named his 'Zulu Nation' after the 1964 British film *Zulu* directed by Cy Endfield and starring Michael Caine. The motion picture clearly intended to depict the Zulus as predatory savages opposed to the 'civilizing mission' of the British empire. But as an American Black whose mother and aunts had migrated to New York from Barbados, Bambaataa saw it another way. In his eyes, the Zulus were heroic warriors resisting oppression. He used their example to inspire his efforts to respond to racism and class oppression in the U.S.A. 'Planet Rock' reached a world audience through the same mechanisms of commercial culture that brought *Zulu* from Britain to the Bronx twenty years earlier, but instead of celebrating Western imperialism, the song hailed the utopian potential of Black music to transform the entire world into 'a land of master jam.'[2]

In lyrics written and rapped by MC Globe, 'Planet Rock' celebrated the ability of music to take listeners to the past and to the future, but it also urged them to enjoy the present, to 'chase your dreams' and 'live it up,' because 'our world is free.' The song located listeners and dancers 'on this Mother Earth which is our rock,' and combined new styles of rapping with a wide variety of Bambaataa's samples, including the theme music from the film *The Good, the Bad, and the Ugly*, sounds from the German techno band Kraftwerk, and cuts from the British band Babe Ruth over a Roland TR 808 drum synthesizer. Bambaataa and his nation inserted themselves into international commercial culture through 'Planet Rock,' which one perceptive reviewer described as 'an unlikely fusion of bleeping, fizzing, techno-rock, Zulu-surrealism, and deep-fried funk.'[3]

Afrika Bambaataa's 'Planet Rock' and Queen Latifah's 'Ladies First' testify to the vitality of what Paul Gilroy calls 'diasporic intimacy' in the Black Atlantic world. Their efforts are only a small part of an international dialogue built on the imagination and ingenuity of slum dwellers from around the globe suffering from the effects of the international austerity economy imposed on urban areas by transnational corporations and their concentrated control over capital. In recent recordings, Jamaican toaster Macka B raps an English language history of Senegal over the singing of Baaba Maal, who speaks the Pulaar language of his native land. Cameroon expatriate Manu Dibango has recorded jazz albums with British rapper MC Mello and Parisian rapper MC Solaar—Solaar appeared on the recent hip hop jazz fusion recording by Guru of the U.S. rap group Gang Starr, while local rap artists in South Korea, Japan, Germany, France, and New Zealand have found significant popularity imitating the African-American styles mastered by Afrika Bambaataa and Queen Latifah.[4]

The significance of these seemingly ephemeral works of popular culture goes far beyond their role as commodities. The diasporic conversation within hip hop, Afro-beat, jazz and many other Black musical forms provides a powerful illustration of the potential for contemporary commercialized leisure to carry images, ideas, and icons of enormous political importance between cultures. Whatever role they serve in the profit-making calculations of the music industry, these expressions also serve as exemplars of post-colonial culture with direct relevance to the rise of new social movements emerging in response to the imperatives of global capital and its attendant austerity and oppression. [...]

## Post-Colonial Culture

During the great global struggle against colonialism in the years following World War II, national self-determination and anti-colonialist internationalism engaged the attention of intellectuals throughout Africa, Asia, and Latin America. From Che Guevara's *Reminiscences of the Cuban Revolution* to Sembene Ousmane's *God's Bits of Wood*, from Chairman Mao's *Yenan Program* to Frantz Fanon's

*The Wretched of the Earth*, nation building occupied center stage as the crucial element in anti-colonial emancipation. Although often somber and self-critical, anti-colonial expressions nonetheless contained an irrepressible optimism about the inevitability of liberation and about the potential achievements of post-colonial nationalism.

Forty years later, a literature of disillusionment and despair calls attention to conditions of austerity and oppression operative everywhere in the Third World. This 'post-colonial' literature seems to confirm in the sphere of culture the failure of nationalist anti-colonial movements around the globe to translate national independence into something more than neo-colonial economic, cultural, and even political dependency. Defenders of colonialism point to the pervasive poverty and political problems of post-colonial countries as proof that independence came too soon. Anti-colonialists generally charge that colonialism itself continues to be the problem, that colonial practices did little to prepare people and institutions for independence. Yet both of these arguments hinge on outdated premises with little relevance for the present.

In this debate, anti-colonialists and neo-colonialists both presume that the nation state still holds the key to self-determination, that the 'quality' of government officials determines the well-being of the nation. But a combination of political, techno-logical, and cultural changes since the 1970s has undermined the authority of the nation state while making multinational corporations, communications networks, and financial structures more powerful than ever before. In an age when capital, communications, and populations travel across the globe at an accelerated pace, the ability of any one nation state to determine its people's life chances has become greatly constrained. Capitalist transnational corporations have gained great advantages by separating management from production with the aid of computer-generated automation, containerization in shipping, and the new technologies ushered in through fiber optics, computer chips, and satellites. Strategies to extract concessions from capitalists through taxation and regulation fail because of the extraordinary mobility of capital that makes it easy to play one country or region against another. At the same time, the need for capital compels formerly colonized nations to accept the compulsory austerity measures required by the International Monetary Fund and the World Bank as the price of securing loans. [...]

Thus, the failures of newly independent regimes that pervade post-colonial literature stem as much from fundamentally new conditions in world politics, economics, and culture as they do from the legacy of colonialism or the short-comings of the struggles against it. Without denying the very important critiques of corruption and political oppression that appear in post-colonial culture, it is also important to understand that post-colonial expressions address emerging problems in the present as well as the failures of the past. The post-colonial era is one of displacement and migration, of multi-culturalism and multi-lingualism, of split subjects and divided loyalties. Post-colonial culture exposes the impossibility of *any* national identity incorporating into a unified totality the diverse and diffuse elements that make up a nation. While valuable for its insights into the failures of particular anti-colonial liberation movements, post-colonial art also exposes the inadequacy of national 'imagined communities' to monitor, regulate, and remedy the explosive contradictions of global structures of economic, political, and cultural power. [...]

The crisis signaled by the emergence of post-colonial literature, art, and music is the crisis confronting movements for progressive social change all around the world. For more than a century, aggrieved populations have pinned their hopes on seizing control of the nation state, or at least on using its mechanisms to extract concessions from capital. But these traditional strategies for social change have been confounded by the emergence of 'fast capital' and the equally rapid mobility of ideas, images, and people across national boundaries.

Yet new forms of domination also give rise to new forms of resistance. Rather than viewing post-colonial culture as a product of the *absence* of faith in yesterday's struggles for self-determination, it might be better to view it as product of the *presence* of new sensibilities uniquely suited for contesting the multinational nature of capital. The disillusionment and despair with politics in post-colonial writing may prove extraordinarily relevant beyond the former colonies; it may in fact be a strategically important stance for people around the globe in an age when centralized economic power has rendered many of the traditional functions of the nation state obsolete. [...] Of course, the state still serves as a source of repression, and still serves as an important instrument for people interested in using politics to address the rampant austerity and injustice of our time. But the state can no longer serve as the sole site of contestation for movements that find they have to be cultural as well as political, global as well as local, transnational as well as national.

One reason for the popularity of post-colonial art among readers in post-imperial countries comes from a shared disillusionment with the nation state and its failed promises. Similarly, stories of exile and return often employ the historical displacement of formerly colonized populations to express a more general sense of cultural displacement engendered everywhere by mass communications, population migrations, and the destructive effects of 'fast capital' on traditional communities. Of course consumers of post-colonial cultural artifacts have many different motivations. A search for novelty, boredom with familiar paradigms, and traditional European and American practices of fascination with (but not respect for) the 'exotic' also account for the recent 'emergence' of post-colonial art in Western consciousness. But while it would be a mistake to ever underestimate the venal intentions and effects of Euro-American appropriations of the cultures of Asia, Africa, and Latin America, it would also be a major error to overlook the strategic importance of post-colonial perspectives for theorizing the present moment in world history. [...]

The present moment in world history is marked by the failure of two grand narratives – the liberal faith in progress, modernization, and the bureaucratic state, and the conservative faith in free trade, de-regulation, and the 'free market.' The global struggles for democratic change and national independence that reached their apex in the 1960s seriously discredited social theories associated with social democracy and liberal capitalism. There was a rapid unraveling of the post-war 'consensus' in industrialized nations that posited a universal stake in the advance of technology, Keynesian economics, and bureaucratic rationality. From 'modernization' theory in sociology to 'modernism' in the arts, ways of explaining the world that had seemed incontrovertible in the 1950s suddenly seemed totally inadequate for explaining the revolutionary ruptures, clashes, and conflicts of the 1960s. But the inadequacy of existing liberal social theory, coupled with the inability among aggrieved groups to propose or implement credible radical alternatives, created an opportunity for conservatives and plutocrats.

De-industrialization and economic restructuring in capitalist countries in the 1970s and 1980s caused the re-emergence of theories lauding the free market (which themselves had been discredited since the Great Depression) as a frame for interpreting world politics and culture. Neo-conservative policies in all industrialized countries encouraged and subsidized the creation of a world economy under the control of multinational corporations and institutions. The dismantling of social welfare structures in the metropolis and the externalization of class tensions onto unprotected workers and consumers at the periphery served to unite capital while fragmenting its potential opponents. The ideology of free market economics appears to have triumphed all around the world, but rather than prosperity and freedom for all, it has produced extravagant wealth for the few and mostly austerity, corruption, and instability for the many.

Yet the relentlessness of capital in seeking new areas for investment has also led to unexpected emergences and convergences in the field of culture. The reach and scope of commercial mass media unite populations that had previously been divided. The spread of commodities into new areas often creates new economies of prestige and undermines traditional hierarchies. The accelerated flow of commerce, commodities, and people across national boundaries creates new social and political realities that enable some people in colonized countries to create new opportunities and alliances. Moreover, the very obsolescence of previous theories of social organization serves as an impetus for creating new ways of looking at the world.

The contemporary crisis of social theory comes largely from the inability of either the nation state or the free market to address adequately the grim realities of the emerging global economy and culture. Post-colonial culture has emerged in the context of this stalemate between two discredited theories. Important on its own terms as art, it also holds significance because of its potential to become one of the sites where social theory becomes reconstituted on a global scale. Post-colonial cultural expressions are based in the experiences of people and communities, rather than on the master narratives of the nation state. They foreground questions of cultural and social identity, rather than direct struggles for political power. They are pragmatic, immediate, and non-ideological, seeking to change life but putting forth no single blueprint for the future. In short, post-colonial culture contains all of the aspects identified by social theorists as characteristic of the 'new social movements.'

## The New Social Movements

Theorists Manuel Castells and Alain Touraine stress that new social movements are often locally based and territorially defined. Hip hop and other forms of diasporic African music participate in constructing these local identities, but they bring to them a global consciousness.[5] They play out local rivalries (for example between New York and Los Angeles rappers) and speak powerfully to local politics (in the Caribbean, Europe, Africa, and North America), but they also situate themselves within international concerns. They have inverted prestige hierarchies around the world, and established new centers of cultural power from Kingston, Jamaica to Compton, California. But hip hop and reggae have also played roles in political movements opposed to apartheid in South Africa, in struggles for educational and curricular reform, and in battles against police brutality around the globe. [...]

Like the influence of Central American magic realism on novels by African-American women, like the importance of novels questioning categories of identity by Asian-American and Native American women for feminists from many ethnicities, or like the growing recognition by indigenous populations of congruent realities in diverse national contexts, the music of the African diaspora testifies to the capacity of post-colonial culture to illumine families of resemblance illustrating how diverse populations have had similar although not identical experiences. By virtue of a shared skepticism about the nation state, an identification with the lived experiences of ordinary people, and an imaginative, supple, and strategic reworking of identities and cultures, post-colonial culture holds great significance as a potential site for creating coalitions to pose alternatives to the discredited maxims of conservative free-market capitalism or liberal social democracy. [...]

Among diasporic communities especially, traditional aesthetic, philosophical, moral, and political principles serve as resources in struggles against centralized systems of power. For these populations there have never been any 'old social movements,' because questions of identity and community always superseded the potential for making claims on the state through ideological coalitions. Their distance from state power and their experiences with cultural exclusion forced upon diasporic communities political practices rooted in the realities of what we have now come to call the 'new social movements.'[6]

Oppositional practices among diasporic populations emerge from painful experiences of labor migration, cultural imperialism, and political subordination. Yet they are distinguished by an ability to work within these systems. In contemporary culture, artists from aggrieved communities often subvert or invert the very instruments of domination necessary for the creation of the new global economy – its consumer goods, technologies, and images. Post-colonial literature, Third Cinema, and hip hop music all protest against conditions created by the oligopolies who distribute them as commodities for profit. They express painful recognition of cultural displacements, displacements that their very existence accelerates. Yet it is exactly their desire to work *through* rather than *outside* of existing structures that defines their utility as a model for contemporary global politics.

One might conclude that this reliance of post-colonial culture on existing economic and cultural forms can at best lead only to subordinate rather than autonomous reforms. That possibility certainly exists. But the desire to work through existing contradictions rather than stand outside them represents not so much a preference for melioristic reform over revolutionary change, but rather a recognition of the impossibility of standing outside totalitarian systems of domination. [...]

[...] Rather than stand outside of society, the new social movements and their cultural corollaries immerse themselves in the contradictions of social life, seeking an immanent rather than a transcendent critique.

Thus, although they seem 'new' to theorists of the new social movements, the techniques of immanent critique have a long history among aggrieved populations.

People can take action only in the venues that are open to them; oppressed people rarely escape the surveillance and control of domination. Consequently they frequently have to 'turn the guns around,' to seize the instruments of domination used to oppress them and try to put them to other uses. [...]

The global popularity of hip hop culture – rap music, graffiti, break dancing, B Boy fashion etc. – has been perhaps the most important recent manifestation of post-colonial culture on a global scale. The 'diasporic intimacy' linking cultural production and reception among people of African descent in the Caribbean, the United States, Europe, and Africa has resulted in a cultural formation with extraordinary political implications. Although hip hop circulates as a commodity marketed by highly centralized monopolies from metropolitan countries, it also serves as a conduit for ideas and images articulating subaltern sensitivities. At a time when African people have less power and fewer resources than at almost any previous time in history, African culture has emerged as the single most important subtext within world popular culture. The popularity of hip hop reflects more than cultural compensation for political and economic domination, more than an outlet for energies and emotions repressed by social power relations. Hip hop expresses a form of politics perfectly suited to the post-colonial era. It brings a community into being through performance, and it maps out real and imagined relations between people that speak to the realities of displacement, disillusion, and despair created by the austerity economy of post-industrial capitalism.[7]

## Hip Hop and the Politics of Sound

Hip hop culture brings to a world audience the core values of music from most sub-Saharan African cultures.[8] It blends music and life into an integrated totality, uniting performers, dancers, and listeners in a collaborative endeavor. As ethnomusicologist John Miller Chernoff observes, 'the model of community articulated in an African musical event is one that is not held together by ideas, by cognitive symbols or by emotional conformity. The community is established through the interaction of individual rhythms and the people who embody them.[9] African music is participatory, collective, and collaborative. Rhythms are layered on top of one another as a dialogue – hearing one enables the others to make sense. The incorporation of these African elements into hip hop raises challenges to Western notions of musical (and social) order. As the great jazz drummer Max Roach explains,

> The thing that frightened people about hip hop was that they heard rhythm – rhythm for rhythm's sake. Hip hop lives in the world of sound – not the world of music – and that's why it's so revolutionary. What we as black people have always done is show that the world of sound is bigger than white people think. There are many areas that fall outside the narrow Western definition of music and hip hop is one of them.[10]

While clearly grounded in the philosophies and techniques of African music, the radical nature of hip hop comes less from its origins than from its uses. The flexibility of African musical forms encourages innovation and adaptation – a blending of old and new forms into dynamic forward-looking totalities. In her important scholarship on rap music, Tricia Rose has argued against reducing hip hop to its origins in African music or African-American oral traditions, but instead calls for an understanding of hip hop as 'secondary orality,' the deployment of oral traditions in an age of electronic reproduction.[11] As a cultural discourse and political activity, it thus speaks to both residual and emergent realities.

Digital sampling in rap music turns consumers into producers, tapping consumer memories of parts of old songs and redeploying them in the present. It employs advanced technology to reconstruct the human voice, and features robot-like movements and mechanical vocals that simulate machines.[12] Sampling foregrounds the fabricated artifice of machine technologies, calling attention to them through repetition, scratching, and mixing. But at the same time, these tactics humanize the machine by asking it to do the unexpected, and they allow for human imitations of machine sounds – as in the vocals by Doug E. Fresh, 'the original human beat box.'[13] Hip hop calls into question Western notions of cultural production as property through its evocation, quotation, and outright theft of socially shared musical memories. Yet it also illumines the emancipatory possibilities of new technologies and the readiness of marginalized and oppressed populations to employ them for humane ends – for shedding restricting social identities and embracing new possibilities of a life without hierarchy and exploitation.

Kobena Mercer and others have warned us against the folly of thinking that some cultural forms are innately radical – that the right combination of notes or colors or words can be socially or politically radical by themselves. Culture functions as a social force to the degree that it gets instantiated in social life and connected to the political aspirations and activities of groups.[14] It is here that hip hop holds its greatest significance and its greatest challenge to interpreters.

For example, in the mid-1980s, the New York graffiti artist, style leader, and hip hop entrepreneur Fab Five Freddy learned an important lesson about the politics of sound from Max Roach, the great jazz drummer from the bebop era.[15] Separated by decades and musical styles (Fab Five Freddy's father was once Max Roach's manager), the two men shared a common admiration for the energy and artistry of rap music. But one day Roach baffled his young friend by describing LL Cool J's music as 'militant.' Freddy later recalled, 'I thought it was funny he should say that because I thought LL was an ego rapper, and political rap seemed out of fashion.' But Roach persisted, claiming that:

> The rhythm was very militant to me because it was like marching, the sound of an army on the move. We lost Malcolm, we lost King and they thought they had blotted out everybody. But all of a sudden this new art form arises and the militancy is there in the music.

Once Roach had directed his attention away from the lyrics and toward the rhythm, Fab Five Freddy understood the drummer's point. 'LL Cool J doesn't seem to like political music,' he later explained in describing the incident, 'but the politics was in the drums.'[16]

The 'politics in the drums' that Max Roach disclosed to Fab Five Freddy pervade hip hop. They express the restlessness and energy described by Frantz

Fanon in his now classic anti-colonial text, *The Wretched of the Earth*. Speaking about times when desires for radical change permeate popular culture even though no political movement has yet arrived to challenge the established order, Fanon argues:

> Well before the political fighting phase of the national movement, an attentive spectator can thus feel and see the manifestation of a new vigor and feel the approaching conflict. He [sic] will note unusual forms of expression and themes which are fresh and imbued with a power which is no longer that of an invocation but rather of the assembling of the people, a summoning together for a precise purpose. Everything works together to awaken the native's sensibility and to make unreal and unacceptable the contemplative attitude or the acceptance of defeat.[17]

Hip hop's energy originates in many sources, but a crucial component of its power comes from its ability to respond to the realities of the African diaspora. Most commentators in the U.S.A. have portrayed diasporic consciousness as essentially a one-way process of preserving African elements in America or maintaining Afro-Caribbean traditions in New York. To be sure, African and Caribbean elements appear prominently in U.S. hip hop, and many of the originators of hip hop in New York during the 1970s had Caribbean backgrounds. [...] But these claims place a value on origins that distorts the nature of Black Atlantic culture. The flow of information and ideas among diasporic people has not been solely from Africa outward to Europe and the Americas, but rather has been a reciprocal self-renewing dialogue in communities characterized by upheaval and change. The story of the African diaspora is more than an aftershock of the slave trade, it is an ongoing dynamic creation. The radicalism of diasporic African culture comes not only from the contrast between African and Euro-American values, but also from the utility of exploiting diasporic connections as a way of expanding choices everywhere – in Africa as well as in Europe, the Caribbean, and the Americas. Just as American and European Blacks have drawn on African traditions to contest Euro-American power relations, Africans have drawn upon cultures of opposition and strategies of signification developed by diasporic Africans as a form of struggle on the African continent.

For example, Fela Kuti, the founder of Nigeria's radical Afro-beat music subculture, learned part of his political radicalism in Los Angeles. His mother had been an activist, a friend of Ghana's President Kwame Nkrumah, and a founder of the Nigerian Women's Union and a leader in the successful struggle to gain the right to vote for women in her country.[18] For ten months in 1969–1970, Fela played music in Los Angeles at the Citadel de Haiti night club on Sunset Boulevard (owned by Black actor Bernie Hamilton, later featured in the television program 'Starsky and Hutch'), but his main focus was on learning about Black nationalism. Sandra Smith (now Sandra Isidore), a woman active in the Black Panther Party, gave Fela a copy of *The Autobiography of Malcolm X* which introduced him to ideas about Pan-Africanism that had been censored in Nigeria.[19] 'Sandra gave me the education I wanted to know,' he recalled years later. 'I swear man! She's the one who spoke to me about ... Africa! For the first time I heard things I'd never heard before about Africa! Sandra was my adviser.'[20]

Fela told friends he learned more about Africa in Los Angeles that he had in Lagos, and insisted that 'The whole atmosphere of Black Revolution changed me, my consciousness, my thinking, my perception of things. I was educated.'[21] Sandra Smith recalls that she introduced him to poems by Nikki Giovanni and the spoken-word art of The Last Poets, as well as to writings by Angela Davis, Jesse Jackson, Stokely Carmichael, and Martin Luther King. In addition, she introduced him to music by Nina Simone and Miles Davis, and connected him with a circle of friends that included singer Esther Phillips, actors Melvin van Peebles and Jim Brown, and the comedian Stu Gilliam.[22] 'For the first time, I saw the essence of blackism,' he later told an interviewer. 'I was exposed to awareness. It started me thinking. I saw how everything worked there. I realized that I had no country. I decided to come back and try to make my country African.'[23]

Experiences in the U.S.A. made Fela Kuti more radical politically, but they also changed his music by informing it with a diasporic consciousness. As he explained, 'Most Africans do not really know about life. They think everything from overseas is greater, but they do not know also that everything from overseas could have gone from here to overseas and come back to us. America gave me that line of thought.'[24] Kuti has subsequently collaborated with Black American musicians including trumpeter Lester Bowie and vibraphonist Roy Ayers. Bowie went to Nigeria and lived with Fela during a particularly difficult time in his life, and admired both the music and politics that the Nigerian produced. 'Fela's stubborn about the right things,' Bowie explained to an interviewer. 'He wants freedom, he wants to get away from oppression. The inequality of wealth in his country is unbelievable, and he's trying to address that. So did Martin Luther King, Jr., so did Malcolm X and so did the founding fathers of America.'[25]

Similarly, Roy Ayers credits Fela for deepening his understanding of Africa during their collaborations. Kuti and Ayers toured Africa and recorded together in 1979. Ayers had been a frequent visitor to Africa, but even in the U.S.A. his deep interest in Afro-Cuban jazz gave his music a diasporic flavor. The recordings made by Fela Kuti and Roy Ayers showed traces of the Afro-Cuban influences on North American jazz as well as of Cuban 'rhumba' bands on African, especially Congolese, music.[26] In turn, Ayers's 1970s jazz-funk albums (especially his Black nationalist *Red, Black, and Green* from 1973) have been a prime source of samples in recent years for hip hop djs and producers. [...]

Diasporic dialogue has also extended far beyond binary exchanges between Africa and North America. For example, Alpha Blondy from Côte d'Ivoire in Africa learned French reading the bible and mastered English from his school lessons and from playing American rock'n'roll in high school.[27] He went to Columbia University in New York in 1976 to study world trade. There he discovered a Jamaican-American reggae band, Monkaya, which he joined, singing his native Mandinka lyrics to the reggae beat. Blondy has become one of the best-selling reggae artists in the world, having recorded reggae songs in English, French, Dioula, and Mandingo. Explaining his interest in what most would consider West Indian music, Blondy argues: 'In Africa, the new generation, my generation, is a mixture of Western and African culture. Reggae has succeeded in a musical unification, it's a good therapy to bring people together.'[28] As part of this 'therapy,' Blondy's band includes musicians from Africa and the Caribbean, and he has performed songs in Arabic during concerts in Israel and songs in Hebrew during concerts in Arab countries. He played a concert in 1986 dedicated to encouraging good relations between Mali and Burkina-Faso, and drew 10,000 fans at the Moroccan International Festival of Youth and Music in Marrakech that same year to hear him play reggae.[29]

Reggae itself originated in Afro-Jamaican religious Burru music, especially its bass, funde, and repeater drums, but the form also drew upon African-American soul music, on records smuggled back to the island by Jamaican migrant workers employed to cut sugar cane in the southern U.S.A. (including Coxsone Dodd, founder of Kingston's Studio One), as well as on broadcasts by U.S. radio stations including WINZ in Miami.[30] Africans like Alpha Blondy, who were familiar with American soul music, took to reggae in part because it contained elements of music they were already familiar with from America as well as from Africa.

On the other hand, when Jamaican singer Jimmy Cliff first heard the yelle music of Baaba Maal from Senegal, it struck him as structurally connected to the rhythms of reggae. Rap music's popularity in Korea stems in part from the close cultural connections built between the U.S.A. and that country since the mass exodus following the Kwangju uprising of the early 1980s, but also from the similarities between rap and traditional Korean sasui lyrics which are recited to the accompaniment of drums.[31]

Manu Dibango, a singer-composer-arranger-reed-piano player from Cameroon, moved to Paris in the 1960s where he started making records, including a tribute to the U.S. rhythm and blues saxophone player King Curtis. In 1972 Dibango's 'Soul Makossa' became an international hit. He moved to New York in the early 1970s where he played the Apollo Theatre in Harlem along with the Temptations and Barry White, and he also collaborated there with Afro-Caribbean musicians including Johnny Pacheco and the Fania All-Stars.[32] By the mid-1980s Dibango brought Antillean musicians into his band and expanded his repertoire to include the zouk music of the Francophone West Indies.[33] [...]

Hip hop employs the legacy of similar instances of diasporic dialogue. Jazzie B of the British group Soul II Soul remembers the lessons he learned in his youth from African American artists. 'People like Curtis Mayfield were a very strong part of my life,' he remembers. 'His songs weren't just songs to me. They were knowledge. I used to carry my records right along with my school books.' But at the same time, Jazzie B also credits the 'African' community in Britain for having a formative influence on his music. 'I don't just remember the music at the Africa Centre [dances], I also remember the people. It was like a religion, all those people sweating and dancing and partying together. It was very inspiring. That's what I tried to put on our album – that same sense of unity and spirit.'[34]

The dynamism of diasporic interchanges in music confirms Peter Linebaugh's wry observation that long-playing records have surpassed sea-going vessels as the most important conduits of Pan-African communication.[35] But it is important to understand that diasporic dialogue in music builds on an infrastructure with a long history. For example, in the 1930s, Paul Robeson galvanized the black population of Britain (and other countries) with theatrical performances that complemented his role as a spokesperson for causes like the defense of the Scottsboro boys.[36] His films *King Solomon's Mines* (1937) and *Sanders of the River* (1934, featuring Jomo Kenyatta) brought certain aspects of African culture to world audiences accustomed to only the most caricatured views of the continent. Many Africans encountered Pan-Africanism the way Fela Kuti did, through the writings of diasporic Africans including Malcolm X, Aimé Césaire, Marcus Garvey, George Padmore, and W.E.B. DuBois.[37] As a foreign student, Kwame Nkrumah learned some lessons in politics attending Adam Clayton Powell's activist church in New York City, while Ghanaian activists used the U.S. abolitionist hymn 'John Brown's Body' to protest Nkrumah's imprisonment during the struggle for independence.[38] These political connections had deep cultural roots; Manu Dibango remembers how important it was for him to hear Louis Armstrong on the radio when he was growing up in Cameroon. 'Here was a black voice singing tunes that reminded me of those that I had learned at the temple. I immediately felt at one with the warmth of that voice and with what it was singing.'[39]

More recently, post-colonial writers in Africa have expressed their indebtedness to African-American writers. Ngugi Wa Thiong'o asserts:

> There's a very vibrant connection between Afro-American traditions in literature and those from many parts of the third world. I know that African literature as a whole has borrowed quite heavily from the Afro-American literary tradition, and I hope vice-versa. Writers like Langston Hughes, Richard Wright, Amiri Baraka, and Alice Walker are quite popular in Africa.[40]

Nigerian writer Buchi Emecheta adds: 'To me, the greatest writers who come from ethnic minorities writing in English come from America. I think the deep, the real deep thinkers now writing in the English language are the black women, such as Toni Morrison, Gloria Naylor, Alice Walker, etc.'[41]

The dialogue of the African diaspora informs the politics and culture of countries across the globe. It draws upon ancient traditions and modern technologies, on situated knowledge and a nomadic sensibility. Generated from communities often criminally short of resources and institutions, it commands prestige from multi-national corporations and other bastions of privilege. It flows through the circuits of the post-industrial austerity economy, and yet still manages to bring to light inequities and injustices.

From Queen Latifah's 'Ladies First' with its images of Africa and the Americas to Thomas Mapfumo's 'Hupenyu Wanyu' which appropriates the African-American 'Bo Diddley' beat for radical politics in Zimbabwe, diasporic intimacy secures space for oppositional expressions obliterated by much of mass media and electoral politics. In a world coming ever closer together through the machinations of global capital, it displays a situated but not static identity. Rooted in egalitarian and democratic visions of the world, diasporic intimacy nonetheless embraces contradiction, change, and growth. It serves notice of the willingness and ability of millions of people to play a meaningful role in the world that is being constructed around us.

In culture and in politics, diasporic expressions constantly come back to what Frantz Fanon called 'the seething pot out of which the learning of the future will emerge.'[42] A sense of urgency about the future permeates the practices of popular music. Salif Keita of Mali locates his interest in making popular music as more than a matter of style. In his own performances he blends traditional Malian music with things he learned listening to Western artists ranging from Pink Floyd to Stevie Wonder, from James Brown to Kenny Rogers. Defending his eclecticism, Keita explains, 'At home, we are traditionalists. It's an attitude I disapprove of.

It's we who make the history, and if we refer only to what has passed, there will be no history. I belong to a century that has little in common with the time of my ancestors. I want society to move.'[43]

Manu Dibango sums up the problem with characteristic eloquence (although with unfortunately sexist pronouns) in a statement that might serve as the motto of the post-colonial project. He asserts:

> People who are curious search for sounds; they seek out harmony and melody because they are curious. Your curiosity can be limited by your environment, or you can expand it to take in things from outside; a bigger curiosity for a bigger world. The extent of your curiosity should not be determined by the village, or the town, or a city in another continent. The musician moves in these circles, but he moves to break out of his limits.[44]

## Notes

1. Mark Dery, 'Rap,' *Keyboard* (November) 1988, 34.

2. David Toop, *Rap Attack 2: African Rap to Global Hip Hop* (London: Serpent's Tail, 1991), 19, 39, 37, 56–60; Lawrence Stanley, ed., *Rap: The Lyrics* (New York: Penguin, 1992), 8; Joel Whitburn, *Top R&B Singles, 1942–1988* (Menomonee Falls, Wl: Record Research, 1988), 33.

3. Mark Dery, 'Rap,' 46.

4. Larry Birnbaum, 'Baaba Maal Sings Blues from the Real Heartland *Pulse* (September) 1993, 39; Jay Cocks, 'Rap Around the Globe,' *Time* October 19, 1992, 70; Michael Jarrett, Guru, *Pulse* (September) 1993, 39.

5. Manuel Castells, *The City and the Grass Roots* (London: Edward Arnold, 1983); Alain Touraine, *The Voice and the Eye: An Analysis of Social Movements* (Cambridge: Cambridge University Press, 1981). See Paul Gilroy, *'There Ain't No Black in the Union Jack': The Cultural Politicis of Race and Nation* (Chicago, IL: University of Chicago Press, 1987), esp. ch. 6.

6. For 'new social movement' activity within old social movements see Robin D.G. Kelley, *Hammer and Hoe* and Vicki Ruiz, *Cannery Women, Cannery Lives* (Albuquerque: University of New Mexico Press, 1987).

7. For discussion of hip hop and the 'new social movements' see Paul Gilroy, *'There Ain't No Black in the Union Jack,'* 223–50.

8. It is important not to assume one unified African system of thought, politics, or culture. But especially in comparison to Western music, certain social and stylistic features from West Africa provide a vivid contrast.

9. John Miller Chernoff, 'The Rhythmic Medium in African Music,' *New Literary History* vol. 22 no. 4 (Autumn) 1991, 1095. See also J.H. Kwabena Nketia, *The Music of Africa* (New York: Norton, 1974), 21–50.

10. Frank Owen, 'Hip Hop Bebop,' *Spin* vol. 4 (October) 1988, 61.

11. Tricia Rose, 'Orality and Technology: Rap Music and Afro-American Cultural Resistance,' *Popular Music and Society* vol. 14 no. 4 (Winter) 1988, 35–44. See also her *Black Noise* (Hanover: Wesleyan/University Press of New England), 1994.

12. High-tech and science-fiction themes played an important role in 1970s African-American music as a way of imagining a space outside of Euro-American racism, especially in the work of George Clinton and Funkadelic.

13. Paul Gilroy, *'There Ain't No Black in the Union Jack,'* 214.

14. I thank Mercer for bringing this to the attention of the Minority Discourse Group at the University of California Humanities Research Institute many times during the Fall of 1992.

15. Fab Five Freddy (Braithwaite) had long known Roach because his father was an attorney who served at one time as Roach's manager. David Toop, *Rap Attack 2*, 140.

16. Frank Owen, 'Hip Hop Bebop,' 73.

17. Frantz Fanon, *The Wretched of the Earth* (New York: Grove Press, 1968), 243.

18. Rob Tannenbaum, 'Fela Anikulapao Kuti,' *Musician* no. 79 (May) 1985, 30.

19. Born in Arkansas, Sandra Smith met Fela at an NAACP-sponsored performance featuring Fela's band and her own dance troupe that performed what they believed were African dances: Carlos Moore, *Fela, Fela: This Bitch of a Life* (London: Allison & Busby, 1982), 83, 91–2.

20. Carlos Moore, *Fela, Fela*, 85.

21. Tom Cheney, 'Sorrow, Tears, and Blood: Q&A with Fela Anikulapo Kuti,' *Los Angeles Reader* vol. 8 no. 41 (August 1, 1986), 1; Labinjog, 'Fela Anikulapo Kuti,' *Journal of Black Studies* (September) 1982, 126.

22. Carlos Moore, *Fela, Fela*, 95, 100.

23. John Darnton, 'Afro-Beat: New Music with a Message,' *New York Times*, July 7, 1986, 46.

24. Mabinuori Kayode Idowu, *Fela: Why Blackman Carry Shit* (Kaduna, Nigeria: Opinion Media Limited, 1985), 37.

25. Rob Tannenbaum, 'Fela Anikulapao Kuti,' 30.

26. Graeme Ewens, *Africa O-Ye! A Celebration of African Music* (New York: Da Capo, 1992), 32, 35; Kuti & Ayers, *Music of Many Colours*, Celluloid CD 6125, 1980, 1986.

27. Don Snowden, 'Alpha Blondy's Multicultural Universe,' *Los Angeles Times*, February 21, 1988, calendar section, 76.

28. Jon Pareles, 'African-Style Reggae Crosses the Atlantic,' *New York Times*, March 22, 1988, C 13.

29. Stephen Davis, 'Alpha Blondy,' *The Reggae and African Beat* vol. 7 no. 1 (1987), 33.

30. Wendell Logan, 'Conversation with Marjorie Whylie,' *Black Perspective in Music* vol. 10 no. 1. (n.d.) 86, 88, 89, 92; Dick Hebdige, 'Reggae, Rastas, and Rudies,' in Stuart Hall and Tony Jefferson eds, *Resistance Through Ritual: Youth Subcultures in Post-war Britain* (London: Hutchinson, 1976), 143; Sebastian Clarke, *Jah Music: The Evolution of the Popular Jamaican Song* (London: Heinemann, 1980), 57–8. Coxsone Dodd, founder of Studio One, got his start as a sound system operator with records he brought back to Jamaica from the U.S.A.

31. Byung Hoo Suh, 'An Unexpected Rap Eruption Rocks a Traditional Music Market,' *Billboard* vol. 104 no. 34 (August 22, 1992), S6.

32. Donald Clarke, ed., *The Penguin Encyclopedia of Popular Music* (London: Penguin, 1989), 339–40; Graeme Ewens, *Africa O-Ye!*, 116.

33. Graeme Ewens, *Africa O-Ye!*, 108.

34. Robert Hilburn, 'Tracing the Caribbean Roots of the New British Pop Invasion,' *Los Angeles Times*, calendar section, September 24, 1989, 84. Paul Gilroy's observations about the importance of the U.S.A. and the Caribbean to Black Britain are relevant here. See Paul Gilroy, *'There Ain't No Black in the Union Jack*,' 154.

35. Quoted in Paul Gilroy, 'Cultural Studies and Ethnic Absolutism,' in Lawrence Grossberg, Cary Nelson, and Paula Treichler, *Cultural Studies* (New York: Routledge, 1992), 191.

36. Chris Stapleton, 'African Connections: London's Hidden Music Scene,' in Paul Oliver, ed., *Black Music in Britain: Essays on the Afro-Asian Contribution to Popular Music* (Buckingham: Open University Press, 1990, 92).

37. John Collins, 'Some Anti-Hegemonic Aspects of African Popular Music,' in Reebee Garofalo, ed., *Rockin' the Boat* (Boston, MA: South End, 1992), 189.

38. John Collins, 'Some Anti-Hegemonic Aspects of African Popular Music,' 191.

39. 'Interview with Manu Dibango,' *Unesco Courier* (March 1991), 4.

40. Feroza Jussawalla and Reed Way Dasenbrock, eds, *Interviews with Writers of the Post-Colonial World* (Jackson: University Press of Mississippi, 1992), 41.

41. Feroza Jussawalla and Reed Way Dasenbrock, eds, *Interviews with Writers of the Post-Colonial World*, 93.

42. Frantz Fanon, *The Wretched of the Earth*, 225.

43. Banning Eyre, 'Routes: The Parallel Paths of Baaba Maal and Salif Keita,' *Option* no. 53 (November–December, 1993), 48. Quoted in Neil Lazarus, 'Unsystematic Fingers at the Conditions of the Times: 'Afropop' and the Paradoxes of Imperialism,' in Jonathan White, ed., *Recasting the World: Writing After Colonialism* (Baltimore, MD and London: Johns Hopkins University Press, 1994), 140.

44. Manu Dibango, 'Music in Motion,' in Graeme Ewens, *Africa O-Ye!*, 7.

# Chapter 40

# Lisa Nakamura

## Head-Hunting on the Internet: Identity Tourism, Avatars, and Racial Passing in Textual and Graphic Chat Spaces

Is it accurate to say that on the Internet nobody can tell what race you are? For the large (and increasing) number of people who use the Internet as a social space via chat rooms and other forms of online interaction, this seemingly philosophical question has acquired increasing urgency. Despite claims by digital utopians that the Internet is an ideally democratic, discrimination-free space – without gender, race, age, or disability – an analysis of both textual and graphic chat spaces such as LambdaMOO, Time Warner's The Palace, and Avaterra's Club Connect will reveal that these identity positions are still very much in evidence. Though it is true that users' physical bodies are hidden from other users, race has a way of asserting its presence in the language users employ, in the kinds of identities they construct, and in the ways they depict themselves online, both through language and through graphic images. These depictions of the self, or online identities, have been termed 'avatars.' Avatars are the embodiment, in text and/or graphic images, of a user's online presence in social spaces.

The Internet is a theater of sorts, a theater of performed identities. 'Passing' is a cultural phenomenon that has the ability to call stable identities into question, and in that sense can be a progressive practice, but the fact remains that passing

From: Lisa Nakamura, *Cybertypes: Race, Ethnicity, and Identity on the Internet*. London: Routledge, 2002.

is often driven by harsh structural cultural inequities, a sense that it really *would* be safer, more powerful, and better to be of a different race or gender. Millions of computer users 'pass' every day, and much scholarly work has been devoted to examining how, why, and what it means that this happens in relation to gender. Piles of articles have been written about cross-gender passing, or 'computer cross-dressing,' but very little has been done on the topic of cross-racial passing despite the fact it may be as common, or even more so. [...]

The celebration of the Internet as a democratic, 'raceless' place needs to be interrogated, both to put pressure on the assumption that race is something that *ought* to be left behind, in the best of all possible cyberworlds, and to examine the prevalence of racial representation in this supposedly unraced form of social and cultural interaction.

If race is indeed a cultural construct rather than a biological fact, as Anthony Appiah and others have asserted, then cyberspace is a particularly telling kind of example when we wish to look at the vexed and contested position of race in the digital age. The Internet is literally a 'construct' (as the recent film *The Matrix* terms it); like race itself, it is a product of culture and its attendant power dynamics rather than an object that somehow existed prior to linguistic and cultural definition. Cyberspace is a place of wish fulfillments and myriad gratifications, material and otherwise, and nowhere is this more true than in chat spaces. Both textual and graphic chat spaces encourage users to build different identities, to take on new nicknames, and to describe themselves in any way they wish to appear. Digital avatars, or renditions of self, provide a pipeline into the phantasmatic world of identities, those conscious or not-so-conscious racial desires and narratives that users construct and inhabit during their interactions in cyberspace.

When I first started researching the topic of race and cyberspace in 1993, the World Wide Web was still a text-only phenomenon; no images were available. Thus, early chat room participants had recourse only to text when they constructed their avatars. Nicknames like Asian_Geisha, Big10inch, and GeekKing were accompanied by often floridly written self-descriptions that advertised not who users 'really' *were*, but rather what they wanted (which in some sense may boil down to the same thing). These textual self-portraits had to do all of the work of physical description, since there were no images available. Race was invisible unless a player chose to inscribe it or include it in their character description, and since many did not, a kind of default whiteness reigned. [...]

However, the World Wide Web's dominance of the Internet has transformed cyberspace into a world of visual images, a world in which text has taken a backseat. Graphic avatars are *visible*, and thus race, which was invisible in textual avatars unless specifically put there, became visible as well. Websites that support graphic avatars like Time Warner's The Palace and Avaterra's Worlds Away Club Connect allow users to create images of themselves that they can move through cyberspace and customize. In this way, graphic chat resembles a video game more than it does live action e-mail in the sense that other users can see you and interact with you as an image. [...]

Club Connect, a graphic chat space run by Avaterra, a company specializing in web-based business meeting spaces, can be accessed via its direct link from NetNoir's website. NetNoir is probably the oldest and certainly one of the best-known examples of an ethnic-identity website, which makes it a rare and important example of a minority presence on the web and the Internet in general. NetNoir started out as a text-only bulletin board addressing African-American concerns, and though it is less than five years old, it is still about as venerable as a website can be. [...] I wanted to experience graphic chat through a minority-run website to see if this factor might prove an exception to the overwhelming whiteness I had seen on the Internet in general. I wish I could say that it did, but unfortunately it didn't, or rather only did in fairly limited ways. As Thomas Foster writes, 'Virtual reality privileges vision as a mode of information processing, and visual perception remains inextricably linked to a history of racial stereotyping' (160). When contrasting graphic chat with earlier forms of text-only chat, such as LambdaMOO, it can be seen that the more image-rich 'virtual reality' enabled by the superior band width it employs only intensifies the 'privileging of vision as a mode of information processing,' and consequently produces racial and gendered cybertypes of the body that can come across as potentially and perhaps perniciously more 'real' than their textual counterparts. A case in point: 'Starr Long, cocreator of Ultima Online, remembered his own reaction when he learned prostitution had been introduced. "Awesome!"' (Kolbert 98). This somewhat disturbing reaction makes perfect sense when we consider the game designers' priorities when creating these immensely popular online social environments: Long's jubilance is due to the fact that spontaneous development of such practices as prostitution online attests to the 'realness' of the Internet environment. Prostitution means that the illusion of bodies created in Ultima Online *works* for the players; sex and gender, like race, need bodies – or rather, 'visual perceptions' that readers can *take* as bodies – in order to possess virtual currency. Unfortunately, cybertyping flourishes under these same conditions; racism, prostitution, and other forms of identity-based oppression online become possible (and perhaps inevitable) when visual perceptions are informed by the same sets of objectifying ideologies that inform these activities offline.

## LambdaMOO and Orientalism

A cute cartoon dog sits in front of a computer, gazing at the monitor and typing away busily. The cartoon's caption jubilantly proclaims, 'On the Internet, nobody knows you're a dog!' This image resonates with particular intensity for those members of a rapidly expanding subculture that congregates within the consensual hallucination defined as cyberspace. Users define their presence within this textual and graphic space through a variety of different activities – commercial interaction, academic research, netsurfing, real-time interaction and chatting with interlocutors who are similarly 'connected' – but all can see the humor in this image because it illustrates so graphically a common condition of being and self-definition within this space. Internet users represent themselves within it solely through the medium of keystrokes and mouse clicks, and through this medium they can describe themselves and their physical bodies any way they like; they perform their bodies as text.

[...] The cartoon celebrates access to the Internet as a social leveler that permits even dogs to freely express themselves in discourse to their masters, who are deceived into thinking that dogs are their peers rather than their property. The element of difference, in this cartoon the difference between species, is comically subverted in this image; in the medium of cyberspace, distinctions and imbalances in power between beings who perform themselves solely through writing seem to have been deferred, if not effaced.

This utopian vision of cyberspace as a promoter of a radically democratic form of discourse should not be underestimated. Yet the image can be read on several levels. The freedom of which the dog chooses to avail itself is the freedom to 'pass' as part of a privileged group – human computer users with access to the Internet. This is possible because of the discursive dynamic of the Internet, particularly in chat spaces like LambdaMOO, where users are known to others by self-authored names they give their 'characters' rather than the more revealing e-mail addresses that include domain names. Defining gender is a central part of the discourse – players who choose to present themselves as 'neuter,' one of the several genders available to players on LambdaMOO, are often asked to 'set gender,' as if the choice to have a neuter gender is not a choice at all, or at least one that other players choose to recognize. They are seen as having deferred a choice rather than having made on unpopular one. [...] Gender is an element of identity that must be defined by each player, though the creators of LambdaMOO try to contribute toward a reimagining of gender by offering four choices (two more than are acknowledged in 'real life'); still, one must be chosen. Each player must enunciate a chosen gender, since this gender will be visible to all players who call up other players' physical descriptions on their screens. Race, however, is not an option that must be chosen. Although players can elect to write it into their descriptions it is not required by the programming that they do so.

Nonetheless, race is 'written' in role-playing cyberspaces as well as read by other players. It is crucial to direct critical attention toward the conditions under which race is enunciated, contested and ultimately erased and suppressed online, and the ideological implications of these performative acts of writing and reading otherness. What does the way race is written in cyberspace reveal about the enunciation of difference in new electronic media? Have the rules of the game changed, and if so, how?

Role-playing sites on the Internet offer their participants programming features such as the ability to physically 'set' one's gender, race, and physical appearance, through which one can, and indeed in many cases is required to, project a version of the self that is inherently theatrical. Since true identities of interlocutors at Lambda are unverifiable [...], it can be said that everyone who participates is 'passing,' since it impossible to tell if a character's description matches a player's physical characteristics. Some of the uses to which this in fixed theatricality are put are benign and even funny. Descriptions of self as a human-size pickle or pot-bellied pig are not uncommon, and generally are received in a positive, amused, tolerant way by other players. In contrast to this, players who elect to describe themselves in racially 'othered' terms, as Asian, African American, or Latino, are often seen as engaging in a form of hostile performance, since they introduce what many consider a real-life 'divisive issue' into the phantasmatic world of cybernetic textual interaction. The borders and frontiers of cyberspace, which had previously seemed so amorphous, take on a keen sharpness when the enunciation of racial otherness is put into play as performance. While everyone is 'passing,' some forms of racial passing are practiced and condoned because they do not threaten the integrity of a national sense of self that is defined as white.

The first act a participant in LambdaMOO performs is that of writing a self-description. It is the primal scene of cybernetic identity, a postmodern performance of the mirror stage:

> Identity is the first thing you create in a MUD. You have to decide the name of your alternate identity – what MUDders call your character. And you have to describe who this character is, for the benefit of the other people who inhabit the same MUD. By creating your identity, you help create a world. Your character's role and the roles of the others who play with you are part of the architecture of belief that upholds for everybody in the MUD the illusion of being a wizard in a castle or a navigator aboard a starship: the roles give people new stages on which to exercise new identities, and their new identities affirm the reality of the scenario. (Rheingold 148)

LambdaMOO requires that one choose a gender; though two of the choices are variations on the theme of 'neuter,' the choice cannot be deferred because the programming code requires it. It is impossible to receive authorization to create a character without making this choice. Race, on the other hand, is not only not a required choice, it is not even on the menu. Players are given as many lines of text as they like to write any sort of textual description of themselves that they want. The architecture of belief that underpins social interaction in the MOO – that is, the belief that one's interlocutors possess distinctive human identities that coalesce through and vivify the glowing letters scrolling down the computer screen – is itself built upon this form of fantastic autobiographical writing. The majority of players in LambdaMOO do not mention race at all in their self-description, though most do include eye and hair color, build, age, and pronouns that indicate a male or a female gender. In those cases when race is not mentioned as such, but hair and eye color are, race is still being evoked – a character with blue eyes and blond hair will be assumed to be white. Yet while the textual conditions of self-definition and self-performance would seem to permit players total freedom, within the boundaries of the written word, to describe themselves in any way they choose, this choice is actually an illusion.

This is because the decision to leave race out of self-description does in fact constitute a choice: in the absence of racial description, all players are assumed to be white. This is partly due to the demographics of Internet users; most are white, male, highly educated, and middle class. It is also due to the utopian belief-system prevalent in the MOO. This system, which claims that the MOO should be a free space for play, strives toward policing and regulating racial discourse in the interest of social harmony. This system of regulation does permit racial role-playing when it fits within familiar discourses of racial stereotyping, and thus perpetuates these discourses. I am going to focus on Asian performance within the MOO because Asian personae are by far the most common nonwhite ones chosen by players and thus offer the greatest number of examples for study.

The vast majority of male Asian characters deployed in the MOO fit into familiar stereotypes from popular electronic media such as video games, television, and film, and popular literary genres such as science fiction and historical romance. Characters named Mr. Sulu, Chun Li, Hua Ling, Anjin San, Musashi, Bruce Lee, Little Dragon, Nunchaku, Hiroko, Miura Tetsuo, and Akira invoke their counterparts in the world of popular media. Mr. Sulu is the token Asian American in the television show *Star Trek:*, Hua Ling and Hiroko are characters in the science-fiction novels *Eon* and *Red Mars;* Chun Li and Liu Kang are characters from the video games *Street Fighter* and *Mortal Kombat*; the movie star Bruce Lee was nicknamed 'Little Dragon'; Miura Tetsuo and Anjin San are characters in James Clavell's popular novel and TV miniseries *Shogun;* Musashi is a medieval Japanese folklore hero; and Akira is the title of a Japanese anime film. The name Nunchaku refers to a weapon, as do, in a more oblique way, all of the names listed above. These names all adapt the samurai warrior fantasy for role-playing, and permit their users to perform a notion of the oriental warrior adopted from popular media. The effect of popular media in cyberspace has been to create a bricolage of figurations and simulations. The orientalized male persona, complete with sword, confirms the idea of the Asian man as potent, antique, exotic, and anachronistic.

This type of orientalized theatricality is a form of identity tourism; my research indicates that players who choose this type of racial play are almost always white, and their appropriation of stereotyped male Asian samurai figures allows them to indulge in a dream of crossing over racial boundaries temporarily and recreationally. Choosing these orientalized cybertypes tips their interlocutors off to the fact that they are not 'really' Asian; they are instead playing in a familiar type of performance. Thus, the Orient is brought into the discourse, but only as a token or type. The idea of a nonstereotyped Asian male identity is so seldom enacted in LambdaMOO that its absence can only be read as a symptom of suppression.

[...] The tokens and types of Asian maleness are pressed into service by identity tourists as a means to shore up their own subject positions online. Cyberspace is a disembodied place; the need to create very clear, recognizable personae is thus a practical one; coherent discourse demands that one is able to conceptualize a self that is *different* from its interlocutors. However, in constructing this necessary difference, the subject has recourse only to those markers of difference that already exist within the symbolic order. That is to say, users are drawn to create personae that are culturally coherent and intelligible, and racial cybertypes provide familiar, solid, and reassuring versions of race which other users can readily accept and understand since they are so used to seeing them in novels, films, and video games. This is not to say that online audiences particularly approve of the spectacle of virtual samurai and geishas in online environments; however, their presence does not constitute a threat to the idea of the subject as Western, white, and male. Indeed, the presence of images of the Orient works to enhance a user's sense of himself as the *one*, not the *other*. These images provide the necessary contrast, the dark background, against which the user can feel even more 'himself' than he did before. [...]

## Fantasy Tourism

Tourism is a particularly apt metaphor for describing the activity of racial identity appropriation in cyberspace. The term used to describe movement through cyberspatial sites – that is, 'surfing' (an activity already associated with tourism in the minds of most Americans) – reinforces the idea that cyberspace is a place where travel and mobility are featured attractions, and figures it as a form of travel that is inherently recreational, exotic, and exciting. The choice to enact oneself as a samurai warrior in LambdaMOO constitutes identity tourism that allows a player to appropriate an Asian racial identity without any of the risks associated with being a racial minority in real life. While this might seem to offer a promising venue for non-Asian characters to see through the eyes of the other by performing themselves as Asian through online textual interaction, the fact the personae chosen are overwhelmingly Asian stereotypes blocks this possibility by reinforcing these stereotypes. [...]

Since the incorporation of the computer into the white-collar workplace, the line that divides work from play has become increasingly fluid. It is difficult for employers, and indeed for employees, to differentiate between doing research on the Internet and playing: exchanging e-mail, checking library catalogs, interacting with friends and colleagues through synchronous media like online conferencing and videoconferencing offer enhanced opportunities for gossip, jokes, and other distractions under the guise of work. Time spent on the Internet is a hiatus from real life, or 'RL,' as it is called by most participants in virtual social spaces like LambdaMOO. When that time is spent in a role-playing space such as Lambda, devoted only to social interaction and the creation and maintenance of a convincingly 'real' milieu modeled after an international community, that hiatus becomes a full-fledged vacation. That Lambda offers players the ability to write their own descriptions, as well as the fact that players often utilize this programming feature to write stereotyped Asian personae for themselves, reveals the attractions lying not only in being able to 'go' to exotic spaces, but in co-opting the exotic and attaching it to oneself, to 'becoming' it. The appropriation of racial identity becomes a form of recreation, a vacation from fixed identities and locales. [...]

[...] Identity tourism in cyberspaces like LambdaMOO functions as a fascinating example of the promise of high technology to enhance travel opportunities by redefining what constitutes travel. Logging onto a discursive space where one can appropriate exotic identities means that one need never cross a physical border or even leave one's armchair to go on vacation. In '"McDisneyization"' and "Post-Tourism": Contemporary Perspectives on Contemporary Tourism,' George Ritzer and Allan Liska identify the Internet as a technologically enabled medium that will usher us into the age of 'posttourism': 'whatever happens, tourism will continue to flourish, but the McDonaldization thesis leads us to believe that, at least for some time, anticipatory technologies [...] such as videos, the Internet and especially virtual (or techno-) touring will not only prepare people to travel, but will replace journeys to far off locales' (101). This promise of post-touristic 'ultimate mobility and perfect exchange' is not, however, fulfilled for everyone in LambdaMOO. The suppression of racial discourse that does not conform to familiar stereotypes, and the enactment of cybertyped notions of the oriental that do conform to them, extend the promise of mobility and exchange only to those who wish to change their identities to fit accepted norms.

Performances of Asian female personae in LambdaMOO are doubly repressive because they enact an identity tourism that cuts across the axes of gender and race, linking them in a powerful mix that brings together virtual sex, orientalist stereotyping, and performance. A listing of some of the names and descriptions chosen by players who masquerade as Asian females in LambdaMOO include

Asian Doll, Miss Saigon, Bisexual Asian Guest, Michelle Chang, Geisha Guest, and Maiden Taiwan. They describe themselves as, for example, a 'mystical Oriental beauty, drawn from the pages of a Nagel calendar,' or in the case of Geisha Guest, a character owned by a white American man living in Japan:

> A petite Japanese girl in her twenties. She has devoted her entire life to perfecting the tea ceremony and mastering the art of lovemaking. She is multi-orgasmic. She is wearing a pastel kimono, 3 under-kimonos in pink and white. She is not wearing panties, and that would not be appropriate for a geisha. She has spent her entire life in the pursuit of erotic experiences.

It is commonly known that the relative dearth of women in cyberspace results in a great deal of 'computer cross-dressing,' or men masquerading as women. Men who do this are generally seeking sexual interaction, or 'Netsex,' from other players of both genders. When the performance is doubly layered, and users extend their identity tourism across both race and gender, it is possible to observe a double appropriation or objectification that uses the oriental as part of a sexual lure, thus using passing performances to exploit and reify the Asian woman as submissive, docile, and a sexual plaything. Beyond LambdaMOO, the fetishization of the Asian woman extends into other parts of the Internet. The extremely active Usenet news group called "alt.sex.fetish.orientals' is only one of the infamous alt.sex news groups that overtly focus upon race as an adjunct to sexuality. [...]

## Graphic Chat: Cybertyping and the Tyranny of the Visible

[...] It seems that most users strongly prefer to 'see' who they're interacting with, even if they are aware that what they are 'seeing' may bear no relation to the actual appearance of the user on the other end. Race becomes part of the visual language of graphic chat in a way that it could not be in textual chat, a factor that creates less difference than one might expect in terms of how race is dealt with in these spaces. Discourse about race is still elaborately 'routed around,' at least in terms of much interface design, avatar construction and deployment, and everyday discourse in Club Connect in spite of the fact that graphic avatars make race so visible. And even though the 'club' is linked to an African American ethnic identity website, NetNoir, certain aspects of racial policing that obtain in LambdaMOO, albeit on an informal basis, are still in evidence at Club Connect.

My initial experiences with Club Connect did prove to inject race into graphic chat in ways that I had not seen in text-only environments and interfaces. The architect's dream of a multicultural virtual world is visible from the start. The log-on screen, which is the first thing that you see when you enter the website, features a little cartoon icon of a person's head, which greets you and asks you if you're having a problem with your password. Since it is practically guaranteed that most new users, especially ones who aren't computer-savvy, will have trouble with this step, viewers are given a great deal of exposure to this virtual greeter. The greeter is an icon of a fairly dark male with dreadlocks and African American features. Though it is generally a shaky move to make claims about which visual images look black, Asian, or in other ways 'ethnic' since these judgments are always subjective and can tend to reduplicate the language of essentialism and racialism if not racism, this figure struck me as undeniably African American. This figure's position on this screen figures him as 'tech support': both a servant of sorts and a technological expert. The figure paradoxically merges images of domestic laborers – like butlers and houseboys, images long associated with both blacks and Asians – and the computer geek figure, an image reserved for young white males. The figure looks young and 'hip,' as signified by the dreadlocks. These dreadlocks also gesture toward an ethnicity that is up front and center rather than elided or hidden, which is a real departure from the norm and a genuine innovation. [...]

Once you've gotten past the password screen, Club Connect's software invites you to choose your gender, and then assigns you a 'starter' or default body which you can further customize after getting acquainted with the site. The first time I logged on, I chose the gender 'female' and was given the body and face of a young black woman, with fairly dark skin, African features, and short dark hair. I chose a name for my avatar, and began to explore the site. The first thing I noticed is that I was the only avatar among hundreds who was noticeably dark. While I saw many Asian-presenting female avatars, I saw no Asian-presenting male ones. This disparity can be accounted for, I am sure, by the fact that it isn't really a disparity; images of Asians in popular culture and the mainstream media do tend to be dominated by females, as in television newscasting, though this is slowly changing. On the other hand, I didn't see many strictly Anglo-presenting avatars, either. Many players chose light-skinned black female characters, Latino-presenting male characters, or Asian-presenting female characters, but there were relatively few black-presenting or Asian-presenting male characters.

I found other players to be extremely helpful and friendly. Perhaps this was because they could tell that I was a new player, but on a site this busy and populated, I suspect that their perceptions of me as 'new' were conditioned by another factor. As I have mentioned earlier, I was the only truly dark character I could see anywhere. A friendly blond female, named mspiggy, offered to show me around, and when I expressed interest in exploring the ways I could customize my avatar, actually gave me a new head as a gift! This head, named 'Rebecca,' was one of dozens of models available via virtual vending machines that would take my virtual tokens and, in return, spit out a face for my avatar. Significantly, 'Rebecca' was blonde and white-skinned; in fact, she greatly resembled my new online friend. While a great deal could be read into this psychologically, if one were so inclined, it seems to me indicative of the ways that beauty and race interact together in graphic chat spaces. Mspiggy's assumption that I would want a head that looked less 'ethnic' seemed to project a particular image of beauty that was less, well, dark. Mspiggy showed me how to detach my old head, which I tucked under my arm, and helped me insert the new one. She then pointed out that my skin color and head color didn't match, saying 'lol [laugh out loud] you look like you have a tan only on your arms!' and offered to help me to acquire some 'body spray' so that I could change it. Throughout this exchange no mention of race was made.

Mspiggy led me to vending machines, where I viewed the multitude of different heads available to me. In an unconscious parody of cosmetic surgery and other technological image 'enhancements,' I noticed that these were priced across a wide range. I admit that I have not looked at every head available, but I did notice that none of them were as dark as my old one had been. This commodification of identity is reflected in the chat room's helpscreens on the topic of 'changing and customizing your avatar's head,' part of which reads,

> Each head comes with its own default hair and face colors, which you may be able to customize. If custom face and hair colors are available, look for vending machines that sell or dispense head spray. If your head is sprayable, the popup menus of your avatar and the spray can will give you the necessary options for using the spray. Go ahead and experiment; you'll be able to change and adjust the colors again and again until you find the combination you like.

As hilarious as this description is, it seems to be doing more than simply pointing out the extent to which race has become elective in cyberspace; indeed, the passage omits any mention of race altogether. Instead of inviting you to give your avatar a race, just as you had given it a gender, the passage invites you to 'experiment; you'll be able to change and adjust the colors again and again until you find the combination you like.' Here, race is constructed as a matter of aesthetics, or finding the color that you like, rather than as a matter of ethnic identity or shared cultural referents. This fantasy of skin color divorced from politics, oppression, or racism seems to also celebrate it as infinitely changeable and customizable: as entirely elective as well as apolitical. Clearly, we must look to the subtextual, to the omitted and repressed, to find the place of race in graphic chat.

Implicit statements about race are to be found by looking at the relative pricing of heads, and the avatars of those around me. The marketplace and traffic in heads and bodyspray work in a traditional capitalistic system of supply and demand; that is to say, the types of heads for sale are available because there is demand for them: avatars are market-driven. If more players wanted to buy, for instance, extremely dark or Asian-looking male heads, undoubtedly they would have been on display, but they were not. The prevalent type seemed to be ethnically hybrid along particular lines: Asian-white females and light-skinned black females were quite popular. There were many male-presenting avatars with animal heads such as tigers, cats, and wolves – a fact in which a more inquiring mind than mine could undoubtedly find much meaning. Perhaps players choosing this option wished to defer the question of race permanently. [...]

As in text-only chat, the identities users choose say more about what they want than who they are, or rather, since these are eminently social spaces, what they think *others* want. In some sense Club Connect is a racially diverse space, since players are choosing Asian- and African-American-presenting avatars, but since it is impossible to tell the race and ethnicity of these avatars offline, one must ask what kind of authenticity, integrity, or political efficacy these communities can have. The site's persistent avoidance of race as any kind of factor at all in the buying and selling of avatars that clearly *are* raced indicates a radical repression of what is all too often coded as a 'divisive' subject, one to be avoided in the name of social harmony. However, like LambdaMOO, Club Connect displays a plethora of raced and gendered bodies, Asian and otherwise that gesture toward a complex, multifaceted, and sometimes conflicted awareness of racial diversity. The notion that race can be customized, changed, and taken on or off as easily as one pops the head off a Barbie doll invokes the distinctive features of identity tourism. The metaphor of headhunting in cyberspace is a powerful one, since it also locates identity tourism in a matrix of colonial trophy-getting, a way of 'eating the Other,' to use bell hooks's phrase. Taming and framing the other by buying its signs and signifiers with virtual tokens seems indeed to be a form of virtual tourism, a kind of souvenir acquisition. The tyranny of visibility, of cybernetic 'ways of seeing' in regard to race, has yet to be challenged in spaces like these.

## Multiply Distributed Identities

The Net is, like other media, a reflection of the cultural imagination. It is a hybrid medium that is collectively authored, synchronous, interactive, and subject to constant revision. Because it borrows liberally from other media like television, film, and advertising, it is particularly sensitive to shifting figurations of race, and thus a good place to look to see how race is enacted and performed. I map sociologist Dean MacCannell's theories from *The Tourist: A New Theory of the Leisure Class* (1976) onto cybernetic racial role-players because I see many parallels. The tourist is also an explorer and navigator of sorts,[1] enjoying a recreational privilege reserved for 'first world' leisure classes, just as do those who possess the material and cultural capital to gain access to the Net. The metaphor of travel that pervades the Net also evokes comparison with tourism, which offers no product but pure experience.[2] The most important point of comparison, though, is the relation between tourists and the 'natives' that they see. Tourist desires for cultural authenticity, to encounter the other as they envision it, underpin their own sense of self as culturally authentic. Internet users who adopt other racialized personae can practice a form of tourism by adopting a repertoire of racial cybertypes. They replicate versions of otherness that confirm its exotic qualities and close off genuine dialogue with the pronounced minority of users who are not white and male.

The word *tourist* has a derisive connotation. MacCannell suggests that tourists are 'reproached for being satisfied with superficial experiences of other people and places' (10). I use the term not to condemn those who pass as versions of the other, but rather because I wish to retain a sense of the identity tourist as one who engages in a superficial, reversible, recreational play at otherness, a person who is satisfied with an episodic experience as a racial minority. My fieldwork in role-playing spaces indicates that tourists desire experiences that they can legitimize as authentic. Their sojourns in the world of cyberspatial identity simulation through online role-playing are often used to confirm their ideas and underpin their ideal visions of the other. This passive version doesn't ask questions or challenge traditional stereotyped notions regarding its 'nature.' While gathering information for this project, I described myself as Japanese-American in my cybernetic self-portrait on LambdaMOO for a while, and for weeks until I edited it out of my description I was deluged with the same one-word message – *konmichiwa,* which means 'hello' in Japanese. This vision of the Asian American as somehow *always* irremediably and stereotypically Asian, always knowing the language, and always receptive to the powers of one magical word that proves a type of cultural knowledge, conforms to touristic expectations about the unitarianism and nonhybridity of culture.

Multiply distributed identities allow identity tourists to simultaneously claim two positions, that of the tourist and that of the native; they can be both inside and outside.[3] If they never come across a samurai during their cybernetic travels, they can be one. Peopling the virtual landscape with samurai, homeboys, and sexy Latina women confirms a vision of ethnicity from which many in the offline world are struggling to distance themselves.[4] [...]

In cyberspace, players do not ever need to look for jobs or housing, compete for classroom attention, or ask for raises. This ensures that identity tourists need never encounter situations in which exotic otherness could be a liability, an aspect of racial passing on the Internet that contributes to its superficiality. Players who represent as members of a minority may get the impression that minorities 'don't have it all that bad,' since they are unlikely to find themselves discriminated against in concrete, material ways. This imperfect understanding of the specific 'real life' social context of otherness can lead to a type of complacency backed up by the seemingly unassailable evidence of 'personal experience.'

In Trinh T. Minh-ha's critique of anthropological methodology, *Woman Native Other,* she writes that 'American tourists [...] looking for a change of scenery and pace in a foreign land [...] strike out in search of the 'real' Japan.' For these tourists 'authenticity [...] turns out to be a product that one can buy, arrange to one's liking, and/or preserve' (88). According to Trinh, tourists are searching for 'the possibility of a difference, yet a difference or otherness that will not go so far as to question the foundation of their beings and makings' (88). Similarly, identity tourists perform a version of their ideal other that conforms to familiar stereotypes and does not ask questions or raise difficult, so-called divisive issues like racism: 'No anthropological undertaking can ever open up the other. Never the marrow' (Trinh 73). The problem with believing that direct experience 'as' the other will give access to knowledge about it, its marrow, is that this enterprise devalues actual conversation *with* it. There's a frisson about cultural transvestism that tantalizes identity tourists and makes them believe that, like Trinh's anthropologist, they can better understand the native through assuming a temporary alterity, by experiencing what they think 'native' life is, rather than by acknowledging their reflexive position as an outsider, as other to the other. As Trinh asks, '[H]ow can he, indeed, read into the other knowing not how the other read into him?' Identity tourism is a type of nonreflexive relationship that actually widens the gap between the other and the one who only performs itself as the other in the medium of the cyberspace.

Bernard Gendron describes theories of the effect of technology on the human condition by dividing them into three categories: Utopian, dystopian, and socialist (4–5). Observing racial and ethnic transvestism on the Internet leads me to conclusions that partake of all three of these categories. While the Net has great potential for expanding access to diversity and creating a globalistic point of view, it does not perform these functions as they exist today. The politics and economics of Net access, as well as the ways in which I see race performed in role-playing spaces, lead me to conclude that the advertising promises of Microsoft, IBM, and America Online that 'make the world smaller' are indeed being fulfilled in a disturbing way. Perhaps opening up the Net through government subsidies and infrastructure building in the schools will redress this problem, but the incentives for minorities to opt for default whiteness online will probably exist as long as there are material disadvantages of nonwhiteness. Chat spaces, however nominally democratized they may appear to be, are unlikely to eradicate these disadvantages. The Net is a medium, a reflection of desires, fears, and anxieties that exist in the culture, not a panacea for social ills and inequalities. The Internet is unlikely to lead to an apocalyptic breakdown of literacy or morality, as some claim; rather, it is a laboratory where users are building particular kinds of social environment with words, as well as racialized personae to deploy within those environments. [...]

The links between the history of media and the history of racial stereotyping are strong. The romantic, inaccurate, and sometimes overtly racist visions of the oriental that circulate in contemporary film, video games, television, and other electronic media are part of a vocabulary of signifying practices that are redeployed on the Internet by identity tourists. Role-playing on the Net and elsewhere is often characterized as games, and thus skeptics often claim that they bear no relation to the real world. Yet the specific ways in which Internet users choose to represent themselves online, the masks and personae of alterity that they fashion for themselves from images taken from the media landscape, reveal a great deal about their cultural and ideological investments and their assumptions about both the other and themselves. Racist ideology operates within role-playing spaces on the Net, creating a social matrix that is both 'default white' and peopled with phantasmatic versions of otherness. To have any hope of approaching the utopian 'level playing field' that so many claim is in the Internet's future, attention must be paid to *discourse with* rather than *appropriations of* the other.

## Notes

1. Microsoft's and Netscape's web browser programs, entitled Internet Explorer and Navigator, respectively, emphasize the links between the notion of travel and tourism and the graphical web. The web browser which preceded them, Mosaic, was a tool for browsing the web in the days when it was text based; hence its name emphasizes the image of the hyperlinked or fragmented web rather than the notion of the web as a space to be traversed and colonized in a ship. Netscape's Navigator icon features an imperial-era tallship steering wheel, further reinforcing this imagery. I am indebted to Matthew Byrnie for this observation.
2. Souvenirs are trophies that evoke memories of an experience rather than commodities possessing an independent or exchange value (see MacCannell 124).
3. See Sherry Turkle, *Life on the Screen* (13).
4. In his analysis of ethnic identity websites, Steve McLaine observes that it's often users of EOCs, or ethnic online communities, that create screen names for themselves like 'blacklatindiva, spicygirl, AlatinoLover [...] and hoocheemama' that seem to 'freely flaunt stereotypes as identification' (18). McLaine speculates that this may constitute a form of empowerment, of taking back the discourse of oppression and repurposing it as a form of solidarity, as in the use of the word *nigger* by African Americans. In any case, the deployment of these terms by users of any 'real life' race or ethnicity demonstrates that race must be cybertyped online to be recognizable. Though it is possible that cybertyping could be used as a means to building race-based communities online, its deployment will always be problematic in the same sense that the use of the word *nigger* is.

# References

Foster, Thomas (1999) ' "The Souls of Cyber-Folk" ': Performativity, Virtual Embodiment, and Racial Histories.' *Cyberspace Textuality: Computer Technology and Literary Theory.* ed. Marie-Laure Ryan. Bloomington, IN: Indiana University Press.
Gendron, Bernard (1977) *Technology and the Human Condition.* New York: St. Martins Press.
Kolbert, Elizabeth (2001) 'Pimps and Dragons (Dept. of Gaming).' *New Yorker,* May 28: 80–98.
MacCannel, Dean (1976) The *Tourist: A New Theory of the Leisure Class.* New York: Schocken.
McLaine, Steven (2001) 'Ethnic Online Communities: Between Profit and Purpose.' Paper presented at the Cyberculture(s): Performance, Pedagogy and Politics in Online Spaces Conference, University of Maryland, April.
Minh-ha, Trinh T. (1989) *Woman, Native, Other: Writing Postcoloniality and Feminism.* Bloomington, IN: Indiana University Press.
Rheingold, Howard (1993) *The Virtual Community.* New York: HarperPerennial.
Ritzer, George and Liska, Allan (1997) ' "McDisneyization" and "Post-Tourism": Complementary Perspectives on Contemporary Tourism.' *Touring Cultures: Transformations of Travel and Theory.* ed. Chris Rojek and John Urry. New York: Routledge.
Turkle, Sherry (1995) *Life on the Screen: Identity in the Age of the Internet.* New York: Simon and Schuster.

# Index

Entries in *italics* denote films, publications and television shows.

abortion 228, 239
*Absolutely Fabulous* 433
'abstract labor' 141, 146
academia 42, 221, 250, 260
acid house culture 383–400
action, legibility transformation 454
activism 324–37, 479–80
*The Act of Seeing with One's Own Eyes*
    (Brakhage) 265
Adorno, Theodor W. 6, 13–14, 86,
    103–8, 119
adventure tales 118
advertising 35–6, 155, 156–7
aesthetics
    discrimination 216–19, 220, 221
    race 529
    reification 116, 117, 121–2, 126
    symbolic creativity 243, 244–8
    *see also* high culture
affective films 264–6
African-American culture
    clothing industry 155–7
    entrepreneurship 162–3
    'face of America' 321
    hip hop 401–16
    Ozomatli influence 486
    Tiger Woods 199
    *see also* black culture
African diasporas 290, 296–7, 401–3,
    408–14, 495–519
    *see also* diasporas
Afro-Caribbean culture 296, 301, 401–2,
    408, 412
Afro-diasporas *see* African diasporas
age of mass customization 151–8
AIDS/HIV 324, 329, 330–4,
    336, 337
alethic modalities 455
Alison, Archibald 57

Allen, Woody 380
Almo Sounds record label 485
alternative acts 417–28
'alternative universe' stories 258
Amazulu 379
America 78
    art films in low culture 263–77
    Asian gay video porn 338–48
    black culture 286–7
    cultural displacement 285–6
    hip hop 401–16
    marketing 159–67
    paradox 159–67
    state of emergency 309–23
American Dream 171–2
Americanization 7–9, 35, 311, 314
anal sex 342–4
ancient Egypt 497
androgyny 380–1
animation studios 187–8
*Annie Hall* (Allen) 380
anthropological methodology 531
anticolonialism 131–3, 506–7
    *see also* colonialism
anti-porn movement 224, 231, 237
antiracist movements 144
    *see also* racialization
Apache Indian 300–4,
    305, 307
apparel *see* clothing industry
Arab Americans 202
Aristotle 13
Armstrong, Billie Joe 423
Arnold, Matthew 4, 33
art as culture 27–8
art films 263–77
articulation of identities 279–348
artists in black culture 163–5
'arts of timing' 75, 80

artworks
    'culture industry' 104, 105–6
    discrimination 216–17, 218, 220–1
    instrumentalization 116, 117
    manipulation theory 127
    materialization 120–1
    mechanical reproduction 96–102
    social relations 122
    symbolic creativity 243–5, 247
    technique concept 105
*Asian Knights* 343–4, 346
Asians
    bhangra music 294–308
    gay video porn 338–48
    Internet users 524–5
    sexual stereotyping 338–40, 341–6, 347
assimilation 480
    *see also* merging cultures
asyndeton 456
aura concept 99, 100, 101, 105
authenticity
    acid house culture 397
    artworks 98–9, 100–2
    black culture 289, 290
    drag kings 435
    popular discrimination 218
    punk subculture 418, 420–2
    underground culture 383–5
authorial signatures 218–19
automation of commodities 112
avantgardism 42, 44–5, 219–20
avatars 520–33
Ayers, Roy 514

baby dresses 378–82
Bakhtin, Mikhail 288, 293
Bambaataa, Afrika 505–6
Bananarama 379
*banda* music 489–91
banned music 388
Barbie dolls 148, 168–83
the barrio 486
Barthes, Roland 7–8, 52–3, 124, 212, 357–8
Baudrillard, Jean 48, 52–3, 54, 121
BBC Radio One 387–9, 394
beat culture 376
beauty contests 179, 206
being in the world 454
believability of names 459
Bell, Shannon 437
*Below the Belt* 341–3
Benjamin, Walter 6, 85, 96–102, 309–10
Berlant, Lauren 280–1, 309–23
bhangra music 294–308
Bikini Kill 424–6
biological identities 199–203
Birmingham Centre 84

black culture 77–8, 159–67, 285–93
    artists 163–5
    corporation investments 160–2
    drag kings 432, 435
    films 159, 166
    hip hop 401–16
    iconography 166
    musical forms 444, 496–503
    music industry 160–2
    New York City 404, 405–7
    white businesses 156–7
    women 504–5, 516
Black Power 501
black/white binary 296–7
Bleich, David 253
Blondy, Alpha 514
the body
    American immigrants 315–16
    black culture 290
    'face of America' 317–18
    film genres 264–5, 272
    grounded aesthetics 246
    hip hop culture 410–11
    *Hustler* magazine 225–7,
        236, 240
    skateboarders 469
Bombay's bhangra music 294–308
borrowing terms 258–60
boundary breakdowns 442
Brakhage, Stan 265
breakdancing 402, 403, 408–13, 416
breasts in pornography 228
Brecht-Benjamin aesthetics 126
Breedlove, Lynn 419–21, 424
Brick Lane market 374
bricolage, style 359–61
Britain
    black populations 500
    rave culture 471
    *see also* United Kingdom
'Britishness' 300–3
Broadcasting Act (1990) 394
Bunker Hill East project 463
Buñuel, Luis 271–2, 276–7
Burnside Project 474
Burroughs, Edgar Rice 38
Buster Hymen 435–6, 440
butch drag kings 430–2, 435–6

Cablinasian term 200
camp culture 432–3
Canclini, García 73, 78–80
canon formation 2–3, 11
capitalism
    Benjamin 96–7
    commodity as spectacle 112–13
    feminism 137–41

capitalism *cont.*
  politics of culture 129–46
  postmodernism 142
  reification 116–17, 119–20, 125–6
  symbolic creativity 242–3
  transnational corporations 507
  *see also* Marxism; Marx, Karl
*The Care of the Self* (Foucault) 325–6
Carlyle, Thomas 4
carnivalesque 79, 80, 288, 293
Cashmore, Ellis 159–67
Castell, Manuel 413–14
Castro clones 438
CDs in black culture 496
'challenging' texts 219–20
*The Changing Face of America* (*Time*) 314–16
character rape concept 257, 258
Chicago scene 397–8
Chicano culture 479–94
children 173–4, 176–7, 312–13
  *see also* girls
China 134
Choplin, Jean-Luc 79–80
cinema *see* films
citizenship, America 314, 316–17, 320–2
the city
  conceptualization 451–3
  control 458
  hip hop 401–16
  readability 449–51
  walking 449–61
civilization
  culture distinction 3–5
  development of word 26–7, 28
  mass 33–8
class
  American immigration 320–1
  the body 226–7, 240
  core national values 310
  death of the nation 315
  New York poverty 404–7
  'popular' relationship 70–1
  punk subculture 419
  sexuality 223–4, 230–3, 237–8
  struggle 126
  subcultures 365, 366–7, 369
classification of people 199–203
Clinton, George 502
clothing
  acid house culture 399
  advertising 155, 156–7
  African-American people 155–7
  exploitation 165
  hip hop culture 409
  industry 151–8, 165
  nationalist emblems 157
  punk 361–2, 364
  second-hand 372–82

clubbers' culture 383–400
Club Casanova 432–3
Club Connect chat space 527–30
Coleridge, Samuel Taylor 4
collective identity 490
colonialism 130, 132–3, 135
commercial culture 66–8
  hip hop 402
  mass media 509
  Ozomatli 480
  US sport 198
commodification
  black culture 289
  culture 83–146
  golf/sport 197–209
  hip hop culture 411–12
  multiculturalism 174
  scope 148, 164
  social life 83–146
  style 349
  transnational capitalism 135–6, 141, 143–4
commodities 83–146
  'culture industry' 103–8
  fetishism 89–95, 110
  forms 356–7
  mechanical reproduction 96–102, 105
  reification 115–28
  spectacle 109–14
  subculture incorporation 356–7
  symbolic creativity 241–4
  tastes 211–12
communications
  hip hop culture 412–13, 414
  New York City 405
  popular culture abilities 444
  style 358–9
community performances 297–9
competitive labor 152
Concept-city 452–3
conformity 106–8
  *see also* social control
'consciousness of desire' 114
consumerism
  new subjects 168–83
  second-hand style 373–8
  symbolic creativity 241–4
consumer magazines 396–9
consumption
  Baudrillard 53–4
  children 176–7
  commodity as spectacle 113
  'culture industry' 103, 106
  global attitudes 171
  hip hop culture 409, 411
  India 168–83
  Marxism 51–2
  mass culture 6
  the masses 31

consumption *cont.*
rap music 512
record sleeves 503
reification 117
*Star Trek* fans 251–2
subculture 359
symbolic creativity 243–4
transnationalism 141, 181
ways of consuming 211–78
women 49–50
containment policies 470–1
containment/resistance dialectic 65–7, 71
contradictions
feminism 139–40
Marxism 133, 135–6
modernity 131, 141–2
nationalism 131–2
control
city dwellers 458
Disney tactics 193–4
grounded aesthetics 245
*see also* social control
conventionality 218
copyright issues 184–6
core national values 310, 321–2
corporations
black culture 160–1
difference construction 172–4
investments 160–2
Mattel 172–4
predatory nature 160–1
universality construction 172–4
Cortijo, Rafael 75–7
cosmetic surgery 499
counter-cultures 376–7
counterpublicity 324–37
counter-response to oppression 510–11
couple forms 336
Crazy Legs 408, 409
creativity 241–8
crews, hip hop 407
criminalization of Latinos 487–8
critical discrimination 215, 216, 220–1
cross-dressing 429–40
Cuban-Americans 330, 333
cultivation 28–9
cults, artworks 100, 101–2
cultural capital 220–1
cultural difference 173, 201–2
cultural forms of 'popular' 58–9, 61
cultural hegemony 287
cultural struggle 65–7, 69–71
cultural studies 73
culture
alternative political rationalities 141–3
civilization distinction 3–5
commodification 83–146
delineation 19–82

culture *cont.*
development of word 25–9
Gresham's law 41
inter-ethnic unity 486
merging cultures 42–3
plurality 4, 27, 74
politics 129–46, 484
'sacralization' 266–8
Williams' delineation 25–9
'culture industry' 6, 16, 73, 79, 103–8, 147–50
cyberspace *see* Internet
Cypress Hill 489

Dada 361
*Dallas* 218
dance music 383–400
dancing
hip hop 402, 403, 408–13, 416
punk subculture 362
Davis, Madeline 431
death of the nation 315
death of the social 53
Debord, Guy 86, 109–14
de Certeau, Michel 250–1, 442, 443
decolonization of third world 286
deconstruction of 'popular' 64–71
definition problems 19, 76
de la Rocha, Zack 484
delineation 19–82
Flores 72–82
Hall 64–71
Leavis 33–8
Macdonald 39–46
Modleski 47–54
Shiach 55–63
Williams 25–32
*Demeter* (Land) 255–6
democracy 31, 316
denaturalized masculinity 438–9
Denning, Michael 2
deontic modalities 455
department stores 154
de Sade, Marquis 265
de Saussure, Ferdinand 14
descriptive definitions 68, 76
design competitions 177–8
desire, *Hustler* 223–40
detective stories 118
deterioration in the city 452–3
diasporas
African 495–503, 504–19
black culture 289–91
black/white binary 296–7
engendering 294–308
Hindu nationalist project 304–5
hip hop culture 401–3, 408–13, 414
post-diaspora 305–6
transnational contexts 178–80

'diasporic intimacy' 506
Dibango, Manu 515–16
'dick' practices, punks 417–28
difference
   black communities 290–2
   constructing 172–4
   female sexuality 230
   postmodernism 286–8
   subculture style 359
'difficulty' in discrimination 219
digital sampling 512
dildos 420–1
disciplinary society 453
discourse
   the city 452–3
   dreams similarity 457
discrimination 215–22
disgust, *Hustler* 223–40
disidentifications 279, 281
disjunctions in subculture 367
Disney 79–80, 148–9, 173, 184–96
Disney Look brochure 190
distributing commodities 94, 105
diversity, multiculturalism 174
division of labor 91–2, 93–4, 140–1, 223–4
DJs, hip hop 402, 408–13
D-Mob 388
*dojo* setting, gay porn 341–2
domination systems
   couterpublicity 327–8, 333–4, 336
   Debord 111–12
   Foucault 325–6
   'popular' 60–1
   racialization of sexuality 338–40
double standards, femininity 47
Douglas, Ann 48–50
Douglas, Mary 229, 231–2, 239
drag kings 429–40
drag queens 429, 432–3
dreams 457
Dred 438
dress *see* clothing
drug cultures 388–91, 398–9, 491
dyke culture 419–20
   *see also* lesbianism
dynamic processes 11

East Asian stereotyping 338–48
economic factors
   commodities 110–12, 114
   fandom 220–1
   *see also* capitalism; consumption; monetary
      value; production
Ecstasy (drug) 389–90
EDI *see* Electronic Data Interchange
editorials, subcultures 396–9
education 4–5, 68
Eisner, Michael 79

electoral domination 487
Electronic Data Interchange (EDI) 152–3
electronic mail 395
El Gavilancillo (Saul Viera) 489
Eliot, T.S. 5
elitism 115
   *see also* high culture
Emergency Resources Unit (LA) 483
emergency state of America 309–23
employees, Disney 186–92
Engels, Friedrich 84–5
engendering diasporas 294–308
entrepreneurship 162–3, 375–8
epistemic modalities 455
eroticism 338–48
escapism 50
essentialism 291–2
ethics of the self 324–37
ethnicities
   America 198, 286, 404–7
   marginalization 287
   nationalism 480
   New York poverty 404–7
   selling products 170
   understanding 198
   *see also* black culture
eugenics 319
Europe
   art films 263–77
   displacement of high culture 285–6
   nationalism 131–2
Euro-trash 263–77
everyday life concept 8–9, 241–2, 244–5,
   247, 252
exchange, commodities 90–2,
   94–5, 113
expenditure and production
   449, 452
expertise of immigrants 179–80
explicitness in pornography 225
exploitation
   racialization 132–3
   transnational capitalism 141
   women 139–40
exploitation film companies 264–6, 268–71
Extension Act 1998 185–6

Fab Five Freddy 409–10, 512
Fabian, Johannes 74–5, 76
'face of America' 309–23
fag drags 438
faith, loss of 508
false consciousness 134
families
   commodities 93–4
   diasporas 303–4, 306, 307
   punk subculture 358
   race 320–2

fandom
    fiction 256–8
    gender 252–6, 259–60
    moral economy 256–8
    popular discrimination 220–1
    readers 250, 251–4
    *Star Trek* 249–62
    writing 249–62
'fantasmatic female' 299–300, 307
fantasy tourism 525–7
fanzines 254–5, 260–1, 363, 377, 391–3
Fascism 97, 102
fashion 148
    department stores 154
    design competitions 177–8
    designers 382
    industry 174, 177–8
    internationalization 174
    students 378
    *see also* clothing...
'fast capital' 508
fathers, bhangra music 303–4
female masculinity 429–40
femininity
    disgust 223–40
    Internet users 526–7
    lesbianism 433–4
    masquerade 47–54
    performance 431, 432–3
    politics of culture 138
    punk subculture 425
    reification 237
feminism 137–41, 145–6
    mass culture 47–54
    popular discrimination 219–20
    sexuality 223–4, 227–8, 231–2, 237–8
    *see also* Barbie dolls
femme drag kings 432, 435–6, 440
fetal metaphors 314, 318
fetishism 89–95, 110
fiction, fandom 256–8
films
    American low culture 263–77
    art reproduction 98, 99, 101–2
    black culture 159, 166
    commodity reification 122–3
    'culture industry' 105, 106–7, 108
    femininity 50–4
    influence 35, 38
    marketing 164–5
    merging cultures 43
    standardization 46
financial categories, NRI 179
Fiske, John 212, 215–22
fleamarkets 375
Flores, Juan 21–2, 72–82
flyers 391, 393
Flynt, Larry 234–6

folk art 40, 41, 46, 498
folk culture 4–5, 9, 13, 43–4, 480
    *see also* bhangra music
'folk devils' 356, 357, 368
folklore 72, 74
football hooliganism 358
footsteps 453–7
Ford, Henry 37, 38
forests of gestures 457
Foucault, Michel 325–6, 327–8, 336, 442,
    443, 453
Frankfurt School 6, 84, 87, 116–21, 124
Franklin, Aretha 499–500
Freccero, Carla 2
free market ideology 509
French culture 8, 26
Freud, Sigmund 126–7, 229–31
Fuchs, Cynthia 351, 417–28
functionalism, discrimination
    216–17, 220
Fung, Richard 281–2, 338–48
Futura 408
future of popular music 516–17

garments *see* clothing industry
gay culture
    drag kings 432, 438
    video porn 338–48
    *see also* homosexuality
gay movements 340, 345–6
gender
    black culture 292, 500
    diasporas 294–308
    drag kings 429–40
    fandom 252–6, 259–60
    Hindu nationalist project 304–5
    Internet users 523, 524
    jokes 229–31
    mass culture 47–8
    pornography 223–40
    punk subculture 417–28
    shopping 372–3
    subcultural entrepreneurs 377
    *see also* men; women
gender queens 437
Gendron, Bernard 531
genealogy, race 204
generic forms of culture 122–3
generic texts 218–19
Genosko, Gary 7–8
genre studies 272–3, 277
German culture 26–7, 28–9
Gilroy, Paul 280, 296–7, 306, 444
Ginoli, Jon 422–3
girls
    men's suits 378–82
    second-hand style 376, 377–82
    shopping 373

globalization
  American immigration 319–20
  black culture 286–9
  consumers 170–2
  feminism 140
  Los Angeles 482
  politics of culture 129–30
  production 471
  skateboarders' role 466–74
  tribalism decrease 198
Godard, Jean-Luc 270
golf 197–209
Gopinath, Gayatri 280, 294–308
government, 'popular' 55–7, 61
governmentality 309–10, 322
graffiti artists 402, 403, 408–13, 473–4
gramophone records 496–503
Gramsci, Antonio 6–7, 14, 133–4, 280
grand narratives 508
graphic chat 527–30
Greater Eastside (Los Angeles) 481–2
Greenberg, Clement 6, 40, 41
Green Day 421, 422–3
Gresham's law 41
Grewal, Iderpal 168–83
Griffin, Ada Gay 159, 160
'grossness', *Hustler* 225–7
grounded aesthetics 243, 244–8
Guest Service Fanatics 189–90
Gwaltney, John Langston 166

Habermasian rationality 327
Halberstam, Judith 351–2, 429–40
Hall, Stuart 14, 21, 64–71, 77–8, 169, 181,
    279–80, 285–93
Handlin, Oscar 73
Hanna, Kathleen 424–5, 426
Hawkins, Joan 213, 263–77
hazardous sports legislation 473
Hebdige, Dick 349, 350, 355–71, 409,
    411–12, 419
Hegel, G.W.F. 84
hegemony 6–7, 287
Hendrix, Jimi 500
Henry, William, A. 320
Hershe Bar drag king contests 434–9
heterosexuality 296–7, 320–2, 336
  *see also* sexuality
high culture 39, 40
  academicism 42
  the body 226
  displacement 285–6, 287
  films 263–77
  future of 44–5
  Gresham's law 41
  'low' distinction 288–9
  merging cultures 42–3
  reification and utopia 115, 119–20, 124

high culture *cont.*
  'sacralization' 266–8
  *see also* aesthetics
*High Fidelity* (Hornby) 211
Hilfiger, Tommy 151–8
Hindley, Annie 430
Hindu nationalist project 304–5
hip hop 401–16, 489, 490–1, 504–19
hippy culture 364, 375–7, 399
Hispanics 404, 405–7, 410
historical interest films 268
historiographies 133, 138–9
history
  culture 72–81
  race 197–209
HIV/AIDS 324, 329, 330–4, 336, 337
Hobbes' state 451–2
Hoggart, Richard 7, 8
Holland, Norman 127
Hollywood films 266, 271, 276
homeland fantasy 299–300, 307
homelessness 464–5
homogenized culture 42, 45
homology of style 364–5
homophobia 324–5, 327, 332–3, 343
homosexuality
  Asian gay video porn 338–48
  Kirk/Spock stories 258–60, 262
  Puig 50–2
  punk subculture 417–28
  Zamora 324–37
  *see also* gay…; lesbianism; queer…
hooliganism 358
Horkheimer, Max 6, 86
Hornby, Nick 211
horror films 263–6, 268–77
'house boy' fantasy 344
humour in performance 432–3
Hunter, Kendra 257, 258
*Hustler* magazine 223–40, 265–6
hybrid cultures 78–80
hygienic governmentality 309–10
hyphenated identity 181

IBA *see* Independent Broadcasting Authority
Ice T 422
iconography, black culture 166
identities
  articulation 279–348
  the city 458
  hip hop culture 407, 409
  punk subculture 422
  style 350
  Zamora's activism 326–37
identity tourism 520–33
ideological subculture incorporation 357–8
*i-D* magazine 397, 398–9
'If I had a Dick' (Fuchs) 417–28

images
    commodity reification 117, 125
    Internet 521–2
    record sleeves 497–503
    *see also* spectacle
imagination, role 76–7
immaterial labor 471
immigrants
    expertise 179–80
    'face of America' 310–23
    racialized scapegoating 483
    *see also* migration
imperialism 65–6
The Impressions 502
incorporation of subcultures 356–8, 411–12
Independent Broadcasting Authority
    (IBA) 394–5
India
    consumption 168–83
    liberalization programs 179
    production 175–8
    toy business 175–6
    vanity industry 177
    *see also* Asians
'Indianness' 301–2, 304
*India Today* magazine 180
individualization 242
industrialization
    commodification 83–4
    commodity as spectacle 111
    'culture industry' 6, 16
    literary tradition 4
    the masses 30
    'sacralization of culture' 267
    *see also* 'culture industry'
inequalities, recuperation 174
informal symbolic creativity 242–3
instrumentalization 116–17
intellectual property rights 184–6
intellectuals, definition 45
intentional communication 358–9
inter-ethnic unity 486
internationalization
    commodification of culture 84
    fashion industry 174
    marketing 205–7
    politics of culture 129–30
*International Skin* 344–5
International Wavelength 341
Internet 395, 445, 520–33
invisible operations 454

jackets, androgyny 380
Jackson, Michael 164
Jafa, Arthur 410, 416
Jameson, Fredric 86–7, 115–28, 379
Jazzie, B. 515
Jenkins, Henry 213, 249–62

*Jihad vs McWorld* (Barber) 206
jokes, *Hustler* 229–31
jumping scale, skateboarders 465–7
Juvee 1–2

karate 341–2
Kennedy, Elizabeth 431
'kinging' 432
    *see also* drag kings
King, Rodney 487
Kipnis, Laura 212, 223–40, 265–6
Kirk/Spock (K/S) stories 258–60, 262
KISS-FM radio 394–5
*Kiss of the Spider Woman* (Puig) 50–4
kitsch 6, 40, 41
Kluge and Negt 327–8
Korean rap music 515
Kracauer, Seigfried 13
Kristeva, Julia 366, 370
K/S stories *see* Kirk/Spock stories
Kuti, Fela 513–14

LA *see* Los Angeles
labor
    'abstract' 141, 146
    commodity as spectacle 111–12, 114
    competition 152
    Disney control 186–91
    fetishism of commodities 89–94
    sexuality 223–4
    transnational capitalism 141
    women 139–41
*Ladies First* (Queen Latifah) 504–5
Lambard, William 55
LambdaMOO chat space 522–7
Land, Jane 255–6, 261
landscape genre 217
language
    power 452
    signifiers 366
    topographical metaphor 454–5
Latino culture
    Los Angeles 481–92
    Zamora 324–37
Leavis, F.R. 5, 20, 33–8
Leavis, Q.D. 5
Lee, Stephen 162
Lefebvre, Henri 8, 14
legal issues
    *Hustler* 235, 239–40
    non-white repression 487
    radio stations 394
legal terms 55–6, 61
leggings 381
legibility 454
legislation 487
    *see also* legal issues
leisure time 241–3

Leninism 133, 134
lesbianism 430, 431, 433–4, 438
    *see also* homosexuality
lesbian movements 340
Levine, Lawrence, W. 266–8
Levi-Strauss, C. 355–6
Lewis, Lisa, A. 213
liberalization programs 179
licensing, TOM Inc. 154
listings, club culture 391, 393
literary tradition 4, 58, 104
    *see also* text…
lithography 97
LL Cool, J. 512
Lloyd, David 87, 129–46
local histories 482–4
localisms 170
locating 441–533
logocentricism 289–90
London ragmarkets 374
London Records 397–8
*Looking for Langston* 346
'looking for my penis' (Fung) 338–48
Lorrah, Jean 251–2, 257–8, 261
Los Angeles Conservation Corps 483
Los Angeles (LA) 412–15, 462–5, 479–94
love for nation 313, 318–19
    *see also* nationalism
'low culture'
    art films 263–77
    'high culture' distinction 288–9
    *see also* mass culture
Lowe, Lisa 87, 129–46
Lynd, R.S. and H.M. 34, 38

MacCannell, Dean 530–1
Macdonald, Dwight 20, 39–46, 73
McLaren, Malcolm 373
McLuhan, Marshall 7
McRobbie, Angela 350, 372–82
Madonna 380
Magic Kingdom *see* Disney
mailing lists, club culture 393, 395
mail order films 263–6, 268–74, 341
male desire 223–40
male impersonators 429–31
male mimicry 436–7
manipulation theory 124–5, 126–7
    *see also* social control
Manning, David 14
Maoism 134
maps 454, 455
*maquiladora* workers 140
marginalization 287
markers of specification 77–8
marketing 147–209
    America's paradox 159–67
    Barbie 168–83

marketing *cont.*
    Disney 184–96
    films 164–5
    national diversity 205–7
    Ozomatli 485
    popular culture 147–50
    record sleeves 498
    socio-economics 147–50
markets, second-hand 373–5
market segmentation 170
marriage 313, 319, 321–2
Marxism 15, 133–6, 145, 146
    commodity reification 116, 124
    gender 48, 138
    the masses 43
    Puig 50–4
Marx, Karl 84–5, 89–95, 96–7
masculinist bias 50, 51
masculinity
    black culture 292
    denaturalization 438–9
    drag kings 429–40
    performance 431–3
    punk subculture 425
    *see also* men
masochism 51–2
masquerade of femininity 47–54
'mass'
    delineation 19–82
    development of word 30–1, 32
mass civilization 33–8
mass culture 147–50
    Americanization 7–8
    consumption 6
    'culture industry' 16
    debate (1950s) 73
    feminist approaches 47–54
    folk culture distinction 4–5, 9, 13
    future of 45–6
    nature of 39–40
    reification 115–28
    theory 39–46
    utopia 115–28
    *see also* 'low culture'
mass customization 151–8
the masses 29–32
    Baudrillard 52–3
    'culture industry' 103–4, 108
    development of word 31–2
    problem of 43–4
mass media 103–4, 383, 385–91, 509
mass society 32
mastectomies 228
materialization 120–1
material production 28
Mattel Corporation 169–81
    *see also* Barbie dolls
meaning creation 216–22, 246–8

means/ends differentiation 116–18
mechanical reproduction 6,
    96–102, 105
mechanization 27, 34–5, 37
media
    British multiculturalism 303, 307
    convergence 12
    'culture industry' 103–4
    mass culture 39, 40
    New York City 405, 406–7, 415
    'play lists' 13
    racial stereotyping 532
    Rodríguez Juliá 76
    subculture development 383–400
    subculture relationship 355–8, 363
    tastes 211
mediation 247
Medieval art 450
'melding' cultures 311–22
    see also merging cultures
memory 76–7, 320–1, 459
men
    Asian stereotypes 340
    bhangra music 303–5
    desire 223–40
    Star Trek fans 252–3
    suits worn by girls 378–82
    see also masculinity
Menchú, Rigoberta 326
'Mera Laung Gawacha' (Sagoo) 294–5
merging cultures 42–3, 311–22
metaphors 25–6
Mexican-Americans 140, 332, 337
Mexicanization of LA 483
Miami Vice 216
micromarkets 472
micro-media 383, 391–9
    see also fanzines
Middletown: A Study in Modern America
    (Lynd and Lynd) 34, 38
migration 170, 197–209
    see also immigrants
Minh-ha, Trinh, T. 531
'minor instrumentalities' 453
minoritarian identities 326–37
minority culture 33–8
misogyny 224, 236–7, 438–9
'modern art of everyday expression' 456
modernism 119–23, 125–7, 286–7
modernization 130–43
Modleski, Tania 21, 47–54
mod style 357, 360, 367–8
Mollenkopf, John 413–14
'moments of freedom' 72–5, 80–1
monetary values 92, 94, 113
    see also economic value
moral economy 256–8
morality of immigrants 316

moral panics 356–9
    adults 471–2
    'subculture' development 385–91, 398, 400
moral reform policies 470–1, 474
Morgan, Robin 223–4, 227
Moses, Robert 406
motherhood 300
Mouse House see Disney
movies see films
MTV 326, 327, 328–32, 334
Mullen, Rodney 463–4
multiculturalism
    bhangra music 301–3, 307
    commodification 174
    couterpublicity 327, 330, 335
    diversity 174
    'face of America' 317
    US, history 202
multinationals 168–9
multiple identities, Internet 530–2
multitude 29–30
the mundane 252
Muñoz, José Esteban 281, 324–37
music
    banda 489–91
    bhangra 294–308
    black culture 160–2, 289–90, 444
    hip hop 489–91, 504–19
    industry 160–2
    Ozomatli 479–94
    'popular' 59
    post-colonial culture 504–19
    press 383, 389–90, 392, 396–9
    punk subculture 362–3, 364, 417–18
    rap 489–91
    reggae 500–1
    repetition 123, 128
    subcultures 383–416
    United Kingdom 300–3
Myrdal, Gunnar 165
mystification of commodities 89–95
myths 457–9

names, the city 458–9
narco-corridos 491
narrative reification 118
national diversity 205–7
nationalism 131–3
    advertising 157
    American immigrants 313–14, 318–19
    clothing industry 157
    diaspora relationship 300, 304–5, 307
    emblems 157
    gender 138, 140
National Origins Act 204
national-popular concept 78, 82
national sovereignty 169
national wholes 203–5

nation-building 507
  America 311–22
  core national values 310
  diasporas 295, 300, 302–3, 305–6
  'melding cultures' 311–22
nation-states 130–1, 142–3, 507–8
natives, tourism 530–2
Negt and Kluge 327–8
neo-conservatism 509
neo-lite-punks 419
NetNoir website 521–2
new consumer subjects 175–8
*New Musical Express* 396
New Social Movements 509–11
newspapers 389–91, 392
  *see also* media
*Newsweek* 249–50
'new wave' versus punk 363, 364
New York City 403–7, 414–15, 449–50
niche media 383, 389–90, 392, 396–9
Nike 200, 205–6
nollies 468
nonresident Indians (NRIs) 169,
    170, 179–80
non-white repression 487
'No Reservations' (Apache Indian) 300–3
nostalgia 379
NRIs *see* nonresident Indians
nudity, *Hustler* 236

'official arts' 244, 247–8
ollies 467–70
Onassis, Jackie 236–7
opera 266–7
operational concepts, the city 451–2
opportunities to see (OTS), micro-media 392
opportunity concept 312–13
oppression 480, 510–11
optical knowledge 451
Orientalism 522–5
'Oriental' stereotyping 338–9, 341–2,
    344, 347
the other
  'popular' in dominant discourses 60
  Rodríguez Juliá 75
  subcultures 358
OTS *see* opportunities to see
overexposure of subculture 383–5, 400
ownership of artworks 98
Ozomatli 443–4, 479–94

Pan-Africanism 515–16
panoptic power 452
Pansy Division 417–18, 420, 421–4, 425
paracinema 263–6, 268–77
paradoxes, US 159–67
*Paris Is Burning* 433, 434
'passing', Internet 520–33

patriarchy
  black diasporas 296–7
  feminism 139–40
  immigrants escaping 313–14
Paul, William 271–2
pay *see* salaries
Peace and Justice Center (Los Angeles) 483–4
penis representations
  gay porn 338–48
  *Hustler* magazine 232
  punk subculture 417–28
*Penthouse* 225
the people 29, 31
  classification 199–203
  cultural struggle 71
  definitions 76, 221
  describing/defining distinction 76
  pluralization 74
  'popular' concept 56–7, 61
  populism 73
perceptions 99–100
performance
  bhangra music 297–9, 301–2
  drag kings 429–40
  ethics of the self 324–37
  punk subculture 418, 420
  subculture 349–440
perks of employment, Disney 191–2
personal as political 309–10
phallic sexuality 232
  *see also* penis representations
phatic functions, pedestrian speech
    acts 454–5
phobic ideology 324–5, 327, 332–3
photography
  art reproduction 97–8, 100–1
  'face of America' 314–15, 318
  whitening black artists 499
pirate radio 391, 393–4
place 441–533
place names 458–9
*Planet Rock* (Afrika Bambaataa) 505–6
Plato 4, 5, 13, 107
*Playboy* 225
'play lists' 12–13
poaching texts, fans 249–62
pogo dance 362
political activism 329, 333–4, 336
political art 125–6
political economy 112
political representation
  black culture 291–2
  the masses 53
  'popular' 55–7, 59, 61
political transformations 9–10
politics
  culture relationship 129–46, 484
  hip hop 401–16

politics *cont.*
  *Hustler* magazine 233–4, 236–8
  personalized 309–10
polysemy, style 365–6
pop culture 59, 484–8
pop music 123, 128
  *see also* music
'popular'
  class relationship 70–1
  commercial definition 66–8
  cultural forms 58–9, 61
  deconstruction 64–71
  definitions 9
  delineation 19–82
  descriptive definition 68
  development of word 55–63
  process definition 69
  role of word 288–9
popular discrimination 215–22
popular government 55–7, 61
popular imperialism 65–6
popularity, hip hop 511
popular performance 349–440
popular press 66
popular tastes 211–78
populism 73, 115
pornography
  films 264–5, 274
  gay videos 338–48
  *Hustler* magazine 223–40
positioning in language 366
post-colonial culture 504–19
post-diaspora 305–6
post-industrialism 401–16, 480
postmodernism 126, 128,
    142, 286–8
post-nationalism 197–209, 484–8
poverty, New York City 403–7
power 441–533
practicing 211–78
  art films in low culture 263–77
  *Hustler* magazine 223–40
  popular discrimination 215–22
  spatial versus signifying 459
  *Star Trek* fans 249–62
  style as signifier 365–8
  symbolic creativity 241–8
  urban practices 451–3
Prawer, S.S. 272
predatory corporations 160–1
primary texts/works 123–4
'primitive art' 245
primitive functions, proper names 459
primitivism 287
privacy issues 310, 315, 318–19,
    322, 329
privation, commodification 112, 113
process definition of 'popular' 69

production
  colonialism 135
  commodities 90–4, 110–12, 114
  'culture industry' 105
  expenditure 449, 452
  Marxism 51
  new consumer subjects 175–8
  *Star Trek* fans 251–2
  symbolic creativity 243–4
  women 50
productivity, discrimination 216
profit motives 104
promoting Disney 191–2
proper names 458–9
Proposition 187, 487, 488
prostitution 522
publications 442
'public inclusion' illusion 469
public spaces 468–9
'Pueblo Pueblo' (Flores) 72–82
Puerto Ricans 75–7, 408
Puig, Manuel 48, 50–4
Punjabi culture *see* bhangra music
punk subculture 356–9, 361–70
  queer theory 417–28
  second-hand style 373, 377–81
  skateboarding 472
purity, black culture 290

qualitative commodity traits 110
quantitative commodity traits 110–11
Queen Latifah 504–5
queer clubs 430, 434–9
queercore culture 418, 419–28
queer theory 10, 15–16,
    351, 417–28

race
  genealogy 204
  history 197–209
racialization 144
  American immigrants
      311–12, 318–19
  bhangra music 298–9
  black culture 291–2
  feminism 137–41
  Marxism 135
  nationalism 132–3
  New York poverty 404–7
  sexuality 338–40, 341–6, 347
  white Americans 319, 320–1
racialized scapegoating 483, 487, 492
racial passing 520–33
racism
  Asian gay porn 345–6, 347
  core national values 321–2, 323
  gay and lesbian movements 340
  *Hustler* magazine 237–8

racism *cont.*
   postmodernism 288
   US 165–6
   Zamora's activism 324–5, 327
radio 387–9, 391, 393–4
ragmarkets 372–82
rap music 402–3, 407, 408–13, 489, 490–1
rationality theories 327
rave culture 383, 386–7, 390, 392, 400, 471
   *see also* acid house culture
raw materials of creativity 243–4, 248
*Reader's Digest* 46
reading
   gender 252–4
   *Star Trek* fans 250, 251–4
'reading' cities 449–50
*The Real World* (TV show) 324–37
reconversion concept 79–80
record sales 481
record shops 501–2
record sleeves 363, 377, 444, 497–503
recuperation
   hip hop culture 411–12
   inequalities 174
   subculture 356
reforms 64
reggae music 500–1
regionalization, hip hop 413
reification
   commodity as spectacle 109
   femininity 237
   grounded aesthetics 247–8
   mass culture 115–28
relationship system 74–5
   *see also* social relations; value relations
relevance in discrimination 216–17
relics of meaning 459
Renaissance art 450
repetition 121–3
representations
   Asian sexuality 338–48
   black culture 291–2
repression
   manipulation theory 126–7
   non-whites 487
reproductions 96–102
   *see also* mechanical reproduction
Republican Party 488
rereadings, *Star Trek* 250, 259
'residing rhetoric' 455–6
resistance/containment dialectic 65–7, 71
retro-style 372, 381–2
   *see also* second-hand style
revolting style 361–4
rewritings, *Star Trek* 259
rhetoric of walking 455–7
Richards, I.A. 33–4, 37
riot grrl culture 418, 419–21, 424–6

ritual function of artworks 100–1
Roach, Max 512
Robinson Crusoe 92–3, 94
robot dance 362
de la Rocha, Zack 484
rock music 362, 369
Rodríguez Juliá, Edgardo 75–7
role-playing Internet sites 523–5
*Romy and Michelle's High School Reunion* 433
Root, Deborah 163
Rosenberg, Bernard 14
Rose, Tricia 351, 401–16
Rubin, Gayle 224
ruptures, hip hop 410–11
Rushton, Philippe 338–9
Russell, Gilbert 35, 36
Russia 133, 134
Russ, Joanna 345

'sacralization of culture' 266–8
Sagoo, Billy 294–5, 301
salaries, Disney 191–2
sales 170, 173
*salwar-kameez* clothes 179, 181
samurai warrior role play 524–5
Sangeet, Apna 305–6, 307
Savage, Jon 379
scale concept 466–7
scholarly inquiry 2, 9–11
Sciach, Morag 21
Sconce, Jeffrey 263, 270
*Screen* 10, 15
second-hand style 372–82
security apparatus 465
*Seinfeld* 431
Seldes, Gilbert 45
the self
   ethics 324–37
   identification 279
self-portraits 521, 524
'selling out' 385–91
semantic tropisms 458
semiotics 364–6
sensationalism 383–400
services 112
sexism 438–9
   *see also* misogyny
Sex Pistols 356, 368
Sexpod 417–18, 426
sexuality
   Asian gay video porn 338–48
   bhangra music 294–5
   black culture 292
   diaspora 296–7
   'face of America' 318–19, 320–2
   films 270–1
   Kipnis 223–40

sexuality *cont.*
    Kirk/Spock stories 258–60, 262
    punk subculture 362, 366–7, 417–28
    Zamora 324–37
Shakespeare, William 267
Sheldon, Reverend Louis 331
Shiach, Morag 55–63
shirts, androgyny 381
shopping, gender 372–3
signifiers
    practice 365–8
    style 358–9, 364–5
    swastikas 365
    traditions 70
Simmons, Jon 327–8
Singh, Malkit 299–300
Sinister Cinema 269–70
skateboarding 443, 462–78
skate parks 473
skinhead subculture 366
sleaze mania 263–77
slums, New York City 406, 415
*Smash Hits* magazine 397
Smileys 399
Smith, Patti 380
Smith, Paul 148, 151–8
Smith, Sir Thomas 60
snobbism 105–6
'the social', construction 470
social change strategies 508
social contest 466
social control 55–6, 268
    *see also* conformity; manipulation theory
social formations of capitalism 135–6
'social imperialist' crisis 65–6
socialism 70, 71
social life
    the city 458
    commodification 83–146
social mobility of artworks 221
social movement culture 480
social relations, commodities
        90–5, 122
social service cuts 403–4
socio-economic considerations
    marketing 147–50
    popular culture 147–50
    sales 173
solidarity 31
sons, bhangra music 303–4
sound reproduction 98, 102
South Asian music 294–308
South Bronx 405–7
Soviet Union *see* U.S.S.R.
space 441–533
spatial exclusion 464
spatial organizations 456
specification markers 77–8

spectacle
    commodities 109–14
    *see also* images
Spengler, O. 37, 38
spider analogy, femininity 51
sport 197–209
    *see also* golf
standardization 35, 37, 46, 105
*Star Trek* fans 249–62
state of emergency 309–23
state forms
    feminism 139
    politics of culture 130–2, 133–4
    transnationalism 142–3
stereotypes
    American immigrants 312
    blacks 498
    'face of America' 317
    racial 532
    racialization of sexuality 338–40, 341–6, 347
    tourists 530
Stowe, Harriet Beecher 48–50
strategic essentialism 291
street furniture 467–8
street markets 373–5
structuring principle of 'popular' 68
Strype, W. 56
studio employees 187–8
styling 349–440
    acid house culture 383–400
    alternative acts 417–28
    bricolage 359–61
    drag kings 429–40
    hip hop 401–16
    homology 364–5
    intentional communication 358–9
    practice signification 365–8
    record sleeve influence 499
    revolt 361–4
    second-hand clothes 372–82
    unifying role 501
    walking rhetorics 455
subaltern studies 138
subculture 349–440
    development of word 29
    entrepreneurs 375–8
    forms of incorporation 356–8
    Hebdige 355–71
    media development 383–400
    second-hand style 372–82
    'subversive consumerism' 373–5
Sum Yung Mahn 341–5
superficiality 218
supervision policies 470–1
Surrealism 361, 366
swastikas 70, 365
symbolic creativity 241–8
symbolic inversion 72, 81

symbolic production 28
symbols in the city 458
synecdoche 456

tabloid newspapers 389–91, 392
taste 211–78
tastelessness 228
Taussig, Michael T. 83
Team Disney *see* Disney
Team Dresh 424
technique concept 105
technology, mass culture 39–40
teddy boys 360
teenagers 241
  *see also* youth culture
telecommunications 405
television
  masculinity 431
  popular discrimination 217–18
  *The Real World* 324–37
  repetition 122–3
  *Star Trek* 249–62
  subculture development 385–7
  symbolic creativity 243
*Tel Quel* group 121, 126
text concept
  discrimination 217, 218–19
  reification 122–4
  symbolic creativity 243, 247
textual poaching 249–62
Thailand 206
theatre 43
*The Face* magazine 396–7
theme parks 188–91
third world
  decolonization 286
  oppression 507
Thompson, E.P. 256
Thornton, Sarah 350–1, 383–400, 471–2
Tiger Woods 197–209
time, popular culture in 72–82
*Time* magazine 310–23
togetherness 207
TOM Inc. 153–7
Tompkins, Jane 50
*Top of the Pops* 385–7
Torr, Diane 436–7, 440
tourism
  instrumentalization 117
  Internet metaphor 525–7
toy business 175–6
  *see also* Barbie dolls
trade unions 193
traditions 69–70, 74
  art reproduction 99
  gender 303–4
  nationalism 132–3
  women's labor 139

training programs, Disney 189–90
transcoding 169
transformations 64
transgression, *Hustler* 226
translocal communities 473
transnationalism
  consumption 181
  corporations 507
  diasporic subjects 178–80
  feminism 137–41
  fractions 203–5
  global consumers 170–2
  India 168–83
  localisms 170
  migration 170
  national consumers 170–2
  NRI 180
  politics of culture 129–30, 135–6, 142–4
  Tiger Woods 200
  *see also* globalization
trash cinema 263–77
travel redefinition 526
trees of gestures 457
Trekkies *see Star Trek* fans
tribalism decrease 198
Tribe 8 417–18, 419–21, 426–7
'tricknowlogy' 462–78

UK *see* United Kingdom
*Un Chien andalou* (Buñuel) 271–2, 276–7
'Uncle Sam' system 482
*Uncle Tom's Cabin* (Stowe) 48–50
underground culture 383–5, 397–8, 400
unification in music 510–11
uniqueness in art *see* aura concept
United Kingdom (UK)
  bhangra music 294–308
  black culture 291
  music 300–3
  *see also* Britain
United States (US)
  biological identity 201–3
  ethnicity 198
  market segmentation 170
  multiculturalism 202
  racism 165–6
universalism 216, 245–6
universality of children 173–4
universality construction 172–4
unnaturalness, subculture 355–6
upper-class transnational NRI 180
urban life 401–16, 451–3
urban renewal 405–7, 413, 415
urban space construction 465
US *see* United States
use value, commodities 89, 95, 113
USSR mass culture 40–1
utopia, mass culture 115–28

value relations
  commodities 89–2, 94–5, 115–28
  commodity as spectacle 113
  core national values 310
  fandom 220–1
  films 269
  race 320–2
  reification 115–28
*Vampyr* (Dreyer) 263, 269
vanity industry 177
variable space, skateboarding 468
VaultReport 191, 192, 193
video companies 263–6, 268–73
video confessionals, *The Real World* 326, 337
videos
  Asian gay porn 338–48
  skateboarding 463–4
  *Top of the Pops* 386
Viennese school 99–100
Viera, Saul (El Gavilancillo) 489
violence in pornography 230, 239
virtual reality, Internet 522
voicing 279–348
  Asian gay video porn 338–48
  bhangra music 294–308
  black culture 285–93
  counterpublicity 324–37
voyeurism 449–51

walking 449–61
Walt Disney Company 79–80
  *see also* Disney
Walt Disney World College Program 188–9
*Wandersmänner* 450
*The War Game* (Watkins) 265
Wasko, Janet 184–96
waste products 452, 459
Watkins, Peter 265
Waugh, Tom 342–3
Wesker, Lindsay 395
West, Cornel 166, 285, 290
Western Marxism 133–6, 145
'Western' nationalism 131–2
Westwood, Vivienne 373
Whannel, Paddy 14
white Americans 202, 316–22
white/black binary 296–7
white businesses 156–7
white-collar workplaces 526
white guilt 163
white homosexuality 340–1, 343–6, 347
white identity politics 487
white label records 384

white masculinities 432–3
whiteness commodity 206
Wil-Dog 483–4, 488–9
Williams, Alyson 502
Williams, Linda 264–5, 272
Williams, Raymond 3, 5, 8, 14, 20,
    25–32, 69
Willis, Paul 212–13, 241–8, 364
Wilson, Governor Pete 488
women
  American immigrants 310, 313, 318
  Asian stereotypes 339–40
  bhangra music 303–6
  black diasporas 297
  drag kings 429–40
  'fantasmatic female' 299–300, 307
  fanzines 392
  pornography 345
  punk subculture 419–21, 424–6
  second-hand style 381–2
  shopping 373
  *Star Trek* fans 252–6, 259–60
  *see also* femininity; feminism
woodcuts 97, 101
Wood, Robin 250
Woods, Eldrick *see* Tiger Woods
word-of-mouth, club culture 391–9
working classes
  New York poverty 404–7
  popular press 66
  subcultures 365, 366–7, 369
work/play overlap, Internet 526
works of art *see* artworks
world labor power 151–2
world peace 207
World Trade Center 449–51
writing, fans 249–62

Yates, Paula 379
youth cultures 462–78
  bhangra music 298
  media development 383–400
  second-hand style 372–82
  spatial mobility 470
  symbolic creativity 241, 243, 245
  *see also* subculture
youth-produced history 471
Yuba City, bhangra music 294–308
Yúdice, George 325–6
Yu, Henry 149, 197–209

Zamora, Pedro 324–37
'The Zulu Nation' 505–6

Compiled by Indexing Specialists (UK) Ltd, Regent House, Hove Street, Hove,
East Sussex BN3 2DW.